Praise for Visual books...

This is absolutely the best computer-related book I have ever bought. Thank you so much for this fantastic text. Simply the best computer book series I have ever seen. I will look for, recommend, and purchase more of the same.

–David E. Prince (NeoNome.com)

I have always enjoyed your Visual books, as they provide a quick overview of functions. Visual books are helpful even for technically inclined individuals who don't have the time to read thick books in order to get the job done. As a frequent traveler, I am extremely grateful to you for providing a pdf version of each book on a companion CD-ROM. I can easily refer to your book while on the road without much additional weight.

–Kin C. Wong (Calgary, Alberta, Canada)

I just want to let you know that I really enjoy all your books. I'm a strong visual learner. You really know how to get people addicted to learning! I'm a very satisfied Visual customer. Keep up the excellent work!

–Helen Lee (Calgary, Alberta, Canada)

These Visual Blueprints are great books! I just purchased ASP 3.0 – it could not have introduced programming with ASP any easier!

–Joseph Moglia (St. Louis, MO)

This book is PERFECT for me - it's highly visual and gets right to the point. What I like most about it is that each page presents a new task that you can try verbatim or, alternatively, take the ideas and build your own examples. Also, this book isn't bogged down with trying to "tell all" – it gets right to the point. This is an EXCELLENT, EXCELLENT, EXCELLENT book and I look forward purchasing other books in the series.

–Tom Dierickx (Malta, IL)

I have quite a few of … very pleased with all of them. I love the way the lessons are presented!

–Mary Jane Newman (Yorba Linda, CA)

I am an avid fan of your Visual books. If I need to learn anything, I just buy one of your books and learn the topic in no time. Wonders! I have even trained my friends to give me Visual books as gifts.

–Illona Bergstrom (Aventura, FL)

I just had to let you and your company know how great I think your books are. I just purchased my third Visual book (my first two are dog-eared now!) and, once again, your product has surpassed my expectations. The expertise, thought, and effort that go into each book are obvious, and I sincerely appreciate your efforts.

–Tracey Moore (Memphis, TN)

Compliments to the chef!! Your books are extraordinary! Or, simply put, extra-ordinary, meaning way above the rest! THANK YOU THANK YOU THANK YOU! I buy them for friends, family, and colleagues.

–Christine J. Manfrin (Castle Rock, CO)

I write to extend my thanks and appreciation for your books. They are clear, easy to follow, and straight to the point. Keep up the good work! I bought several of your books and they are just right! No regrets! I will always buy your books because they are the best.

–Seward Kollie (Dakar, Senegal)

Thank you for making it clear. Keep up the good work.

–Kirk Santoro (Burbank, CA)

Feb 03

maranGraphics is a family-run business
located near Toronto, Canada.

At **maranGraphics**, we believe in producing great computer books — one book at a time.

maranGraphics has been producing high-technology products for over 25 years, which enables us to offer the computer book community a unique communication process.

Our computer books use an integrated communication process, which is very different from the approach used in other computer books. Each spread is, in essence, a flow chart — the text and screen shots are totally incorporated into the layout of the spread. Introductory text and helpful tips complete the learning experience.

maranGraphics' approach encourages the left and right sides of the brain to work together — resulting in faster orientation and greater memory retention.

Above all, we are very proud of the handcrafted nature of our books. Our carefully-chosen writers are experts in their fields, and spend countless hours researching and organizing the content for each topic. Our artists rebuild every screen shot to provide the best clarity possible, making our screen shots the most precise and easiest to read in the industry. We strive for perfection, and believe that the time spent handcrafting each element results in the best computer books money can buy.

Thank you for purchasing this book. We hope you enjoy it!

Sincerely,

Robert Maran

President
maranGraphics
Rob@maran.com
www.maran.com

CREDITS

Project Editor
Sarah Hellert

Acquisitions Editor
Jody Lefevere

Product Development Manager
Lindsay Sandman

Copy Editor
Marylouise Wiack

Technical Editor
Steve Wright

Editorial Manager
Robyn Siesky

Senior Permissions Editor
Carmen Krikorian

Media Development Specialist
Travis Silvers

Editorial Assistant
Adrienne D. Porter

Manufacturing
Allan Conley
Linda Cook
Paul Gilchrist
Jennifer Guynn

Book Design
maranGraphics®

Production Coordinator
Maridee V. Ennis

Layout
Beth Brooks
LeAndra Hosier
Kristin McMullan

Screen Artist
Jill A. Proll

Illustrator
Ronda David-Burroughs

Cover Illustration
David E. Gregory

Proofreaders
Laura L. Bowman
John Tyler Connoley
Susan Moritz

Indexer
Joan Griffitts

Vice President and Executive Group Publisher
Richard Swadley

Vice President and Publisher
Barry Pruett

Composition Services Director
Debbie Stailey

ABOUT THE AUTHOR

Scott Barker has been involved with database development for 17 years since he graduated with a BS in Computer Science in 1986. On the original Microsoft Access team, Scott has worked with Access and SQL Server for over 11 years, written seven books, including *F. Scott Barker's Microsoft Access Power Programming,* and *Database Programming with Visual Basic .NET and ADO.NET.* He has trained thousands of developers, and is a frequent speaker at Microsoft conferences around the world.

Scott is the father of five, and can be found in Woodinville, Washington, with his wife Diana. Scott is the owner of AppsPlus, a software development company specializing in database development for both the desktop and the Web. You can reach him at www.appsplus.com.

AUTHOR'S ACKNOWLEDGMENTS

This has been a very enjoyable project, from the first when I looked over the unique design. Included in that is the pleasure that the folks at Wiley have been to work with; thanks for giving me a shot. Thanks to Jody Lefevere for being patient with me as we nailed down the initial contract, and to Sarah Hellert for putting up with me during development. Also, thanks to Steve Wright for keeping me on the ball with his technical edits. A big thanks goes to Marylouise Wiack, who's tough comments made this a much better book.

I want to acknowledge Neil Salkind, the best agent in the world, and StudioB for getting me these opportunities and putting up with me.

Of course, as usual, the biggest acknowledgment goes to my wife, Diana, who puts up with me every time I go into the writing cycle, as well as my five fantastic kids: Chris 16, Kari Anne 13, Nichole 11, David 8, and Joseph 2.

I would like to dedicate this book to my newest son, Joseph. Already you have brought so much happiness to our lives; we are so blessed to have you.

TABLE OF CONTENTS

4) WORKING WITH FORMS

5) UTILIZING CONTROLS ON FORMS

TABLE OF CONTENTS

6) VBA FOR AUTOMATING YOUR APPLICATION

7) USING VBA BEHIND YOUR FORMS

8) CREATING REPORTS

9) ANALYZING DATA USING PIVOTTABLE AND PIVOTCHART VIEWS

10) IMPORTING, LINKING, AND EXPORTING DATA

11) ACCESSING DATA DIRECTLY WITH ADO

12) AUTOMATING OTHER OFFICE PRODUCTS

13) SECURING ACCESS DATABASES

14) REPLICATING YOUR DATABASE

15) PUBLISHING DATA TO THE INTERNET

APPENDIX A)

APPENDIX B)

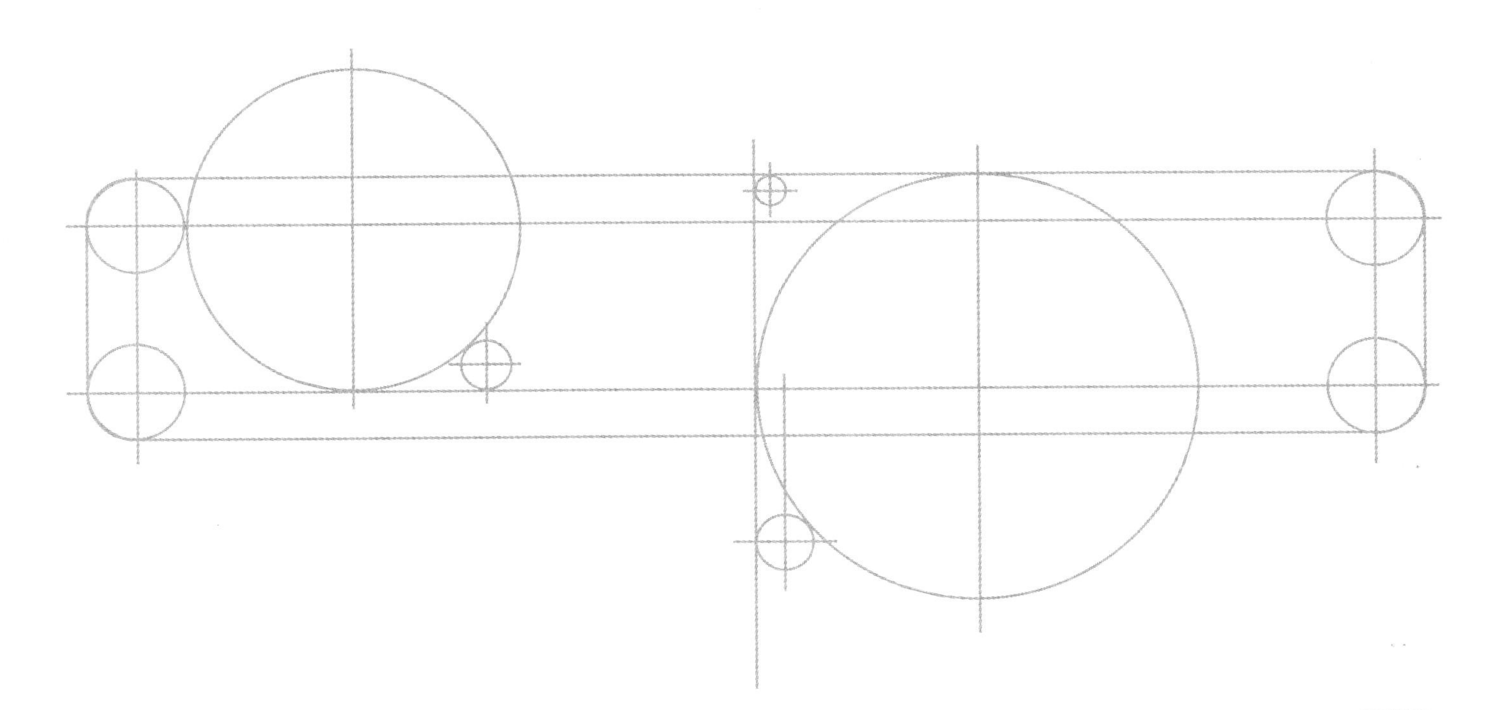

HOW TO USE THIS BOOK

Access 2003: Your visual blueprint for creating and maintaining real-world databases uses simple, straightforward examples to teach you how to take advantage of Access' powerful database features.

To get the most out of this book, you should read each chapter in order, from beginning to end. Each chapter introduces new ideas and builds on the knowledge learned in previous chapters. When you become familiar with *Access 2003: Your visual blueprint for creating and maintaining real-world databases*, you can use this book as an informative desktop reference.

Who This Book Is For

If you are interested in understanding Access, and creating powerful, yet easy-to-use, databases, *Access 2003: Your visual blueprint for creating and maintaining real-world databases* is the book for you.

What You Need to Use This Book

For hardware, you will just need whatever is required by Office to work with the examples in this book. There are a couple of tasks that show how to use Access with SQL Server, so you will need that for those tasks. A couple other tasks show how to use Access with Windows SharePoint Service, so access to a site will be necessary. See Appendix B, "What's on the CD-ROM," for more information about hardware and software requirments.

The Conventions in This Book

A number of typographic and layout styles have been used throughout *Access 2003: Your visual blueprint for creating and maintaining real-world databases* to distinguish different types of information.

`Courier Font`

Indicates the use of code, such as tags or attributes, scripting language code such as statements, operators, and functions, and code such as objects, methods, and properties.

Bold

Indicates information that you must type.

Italics

Indicates a new term.

Apply It

An Apply It section usually contains a segment of code that takes the lesson you just learned one step further. Apply It sections offer inside information and pointers that you can use to enhance the functionality of your code.

Extra

An Extra section provides additional information about the task you just accomplished. Extra sections often contain interesting tips and useful tricks to make working with Access macros easier and more efficient.

The Organization of this Book

Access 2003: Your visual blueprint for creating and maintaining real-world databases contains 15 chapters and two appendices.

The first chapter, "Architect Your Access Database," introduces database concepts that explain how you can create real-world databases using Access. This chapter introduces various Access tools you can use to create your databases, and goes into detail about creating and modifying tables, including ways of validating data that users enter into your tables.

Chapters 2 and 3, "Creating Queries to View Your Information" and "Advanced Queries," respectively, introduce you to using queries to get the most out of your databases. These chapters discuss how to create parameter queries for simple and complex criteria, as well as creating queries to perform bulk operations such as deleting, adding, and editing records. These chapters also show you how to analyze your data using totals and Crosstab queries.

Chapter 4, "Working with Forms," shows you how to create forms that control how users enter data into your tables. This chapter shows you how you can use the different views of forms, and the tools that are available for editing your forms.

Chapter 5, "Utilizing Controls on Forms," takes you further into creating powerful forms by utilizing available controls. You can display multiple pages using the Tab control, limit data that displays using combo and list boxes, display company logos on your forms, and work with the Calendar ActiveX control.

Chapter 6, "VBA for Automating Your Application," explains the how and why of using Visual Basic for Applications, or VBA, in your Access database. It introduces the basics of VBA, and how you can use VBA to get the most from your application. You will work with VBA throughout the rest of the book.

Chapter 7, "Using VBA Behind Your Forms," introduces you to more advanced uses for VBA in Access, for example, showing you how to work with forms and controls at runtime. This chapter discusses enabling and disabling controls, and programming combo boxes and multi-select list boxes. Many other techniques, including error handling, are also presented.

Chapter 8, "Creating Reports," not only shows you how to create basic reports using the report designer, but also how to use VBA in your reports, how to use sub-reports and graphics, how to create running totals, and how to use parameters and forms with your reports.

Chapter 9, "Analyzing Data Using PivotTable and PivotChart Views," shows you how to use Pivot table and PivotChart objects to present and analyze your data. It includes information about adding filters and displaying summary and detail data, as well as how to change the various chart types and display multiple plots.

Chapter 10, "Importing, Linking, and Exporting Data," discusses the various formats to and from which you can import and export data. It shows the steps for performing these tasks, and tells you what to watch out for when importing and exporting data.

Chapter 11, "Accessing Data Directly with ADO," introduces you to ActiveX Data Objects, or ADO, which is the most recent method of accessing data directly while using VBA. Using ADO, you can work with data row by row, using code to manipulate the data down to a field level if necessary.

Chapter 12, "Automating Other Office Products," shows you how to control various Office products from within Access. For example, you can create Word and Outlook documents, and Excel worksheets, and pass data to these files from Access.

Chapter 13, "Securing Access Databases," explains the options that you can use for securing your Access databases. It also goes into detail about how to work with users, groups, and permissions.

Chapter 14, "Replicating Your Database," details how you can create smart copies of your database through a process called replication, how you can update, or synchronize, the copies, and also how you can handle conflicts in the data. It shows you how to perform these tasks using both menus and VBA.

Chapter 15, "Publishing Data to the Internet," helps you place your data on the Web. It shows you how to publish both static and dynamic data to Web pages. It also discusses Data Access Pages, as well as what XML is and how you can take advantage of it in your applications.

What's On The CD-ROM

The CD-ROM included in this book contains the files referenced in each of the book's tasks. The CD-ROM contains trial versions of software that you can use to work with *Access 2003: Your visual blueprint for creating and maintaining real-world databases*. An e-version of the book is also available on the CD-ROM.

UNDERSTANDING RELATIONAL DATABASES

Unlike other Office applications, such as Word and Excel, where you can easily open the application and start using it without much training, Access requires that you have some background information to be able to use the software effectively. For example, with Microsoft Word, you can open the application and start typing. At worst, you may have to retype or reformat some documents after learning more about the software. However, with database software such as Access, the way in which you create or "architect" your database determines how usable the information will be when you go to retrieve that information.

In order to create your database correctly, you must understand two things:

1. What a database is, and
2. What is meant by the term "relational databases"

RELATIONAL DATABASES IN THE REAL WORLD

You deal with databases in the real world all the time. When you deal with customers and do business with them, you record all the information and activities in real-world databases, or an element of one. For example, you track customer information such as company name and contact information. This information is ***related*** to invoice information. Along with tracking information on the invoice such as invoice date, invoice number, line item details, and total due, we must also track the customer to whom the invoice belongs. By putting the customer name or number on the invoice, you are relating the invoice to the customer. At your desk, you track information using manila files, with each file containing all, or part of, the business you do with a client. You may have one file that contains contacts made with a client, and another file that contains invoices. These folders are analogous to tables used in an Access database. There are many similarities between how you track information in the real world and how you track it on the computer. Now, take a look at how real-world information is stored in an Access database.

RELATIONAL DATABASES IN MICROSOFT ACCESS

When starting to work in Microsoft Access, you begin with a single file, called a database file. Within this database file are all the items, or ***objects***, you need to track real-world information.

Tables

The main object you use in a database is a ***table***. Tables store information about a topic or activity. Topics include subjects such as customers, invoices, or students. Activities include meetings, schedules, and other actions you may need to track.

Tables have structures, and those structures are made up of ***fields***. Fields track the individual pieces of data for your tables. For a customer's table, called tblCustomers to use the correct naming convention, you can include fields such as CompanyName, ContactName, Address, City, State, and Zip. For more information on naming conventions, see Appendix A.

When you create a table, and add the fields, you can then add the data. You enter individual customers into the table, field by field. Access stores the individual customer data in ***records***, also called ***rows***, in the table.

RELATIONAL DATABASES IN MICROSOFT ACCESS (CONTINUED)

Tables in the Database

You can store data in the database in which you also keep other objects, such as queries and forms. When working with small- to medium-size databases, with just a few people accessing the database, you can store all the tables in the same database.

Linked Tables

When you have a number of people accessing your database over a network, you may want to split your database so that the tables are in a separate database from other objects, such as queries and forms. You can use linked tables to access data owned by somebody else, either in a separate Access database, or other file types that Access supports, such as Excel worksheets, text files, and SQL Server tables. More about working with linked tables can be found in the last two sections of this chapter.

Primary Keys

Each table should have a ***Primary Key*** field. A primary key makes each row of data you enter into a table unique. This means that when you need to refer to a record within a table, you can do so by using the Primary Key field. You should use a field that is commonly used to individualize records from one another, such as CustomerID, SSN, or MemberID.

Note that while you can use multiple fields that make up a unique value for a primary key, it is not recommended for performance reasons and maintainability of the database. This type of primary key field is called a composite key.

Access provides a method for creating a type of field that automatically increments itself to make it unique for each record. This type of field is called ***AutoNumber***. You should use an AutoNumber for the Primary Key field rather than creating a field you need to maintain yourself. When using an AutoNumber type field for a primary key, you are using a Surrogate Key.

Relationships

Access uses relationships between relational databases to link tables to each other. You can create relationships by telling Access which tables relate to others, and which fields are related. There are three types of relationships that you can use: One-to-Many, One-to-One, or Many-to-Many. Creating the actual relationships in Access can be found in the section "Establish Relationships," later in this chapter.

You create relationships using the Primary Key fields in tables, and relate them to other tables using Foreign Keys. The next few sections discuss the different types of relationships.

One-to-Many

This is the most common type of relationship. An example of a one-to-many relationship would be customers to invoices. One customer can have many invoices. The field on which you would base the relationship is the CustomerID field in both tables. In the invoices table, the CustomerID field is a foreign key to the CustomerID field in the tblCustomers table, where it is the primary key.

One-to-One

Probably the least used, this relationship type relates two tables on a one-to-one basis. An example of this type would be a tblCustomers table that contains common information such as name and address, and a tblCustomersFinancial table that contains more sensitive information such as credit and income information for each customer.

Many-to-Many

This relationship is more complicated in that it is made up of two one-to-many relationships. An example of this would be a student database. In a student database you would have tblStudents, tblClasses, and tblSchedules. Each student, represented by a StudentID field, could have many classes, and each class, represented by a ClassID field, could have many students. The schedule — StudentID, ClassID — would join the other two tables to make a many-to-many relationship.

OVERVIEW OF ACCESS

Access is made up of various "objects" that build on each other. When you open the database window, the object groups appear in a list. The objects are Tables, Queries, Forms, Reports, Pages, Macros, and Modules. While you can use some of these objects by themselves, such as tables, when you use them together they help you to create a much more robust and user-friendly database.

OBJECTS FOR DATA INPUT AND OUTPUT

Pages

Also known as Data Access Pages, or DAPs, pages present your Access data on the Web. Pages are a blend of both forms and reports: You can use them for both data input and information presentation. They are created in HTML, with a link in your Access database.

Pages and other Internet features are discussed in Chapter 15.

Forms

While you can enter data directly into a query or table using Datasheet view, you do not have much control over the way the data is entered. It is preferable to create forms that you base on queries or tables. You can use forms to help the user enter the data entered, and make the user's job much easier. In addition to table fields that you can place in forms, Access also provides an enormous number of controls that you can add to your forms to make entering data a logical and pleasant experience.

Among the controls used for entering data are text boxes, the most common. Text boxes allow you to enter data just as you would in a datasheet, only with more control. Other input controls include list boxes and combo boxes, which present the user with a list of possible data choices for a field. You also have command-button controls that allow you to lead the user through your application and allow the user to perform tasks.

Forms are discussed in many chapters, but the ways to create them are introduced in Chapter 4.

Tables

Discussed in the last sections, a table is the base object in which you store your data. You can enter data directly into a table using the Datasheet view, or use the table as a base for other Access objects.

Working with tables is discussed in this chapter starting in the section "Create a New Table Using Data."

Queries

Queries are used to retrieve information from your tables. With a query, you can limit the data the user can obtain, or update bulk information, such as when you want to update all costs of a sales item by 5%. You can also use a query to delete or add multiple records. Forms, reports, and pages can all be based off a query or a table directly.

Queries are covered in Chapter 2 and Chapter 3.

Reports

Just as forms can help users enter data into your database, reports are used to present information from your database. Access has a powerful report designer that allows you to create professional-looking reports as simple as a mailing list, or as complicated as complete loan documentation.

Reports are discussed in Chapter 8.

AUTOMATING AND DEVELOPMENT

Macros

Access uses macros differently than in other Office applications such as Word and Excel. In the other Office applications, macros are Visual Basic for Applications, or VBA, routines that you can create manually, or by using the Macro Recorder. In Access, macros consist of individual macro actions, created using a menu-driven editor. However, the macros in Access do not allow you to trap any kind of errors that may occur, and have other limitations. Also, you can use the DoCmd object that can be used in VBA modules for performing macro actions, yet control errors. Methods of the DoCmd object used in VBA reflect most macro actions you can use in macros.

Information about converting your macros and the DoCmd object can be found in Chapter 6.

Modules (VBA)

Modules store the VBA code you can create to handle automating your application. While this may seem intimidating if you do not come from a development background, it should not be. Access does supply some tools that create routines for various tasks. For example, if you add a Command Button control to a form, with wizards turned on, a wizard walks you through specifying what you want to accomplish with the control, and creates the code to do it, including error handling.

Using modules and VBA begins in Chapter 6, and continues through the rest of this book.

OTHER FEATURES

Importing and Exporting Data

One of the main features that make Access so popular is the ability to import and export data to or from other data formats such as text files, XML, Excel worksheets, SQL Server data, and others. You can import and export using the menus, or even automate the tasks using code.

Importing and exporting other data formats is discussed in Chapter 10.

Security

While this is a very important part of your database, due to the need for high security for sensitive data, handling security can sometimes be a real pain. Access gives you a couple of ways to secure your database. The easiest way is to use a single password. The more complete, but more difficult way, is to use user, group, and object permissions.

Both ways to secure your database are discussed in Chapter 13.

Automation of Other Office Applications

As with all of the Office products, you can control different Office applications from within Access, increasing the power of the Office platform. This enables you to take data from a table in Access and create a worksheet in Excel, for example.

Automation using VBA is discussed in Chapter 12.

Replication

Replication lets you create copies of your database, have users update data in the copies of the data, and then merge the changes back into your main copy of the database. As with most of the features in Access, this can be performed either using the menus or through code.

You can see how to replicate, or copy, your database by reading Chapter 14.

USING THE ACCESS DATABASE WIZARD

One of the features that make Access such a popular application is its wizards: They do so much to get you started. You can use the Access Database Wizard to create complete database applications. Another term for the various types of databases that can be used is *template*. In Access, a template guides you in creating database applications for a specific topic. You may be familiar with templates in other applications such as Word and Excel.

In Access you find templates for database applications such as Asset Tracking, Contact Management, and Expenses, to name a few.

After the wizard creates the database file, you can specify where you want to store it. In addition, it creates the various tables, queries, forms, reports, and other objects that are necessary for the template that you have chosen. With the wizard, you can choose what columns you want to include for each table, so that you can customize it to your needs. You can also specify formats for forms and reports. The wizard also generates a main switchboard, which allows you to pick various data entry forms you want to access, as well as reports that the database application generates.

The Access Database Wizard is a great way to start using Access because it can give you an idea of what you can create on your own. When you examine the finished product, you can see how to create your own application. You can do this by pressing F11 and walking through the various objects in the database window, after the Database Wizard has completed.

USING THE ACCESS DATABASE WIZARD

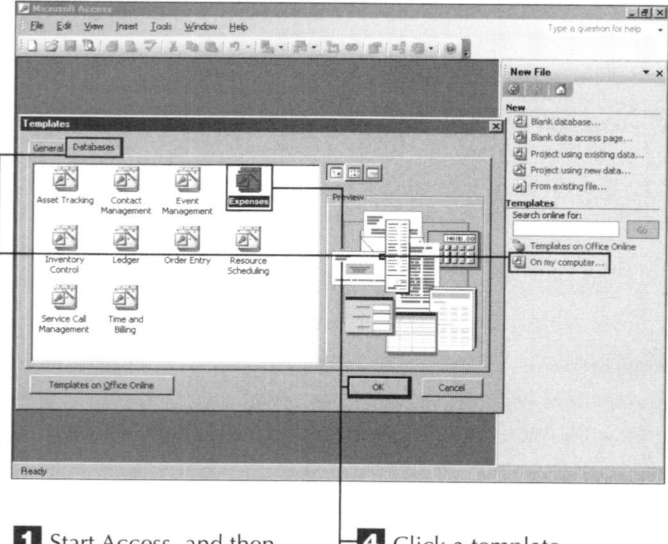

1 Start Access, and then click File ⇨ New.

2 Click On my computer.

■ The Templates dialog box appears.

3 Click the Databases tab.

4 Click a template.

■ This task uses the Expenses template.

5 Click OK.

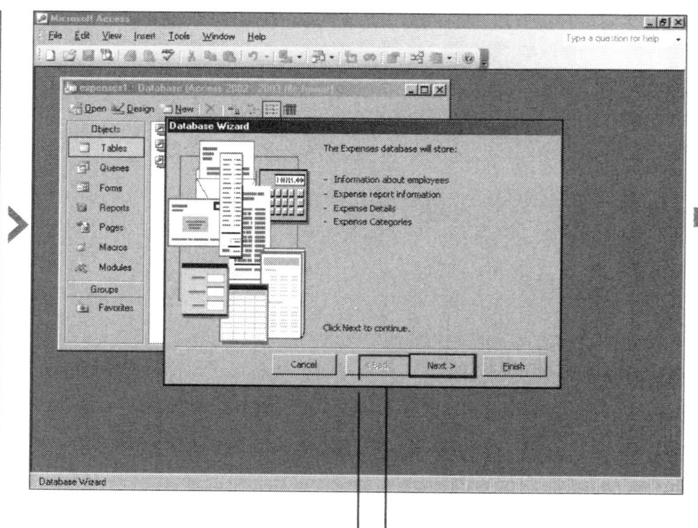

6 In the File New Database dialog box that appears, click Create to accept the default name.

■ The Database Wizard appears.

■ The introduction gives you an idea of what features the new database will include.

7 Click Next.

Extra

After closing your database, the next time you go into it you may see the Disable/Enable macro dialog box. You have probably seen this in prior versions of Word and Excel. If you receive this message, click Enable Macros, and your database opens just fine. In order to not receive this message, click Tools ➪ Macros ➪ Security. The Security dialog box appears. Next, set the Security Level to Low, and click OK.

Warning: A low security setting leaves your database vulnerable to someone sneaking a macro virus in on you in a database. There are also ways to create a VBA certificate for your code, but that is beyond the scope of this book.

The Database Wizard is a non re-entrant wizard. If you use the Database Wizard to create a database, you cannot use the Database Wizard to modify the existing database. Instead, you must create a new database with the wizard, or modify the tables using the Design view of the tables.

You can create tables using a wizard similar to the Database Wizard by clicking Create table using wizard in the Tables list.

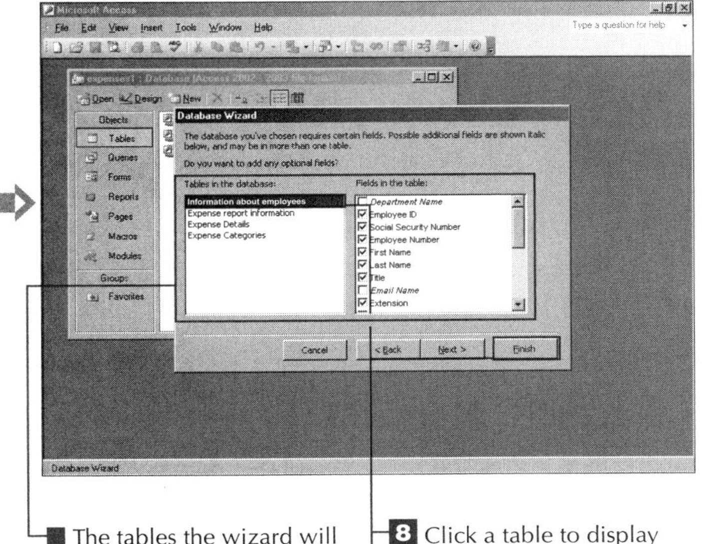

■ The tables the wizard will include in your database appear along with the fields they will contain.

8 Click a table to display the fields in the table, and check any additional fields you want to include.

9 Click Finish.

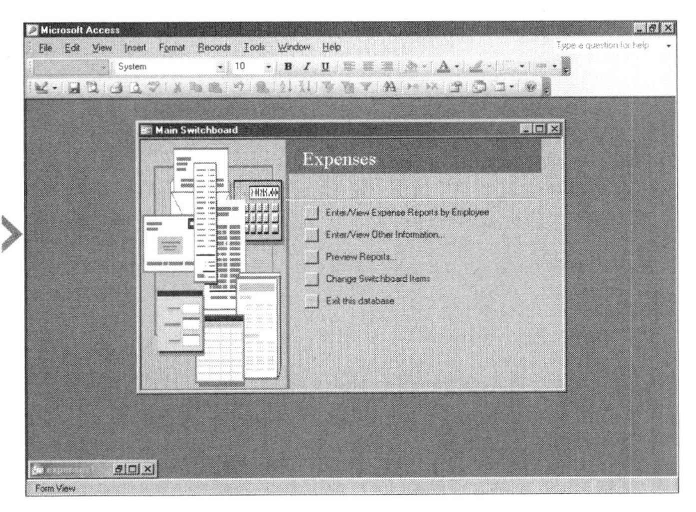

■ After the wizard generates the new database, the Main Switchboard window appears for the new database.

DOWNLOAD ADDITIONAL DATABASE TEMPLATES

Besides the ten templates that are included with the Office package, you can find other templates on the Web, located at the Template home page.

To locate the Access templates on the Web, click Template home page in the New File task pane. On the Template home page, you can search for Access templates, and the templates appear with icons representing the applications in which they are created. Along with Access, you can find templates for Word, Excel, and PowerPoint.

Note that in addition to downloading the .cab file, you have to copy the database out of the .cab file, and set the database file read-only property to false. Cab files are basically self-extracting compressed files.

Although the database files you download are called templates, they are actually sample databases that allow you to get an idea of some of the applications that can be created with Access. This includes giving you examples for creating tables.

Unlike the templates that are included with Access, with the downloaded templates you cannot add extra fields, or specify how you want the forms and reports to look.

Some of the templates found in the Template home page are Inventory Management Database, DVD Collection Database, Resource Management Database, and a Customer Orders Database.

You also have another sample database that comes with Access called Northwind.mdb. The Northwind.mdb database has been supplied with Access since Access 1.0, and can be found under the Office folder, in a folder called Samples. To use the Northwind.mdb database, you need to have told Office to install Sample Databases when you installed Access.

The CD that accompanies this book includes example databases for each chapter, named Chapter??mdb.

DOWNLOAD ADDITIONAL DATABASE TEMPLATES

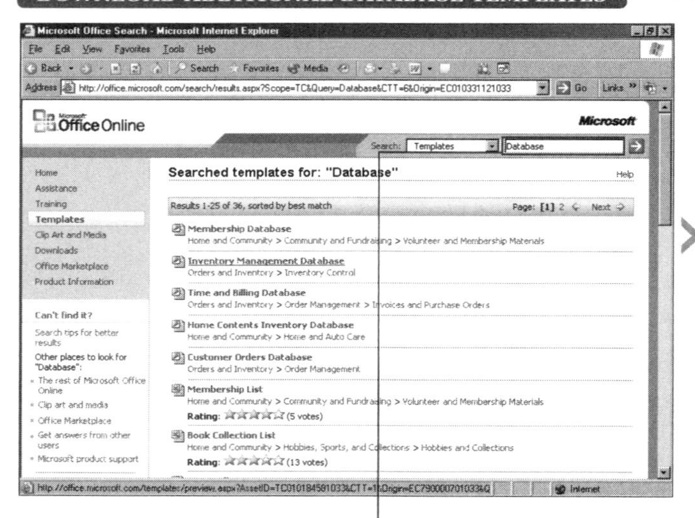

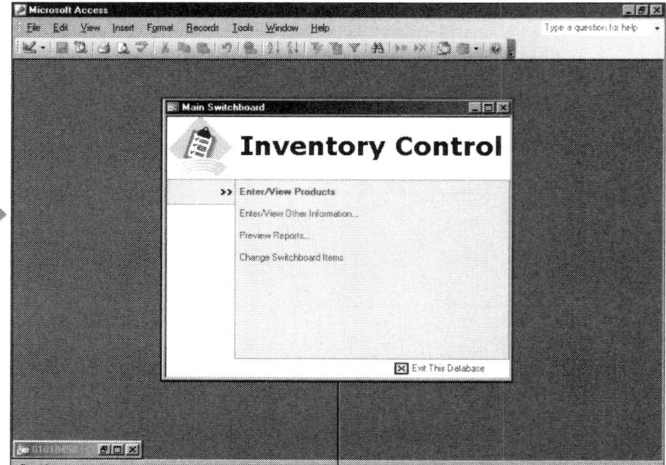

1 Start Access, and then click File ⇨ New.

2 Click Templates home page.

■ Your browser opens to the Microsoft Office Templates home page.

3 Type **Database** in the Search text field and press Enter.

■ A list of templates appears, with three Access templates at the top of the list.

4 Click a database template you want to download.

■ The sample page for the template you chose appears.

5 Click Download on the next two pages that appear.

■ The File Download dialog box appears.

6 Click Open.

■ The .cab file opens.

7 Copy the file onto your system, and open it in Access.

■ The Main Switchboard window of the database you selected appears.

CREATE A BLANK DATABASE

While Access can help you create some standard types of database applications, you may find a subject that is not covered with any of the templates available, on or off the Web. If you find that none of the existing templates meet your needs, you can create your own database, along with tables, queries, and other objects.

Even creating a blank database you must make a decision. With Access, you can create two different types of database file types.

The first database file type is the Microsoft Access Database. This file type, with the extension of .mdb, keeps tables and queries in the same file as forms, reports, macros, and code. You can use this database file type for a single user, or for a file server with the tables in one database on the server, and the rest of the objects in a database on local machines. Using Access in the latter fashion is discussed in the sections "Link Access Tables" and "Link SQL Server Tables."

The second database file type is the Microsoft Access Project. This database type, with the extension .adp, was created in Access 2000 to be a front-end for SQL Server. Using this file format, you can create tables and queries that are stored in an SQL Server database. Your other Access objects are stored in the Access project.

The first file type, Microsoft Access Database, or mdb, appears in the examples throughout this book. Also, most of the examples use single database files containing tables and queries, along with forms, reports, macros, data access pages, and modules.

CREATE A BLANK DATABASE

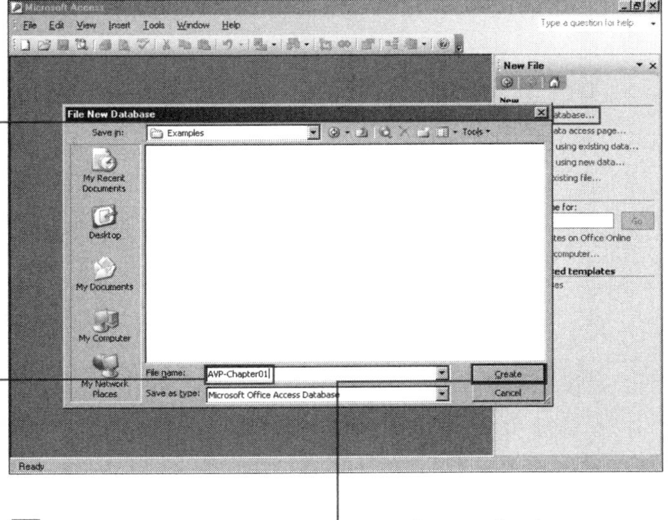

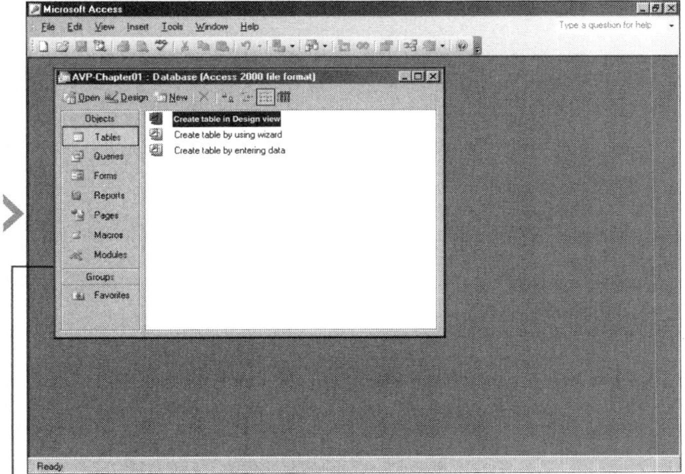

1 Start Access, and then click File ➪ New.

2 Click Blank database.

■ The File New Database dialog box appears.

3 Type the filename for the database.

Note: The extension does not appear if the setting Windows has for displaying extensions of known file types is turned off.

4 Click Create.

■ The new database window appears. You now have a blank database, ready for you to add the new tables and other objects to perform necessary tasks.

CREATE A NEW TABLE USING DATA

When you create a table, you can specify how you want to store your data in the database. In so doing, you are specifying the table structure.

You can create a table using either data or the Table Designer. If you want to use data to create a table, you can choose the Create table by entering data option in the Tables list in the database window. This is a quick way to get your data into a table, without worrying about details such as the length of fields, data types, and validation rules. When you create a table this way, Access makes its best guess as to the type of data you are entering.

As you are entering data into the new table, the fields are named with the default values of Field1, Field2, and so on. Using a right-click menu in the column heading, you can rename columns while entering data. Using the same right-click menu, you can also perform other tasks such as inserting columns, deleting columns, and creating lookup values. See the section "Specify Lookup Values," later in this chapter, for more information on lookup values.

Entering the data feels just like it does when you are entering information into an Excel spreadsheet. You type a value into a column, and then either press the right-arrow key to move into a new field or the down-arrow key to move into a new record.

When you have entered the data desired, you can close the table. Access asks you to name and save the table. It also notifies you that no primary key is defined, and asks if you wish to specify one, or have Access create one.

After creating a table using this method, you can go back and modify the table structure using the table designer.

CREATE A NEW TABLE USING DATA

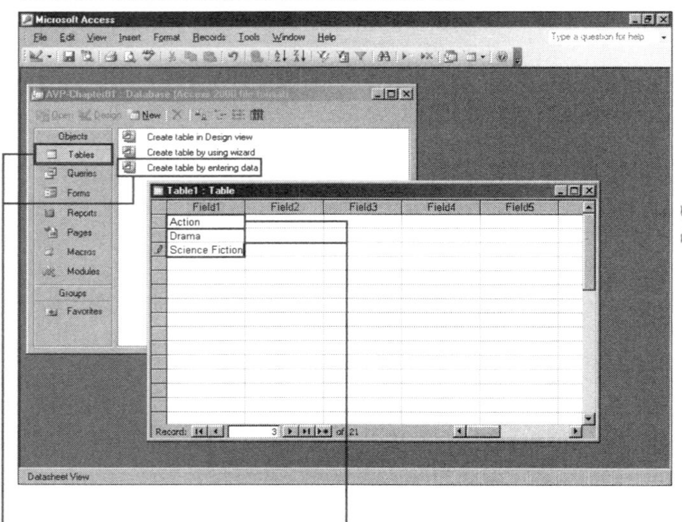

Note: This task uses the database AVP-Chapter01.mdb on the CD-ROM.

1. Open a database for which you want to create a table.
2. Click Tables.
3. Double-click Create a table by entering data.

■ A new table opens in Datasheet view.

4. Type a category name in the first cell of the table.
5. Repeat step 4 to create additional categories.

■ The categories are named Action, Drama, and Science Fiction.

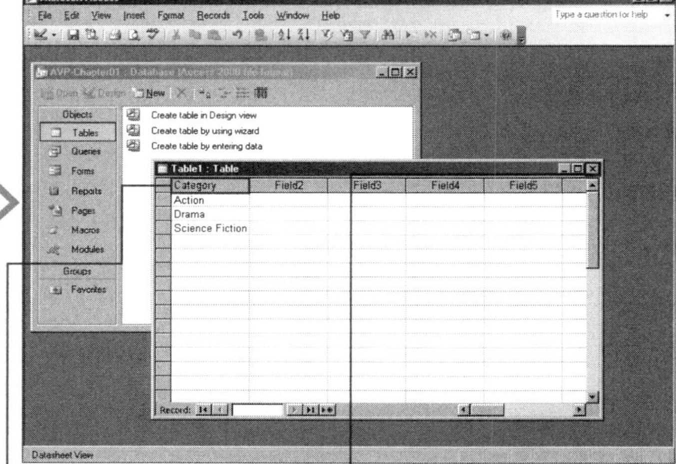

6. Right-click the column heading labeled Field1 and select Rename Column from the drop-down list.
7. Type a name for the column heading.

■ By filling in the column heading with Category, you have also named the field.

■ The name you enter in the column heading becomes the name for the field.

8. Click the Close button.

Extra

While in the Datasheet view entering your data, you can edit the column properties to make entering data easier for yourself and other users. When you click the Format menu option in the Datasheet view of a table, query, or form, the following choices appear:

MENU CHOICE	DESCRIPTION
Font	Set the font attributes when using datasheets.
Datasheet	You can set various properties, other than font, when you are in Datasheet view, such as cell effects and grid lines.
Row Height	Lets you determine the row height for all rows in the datasheet.
Column Width	Lets you resize columns. You can also click between columns, and drag them to control column width.
Rename Column	Renames a column, as shown in this section.
Hide Columns	After you click and drag across a column or columns, you can hide those columns. You can also set a column width to zero for the same effect.
Unhide Columns	Makes hidden columns visible.
Freeze Columns	Freezes a column or columns to the left side of the datasheet.
Unfreeze All Columns	Unfreezes frozen columns.

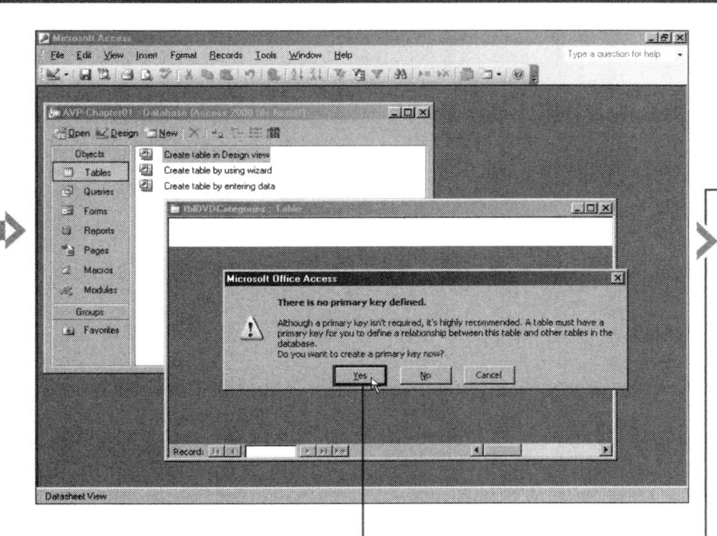

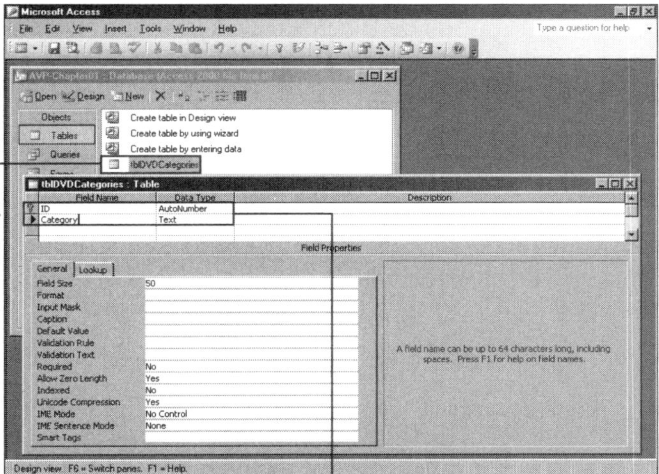

■ A dialog box asking if you want to save changes to the design of the table appears.

9 Click Yes.

■ A Save As dialog box appears.

10 Type a table name, and click OK.

■ In this example, the table is named tblDVDCategories.

■ A dialog box appears, and asks if you want Access to create a primary key for the table.

11 Click Yes.

■ The table now appears in the list of tables in the database window.

12 Click the table.

13 Click Design.

■ You can now see the Text field you created, as well as the new Primary Key field.

CREATE A NEW TABLE WITH THE DESIGNER

You can create a table using the table designer. Creating a table using the table designer takes more time and work than simply inputting data directly into a blank table, but gives you more precise control over the table structure. This is because you are specifying properties instead of letting Access perform this task for you.

The table designer window is divided into two fields, upper and lower. In the upper area you specify the field names, data types, and descriptions of the fields you are adding.

When entering the Name property for the field, you should not include spaces. For example, when you enter a field that tracks the first name of a person, you should specify a field name of FirstName rather than First Name. Note that each word in the name is capitalized. Capitalizing the first letters of each word makes the name easier to read.

The Data Type property tells Access what type of data is going to be put into each field. Choices include Text, Number, and Date/Time. The Description property is important because it allows you to give more information to the user entering the data. It appears on the application status bar in forms and datasheets.

In the lower field you can choose additional properties that control the type of data users enter into the table. Which properties appear depends on the data type you assign to the field. Some properties, such as Caption, appear for all data types. The Caption property is displayed on labels for text boxes, on forms and reports, and column headings for datasheets. For example, you can set the Caption property to First Name for the FirstName field.

CREATE A NEW TABLE WITH THE DESIGNER

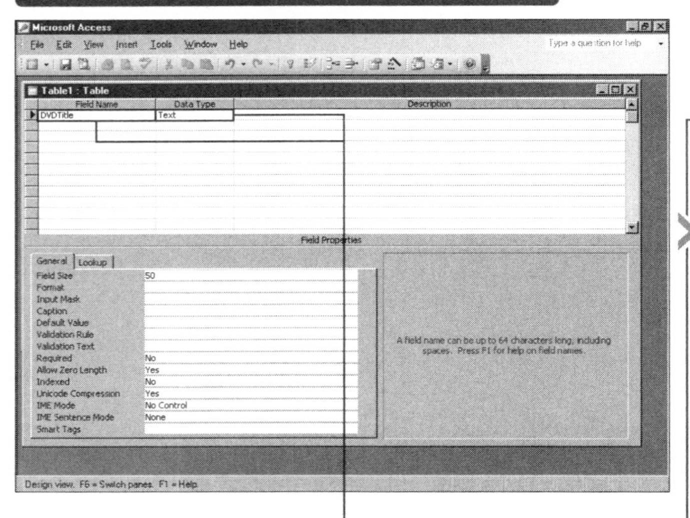

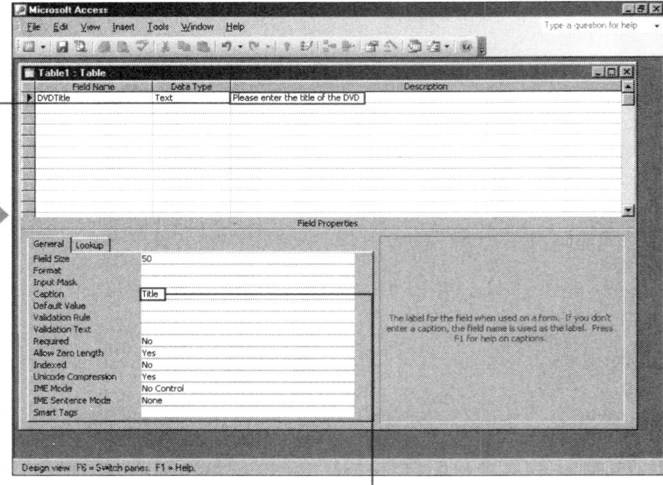

Note: This task uses the database AVP-Chapter01.mdb on the CD-ROM.

1 Open a database and click the Tables group.

2 Double-click Create a table in Design view.

■ A new table appears in Design view.

3 Type the name you want in the Field Name property of the first field.

■ The field is named DVDTitle.

■ This task uses the default Data Type property of Text.

4 Type the description you want to appear in the Description property for the first field.

5 Type the text for the caption in the Caption property field.

Extra

The Data Type property helps you control what type of data goes into a field. The most common data type used, and the default, is the Text data type. This data type accepts alphanumeric type values, such as names, addresses, phone numbers, and zip codes. In other words, it accepts any value that you do not use for mathematical expressions. Other data types can be seen in the table.

DATA TYPE	DESCRIPTION
Text	Alphanumeric values up to 256 characters long.
Memo	Alphanumeric values up to 65,535 characters long.
Number	Various numeric types such as Long, Single, and Integer. The Size property of the field controls the size of the numeric value.
Date/Time	Used to store Date or Time values. The Format property allows you to specify how you want to display Date and Time values with options such as Short Date and Long Date.
Currency	Dollar values that reflect the localized version of Access and Windows that you are using.
AutoNumber	Used to create primary key fields. This Long Integer type number creates unique records.
Yes/No	This is a Boolean value, also represented by True/False and –1/0.
Ole Object	Various objects such as graphic files, Word documents, Excel worksheets.
Hyperlink	Links to Web sites and e-mail can be described with display text.
Lookup Wizard	Creates properties that can be used to display lookup values for a field. See the section "Specify Lookup Values" for more information.

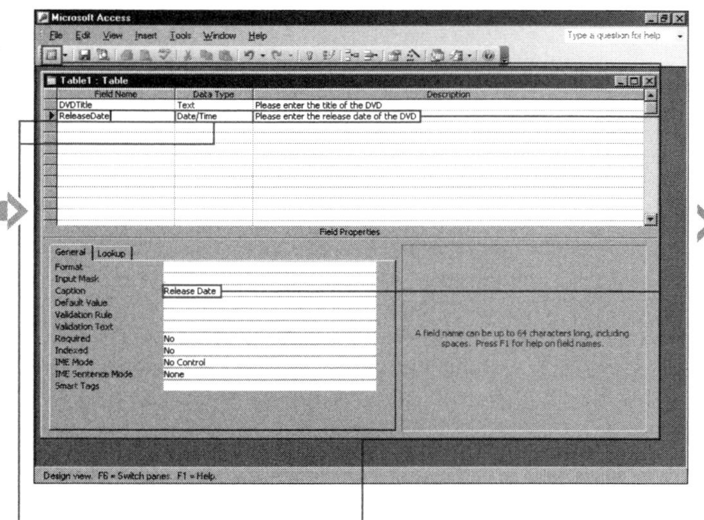

6 Type the name you want in the Field Name property of the second field.

7 Click the Data Type property drop-down list and choose Date/Time.

8 Type the description you want to appear in the Description property for the second field.

9 Type the text for the caption in the Caption property field.

10 Click the View button.

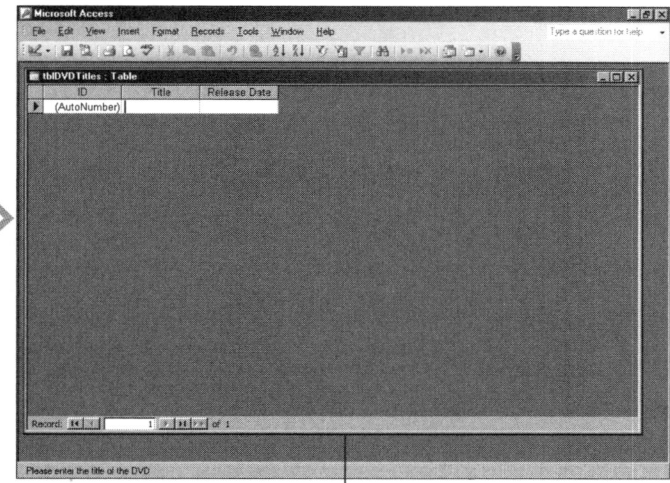

■ A dialog box appears, and asks if you want to save changes to the design of the table.

11 Click Yes.

■ A Save As dialog box appears.

12 Type a name in the Table Name field, and click OK.

■ A dialog box appears, and asks if you want Access to create a primary key for the table.

13 Click Yes.

■ The new table appears in Datasheet view, with the three fields displayed.

CREATE AN INPUT MASK

You can use the Input Mask property to control how users enter data into your tables. For example, you can use this property to ensure that users type phone numbers, zip codes, and Social Security numbers correctly in the fields.

With the Input Mask property, you can specify how to enter the data; which literal characters — dashes used in Social Security numbers for example — to use; and what you want to use as a place marker for data that users enter — an example and default for the place marker is the underscore character, _. For example, the syntax for the Input Mask for a Social Security number is as follows: `000-00-0000;;_`.

The number 0 indicates that users can only enter digits. Access cannot save literal characters with the data, and the underscore is used as a place marker. The semicolons (;) are used to separate the format parameters, much like the comma is used for parameters in routines.

Besides the number 0, which specifies digits only, you can use other character masks. Examples include # for characters or digits, entry not required; and the number 9 for either a digit or a space, entry not required. To see more examples of character masks, you can press F1 while the cursor is within the Input Mask property.

You can also use the Input Mask property to specify a mask for password-type fields. To perform this task, you can type the word PASSWORD into the Input Mask property.

Microsoft supplies an Input Mask Wizard that creates some masks for some of the more common tasks, such as those in this section. The wizard walks you through each of the sections that you can specify. It takes the options you specify, and updates the Input Mask property.

CREATE AN INPUT MASK USING THE WIZARD

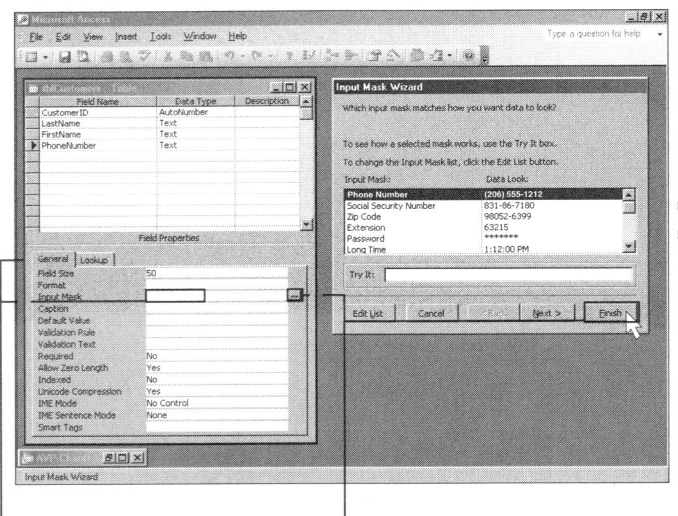

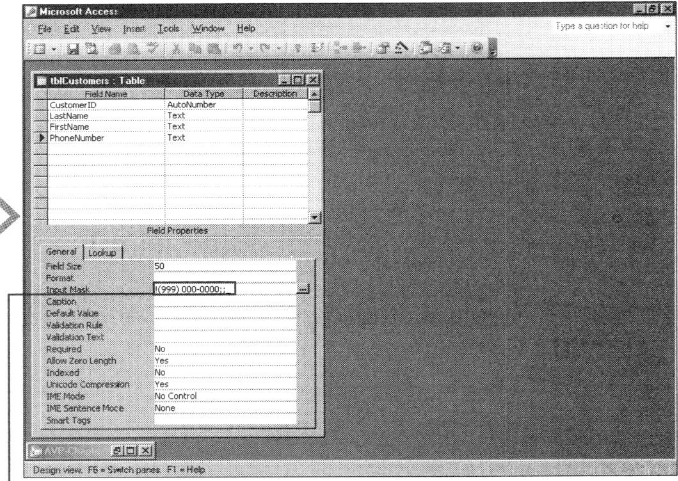

1 Create a new table with multiple fields.

■ Specify Field Names and Data Types for each field.

2 Click in the Input Mask property field.

3 Click the Builder button.

■ A Save Table dialog box appears, and asks if you want to save the table.

4 Click Yes.

■ The Input Mask Wizard appears.

5 Click Finish.

■ Access places the final mask in the Input Mask property.

Extra

The Input Mask Wizard includes a number of other input masks. You can also create your own mask or edit current masks that the wizard supplies. To do this, follow steps 3 and 4 in the section below, and then click the Edit List command button. The individual input masks appear. Be careful when you edit the existing entries because you could make them unusable.

The list of existing input masks includes:

MASK TITLE	
Phone Number	Long Time
Social Security Number	Short Date
Zip Code	Short Time
Extension	Medium Date
Password	Medium Time

Note that if you want the users to have a choice in how they enter date data, but want to display the date in Short Date format, then set the Format property to Short Date, and leave the Input Mask property blank.

CREATE AN INPUT MASK MANUALLY

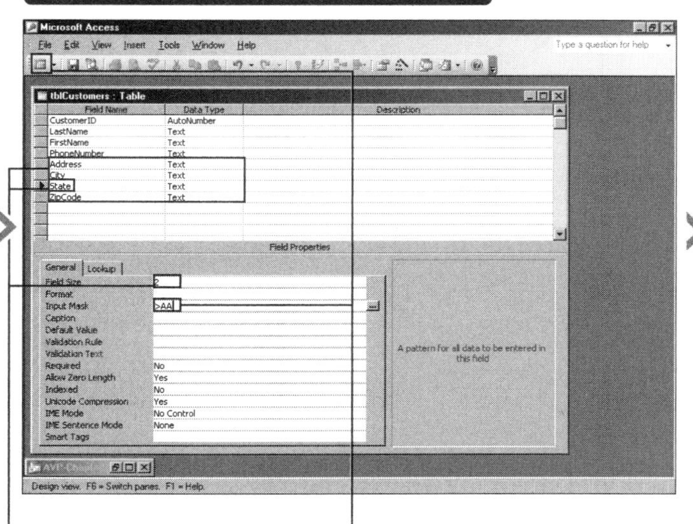

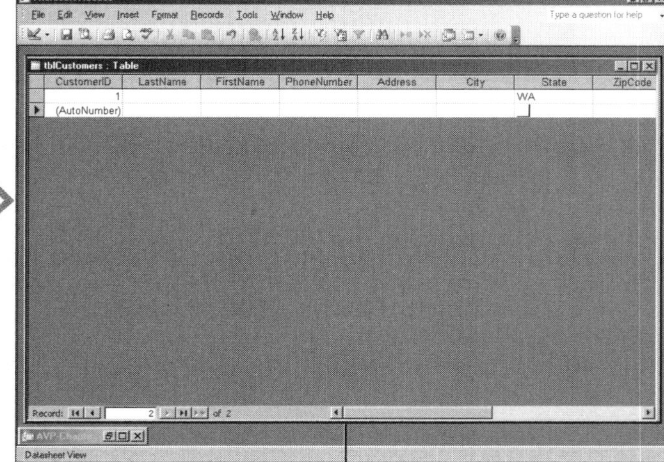

6 Add more fields to your table.

7 Click a field.

8 Type a number in the Field Size property field.

■ This example specifies a field size of two characters for the State field.

9 Type a character format in the Input Mask property field.

■ >AA represents two characters displayed in upper case in the State field.

10 Click the View button.

■ A dialog box appears, and asks if you want to save changes to the design of the table.

11 Click Yes.

12 Type the name in the Table Name field, and click OK.

■ A message box appears, and asks if you want Access to create a primary key for the table.

13 Click Yes.

■ The new table appears in Datasheet view.

ADD A VALIDATION RULE AND VALIDATION TEXT

While the Input Mask does a good job controlling how users enter data, there may be cases where you need to be more precise within the masked data. For example, you may want to limit dates that users enter into a date field such as an invoice date. You can add a Validation Rule to limit the date that the users enter to ensure that the date is either today or after. To do this you can type **>=Date()** in the Validation Rule property of the desired field.

As with a number of other table field properties, when you add a Validation Rule at the table level, forms, queries, and even importing data must pass the validation rule.

You can also make the Validation Rule more precise by using And, Or, or even Between, as shown here:

```
Between Date() and Date()+10
```

When the data does not pass the validation rule, Access returns a default message that may confuse the user. For example, if the user types an incorrect invoice date, this message appears:

```
One or more values are prohibited by
the validation rule '>=Date()' set for
'tblInvoices.InvoiceDate'. Enter a value
that the expression for this field can
accept.
```

This is not a user-friendly message. It includes information the user does not need to know, such as the table to which the field belongs. Use Another property, Validation Text, instead. By entering **Please enter a date that either is on or after today's date.** into the Validation Text property, a message box displays the text when the data does not pass the Validation Rule's setting.

ADD A VALIDATION RULE AND VALIDATION TEXT

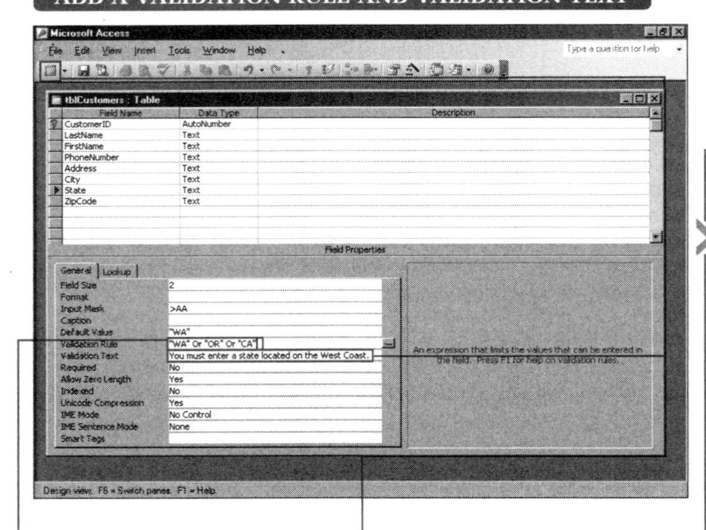

Note: This task uses tblCustomers in AVP-Chapter01.mdb on the CD-ROM.

1 Open a table in Design view.

2 Type values in the Validation Rule property field.

■ This validation rule limits state choices to WA, OR, or CA. Access adds the quotes.

3 Type a message in the Validation Text property field.

4 Click the View button.

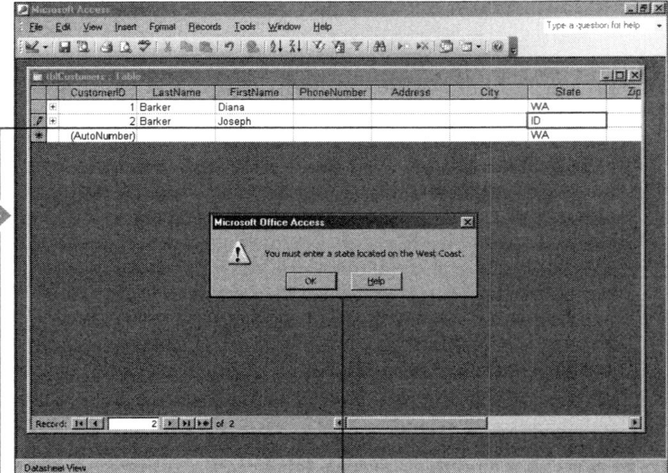

■ A dialog box asks if you want to save changes to the design of the table.

5 Click Yes.

6 Type an incorrect value into the column for which you added a Validation Rule, and press Enter.

■ This example uses the incorrect value ID in the State field.

■ A dialog box appears with the text you typed in step 3.

ADD THE DEFAULT VALUE AND REQUIRED PROPERTIES

When users enter data into your database, you may want to ensure that certain fields always contain data, and that the data is appropriate. To do this, you can use the Default Value and Required properties to guide the user in entering data correctly.

The Default Value property lets you specify a value that automatically appears in new records. This is useful for entries that usually require the same value. For example, an invoice may need the current date. If so, then you can type **=Date()** in the Default Value property field. You can use built-in functions, such as Date(), in your Default Value property, but you cannot use user-defined functions.

When you specify a value for the field's Default Value property, that value automatically appears in that field in the form. If you change the form control's Default Value property for the field, Access uses that value rather than the field level Default Value. For example, you can type **=Date()** at the table field level, and then overwrite the value on a form's text box control that uses the field as the ControlSource by typing **=Date()+1**.

The Required property tells Access that the user must enter a value into the field. You can activate this feature by setting the Required property for that field to True. When the Required property is set to True, and the user enters data into the field in either Datasheet view or Form view, then Access requires the user to enter data into this field as well. The same is true when data is being imported: An error occurs in those records that have null in the required field.

When the Required property is set to True on a field that is Text data type, and the user presses the space bar as the only character while editing data in the field, by default Access allows the entry in the field. If you want to make sure that the user enters more data than just a space, then you can set the Allow Zero Length property to False.

ADD THE DEFAULT VALUE AND REQURED PROPERTIES

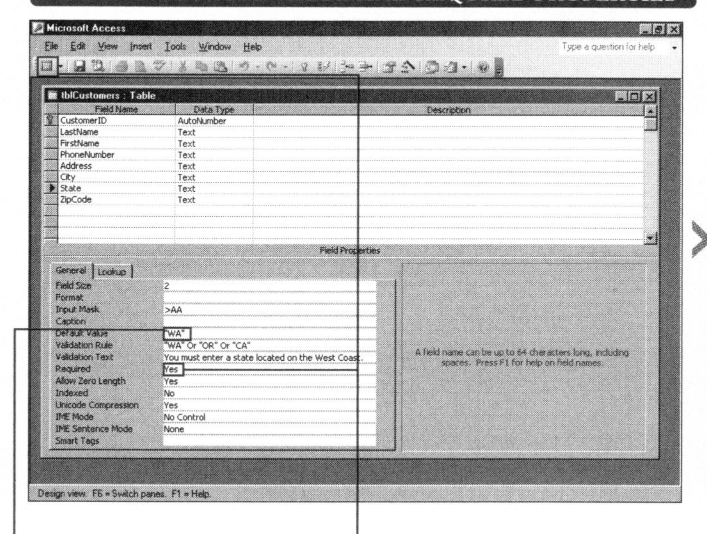

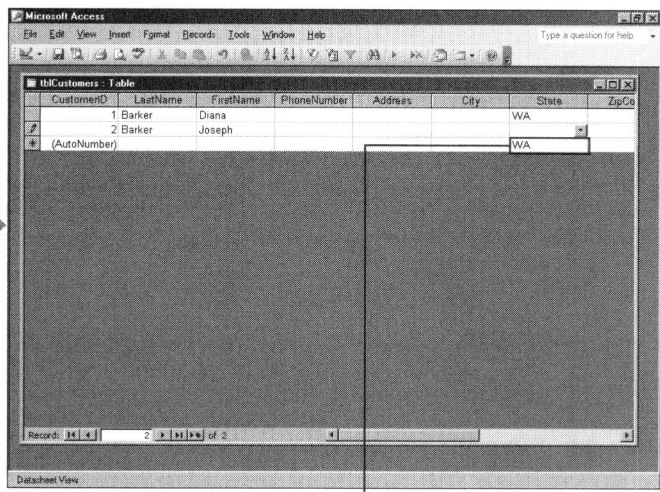

Note: This task uses tblCustomers in AVP-Chapter01.mdb on the CD-ROM.

1 Open a table in Design view.

2 Type a value in the Default Value property field of the field you select.

■ This example uses WA in the State field. Access adds the quotes.

3 Type **Yes** in the Required field.

4 Click the View button.

■ A dialog box asks if you want to save changes to the design of the table.

5 Click Yes.

6 Click in a cell for a new record.

■ The default value you specified in step 2 appears in the appropriate column by default.

■ If you delete the value from the field and try to save the record, an error message appears.

SPECIFY LOOKUP VALUES

In the continuing effort to control what data goes into your database, you can direct users as to what data you want them to enter. Although you can achieve this control through various properties such as Validation Rule and Input Mask, you can use another powerful tool to specify lookup values at the table field level. When you specify a lookup value, Access points the user to data in another table, and limits the user's entry to that table's data.

For example, you can use a lookup value to offer a limited selection of states that the user can enter in a field. If you use Validation Rule and Valuation Text, you specify that you want the State field Validation Rule to be "WA," "OR," or "CA." This is what you did in the table tblCustomers in the previous section. However, if you want to add another state, then you must go into the Validation Rule property and change it. A better way is to create a separate table, called tblValidStates for example, and enter each of the valid states into it. Another difference between lookup values and setting the Validation Rule property is that you can let the user add values to the fields using the lookup value if you choose to, but not to the field using the Validation Rule.

After creating the table, you can then change the Data Type of the State field to be Lookup Wizard in the tblCustomers table. When you do this, the Lookup Wizard helps you specify the table you want to use as the lookup table, and asks you to specify which fields to use from the lookup table for the combo box you create.

The resulting combo box displays a drop-down list filled with values from the lookup table when the table that uses the lookup value is viewed in Datasheet view or used in queries. Access also creates the combo box when you drop the field onto forms.

SPECIFY LOOKUP VALUES

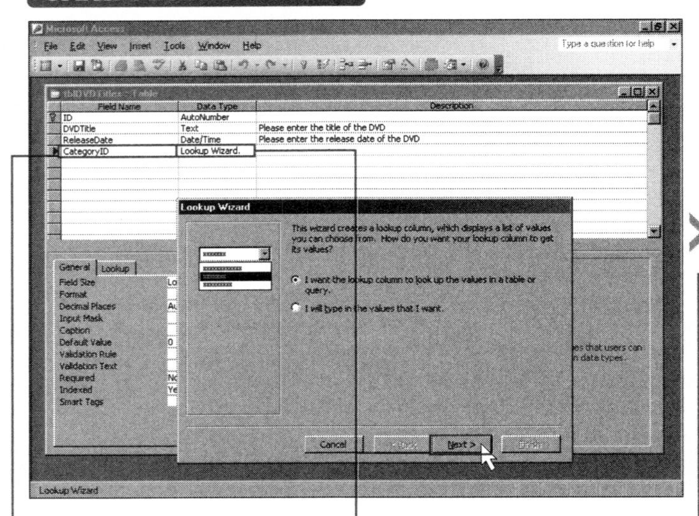

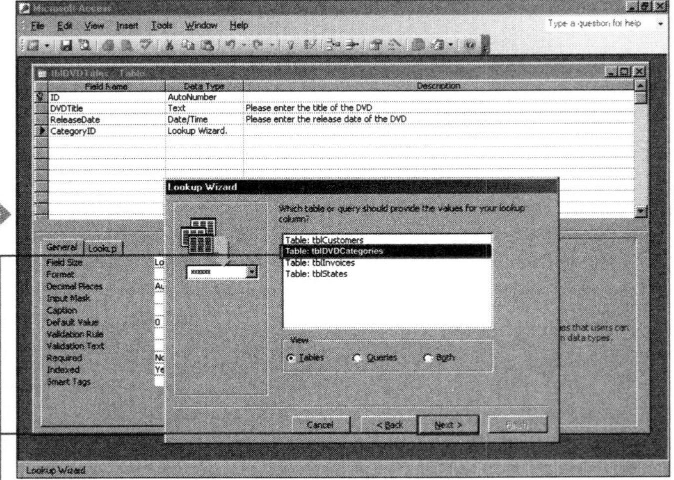

Note: This task uses tblDVDTitles in AVP-Chapter01.mdb on the CD-ROM.

1 Open a table in Design view.

2 Add a new field.

3 Click the Data Type drop-down list and select Lookup Wizard.

4 In the Lookup Wizard, click Next to accept the default of the wizard looking up the values in a table or query.

5 Click the table.

6 Click Next.

■ The wizard displays the list of fields from the table, tblDVDCategories in this example.

7 Click >> to select all fields.

■ The fields move to the right-hand column.

8 Click Next.

9 Click the field you want to sort. This example uses the Category field.

10 Click Next.

Extra

When you establish a field as being a lookup value, you can use a number of properties to change how the lookup is displayed. For example, you can use a list box instead of a combo box. The Properties section of the table designer includes two tabs, General and Lookup. Sections in this chapter show you the properties listed in the General tabs. If you go to the Lookup tab, you see the properties shown in the table below. These are common properties for list boxes and combo boxes and are discussed in Chapter 5.

PROPERTY	DESCRIPTION
Display Control	Text Box (no lookup), List Box, or Combo Box.
Row Source Type	Table/Query, Value List, or Field List.
Row Source	Table Name, Query Name, or SQL Select statement.
Bound Column	Column you want to use for the lookup value.
Column Count	Number of columns that the lookup uses.
Column Heads	Whether or not to display column headings in the list.
Column Widths	Widths for each of the columns in the list. Note that to hide a column, you can specify zero.
List Rows	Number of rows to display in the column.
List Width	Overall width of the displayed list.
Limit To List	Have Access limit the user's input to the list.

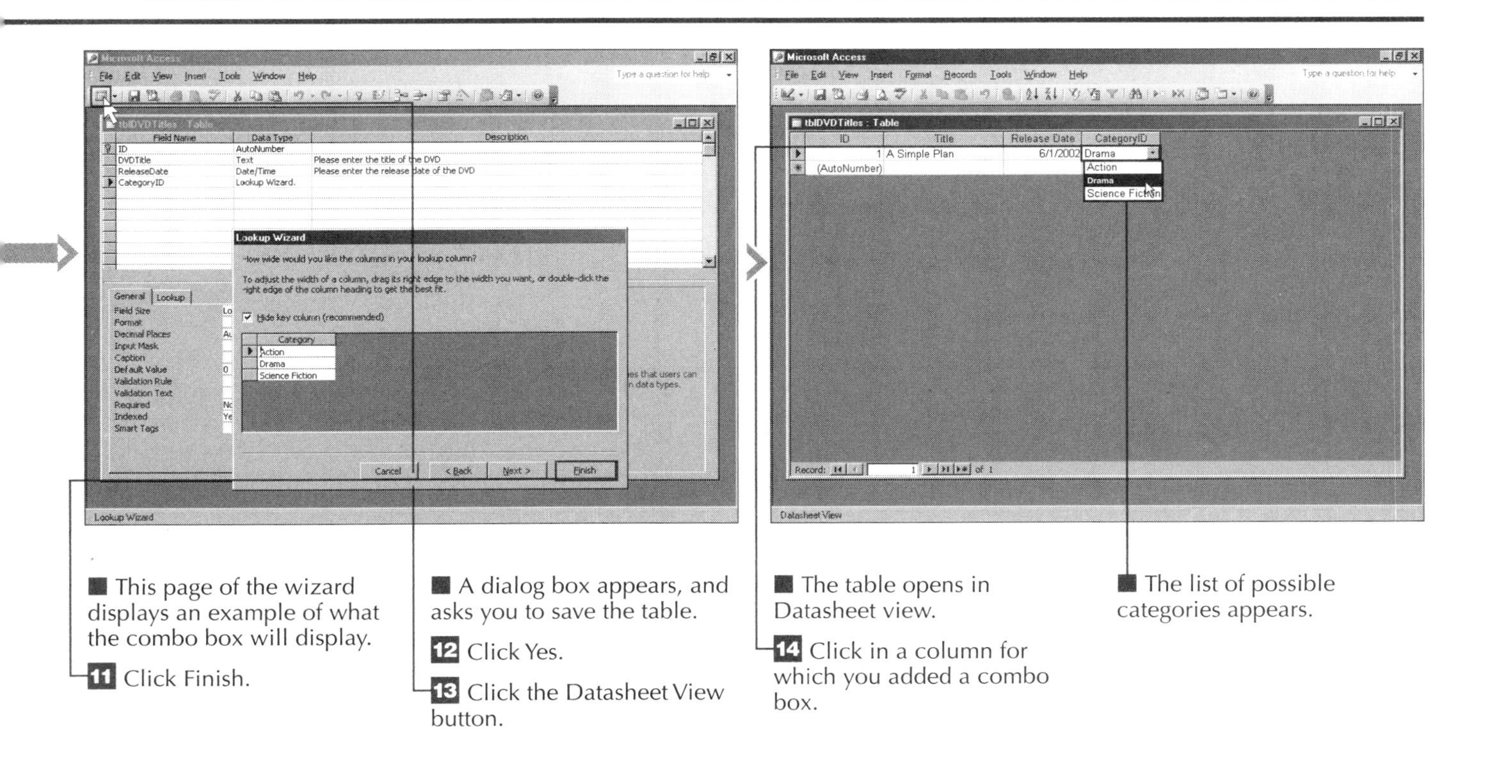

■ This page of the wizard displays an example of what the combo box will display.

11 Click Finish.

■ A dialog box appears, and asks you to save the table.

12 Click Yes.

13 Click the Datasheet View button.

■ The table opens in Datasheet view.

14 Click in a column for which you added a combo box.

■ The list of possible categories appears.

ESTABLISH RELATIONSHIPS

You can establish relationships between all tables in Access, as well as the referential integrity you want to specify between two tables. Referential integrity is used in a database to help make sure that data only goes into tables when records in a related table exist. For example, you may have a table that contains categories of DVDs and another that contains titles of DVDs. The relationship between these two tables is a one-to-many type, where you can assign many titles to one category.

To join two tables, you must first open the Relationships window, and then add the tables to the window. Next, you can create a line that represents a relationship between the tables. Based on which tables and fields you are joining, Access determines which type of relationship it is.

Note that Access creates relationships for you when you specify lookup tables. See the section "Specify Lookup Values" for more information.

After you create a join line between two tables, you can double-click the line and then specify how you want Access to handle your referential integrity. After you click the referential integrity check box, you can then select either the Cascade Update Related Fields option, or the Cascade Delete Related Records option. The Cascade Update option updates fields in related tables if you change a value in the Primary Key field. The Cascade Delete option deletes matching records in related tables when you delete a record. For example, if you delete a customer record, then Access deletes all of the invoices for that customer.

Note that when you have an AutoNumber data type for your Primary Key field and you set a relationship between that and another table, you do not need to worry about the Cascade Update Related Fields option: AutoNumber fields cannot be updated.

ESTABLISH RELATIONSHIPS

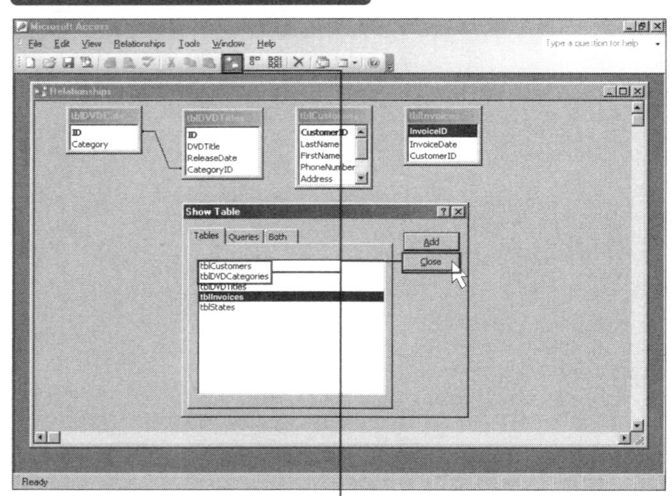

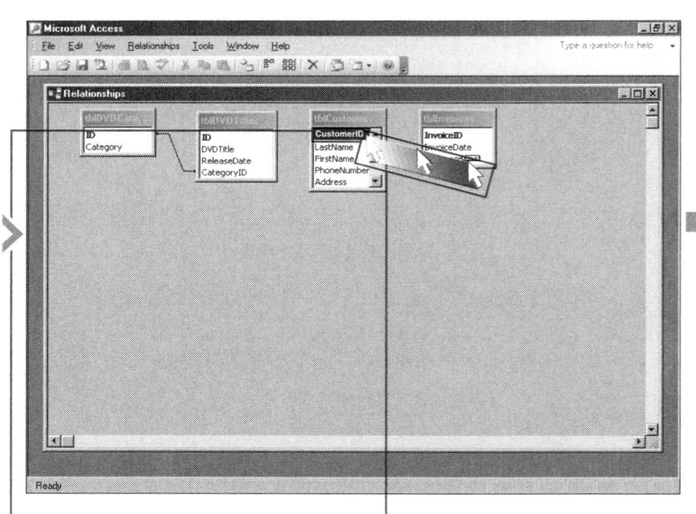

JOIN TABLES

Note: This task uses AVP-Chapter01.mdb on the CD-ROM.

1 Click Tools ➪ Relationships.

■ tblDVDCategories and tblDVDTitles are already in your database.

2 Click the Show Table button.

■ The Show Table dialog box appears.

3 Double-click tblCustomers and tblInvoices.

■ Access adds them to the Relationships window.

4 Click Close.

5 Click the CustomerID field in the tblCustomers table, holding the left mouse button down.

6 Drag the mouse over to the CustomerID field in the tblInvoices table.

Extra

In order to appreciate the changes you just made to the database, go into the Datasheet view of the tables and perform some tasks.

At this point, if you try to enter a value into the tblInvoices CustomerID field that does not match one found in tblCustomers, you get the following error message:

```
You cannot add or change a record because a
related record is required in 'tblCustomers'.
```

In the same manner, if you try to delete a record in tblCustomers that has invoices in tblInvoices, you get the following message:

```
Relationships that specify cascading deletes
are about to cause 1 record(s) in this table
and in related tables to be deleted.
```

When you create relationships between tables, the relationships help Access to query your database more efficiently, as discussed in the next chapter.

There are situations when you will want to choose Cascade Update Related Fields (☐ changes to ☑) in the Edit Relationships dialog box. When you have a primary key made up of an updatable field in a table, such as a social security number, and a related table that uses the same field as a foreign key, you can update the field in the primary table, and Access automatically updates the fields in the foreign table.

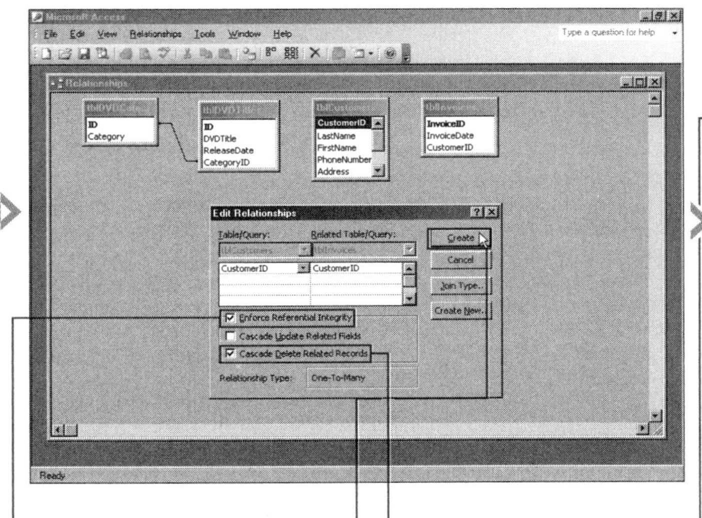

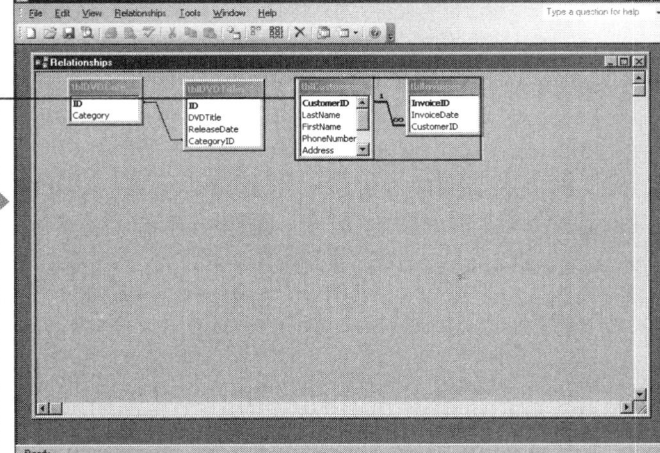

SPECIFY REFERENTIAL INTEGRITY

■ Access creates a one-to-many relationship between tblCustomers and tblInvoices.

■ The Edit Relationships dialog box appears.

7 Click Enforce Referential Integrity.

8 Click Cascade Delete Related Records.

Note: You do not need to check Cascade Update Related Fields because CustomerID is an AutoNumber field, which you cannot update.

9 Click Create.

■ A line appears between the fields, indicating a one-to-many relationship.

10 Click File ➪ Close.

■ The Relationships window closes.

LINK ACCESS TABLES

You may occasionally want to use data that belongs to somebody else, but rather than import the data, which brings the data into your database, you may just want to link to the data. You can link to another database, and that database becomes the back-end database, and the current database you are in becomes the front-end database.

Thus far you have worked with tables that are in the current database in which you are working. While this works great for small databases with which you or a couple of users are working, for larger databases with many users, it is sometimes better to break out the tables from the queries, forms, reports, and other Access objects.

To link to a table, you can click File ➪ Get External Data ➪ Link Tables. The Link dialog box appears and walks you through linking the table. It asks you the file you want to link to, with Access databases being the default. It then asks you to specify the files. After you link your Access table, an icon appears in the table list that looks like a regular Access table, but with an arrow pointing to it.

When you link to data from an Access database, you can update and query the data as if it were in your current database. This means that you can use the table as a record source for both forms and reports. The only task you cannot perform on the linked table is to modify the structure of the table. You can only view the structure of the table.

LINK ACCESS TABLES

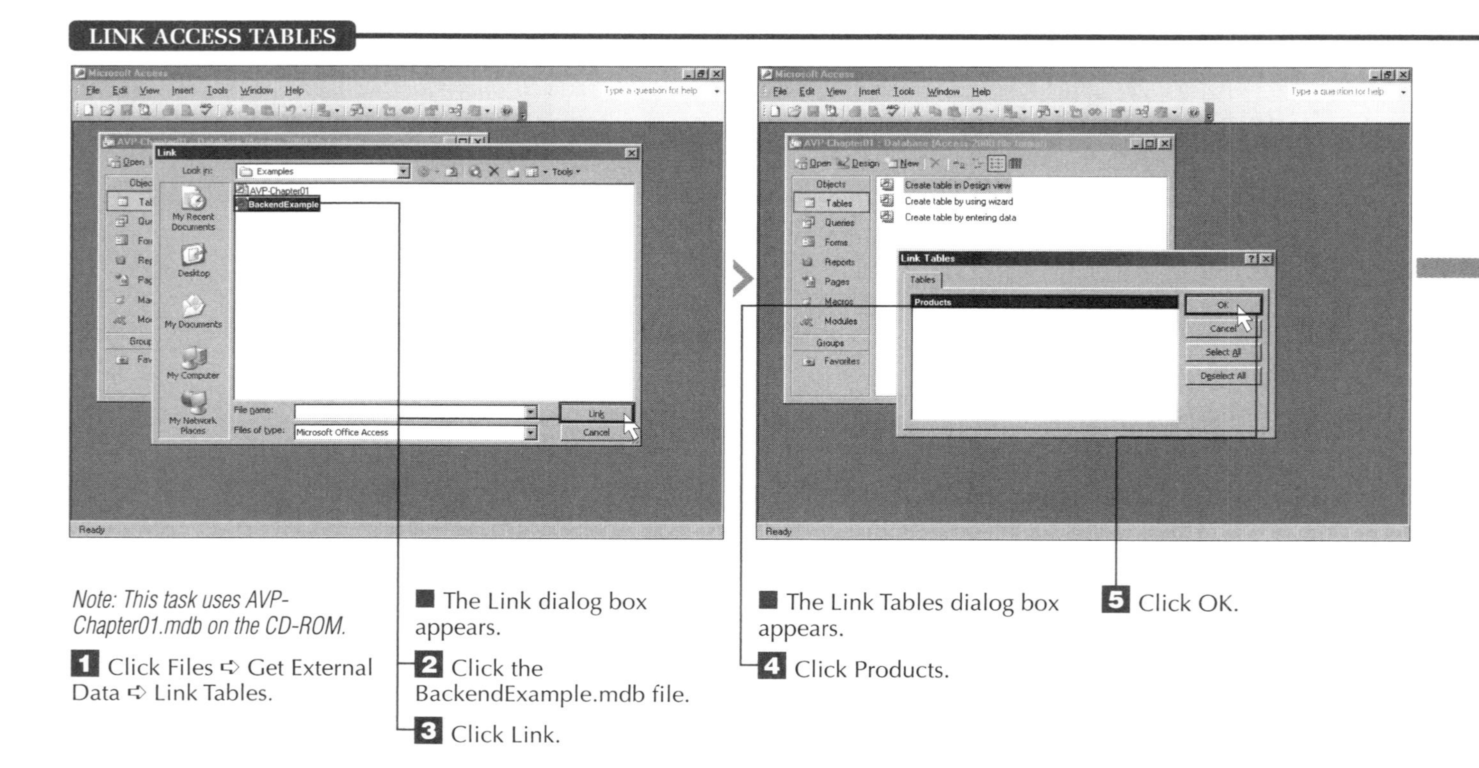

Note: This task uses AVP-Chapter01.mdb on the CD-ROM.

1 Click Files ➪ Get External Data ➪ Link Tables.

■ The Link dialog box appears.

2 Click the BackendExample.mdb file.

3 Click Link.

■ The Link Tables dialog box appears.

4 Click Products.

5 Click OK.

Extra

The links in your database can occasionally break. For example, this can occur if the linked database, or table, is deleted or moved. If you unintentionally delete the back-end database or table, then you must restore it from a backup, if you have one. If the back-end database is on a file server, and the network is down, then you must wait until the network reconnects.

If the back-end database has been moved, then you get the following error message:

```
Could not find file 'file path\filename.mdb'
```

When this happens, you can use a utility included in Access called the Link Table Manager. You can open the Link Table Manager by clicking Tools ➪ Database Utilities ➪ Link Table Manager. When the Link Table Manager dialog box appears, check the link (☐ changes to ☑) you want to manage from the list of linked tables in the database, and then click OK. The Open File dialog box appears. When you locate the file, click OK. The table then re-links.

Note that you can also right-click the tables list, and choose Link Table Manager, located at the bottom of the menu.

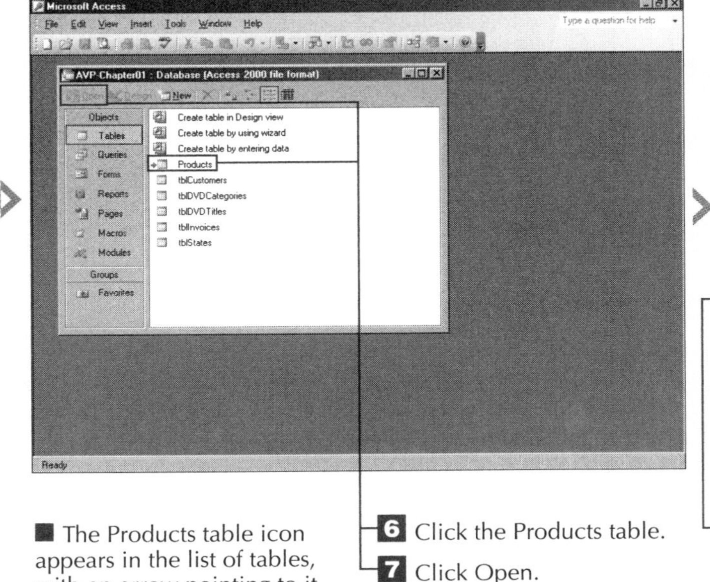

■ The Products table icon appears in the list of tables, with an arrow pointing to it.

6 Click the Products table.

7 Click Open.

■ The Products table window appears in Datasheet view.

■ You can update the data as if it were in the same database.

LINK SQL SERVER TABLES

You can link to several different file formats in Access. Along with Access files, you can link to text files, Excel worksheets, FoxPro database files, and SQL Server tables.

SQL Server is a very large database system. It is also called Client Server. A client server system performs work such as querying on the server where it is located. Although you can link to a client server system such as SQL Server, when you link to the tables, you are not really taking advantage of the client server.

Linking to an SQL Server database requires a bit more work than linking Access tables. To link to an SQL Server table you need to use a Data Source, or DSN. When you create a DSN, a file is created that tells Access the database file type to which you are connecting. When you create a DSN for SQL Server, you must also specify which SQL Server and database to which you are connecting. Lastly, you must also specify which kind of security you want to use, Windows Authentication, SQL Server security, or Mixed.

Note also that in order to perform these tasks you must have access to an SQL Server database. Talk with your network administrator for help locating an SQL Server database to use. For this book, a locally installed version of SQL Server is used with the Northwind database that now comes with SQL Server Developer Edition. Also, the Windows Integrated option is used. Another option is to use the Microsoft SQL Server Desktop Edition, or MSDE, which comes with your Office CD-ROM. However, the client tools are not included.

LINK SQL SERVER TABLES

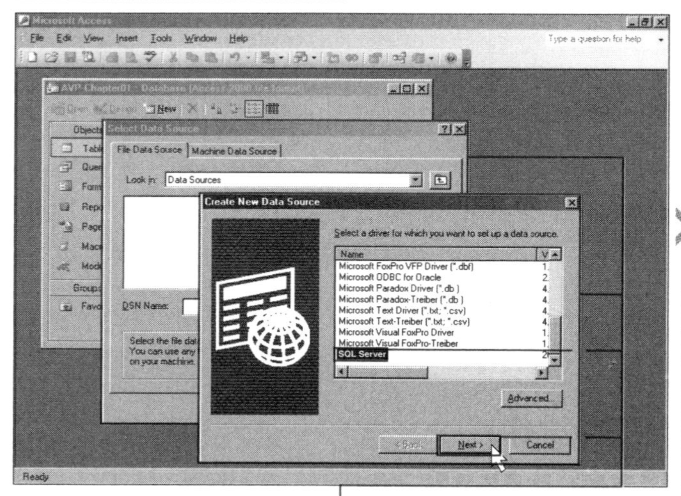

Note: This task uses AVP-Chapter01.mdb on the CD-ROM.

1 Click Files ➪ Get External Data ➪ Link Tables.

■ The Link dialog box appears.

2 Choose ODBC Databases in the Files of type field.

■ The Select Data Source dialog box appears.

3 Click New.

■ The Create New Data Source dialog box appears.

4 Click SQL Server

5 Click Next.

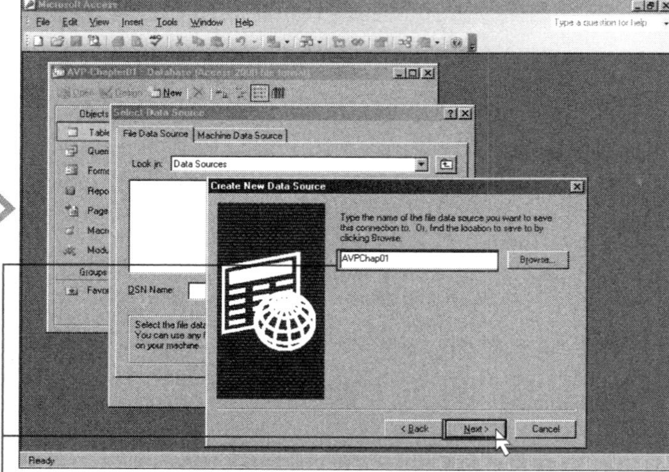

■ A new dialog box appears, and asks you for the filename of the new DSN.

6 Type **AVPChap01**.

7 Click Next.

■ The final page of the Create New Data Source dialog box appears.

8 Click Finish.

Extra

The way in which your administrator sets up your SQL Server security can affect how difficult it is for you to access the SQL Server. If the security is set up using Windows NT authentication, then SQL Server simply uses the network login that the administrator assigns to you. If you use the SQL Server security or Mixed, then, depending on which version of SQL Server you use, you must have a separate login and password whenever you need to utilize the SQL Server, which can be inconvenient.

If you use SQL Server security, then the default user is "sa" with a blank password. However, many administrators change this user and password for security reasons.

When you use Windows NT authentication, you, or the Windows group to which you belong, still need to be added to the SQL Server users and groups to access the database. Again, your SQL Server administrator should take care of this for you.

Another choice for security is mixed SQL Server and Windows authentication, which allows for different databases in an SQL Server, each using one or the other security methods. Generally, this is an option for older servers that are upgraded to the later operating systems and versions of SQL Server.

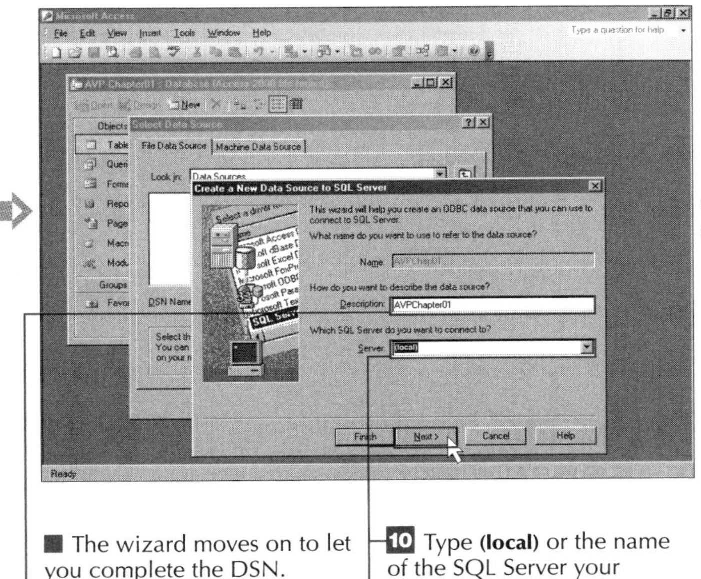

■ The wizard moves on to let you complete the DSN.

9 Type **AVPChapter01** for the Description of the DSN.

10 Type **(local)** or the name of the SQL Server your administrator has given you.

11 Click Next.

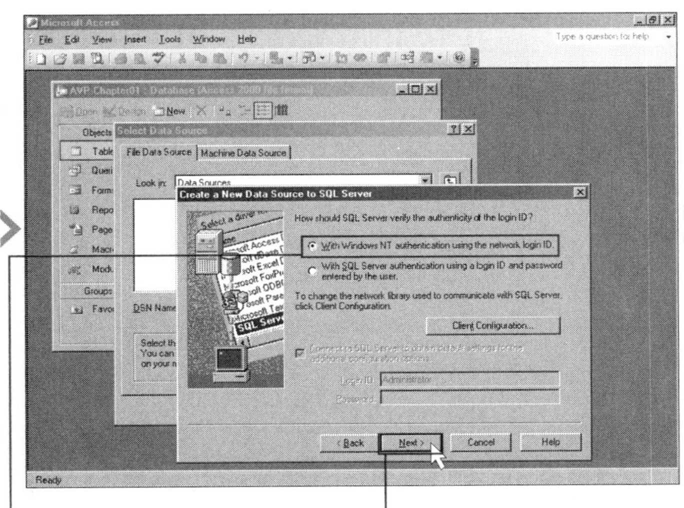

■ A dialog box appears, and asks how you want to handle SQL Server security for the database.

12 Select With Windows NT authentication using the network login ID.

13 Click Next.

Note: Again, this depends upon how your administrator has set up your SQL Server.

CONTINUED

LINK SQL SERVER TABLES (CONTINUED)

After you select the type of security you want to use, you can specify which database you want SQL Server to attach using this connection. If you want to attach multiple databases, then you can use multiple DSNs as well.

After you create the DSN, you must go through the same basic steps that you would to link to Access tables. You can select one or multiple tables at a time when using the Link Table dialog box. Whenever you need to link future tables to the same SQL Server database from any of your Access databases, you can use the same DSN file.

When you are using SQL Server tables, you must establish a primary key for the table in order to update the table. If you link to a table in SQL Server that does not have a unique field, then a dialog box appears, and asks you to specify a unique field.

Remember that although you are connecting to an SQL Server database, you cannot really take advantage of the power of the database when you use linked tables, because the Access database engine, called JET, actually performs the queries on the front-end. If you want to take full advantage of SQL Server-enhanced performance for large amounts of data while using Access, then you can create an Access Data Project, or ADP. ADPs are not covered in this book, because you would then need to use SQL Server's views and stored procedures, and other data elements.

LINK SQL SERVER TABLES (CONTINUED)

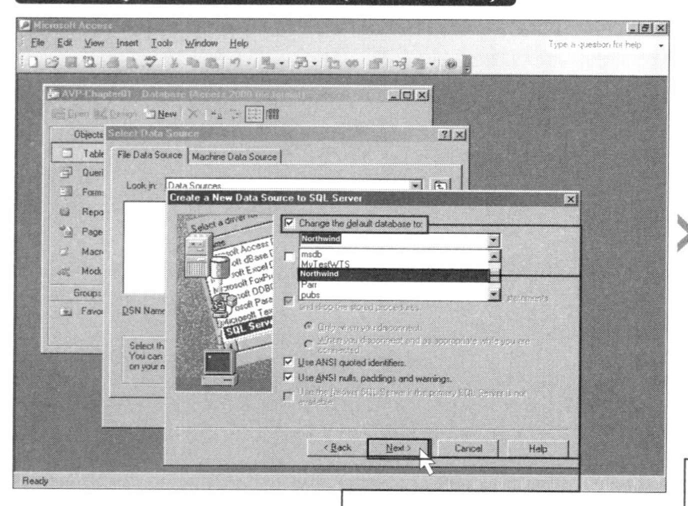

■ A dialog box appears, and asks you to select the database to which you want to connect.

14 Click the Change the default database to check box.

15 Click Northwind.

16 Click Next.

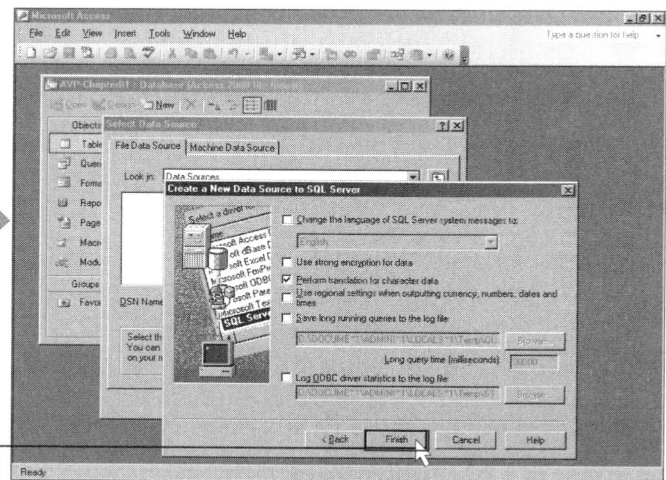

■ A dialog box appears, with a selection of default values you can use for the database.

17 Click Finish.

■ A dialog box appears, displaying information about the DSN that Access is creating.

18 Click OK.

■ You return to the Select Data Source dialog box.

19 Click OK.

■ Access selects the new DSN you just created.

Extra

Open Database Connectivity, or ODBC, drivers are available for various file formats, and companies can create their own drivers to help Access users connect to their file formats. With the drivers, Access users avoid having to learn all the specific commands necessary for accessing data from the various file formats, and so they can access the data using the same tools as the native file format.

You can now use the DSN that you create in the steps below, when linking other Northwind SQL Server tables from this, or other, Access tables. To do this, create a new Access database, and then click File ⇨ Get External Data ⇨ Link Tables.

In the Link dialog box, select ODBC Databases and click OK. You can choose the same DSN that you have already created, by looking in the File Data Source tab, and clicking AVPChap01, then OK. Select dbo.Employees from the list of tables, and then click OK.

You should now see dbo_Employees in the list of tables in Access.

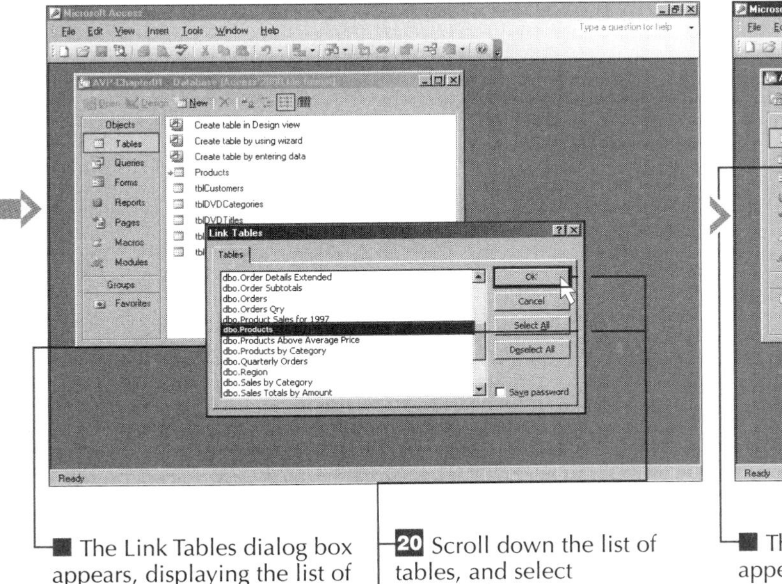

■ The Link Tables dialog box appears, displaying the list of tables from the Northwind database.

20 Scroll down the list of tables, and select dbo.Products.

21 Click OK.

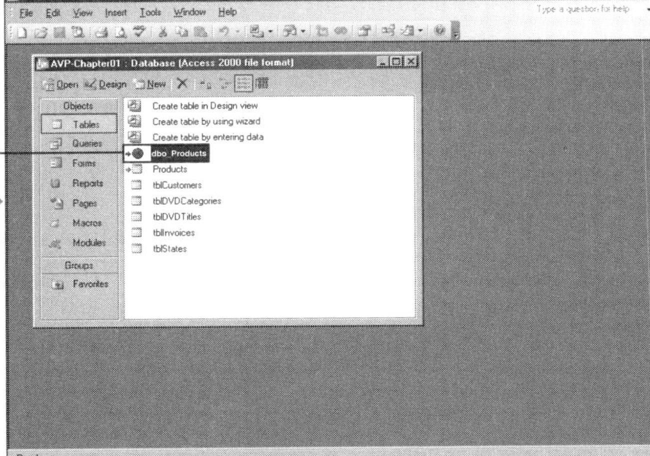

■ The dbo_Products icon appears in the Tables list in your database, with a world icon and an arrow beside it.

UNDERSTANDING SQL

After you enter data into your database, you need to have a means for retrieving that information. In order to accomplish this task in Access you can use queries. Access includes a query designer to help you create your queries. As in many other relational databases, queries in Access are made up of commands, called statements, in a language called SQL, or Structured Query Language.

Access uses SQL for many purposes, including as record sources for forms and reports, and as row sources for combo and list boxes.

SYNTAX OF AN SQL STATEMENT

While you can use the query designer for the majority of the tasks you need to perform, you may sometimes want to type in SQL directly, so it is a good idea to learn the basics. SQL statements are not case sensitive; this Query Design view formats SQL statements its own way, by capitalizing key statements, and placing the semicolon at the end. The semicolon (;) is not required, and in fact causes problems if you use the SQL statement directly in SQL Server.

Basic SQL Statements

SQL statements are somewhat like the English language in how you tell the database what information you want from the tables. For example, if want to retrieve all the company names of the customers in the tblCustomers table, you can type a SELECT statement like this:

```
SELECT tblCustomers.CompanyName FROM
tblCustomers;
```

In the statement above, CompanyName is a field from the tblCustomers table. When using a single table, the table name is not required by SQL when specifying individual field names.

The SELECT statement is the most common statement used in SQL, and while it can be used as shown above by itself, it can also be used as part of some other type of query.

Additional Clauses

You can also add additional operators and clauses onto the basic SELECT statement. For example, when you need to sort the results, you can use the `ORDER BY` clause with the field name. So if you want to sort the results of the last SELECT statement displayed by the Region field, you can type the following:

```
SELECT tblCustomers.CompanyName,
tblCustomers.Region FROM tblCustomers
ORDER BY tblCustomers.Region;
```

Additional Clauses (continued)

When you need to use criteria, which allow you to compare fields to specified values, and return records based on them, you can use the WHERE clause. Shown here is a SELECT statement that displays companies located in Seattle.

```
SELECT tblCustomers.CompanyName,
tblCustomers.City FROM tblCustomers WHERE
(((tblCustomers.City)="Seattle"));
```

Using criteria is discussed further, starting in the section "Add Simple Criteria to a Query." Additional clauses will be introduced throughout this and the next chapter.

Including All Fields

When you want to use all the fields in the table, you can include an asterisk (*), as shown here:

```
SELECT tblCustomers.* FROM tblCustomers;
```

You should include only those fields that are necessary from a table for both security and performance reasons.

Access, SQL, and ANSI

The default used by Access is a version of SQL called ANSI-89; SQL Server uses ANSI-92. In Access versions 97 and before, only ANSI-89 could be used, but in Access 2000 and after, you can use ANSI-92. To set this feature you can click Tools ⇨ Options, click the Tables/Queries tab, and then choose ANSI-92. With ANSI-92 you can make your SQL more SQL-Server compatible, and take advantage of some of the new SQL features in ANSI-92. However, if SQL Server compatibility is not an issue, you can just use the default.

TYPES OF QUERIES FOUND IN ACCESS

To modify and use information in your database, Access, and SQL, supply different types of queries. Which query type you use depends on your need.

SELECT QUERY

Use this as a base for forms and reports, and for simply displaying information.

AGGREGATE QUERIES

Aggregate queries summarize and total information. The results that are returned are read-only and can be used for reports.

Totals Query	Crosstab Query
Use this to summarize data. Functions available are Sum, Count, STD, and First and Last (occurrence).	Using this, you can cross-tabulate your totals. Crosstab queries are similar to, but not as flexible as Excel's pivot table.

BULK OPERATION QUERIES

You can use Bulk Operation queries, also called Action queries, when you need to perform tasks against a number of records based on criteria.

Update Query	Make Table Query
Use this to update individual fields in one or more tables.	This creates a new table in either the current database or a different database.
Append Query	**Delete Query**
Use this to add additional records to an existing table.	Use this to delete records based on criteria you specify.

SQL SPECIFIC QUERIES

These queries are not available in Query Design view.

Union Query

You can combine two or more separate record sources that have the same number of fields into one set of results. For example, you can combine records containing the LastName and FirstName fields from tblEmployees with the same fields in tblImportedEmployees. If you have nine records in tblEmployees, and two records in tblImportedEmployees, Access returns 11 records in the query results. The SQL looks like this:

Union Query (continued)

```
Select LastName, FirstName FROM
tblEmployees UNION SELECT LastName,
FirstName FROM tblImportedEmployees;
```

Data Definition Query

You can use this to create tables, relationships, and other data structures in your database

Pass-Through Query

You can use this to call stored procedures directly through to an SQL Server. This book does not cover Pass-Through queries in detail.

CREATE A BASIC QUERY

You can use the Query Designer in Access to create the necessary SQL statements by pointing and clicking, rather than by using the SQL statements directly.

When you use the Query Designer, Access first asks you to choose the table or tables that you want to include in the query results. You can also use other queries as well.

After you choose the tables and/or queries to include, the Query Designer appears. The Query Designer window has two main areas: The upper part displays the record sources for the query, and the lower part displays the query design grid. For each of the record sources included, you see a field list. The field list lets you select which fields to include: You can click and drag the fields onto the query design grid. The query design grid is where you specify the information you want the query to display, such as which columns you want to include in the results, what criteria you want to use, or how you want to sort it. You can also add columns by double-clicking the fields in the field lists.

In the query design grid, you can rearrange the order of the columns by clicking the top of a column and dragging it to the desired location in the designer. Note that when you rearrange the columns, the new arrangement is not necessarily reflected in the datasheet results when it is displayed in Datasheet view.

When you are ready to view your query results, you can click the View toolbar button, which shows the results in Datasheet view. You can then rearrange the columns when you are in Datasheet view.

CREATE A BASIC QUERY

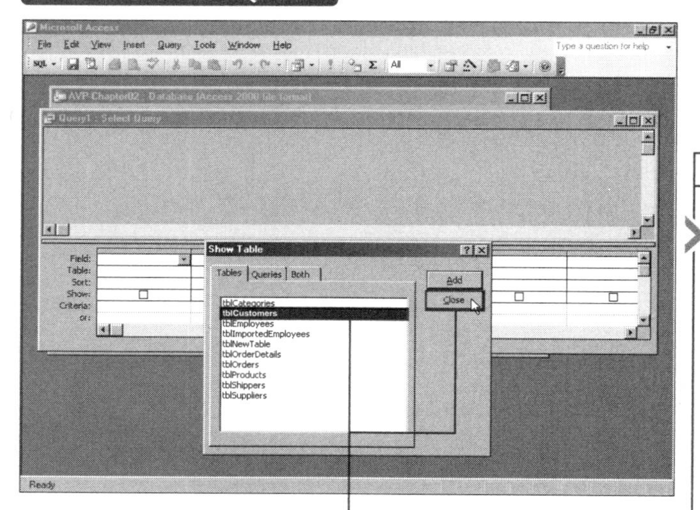

Note: This task uses the database AVP-Chapter02.mdb on the CD-ROM.

1 Open a database.

2 Click the Queries group.

■ The list of existing queries appears.

3 Double-click Create query in Design View.

■ The Show Table dialog box appears.

4 Double-click a table.

■ This example uses the tblCustomers table.

5 Click Close.

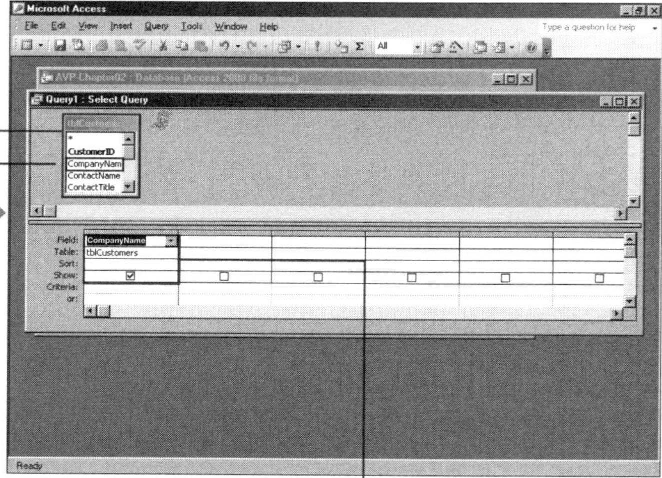

■ The table you chose is now displayed in the upper pane of the Query Designer.

6 Double-click a field in the table's field list.

■ That field is now displayed in the query design grid.

Extra

There are a number of rows in the query design grid where you create the various types of queries, including Select. The first row is the Field row, which contains the fields you select, CompanyName and ContactName in this example. The second row is also self-explanatory, listing the table or query from which each of the columns comes. Here are the other rows in the Select type query:

ROW TITLE	DESCRIPTION
Sort	Allows you to specify the sort order of the columns, discussed in the next section, "Sort Columns."
Show	Enables you to display or hide individual columns. Useful when you want to hide a column that is being used for criteria.
Criteria	This row lets you control which data, or rows, are included in the results. Discussed further starting in the section "Add Simple Criteria to a Query," later in this chapter.

These rows change depending on which type of query you are using. In the following sections in this chapter, the different query types will be discussed, as well as which rows are displayed in the query design grid for each type.

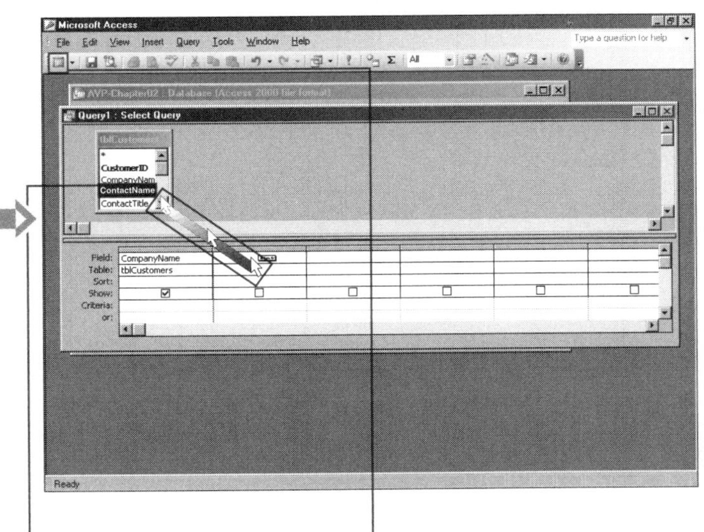

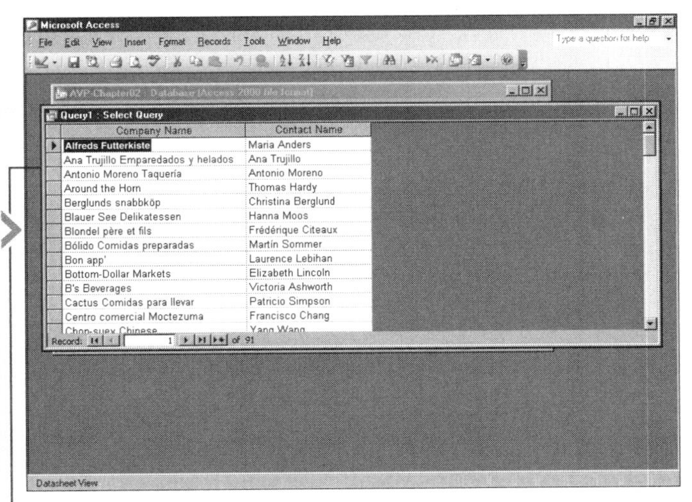

7 Click and hold the left mouse button on a field in the tblCustomers field list.

■ This example uses the ContactName field.

8 Drag the mouse to the first open column in the query design grid.

■ The field appears in the column.

9 Click the Datasheet View button.

■ The results datasheet appears, showing the fields you selected as columns.

■ When you close the datasheet, Access asks if you want to save the query. You can name and save the query, or click the Design View button (⧉) for the next task.

SORT COLUMNS

When you pull fields into your queries, and then view the results, records are listed in the order of the primary key field for the record source of the query. However, you can tell Access to order your results using a specific field, or fields, that you specify. To accomplish this, you can use the Sort row in the query design grid.

When you want to specify the sort order based on a column, you can set the sort order in the column to either Ascending or Descending.

If you want to include two fields in the sort order, you can specify the sort order in the two fields. Note that Access sorts the fields from left to right, so if you want to sort using one field first, put that field to the left of the other field in the query design grid. For example, if you want to sort using first the Region and then the City fields in the tblCustomers table, then you must place the Region field to the left of the City field in the query design grid.

When you set the order using two fields, you can set the first column to Ascending and the second column to Descending if desired.

There is no limit to the number of columns you can sort, but remember to have them in the correct order in the query design grid.

You can hide a sorted column if you want the results in a certain order but do not want the sort column or columns displayed. However, if you do this it may be somewhat confusing to the person who is viewing the results and is not aware of the sort order.

SORT COLUMNS

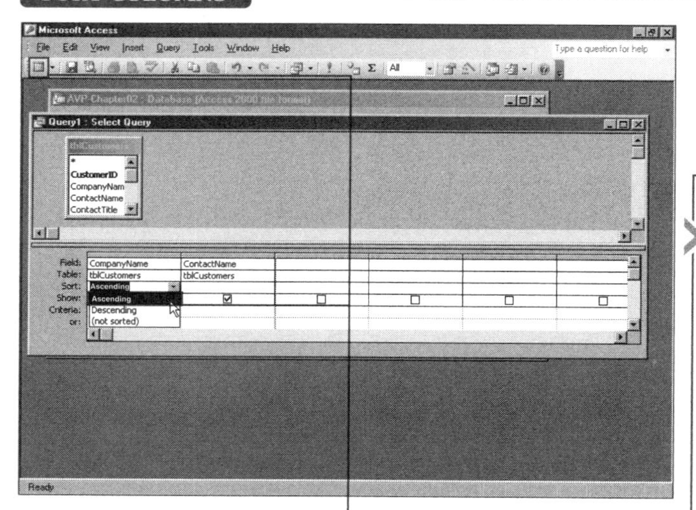

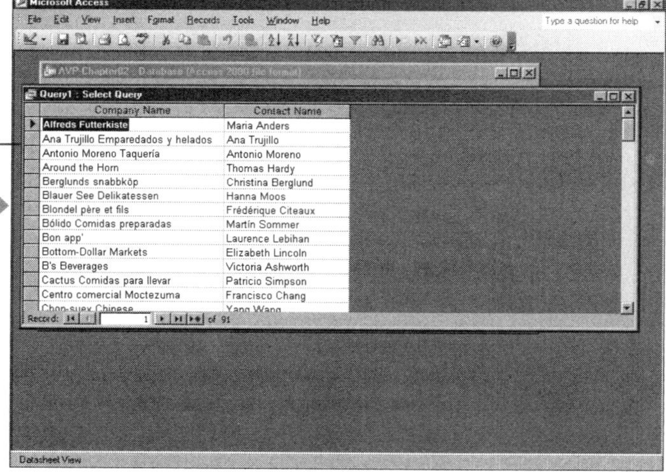

Note: This task uses the query qrySortColumns in the database AVP-Chapter02.mdb on the CD-ROM.

1 In Design view, open a database, and open a query.

2 Select a sort order from the Sort row.

3 Click the Datasheet View button.

■ The results datasheet appears in the new order. In this example, the records are sorted alphabetically by company name.

VIEW AND MODIFY SQL DIRECTLY

Although you can create queries in the Query Design view without reference to SQL, you may sometimes want to view and modify SQL directly. While Access does a great job of protecting you from SQL in day-to-day interaction with your databases, it is a good idea to become comfortable with reading SQL directly, and even modifying it.

There are benefits of having some knowledge of SQL statements. Even though Access lets you modify SQL using the Query Design view, when Access displays your query in form and control properties, it displays the SQL, unless you have saved your SQL to a named query. Form and control properties are discussed starting in Chapter 4.

After you save your query in the Query Design view, you can change to the SQL view to see the syntax of your query by clicking View ➪ SQL View.

Besides viewing the SQL, you can edit the SQL when in the SQL view. You want to be careful when editing your query, because you can break your query by having the wrong syntax in the SQL itself.

When you modify SQL statements using the SQL view, you can switch back to the Query Design view, and your changes are reflected immediately. Writing the SQL statements directly and switching to the Design view is a great way to practice writing your SQL statements.

Also, if you want to learn SQL, you can design some queries using the Query Design view, and then switch over to SQL view to read them. What you will find is that the SQL statements get easier to read the more you read them. As you create more complex queries, however, the SQL statements do get tougher to read.

Note that when you save a query in SQL view, the next time you open the query for modification, it will still be in SQL view.

VIEW AND MODIFY SQL DIRECTLY

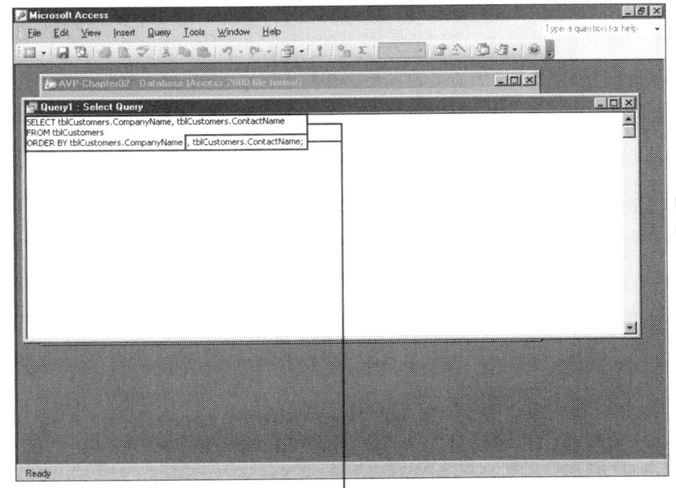

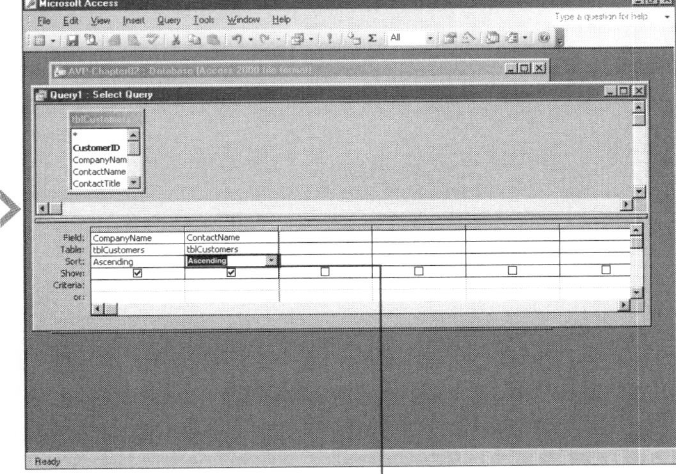

Note: This task uses the query qryViewModifySQLDirectly in AVP-Chapter02.mdb on the CD-ROM.

1 In Design view, open a database, and open a query.

2 Click View ➪ SQL View.

■ The SQL for the query appears.

3 Type the field names that you want to determine sort order between other field names. Begin with a comma to use SQL syntax.

■ This example uses tbl Customers.ContactName.

4 Click the Design View button (▣).

■ The field you specified in step 3 has the Sort row set to Ascending.

ADD SIMPLE CRITERIA TO A QUERY

Thus far you have been using data from a complete table. While this is fine when you want all the data, it is not very convenient when you only want a certain set of records. That is where criteria come in. You can add simple criteria to your query to find specific records in your database. For example, you may want to obtain a list of customers in a particular state from a database that contains a list of all your customers.

Just as in the real world where you sometimes ask for information based on certain criteria, you can have Access perform the same task. You can do this using the Criteria rows in the query design grid. The reason there are multiple rows is that you have the capability to use multiple criteria.

When you use multiple criteria, it is called using complex criteria. This is discussed in the next section, "Add Complex Criteria to a Query."

For now, to add criteria to your query you first add the field on which you want criteria based into the query design grid. Next, in the Criteria row, you can type the criteria against which you want to compare the field. For example, if you want to see all the companies in Washington state, you type WA into the Criteria row of the Region column.

When you type WA, you are telling Access to return all the records in the tblCustomers table where the Region field contains the value WA. The SQL SELECT statement for this query looks like this:

```
SELECT tblCustomers.CompanyName,
tblCustomers.Region FROM tblCustomers WHERE
(((tblCustomers.Region)="WA"));
```

Note that Access adds the parentheses, double quotes, and semicolon for you.

When you enter criteria for different types of data, you can use different characters, called *delimiters*, around your criteria. When you specify strings, use either single or double quotes, and for dates use the pound sign, #. You do not use delimiters when using numbers.

ADD SIMPLE CRITERIA TO A QUERY

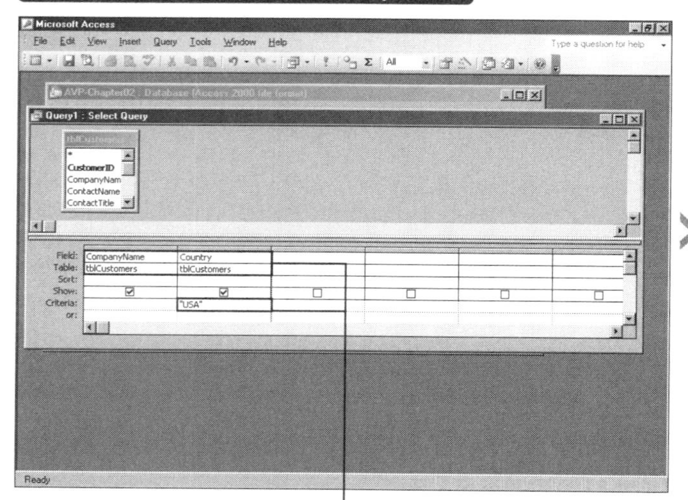

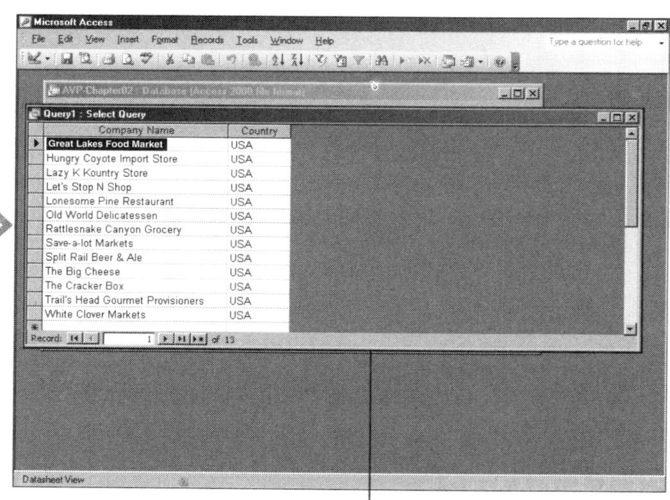

ADD STRING CRITERIA

Note: These steps use tblCustomers in AVP-Chapter02.mdb on the CD-ROM.

1 Open a database.

2 Create a new query in Design view, adding a table.

3 Add the fields you want from the table to the query design grid.

4 Type the criteria you want in the Criteria row of the field.

■ This example uses USA for the Country field criteria.

■ Access adds the quotes.

5 Click View ⇨ Datasheet View.

■ You now see the records that meet your criteria.

Extra

The steps in this task show an exact match, but there may be times when you will want to match only a portion of the string, or even a range of numbers or dates. There are quite a few ways to accomplish this.

When you want to match a portion of a string, you can use the LIKE operator combined with the wild card symbol, *. For example, if you want to see all the companies whose name starts with the letter B, you can use the criteria:

```
LIKE "B*"
```

The entire SQL SELECT statement is:

```
SELECT tblCustomers.CompanyName FROM
tblCustomers WHERE tblCustomers.CompanyName
LIKE "B*"
```

You can also use one or more of these wild cards:

WILD CARD	DESCRIPTION
*	Match any pattern of strings
?	Single character match
`[char list]`	Any single character in `char list`
`[!char list]`	Any single character not in `char list`

The wild card bracket is useful when, for example, you want those companies whose name starts with an A or B. In this case, you can type either

```
LIKE "[a-b]*"
```

or

```
LIKE "[ab]*"
```

Note that none of these commands is case-sensitive.

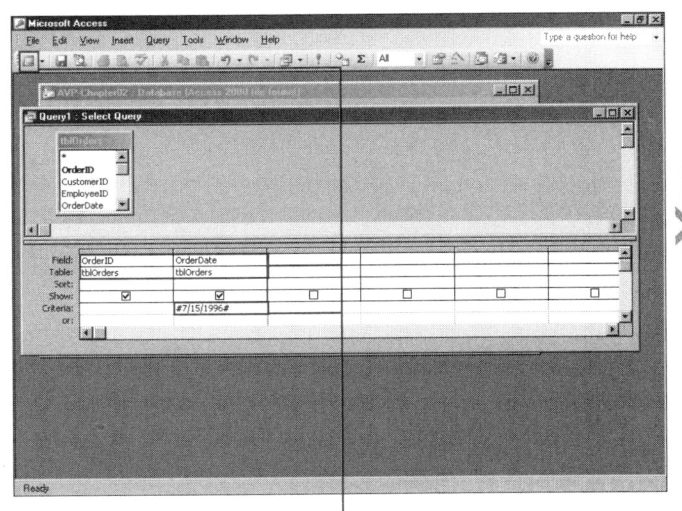

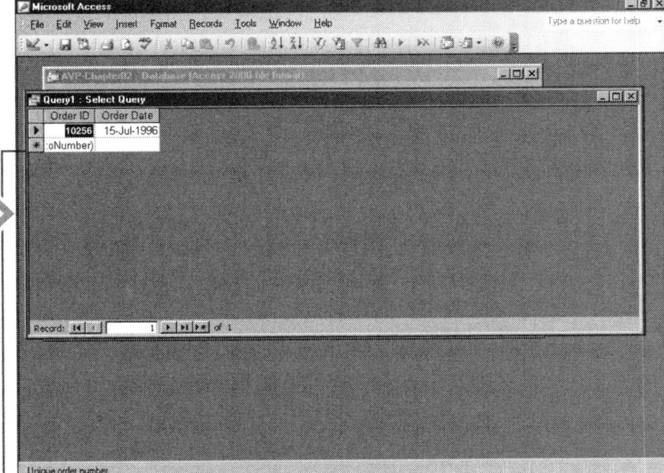

ADD DATE CRITERIA

Note: These steps use qryAddDateCriteria in AVP-Chapter02.mdb on the CD-ROM.

1 Open a database.

2 Create a new query in Design view, adding a table from the database.

3 Add the fields you want to the query design grid.

4 Type the date you want in the Criteria row of the date/time type field.

■ Access adds the pound signs, #.

5 Click the Datasheet View button.

■ The records for the date you entered appear.

ADD COMPLEX CRITERIA TO A QUERY

You can use multiple criteria to find records in your database using the OR and AND conditions. The OR condition looks for records that meet at least one of the criteria you specify, while the AND condition looks for records that meet all of the criteria you specify. When you use the use of OR and AND operators, you are using complex criteria.

The easiest way to understand how to use complex criteria is to read the query in English, and then view the SQL for it. For example, as specified here in English: If you want to see all the records in a database for companies and contacts located in the United States and whose contact title is Owner, the SQL SELECT statement would look like this:

```
SELECT tblCustomers.CompanyName,
tblCustomers.ContactName,
tblCustomers.ContactTitle,
tblCustomers.Country FROM tblCustomers WHERE
(((tblCustomers.ContactTitle)="Owner") AND
((tblCustomers.Country)="USA"));
```

For the above example, you would place your criteria on the same row of the query design grid. That is how Access knows to create an AND relationship between your criteria. This query would bring back records that meet both criteria: in the United States and having Owner for the contact title.

If, instead, you want all the records that are either in the United States or have Owner for the contact title, then you can place the criteria on separate lines in the query design grid, under the appropriate columns. If you do run the query with these criteria on tblCustomers, Access returns 28 records.

You can also use the OR operator with the same field. For example, if you want to find companies that are either in the United States or the United Kingdom, you can either type the criteria in two rows underneath each other in the Country column, or type **USA OR UK** in the same criteria cell. Access understands it either way.

To help you remember that OR is used going down the rows in the criteria area, you can see the word "or:" underneath the criteria label, beside the query grid.

ADD COMPLEX CRITERIA TO A QUERY USING AND

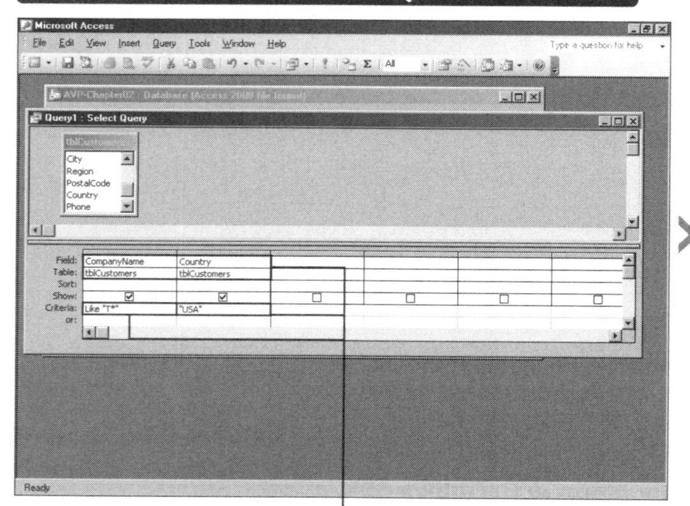

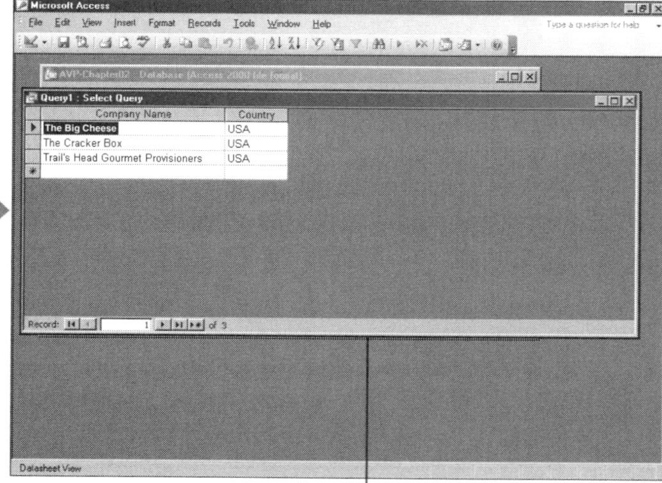

Note: This task uses qryAddComplexCriteriaUsingAND in AVP-Chapter02.mdb on the CD-ROM.

1 Open a database.

2 Create a new query in Design view, adding a table.

3 Add the fields you want to the query design grid.

4 Type the criterion you want in the Criteria row of desired field.

5 Type the other criterion you want in the Criteria row of another field.

6 Click the Datasheet View button (▦).

■ The records that appear reflect the criteria that you specified.

■ In this example, the companies that are in the USA and have names that start with T appear.

Extra

You can combine AND and OR operators in various combinations with each other. Just make sure that the operators are in the correct order for the desired results.

Parentheses can be used to set the order in which the ANDs and ORs are used. Access applies parentheses as seems best, but it tends to throw in some extra parentheses, making the code confusing.

When using AND with multiple OR criteria, repeat the AND criteria for each OR criteria. Alternatively, you can use parentheses around the OR criteria. For example, you can change the query in the steps below to companies whose name starts with T and are located in the United States or the United Kingdom with this SELECT statement:

```
SELECT tblCustomers.CompanyName, tblCustomers.Country FROM
tblCustomers
WHERE (tblCustomers.CompanyName Like "S*") AND
        (tblCustomers.Country="UK" Or tblCustomers.Country="USA");
```

Note that if you do not add the parentheses, Access adds them for you. In the above code, the parentheses that Access adds were omitted to make it easier to read, as well as to improve performance. However, entered as seen above, the SELECT statement still works correctly.

ADD COMPLEX CRITERIA TO A QUERY USING OR

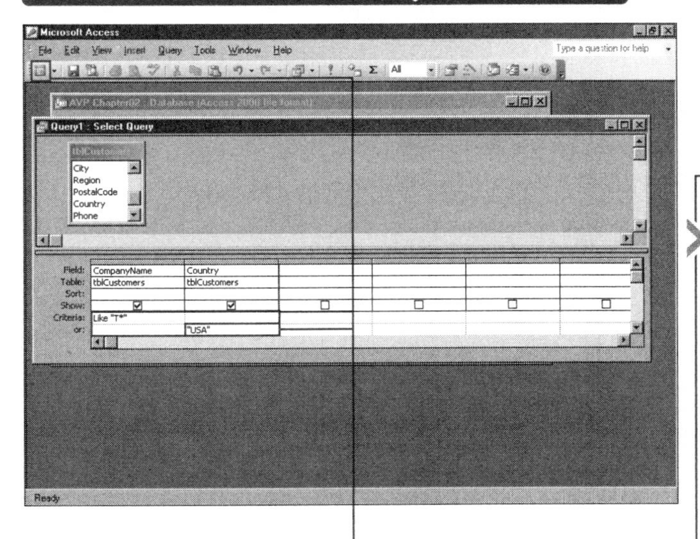

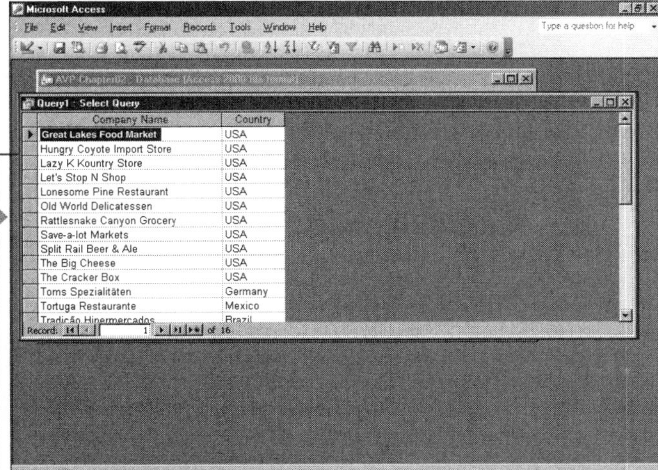

1 Repeat steps 1 to 5 from the preceding page.

2 Highlight the text in the Criteria row, and click Edit ➪ Cut.

3 Click in the Criteria row, below the original location, and click Edit ➪ Paste.

■ The two criteria now appear on separate Criteria rows.

4 Click the Datasheet View button.

■ The records that appear reflect the criteria that you specified.

■ In this example, the companies that are in the USA or have names that start with T appear.

CREATE A PARAMETER QUERY

You can specify criteria in Design view; however, in order to change the results returned you must open the query in Design view, and modify the criteria. You can create a parameter query, without going into Design view, to modify your query. This is useful when you want other users to take advantage of your queries.

When you specify a parameter, Access displays an input box or boxes if you specify more than one parameter. At runtime, Access retrieves the value that you want to compare in the criteria. You surround your parameter, which also doubles as the input box's prompt, with brackets, []. An example of a parameter can be seen here, where the user is asked to enter a region:

```
[Please enter a region to query:]
```

Access places this code in the Criteria row of the Region column. Also, if you want to use the LIKE operator, you can type the following:

```
Like [Please enter a region to query:] & "*"
```

You can also use multiple parameters. For example, the BETWEEN operator allows you to specify a range of dates or numbers for criteria. If you want to retrieve a set of orders between two dates, you can type the following:

```
Between [Enter Begin Date] And [Enter End
Date]
```

When you use two parameters, two boxes open sequentially after you enter each parameter.

Besides the convenience parameters provide of not having to modify the query itself, parameters save on compile time. Access compiles queries after they are modified, and before the first time they are run. The compile time, while not great, is not incurred each time you open and run the query.

CREATE A PARAMETER QUERY USING AN EXACT MATCH

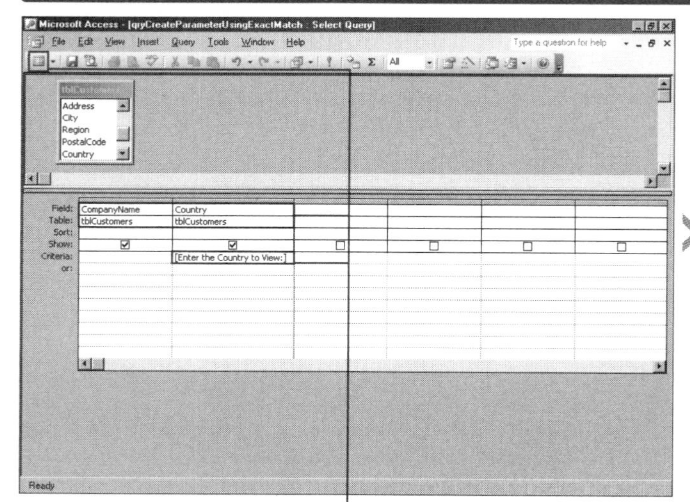

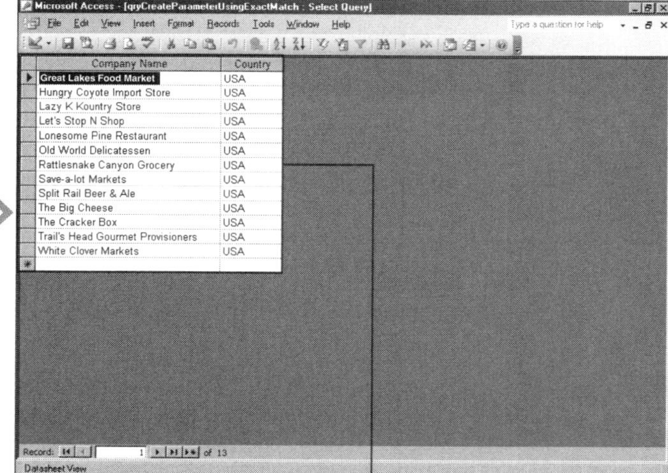

Note: These steps use qryCreateParameterUsingExactMatch in AVP-Chapter02.mdb on the CD-ROM.

1. Open a database.
2. Create a new query with the tables you want in Design view.
3. Click and drag the fields you want in the query onto the query design grid.
4. Type a prompt in the Criteria row of the Country field.
5. Click the Datasheet View button.

■ A parameter input dialog box appears, with the prompt you typed in step 4.

6. Type a parameter in the dialog box.
7. Click OK.

■ The records that appear reflect the parameters you chose in step 6.

■ For this example, all companies in the USA appear.

Extra

When you frequently use a particular field for your queries, whether specifying the field as Sort field or using criteria against it, you may want to create an index for that field. Access, or more accurately the database engine Jet used by Access, uses the index to optimize performance for querying and sorting when you are using that field.

To create an index, open the table that contains the field in Design view, and then set the Index property of the field, located in the Properties section of the table design, to Yes (Duplicates OK). You can also select Not Indexed and Yes (No Duplicates). Duplicates OK hides any records that have duplicates in the indexed field. Not Indexed removes any indexes.

Access automatically creates indexes when you create relationships, when you specify lookup values, and for Primary Key fields. Primary Key fields use indexes with No Duplicates, because that field needs to be unique for each record.

You can also set up an index in Design view by clicking View ⇨ Indexes. In the Indexes dialog box that appears, you can specify indexes on individual fields, or create composite indexes. For example, you can create a composite index for LastName and FirstName fields if you use both fields in an expression on which you sort. However, it is more efficient to create single indexes for each field you use in the expressions.

CREATE A PARAMETER QUERY USING LIKE

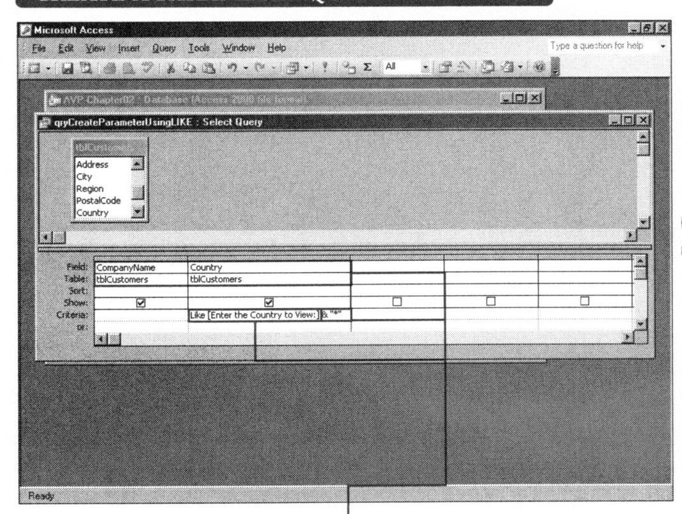

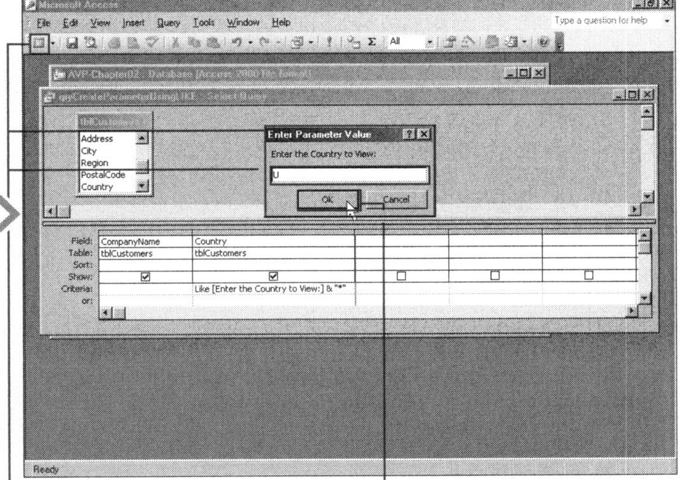

Note: These steps use qryCreateParameterUsingLIKE in AVP-Chapter02.mdb on the CD-ROM.

1 Open a database.

2 Create a new query with the tables you want in Design view.

3 Click and drag the fields you want in the query onto the query design grid.

4 Type **LIKE**, followed by a space, and then a prompt in brackets.

5 Type **& "*"**.

6 Click the Datasheet View button.

■ A parameter input dialog box appears, with the prompt you typed in steps 4 and 5.

7 Type the first letter of the parameter in the dialog box.

8 Click OK.

■ The records that appear reflect the criteria you chose in step 7.

■ For this example, all countries that start with U appear.

DISPLAY A CALCULATED COLUMN

With Access, you can display calculated fields, or expressions, in your query results. For example, you may want to combine the FirstName and LastName fields from tblEmployees into full names that you can display in a single column. To accomplish this, you use the following syntax in the Field row of a new column in the query:

```
CalculatedColumnName: expression
```

To display the full name of the employee, you can type the following:

```
FullName: LastName & ", " & FirstName
```

By using the ampersand, you are telling Access to concatenate the LastName and FirstName fields to the literal string of a comma and space. By using the ampersand rather than the plus symbol, which also works if Null values are entered, the rest of the expression after the ampersand will still be displayed. When you use the plus symbol, you are adding the two strings together, and anything added to a Null value is null.

You can also create a calculated column to display the total quantity of an item, multiplied (*) by the price of each item. You can use the Quantity and UnitPrice fields from tblOrderDetails to create a new field called TotalCost with this expression:

```
TotalCost: Quantity*UnitPrice
```

Access also supplies some functions that can be used with dates to help format the output of the dates, and then use them in calculated expressions. A function takes parameters, and returns a value. Access includes functions that, let you add and subtract from dates, or use different time intervals such as days, weeks, and years. Another function allows you to display dates and numeric values as formatted strings.

Here is an example of specifying a date column in a European format of showing day first, month second, and year last, with periods separating the numbers:

```
EuroDate: Format (OrderDate, "DD.MM.YY")
```

DISPLAY A CALCULATED STRING

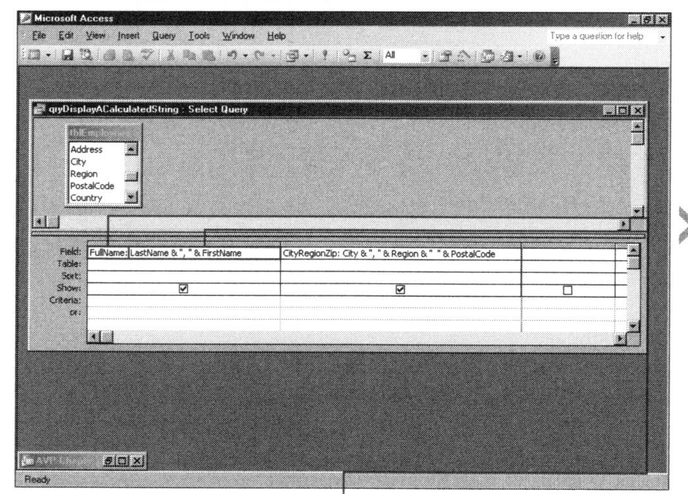

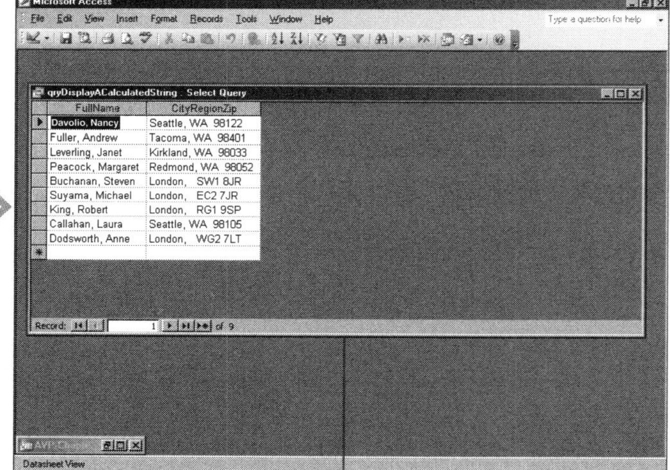

Note: These steps use qryDisplayACalculatedString in AVP-Chapter02.mdb on the CD-ROM.

1 Open a database.

2 Create a query in Design view, adding a table.

3 Add the fields you want to the query design grid.

4 Type a name for the calculated column, and then **:**.

5 Type a field name, **& ","** **&**, and then another field name.

6 Repeat steps 4 and 5 for other calculated columns.

7 Click the Datasheet View button (▦).

■ The records appear, listed as specified in steps 4 to 6.

Extra

Notice that all the names of the calculated column have no spaces in them, just as field names in tables should not have spaces in them. Neither, in the author's opinion, should calculated columns have spaces in them. If you want the datasheet, or forms, to display spaces in column headings, then you can specify this in the Caption property of the calculated expression. To accomplish this, do the following. In the query design grid, click in the column of the calculated expression, and then click View ⇨ Properties. The property sheet for the calculated column appears, and you can then specify the Caption property as one of the possible properties for query columns.

Along with the Caption property, you can also set the Description, Format, Input Mask, and Smart Tags.

When you set these properties at the query level, they take precedence over the same properties set at the table level. You need to be careful, however, especially if you have set the Input Mask property to mask the field a certain way. It is generally a good idea to use these properties for calculated expressions only.

DISPLAY A CALCULATED VALUE

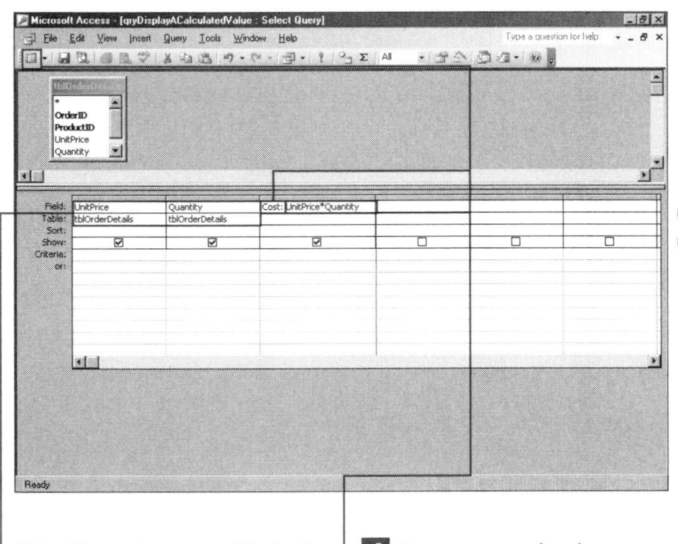

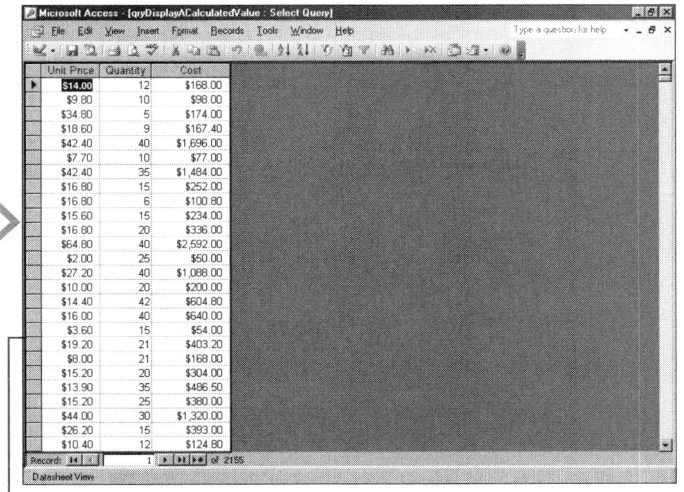

Note: These steps use qryDisplayACalculatedValue in AVP-Chapter02.mdb on the CD-ROM.

1 Open a database.

2 Create a query in Design view, adding a table.

3 Add the fields you want to the query design grid.

4 Type a name for the calculated column, and then **:**.

5 Type a field name, *****, and then another field name.

6 Click the Datasheet View button.

Note: It is not required that the fields appear in the lower half of the query design grid to use them; they just need to be in the tables.

■ The records that appear display the columns you chose in steps 4 and 5.

■ For this example, UnitPrice, Quantity, and Cost are displayed in a datasheet.

USING MULTIPLE TABLES

When using relational databases, Access allows you to view the data that has been split out into separate tables, such as customers and orders, as if they were combined into single records again. This is especially useful when you create reports and view data.

To accomplish this, you can add additional tables to your queries, and join all the tables together. Access joins the tables together for you, based on the relationships you have created, and the names of the fields in the tables.

To add multiple tables to your query, you select multiple tables, or queries, and click Add Table in the Show Table dialog box. After you add the tables and close the Show Table dialog box, the tables appear in the top pane of the Query Designer, with lines joining them.

If you have set up your relationships, then Access shows you what kind of relationships they are, based on the symbols on the join lines.

You can then add the fields from the various tables to the query design grid in the same manner as when you are using a single table. As you add fields from the various tables, the Table row in the query design grid comes in handy, showing you the table from which each field comes.

When you are using multiple tables, you can use criteria-based fields from any of the tables you use in the query.

Note that when you use one-to-many relationships, such as customers to invoices, the one side repeats in the results for each of the matching records on the many side.

USING MULTIPLE TABLES

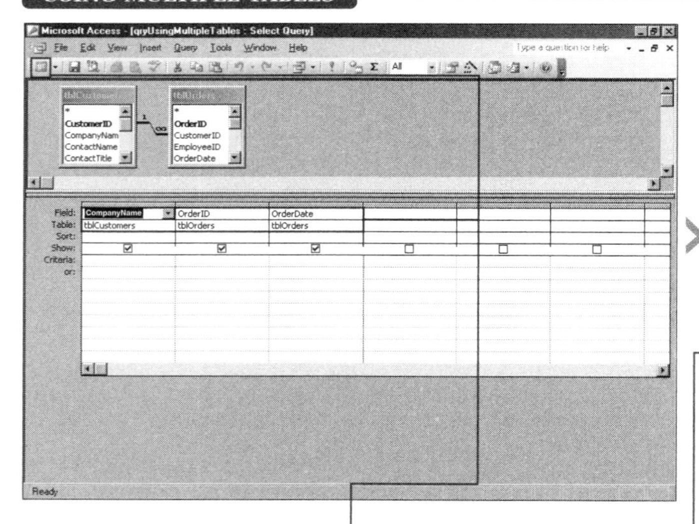

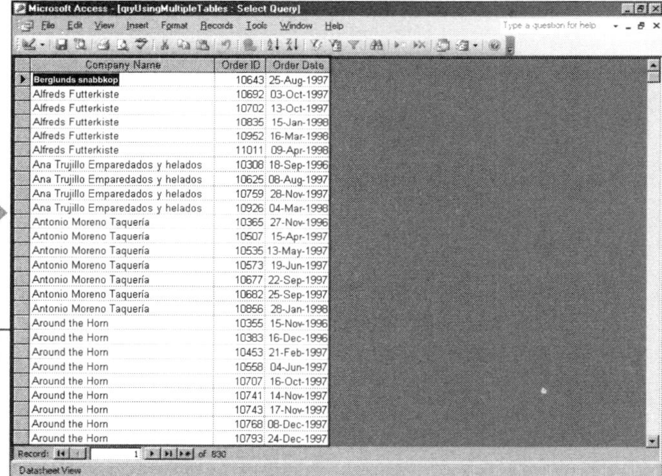

Company Name	Order ID	Order Date
Berglunds snabbkop	10643	25-Aug-1997
Alfreds Futterkiste	10692	03-Oct-1997
Alfreds Futterkiste	10702	13-Oct-1997
Alfreds Futterkiste	10835	15-Jan-1998
Alfreds Futterkiste	10952	16-Mar-1998
Alfreds Futterkiste	11011	09-Apr-1998
Ana Trujillo Emparedados y helados	10308	18-Sep-1996
Ana Trujillo Emparedados y helados	10625	08-Aug-1997
Ana Trujillo Emparedados y helados	10759	28-Nov-1997
Ana Trujillo Emparedados y helados	10926	04-Mar-1998
Antonio Moreno Taquería	10365	27-Nov-1996
Antonio Moreno Taquería	10507	15-Apr-1997
Antonio Moreno Taquería	10535	13-May-1997
Antonio Moreno Taquería	10573	19-Jun-1997
Antonio Moreno Taquería	10677	22-Sep-1997
Antonio Moreno Taquería	10682	25-Sep-1997
Antonio Moreno Taquería	10856	28-Jan-1998
Around the Horn	10355	15-Nov-1996
Around the Horn	10383	16-Dec-1996
Around the Horn	10453	21-Feb-1997
Around the Horn	10558	04-Jun-1997
Around the Horn	10707	16-Oct-1997
Around the Horn	10741	14-Nov-1997
Around the Horn	10743	17-Nov-1997
Around the Horn	10768	08-Dec-1997
Around the Horn	10793	24-Dec-1997

Note: This task uses the tables tblCustomers and tblOrders in the database AVP-Chapter02.mdb on the CD-ROM.

1 Open a database.

2 Create a new query in Design view, and add tables from the database.

3 Click and drag the fields you want from both tables to the query design grid.

4 Click the Datasheet View button.

■ Records that appear display the columns you chose in step 3.

■ For this example, companies with OrderID and OrderDate appear in a datasheet.

Extra

Besides basing queries on tables, you can also base queries on other queries. This is useful because queries can get complicated as you add the features, such as Order By statements and parameters, that have been discussed in this chapter alone.

It is also useful to base a query on another query when you are performing the same basic steps in a number of different queries, and these steps use the same table or expressions. It makes sense to create a model query, and then use that query as a base for other queries. This way, if you must change something in the base query, all the other queries can reflect the change made in that base query.

To base a query on a query, create the query using the Design view, just as you would if you were basing the query off a table, except that in the Show Table dialog box, click the Queries tab. You can then select the query on which you want to base the new query by double-clicking the query, just as you did tables.

Queries and tables can be mixed if needed, and Access creates the join lines if it can. If Access cannot add the join lines, the user can add them. Also, you can remove the join lines that Access creates and create your own instead.

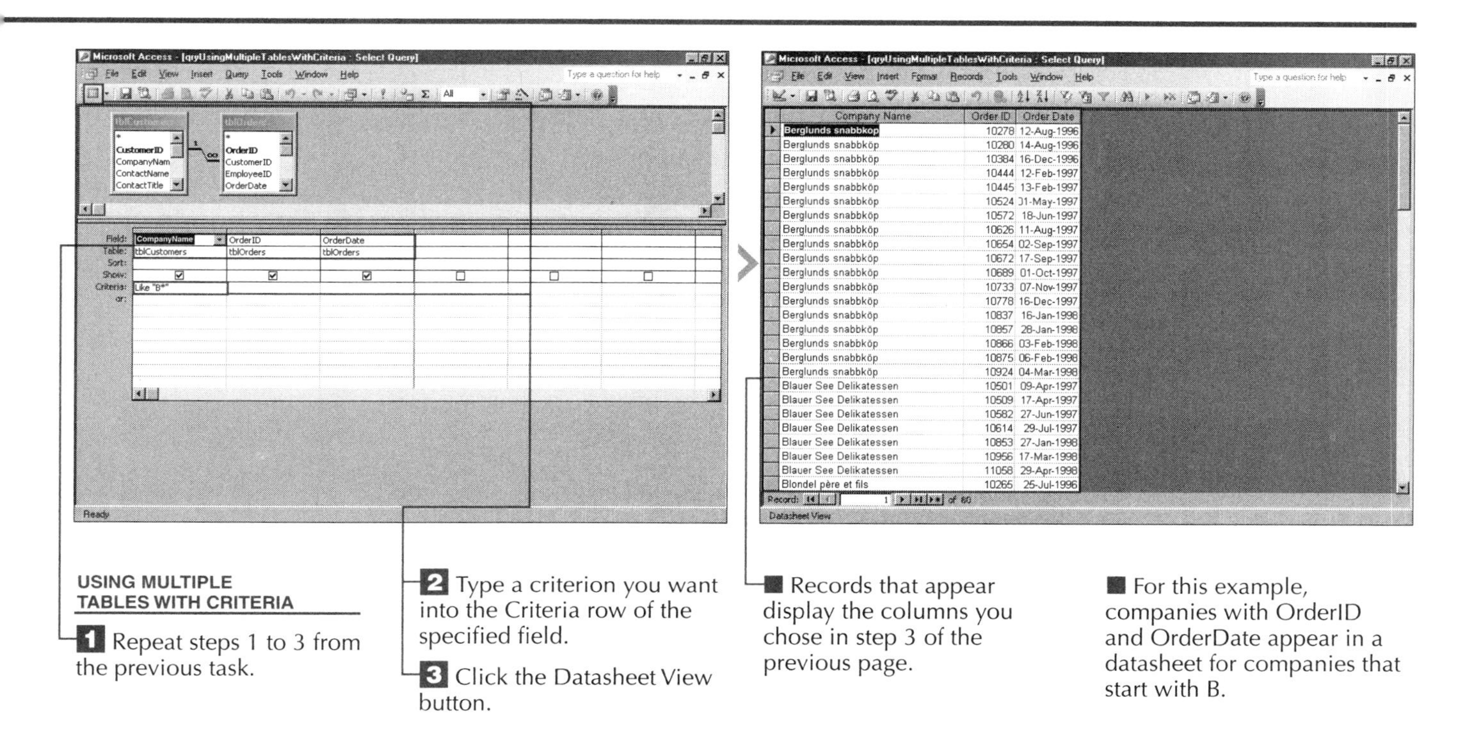

USING MULTIPLE TABLES WITH CRITERIA

1 Repeat steps 1 to 3 from the previous task.

2 Type a criterion you want into the Criteria row of the specified field.

3 Click the Datasheet View button.

■ Records that appear display the columns you chose in step 3 of the previous page.

■ For this example, companies with OrderID and OrderDate appear in a datasheet for companies that start with B.

UPDATE EXISTING RECORDS

You can update existing records using a query. You can use all of the features available for queries, including criteria and calculated fields, to update records.

For example, if you want to update prices for a category of products by 2%, you can include criteria that use the CategoryID to limit the records. The SELECT statement for such an Update query looks like this:

```
UPDATE tblProducts SET tblProducts.UnitPrice
= [tblProducts].[Unitprice]*1.02 WHERE
(((tblProducts.CategoryID)=1));
```

After you create a Select query that uses the table and fields you want to update, you can use this query as a base for other queries. To do this, you can use the Update Query feature from the Query Type toolbar button.

When you have set the query type to Update query, the Sort row disappears and the Update row appears.

The Fields row contains the fields that you want to update, and the Update To field contains the values with which you want to update the Fields row columns.

When you add the values into the Update row, Access places the correct delimiters around the value: double quotes for text, pound signs (#) for dates, and nothing for numeric values. You can also use functions such as those discussed in the section "Display a Calculated Column."

You can join another table, and then when specifying fields to be updated in the original table, use values from the joined table. When you specify a field from which you are updating, include the table name, a period, and then the field name in the Update row of the column you want to update.

UPDATE EXISTING RECORDS

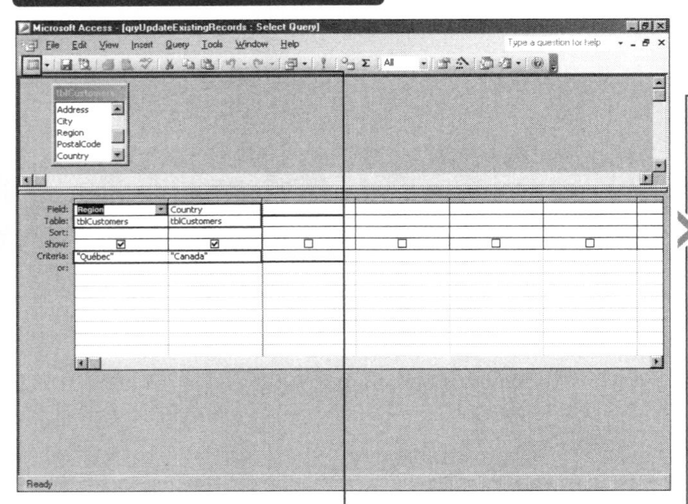

Note: This task uses the query qryUpdateExistingRecords in the database AVP-Chapter02.mdb on the CD-ROM.

1 Open a database.

2 Create a new query in Design view, and add a table from the database.

3 Click and drag the fields you want into the query design grid.

4 Type the criteria you want in the Criteria rows.

5 Click the Datasheet View button.

■ Records that appear reflect the criteria you chose in step 4.

■ For this example, one record should appear in the results datasheet.

■ If you have run this task's complete Update query more than once, then you will not have any records returned, because they will have been updated.

6 Click the Design View button.

Extra

You may notice that in the steps below you do not execute the query by clicking the same Datasheet View button (▦) you have used in all the prior tasks. This is because you must click the Run button (!) to execute one of the Action queries. You can still use the Datasheet View button to test your action queries even after you specify them to be an Action query versus a Select query.

This being said, it is still a better habit to test your query as a Select query prior to changing it to an Action query. This applies especially to Delete queries, which can be destructive.

After you have made it into an Action query, you should view the query before you execute it. You can view the query results in the target table. When you use an Update query, you view the table you are updating, and when you use an Append query, you view the table to which you are appending, and so on. You will see more about this in the sections that follow.

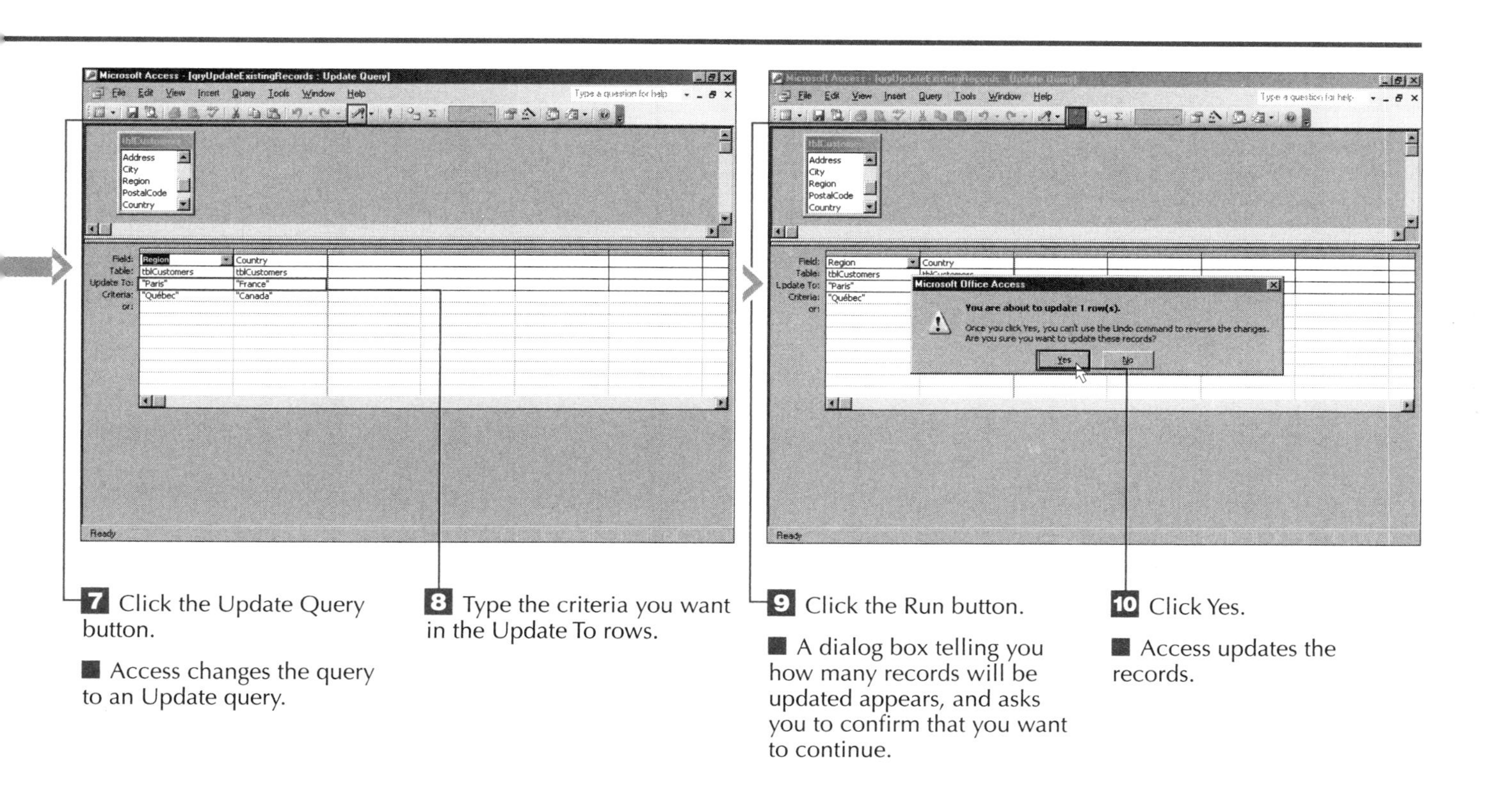

7 Click the Update Query button.

■ Access changes the query to an Update query.

8 Type the criteria you want in the Update To rows.

9 Click the Run button.

■ A dialog box telling you how many records will be updated appears, and asks you to confirm that you want to continue.

10 Click Yes.

■ Access updates the records.

APPEND NEW RECORDS

While you can add individual records to tables in Datasheet view, you may also want to add multiple records. You can add, or append, records from one or more tables to another, or create new records altogether, using an Append query.

For example, you may want to import some records from another system and append them to an existing table. You can import them into a new table to look through the data first, and to do any necessary cleanup. After cleaning up the data, you can then append the records into an existing table, even adding data to fields as Access appends the records.

When you are creating an Append query, you again create a Select query that displays the data you want to append. You then click Query ⇨ Append Query. After you type the name of the table to which to append the record(s), an Append To row appears in the query design grid. In this row you tell Access which fields you want to be filled with the source data. When you append data from one table to another, Access fills in the field names for you if there is a matching field name between the two, or more, tables.

For example, when adding new rows to the tblCustomers table from an imported table called tblImportedEmployees, the Append query looks like this:

```
INSERT INTO tblEmployees ( LastName,
FirstName )

SELECT tblImportedEmployees.LastName,
tblImportedEmployees.FirstName

FROM tblImportedEmployees;
```

As you can see, the actual SQL statement is the INSERT INTO statement.

APPEND NEW RECORDS

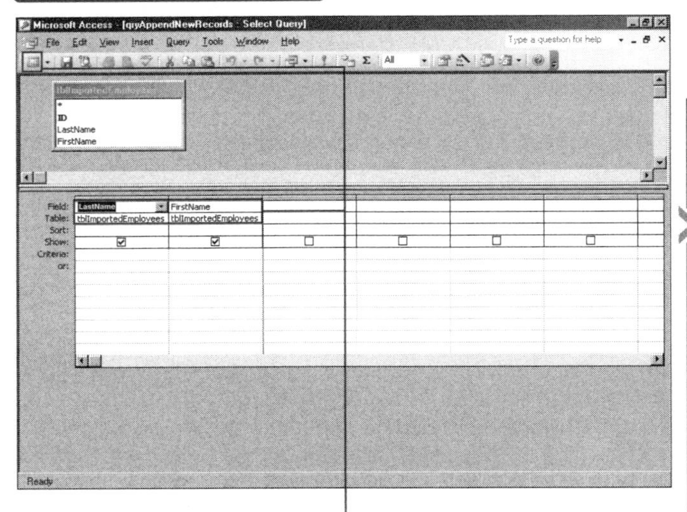

Note: This task uses the query qryAppendNewRecords in the database AVP-Chapter02.mdb on the CD-ROM.

1 Open a database.

2 Create a new query in Design view, and add a table from the database.

3 Click and drag the fields you want into the query design grid.

4 Click the Datasheet View button.

■ The records to be added appear in the results datasheet.

5 Click the Design View button.

Extra

When using an Append query to add new records, you may want to fill in one of the fields with values of your own. To do this, you can create a calculated column just as you would in a Select query. For example, if you want to change the Title column in the tblEmployees table to New Employee, you can type Title: "New Employee" in the Field row of an empty column.

After you change the Select query into an Append query, you can choose Title from the list of possible fields in the tblEmployees table. Here is the SQL statement:

```
INSERT INTO tblEmployees ( LastName, FirstName, Title )
SELECT tblImportedEmployees.LastName,
tblImportedEmployees.FirstName, "New Employee" AS Title
FROM tblImportedEmployees;
```

When you create the calculated column, the name of the calculated column does not need to match the name of the field into which you are importing the calculated field. In fact, you can just leave the name of the calculated column blank, and Access adds a name for you.

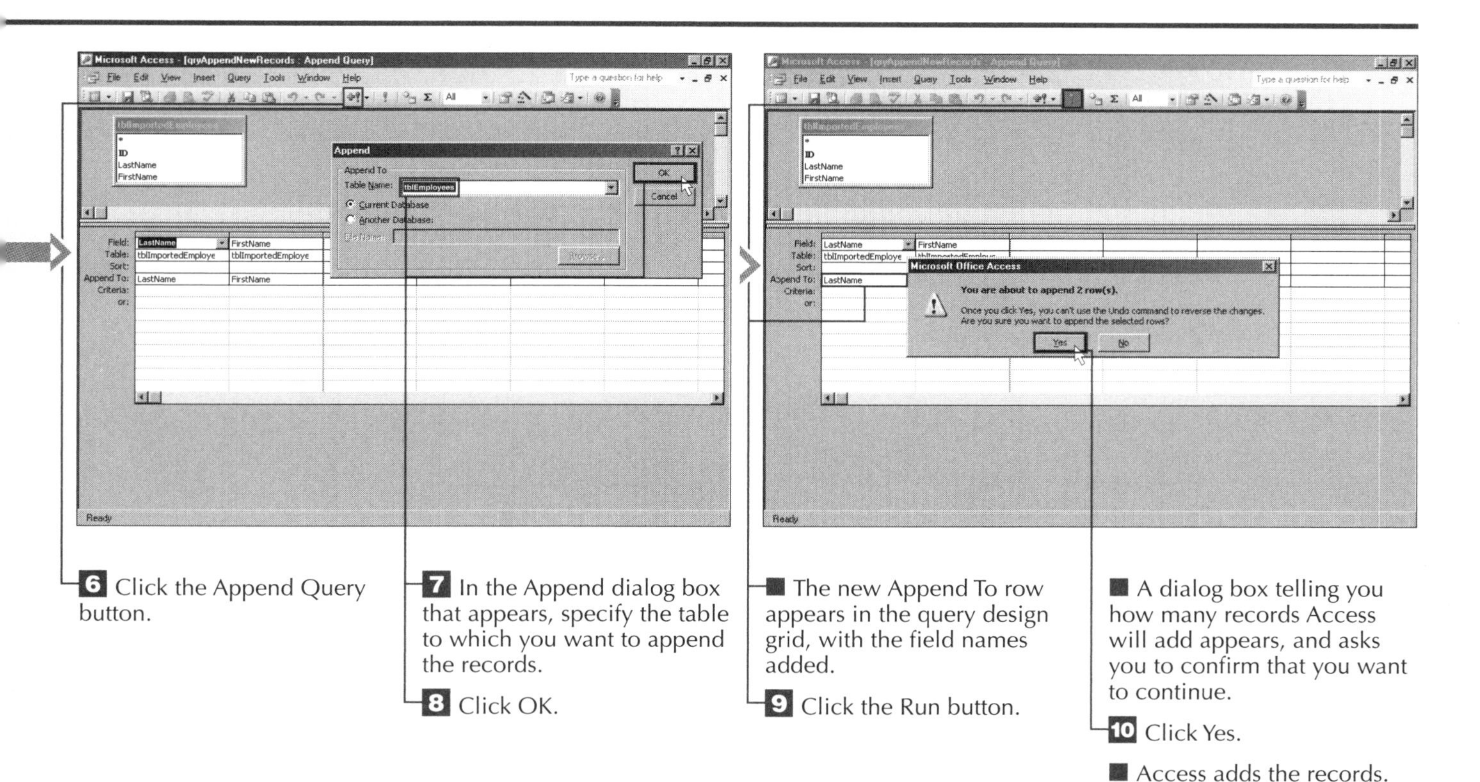

6 Click the Append Query button.

7 In the Append dialog box that appears, specify the table to which you want to append the records.

8 Click OK.

■ The new Append To row appears in the query design grid, with the field names added.

9 Click the Run button.

■ A dialog box telling you how many records Access will add appears, and asks you to confirm that you want to continue.

10 Click Yes.

■ Access adds the records.

MAKE A NEW TABLE USING A QUERY

You can use a query to create a new table, for example when you want to generate a temporary table. To do this, you create a Select query and test it to verify the results. You can then create the table using the Make-Table query feature from the Query Type toolbar.

When you choose the Make-Table query type, you can specify a name for the new table using the Make Table dialog box. Remember to use a standard naming convention when naming the table. You can also specify whether you want to create the table in the current database, or in another Access database. For further information on naming conventions, see Appendix A, "Leszynski Naming Conventions for Microsoft Access."

After you specify what you want to call the table and where you want to put it, you are presented with the Query Design view.

As with most other query types, you can use calculated fields. When you use a calculated field, Access makes its best guess of data type to create for the new field.

Here is an example of the SQL generated for a typical Make-Table query that contains a calculated field:

```
SELECT tblCustomers.CustomerID,
tblCustomers.CompanyName, tblCustomers.
ContactName, 7000 AS Test INTO tblTest;

FROM tblCustomers;
```

If you have created the table more than once, Access lets you know it and asks if you want to replace the table.

Note that when you create a new table using a Make-Table query, neither your indexes nor your the primary key are created. In fact, the data type and size of the field are the only features that appear in the new table.

Generally, you want to use the Make-Table query only when necessary, and use Select queries to act as record sources for forms and reports.

MAKE A NEW TABLE USING A QUERY

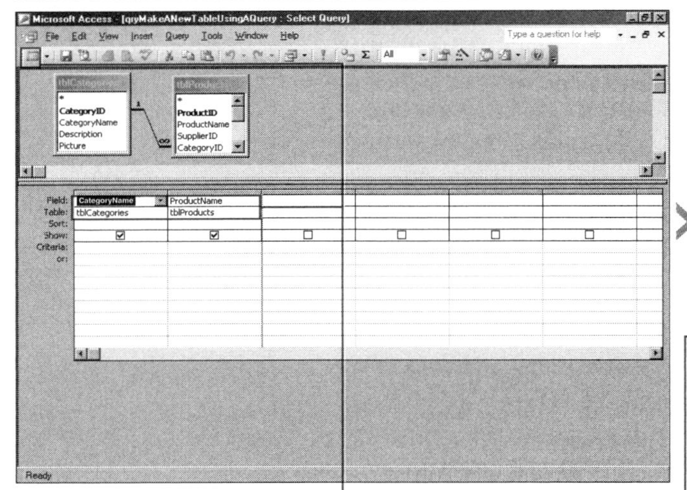

Note: This task uses the query qryMakeANewTableUsingAQuery and tblProducts in the database AVP-Chapter02.mdb on the CD-ROM.

1 Open a database.

2 Create a new query in Design view, and add tables from the database.

3 Click and drag the fields you want into the query design grid.

4 Click the Datasheet View button.

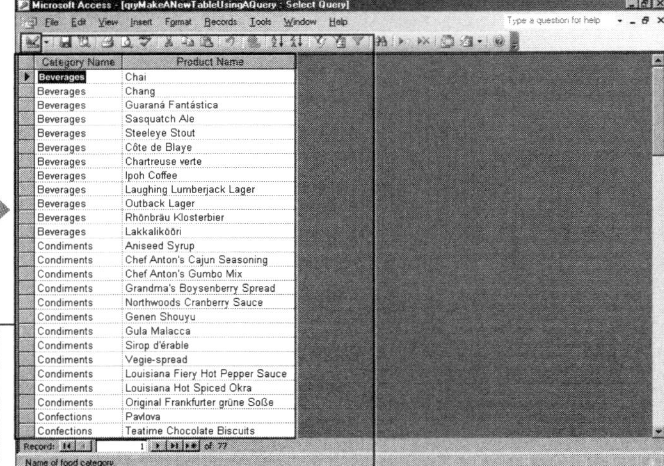

■ Access displays the records that will be added in the results datasheet.

5 Click the Design View button.

Extra

You can also specify another database for both Make-Table queries and Append queries. When you choose to create these types of queries, a dialog box appears in which you can specify whether you want to create a table or append records to a table, as well as an option for another database.

You can select an existing database, either by typing the path and name, or browsing to the file. Access adds an IN clause to the SQL statement created. For example, you may want to make a new table using the base query that you created below. To import the new table into a database with the path and filename D:\Documents and Settings\Administrator\My Documents\db1.mdb, the SQL statement for the Make-Table query looks like this:

```
SELECT tblCategories.CategoryName, tblProducts.ProductName INTO
tblNewTable IN 'D:\Documents and Settings\Administrator\My
Documents\db1.mdb'

FROM tblCategories INNER JOIN tblProducts ON tblCategories.
CategoryID = tblProducts.CategoryID;
```

You are limited to Access-type databases, including both .MDB and .ADP. Note that by choosing an .ADP database, you can create a new table in an SQL Server database. Remember that .ADP acts as a front-end for SQL Server back-ends.

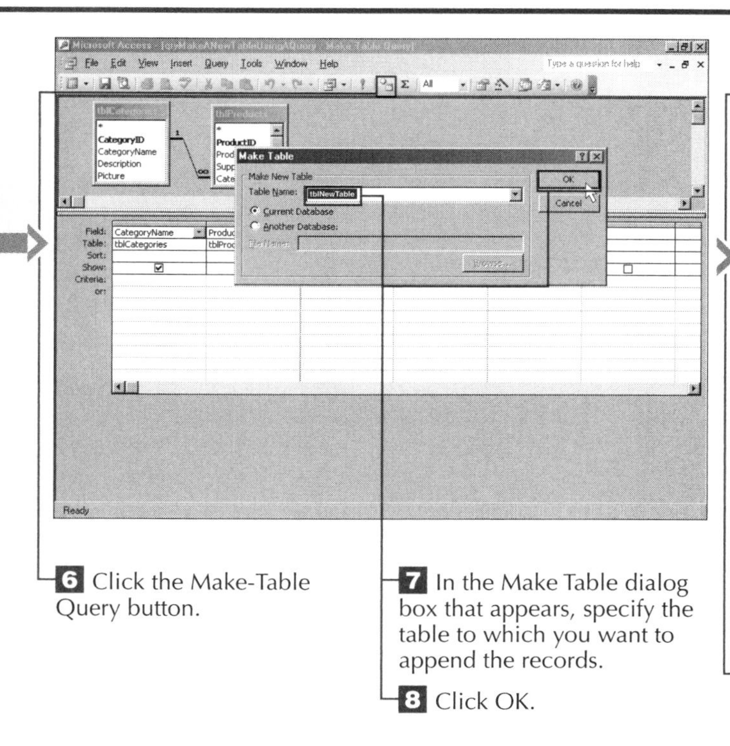

6 Click the Make-Table Query button.

7 In the Make Table dialog box that appears, specify the table to which you want to append the records.

8 Click OK.

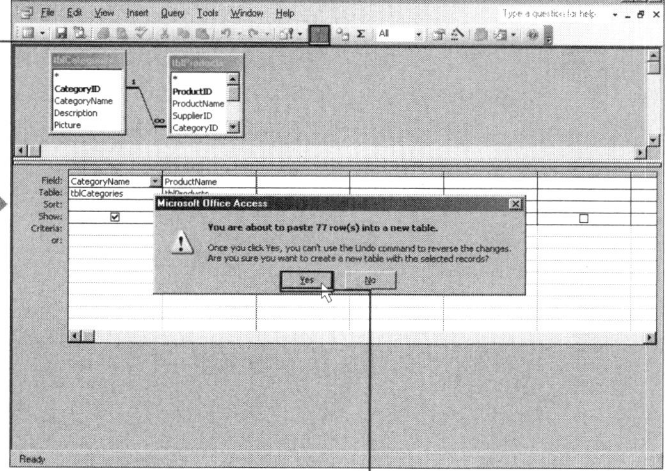

■ The caption in the designer window changes to Make Table Query.

9 Click the Run button.

■ A dialog box appears, telling you how many records Access will add, and asks you to confirm that you want to continue.

10 Click Yes.

■ Access creates the new table.

Note: If you have run this query more than once, then Access notifies you that the table already exists. Click Yes to re-create the table.

DELETE RECORDS

Just as you can add and update records using queries, you can also use a query to delete records. Unlike other query types that let you update individual fields, with the Delete query you can only delete an entire record, not individual fields. It is the whole record or nothing.

As with all the other query types, you can use multiple tables and criteria when you use a Delete query. Again, as with the other bulk operation queries, you should also create a Select query first to show the records that your query will affect. You can then use the Datasheet View button to test the query.

When the Select query displays the records you want to delete, you can use the Delete Query feature from the Query Type button.

When you change a query to a Delete query, the Show and Sort rows disappear from the query design grid, and are replaced by a new row labeled Delete, which offers two choices: From and Where.

Access turns the column containing the asterisk into the From column, and all other fields into Where columns.

For example, if you want to delete the records in the tblEmployees table for all employees who live in Seattle, the Delete query SQL looks like this:

```
SELECT tblEmployees.*, tblEmployees.City
FROM tblEmployees WHERE
(((tblEmployees.City)="Seattle"));
```

If referential integrity is in place and there are related records, then the records must abide by the relationship rules, such as having Cascade Delete set to True for related records.

DELETE RECORDS

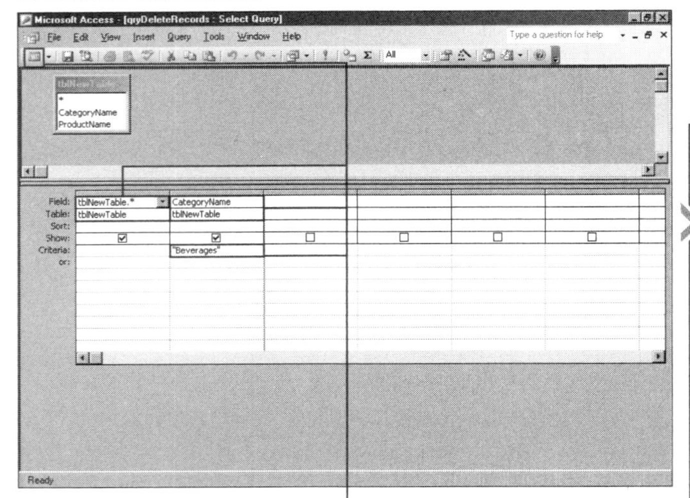

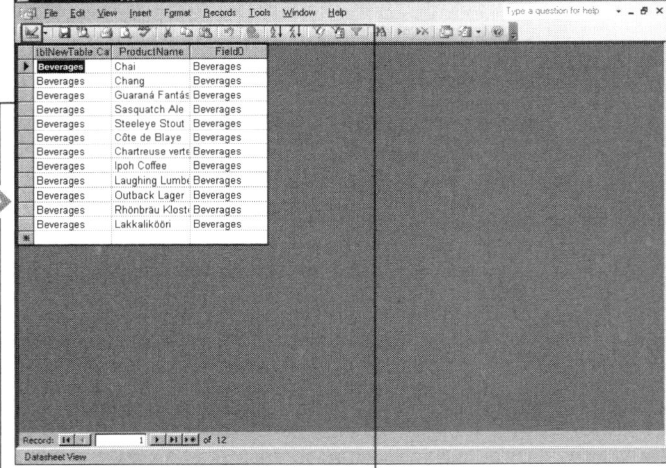

Note: This task uses qryDeleteRecords in the database AVP-Chapter02.mdb on the CD-ROM.

1 Open a database.

2 Create a new query in Design view, and add the table from the database.

3 Click and drag the asterisk, *, into the query design grid.

4 Click and drag the field that you want into the query design grid.

5 Type a criterion for the Criteria row.

6 Click the Datasheet View button.

■ The records that Access will delete appear in the results datasheet.

7 Click the Design View button.

Extra

You can include multiple tables or queries in a Delete query, and specify the table from which you want to delete the records.

For example, if you want to delete all the orders for companies that are located in France, you must use both the tblCustomers and tblOrders tables. After adding the tables to the query, you can then set a criteria on the tblCustomers.Country column to France. You can then click and drag the tblOrders.* table into the query design grid. When you change the Select query into a Delete query, the From option appears in the tblOrders.* column, and the Where option appears in the tblCustomers.Country column. The SQL statement looks like this:

```
DELETE tblCustomers.Country, tblOrders.*
FROM tblCustomers INNER JOIN tblOrders ON tblCustomers.CustomerID =
tblOrders.CustomerID
WHERE (((tblCustomers.Country)="France"));
```

Note that the table containing the Where option does not have records deleted: It is the From option that has records deleted.

When you delete the tblOrders records, Access automatically deletes any records related to the tblOrdersDetails records. These records are automatically deleted because of the relationship settings between the tables. To review relationships, see Chapter 1.

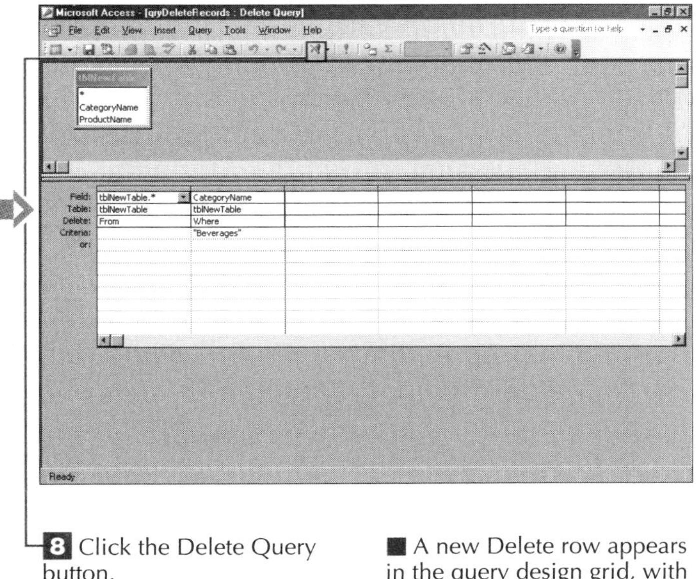

8 Click the Delete Query button.

■ A new Delete row appears in the query design grid, with From displayed for the * column, and Where for the other column.

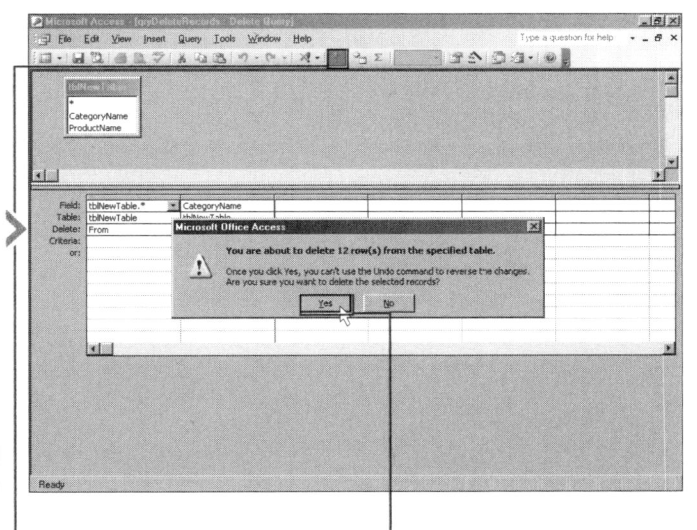

9 Click the Run button.

■ A dialog box appears, telling you how many records Access will delete, and asks you to confirm that you want to continue.

10 Click Yes.

■ Access deletes the records.

UNDERSTANDING JOIN TYPES

You can use Joins whenever you bring more than one record source from a table or query into another query. Access designates the joins by drawing lines in the Query Design view. Joins show how Access will use the record sources in relation to each other.

Although you usually specify a formal relationship using Access relations when you join record sources, it is not always the case. Unlike relations, when you create joins it is for a specific query or SQL statement.

INNER JOIN, LEFT AND RIGHT OUTER JOINS

You can join record sources in different ways, depending on what information you want to present. These joins limit records based on which type of join you use. The three types of joins are Inner Join, Left Outer Join, and Right Outer Join.

Inner Join

Inner Joins are the most common type of join, and the default join type in Access. When you specify that you want to create an Inner Join between two record sources, you are saying that you want to display records in each record source only when there is a related record in the other joined record source. For example, you may want to see only those customers who have orders.

Left Outer Join

You can use Left Outer Joins when you want all records to display in the first record source, regardless of matching records in the second record source. Records in the second record source only display if there is a matching record in the first record source. In this case, all customers would be displayed, but the only orders that display are those you assign to a customer.

Right Outer Join

You can use Right Outer Joins when you want all records to display in the second record source, regardless of matching records in the first record source. Records in the first record source only display if there are matching records in the second record source. For example, you may want to see all the orders you have entered, even if the orders do not have a matching customer.

You can use this join type primarily when you want to check for data that you may have entered erroneously, such as orders you have entered without a customer. Sometimes these errors occur if you have not set up referential integrity correctly. See Chapter 1 for more about referential integrity.

SELF JOINS

When you join a record source to itself, you are creating a Self Join. To do this you can add two instances of the same record source to a query, and draw a line in between them. For example, when you list employees with their supervisor, and you store the supervisors in the same table as the employees, the SupervisorID then refers back to the EmployeeID.

CARTESION PRODUCT JOINS

You may occasionally want to display two record sources in the same query, without a join line between them. When you do, Access displays a record for each record in the first record source, multiplied by each record in the second record source. For example, if you have four tblDepartment records and three tblProduct records, then the query displays 12 records in the results.

ADHOC JOINS

You can create an Adhoc Join in the Query Designer when there is not an existing relationship between two tables.

CREATE AN INNER JOIN

You can create an Inner Join to limit the data returned to just those records that have matching records in each of the joined tables. This lets you control what data is displayed in your results. Usually when you create an Inner Join, there is not much work to do. Because this is the default type of join, Access creates it for you automatically. When you place two tables onto the Query Design view from the Add Tables dialog box, Access creates the line between the two record sources for you.

In the SQL statement for the Inner Join, the INNER JOIN clause appears along with the ON clause, which uses the fields in each of the record sources to join them. For example, the following SQL statement takes the customers and orders and displays information where both have existing records.

```
SELECT tblCustomers.CompanyName, tblOrders.
OrderDate FROM tblCustomers INNER JOIN
tblOrders ON tblCustomers.CustomerID =
tblOrders.CustomerID;
```

To examine or change the type of join, you can double-click the join line between two record sources to open the Join Properties dialog box. This dialog box offers three choices: Inner, Left Outer, or Right Outer joins. These options are presented with explanations: 1: Only include rows where the joined fields from both tables are equal (Inner); 2: Include ALL Records from 'tblCustomers', and only those records in 'tblOrders' where the joined fields are equal (Left Outer); and lastly, 3: Include ALL Records from 'tblOrders', and only those records in 'tblCustomers' where the joined fields are equal (Right Outer).

CREATE AN INNER JOIN

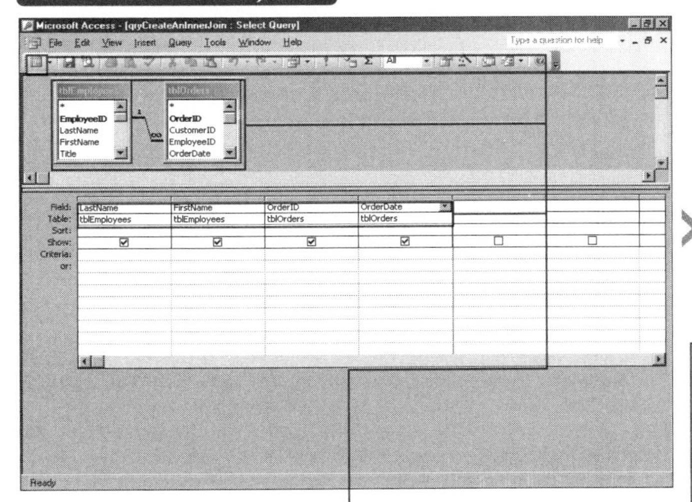

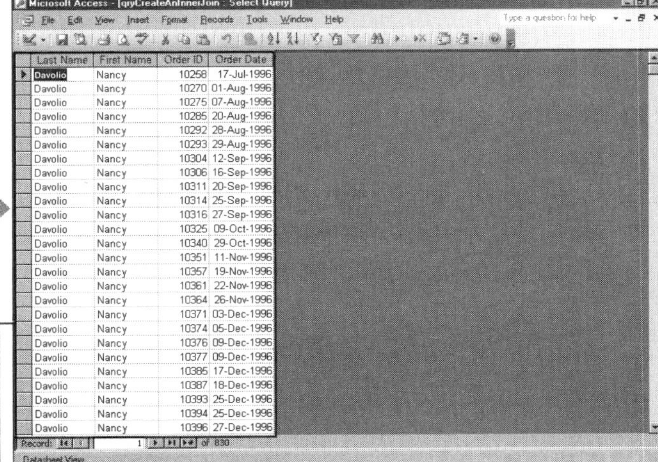

Note: This task uses qryCreateAnInnerJoin in AVP-Chapter03.mdb on the CD-ROM.

1 Create a new query in Design view.

2 Add the two tables you want to join using the Show Table dialog box.

■ The two tables appear with an inner join line between them.

3 Click and drag the fields you want from each of the tables into the query design grid.

4 Click the Datasheet View button.

■ The results datasheet appears, showing records from each table that has a matching record in the other table.

■ In this example, records from both tblOrders and tblEmployees are displayed when each has a matching entry.

CREATE LEFT AND RIGHT OUTER JOINS

You can create Left and Right Outer Joins to locate those records without matching records in another table. Creating Left and Right Outer Joins takes a bit more work than the Inner Join, because they are not the default. When you create a query that uses either Inner or Outer Joins, you must first add the record sources that you want to use. When you add the record sources, a join line appears between the tables, representing the Inner Join. When you double-click the join line, the Join Properties dialog box appears, displaying three choices: Inner, Left Outer, or Right Outer joins.

If you want to create a Left Outer Join, choose 2: Include ALL Records from 'tblCustomers,' and only those records in 'tblOrders' where the joined fields are equal. If you want to create a Right Outer Join, choose 3: Include ALL Records from 'tblOrders,' and only those records in 'tblCustomers' where the joined fields are equal.

After you select either the Left Outer Join or the Right Outer Join, and close the Join Properties dialog box, an arrow appears at one end of the join line. The arrow points from left to right for the Left Outer Join, and right to left for the Right Outer Join.

The usefulness of Outer Joins becomes apparent when you use criteria with them. For example, if you want to see which customers do not have any invoices, you can choose a Left Outer Join for the join type, and type **Is Null** in the OrderID Criteria row. By adding this, the resulting SQL statement looks like this:

```
SELECT tblCustomers.CompanyName, tblOrders.
OrderID, tblOrders.OrderDate FROM tblCustomers
LEFT JOIN tblOrders ON tblCustomers.
CustomerID = tblOrders.CustomerID WHERE
(((tblOrders.OrderID) Is Null));
```

This command returns only those records in tblCustomers that do not have any matching records in tblOrders.

CREATE A LEFT OUTER JOIN

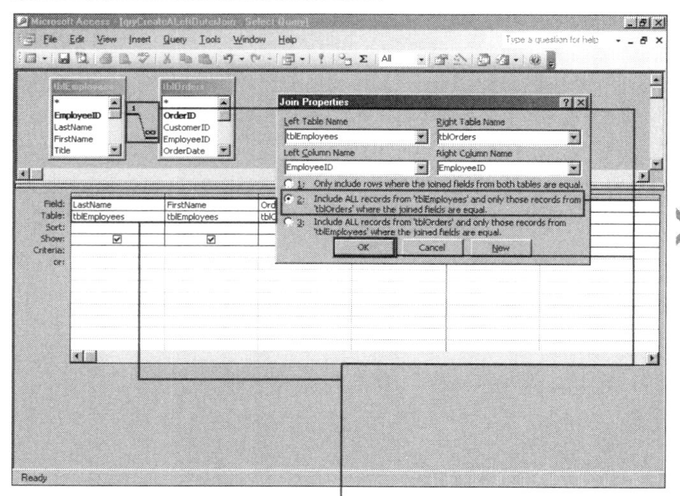

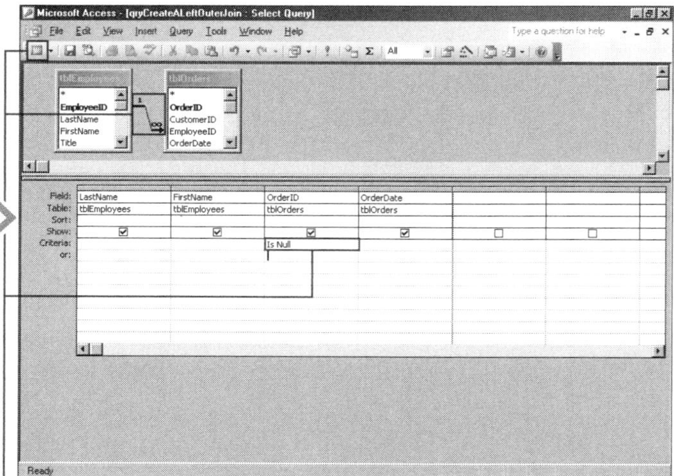

Note: These steps use qryCreateALeftOuterJoin in AVP-Chapter03.mdb on the CD-ROM.

1 Create a new query, and add two tables using the Show Table dialog box.

2 Click and drag the fields you want into the query design grid, including the Primary Key field from the second table.

3 Double-click the join line.

4 In the Join Properties dialog box, click the second option.

5 Click OK.

■ An arrow pointing to the second table appears.

6 Type **Is Null** in the Criteria row of the column that contains the Primary Key field.

7 Click the Datasheet View button.

■ Access displays the records in the first table that do not have matching records in the second table.

■ In this example, the results show those employees who do not have any orders.

Extra

When you use either a Left or Right Outer Join, and have more than two tables making up the query, you should pay attention to what combination of joins you use between the three or more tables. For example, if you have a Left Outer Join going from table one to table two, and an Inner Join or a Right Outer Join between table two and table three, an error message appears, telling you that you have created ambiguous joins.

In order to use the Left Outer Join, you need to be consistent, and create a Left Outer Join between tables two and three, as well as between tables one and two.

Using the Right Outer Join is a great way to test for data that was entered without the use of relationships and referential integrity in place. Erroneous data can get into your database when you import data, or when you clean up somebody else's data. By creating queries as described in these last steps, you can greatly enhance the integrity of the data. In a perfect world with referential integrity in place, you should not ever have to create Right Outer Joins going from a parent table, Customers in this example, and child tables, Invoices in this example. For more information on referential integrity, see Chapter 1.

CREATE A RIGHT OUTER JOIN

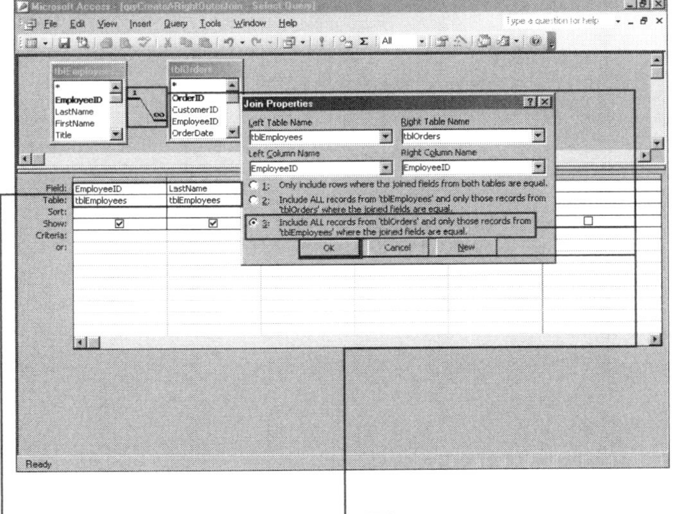

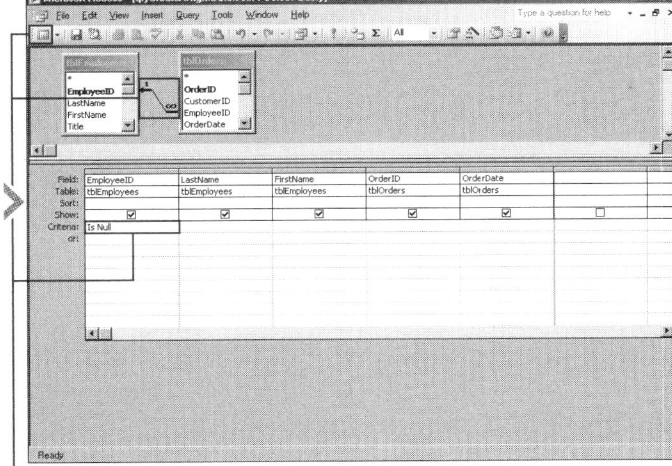

Note: These steps use qryCreateARightOuterJoin in AVP Chapter03.mdb on the CD-ROM.

1 Create a new query, and add two tables using the Show Table dialog box.

2 Click and drag the fields you want into the query design grid, including the Primary Key field from the first table.

3 Double-click the join line.

■ The Join Properties dialog box opens.

4 Click the third option.

5 Click OK.

■ An arrow pointing to the second table appears.

6 Type **Is Null** in the Criteria row of the column that contains the Primary Key field.

7 Click the Datasheet View button.

■ Access displays the records in the second table that do not have matching records in the first table.

■ In this example, the results show those orders that do not have an employee assigned to them.

SUMMARIZE DATA USING A TOTALS QUERY

In previous sections, you have used queries to display individual results, based on one or more record sources. While this is powerful, you can use the Totals query, also called an Aggregate query, to analyze your data. The Totals query uses various functions on your data, such as summing up columns, averaging values, counting records, and displaying minimum and maximum values for a set of results.

To create a Totals query, you can select a field or fields on which you want to group data, and the fields to which you want to apply functions. Then, click the Totals button, which adds a new row, called Totals, to the query design grid.

The Totals row offers you options including Group By, which you use to specify the field or fields for which you want to aggregate data, Sum, Avg, Min, and Max. In addition to the standard functions, you can also select Expression, which allows you to create your own expression, and Where, which instructs the field not to display, and to act as a criteria field only.

When you create a Totals query, Access adds the function to the SQL statement along with a GROUP BY clause. For example, if you create a Totals query to sum up quantities sold (tblOrderDetails.Quantity) for each product (tblProducts.ProductID), then the SQL statement looks like this:

```
SELECT tblProducts.ProductID,
Sum(tblOrderDetails.Quantity) AS
SumOfQuantity FROM tblProducts INNER JOIN
tblOrderDetails ON tblProducts.ProductID =
tblOrderDetails.ProductID GROUP BY
tblProducts.ProductID
```

In the example above, the GROUP BY clause applies to the tblProducts.ProductID field, and the Sum function applies to the tblOrderDetails.Quantity field.

SUMMARIZE DATA USING A TOTALS QUERY

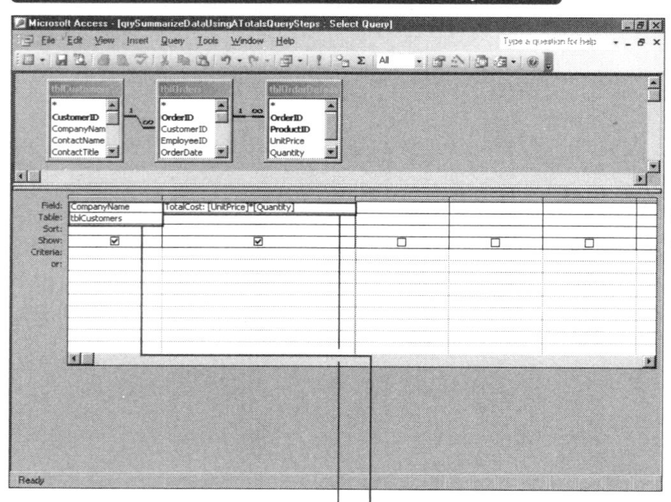

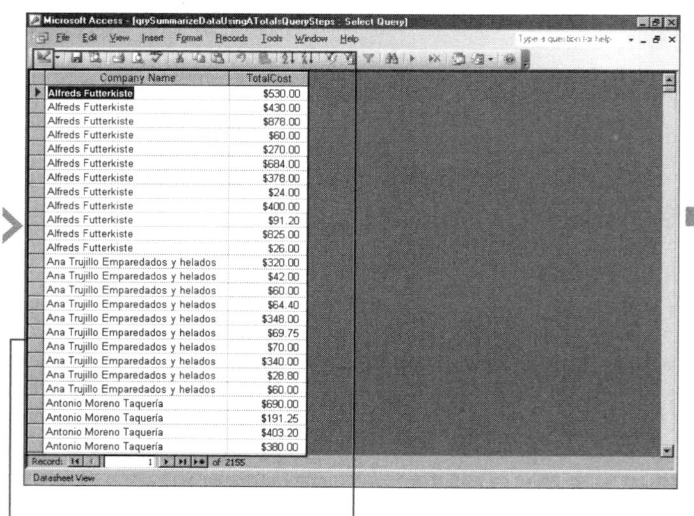

Note: This task uses qrySummarizeDataUsingATotalsQuerySteps in AVP-Chapter03.mdb on the CD-ROM.

1 Create a new query in Design view, adding the tables you want to include in the Totals query.

2 Add the fields that you want to use to group data.

3 Add the fields that you want to use with functions.

■ This example uses the expression TotalCost for the Sum value.

4 Click the Datasheet View button ( ).

■ The Select Query window appears, with the results of the Totals query that Access creates from your base data.

■ You can now verify that the base recordset is what you want for the totals query.

5 Click the Design View button.

Extra

When you use criteria with Totals queries, you should pay attention to where you place the criteria. For example, if you place the criteria on a column by setting the Totals row value to Where and add criteria, rather than placing an entry into the Criteria row of a column containing a function, you get two different answers. This is because you are comparing the criteria against the values using the individual records instead of values from the aggregated results.

In the query below, for example, if you add criteria to the column that contains the Sum function, the SQL statement now includes the HAVING clause, and returns 19 records in the results. With the HAVING clause, the criteria looks at the summed values, rather than the individual values.

```
SELECT tblProducts.ProductName, Sum(tblOrderDetails.Quantity) AS
SumOfQuantity

FROM tblProducts INNER JOIN tblOrderDetails ON tblProducts.ProductID =
tblOrderDetails.ProductID GROUP BY tblProducts.ProductName HAVING
(((Sum(tblOrderDetails.Quantity))<400));
```

However, if you place the criteria in a separate field, setting the Totals row to Where for the individual Quantity column, the SQL statement returns 77 records:

```
SELECT tblProducts.ProductName, Sum(tblOrderDetails.Quantity) AS
SumOfQuantity FROM tblProducts INNER JOIN tblOrderDetails ON
tblProducts.ProductID = tblOrderDetails.ProductID WHERE
(((tblOrderDetails.Quantity)<400)) GROUP BY tblProducts.ProductName;
```

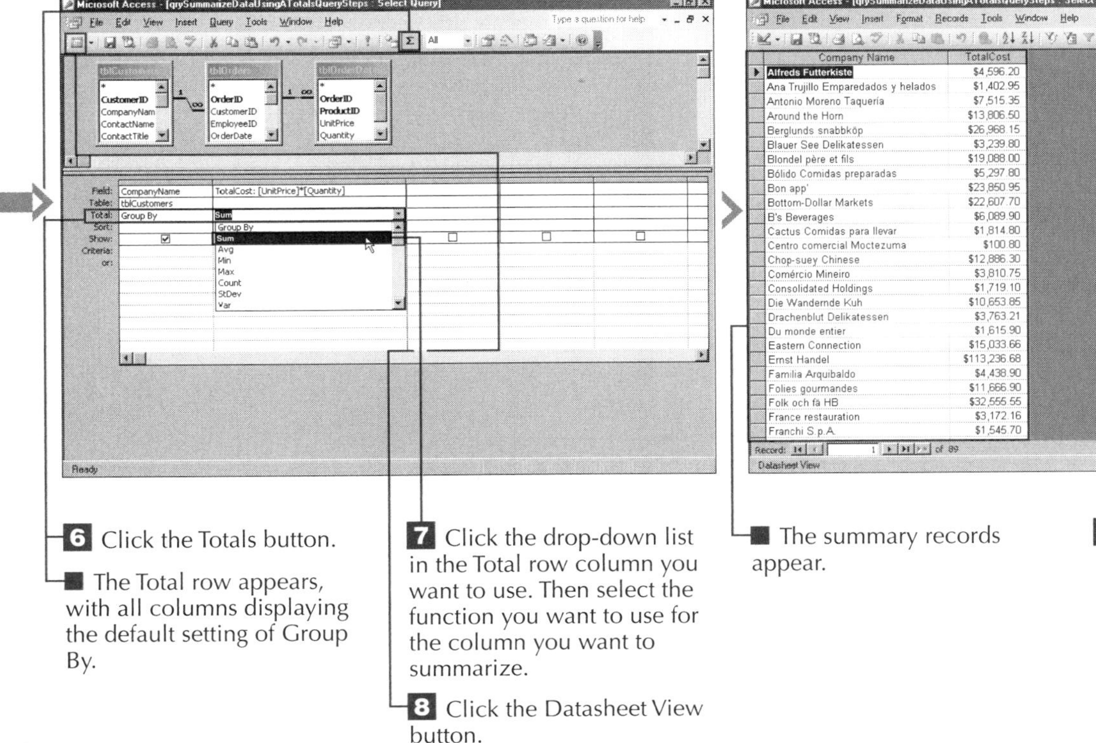

6 Click the Totals button.

■ The Total row appears, with all columns displaying the default setting of Group By.

7 Click the drop-down list in the Total row column you want to use. Then select the function you want to use for the column you want to summarize.

8 Click the Datasheet View button.

■ The summary records appear.

9 Save and close the query.

RETRIEVE THE TOP VALUES

When you use queries to analyze your data, Access allows you to specify either the top or bottom percent or number of records to return. You can use this feature on either individual records, or when utilizing the Totals query.

For example, you can use the Total query to display the total quantities sold for each product your company offers, and then apply the Top Value property with this query. Access offers two options that determine which information appears, and in what quantity.

The first option is whether you want Access to display the bottom or top values. You can set this option by setting the Sort row in the query design grid as Ascending, for bottom values, or Descending, for top values.

The second option is the quantity of records that you want to see. You can set this option by clicking View ➪ Properties while in the upper pane of the Query Design view. In the Query Properties dialog box, you can choose from a list of the Top Value properties, including 5, 25, 100, 5%, 25%, or All. The first three values represent rows, and the last are percentages. You can also enter your own values. For example, if you want to see the top 50%, you can type **50%** in the Top Values field.

This SQL statement tells Access to display the top 5% of products your company sells:

```
SELECT TOP 5 PERCENT qrySummarizeDataUsing
ATotalsQueryIntro.ProductName, qrySummarize
DataUsingATotalsQueryIntro.SumOfQuantity

FROM qrySummarizeDataUsingATotalsQueryIntro

ORDER BY qrySummarizeDataUsingATotalsQuery
Intro.SumOfQuantity DESC;
```

The statement uses the TOP clause, and the DESC option to specify the sort order.

To use this statement on individual records, you can use the table directly instead of using the Totals query.

RETRIEVE THE TOP NUMBER OF RECORDS

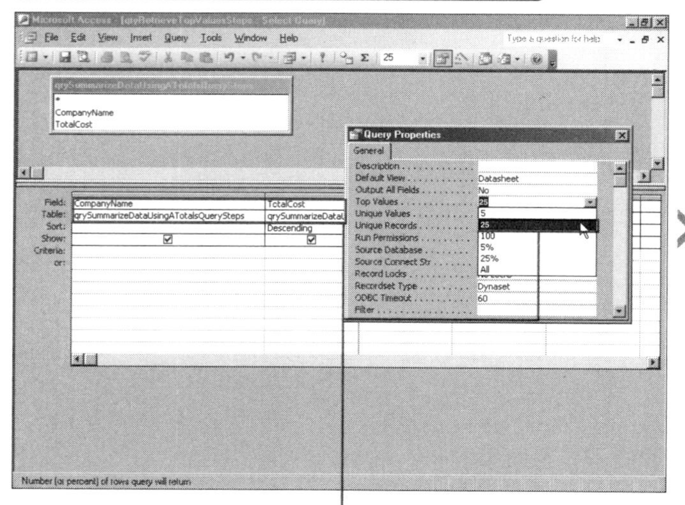

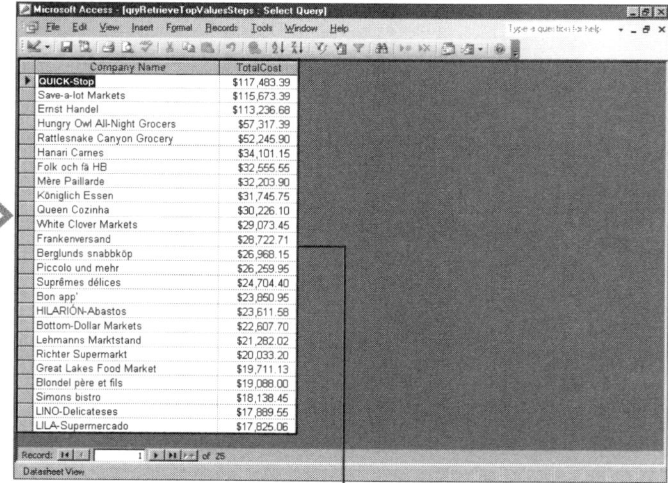

Company Name	TotalCost
QUICK-Stop	$117,483.39
Save-a-lot Markets	$115,673.39
Ernst Handel	$113,236.68
Hungry Owl All-Night Grocers	$57,317.39
Rattlesnake Canyon Grocery	$52,245.90
Hanari Carnes	$34,101.15
Folk och fä HB	$32,555.55
Mère Paillarde	$32,203.90
Königlich Essen	$31,745.75
Queen Cozinha	$30,226.10
White Clover Markets	$29,073.45
Frankenversand	$28,722.71
Berglunds snabbköp	$26,968.15
Piccolo und mehr	$26,259.95
Suprêmes délices	$24,704.40
Bon app'	$23,850.95
HILARIÓN-Abastos	$23,611.58
Bottom-Dollar Markets	$22,607.70
Lehmanns Marktstand	$21,282.02
Richter Supermarkt	$20,033.20
Great Lakes Food Market	$19,711.13
Blondel père et fils	$19,088.00
Simons bistro	$18,138.45
LINO-Delicateses	$17,889.55
LILA-Supermercado	$17,825.06

Note: This task uses qrySummarizeDataUsingATotalsQuerySteps and qryRetrieveTopValuesSteps in AVP-Chapter03.mdb on the CD-ROM.

1 Create a query based on the query from the last task.

2 Drag the fields you want from the field list into the query design grid.

3 Click View ➪ Properties.

4 Click in the Top Values field, and select the value to use for Top Value.

5 Close the Query Properties dialog box.

6 Set the Sort row of the column of values to Descending by clicking in one of the fields, and choosing Descending from the list that appears.

7 Click View ➪ Datasheet View.

■ The top number of records appear.

Extra

There are two ways to use the Top Values property to determine which data appears. The first way involves using criteria to control which records you want to include in the top values. Note that where you place the criteria affects the results presented.

The second way involves the Sort order of the records in the query. To view top values (largest), you set the Sort order to Descending. For bottom values (least), you set the Sort order to Ascending. For example, if you want to target a mailing to those customers who have bought the least amount of product, you can set the Top Value property to either the number of records or percent you want to target, and set the Sort order to Ascending. The SQL SELECT statement looks like this:

```
SELECT TOP 5 PERCENT tblCustomers.CompanyName,
UnitPrice*Quantity AS TotalCost FROM (tblCustomers INNER
JOIN tblOrders ON tblCustomers.CustomerID =
tblOrders.CustomerID) INNER JOIN tblOrderDetails ON
tblOrders.OrderID = tblOrderDetails.OrderID ORDER BY
UnitPrice*Quantity;
```

The statement above indicates Ascending order by the absence of the DESC option on the ORDER BY clause.

RETRIEVE THE TOP PERCENT OF RECORDS

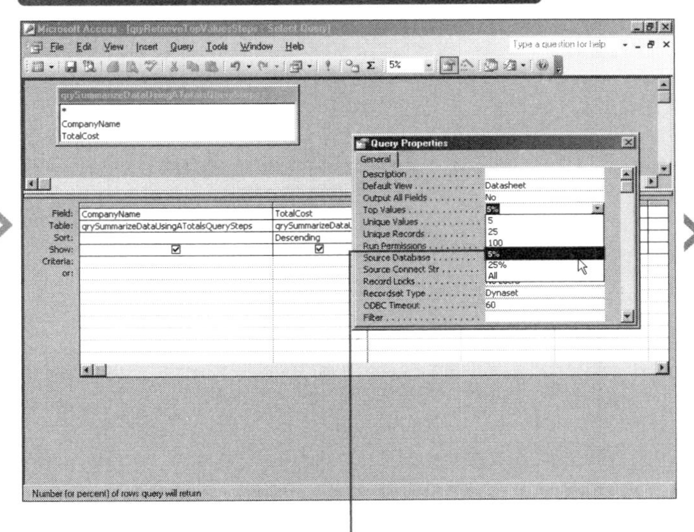

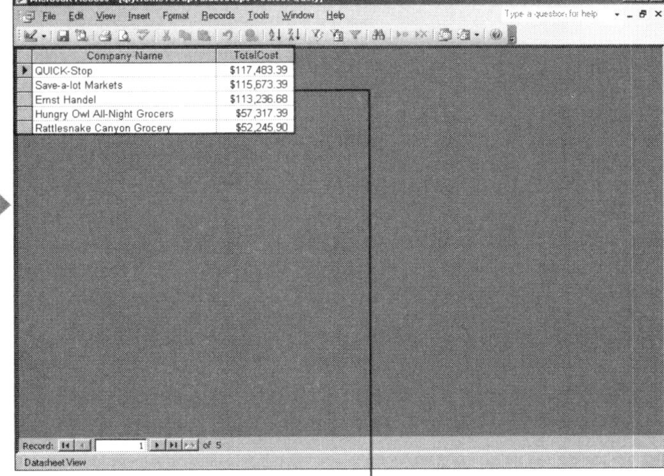

8 Click View ➪ Properties while in a blank spot in the upper pane of the query design grid.

■ The Query Properties dialog box appears.

9 Click in the Top Values field, and select the percent you want to use for Top Value from the list that appears.

10 Click View ➪ Datasheet View.

■ The top percent of records appear.

CREATE A SIMPLE CROSSTAB QUERY

With a Totals query you can see total values for a single topic, such as total amount sold. However, if you want to see totals for two topics, you can create a Crosstab query. For example, you may want to see the total sold by each employee and the total sold by years. To get this total, you need a cross tabulation of the values, which you can get from a Crosstab query.

When you create a Crosstab query, the first topic you specify appears down the left-hand side of the datasheet, and the second topic appears across the top. In the example from the previous paragraph, you would see employees listed on the left-hand side of the datasheet, and month and years across the top.

To create a Crosstab query, you can add the tables and drag the fields you want to use into the query design grid, just as you would the other types of queries. The first field you drag to the query design grid is displayed in the rows of your final datasheet. The second field is displayed across the datasheet, and the third field calculates the values.

For example, you may want to add the tblEmployees, tblOrders, and tblOrderDetails tables to a query. Click and drag the employee name from the tblEmployees table, create an expression of Format from the tblOrders table (OrderDate, "yy' mmm"), and then create an expression (UnitPrice*Quantity) for the last value you want to use. When you activate the Crosstab query feature, new rows called Totals and Crosstab appear in the query design grid. You can place Sum for the Totals row of the UnitPrice*Quantity column, and set Row Heading, Column Heading, and Value for the three columns in the Crosstab row.

As with other types of queries, you can base a Crosstab query on tables or other queries to make them easier to use.

CREATE A SIMPLE CROSSTAB QUERY

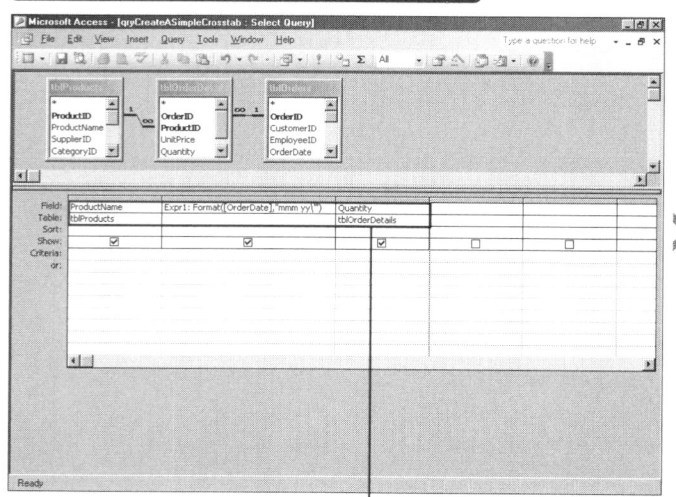

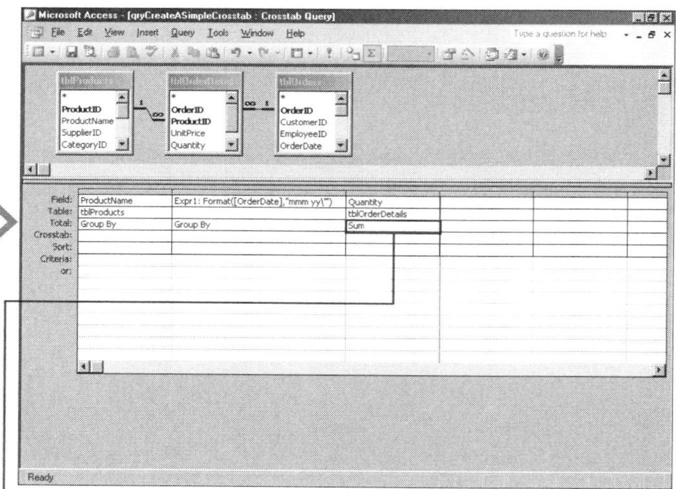

Note: This task uses the query qryCreateASimpleCrosstab in the database AVP-Chapter03.mdb on the CD-ROM.

1 Create a new query in Design view, and add the tables you want to include in the Crosstab query.

2 Click and drag the fields you want to use for the Row Heading, Column Heading, and Value columns.

■ For the query to work properly, you must add the fields in the exact order indicated in step 2.

3 Click Query ➪ Crosstab Query.

4 Click in the Total row of the column you want to use as the value, and select the function you want the query to perform from the drop-down list.

■ In this example, Sum is used for the Quantity column.

Extra

When you create a Crosstab query, you are also using the Totals query features. When you set columns to Row Heading and Column Heading, you must leave the Total row set to Group By. However, you can choose from several functions for the Value column, including those shown in the table, in addition to the Sum function used in the steps.

FUNCTION	DESCRIPTION
Sum	Sums up the values for the Group By columns.
Avg	Averages the values for the Group By columns.
Min	Retrieves the minimum value in the Group By columns.
Max	Retrieves the maximum value in the Group By columns.
Count	Counts the records for the Group By columns.
StDev	Returns the standard deviation of the values for the Group By columns.
Var	Returns the variance of the values for the Group By columns.
First	Retrieves the first value in the Group By columns.
Last	Retrieves the last value in the Group By columns.
Expression	Allows you to use your own expression.

You can set the Total row to Where, in which case the column is simply used for criteria.

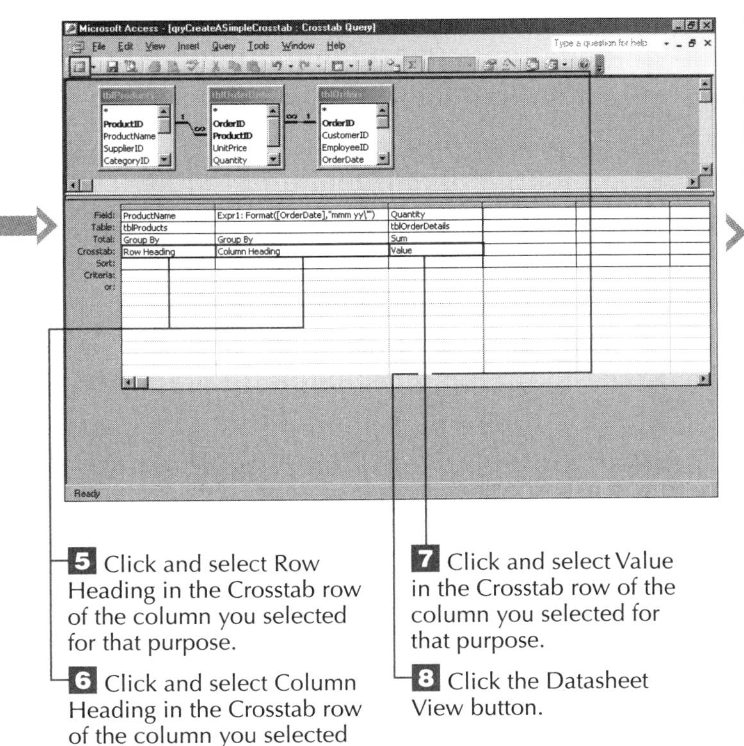

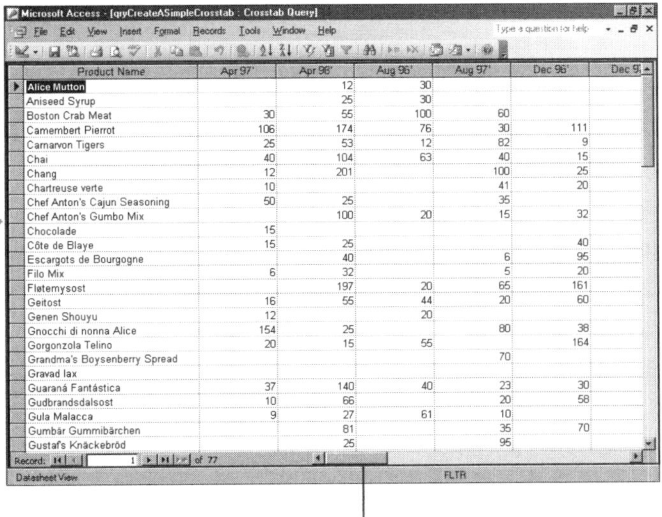

5 Click and select Row Heading in the Crosstab row of the column you selected for that purpose.

6 Click and select Column Heading in the Crosstab row of the column you selected for that purpose.

7 Click and select Value in the Crosstab row of the column you selected for that purpose.

8 Click the Datasheet View button.

■ For this example, Access displays the products by month.

■ The completed results appear.

CONTROL ORDER OF HEADINGS

When initially creating Crosstab queries, simply getting data to display approximately as you intended can be exciting. However, when there is no data for a given column, or when the query uses a certain format, the columns may not appear as you want them to. You can control the order of headings that appear in the results of your Crosstab queries with the Column Heading property field.

For example, when you create a Crosstab query that uses the format of year and month name for the columns, by default the columns are be alphabetized by year, and then by month name. However, you will probably want the columns to appear in the correct year and month order, that is, numerically, not alphabetically.

Another problem arises when you do not have data for a particular month. By default, this month is totally excluded from the results, which may not be what you want.

To solve these problems, you can set the column headings by clicking Query ⇨ Query Properties after you create the Crosstab query. Next, you can set the Column Headings property of the query with the text and order you want to display. For example, you can type the following text into the Column Headings property field: **"96' Aug","96' Sep","96' Oct", "96' Nov", "96' Dec", "97' Jan".**

The columns in this example now appear, regardless of whether they contain any data. Keep in mind that you have to specify the column headings exactly as the query will create them. This is because only those headings that you specify in the Column Headings property field actually appear. Thus, if columns do not match, they do not display, with the result that misspelled column headings that you specify in the Column Headings property field will appear blank.

CONTROL ORDER OF HEADINGS

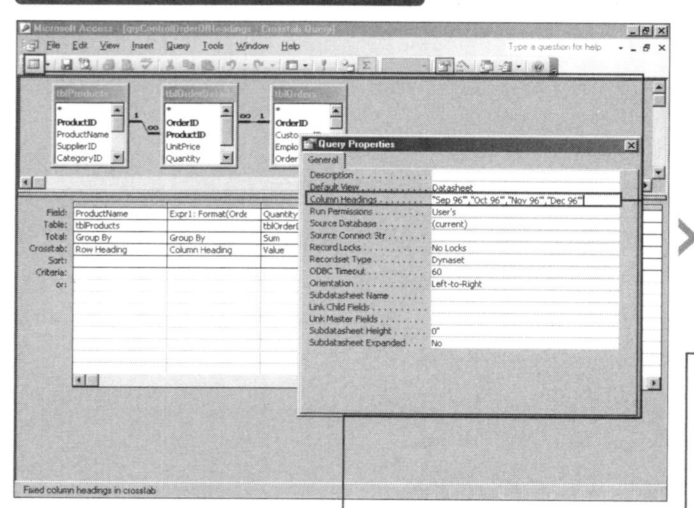

Microsoft Access - [qryControlOrderOfHeadings : Crosstab Query]

Product Name	Sep 96'	Oct 96'	Nov 96'	Dec 96'
Alice Mutton	40	98	36	
Aniseed Syrup				
Boston Crab Meat	50		4	
Camembert Pierrot			143	111
Carnarvon Tigers	25	60		9
Chai	20		27	15
Chang	40	56		25
Chartreuse verte	90	4	104	20
Chef Anton's Cajun Seasoning	20	52	35	
Chef Anton's Gumbo Mix				32
Chocolade				
Côte de Blaye		20	80	40
Escargots de Bourgogne	30	30		95
Filo Mix		28		20
Fløtemysost	5	70	5	161
Geitost		8		60
Genen Shouyu		5		
Gnocchi di nonna Alice	24	12	20	38
Gorgonzola Telino		85	120	164
Grandma's Boysenberry Spread	30	6		
Gravad lax		28		
Guaraná Fantástica			45	30
Gudbrandsdalsost	23		68	58
Gula Malacca			77	
Gumbär Gummibärchen		74	16	70
Gustaf's Knäckebröd				

Record: 1 of 77

Datasheet View

1 Open the query qryControlOrderOfHeadings on the CD-Rom.

2 Click View ⇨ Properties.

3 In the Query Properties dialog box, type the column headings you want to appear in the Column Headings property field.

4 Click the Datasheet View button.

■ The columns appear in the order you specified in the Column Headings property field.

ADD ROW TOTALS TO YOUR CROSSTAB QUERY

When you summarize your data across columns, you can also create totals for each row. To do this you must add another Row Heading column to your Crosstab query.

After you make a copy of the current Value column, you can change the name of the column to Row Total and add a title such as Employee Total. You can then change the Crosstab row entry to Row Heading. You can now position the new Row Heading column before the individual columns by placing the new Row Heading column directly after the first Row Heading column. If you place the new Row Heading column after the Value column, the new total appears after the individual columns. You can also adjust the columns when you are in Datasheet view.

This SQL statement shows how complicated your queries can become as you add features to your Crosstab query:

```
TRANSFORM Sum(UnitPrice*Quantity) AS Expr1

SELECT LastName & ", " & FirstName AS
Employee, Sum(UnitPrice*Quantity) AS
[Employee Total]

FROM (tblEmployees INNER JOIN tblOrders ON
tblEmployees.EmployeeID =
tblOrders.EmployeeID) INNER JOIN
tblOrderDetails ON tblOrders.OrderID =
tblOrderDetails.OrderID

GROUP BY LastName & ", " & FirstName

PIVOT Format(OrderDate,"yy"" ""mmm");
```

TRANSFORM and PIVOT are added as part of the Crosstab query, and tell the database to use the Sum for the value (TRANSFORM) and the Format statement for column headings (PIVOT) .

The new PivotTable view of queries allows you to change the arrangement of the data you are viewing. See Chapter 9 for more information.

ADD ROW TOTALS TO YOUR CROSSTAB QUERY

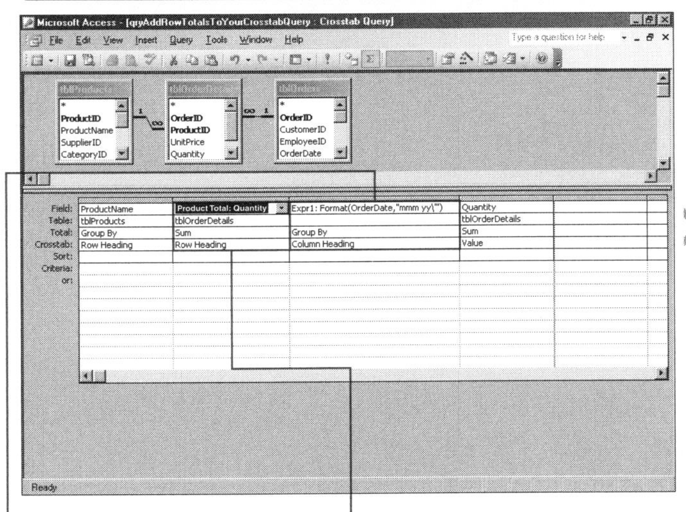

Product Name	Product Total	Apr 97'	Apr 98'	Aug 96'	Aug 97'	Dec 9
Alice Mutton	978		12	30		
Aniseed Syrup	328		25	30		
Boston Crab Meat	1103	30	55	100	60	
Camembert Pierrot	1577	106	174	76	30	
Carnarvon Tigers	539	25	53	12	82	
Chai	828	40	104	63	40	
Chang	1057	12	201		100	
Chartreuse verte	793	10			41	
Chef Anton's Cajun Seasoning	453	50	25		35	
Chef Anton's Gumbo Mix	298		100	20	15	
Chocolade	138	15				
Côte de Blaye	623	15	25			
Escargots de Bourgogne	534		40		6	
Filo Mix	500	6	32		5	
Fløtemysost	1057		197	20	65	
Geitost	755	16	55	44	20	
Genen Shouyu	122	12		20		
Gnocchi di nonna Alice	1263	154	25		80	
Gorgonzola Telino	1397	20	15	55		
Grandma's Boysenberry Spread	301				70	
Gravad lax	125					
Guaraná Fantástica	1125	37	140	40	23	
Gudbrandsdalsost	714	10	66		20	
Gula Malacca	601	9	27	61	10	
Gumbär Gummibärchen	753		81		35	
Gustaf's Knäckebröd	348		25		95	

1 Open the query AddRowTotalsToYourCrosstabQuery on the CD-ROM.

2 Click the Column Heading column.

3 Click Insert ⇨ Rows.

4 Copy and paste the Value column into the blank column.

5 Change the Field Name to the row title, and change the Crosstab row entry to Row Heading.

■ This example uses Product Total: Quantity as the row title.

6 Click the Datasheet View button (▦).

■ The results with the new Row Heading appear.

TOTAL UP CROSSTAB COLUMNS

While you can total up and display column totals across the rows, Access does not automatically summarize and display the column data down the columns of a table. To do this, you can create a separate Totals query that displays the totals, and then combine the Totals query with the Crosstab query. Although this may sound complicated, it is not.

After opening an existing Crosstab query, you can save it as a new query, with the text Totals attached to the original name.

Next, after opening the new query in Design view, you can change the Field entry in the Row Heading column. For example, if the Field entry is:

```
Employee: LastName & ", " & FirstName
```

then you can change it to:

```
Employee: "Total Employees"
```

You can then save and close the new Totals query. If you open the query in Datasheet view, the first row displays Total Employees in the first row, followed by the columns that are in the original Crosstab query.

Note that you must ensure that both the original and new Crosstab queries have the Column Headings property set to the same values. Otherwise problems can occur.

After creating the Totals query, you can create a new Union query that combines the two other Crosstab queries. The SQL statement for the Union query is:

```
Select * From qryTotalUpCrosstabColumnsIntro
Crosstab UNION Select * From qryTotalUp
CrosstabColumnsIntroTotals;
```

In the employee example above, the Total Employee row shows up at the bottom of the results. This happens because there are no employees whose name starts with the letter T. To solve this issue, see the Extra area in this section.

TOTAL UP CROSSTAB COLUMNS

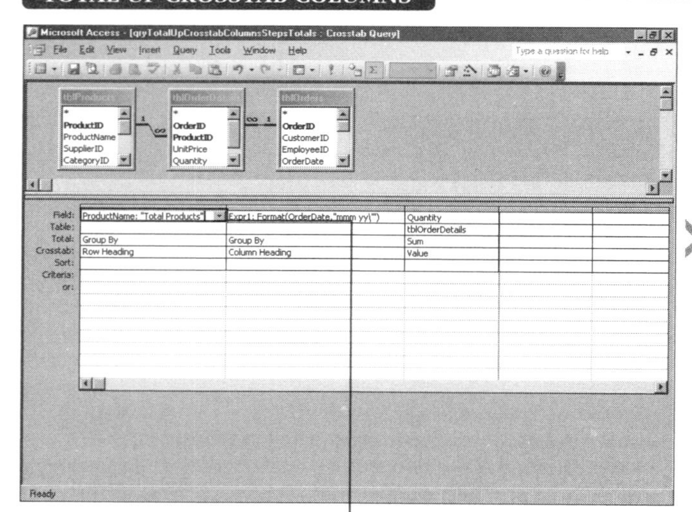

CREATE THE CROSSTAB ROW TOTALS

Note: This task uses qryTotalUpCrosstabColumnsSteps in AVP-Chapter03.mdb on the CD-ROM.

1 Create a Crosstab query, and then save the query.

2 Re-open the query, and click File ⇨ Save As.

3 Type the name of the query, followed by Totals, and then click Save.

4 After the Field name, type **Total Row**.

■ For this example, type **Total Products**.

5 Click the Datasheet View button ( ).

■ A summary of rows appears.

6 Save and close the new query.

Extra

When you combine two Crosstabs queries to display both the Detailed rows and a Totals row, the Totals row displays alphabetically because of the automatic sorting of the Union query. To fix this problem, you can modify the Union query.

You must add an extra column to each of the SELECT statements, with 0 for the Detail crosstab and 1 for the Totals crosstab. You can then sort on this new column, and then the Row Heading column, so that Access sorts the records, with the total row coming last, and the rest of the entries sorted appropriately.

The Union query looks like this:

```
Select *, 0 as Display From qryTotalUpCrosstabColumnsSteps
Crosstab UNION Select *, 1 as Display From qryTotal
UpCrosstabColumnsStepsTotals Order By Display, ProductName;
```

The results are displayed in the extra column, although you can hide this column if you want. For more about hiding columns in datasheets, see Chapter 4.

Microsoft Access - [qryTotalUpCrosstabColumnsSteps : Union Query]

ProductName	Apr 97'	Apr 98'	Aug 96'	Aug 97'	Dec 96'	Dec 97'
Röd Kaviar			25	35		
Røgede sild	21	20		20	15	
Rössle Sauerkraut	66	90	20	45	26	
Sasquatch Ale		180	20		10	
Schoggi Schokolade	120		15			
Scottish Longbreads	6	44	3	33	68	
Singaporean Hokkien Fried Mee	70	112		5		
Sir Rodney's Marmalade	39	15	26		40	
Sir Rodney's Scones	52	103		97	10	
Sirop d'érable	40	97		20		
Spegesild	9	48	15	23	73	
Steeleye Stout	3	117	104	30	70	
Tarte au sucre	3	33	52	95	30	
Teatime Chocolate Biscuits		85	19	50		
Thüringer Rostbratwurst	36	122	15	26	34	
Tofu	70			24	57	
Total Products	**1912**	**4680**	**1322**	**1861**	**2200**	**26**
Tourtière	20	10	10	30	10	
Tunnbröd	10	10		10	40	
Uncle Bob's Organic Dried Pears	50	124		35	10	
Valkoinen suklaa				25	15	
Vegie-spread		42	13		16	
Wimmers gute Semmelknödel		45	9	9	30	
Zaanse koeken	6					

Record: 71 of 78

Datasheet View

COMBINE THE TWO CROSSTABS

7 Create a new query without adding any tables.

8 Click the SQL View button (SQL).

■ The SQL editor appears.

9 Type the SQL statement that creates the Union query.

■ For this example, type **Select * From qryTotalUp CrosstabColumnsStepsCrosstab UNION Select * From qryTotal UpCrosstabColumnsStepsTotals;**.

10 Click View ➪ Datasheet View.

■ The new row appears in the results, displaying the totals for each column.

CREATE DATA DEFINITION QUERIES

You may sometimes want to create or modify table structures using code rather than using the Design view of the tables. To do this you can use Data Definition queries.

Data Definition queries are useful for a number of situations. For example, if you are importing a large amount of data, it is a good idea to remove indexes, import the data, and then recreate the indexes after you have imported the data. You can do this with Data Definition queries. They are also useful when you need to create a new table to receive data, and you want to have the table already in the database. For more information on importing and exporting data, see Chapter 10.

Data Definition queries require SQL, and you must enter the SQL statements directly into the SQL view, because the Design view cannot display Data Definition queries.

You can use a number of commands when you work with tables, relationships, and indexes. The commands you use depend on what you want to do.

Three important commands are Create Table, Create Index, and Drop Index.

For example, if you want to create a table that contains a Text field and an Integer field, you can type:

```
CREATE TABLE tblMyTest (FirstField TEXT(5),
SecondField INTEGER);
```

This statement creates a new table called tblMyTest, with two fields, called FirstField and SecondField.

Next, if you want to add an index to the FirstField field, you can create the following SQL statement in a query:

```
CREATE INDEX MyIndex ON tblMyTest
(FirstField)
```

To delete the index that you just created, you can type:

```
DROP INDEX MyIndex ON tblMyTest
```

CREATE DATA DEFINITION QUERIES

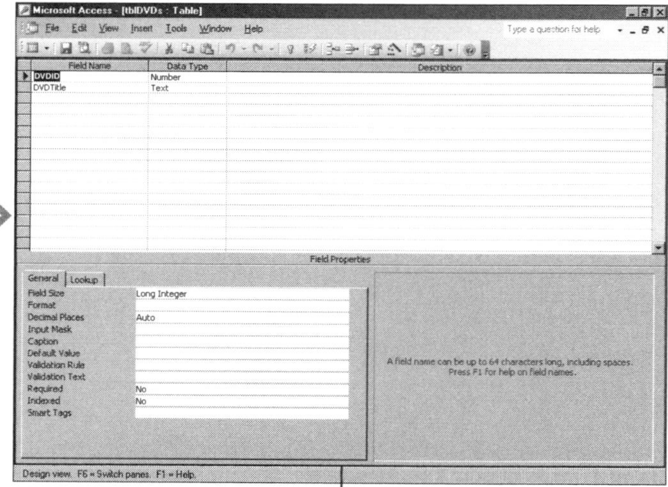

CREATE A TABLE DATA DEFINITION QUERY

1 Create a new query, but do not add any tables.

2 Click View ➪ SQL View.

3 Type a Create Table statement to create the table you want.

■ For this example type **CREATE TABLE tblDVDs (DVDID INTEGER, DVDTitle TEXT(30));**.

4 Click the Run button (!).

■ Access creates a new table.

5 Save and close the query.

6 Click Tables, and open the new table in Design view.

■ The structure of the new table appears in Design view.

Apply It

You can modify the structures of existing tables with the ALTER TABLE statement. You can add ADD COLUMN, ALTER COLUMN, or DROP COLUMN to the ALTER TABLE statement to modify fields in the table. Remember that you are modifying the structure of a column, not the data within the table.

For example, if you want to add a new column called ThirdField to the tblMyTest table, the SQL statement looks like this:

```
ALTER TABLE tblMyTest ADD COLUMN ThirdField TEXT(10)
```

If you want to resize one of the existing columns, such as FirstField, to the length of 50 characters, you can use the following SQL statement:

```
ALTER TABLE tblMyTest ALTER COLUMN FirstField TEXT(50)
```

You can also use the ALTER TABLE command to delete columns using the DROP COLUMN clause. You can remove the ThirdField column using the DROP COLUMN clause on the Alter Table statement. You can follow the format of the ALTER COLUMN clause, without designating a data type or length.

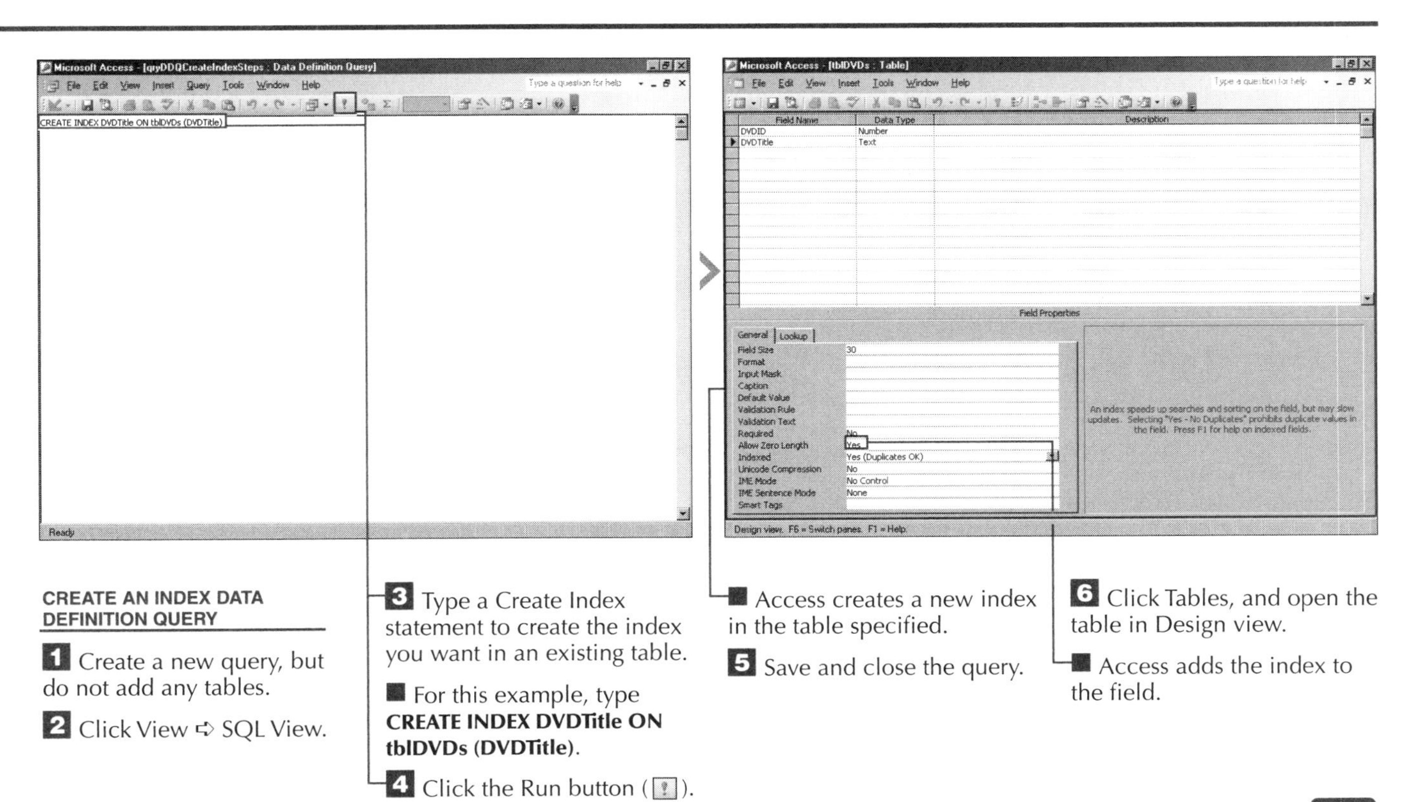

CREATE AN INDEX DATA DEFINITION QUERY

1 Create a new query, but do not add any tables.

2 Click View ➪ SQL View.

3 Type a Create Index statement to create the index you want in an existing table.

■ For this example, type **CREATE INDEX DVDTitle ON tblDVDs (DVDTitle)**.

4 Click the Run button (!).

■ Access creates a new index in the table specified.

5 Save and close the query.

6 Click Tables, and open the table in Design view.

■ Access adds the index to the field.

FORM BASICS

You can create forms that help you control the way users enter data into a database. While you can simply enter data directly into tables or obtain information from tables by using queries, there are a number of reasons why you may want to use forms.

REASONS FOR USING FORMS

Control

You can set validation clauses and default values for entering data into your tables, but if a user can enter data directly into the table, he may accidentally change the table structure or data. By using forms in your database, you can hide the tables from the user, giving you greater control over the data. With forms, you can also control how a user enters data. For example, when a user fails to enter a required value into a record, you can return him to the required field on the form.

By using forms, you can also direct users to input the data in a method that is more appropriate to the data being entered. For example, you can add an Option Group control to give the user a limited list of options for the data being entered. See Chapter 5 for more about Option groups.

Aesthetics

You can arrange your data in a logical manner to reflect the way the user performs a similar task on paper. You do this with the Tab control. For more about Tab controls, see Chapter 5.

ANATOMY OF A FORM

A form can consist of three possible sections. Which sections you use depends on the purpose you have for that form. Forms also have a number of features that you may also want to use, or not use, depending on the purpose of the form.

Form Header Section

The Form Header section displays information or controls at the top of a form, and remains the same, regardless of which record is currently being displayed on the form.

Form Footer Section

This section performs the same purpose as the Form Header section, except at the bottom of a form.

Form Detail Section

This section allows display and editing of individual rows in the record source.

Record Selectors

These are located on the left-hand side of the form. You can click the Record Selector to perform actions on the entire record, such as deleting or saving the record.

Navigation Buttons

These buttons at the bottom of a form help the user navigate around the records in the record source. Users can move to the next record, previous record, first and last records, and new records.

Scroll Bars

You can use scroll bars to scroll either vertically or horizontally on a form when the data goes beyond the visible space on a form. Rather than relying on scroll bars, you should create forms for the lowest screen resolution being used.

Events

Events allow you to add macros or VBA code to your forms. In these macros, or code, you can react to: an action, such as pressing a key, from the user; the form or controls on the form; or the computer itself.

DIFFERENT VIEWS OF FORMS

Access has several form views that you can use for your database applications. You can create some of the form views by setting properties on the forms, while some of the views are default views for when you are creating or modifying your forms.

You can set all the views discussed in this section, except the Mainform/ Subform view, by using the Default view property of a form.

Datasheet View

You should be fairly familiar with this view. A form in Datasheet view looks exactly like tables and queries in the Datasheet view. However, with forms you can add code behind the form datasheet, as well as use form events.

Continuous Form View

As with the Datasheet view, Continuous Form view allows you to see more than one record on the screen at a time. However, unlike the Datasheet view, you can display more than one line of controls for a record at a time, as well as include command buttons and other useful controls. Forms in Continuous Form view are particularly useful in subforms.

Single Form View

This form view is the most useful for managing data input. Single Form view displays one record at a time. With it you can display a lot of information for that record, as well as use subforms and the tab control to manage the way users enter data.

You can use a form in Single Form view with a record source such as a table or query. When you use a form with a record source, the form becomes a bound form. An unbound form does not have a record source. You can use unbound forms for opening reports or as dialog boxes, among other uses.

Mainform/Subform View

Mainform/Subform view is extremely useful in allowing you to display and edit related data using a single form. For example, you may want to create a form that is for customer orders. On the mainform, the order header can contain information such as order date, order number, and customer number. The mainform can be based on a table such as tblOrders. The subform, displayed on the mainform, can then contain the order details, such as individual records for products, quantities, and prices. The table that you use with the subform can be called tblOrderDetails.

Subforms can also be forms on their own, and can be brought into a mainform for a specific use. Information on using subforms can be found in Chapter 5.

PivotTable View

The PivotTable view presents data in the same format as a Pivot Table used in Excel. You can manipulate and filter data to analyze the data. As with Datasheet view, the PivotTable view of a form looks just like the PivotTable view of tables and queries. However, there are some events that you can use with the form's PivotTable view that you do not have with tables and queries.

PivotChart View

This view allows users to chart information based on a record source. The similarities and differences apply to the Form view as opposed to tables and queries that apply to the PivotTable and Datasheet views.

For more about both PivotTable and PivotChart views, see Chapter 9.

CREATE A DATASHEET VIEW FORM USING AN AUTOFORM

Although you can create a form using the Design view or the Form Wizard, the quickest way to create a form is to use an AutoForm. When using the AutoForms you can create a form quickly in the Design or Datasheet view.

One way to create a form using the AutoForm method is to click the New button after you select Forms in the Object group. The New Form dialog box appears, listing the various methods for creating a form. After you select a record source, you can then select which method you want to use to create the form, such as AutoForm: Datasheet.

Another way to create a form using an AutoForm method is to highlight a table or query in its respective group, and then click Insert ➪ AutoForm. When you create a form in this way, Access creates a Single Form view or Mainform/Subform view form.

When you create a form using an AutoForm, you are accepting whatever Access sets as defaults for the various types of views, such as columnar, tabular, and datasheet. Access sets the form to the theme that you used the last time you ran the Form Wizard. Although the theme is not apparent in the Datasheet view, the theme takes effect when you are in Design view or in Single Form and Continuous Forms views. For more information about the Form Wizard, see the section "Using the Form Wizard," later in this chapter.

After you create the form using an AutoForm, the form opens in the Datasheet view. When you close the form, Access asks if you want to save the form.

CREATE A DATASHEET VIEW FORM USING AN AUTOFORM

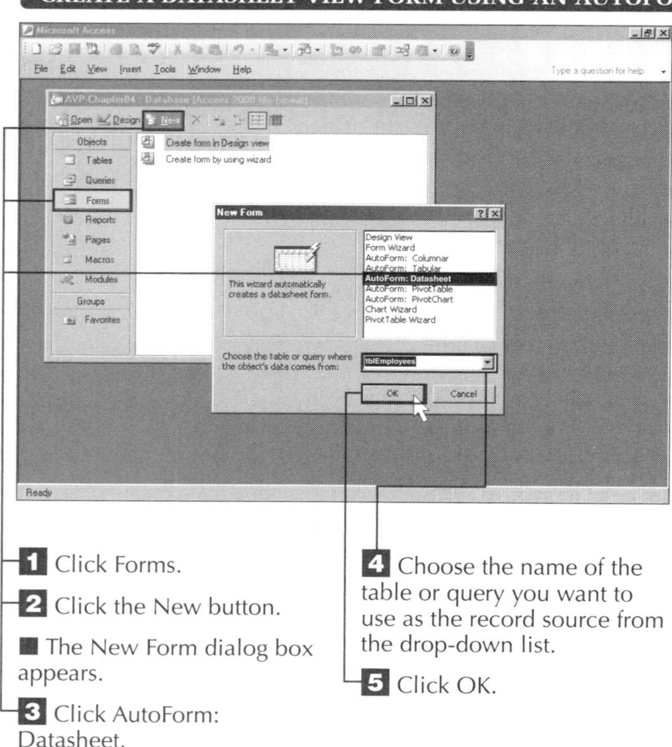

1 Click Forms.

2 Click the New button.

■ The New Form dialog box appears.

3 Click AutoForm: Datasheet.

4 Choose the name of the table or query you want to use as the record source from the drop-down list.

5 Click OK.

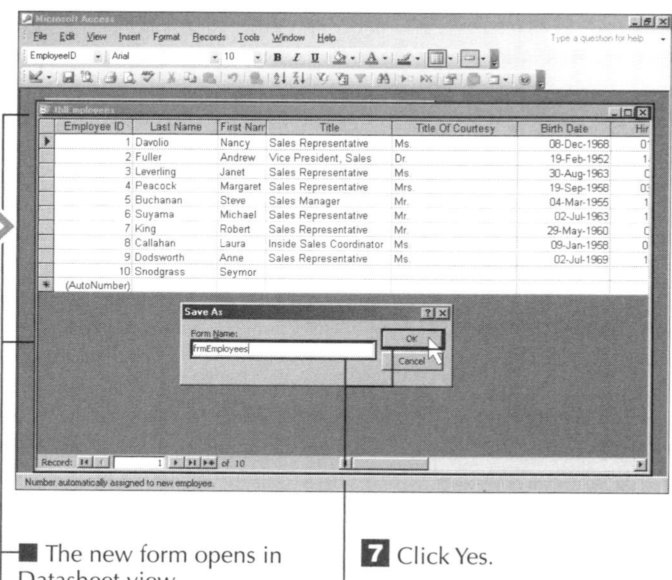

■ The new form opens in Datasheet view.

6 Click the Close button.

■ A dialog box appears, and asks if you want to save the new form.

7 Click Yes.

■ The Save As dialog box appears.

8 Type a name for the new form.

9 Click OK.

MOVE THROUGH THE DATASHEET

There are a number of ways to move through a datasheet so that you can review and edit your data. You can use the arrow keys, Page Up and Page Down keys, or Navigation buttons.

The Navigation buttons are located at the bottom of the form, and you can use them to move around the datasheet. Along with the Navigate To text field are the following buttons: First Record, Previous Record, Next Record, Last Record, and New Record.

The Navigate To text box is a useful tool because it allows you to move around your records by entering the absolute location of the record. Keep in mind that the value you enter is not the key field value; it is a record number of the current record set being displayed in the datasheet. For example, if a user sorts the datasheet, by choosing either the Sort Ascending or Sort Descending buttons, and then enters a value into the Navigate To text field, he goes to a different record than before he sorted the datasheet.

There are some other things to keep in mind when you use Datasheet views in tables and queries, or open a Mainform/Subform type form in Datasheet view. When you have related tables, those tables appear in the datasheet as a plus sign next to the record selector. You can click the plus sign and move around in the related table. Note that the values shown in the Navigation buttons reflect the record source in which you are working.

MOVE THROUGH THE DATASHEET

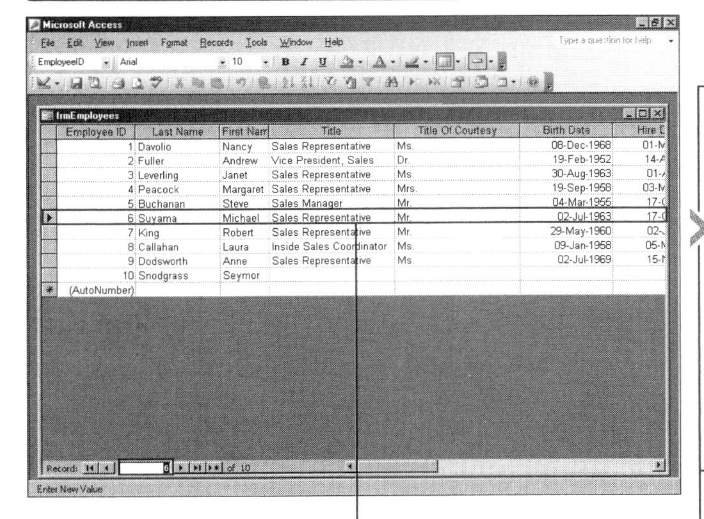

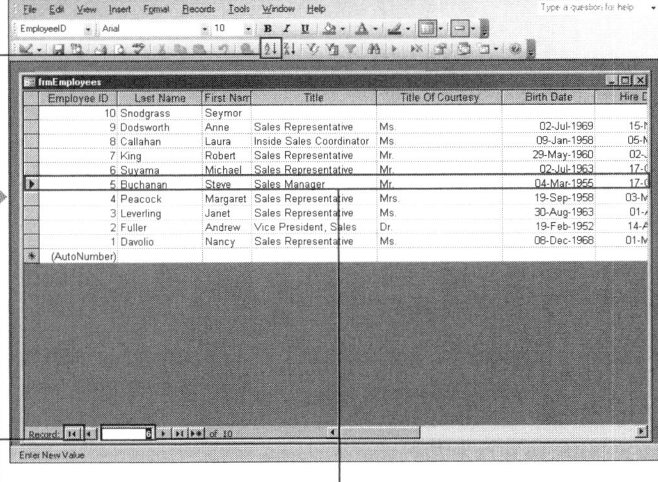

Note: This task uses frmEmployees in AVP-Chapter04.mdb on the CD-ROM.

1 In Datasheet view, open a form, or create a new one.

2 Click in the Navigate To text field, type a record number to which you want to navigate, and then press Enter.

■ The record pointer appears in the record you requested.

■ Make a note of the record you are on.

3 Click the First Record button.

4 Click the Sort Ascending button.

5 Type the same value you entered in step 3 into the Navigate To text field and press Enter.

■ The record pointer points to a different record.

FILTER BY SELECTION

While you can use queries to filter your data down to specific records, you can also filter your data while you are working in a form in Datasheet view. There are two types of filtering options: Filter By Selection and Filter By Form. The first option is discussed in this section, and the second option is discussed in the next section.

As the name suggests, with the Filter by Selection option you can place the cursor in the cell of the data that you want to filter by. After you click the Filter By Selection button, Access displays only those records that match the value you selected. For example, in a form displaying customer records, if you place the cursor in the state column with the particular cell containing WA, and then click the Filter by Selection button, Access displays only those records having WA for the state.

If you then place the cursor in another column's cell, such as the city column, with the value of Seattle, and then click the Filter by Selection button again, the filter narrows down the records even further. As you keep doing this, Access continues to reduce the records displayed.

Another important button is the Apply/Remove Filter button. This button toggles the filter either on or off, depending on the filter's status. If you have chosen a field to filter on, and you want to change the filter, you can click the Apply/Remove Filter button, and then select another field to filter on. You can also turn on and off the same filter by just clicking the Apply/Remove Filter button.

FILTER BY SELECTION

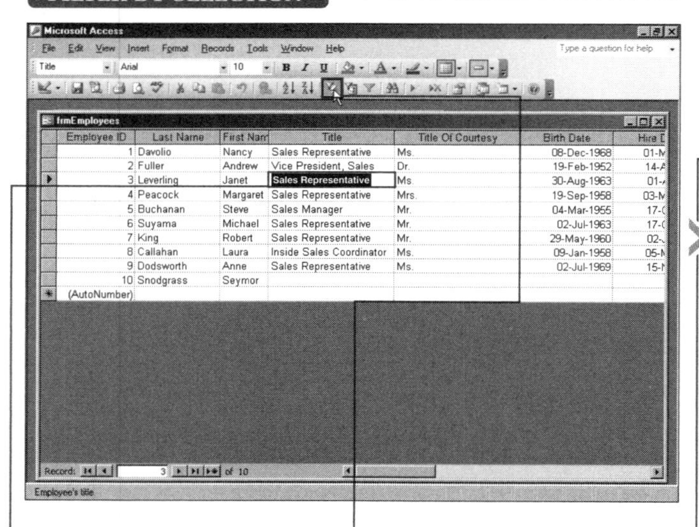

Note: This task uses frmFilterBySelection in AVP-Chapter04.mdb on the CD-ROM.

1 In Datasheet view, open a form, or create a new form.

2 Click in the column and cell that contain the data you want to filter on.

■ In this example, the text Sales Representative in the Title column is hightlighted.

3 Click the Filter By Selection button.

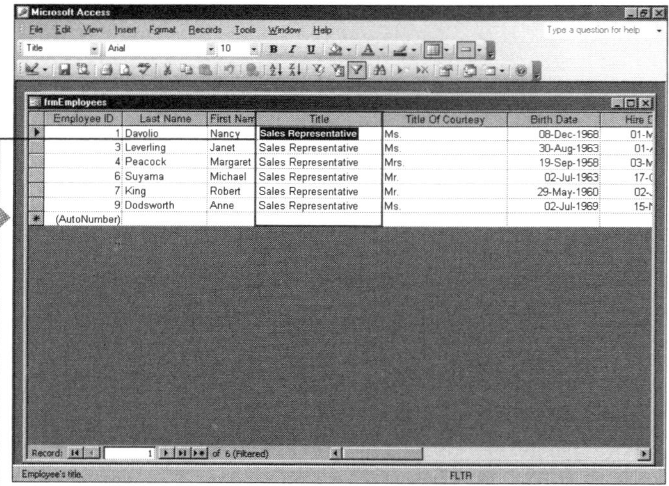

■ Access narrows the records to the value you chose.

Extra

When you click the Filter by Selection button (), you set two properties on the form: Filter, which you can view in the property sheet on the Data tab, and FilterOn, which you can modify using VBA. For more information on using both of these properties in VBA, see Chapter 7.

The Filter property in the property sheet looks similar to criteria in an SQL statement. For the steps below, the expression looks like this:

```
((tblEmployees.Title="Sales Representative"))
```

The rules of criteria delimiters also apply here: Text is surrounded by double quotes, and dates by the pound sign.

If you apply another Filter by Selection, the Filter property looks like this:

```
 (((tblEmployees.Title="Sales Representative"))) AND
((tblEmployees.TitleOfCourtesy="Mr."))
```

You can set the Filter property manually by typing the code on your own, or you can open the form in Design view, and set the property there.

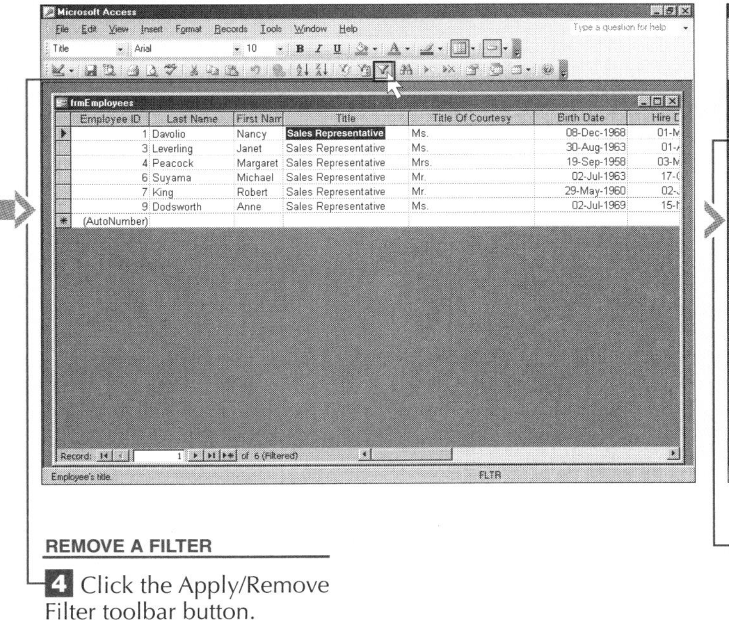

REMOVE A FILTER

4 Click the Apply/Remove Filter toolbar button.

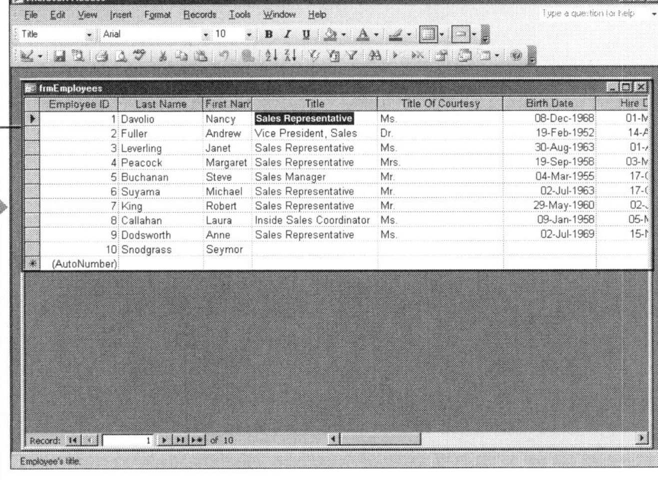

■ The original records are displayed.

FILTER BY FORM

You can use the Filter by Form feature to view database records that meet certain criteria that you specify. When you click the Filter by Form button, a blank form appears, with the column headings containing the field names from your table. Below each heading is a blank field with a drop-down list that contains all the possible choices for each column in the form record source.

If you choose entries from more than one column, Access automatically applies the And operator between the criteria. To use an Or operator, you can click the Or tab after you select an item from a drop-down list.

The Or tab appears at the bottom left corner of the Filter by Form window, to the right of the Look For tab. The Look For tab is the default tab that appears when you input your first criteria for the filter feature. When you click the Or tab, the form clears, and you can select another item to add to the filter. You can combine the ANDs, by picking multiple columns on the same Or page, or with multiple Or pages.

After you select the criteria, you can click the Apply Filter button. Access applies the filter and displays the records that match your criteria.

Access displays the Filtered statement beside the Navigation buttons at the bottom of the form when the results of the filter appear. When you return to displaying all records, the Filtered statement disappears.

You can use the Apply/Remove button to remove a filter. When you create the filters using Filter by Form, Access sets the Filter and FilterOn properties, which you can access by code.

FILTER BY FORM

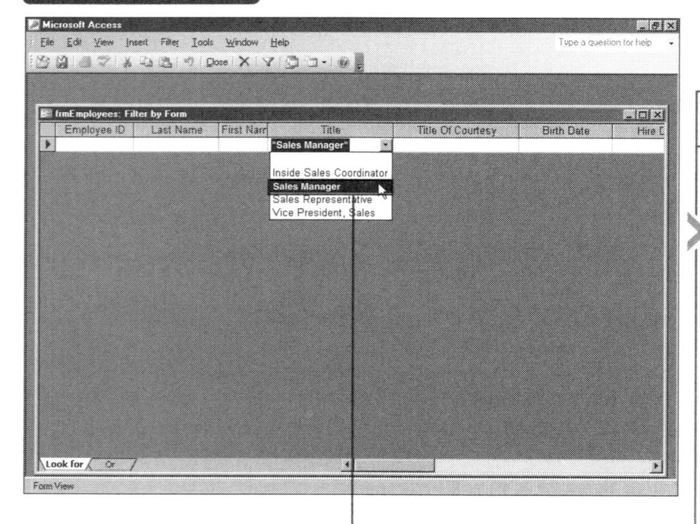

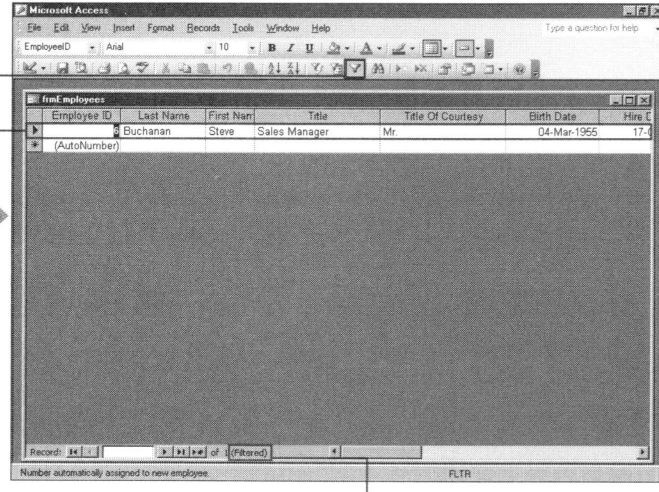

SINGLE VALUE FILTER BY FORM

Note: This task uses frmFilterByForm in AVP-Chapter04.mdb on the CD-ROM.

1 Open a form in Datasheet view.

2 Click the Filter By Form button ( ).

■ The Filter by Form window appears.

3 Click in a field, and select a value from the drop-down list.

4 Click the Apply Filter button.

■ Access filters the records and displays the records that meet the criteria you specified in step 3.

■ The word Filtered appears here, indicating that Access is displaying filtered records.

Extra

When you use the Filter by Form feature, you can use these additional commands from the Filter by Form toolbar. The Load from Query button (icon) and the Save As Query button (icon) are the first two buttons on the Filter By Form toolbar.

The Load from Query command allows you to load the criteria for your filter from a saved query in your database. When you click the Load from Query button, the Applicable Filter dialog box appears, displaying currently saved filters. These filters are actually queries that contain whatever record source you are using for the form in which you are working. For example, if you use tblEmployees for the record source, then those queries that use tblEmployees appear.

The Save as Query command saves the current filter as a query. When you click the Save as Query button, the Save As Query dialog box appears. After saving the filter, you can view and edit the filter along with your other queries.

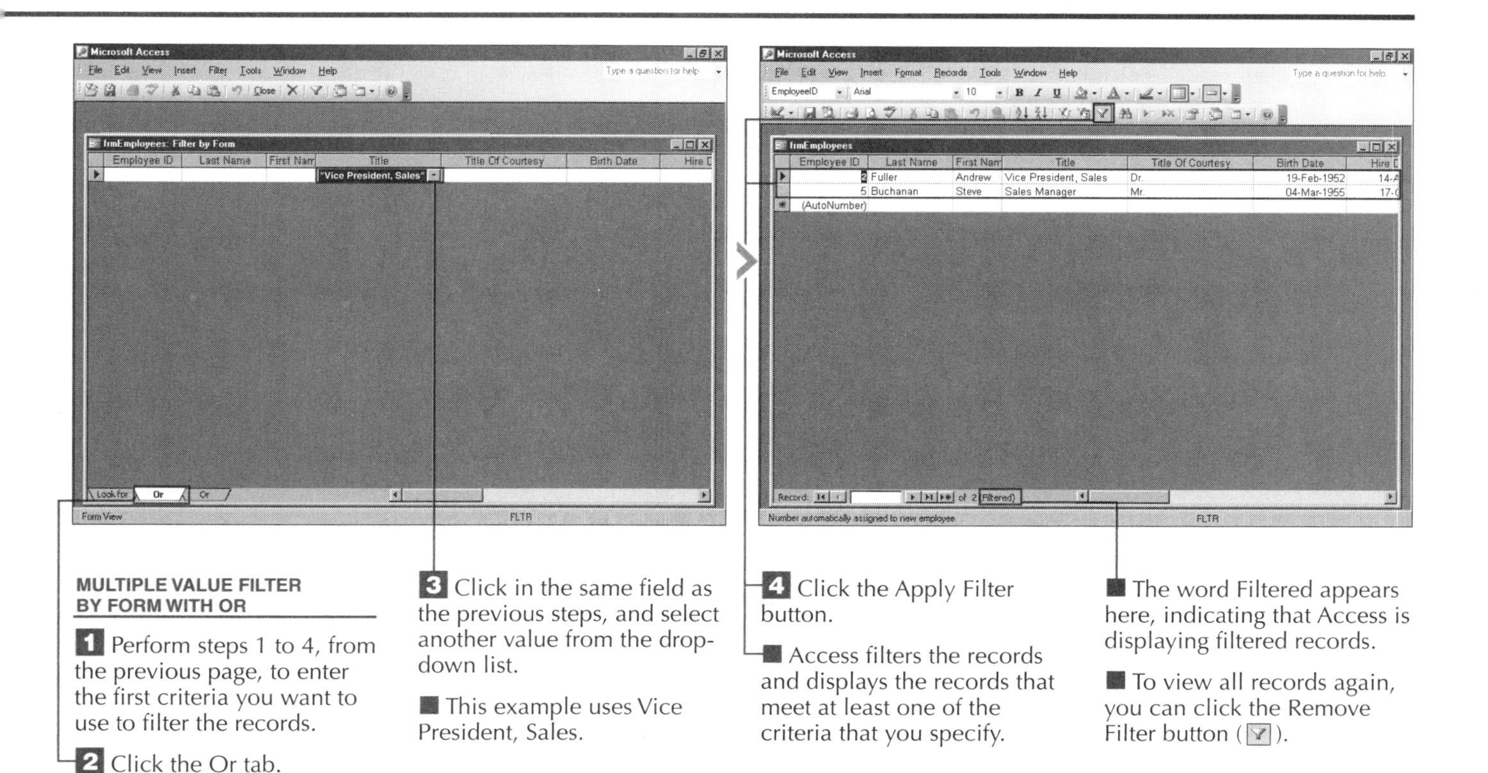

MULTIPLE VALUE FILTER BY FORM WITH OR

1 Perform steps 1 to 4, from the previous page, to enter the first criteria you want to use to filter the records.

2 Click the Or tab.

3 Click in the same field as the previous steps, and select another value from the drop-down list.

■ This example uses Vice President, Sales.

4 Click the Apply Filter button.

■ Access filters the records and displays the records that meet at least one of the criteria that you specify.

■ The word Filtered appears here, indicating that Access is displaying filtered records.

■ To view all records again, you can click the Remove Filter button (icon).

FIND AND REPLACE DATA IN YOUR DATASHEET

You can search for and replace data in your records, tables, queries, and forms. The Access Find and Replace feature is similar to that of Microsoft Word, except that you are searching for data in a table, and not in a document.

To locate data in a datasheet, you must first open that datasheet. If you know which column contains the data, you can place the cursor in that column. Next, you can click Edit ⇨ Find to open the Find and Replace dialog box.

In the Find and Replace dialog box, there are two tabs labeled Find and Replace.

On the Find tab, in addition to the text you want to locate, you can specify whether to search for the text within the current field, or to use all fields in the form.

Next, you can choose how you want to match the text for which you are looking. Access offers the following choices: Any Part of Field, Whole Field, or Start of Field. You can also specify in which direction you want to search for the data, Up or Down. Access also offers you the Match Case capitalization option, or the Search Fields as Formatted option.

When you specify all the options you want to use, you can click the Find Next button to perform the search.

When you need to perform a replace, you can click the Replace tab. A new text field appears, allowing you to enter the data you want to replace the data you are locating. Two additional buttons appear: Replace, which replaces a single instance of the data, and Replace All, which replaces all instances of the data.

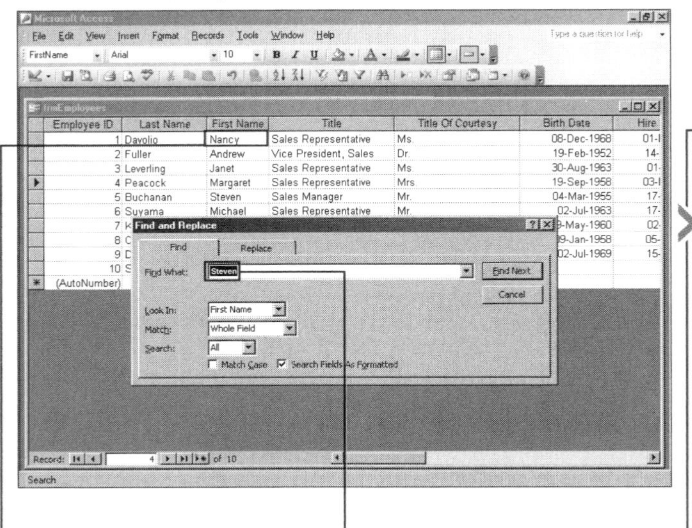

Note: For this example you can use any form in your database.

1 Open a form in Datasheet view.

2 Click in the column you want to search.

Note: Step 2 is not required but makes for better performance.

3 Click Edit ⇨ Find.

4 Type a value you want to find.

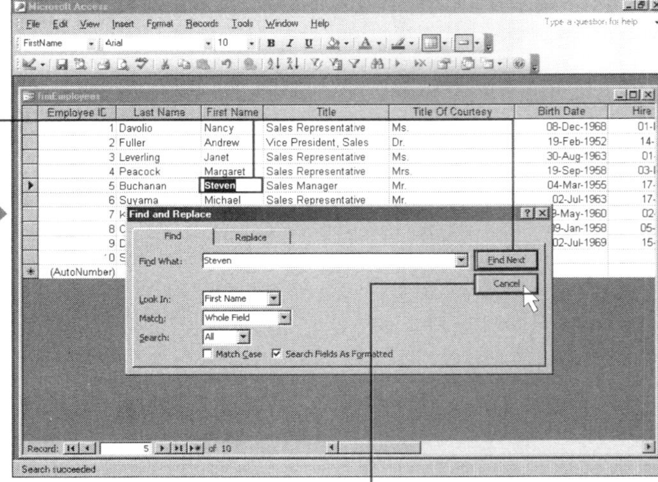

5 Click Find Next.

■ If Access finds a match for the value, it highlights the value in the table.

6 Click Cancel to close the Find and Replace dialog box.

Extra

Here are a few ideas to increase performance of your searches:

- While you are not required to specify a particular field in which to search, for performance reasons it is a good idea. If you have a large number of records with many fields to search, Access must search each one of the fields for each record, slowing your search.
- Limit your searches to exact matches. Instead of using Any Part of Field or Start of Field for the Match setting, use Whole Field. The first two choices widen the scope of your search.
- If you know your text is in one half of the set of records, either before or after your current location, then only pick that direction to search in. For example, if the record pointer is on the 500th record in a set of 1000 records, and you know the record you are searching for is between the current location and the end of the table, use Down for the Search setting. If the record is between the record pointer and the beginning of the table, then use Up. If you do not know where the record is, then use All for the Search setting.

REPLACE THE DATA

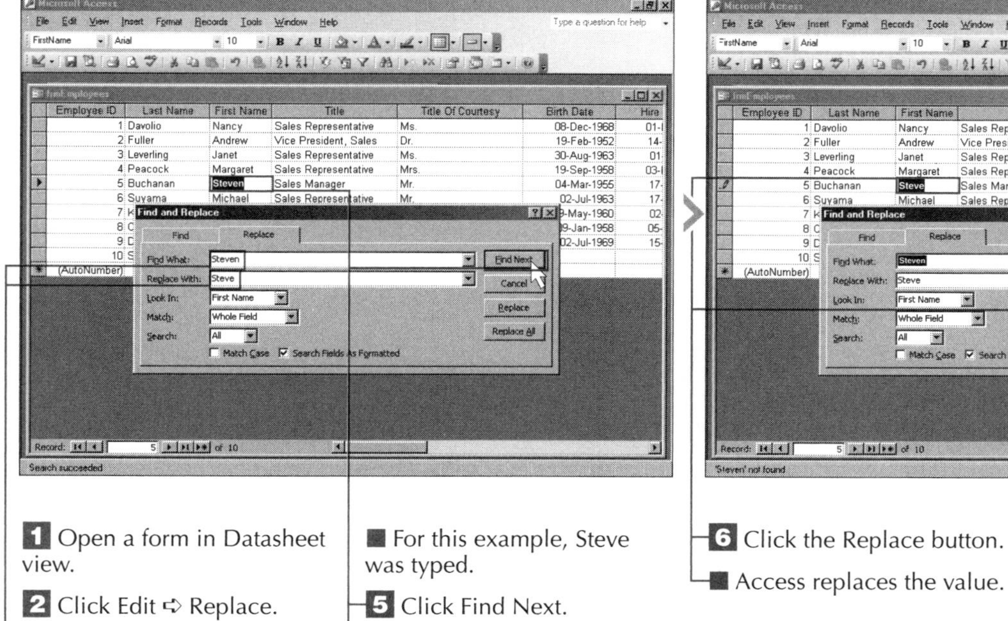

1 Open a form in Datasheet view.

2 Click Edit ➪ Replace.

3 Type a value to find.

4 Type the value with which you want to replace the original value.

■ For this example, Steve was typed.

5 Click Find Next.

■ If Access finds a match for the value, it highlights the value in the table.

6 Click the Replace button.

■ Access replaces the value.

■ When you click Replace All, Access finds and replaces all occurrences of the value in the Find What text field.

USING THE FORM WIZARD

Access offers a Form Wizard that automates the process of creating a form. You can use the Form Wizard to create forms and also to learn how to create forms on your own. As you become more familiar with creating forms, and begin developing your own style, you can start to copy your own forms, and use them as starting points. But for now, you can use the Form Wizard.

You can use the Form Wizard by clicking the Forms group, and then clicking Create form by using wizard. The Form Wizard starts by asking you which tables, or queries, you want to use to create the form, as well as which fields.

The wizard then asks you which type of form you want to create. See the section "Forms Basics" for a list of available form types.

Next, the wizard asks you which style you want to apply to your form. When you select a theme, Access sets various aspects of the appearance of your form, such as background, color, and effects for controls. The effects include flat, sunken, ridged, and shadowed. When you select a theme, you should use it for all your forms in an application. This is because if you have a different theme for each form, the user may find the different themes to be confusing. The Standard theme, although basic, is easy to maintain.

After you select your theme, Access asks you for a title for your form. Access then creates your form.

USING THE FORM WIZARD

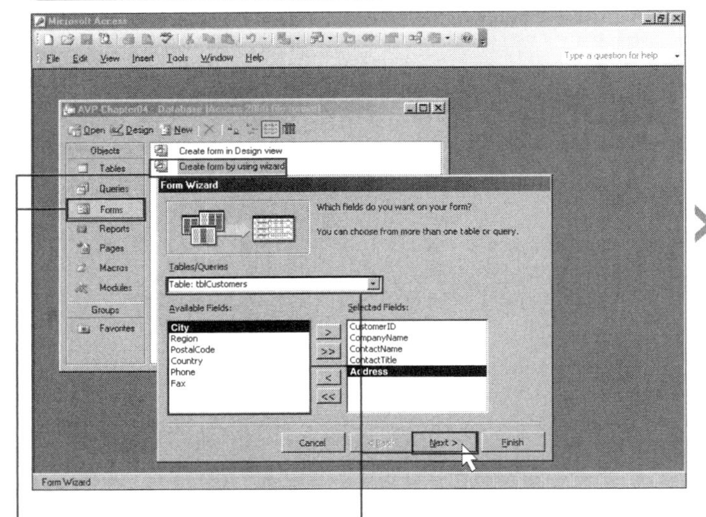

Note: This task uses frmUseTheFormWizard in AVP-Chapter04.mdb on the CD-ROM.

1 In a database, click Forms.

2 Double-click Create form by using wizard.

3 Select the table or query to use as the new form's record source.

4 Double-click each field to include in the form.

■ You can also click each field in the left-hand list, and then click >.

5 Click Next.

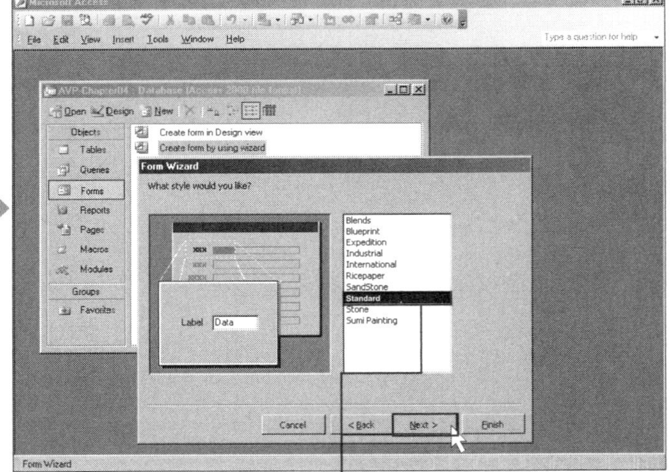

■ A list of AutoForms types appears. The default is columnar.

6 Click a type of form view to use.

7 Click Next.

■ A list of styles appears.

8 Click a theme.

9 Click Next.

Extra

You can create a Mainform/Subform view form by choosing fields from two related sources in the first page of the Form Wizard. When you choose fields from the two different sources, such as tblOrders and tblOrderDetails, the next page of the Form Wizard asks you on which record source you want to base the mainform. The Form Wizard also gives you the choice whether to use a subform, or link another form that it creates for you.

Next, the wizard asks what kind of layout you want for your subform, giving you the choices of Tabular, or continuous form, Datasheet, PivotTable, or PivotChart.

Access then asks you to choose a theme as you would for a single form.

Lastly, Access asks you to name both the mainform and subform.

A good way to learn how to create a Mainform/Subform view form is to look at the mainform in Design view. For more information, see Chapter 5.

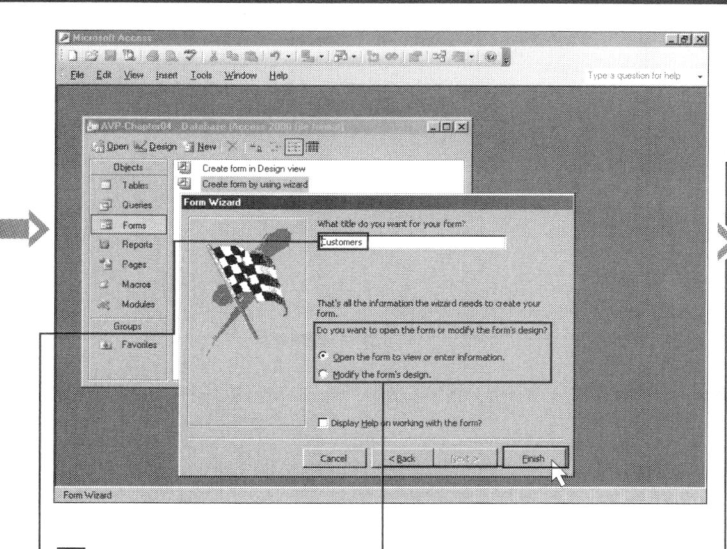

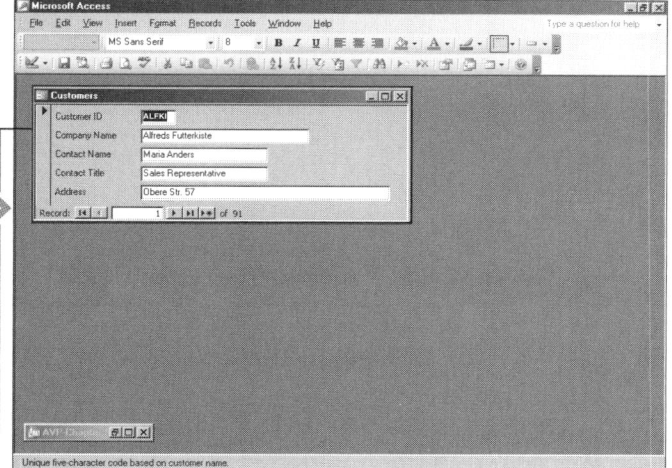

10 Type in a title for your form.

■ Access uses this name for both the top of the form, and the name of the form.

■ By default, Access opens the form to let you view or enter information after it creates the form. If you want to modify the design of the form, you can select that option instead.

11 Click Finish.

■ The form appears, displaying the field names you selected and the first record.

■ To follow naming conventions, you may want to rename the new form by appending the text frm to the beginning of the name, as with frmCustomers in this example.

Note: See Appendix A, "Leszynski Naming Conventions for Microsoft Access," for more about naming conventions.

TOOLS OF FORM DESIGN VIEW

You can use the Access Form Design view to create organized and attractive forms. Access has four main tools that help you to do this. They are the Form Design Layout window, the Controls Toolbox, the Field List, and the Property Sheet.

FORM DESIGN LAYOUT WINDOW

You can use the Form Design Layout window, also called the Layout window, to specify which sections you want to use in your form, such as the Form Header, Form Footer, and Detail sections. Within these sections, you can place the controls that you want to appear in your form exactly as they will appear when the form is opened for use.

In the Layout window, there are two rulers that give you the vertical and horizontal measurements of the form. One is located at the left side of the Layout window, and the other at the upper edge of the Layout window.

You can add controls from the Controls Toolbox to your form to take advantage of the Layout window, by placing the controls where you need them.

CONTROLS TOOLBOX

The Controls Toolbox, or Toolbox, contains various types of controls that you can use on your forms. When you want to add a control, you can click and drag the control from the Toolbox to your form. By default, the Toolbox is located on the left side of the Layout window. If you do not see the Toolbox, you can click View ⇨ Toolbox to display it.

You can use controls in your forms to do everything from displaying static information using a Label control, to prompting the user to input text information into a field of a table using a Textbox control. For more information about controls, see Chapter 5.

FIELD LIST

You can use the Field List to list fields of the record source the form is bound to. You can drag a field from the list to your form in the same way that you would in the Query Designer.

If the Field List is not visible, then you can click the Field List button ( ), or you can click View ⇨ Field List to display it. If the form is not bound to a record source, then both of these options are disabled. If the Field List is left open, and you open a form that is unbound in Design view, the Field List remains blank.

PROPERTY SHEET

The Property Sheet allows you to edit various properties that pertain to both the form and to the controls on the form. To display or hide the Property Sheet, you can click the Property Sheet button ( ) or click View ⇨ Property Sheet. For more information about properties and the Property Sheet, see the section "Introducing Form Properties."

INTRODUCING FORM PROPERTIES

Just like tables, fields, and queries, forms also have properties. Form properties allow you to specify how you want the form to look and perform for the user. When you click View ➪ Properties, the form's property sheet appears, with tabs for the form's property categories: Format, Data, and Other. For more information about the fourth tab, Events, see Chapter 6.

FORMAT PROPERTIES

You can use Format properties to tell Access how you want the form to look.

PROPERTIES	DESCRIPTION
Caption	Text that appears at the top of your form when you open the form.
Default View	Sets the view you want to appear when a user opens the form.
Scroll Bars	Displays scroll bars horizontally or vertically on the form.
Record Selectors	Displays record selectors at the left side of the form.
Navigation Buttons	Displays Navigation buttons at the bottom of the form.
Auto Center	When True, the form automatically centers on the screen. The default is False.

DATA PROPERTIES

These properties determine how users can interact with the form.

PROPERTIES	DESCRIPTION
Record Source	Specifies which table or query the form is bound to.
Filter	Sets the current filter at the form level. You must first set the Allow Filters property to True.
Allow Filters	Specifies whether filters can be used.
Allow Edits	Specifies whether users can edit records.
Allow Additions	Specifies whether users can append records.
Allow Deletions	Specifies whether users can delete records.
Data Entry	If set to True, then a user can only add records using the form, and cannot edit records that were added prior to opening the form.

OTHER PROPERTIES

PROPERTIES	DESCRIPTION
Pop-up	When a form is open, the form remains in front of other forms, even if other forms have the focus.
Modal	When a form is open, you cannot click outside the form until you close the form. If you set both the Pop-up and Modal properties to True, then you must ensure that the user is able to close the form.
Cycle	Determines where the tab moves the focus when you are at the end of the record.
Allow Design Changes	Specifies whether to display the property sheet in different views. Design Only is recommended.

CREATE A SINGLE PAGE FORM USING THE DESIGN VIEW

Although the Form Wizard is an excellent tool for creating forms, as you become comfortable with Access, you may want to create your own forms. After you create your form, you can modify it using the Form Design view.

To create a form using the Form Design view, you can click the New button while in the Forms group in the database window. Then, if you are creating a bound form, you can specify the record source. Then, after making sure that Design view, the default, is selected, you can click OK.

Instead of using a wizard to create your form, you can now start from a blank form. You can begin by dragging the fields you want from the Field List to the Layout window. If the Field List is not visible, you can click the Field List button to make it appear.

You can click multiple fields in the Field List while holding down the Ctrl key, and then drag them all to the form Layout window. The fields use the underlying grid to align with each other.

The majority of the fields that you use in your form are text boxes. In addition to the controls you choose, most controls also include a Label control, which displays the field's Caption property.

To view the form, you can click the View button, which displays the Form View icon. Your form appears, complete with Navigation buttons at the bottom.

To switch back to Design view, you can click the View button, which now displays the Design view icon. In the Design view, you can modify your form by adding fields and other controls, and modifying properties. For more information about modifying form properties, see the section "Set Form Properties."

CREATE A SINGLE PAGE FORM USING THE DESIGN VIEW

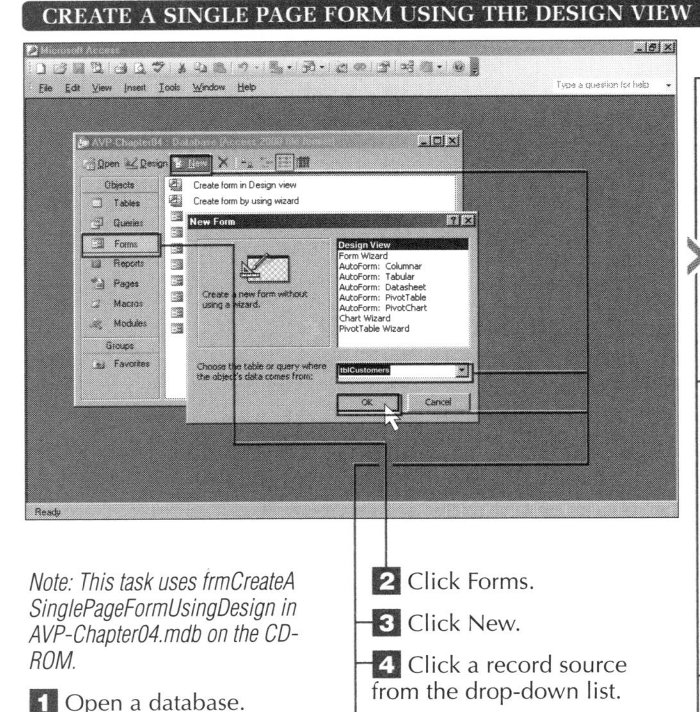

Note: This task uses frmCreateA SinglePageFormUsingDesign in AVP-Chapter04.mdb on the CD-ROM.

1 Open a database.

2 Click Forms.

3 Click New.

4 Click a record source from the drop-down list.

5 Click OK.

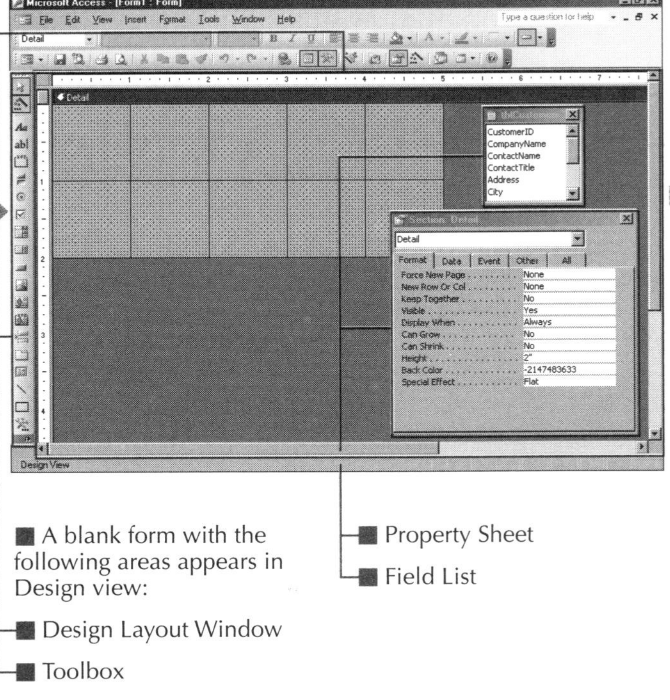

■ A blank form with the following areas appears in Design view:

■ Design Layout Window

■ Toolbox

■ Property Sheet

■ Field List

Extra

Here are a few tips about using controls on your forms:

- When you drag a field to the Layout window, Access uses the control that is most suitable to the data type. For example, if you use a text field, then Access uses a Text Box control. If you use a Yes/No field, then Access uses a Check Box control.
- When you create controls from the Field List, all of the properties that you set at the table level apply to the controls. Some of the properties, such as Format, can be overwritten. However, some properties, such as Validation Rule, use a combination of the settings. Because this may cause unexpected results, the best option is to use the Property settings as they are from the table.
- When you have a Label control, you can click the cursor in the text, and then type new text over the original text. You can use this control if you have not added the Caption property to the table level of the field, and want to change the displayed text.

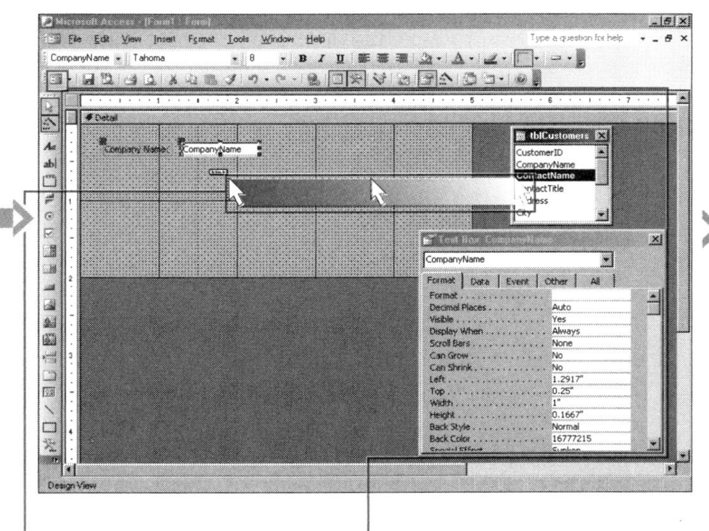

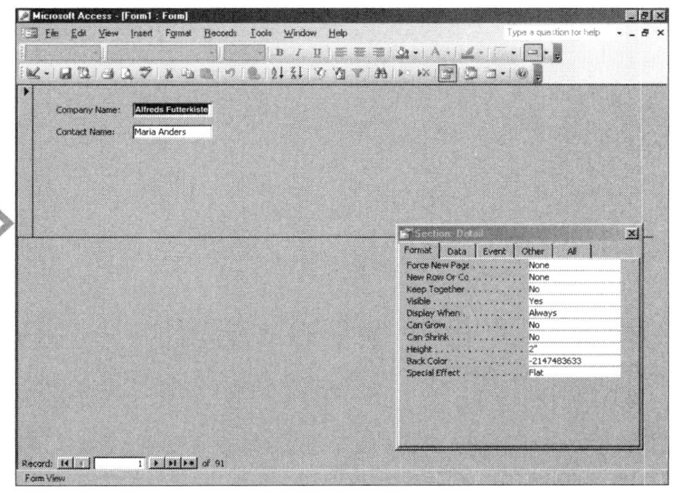

6 Click and drag a field from the Field List to the Layout window.

■ The cursor turns into a field symbol.

7 Repeat step 6 for any additional fields you want to use.

8 Click the View button.

■ By default, the form is displayed in Single Form view.

■ The Property dialog box remains open if the Allow Design Changes property is left in the default setting of All Views.

SET FORM PROPERTIES

You can set form properties in a number of ways, depending on the property you want to set. If the property sheet does not already appear while you are in the Design view of the form, you can click View ➪ property sheet. Depending on the property you are using, you can choose from a list of settings, open another dialog box to change the property, or simply type in the values you want.

To make sure you are setting a property for the correct form, you can look at the top of the property sheet. It displays one of the following: Form, Section: *SectionName*, or *Control Type*: *Control Name*, depending on where the focus is on the form.

When you want to focus on the actual form, you can click the form selector, which is the small box located where the two rulers meet in the top, left-hand corner of the Layout window.

When the property sheet appears for the form, you can click the Format tab of the property sheet to view the properties that determine how Access formats the form. If you make a change to one of these properties, and switch to Form Design view, the change appears immediately.

For example, Auto Center is a format property that appears in the Format tab of the property sheet. If you want to set the Auto Center property to True, then you can type **True**, or double-click the property to make it switch values. When you save and close the form and reopen it in the Form Design view, the form appears centered in the middle of your screen, regardless of your screen resolution.

SET THE CAPTION PROPERTY OF A FORM

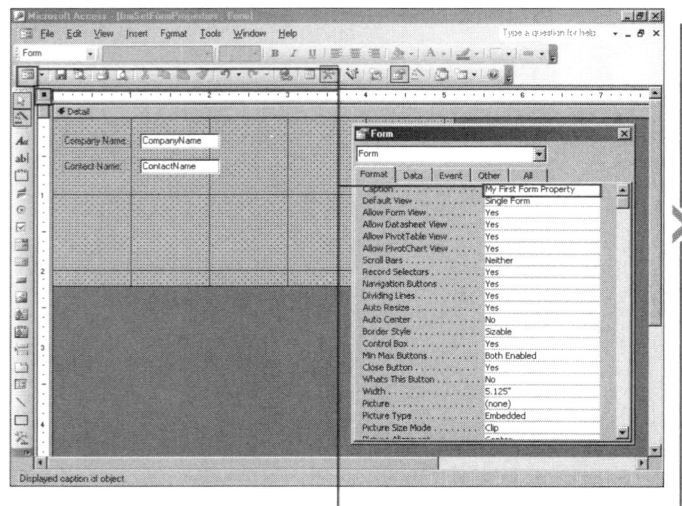

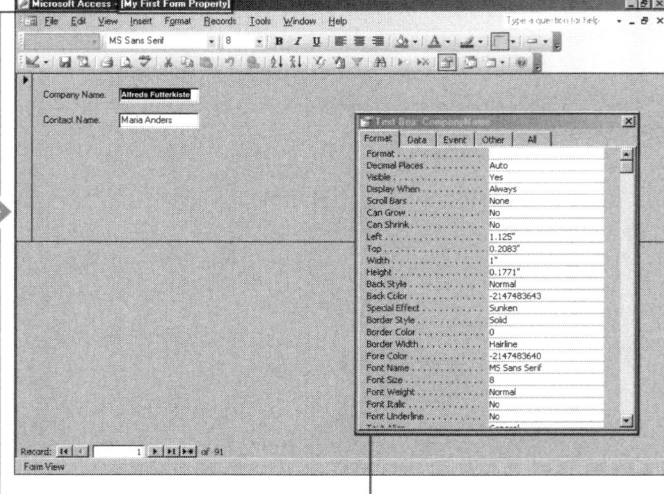

Note: This task uses frmSetFormProperties in AVP-Chapter04.mdb on the CD-ROM.

1 Click a form in your Forms group, and click the Design View button ( ).

2 Click View ➪ Property Sheet.

3 Click the Form Selector.

4 In the form's property sheet, type the text you want in the Caption field.

5 Click the View button.

■ The text you typed in step 4 appears in the title bar of the form.

■ The property sheet remains in front of the other windows. Perform the following steps to disable this feature.

Extra

You can set properties using various methods. For example, you may want to change the Back Color property for the Detail section of a form. When you click in the Detail section, the top of the property sheet indicates that you have moved the cursor over Section: Detail.

Back Color is one of the Format properties for the Detail section. There are four ways to change this color:

- Click the Fill/Color button (), located on the Format toolbar.
- Use VBA to change the property at runtime.
- Type the number value of the color you want into the Back Color property in the property sheet. For example, 16711680 is blue.
- Click the Builder button (...) next to the Back Color property in the property sheet. You can then specify the color you want in the color palette that appears.

SET THE ALLOW DESIGN CHANGES PROPERTY OF A FORM

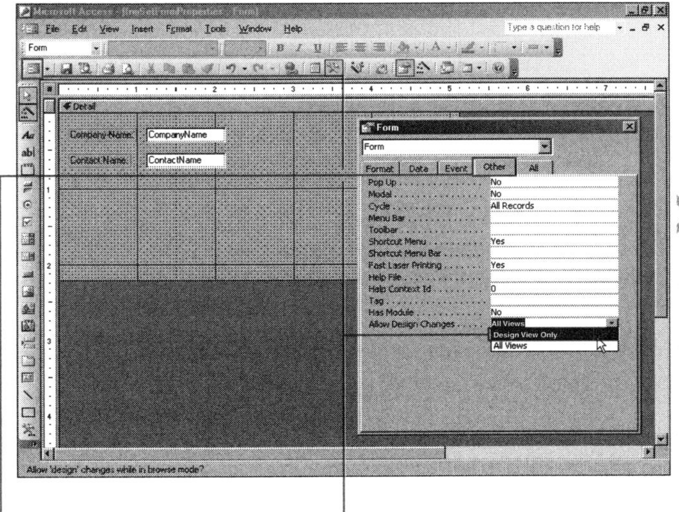

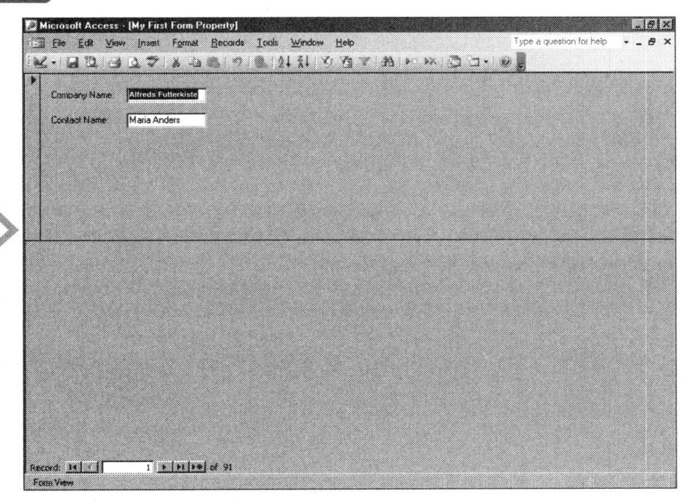

1 Repeat steps 1 to 3 from the previous steps.

■ The property sheet appears for the form.

2 Click the Other tab.

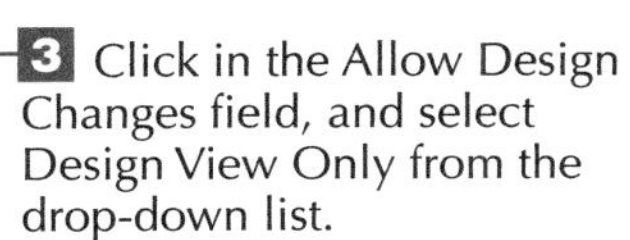

3 Click in the Allow Design Changes field, and select Design View Only from the drop-down list.

4 Click the View button.

■ The property sheet closes.

WORK WITH MULTIPLE CONTROLS

When you are creating and modifying forms in the Layout window, you spend much of your time working with multiple controls. You can move groups of controls around, and you can resize and align the controls to create appealing forms.

It is very distracting to see a text box that is out of alignment with other text boxes on a form. Nothing draws the eye more quickly. To prevent this, Access provides a grid that helps you to align your text boxes.

Access provides a few ways to work with multiple controls. One way is to draw a selection box around a group of controls. You can do this by clicking and holding the left mouse button, and dragging the mouse over the controls you want to select. When you release the mouse button, all the controls within the selection box you have drawn are highlighted. The selection box captures all the controls, even those that it only covers partially.

After you select the controls you want, you can modify the controls. For example, you can resize the controls to make them all the same size, and align the controls to an edge of one of the controls.

When you want all of the controls to conform to a single size, you have four resizing options, To Tallest, To Shortest, To Widest, To Narrowest, To Fit, and To Grid.

When you want to align multiple controls with one another, you have four alignment options, Left, Right, Top, and Bottom.

You also have two other options when modifying multiple controls: You can space them horizontally or vertically to one another.

You can find all these formatting commands on the Format menu bar.

WORK WITH MULTIPLE CONTROLS

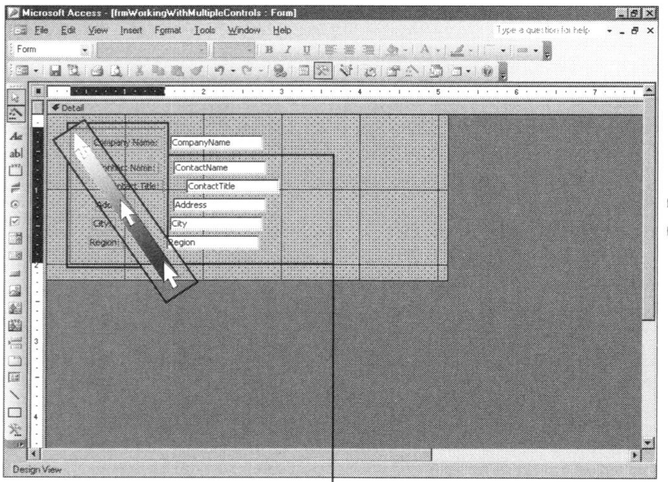

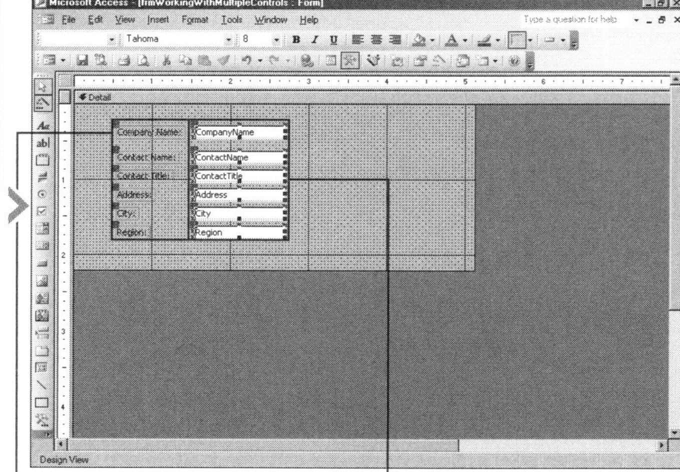

ALIGN CONTROLS

Note: This task uses frmWorkingWithMultipleControls in AVP-Chapter04.mdb on the CD-ROM.

1 In Design view, open a form that contains multiple fields.

2 Click and drag the cursor across the controls you want to select.

■ A selection box appears around the items.

3 Release the mouse.

4 Click Format ➪ Align ➪ Left.

■ The labels align with the left-most label.

5 Repeat steps 2 to 4 for the next group of controls.

■ The text boxes align with the left-most text box.

Extra

Here are a few tips about working with multiple controls:

- When you use the selection box around a group of controls, you may not need to select all of the controls within the selection box area. If you want to work with just some of the controls, you can click the controls that you do not want while holding down the Shift key. When you hold the Shift key down, you can click individual controls to select them as well as deselect them.
- When you are sizing and aligning controls, you should also create a selection box around the labels, so that they follow the controls to which they belong.
- When you select the controls with which you want to work, you can move the entire group by clicking and dragging the group to where you want it to go. When you place the cursor over the multiple selections, the cursor becomes a flat hand icon (✋).
- To resize a control using the mouse, click one of the outside handles. The cursor turns into a two-way arrow, indicating that you can resize the control.
- Click Edit ⇨ Undo option to undo any changes you make.

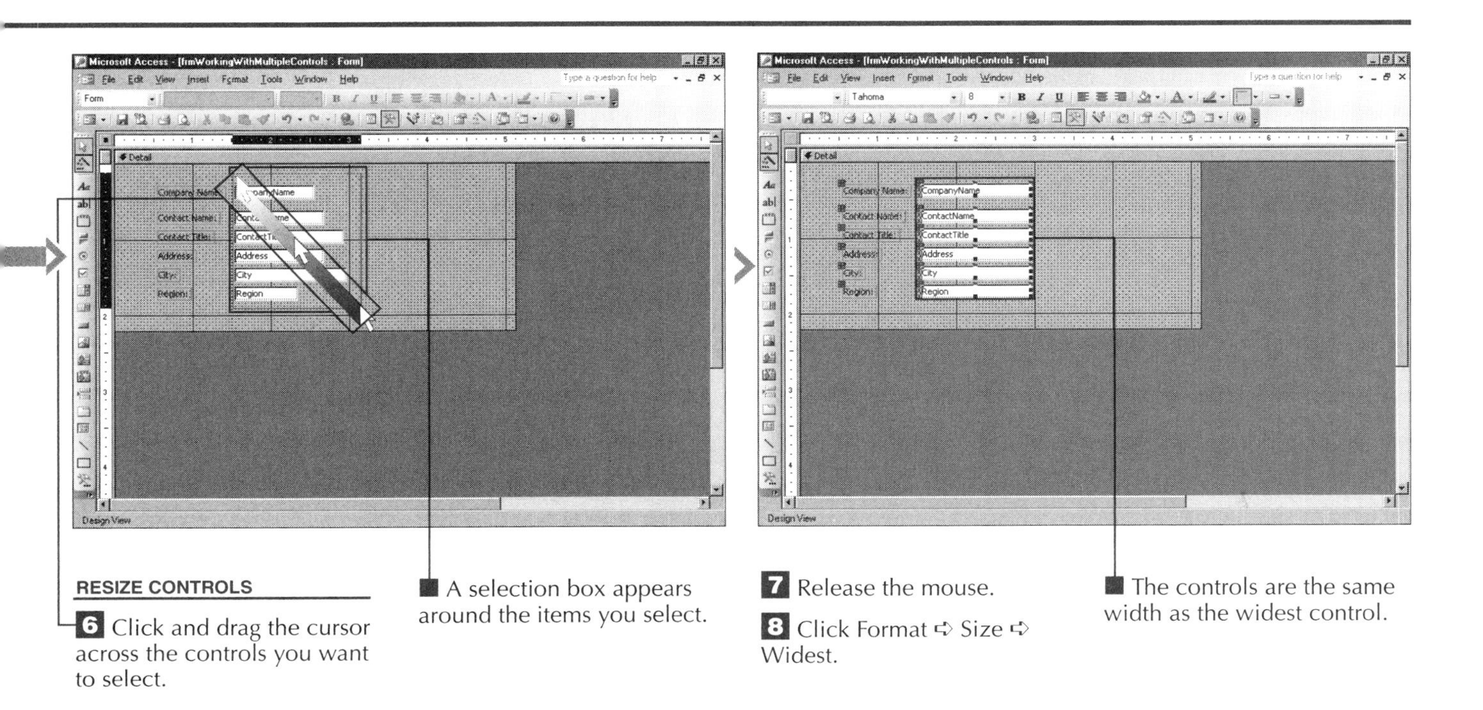

RESIZE CONTROLS

6 Click and drag the cursor across the controls you want to select.

■ A selection box appears around the items you select.

7 Release the mouse.

8 Click Format ⇨ Size ⇨ Widest.

■ The controls are the same width as the widest control.

CREATE A FORM IN THE CONTINUOUS FORM VIEW

In addition to the Datasheet and Single Form views, you can also create a form in the Continuous Form view. The Continuous Form view is used quite often in the subform part of the Mainform/Subform view forms, which will be discussed in the next chapter.

The Continuous Form view is very useful when you want to be able to see multiple records in a form, but do not want the records to appear in the datasheet format.

When you create a form in Continuous Form view, you can create the form as you would a Single Form view form. You can place the form controls in the format in which you want the user to input the data. Usually you can format the controls so that they require less vertical space, and use more horizontal space. This is because you want to be able to see multiple records in the form, and if you use a vertical alignment, as you would with a Single Form, you cannot see many records.

When you format the controls the way you want them, you can set the Default View property of the form to Continuous Forms. When you view the form, you will see multiple records displayed in the form, instead of the single form that you would see in the Single Form view.

With the Continuous and Single Form views, you can also include command buttons on your form, as well as pictures, using the Image control, and other controls that you cannot use if you create the form in Datasheet view.

You may want to adjust the size of the form by clicking and dragging the border of the form, and then saving it in the size you want it to be when you open the form in Continuous Form view.

CREATE A FORM IN THE CONTINUOUS FORM VIEW

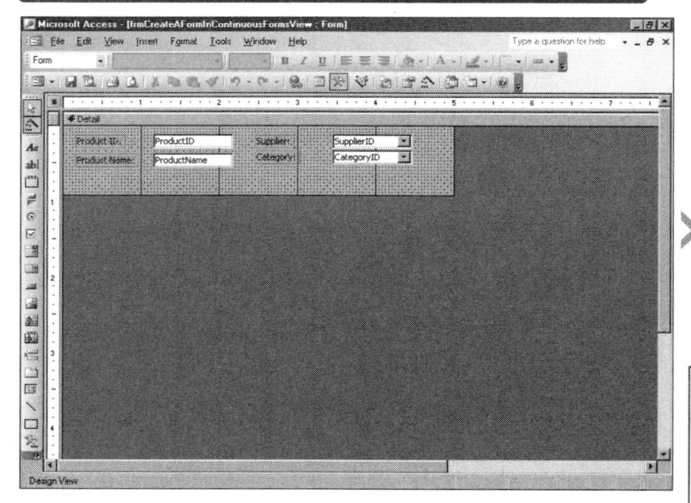

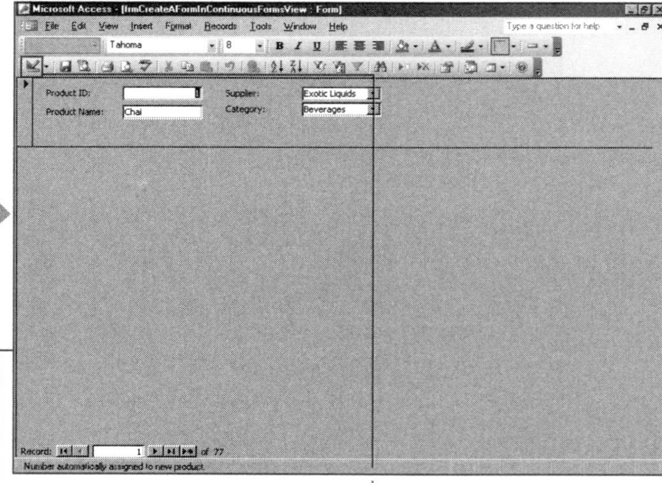

Note: This task uses frmCreateAFormInContinuousFormsView in AVP-Chapter04.mdb on the CD-ROM.

1 In Design view, open a form that contains multiple fields.

2 Arrange the fields you want into a horizontal format.

3 Save the form, and then reopen it.

■ The form appears in Single Form view.

4 Click the Design View button.

Extra

Although you can choose the Default view for your forms, users can also choose other views by clicking the View button, and selecting a different view. You can also set which view you want to display at runtime. For example, when you open Form B from Form A, you can specify one view, and then when you open Form C, you can specify a different view.

If you do not want to prevent users from selecting other views, you can set properties that allow them to use one or all other views. The properties that you can set are Allow Form View, Allow Datasheet View, Allow PivotTable View, and Allow PivotChart View. By default, all the views are set to True, allowing users to choose them.

Some good reasons to prevent users from switching from one view to another are:

- If you have controls that cannot be displayed in some views, such as command buttons, then the users may miss the features that these buttons represent.
- Users sometimes switch between views by accident, which can lead to confusion and frustration.

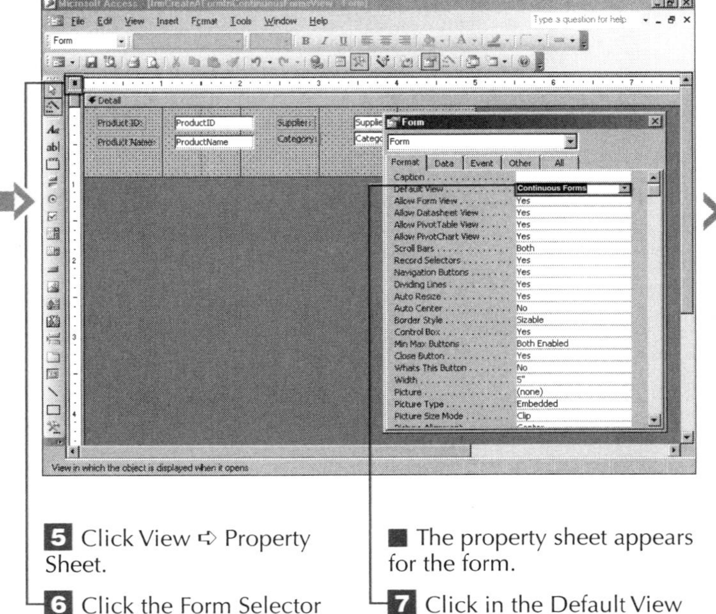

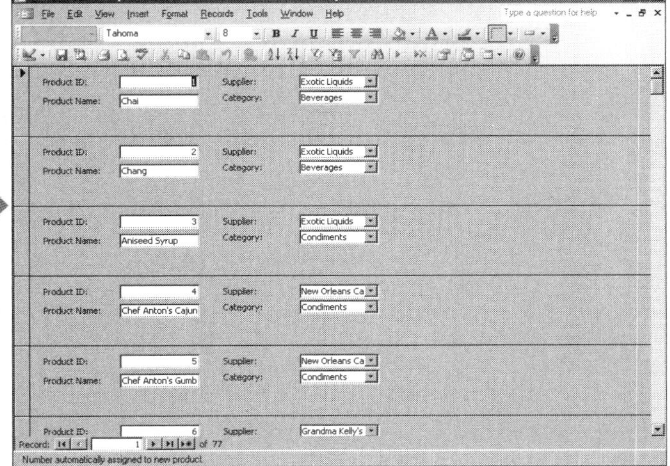

5 Click View ➪ Property Sheet.

6 Click the Form Selector button.

■ The property sheet appears for the form.

7 Click in the Default View field, and choose Continuous Forms from the drop-down list.

8 Save and close the form.

9 Open the form in the Form view.

■ The form appears, with multiple records displayed.

MATCH THE CONTROL WITH THE CORRECT PURPOSE

When you create forms in Access, you can make them more useful and powerful by adding controls. Before you add a control to your form, you need to consider how you want to use the control. For example, you do not want to display static text using a Textbox control when you can use a Label. This is because whenever a form is refreshed, the Textbox is recalculated, whereas a Label is not.

It is a good practice to become familiar with controls so that you know which control to use for which purpose. For example, the Label control is best for static text. With this control, you do not need to worry about recalculating for each record. The Textbox lets you use dynamic data or expressions in your forms. See the next section for more about creating expressions using Textbox controls.

THE ACCESS CONTROLS TOOLBOX

While you can use text boxes to input data and display results, you can make the text boxes more useful by adding controls to them. All the controls below can be found in the toolbox of the Form Design view, and all are discussed in more detail in this chapter.

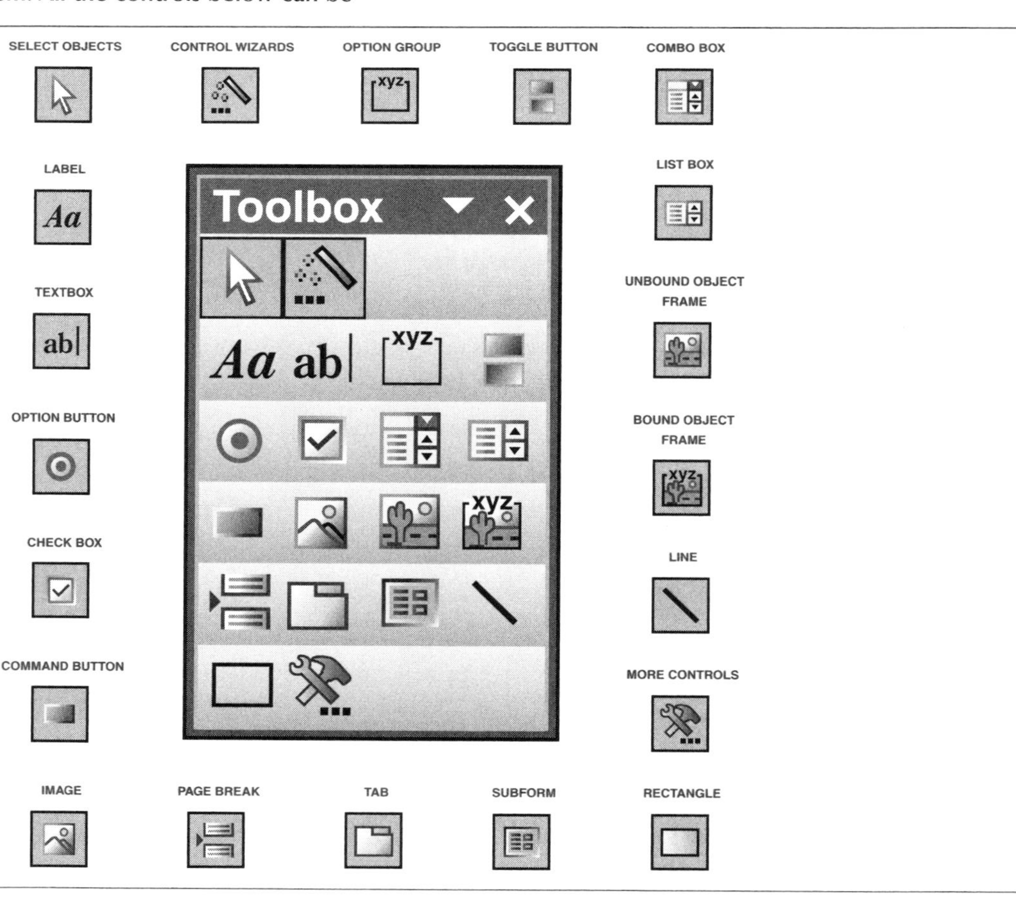

CONTROLS TO USE FOR DIFFERENT TASKS

Limited List Choices

When you have a limited number of options, for example five or less, and you know that they will not change, you can use an Option Group. The Option Group allows you to display a list of choices, with three different types of controls to accept the user's mutually exclusive choices. The three control types are radio buttons, check boxes, and option buttons. Check boxes are not recommended because they are generally used for selecting multiple items. For more about the Option Group, see the section "Create an Option Group Control."

Unlimited List Choices

When you have a list of choices that may change, or the choices include more information than can be displayed in an Option Group, such as data from a lookup table, then you can choose either the List Box or Combo Box controls.

While both controls serve the same purpose, there are certain factors that will direct your choice. The List Box control can display some of the choices in the list, and can also allow the user to select multiple choices. The Combo Box control is a drop-down style list, and only allows a user to choose one item from the list.

Yes/No Choices

The Check Box control is the logical choice when you want the user to answer a Yes or No question. The check box contains a check for a Yes answer, and no check for a No answer. The check box appears grayed out when no choice, or a Null answer, is made. Some people also use the List Box or Combo Box to display Yes and No choices. In tables, the values of 0 (No) and –1 (Yes) are displayed.

Visual/Graphics

When you want to display images on the form, you can choose from one of three controls. If you are using graphics stored in a table, you can use the Bound Object Frame control. If you are using an unbound graphic such as a logo, then you can use the Image control or Unbound Object Frame control.

When you want to add visual effects, such as lines and panels to give the impression of grouping controls, you can use the Line and Rectangle controls.

Data Choices

The Subform control helps you display additional data on a form. The Tab control also helps you display additional data. With the Tab control, you can display and edit multiple pages of data on your forms.

ActiveX Controls

ActiveX controls are not native to Access, but can be used within Access, as well as in other development environments such as Visual Basic and C. They have properties, methods, and events just like native Access controls. For more about ActiveX controls, see the section "Using the ActiveX Calendar Control."

DISPLAY A CALCULATED EXPRESSION IN A TEXT BOX

Like bound and unbound forms, a bound control is a control that is bound to either a field in the record source of the form, or a calculated expression. When you create a query, you can display a calculated expression in a query column. For example, you are creating a calculated expression when you type the following:

```
FullName: LastName & ", " & FirstName
```

You can do the same using the Textbox control on a form. The syntax is a bit different from the syntax of a calculated expression in a query. For example, instead of typing the name of the expression as you would in a query, you can use the equal sign, =. Thus, if you want to display the full name in a text box on a form, you can display it using the following expression:

```
=LastName & ", " & FirstName
```

If you forget the equal sign in the expression, Access displays "#Name?" in the text box field when you view the form.

Most controls that can be bound to data have two properties that control whether you can edit the data within the control. The properties are Enabled and Locked. After you create a calculated expression, you may also want to set the Enabled property to False and the Locked property to True so that the user does not try to edit the data in the text box. The Locked property allows the focus to be set to the control, but the data cannot be updated. The Locked property does not affect the color of the control. The Enabled property does not allow the focus to be set to the control at all, but it also grays out the control. If you do not want to have the user go into the field at all, but not affect the control color, you can combine the two by setting the properties as described above.

DISPLAY A CALCULATED EXPRESSION IN A TEXT BOX

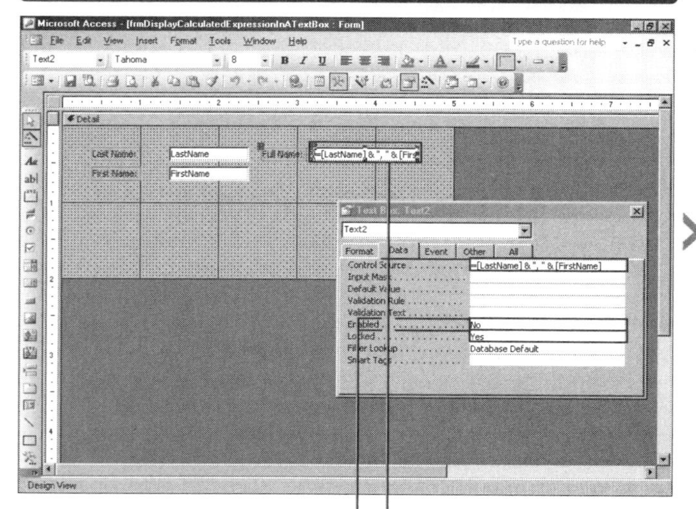

Note: This task uses frmDisplayCalculatedExpressionInATextBox in AVP-Chapter05.mdb on the CD-ROM.

1 Create a form with a record source.

2 Add bound controls from the Field List.

3 Add a Textbox control from the toolbox, and set the Control Source property to a calculated expression.

4 Type **No** to set Enabled to False.

5 Type **Yes** to set Locked to True.

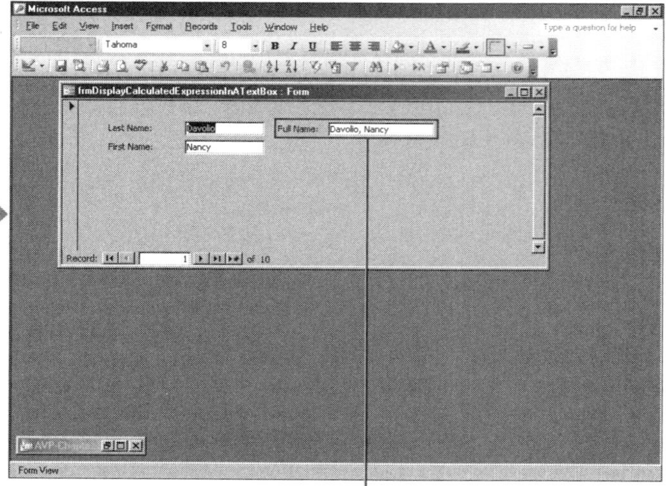

6 Click the View button ( ).

■ The new expression appears.

CORRECT CONTROL ERRORS

With a new feature in Access 2003, you can check errors on forms. You can use this feature to correct errors that occur when you are creating forms, such as when you forget to type an equal sign in your expression.

There are four types of errors that you can tell Access to track: unassociated labels and controls, new unassociated labels, keyboard shortcut errors, and invalid control properties. When you forget the equal sign in your expression, this is an example of an invalid control property.

You can set which errors you want to track by clicking Tools ⇨ Options, and then clicking the Error Checking tab. The tracking options appear, and you can turn them on or off individually, as well as choose the colors for the error message. You can also specify whether you want to enable error checking at all.

When an actual error occurs, the color you choose in the Error Checking tab appears in the top-left corner of the control field; by default, the color is green. If you click the colored area, a pop-up menu appears, describing the problem, and offering a list of possible fixes.

You can select one of the fixes, and depending on which fix you choose, Access leads you through the repair process. In some cases, such as the missing equal sign error, Access offers a solution to the problem, and asks if you want to edit the control source. For an error such as an unassociated label, Access lists possible unassociated controls from which you can choose.

Access also offers you a Help option in the pop-up menu, which describes the error in greater detail.

CORRECT CONTROL ERRORS

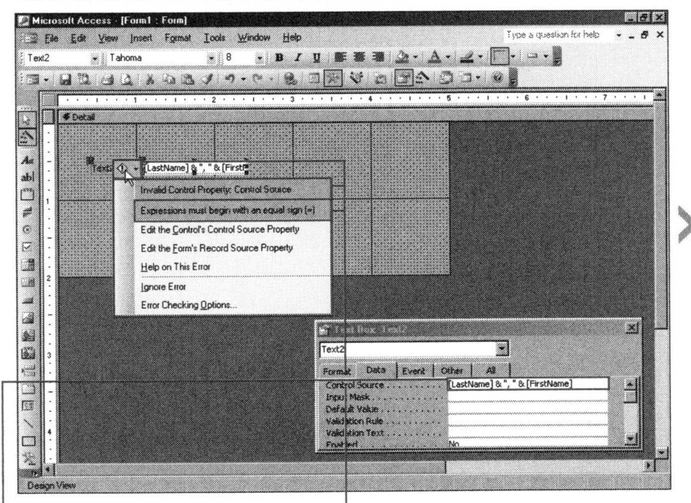

Note: This task uses frmControlFormErrors in AVP-Chapter05.mdb on the CD-ROM.

1 Create a form with a record source.

2 Type an expression with no equal sign and press Enter.

■ A green icon appears in the top left of the control.

3 Click the control, and then click the exclamation point.

■ Errors and solutions appear.

4 Click a suggestion and then press Enter.

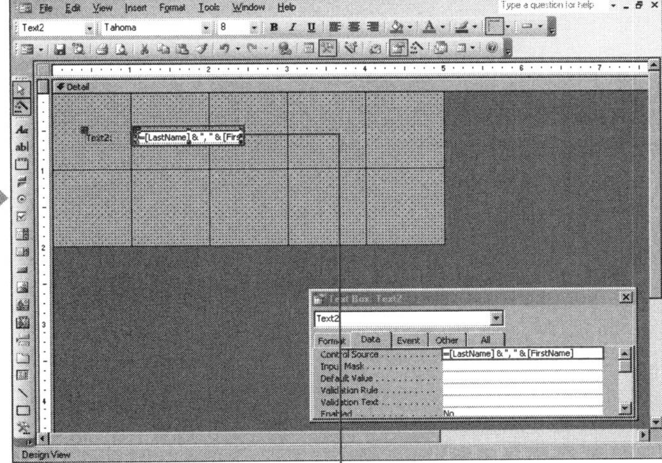

■ In this example, Access suggests correcting the error by adding an equal sign to the expression.

5 Type = and press Enter.

■ The green icon disappears, indicating that the error has been corrected.

CREATE AN OPTION GROUP CONTROL

You can use Option Group controls when you have a limited list of mutually exclusive items. For example, you may want to track three different employee types in a tblEmployees table. You can specify the employee types in a field called EmployeeType, with the following three values: 1 for FullTime, 2 for PartTime, and 3 for Contract. When you create an option group, you may want to use the Option Group Wizard, which guides you through the setup. When you use an option group, you are actually using two different types of controls: the option group frame, followed by a control you want to use inside the frame, such as option buttons, radio buttons, and check boxes.

After you ensure that the control wizards are enabled by checking that the control is activated in the toolbox, you can click the Option Group control, and drag it into the form. When you release the mouse button, the Option Group Wizard appears, and you can specify the labels that you want to display for each option.

After you choose the labels, the wizard asks which choice, if any, you want as the default option. Next, you can change the values of the options if you want, although the default values of 1, 2, and 3 are usually adequate.

Then, you can decide which field contains the result from the option group, setting the Control Source property.

You then choose which type of control you want to use for the options, and what special effects you want to use. The choices are Etched, Flat, Raised, Shadowed, and Sunken. These are the same special effects you can choose for most of the controls on your forms.

You then enter the caption for the entire option group.

CREATE AN OPTION GROUP CONTROL

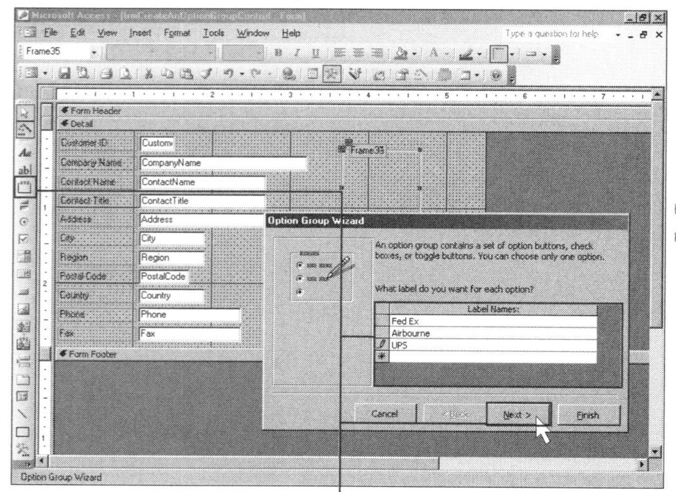

Note: This task uses frmCreateAnOptionGroupControl in AVP-Chapter05.mdb on the CD-ROM.

1 Create or open a form to which you want to add a new option group.

2 With the control wizards ( ) on, click the Option Group control, and then drag the control to the form.

3 In the Option Group Wizard, type the values you want to use for the option group items.

4 Click Next.

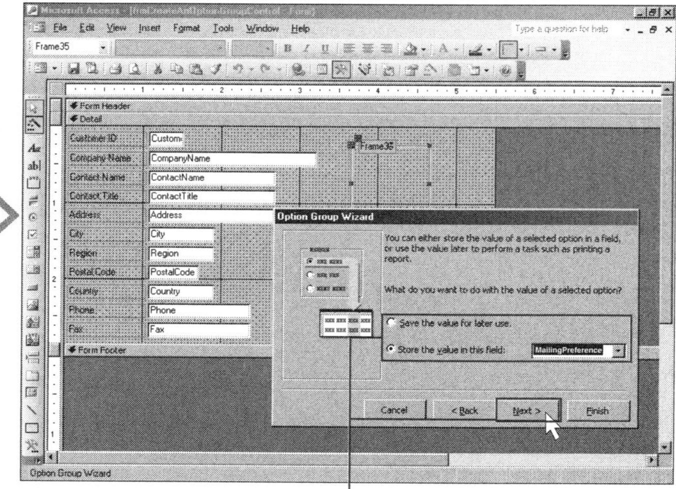

■ The wizard asks you which option, if any, you want to use as a default.

5 Click the option you want, and click Next.

■ The wizard displays the values that Access will use.

6 Click the option you want.

7 Click Next.

Extra

When you use text boxes in your forms, you can drag the text boxes from the Field List into your forms. You can use the same method for other types of controls, such as the Option Group control, discussed in this section, and the Combo Box control, discussed in the next section.

When you want to base one of the controls from the toolbox on a field in the Field List, you can start by clicking the control. Instead of dragging the control directly into the form, move the mouse over to the Field List, and drag the field into the form.

Because you click the type of control you want in the toolbox, Access still performs the task and builds the control you choose. However, the Control Source property of the control is now set to the field name of the field you choose from the Field List.

If you have already created a control without assigning a control source, you can assign a control source by updating the Control Source property using the property sheet in the Data property tab.

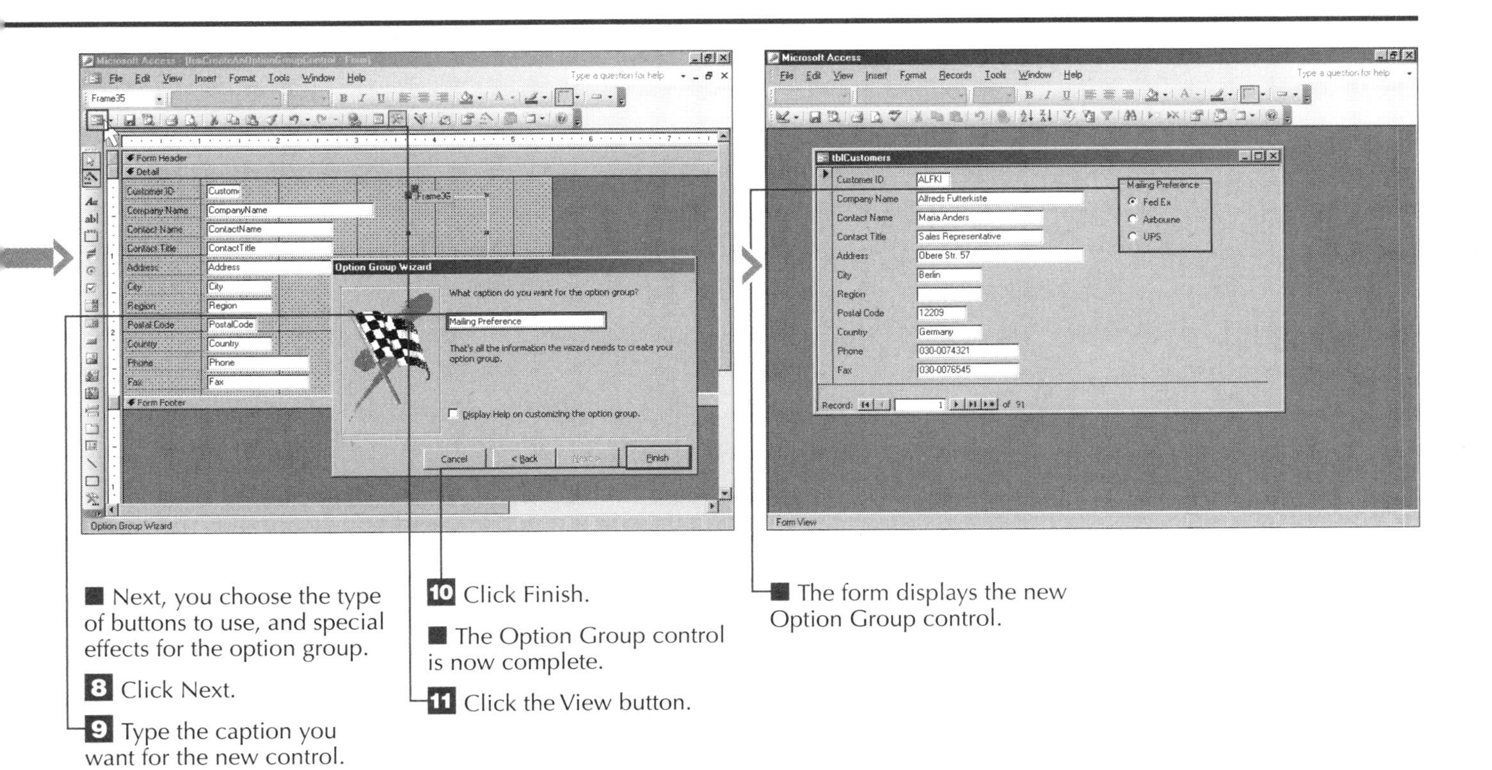

■ Next, you choose the type of buttons to use, and special effects for the option group.

8 Click Next.

9 Type the caption you want for the new control.

10 Click Finish.

■ The Option Group control is now complete.

11 Click the View button.

■ The form displays the new Option Group control.

ADD A COMBO BOX CONTROL TO LIMIT DATA

The Combo Box control is an effective way to display lookup values for users. It limits the data that the user can enter, although you can also program a combo box to allow the user to add new values.

You can create a combo box using a wizard. This is a good method to use until you become familiar with the properties of the Combo Box controls.

When you add a combo box to your form with the control wizards on, the Combo Box Wizard appears, asking whether you want to use a record source for the values in the combo box, or type the values into the combo box yourself.

If you decide to use a record source, you can select from the existing tables and queries in your database. After you select the source, Access displays the possible fields you can include in the combo box. You can select the key field of the lookup table, along with any fields you want to display in the combo box.

After the wizards asks you which field you want to sort on, it then displays a preview of the combo box list. The wizard automatically hides the key field value. You can drag the columns over if you want some of the columns hidden. For more information about hidden columns, see the section "Utilize Hidden Columns in a Combo Box."

Finally, you can specify the label for the combo box you create.

When the combo box appears in the form, you can click the combo box to display the drop-down list. You can set the Control Source property of the combo box to the field in which you want to store the value returned by the combo box.

ADD A COMBO BOX CONTROL TO LIMIT DATA

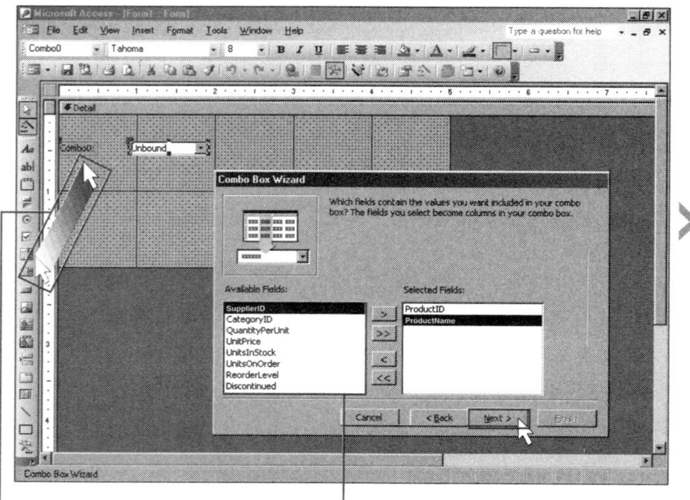

Note: This task uses frmCreateAComboBox in AVP-Chapter05.mdb on the CD-ROM.

1 Create or open a form in Design view.

2 Click the Combo Box control and drag it into the form.

3 In the Combo Box Wizard, click a record source, and then click Next.

■ The wizard displays a list of fields you can include in the combo box.

4 Double-click the fields you want to include.

5 Click Next.

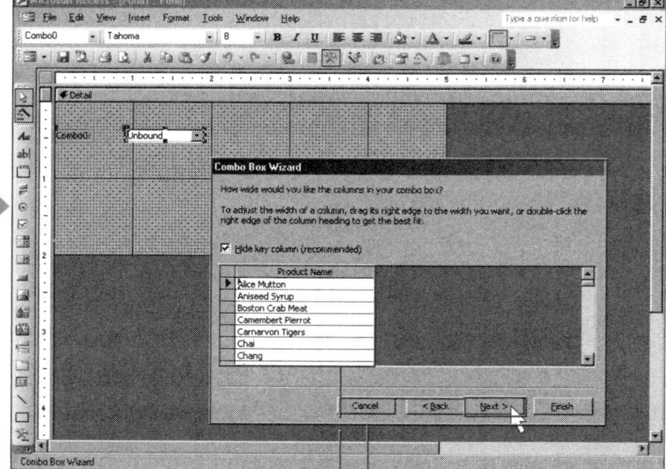

■ The wizard displays a list of fields on which you can sort.

6 Click a field and then click Next.

■ The wizard displays a preview of the combo box list.

7 Adjust the column width.

8 Click Next.

Extra

It is a good idea for you to become familiar with the properties that have important roles in specifying how your combo box behaves. Although the Combo Box Wizard does a good job of creating your combo box, when you want to adjust certain features of the combo box, or use more advanced features, you may want to know which properties to modify.

Here is a list of properties for the Combo Box control:

PROPERTY	TYPE	DESCRIPTION
Column Count	Format	Specifies the number of columns in the combo box, including any hidden columns.
Column Heads	Format	Specifies whether you want column headings displayed.
Column Widths	Format	Determines the width of each of the columns that appear in the combo box.
Row Source Type	Data	Values are Table/Query, Value List, and Table List. When using Value List, you can specify the values, separated by commas. Table/Query and Field List require a table or query in the Row Source. Field List displays the fields in the table.
Row Source	Data	You base your combo box on a table, query, or SQL statement when you use Table/Query in Row Source Type.
Bound Column	Data	Sets which column of the combo box you want to store the control source.

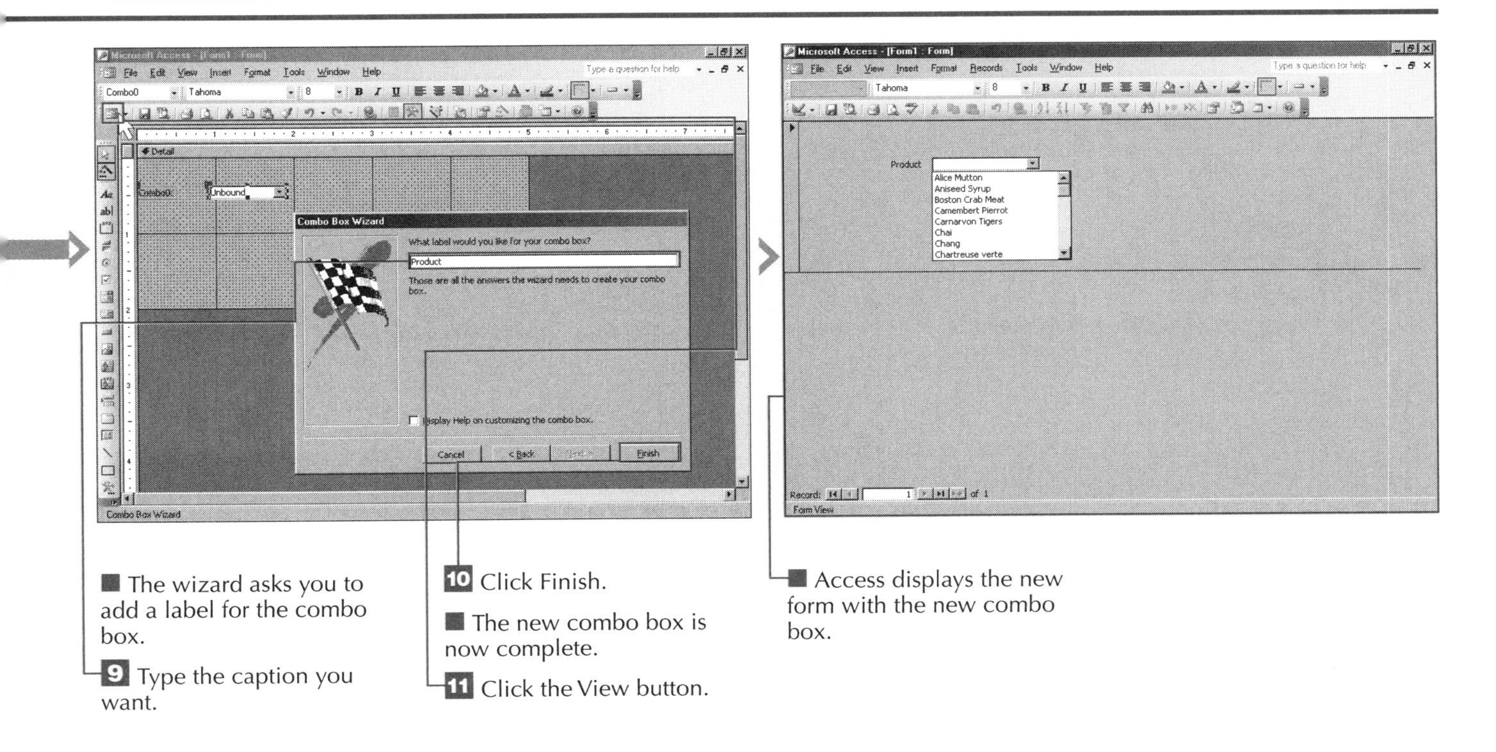

■ The wizard asks you to add a label for the combo box.

9 Type the caption you want.

10 Click Finish.

■ The new combo box is now complete.

11 Click the View button.

■ Access displays the new form with the new combo box.

UTILIZE HIDDEN COLUMNS IN A COMBO BOX

You can display values in the lookup table on your form, and not actually show them in the combo box itself. You can use hidden columns in a combo box when you want to include additional data on a form, but not display it in the combo box.

To use the hidden column feature, you must modify the Row Source property, which contains the table, query, or SQL SELECT statement that you use to make the Combo Box list. You must then include the hidden column value in the property.

You can then increase the value of the Column Count property to include the new column. Because you add a column, but want it hidden, you must type an entry into the Column Widths property for the new column, setting it to 0. When you make a column width 0, the column is not visible in the list when the user clicks the combo box, but is accessible when you need to view or change it.

You can then create a new text box that uses the hidden column as the Control Source. The syntax for the Control Source property is:

```
=ComboBoxName.Column(ColumnNumber)
```

By setting the Control Source property of a text box to point to a column in the combo box, you are pulling the column value that you need from the combo box.

The ColumnNumber values start at 0 instead of 1 to represent the first column, and continue through ColumnCount –1. For example, if you have a combo box called cboCustomer, and you want to display the third column, you can type the following in the Control Source property of the text box in which you want to display the value:

```
=cboCustomer.Column(2)
```

When the user selects a new value in the combo box, the value that appears in the text box is updated as well.

UTILIZE HIDDEN COLUMNS IN A COMBO BOX

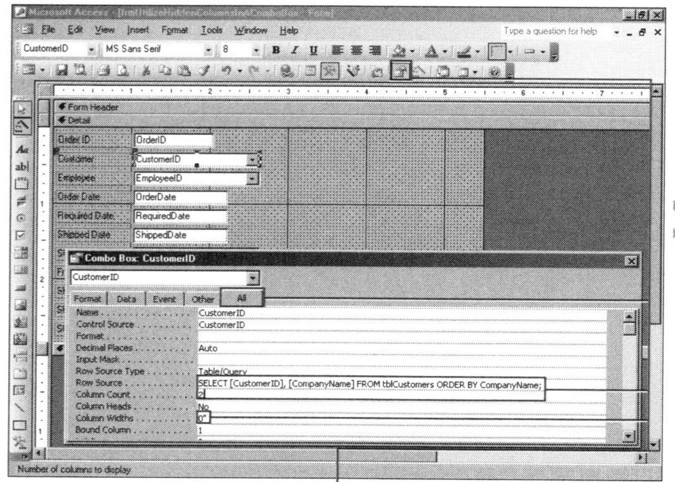

Note: This task uses frmUtilizeHiddenColumnsInAComboBox in AVP-Chapter05.mdb on the CD-ROM.

1 Create a form that includes a combo box.

2 Open the property sheet by clicking the Property Sheet button.

3 Click the All tab.

4 Make a note of all the current settings for Row Source, Column Count, and Column Widths.

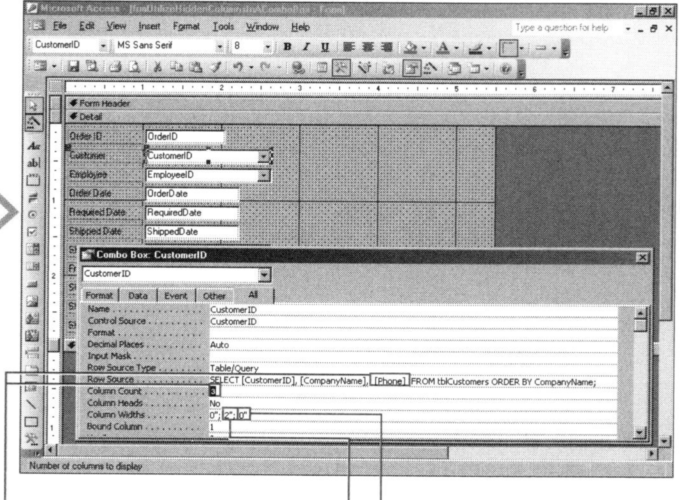

5 Modify the Row Source to include the field you want to add.

6 Add 1 to the Column Count property field.

7 Modify the Column Widths so that another field is included, but set to 0.

8 Add a value for the existing field that is displayed.

Extra

The steps below describe how you can pull data from a combo box. You can also push data to a text box. To do this, you can perform the steps below, except that, instead of setting the Control Source of the text box, you add an event procedure to the combo box. For more information about event procedures, see the next chapter.

In the property sheet, click the Events tab, and then click the Builder button (...) in the After Update property field. In the Choose Builder dialog box, click Code Builder, and then click OK. Type the following in the blank line between the two lines that start with Private Sub and End Sub:

```
TextBoxName = ComboBoxName.Column(ColumnNumber)
```

Save and close the form, and then reopen the form. The text box updates as you choose new values from the combo box.

If you only need a single hidden column from a combo or list box, use the Push method described in the steps below, but if you want to use additional fields, then you can use the Pull method.

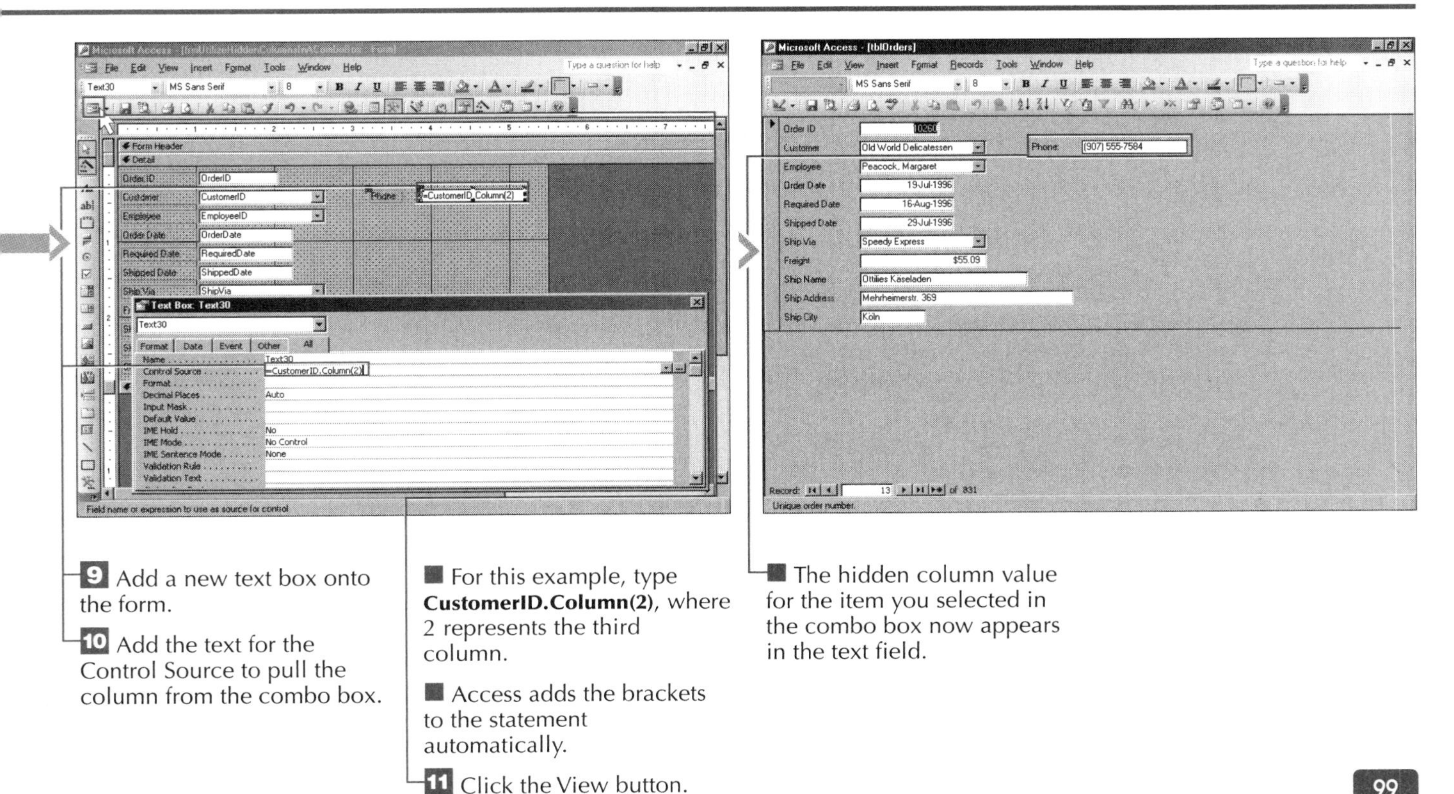

9 Add a new text box onto the form.

10 Add the text for the Control Source to pull the column from the combo box.

■ For this example, type **CustomerID.Column(2)**, where 2 represents the third column.

■ Access adds the brackets to the statement automatically.

11 Click the View button.

■ The hidden column value for the item you selected in the combo box now appears in the text field.

ADD A LIST BOX CONTROL

You can add a List Box control to your form to limit the data the user can enter, and let the user see more that just the chosen entry. List Box controls are very similar to Combo Box controls, in that you use the same properties to create them, and they both display lists of data for the user. The List Box Wizard is nearly identical to the Combo Box Wizard, page for page.

You can set the properties manually to create a List Box control. After you open your form in Design view, you can turn off the control wizards by clicking the control in the toolbox. Next, you can drag a List Box control into the form from the toolbox.

You can now set the necessary properties for the list box: Control Source, Row Source Type, Row Source, Column Count, and Column Widths. If you set up your table or query with the lookup key value in the first column, you do not need to modify the Bound Column property.

Unlike the combo box, which only displays the first column in the list, after you select a value in a list box, the list box displays all the columns. You can still use the hidden columns shown in the last section, but you should ensure that those columns that are visible look good. To do this, you can adjust the Column Widths property. You can also turn on the column headings with the Column Heads property.

One big difference between the List Box and Combo Box control types is that you can set the list box to accept multiple selections. To use the multi-select feature, you must use VBA code to actually read the values chosen from a multi-select list box. For more information, see Chapter 7.

ADD A LIST BOX CONTROL

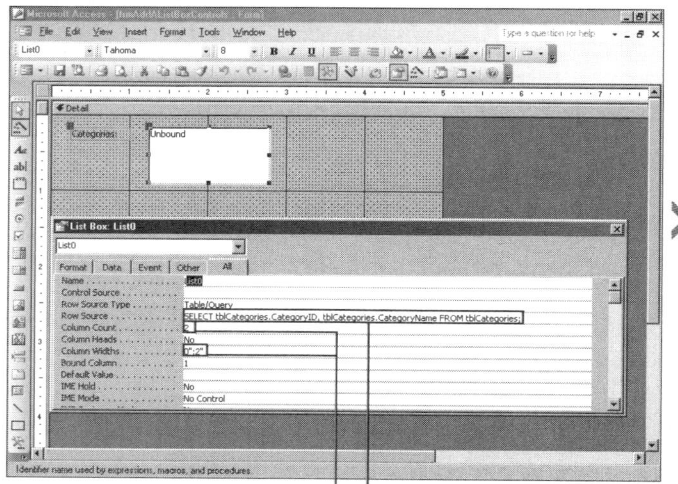

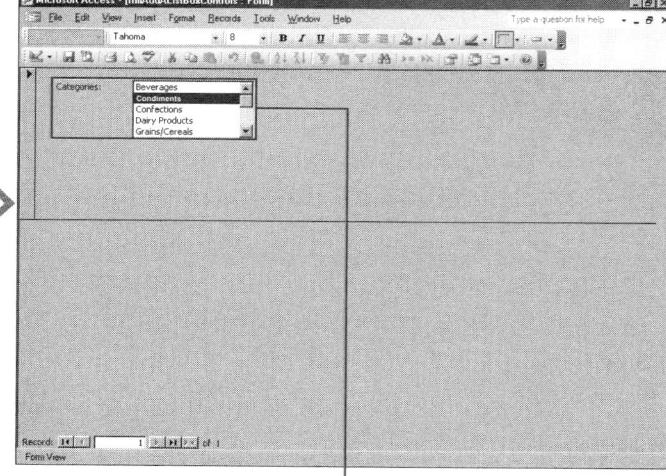

Note: This task uses frmAddAListBoxControls in AVP-Chapter05.mdb on the CD-ROM.

1 Create or open a form in Design view, and then turn off the control wizards (). Click and drag a List Box control onto the form.

2 After opening the property sheet for the control, type a value for the Row Source property.

3 Type a value for the Column Count property that matches the number of columns included in the row source.

4 Type a value for the Column Widths.

5 Type the Caption for the List Box Label control, which is attached to the List Box control.

6 Click the View button ().

■ The list box appears with values.

ADD SMART TAGS TO CONTROLS

The Microsoft Office applications all use a feature called Smart Tags. You can add Smart Tags to fields, controls, cells, or words, depending on which application you are using. When you add a Smart Tag to a field in Access, a purple triangle appears in the bottom-right corner of the field. When you move the mouse over a tagged field that contains data, a pop-up menu appears, displaying a list of tasks that you can perform using the data.

The tasks that appear on a control depend on the type of Smart Tag that you have set up. For example, you can use a Date type Smart Tag, and have it schedule meetings or show your calendar in Outlook.

You can assign Smart Tags at either the table-field level, or form-control level. If you want to use the Smart Tag on all your forms and Datasheet views, you can assign it at the table-field level. Otherwise, you can assign it to a control on your form.

To create a Smart Tag, you can use the Smart Tag property, found under the Data category of the property sheet.

When you click the Builder button next to the Smart Tag property, a list of Smart Tag types that are available with Access appears. You can also use a Web link labeled More Smart Tags. This link takes you to the Microsoft Web site that contains new Smart Tags. The majority of the Smart Tag sites are for Word, Excel, and Outlook Smart Tags.

After you choose a Smart Tag, you can open the form. When a user enters data into the field, the Smart Tag menu of tasks appears.

ADD SMART TAGS TO CONTROLS

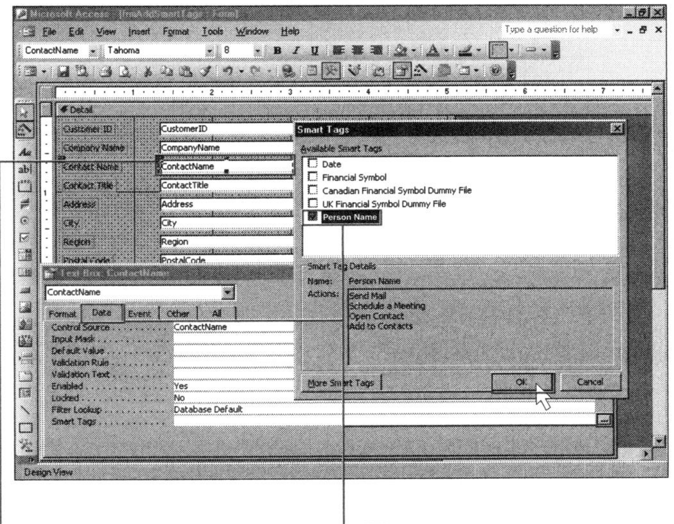

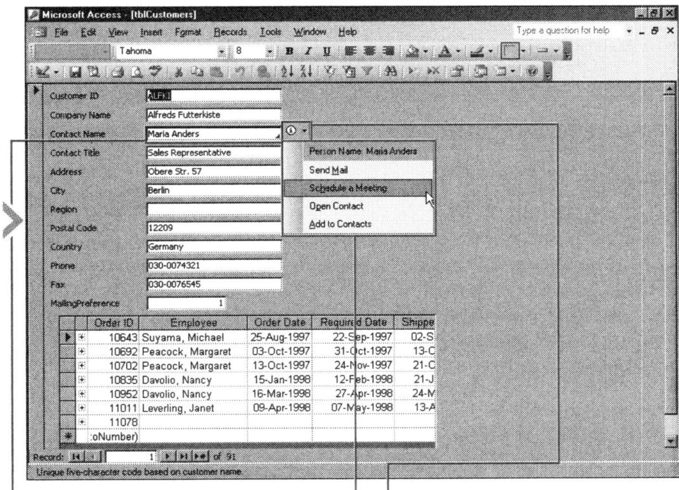

Note: This task uses frmAddSmartTags in AVP-Chapter05.mdb on the CD-ROM.

1 Create or open a form that is based on a record source.

2 Click a field to which you want to add a Smart Tag.

3 In the property sheet, click the Data tab.

4 Click the Builder button.

5 Click a Smart Tag.

6 Click OK.

7 Click the View button ( ).

■ The form appears.

8 Move the mouse over the field that contains the Smart Tag.

9 Click in the Information box that appears.

■ The Smart Tag menu displays your options.

ADD A TAB CONTROL TO A FORM

Controls make Access forms both powerful and easy to use. The standard controls, such as Textbox and Label controls, are relatively easy to add and use. The Tab control, although more difficult to implement, makes it much easier for a user to navigate through a form.

When you create your form, you may sometimes have more information than can fit on a single screen. You can set up the form to scroll down the page to the data you want to use. However, this method can be confusing if the form is lengthy and detailed. You can use the Tab control to navigate easily through your form. Tabbed screens in Access are similar to the various Option dialog boxes that you use in applications such as Word and Excel. When you add a Tab control to a form, you can then use the other controls, such as Textboxes, on the different pages of the form.

After you add a Tab control to your form, you can specify the number of pages the form requires. For example, if you were maintaining data in the Employees table, located in the Northwind.mdb database, you could set up pages for company information, personal information, and even for notes.

You can take advantage of additional features, such as using VBA code in your form. You can also control the visibility of the individual tabs, and you can set the Tab control to display tabs in multiple rows when you have a large number of tabs.

ADD A TAB CONTROL TO A FORM

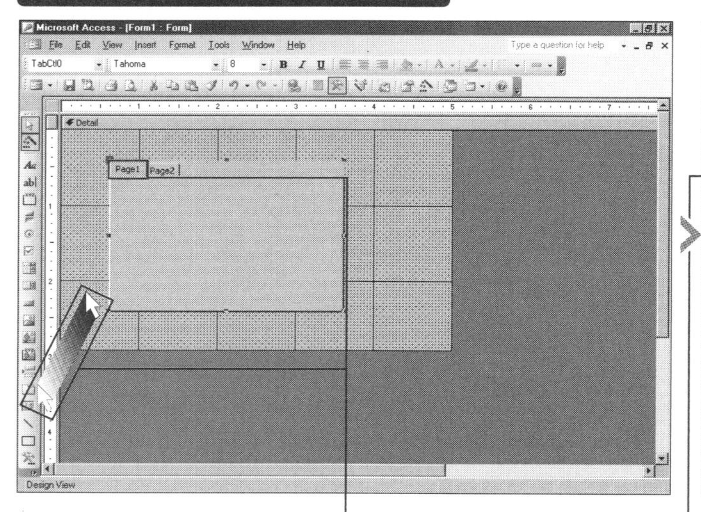

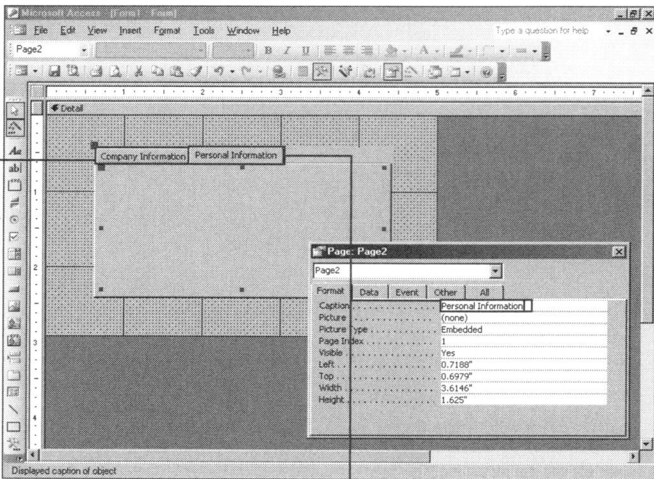

Note: This task uses frmAddATabControlToAForm in AVP-Chapter05.mdb on the CD-ROM.

1 Create or open a form, with a record source you specify.

2 Click the Tab control and drag it into your form.

3 Double-click the Page1 tab.

■ The property sheet for Page1 appears.

4 Click the Format tab.

5 Type a caption in the Caption property field.

■ The caption for the first tab appears.

6 Click the Page2 tab.

7 Type a caption in the Caption property field.

■ The caption for the second tab appears.

Extra

In addition to adding new pages, you can also perform other tasks when you right-click the Tab control. Those tasks are:

MENU ITEM	USE
Insert Page	Inserts a page into the Tab control.
Delete Page	Deletes a page from the Tab control. This action deletes whatever page you have highlighted.
Page Order	Rearranges the order of the pages in the Tab control.
Tab Order	After highlighting a page, you can set the Tab order of the controls on that page.

A Tab control has two distinct sets of properties, and property sheets, that you use: those for the Tab control, and those for the individual pages of the Tab control. When you want to work with a specific page on the Tab control, you must ensure that you click that tab's caption. If you want to modify the properties of the entire Tab control, then you must click the edge of the control. When the property sheet appears, the title reflects whether you are modifying the Tab control, or an individual page.

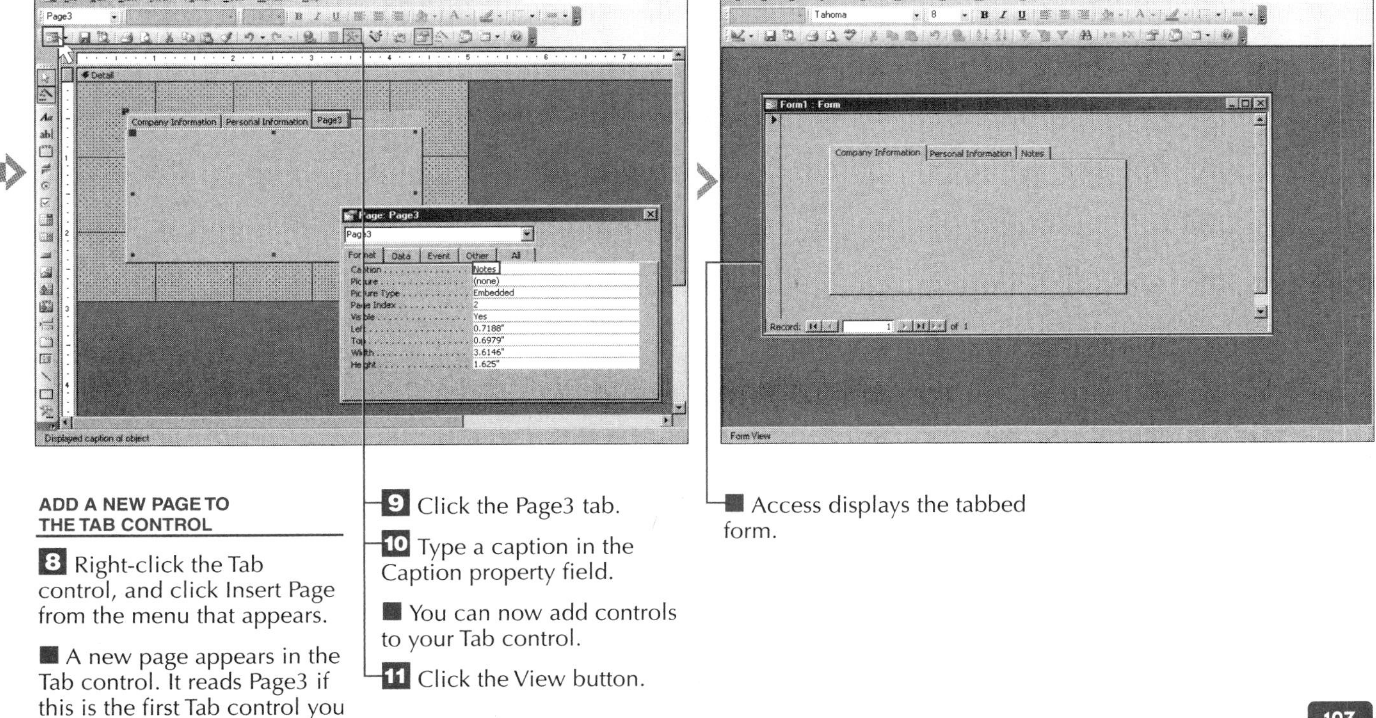

ADD A NEW PAGE TO THE TAB CONTROL

8 Right-click the Tab control, and click Insert Page from the menu that appears.

■ A new page appears in the Tab control. It reads Page3 if this is the first Tab control you have added to your database.

9 Click the Page3 tab.

10 Type a caption in the Caption property field.

■ You can now add controls to your Tab control.

11 Click the View button.

■ Access displays the tabbed form.

ADD DATA TO THE TAB CONTROL PAGES

After you create a Tab control, you need to add other controls, such as text boxes and combo boxes, to the Tab control. These controls add functionality to your Tab control.

You can add controls to the Tab control by pulling fields from the Field List into the Tab control pages. You must first click the tab of the page to which you want to add the field. When you drag the cursor over the Tab control page, the page turns black. This tells you that you are on the specific tab page, and not the form or Tab control.

After you position the control field in the general area of the tab page where you want to place it, you can release the mouse button. Access adds the control field to the tab page. Some examples of control fields that you can add are textboxes, combo boxes, and check boxes. You can then reposition the control field to where you want it on the tab page.

You can follow the same steps when adding controls from the toolbox. Note that you can add any of the controls in the toolbox, except for another Tab control. To add another Tab control, you would need to add a Subform control, and then place the additional Tab control on the form that you would use in the subform.

When you add the controls you want, you can open the form in Form view, and test the tab page. You may also want to adjust and reposition the controls on the tab page. If you move a control over the edge of the tab page, Access adjusts the Tab control size to compensate.

If you move or add a number of controls in the Tab control, you may need to change the tab order of the controls on the form. You can do this by right-clicking the tab page, choosing Tab Order from the drop-down list, and modifying the tab order in the Tab Order dialog box.

ADD DATA TO THE TAB CONTROL PAGES

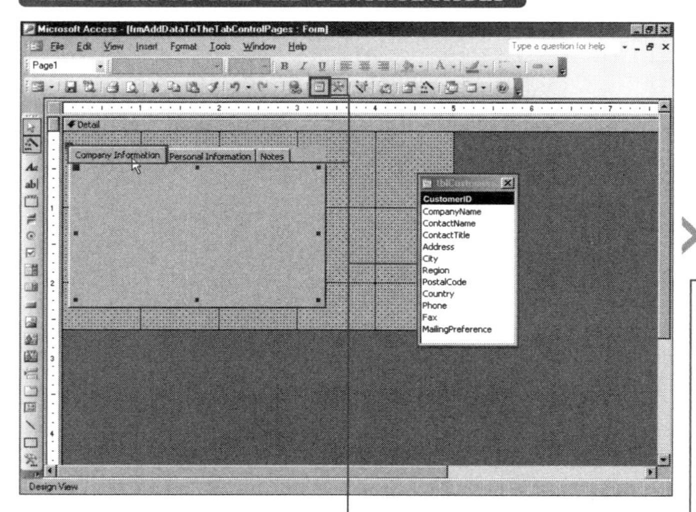

Note: This task uses frmAddDataToTheTabControlPages in AVP-Chapter05.mdb on the CD-ROM.

1 Create or open a form.

2 Add a Tab control.

3 Click the Field List button.

■ The Field List appears.

4 Click the tab for the tab page to which you want to add fields.

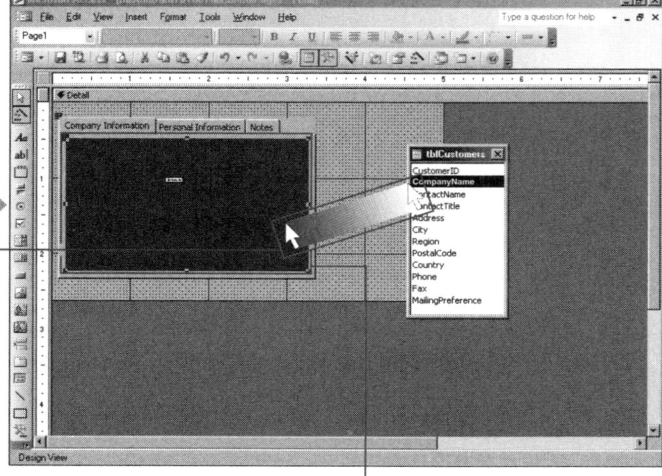

5 Click the field you want to add, and drag it to the tab page where you want to add it.

■ The tab page turns black.

Extra

You may want to use the Tab control to navigate through a lengthy form. To do this, you can place the Tab control on the form, and select the controls for the first tab you want to populate. Draw a selection box around the controls you want by clicking and holding the left mouse button, and dragging the mouse over the controls you want to select. Then, click Edit ➪ Cut.

Click in the page of the Tab control where you want to add the controls, and click Edit ➪ Paste. The controls appear in the tab page. Create any additional pages you need, and repeat the process until all controls are assigned to tab pages.

If you try to click and drag the controls from the form into the tab pages, they either sit on top of or underneath the Tab control. You can determine whether the Tab control is above or beneath the other controls by clicking the tabs to see if the controls respond properly.

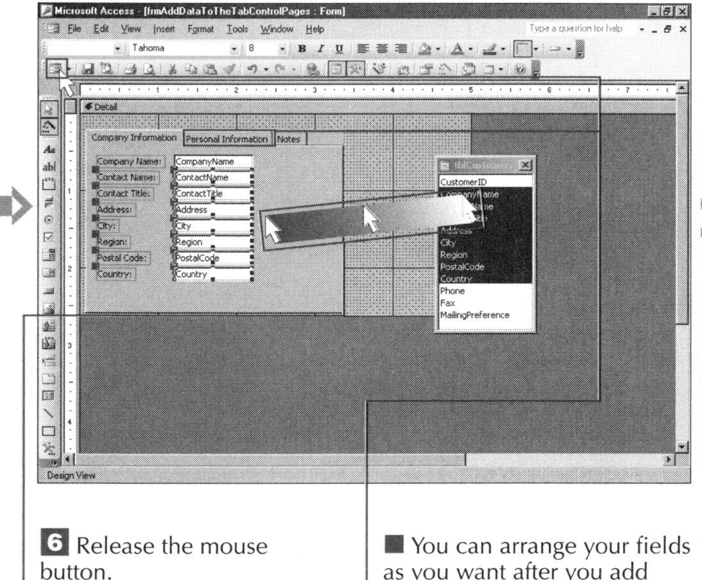

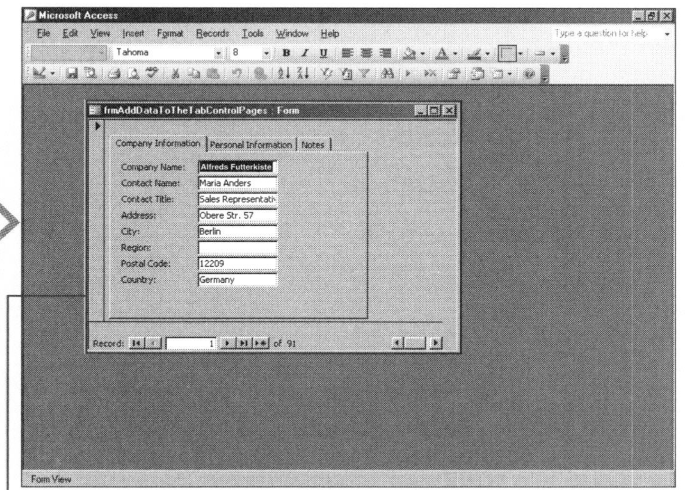

6 Release the mouse button.

7 Repeat steps 5 and 6 for any additional fields that you want to add to the tab page.

■ You can arrange your fields as you want after you add them.

8 Click the next tab, and add additional fields.

9 Click the View button.

■ Access displays the tabbed form with data on it.

■ You can click any tab to display the data for that tab.

ADD GRAPHICS TO A FORM

You can add graphics, such as your company logo, to your forms, enhancing the look of your forms. However, keep in mind that graphics can affect the performance of your forms by slowing them down if you have low memory. It is a good idea to keep the graphics and colors to a minimum, so that users are not distracted from the purpose of your form.

You can add graphics to a form with the Image control. After you click the Image control and drag it into the form, the Insert Picture dialog box appears, and you can locate your logo file.

After you have added the image you want in the form, you can set properties that affect how your image appears on your form.

Along with the standard formatting properties such as border colors and size, there are specific properties for Image control.

The Picture property contains the path and filename of the graphic you choose. The value that this property stores depends upon the Picture Type property, with which you can embed — the default — or link an image.

When you embed an image, the form contains a bitmap of the image. When you link an image, the Picture property contains the file path and filename of the image. When you use the Link feature and then update the original graphic file, the Image control reflects the changes the next time you open the form. However, if you delete or move the graphic file, then the link is broken, and the graphic disappears from the form.

You can use three properties to affect how the graphic appears on the form. They are Size Mode, Picture Alignment, and Picture Tiling.

You can also assign your Web URL to the Hyperlink Address property, so that when a user clicks the graphic, the Web browser opens, and your Web site appears.

ADD AN UNBOUND GRAPHIC TO A FORM

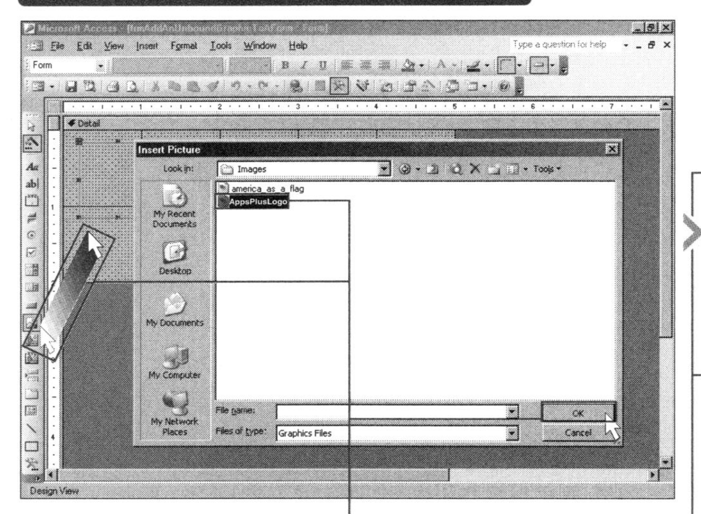

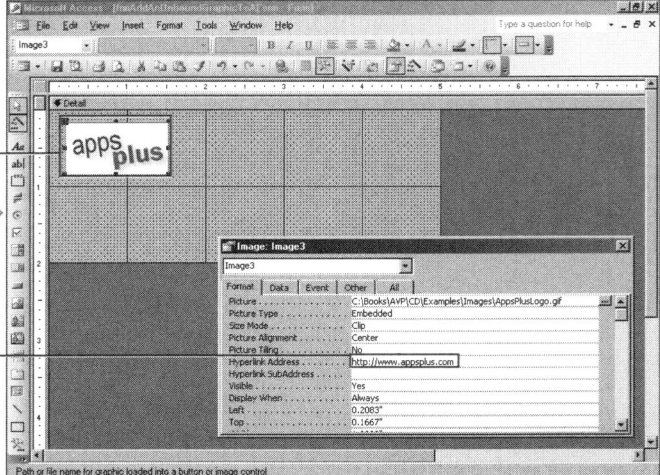

Note: This task uses frmAddAnUnboundGraphicToAForm in AVP-Chapter05.mdb on the CD-ROM.

1 Create or open a form to which you want to add a graphic.

2 Click the Image control, and then click the mouse where you want the image on the form.

3 In the Insert Picture dialog box, click the graphic file you want to use.

4 Click OK.

■ The graphic appears on the form.

5 With the property sheet open, type a URL in the Hyperlink Address property field.

■ This example uses the URL for my Web site.

■ When you click the graphic in your form, your Web browser opens, and takes you to the URL you entered in step 5.

Extra

When you have graphics in a table, and want to display them in a form, you can do so just as you would any other type of data. You can do this by clicking and dragging the field from the Field List to the form.

Access can create the Bound Object Frame control to work with the data. This control is different from the Image control. Both controls use the Size Mode to adjust the size of the graphic, but the other properties that are used by the Image control do not apply here.

When you switch records, the new picture is displayed. You can also update the picture by choosing Insert Object from the right-click menu. Access asks you to point to the graphic you want to insert. Access then adds the graphic to the table.

If you want to make sure that the user cannot update the graphics in your table, you can set the Locked property of the control to True.

DISPLAY GRAPHICS FROM A TABLE

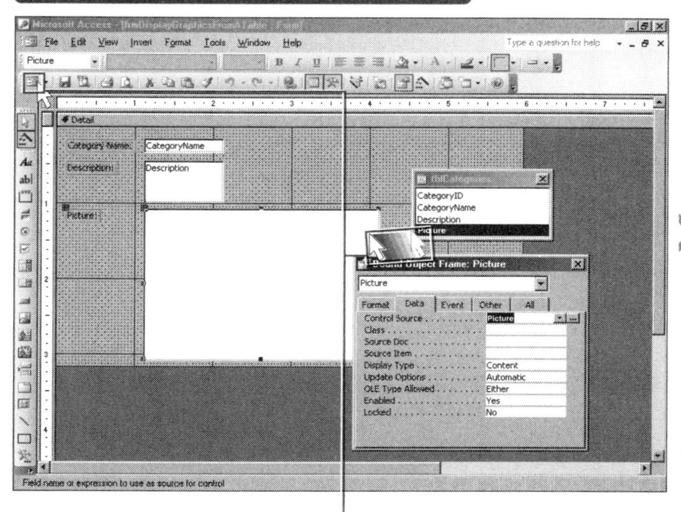

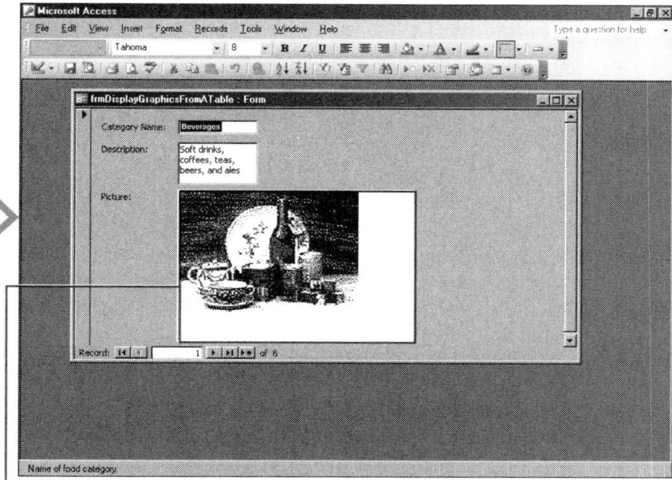

1 Create or open a form, based on a record source that includes a field that contains graphics.

■ For this example tblEmployee was used from the sample database.

2 Click and drag the graphic field from the Field List to the form.

3 Click the View button.

■ The graphic appears on the form.

USING A SUBFORM TO DISPLAY MAIN/DETAIL DATA

You can organize data on a form with a subform section that displays related tables in the same window, or you can link data from a table that displays in a separate window.

With Access, you can create the two forms separately, and then use one form as a Subform control in the other form, which becomes a mainform. Access guides you through the connection process with a wizard.

When you create the forms, you should keep in mind the layout you want to use for each form. For example, you may want to use the mainform in Single Form view, and the subform in another view, such as Datasheet view.

Access creates all the forms for you through the Form Wizard, and selects fields from the two different record sources. If you prefer, you can also create your own forms.

The SubForm Wizard appears when you turn on the control wizards. The wizard first asks you whether you want to use tables or queries for your subform. It then uses the tables or queries to create a form, or adds them to an existing form.

You can select a form that you want to link to another form. The wizard asks you which fields you want to use to link the two forms. This is the same set of fields that relate the record sources underlying the forms. For example, if you want to create a mainform/subform using tblOrders as the mainform and tblOrderDetails as the subform, then the key field in each table is OrderID, because this is the field that relates the two tables. You can use the combination that Access suggests to you.

Lastly, you must specify a name for the subform. The wizard then completes the process, and creates the Subform control.

USING A SUBFORM TO DISPLAY MAIN/DETAIL DATA

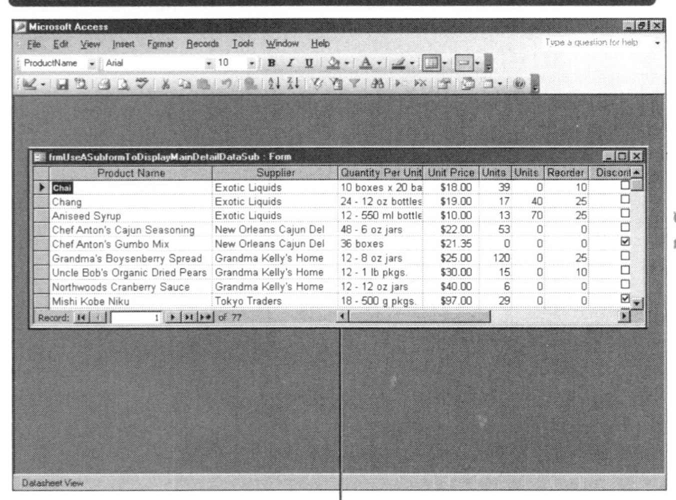

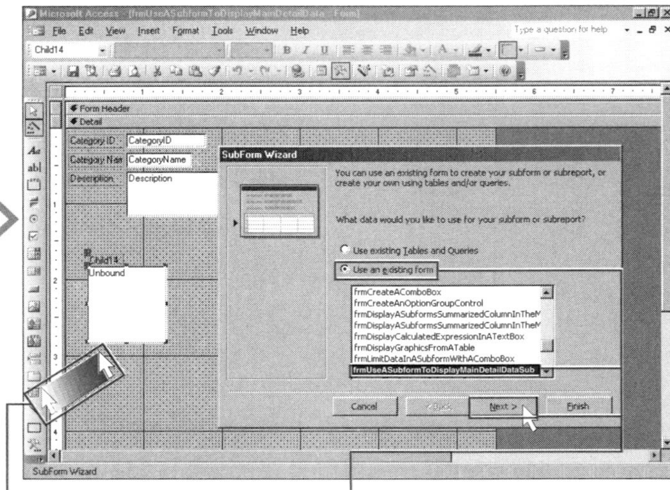

Note: This task uses frmUseASubformToDisplayMainDetailData and frmUseASubformToDisplayMainDetailDataSub in AVP-Chapter05.mdb on the CD-ROM.

1 Create or open the form that you want to use for the subform.

2 Click the View button (▤) to see the form in view mode, and make sure the layout is what you want.

■ This example uses the Datasheet view.

3 Create the mainform, using Single Form view.

4 With the control wizards (🪄) on, click the Subform control, and drag it into the form.

■ The Subform Wizard appears.

5 Click Use an existing form.

6 Click the form you created or opened in steps 1 and 2.

7 Click Next.

Extra

There are three important properties on the Subform control. They are listed in the following table:

PROPERTY	DESCRIPTION
Source Object	Name of the form that you are using for the subform. You are given the list of forms in the database from which to choose.
Link Child Fields	Fields that you want to link, located in the subform's record source. You can specify more than one field, separated by a comma.
Link Master Fields	Fields that you want to link from the mainform. Even though the name of the property is Link Master Fields, you can use Unbound controls to link from the mainform, not just controls bound to fields in the master form's record source. For more information about using Unbound controls, see the next chapter.

If you click the Builder button, which appears next to the last two properties, the Subform Link Finder appears to help you find the correct link.

When you use the Subform Wizard to set up your Subform control, take a look at these properties to become more familiar with them. Also, keep in mind that the problems between mainforms and subforms may result in one of these properties being incorrect. The new Form Control Error feature of Access does not find these types of errors.

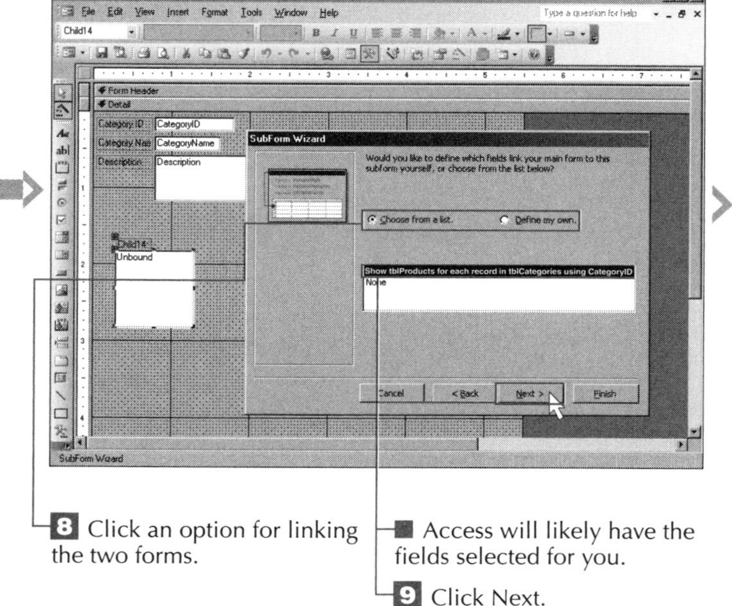

8 Click an option for linking the two forms.

■ Access will likely have the fields selected for you.

9 Click Next.

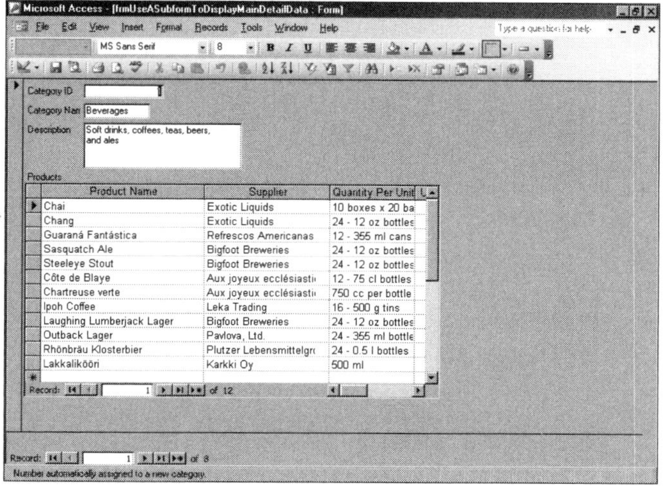

10 Type the caption you want for the subform, and click Finish.

11 Adjust the subform to fit the form by placing the cursor at the edge of the form, holding down the left mouse button, then expanding the form as desired.

12 Click the View button (▣).

■ The new mainform/subform appears.

LIMIT DATA IN A SUBFORM WITH A COMBO BOX

You can link a subform to a combo box in a form to display limited query results. When a user selects the value from a combo box, Access compares the link in the subform with that value. All of this is done without a single line of code.

When you create a combo box, the combo box lists the main items you want to display in the subform. For example, if you want to display all the orders for different customers, you modify the properties of the combo box so that it displays the customer list. The Row Source for the combo box would contain the following statement:

```
Select CustomerID, CompanyName from
tblCustomers
```

You can then create a subform that lists any order information you want to include. After this, you can place a Subform control on the mainform that contains the combo box. You should adjust the Subform control in the form to ensure that all the data displays properly.

Next, you can set the three properties in the subform: The Object Source property specifies the subform name; the Link Child Fields property, CustomerID in the example above, specifies the field to which you want to link in the subform; and the Link Master Fields property specifies the name of the combo box.

You can now save and close the form. When you reopen the form and select new values in the combo box, the subform is re-queried.

LIMIT DATA IN A SUBFORM WITH A COMBO BOX

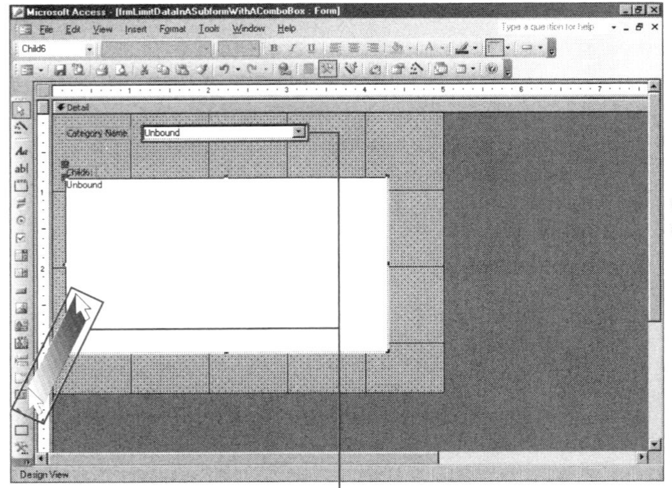

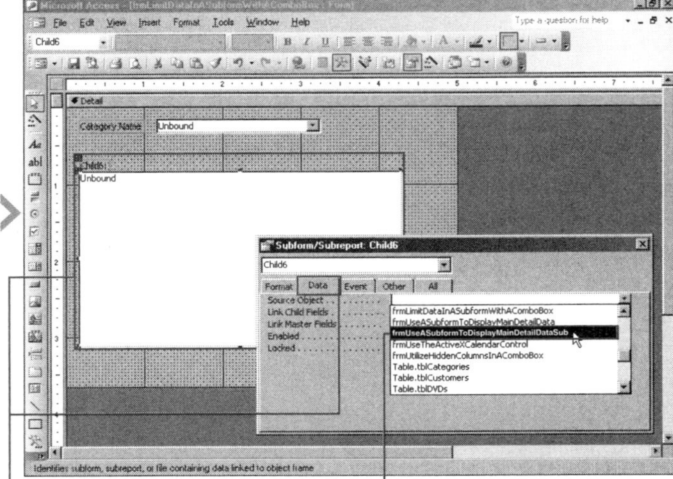

Note: This task uses frmLimitDataInASubformWithAComboBox and frmUseASubformToDisplayMainDetailDataSub in AVP-Chapter05.mdb on the CD-ROM.

1 Create the form you want to use as the subform.

2 Create an unbound form, and place the combo box you want to use on the form.

3 Set the Name property using the property sheet.

4 With the control wizards off, click and drag the Subform control into the form.

5 Double-click the new Subform control.

■ The property sheet for the Subform control appears.

6 Click the Data tab.

7 Select the form being used as a subform in the Source Object property field from the drop-down list.

Extra

Instead of using the Link Child and Link Master field properties, you can also include criteria in a query, which would point to the combo box. In the example below, you can leave the Link Child and Link Master Fields properties blank, and in the CategoryID field of the tblProducts table, you can use the following criteria:

```
=Forms!frmLimitDataInASubformWithAComboBox!cboCateg
ories
```

You must also add an event procedure to the combo box.

You can click the Builder button in the After Update event, located in the Events tab of the combo box property sheet. In the Choose Builder dialog box, you can select Code Builder, and click OK. You can then type **subFormName.Requery** in the blank line between the two lines that start with Private Sub and End Sub.

When you save and reopen the form, the subform works as if you were using the Link Child and Link Master Field properties. You can use this feature when you are using different forms as subforms.

You can set the Default Value property of the combo box to point to the first value. Otherwise, the subform display points to a new record, because there are no matching records if the combo box value is NULL.

To set the Default Value property to the first value in the combo box, you can type **=*ComboBoxName*.ItemData(0)** in the property field. In the example below, you would type **=cboCategories.ItemData(0)** in the property field.

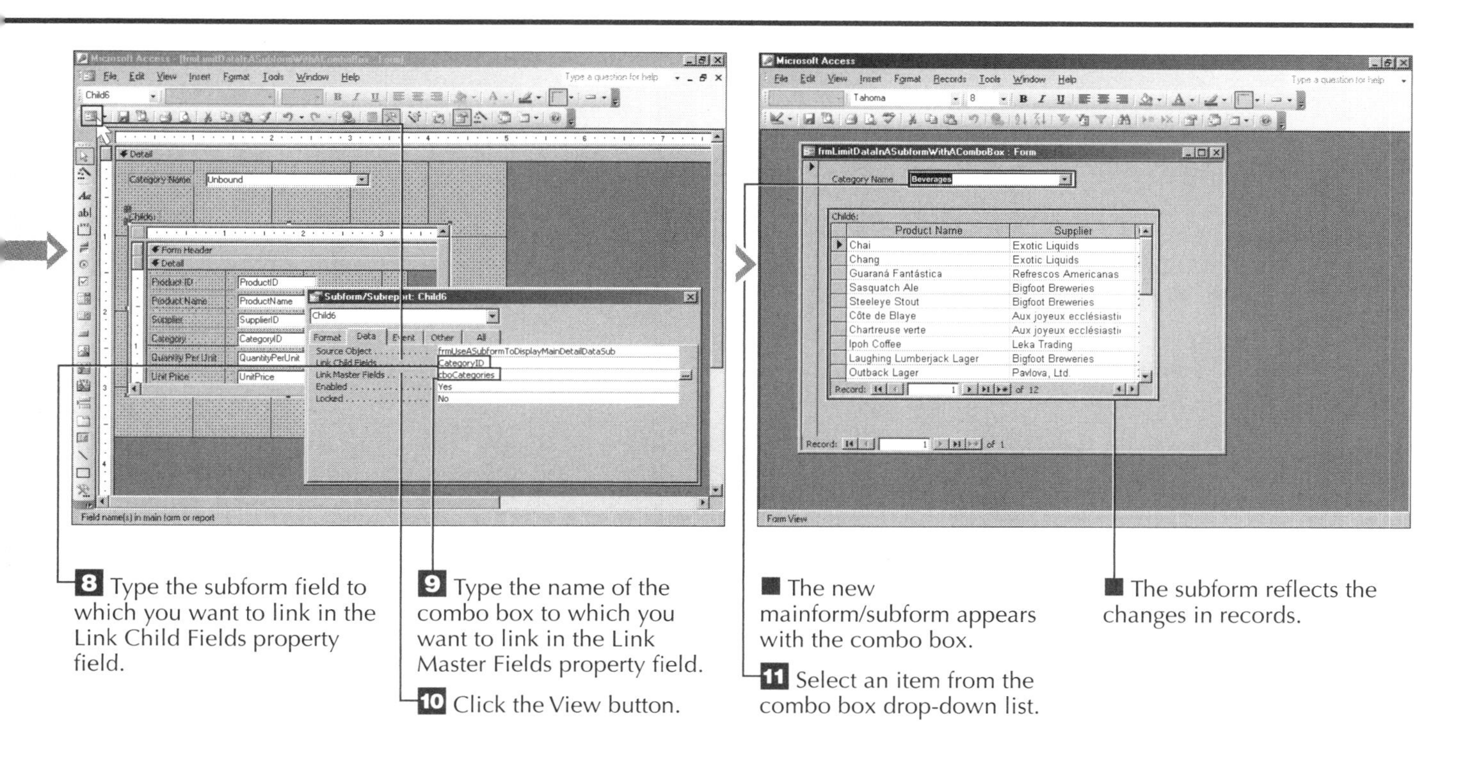

8 Type the subform field to which you want to link in the Link Child Fields property field.

9 Type the name of the combo box to which you want to link in the Link Master Fields property field.

10 Click the View button.

■ The new mainform/subform appears with the combo box.

11 Select an item from the combo box drop-down list.

■ The subform reflects the changes in records.

DISPLAY A SUMMARIZED SUBFORM COLUMN IN THE MAINFORM

You can summarize a column or columns from the subform and display the results on the mainform.

For example, when you create an invoice using the Mainform/Subform type form, you can use the mainform for the header section of the invoice, and the subform for the line item details. You can tell Access to calculate totals for items in the subform, and then to display those totals on the mainform.

You must first create your subform in Datasheet view, including the quantities and prices. Then, you can add a Textbox control to the Form Footer section of the form. The Control Source property for the text box must contain the following syntax:

=Sum(*fields*)

When you set the Name property of the new text box, you need to remember the exact name. Although you place this text box in the Form Footer section of the form, when you display the form in Datasheet view, the Form Footer section is not visible. However, the control is still calculating the sums of the fields in the background.

After you place the subform on the mainform, you can then add a Textbox control in which you set the Control Source property to the name of the text box located on the subform. The syntax is as follows:

=*subformcontrolname*!*textboxname*

You want to ensure that you use the Subform control name, and not the name of the form that is set in the Source Object property field of the subform.

CREATE THE TEXT BOX IN THE SUBFORM

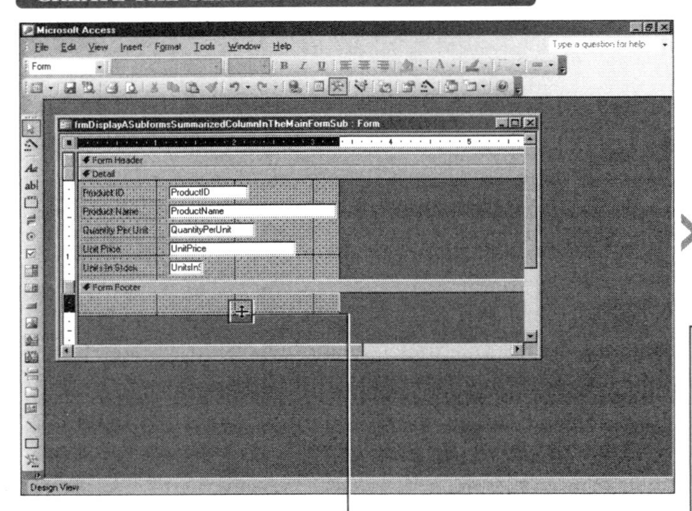

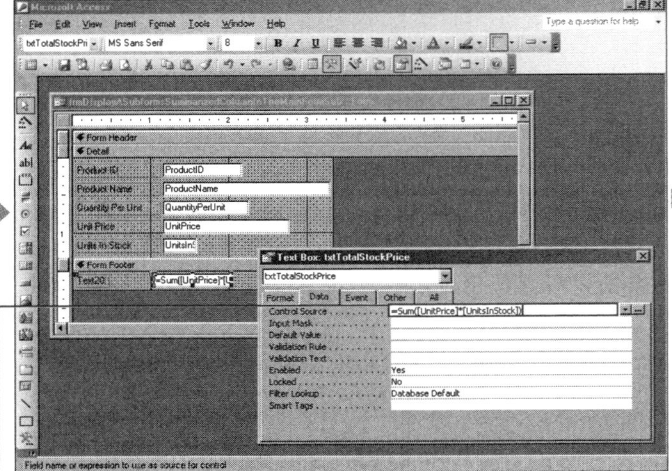

Note: This task uses frmDisplayASubformsSummarizedColumnInTheMainForm and frmDisplayASubformsSummarizedColumnInTheMainFormSub in AVP-Chapter05.mdb on the CD-ROM.

1 Create the subform that you want to use.

2 Expand the Form Footer section by clicking and dragging the edge of the section.

3 Add a new text box.

4 Set the Name property for the text box using the property sheet.

5 Type the criteria you want for the Control Source property.

6 Save and close the form.

■ The subform is now created, and ready to use for the mainform.

Extra

Along with the `Sum()` function, you can use any of the mathematical functions that you want, by clicking the Builder button next to the Control Source property. The Expression Builder dialog box appears, and you can click Functions, and then Built-In Functions in the first column. In the second column you can choose SQL Aggregate. A list appears, displaying the possible aggregate functions that you can use. You may want to experiment with the other available functions.

When you find the function you want to use in the text box, click the function, and then click OK. Access copies the shell, or syntax, of the function into the Control Source property field, and you can then modify the arguments to use the expression.

By default, the number that appears in the text box does not use any kind of formatting. You can set the formatting on the Textbox control that you add on the mainform. You can set the Format property, just as you can at the query or table field level, using the Currency format.

CREATE THE TEXT BOX IN THE MAINFORM

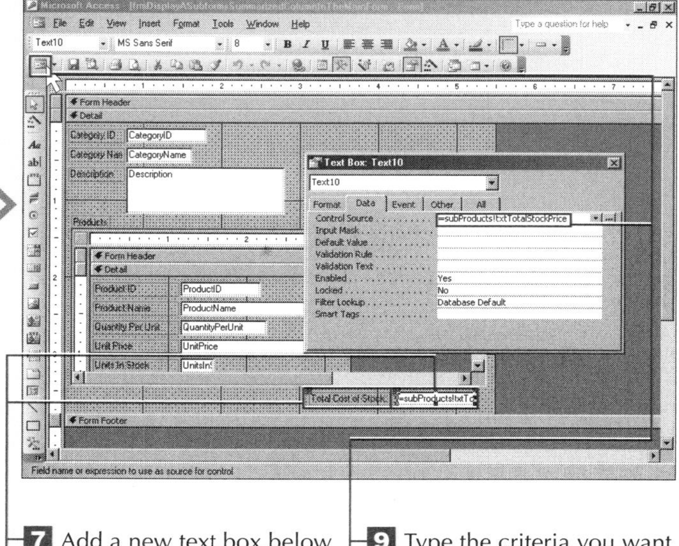

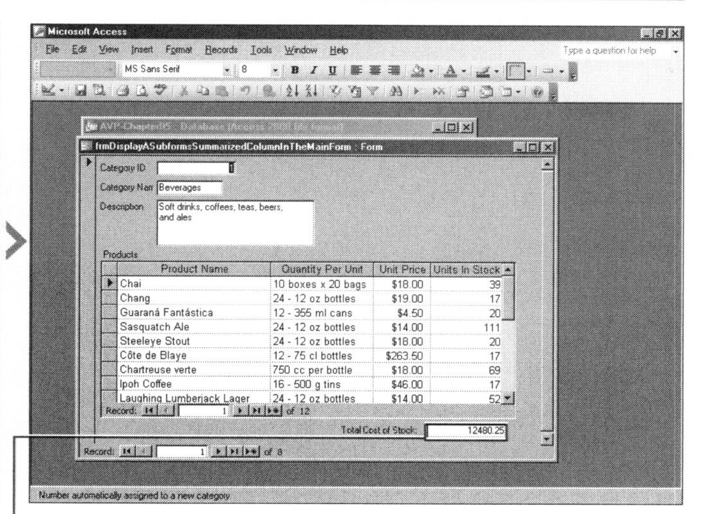

7 Add a new text box below the subform.

8 Type descriptive text into the label of the new text box.

9 Type the criteria you want for the Control Source property.

■ You must accurately type the name of the Subform control.

10 Click the View button.

■ The new mainform/subform appears, with the new text box displaying the subform total.

USING THE ACTIVEX CALENDAR CONTROL

Access offers a number of controls to add functionality to your forms, there are even more controls that you can use that come from sources other than Access. Those controls are called ActiveX controls.

ActiveX controls are created to a standard that various development environments can work with, including Visual Basic, C, Delphi, and anything that uses VBA.

You can generally use ActiveX controls just as you would Access controls. Some ActiveX controls can even be bound to your data using the Control Source property. One of these controls, the Calendar control, is included with Access.

To determine whether you have the Calendar control installed on your computer, you can click Insert ➪ ActiveX Controls while in a form in the Design view. The Calendar control should appear in the list alphabetically, with the title, Calendar Control 11.0. If you do not see the control, you may need to use the Windows Add/Remove Program utility to locate the Calendar control under the Access application.

When you place the Calendar control on your form, you can then set the control properties through either the Access property sheet, or the property sheet that belongs to the ActiveX control. The properties that are specific to each ActiveX control appear on the Access property sheet in the Other tab. When you place the Calendar control on a form, you need only set the Control Source property to the field you want to use, and it is ready to work.

When you view your form, and make a selection in the calendar, the field to which you have bound the control updates in the table.

USING THE ACTIVEX CALENDAR CONTROL

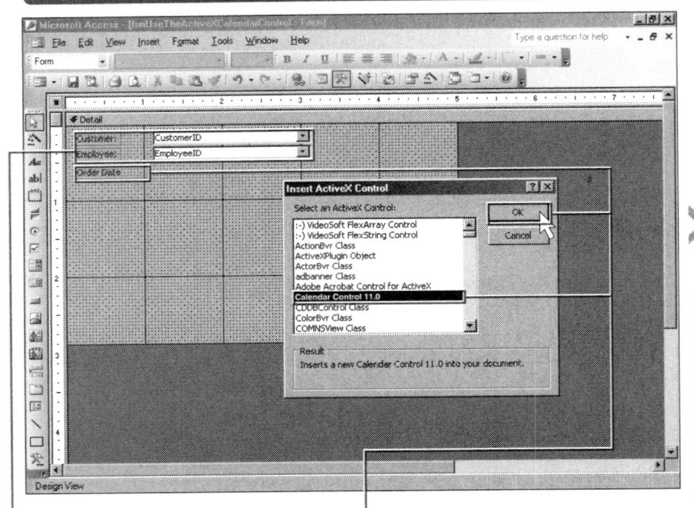

Note: This task uses frmUseTheActiveXCalendarControl in AVP-Chapter05.mdb on the CD-ROM.

1 Create a form, based on a record source with a Date/Time data type field.

2 Add fields to the form, except for the field that will contain the Calendar control.

3 Add a label and a caption to the ActiveX control.

4 Click Insert ➪ ActiveX control.

5 Click Calendar Control 11.0.

6 Click OK.

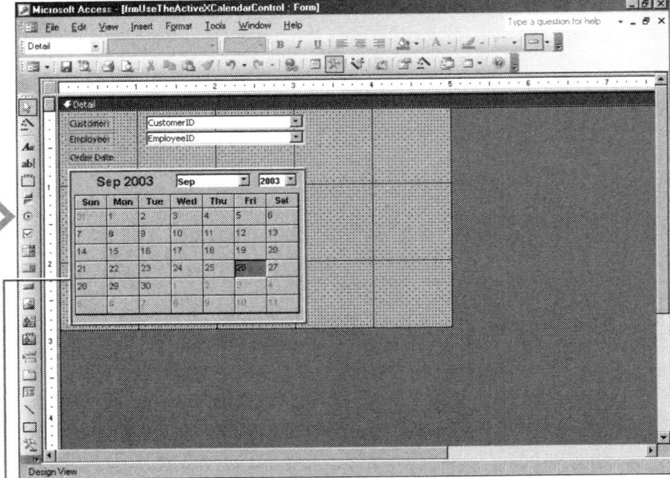

■ The Calendar control appears on the form.

7 Click and drag the control to where you want it on the form.

Extra

Along with the Control Source property, there are a number of properties that you can use with the Calendar control. These properties appear in the Other tab of the property sheet for the control, under the Custom property.

PROPERTY	DESCRIPTION
DayFont	Font used to display the days of the week.
DayFontColor	Color used to display the days of the week.
DayLength	Format used to display the days of the week.
FirstDay	First day of the week.
MonthLength	Format used to display the months of the year.
ShowDateSelectors	Visibility of the month and year date selectors.
ShowDays	Visibility of the days of the week.
ShowTitle	Visibility of the month/year title.
TitleFont	Font used for the month/year title at the top of the calendar.
TitleFontColor	Color used for the month/year title.

You can set these values using either the property sheet, or VBA code. The control also has methods and events. For more information on methods and events, see Chapter 6.

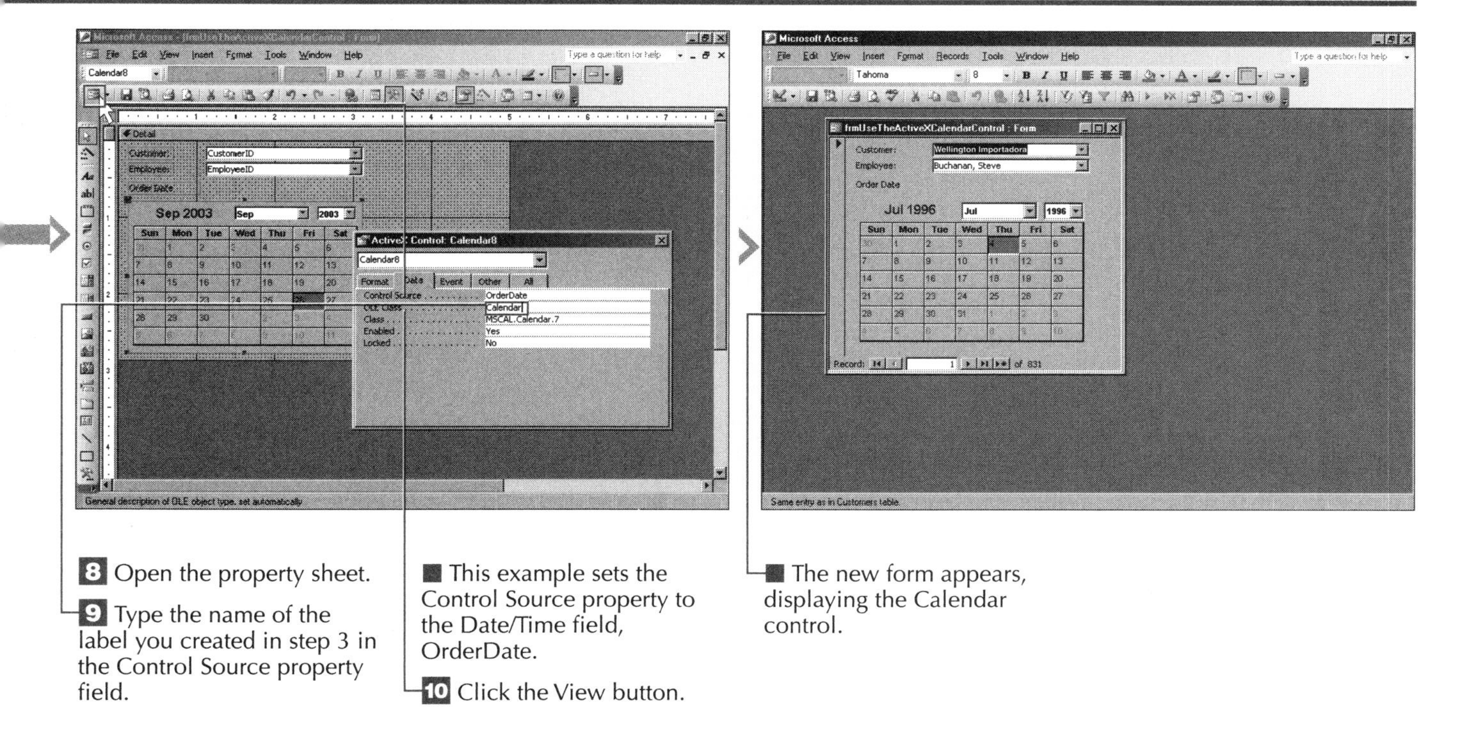

8 Open the property sheet.

9 Type the name of the label you created in step 3 in the Control Source property field.

■ This example sets the Control Source property to the Date/Time field, OrderDate.

10 Click the View button.

■ The new form appears, displaying the Calendar control.

UNDERSTANDING VBA BASICS

Visual Basic for Applications, or VBA, is a programming language you can use to automate your database applications. You can write code — commands that the computer understands — to tell Access to perform various tasks for you. When you type lines of commands into routines, then call those routines from different areas of Access, VBA works in the background, manipulating objects, such as forms, reports, and queries. For example, you can use VBA to open a form, or run update queries within a form.

Access automatically creates some code for you when you place Command Button controls into your forms. For more information on this, see the section "Learn to Code from the Command Button Wizard."

TYPES OF VBA ROUTINES

There are two types of VBA routines, Function and Sub. The routine type that you use depends on your purpose and the location from where you are calling it. Note that both routine types use parameters in a way similar to queries. You supply a parameter, which delivers arguments on the calling side, and the routine uses the parameter to perform its task.

Functions

You can use functions when you want to return a value after performing a task. For example, you can pass values to the DateAdd() and DateDiff() built-in VBA functions. When you are calling functions, the values you pass are called arguments. The functions then send back a return value.

You can create your own functions in Access; in fact, in some cases Access can only use functions, instead of subroutines.

Here is the syntax for a function:

```
Function FunctionName(parameter1 AS
datatype,...) as ReturnDataType

        '--- comments

        ' code within the function

        FunctionName = ValueToReturn

End Function
```

Here is an example of a function that returns a full name for a last name and first name passed into the function:

```
Function FullName(strLastName As String, _

         strFirstName As String) As String

     FullName = strLastName & ", " &
strFirstName

End Function
```

Functions (continued)

The FullName() function that concatenates the two strings together should look familiar because it uses the same syntax that Access uses in calculated columns in queries, and for calculated controls in forms. In fact, you can use the FullName() function identically for both purposes.

Subroutines

When you have tasks to perform but do not need return values, you can use a subroutine. Subroutines have a similar syntax to functions, but they do not return a value.

```
Sub SubName(parameter1 AS datatype,...)

        '-- comments

        ' code within the subroutine

End Sub
```

Here is an example of a subroutine that displays a message passed to it:

```
Sub DisplayMsg(strMessage As String)

     MsgBox strMessage, vbInformation,
"Example"

End Sub
```

This subroutine takes the value passed in the strMessage string, and displays it using the MsgBox statement. Note that the routine does not return a value.

HOW ACCESS STORES VBA CODE

Access stores VBA routines in modules. There are three types of modules: Standard, Form/Report, and Class.

Standard Modules

When you want to use VBA code throughout your application, you can place the code in Standard modules. These modules are routines that you can call from more than one place in your application. These modules are located under the Module group in the database window. When you open the database application, Access loads routines that use code in Standard modules.

Class Modules

These are special modules that allow you to create your own classes. With these classes, you can create objects that have their own properties and methods. Class modules are beyond the scope of this book.

Form/Report Modules

Form/Report modules are special Class modules that you can use specifically for forms or reports. When you create routines in a Form/Report module, by default only that form or report accesses those routines. Access only loads routines that use the Form/Report modules into memory when you open the form or report.

You can open these modules by going to the form or report for which you want to access the routines, and then clicking View ➪ Code; you can also open the property sheet to the Event tab, and click the individual events.

WHERE ACCESS USES VBA

Access can use VBA routines in a number of areas. Over the many versions of Access, Microsoft has used the input of many developers to determine the most effective ways to use VBA to improve Access.

Form/Report/Control Events

Forms, reports, and controls have three things in common:

- They use properties, which describe something about objects.
- They use methods, which are tasks that an object performs. For more information about methods, see Chapter 7.
- They use events to call VBA code routines that you create. Events are actions that occur with or because of objects, such as forms, reports, and controls.

An event procedure is an action that occurs as a result of a specific event occurring for an object. You can tell which events an object has by looking in the property sheet for the object, under the Events tab. Two examples of events are the Click event for a command button and the Open event for a form or report.

Control Source Property for Controls

You can use functions for the Control Source property of controls in both forms and reports. To do this, you must precede the function call with an equal sign, =.

Queries

You can call VBA routines that you create, from calculated expressions in query columns, or for criteria.

Other Routines

VBA routines can be called from one another. Access determines how the routine is called, based on which type of routine, subroutine, or function you are using.

WHY USE VBA AND NOT MACROS?

Although you can use macros to quickly automate many of the features in the other Office applications, it is a good idea to become familiar with VBA code so that you do not need to rely on macros for all of your tasks in Access. This is because macros in Access are different from macros in Excel, Word, and other Microsoft Office applications.

ACCESS MACROS VERSUS MACROS IN OTHER OFFICE APPLICATIONS

When you create macros in Office applications other than Access, you are in fact creating VBA routines that you can view, edit, and run. When you create a macro in Access, you are using a set of menu-driven commands called Macro Actions, which Access groups together in the Macro list of the database window.

While Access macros can help you perform a task quickly, they cannot be error trapped. This means that your applications respond poorly if someone enters bad data or commands.

One of the reasons people may hesitate to switch from macros to VBA is their concern that they would have to learn an entire programming language. However, you may find that VBA code is actually much easier to read than macros, especially when documented correctly using comments.

SWITCHING FROM MACROS TO VBA

If you have been working with macros in Access for a while, you can use a menu command, discussed in the next section, to convert your macros into VBA code. You can also learn VBA by reading the code that the control wizards generate. For more about the control wizards, see the section "Learn to Code from the Command Button Wizard," later in this chapter.

Using the DOCMD Object

The DoCmd object has methods that perform most of the macro actions that you can do using Access macros.

For example, you can open forms in macros using the OpenForm macro action, supplying the form name, possible filter, Where clause, and other optional parameters.

The same macro action is a method on the DoCmd object, and uses exactly the same parameters. For example, in VBA, the command to open a form called frmCustomers looks like this:

```
DoCmd.OpenForm "frmCustomers"
```

You can also supply some or all of the other parameters. For more information on the DoCmd object, see the section "Using DoCmd to Open Forms and Queries."

Other VBA Statements

VBA statements that are not included in the DoCmd object are included in some other way. For example, the MsgBox statement takes the place of the MsgBox macro action. Like the macro action, you can use the MsgBox statement as a simple message box display. However, you can also use the MsgBox statement as a function that returns values that the user inputs. Instead of simply displaying a message that tells the user that he has made an error, you can ask whether he wants to correct the error. For more information, see the section "Using the MsgBox Statement."

CONVERT YOUR MACROS

If you have macros that you use in your database applications, you may want to convert your current macros to VBA code. When you convert your current macros to VBA code, you can learn a great deal about VBA programming.

To convert existing macros, you can select the macro group you want to convert. Access lists them under Macros in the database window. You can then click File ➪ Save As. The Save As dialog box appears. Access automatically gives the module the filename Converted Macro: *MacroName*. In the As drop-down list, you can choose Module, and then click OK.

In the Convert macro dialog box that appears, you can add error handling to the code generated, along with comments from your macro descriptions. It is recommended that you use the default setting, which selects both options. You can then click Convert.

After Access generates the VBA module, you must now find all the places that you call your macros, and change them to calls to your newly created functions. You can locate them in the Event tab of property sheets, along with some of the macros that call other macros. You should begin by converting small macros. If you have large macros, you may not want to convert them, and instead create the VBA code yourself.

To look at your new VBA code, you can double-click the new module in the Modules list. For more information on the module editor, called the Integrated Development Environment, or IDE, see the next section.

CONVERT YOUR MACROS

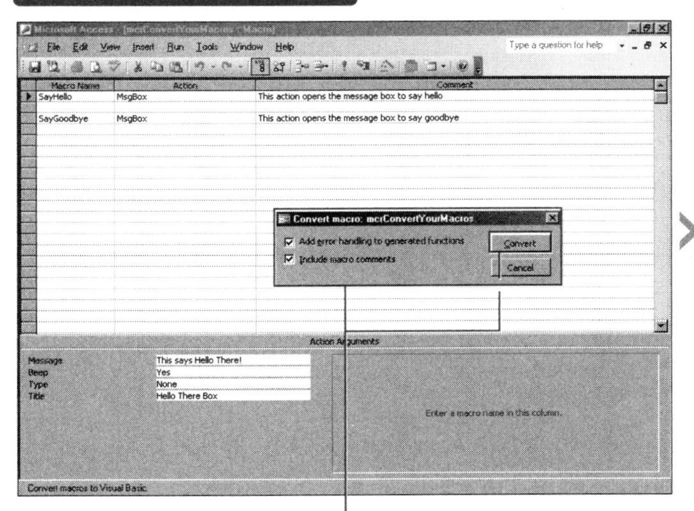

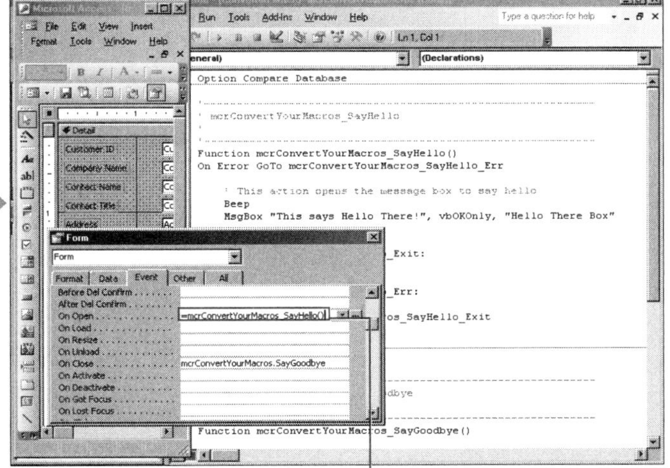

Note: This task uses mcrConvertYourMacros in AVP-Chapter06.mdb on the CD-ROM.

1 Open a macro that you want to convert, and then click File ➪ Save As.

■ The Save As dialog box appears.

2 Select Module for the As field.

3 Click OK.

■ The Convert macro dialog box appears.

4 Click Convert.

■ A message box appears, stating that Access has created the module.

5 Open the newly created module in the database window.

6 Locate the events where the macros are called.

7 Type = before the call, replace the period with an underscore, and add () at the end.

■ In this example, mcrConvertYourMacros. SayHello is replaced with =mcrConvertYourMacros _SayHello().

SET UP THE INTEGRATED DEVELOPMENT ENVIRONMENT

In order to create and modify code, you must use an editor application. In Access, you can use the editor in the Integrated Development Environment, or IDE. With the IDE, you can edit your code as well as debug and test your code.

To access the IDE you can double-click a module, or click View ⇨ Code from a form or report. The main areas of the IDE are the Project Explorer, the property sheet, and the main editor. If you use VBA in the other Office applications, such as Excel or Word, or even Visual Basic 6.0, then the interface should look familiar because they use the same IDE.

Even if you open a specific module for editing, the Project Explorer lets you open other modules. The Project Explorer displays a tree view, listing Access forms and report modules first, under the heading of Microsoft Access Class Objects. The next heading is Modules, which is where you can find standard modules. You can double-click a module to open it for editing.

Because you will probably not need to use the property sheet, you may want to close it to leave space for another window. To close the property sheet, you can click the Close button in the upper-right corner.

At the top of the main editor window are two drop-down lists. The first list appears at the top-left corner of the editor window, and you can use it to switch between objects in a form or report module. The second drop-down list, located to the right of the first drop-down list, includes general subroutines you have created for standard modules, and events for the highlighted objects in form and report modules. You can use it to move to the various routines within the current module with which you are working.

There is another window called the Immediate window. You can open it by clicking View ⇨ Immediate Window, and then reposition it to where the property sheet window was.

SET UP THE INTEGRATED DEVELOPMENT ENVIRONMENT

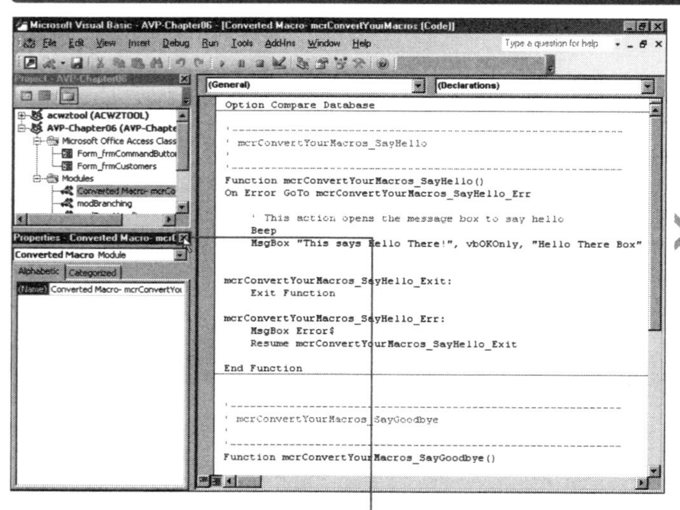

1 Open the IDE by double-clicking an existing module, or click New in the Module listings in the database window.

2 Close the property sheet by clicking the Close button.

■ The property sheet pane disappears.

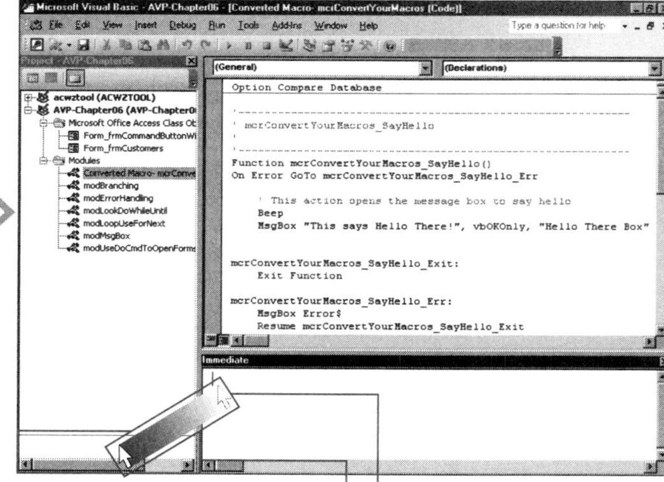

■ The Project Explorer window expands to the full length of the editor window.

3 Click View ⇨ Immediate Window.

■ The Immediate window appears below the editor window.

4 Click the title bar of the Immediate window, and drag it to the bottom of the Project Explorer.

■ The outline of the new location appears.

5 Release the mouse.

Apply It

You can use the Immediate window for testing and debugging your applications. The Immediate window lets you view expressions and update variables. For more information on variables, see the section "Using Variables and Constants," later in this chapter. The following are some expressions you can use in the Immediate window.

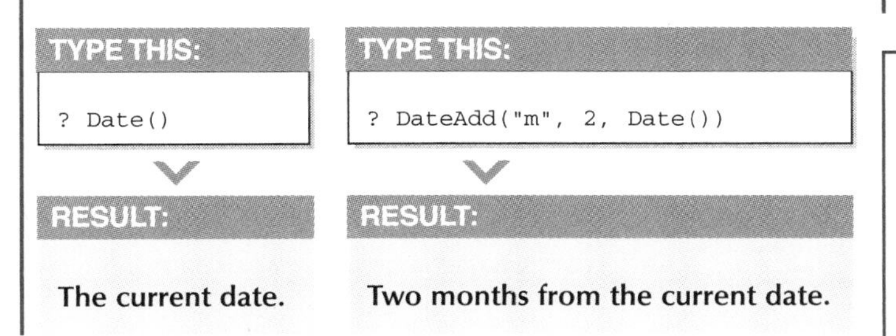

TYPE THIS:

```
? Date()
```

RESULT:

The current date.

TYPE THIS:

```
? DateAdd("m", 2, Date())
```

RESULT:

Two months from the current date.

If you want to view routines one at a time rather than continuously in the editor, you can click the Procedure View button (▤), located in the bottom-left corner of the main editor window. To switch back, click the Full Module View button (▤).

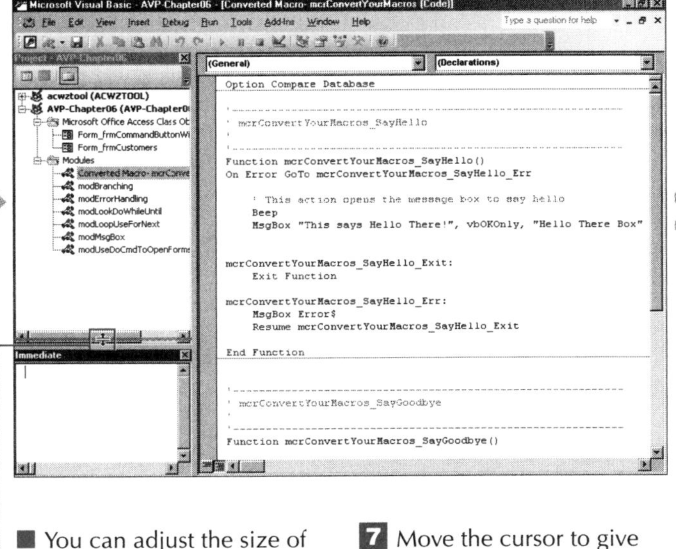

■ You can adjust the size of the Immediate window relative to the Project Explorer.

6 Click and hold the mouse on the border between the Project Explorer and the Immediate window.

7 Move the cursor to give either window more space.

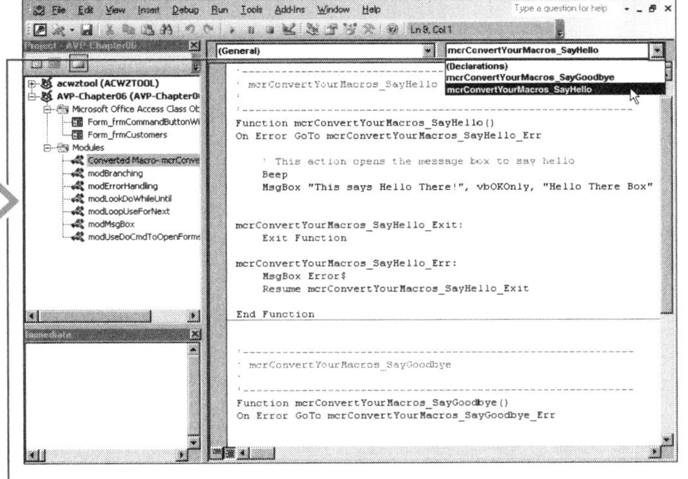

8 Click ▾.

■ A list of routines, both functions and subroutines, appears for the current module.

LEARN TO CODE FROM THE COMMAND BUTTON WIZARD

The quickest way you can learn VBA coding, and also learn some of the more common tasks that you can perform using VBA, is to examine the code that the control wizards create for you.

When you add a Command Button control from the toolbox in Form design view, and the control wizards are active, Access opens the Command Button Wizard. This dialog box guides you through selecting the type of task you want the command button to perform. For example, if you want to have the command button open a form, you can select Form Operations in the wizard, and then select Open a Form from the list that appears.

After you click Next, you can choose the form you want to open with the command button. Finally, you can specify the caption for the command button, and then click Finish.

Access creates the code for the command button, attached to the Click event for the form. Here is the code that Access creates to open a form:

```
Private Sub cmdOpenEmployees_Click()

On Error GoTo Err_cmdOpenEmployees_Click

    Dim stDocName As String

    Dim stLinkCriteria As String

    stDocName = "frmEmployees"

    DoCmd.OpenForm stDocName, , ,
    stLinkCriteria

Exit_cmdOpenEmployees_Click:

    Exit Sub

Err_cmdOpenEmployees_Click:

    MsgBox Err.Description

    Resume Exit_cmdOpenEmployees_Click

    End Sub
```

LEARN TO CODE FROM THE COMMAND BUTTON WIZARD

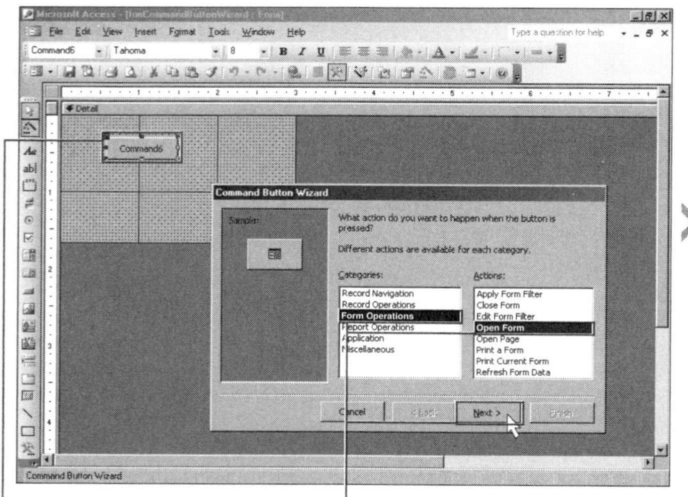

Note: This task uses frmCommandButtonWizard in AVP-Chapter06.mdb on the CD-ROM.

1 Create a form without a record source.

2 Drag a Command Button control into the form.

■ The control wizards (icon) should be toggled on.

3 On the first page of the Command Button Wizard, click Form Operations.

4 Click Open Form.

5 Click Next.

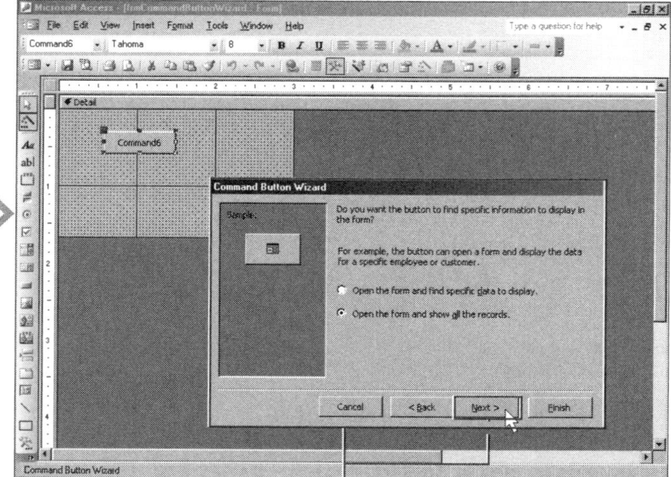

■ The next page of the wizard displays a list of forms.

6 Click a form, and click Next.

■ On the next page of the wizard, you can choose whether to open the form from a single record or all records.

7 Click Next to accept the default of all records.

Extra

If you create code using the Command Button Wizard, and then rename the control, the code does not run. This is because when you change the name of a control that has links to event procedures, you break the link to the events.

There are two methods you can use to correct this problem. You can rename the event procedure to match the name of the control. With Access 2002 and after, this is all you have to do. Access can match the control with the event procedures. For more information on event procedures, see Chapter 7.

The other way to correct the problem is to click the Builder button (...) next to the event in the property sheet pane. The IDE opens to a new event procedure that does not contain any lines of code between the Sub and End Sub lines. You can then cut and paste the code from the original event procedure into the new event procedure. Clean up the old code by deleting the entire event procedure, but be careful to only delete the old code.

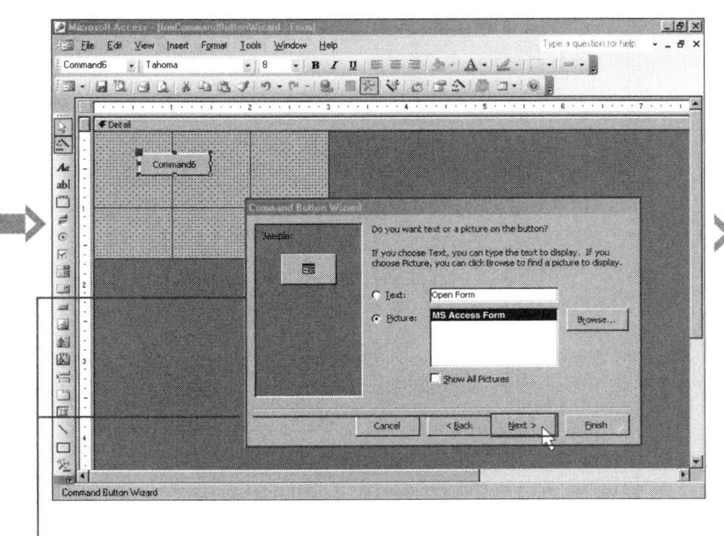

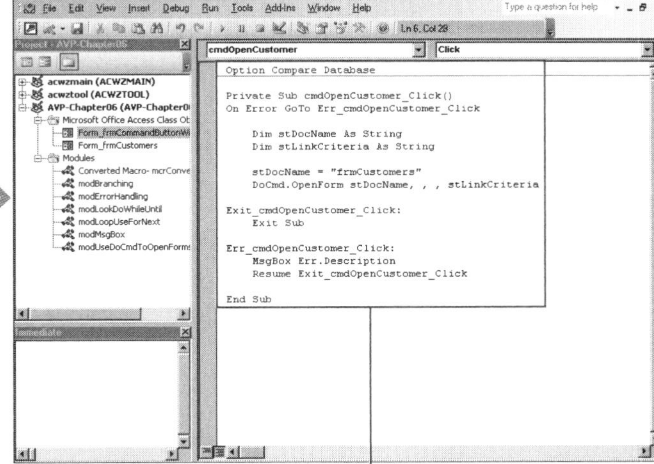

■ On the next page of the wizard, you can specify whether to use text or a graphic on your command button.

8 Click Next to accept the graphic.

■ On the last page of the wizard, you can specify the name of the new Command Button control.

9 Type the name of the command button, starting with **cmd**.

10 Click Finish.

■ Access adds the button to the form.

11 Click the View Code button ( ).

■ Access displays the code created by the Control Button Wizard.

USING DOCMD TO OPEN FORMS AND QUERIES

Two tasks you can perform using the DoCmd object are opening forms and queries. The two methods to perform these tasks are called OpenForm and OpenQuery. The syntax for the OpenForm method is:

```
DoCmd.OpenForm FormName, View, FilterName,
WhereCondition, DataMode, WindowMode,
OpenArgs
```

FormName is the name of the form. View can be acDesign, acFormDS, acFormPivotChart, acFormPivotTable, acNormal, or acPreview. The default View is acNormal, which takes the value you have for the Default View of the form. FilterName is the name of a filter that you can apply to the form.

WhereCondition is a criteria string that you can apply to the form as it opens. DataMode can be acFormAdd, acFormEdit, acPropertySettings, and acFormReadOnly. acPropertySettings is the default constant.

WindowMode can be acDialog, acHidden, acIcon, or acWindowNormal. acWindowNormal is the default constant. OpenArgs is a string value that you can send the form, and then write code to read the value when you are inside the form.

When you type **DoCmd** and then a period, the list of methods appears. As you continue, the various parameters are listed. This feature is called Intellesense, and it will help you remember commands and methods.

It is convenient for users to view queries without having to go into the database window under queries. You can use the OpenQuery method to do this. The syntax for the OpenQuery method is:

```
DoCmd.OpenQuery QueryName, View, DataMode
```

QueryName is the name of the query. As with OpenForm, View can be acDesign, acFormDS, acFormPivotChart, acFormPivotTable, acNormal, or acPreview. The default for View is acNormal, which takes the value you have for the Default View of the form. DataMode can be acFormAdd, acFormEdit, or acFormReadOnly. acFormEdit is the default criteria.

OPEN A FORM USING DOCMD

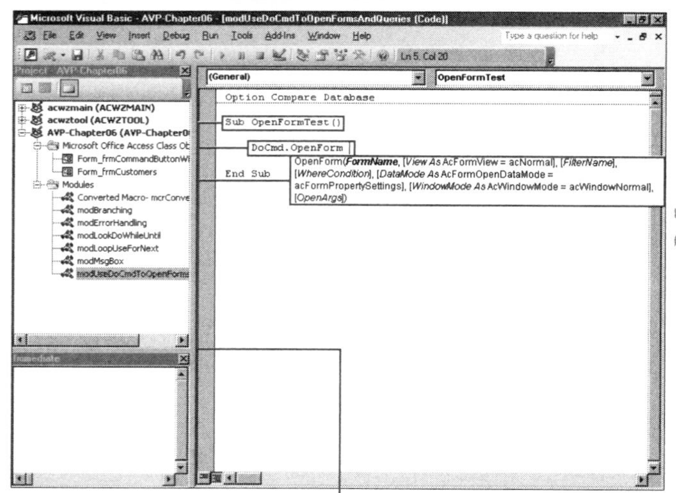

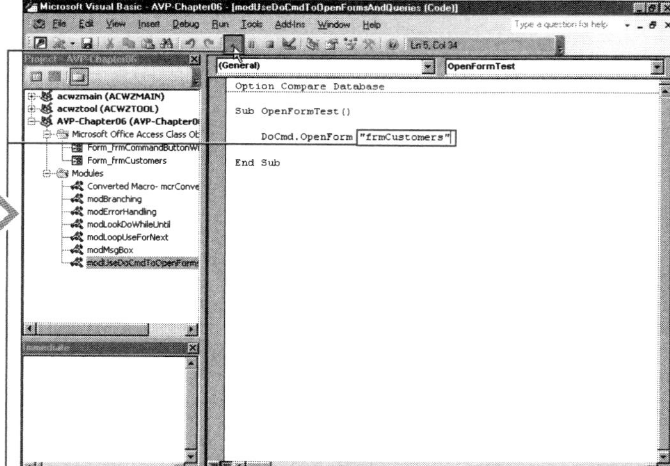

Note: This task uses modUseDoCmdToOpenFormsAndQueries in AVP-Chapter06.mdb on the CD-ROM.

1 Create or open a form, and then click New in the Modules list.

2 Type **Sub**, a space, a subroutine, and then press Enter to create a subroutine.

3 Add blank lines between Sub and End Sub, type **DoCmd.OpenForm**, and then a space.

■ Intellesense displays the parameters for the method.

4 Type the name of the form you want to open in double quotes.

5 Click the Run button.

■ Access tests the new routine, and the form opens.

Extra

The IDE has a very helpful feature called Intellesense. When you are typing methods using the editor, Intellesense lets you know the parameters for the code you are developing, and what values are acceptable. For example, when you type **DoCmd.**, Access displays a list of methods for the DoCmd object as soon as you type the period after DoCmd.

You can either use the arrow keys to move up and down the list, or type letters to narrow down the selection. When you choose a method, Intellesense displays the parameters for that method. As you supply the parameters and type commas between them, Intellesense monitors your progress, displaying the options for each parameter, with the default value appearing in bold.

Intellesense can also save you time when you begin to type a method or parameter option. If Intellesense has highlighted the correct value you are looking for, you can either press the spacebar, Tab, or Enter, or type a comma. Intellesense then completes the entry for you.

OPEN A QUERY USING DOCMD

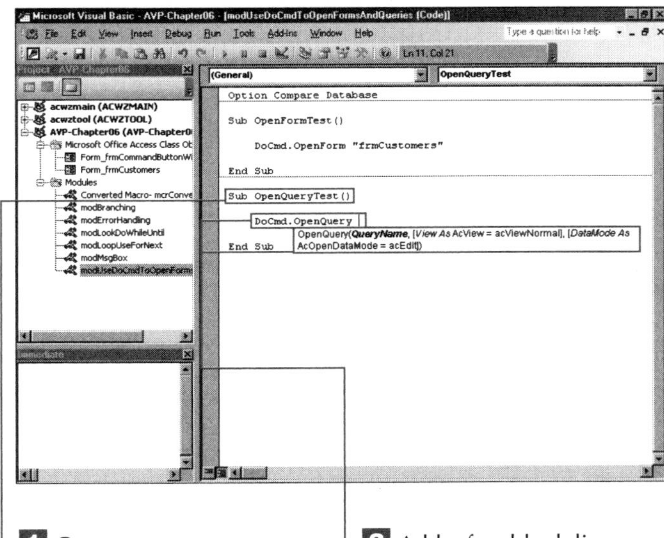

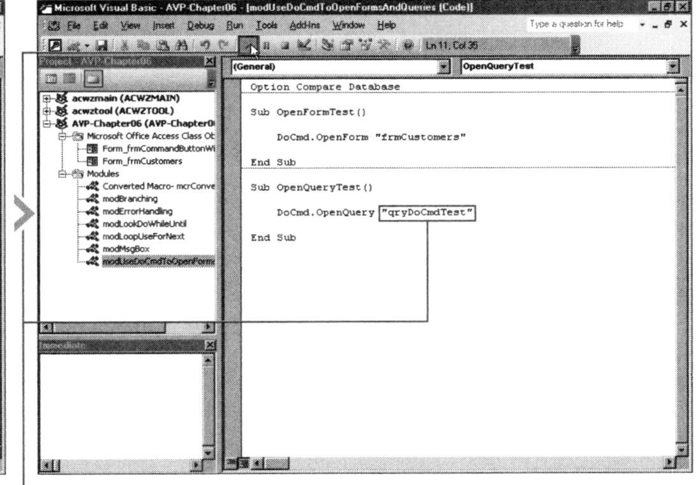

1 Create or open a query.

2 Type **Sub**, a space, a subroutine, and then press Enter.

■ Access creates a new subroutine.

3 Add a few blank lines between the Sub and End Sub lines.

4 Type **DoCmd.OpenQuery** and then a space.

■ Intellesense displays the parameters for the method.

5 Type the name of the form you want to open in double quotes.

6 Click the Run button.

■ Access tests the new routine, and the query opens.

■ You may need to close the IDE to view the query.

USING VARIABLES AND CONSTANTS

As you are writing code to perform various tasks, you may want to store temporary values in memory. While you can store data in your database, when you want to manipulate data and only need to keep it temporarily, you can store the data in variables.

When you use values that do not change throughout your application, but you need to use them in code, you can create constants to handle these values.

VARIABLES

You can store variables in memory, but you must declare them in your code. Below is an example of variable declaration and usage, a portion of the code created by the wizard in the section "Learn to Code from the Command Button Wizard."

```
Dim stDocName As String
Dim stLinkCriteria As String

stDocName = "frmCustomers"
DoCmd.OpenForm stDocName, , ,
stLinkCriteria
```

The stDocName is declared, and then used later in the statement.

Declaring Variables

There are a number of ways to declare a variable. How you declare a variable depends on the lifetime of the variable and the scope of the variable.

Lifetime

The lifetime of a variable refers to how long the variable exists. You can choose to have a variable exist for the duration of a single routine, or for the entire time an application is open. If you use the variable for only a single routine, then you can use the Dim statement, as shown above. When the routine is over, the variable ceases to exist. The next time the single routine runs, Access creates the variable again.

Private variables retain their values when you enter, leave, and then re-enter a routine when you declare a variable as Static. Static variables can be set as follows:

```
Static EmployeeNumber(200) As Integer
```

When you want to use a variable throughout an entire application, you can declare the variable using either a Private or Public statement. Which statement you use depends on the scope of the variable.

Precedence

If you have a variable that you declare at the routine level, and a variable that you declare at the module level with the same name, the variable at the routine level takes precedence. The variable you declare as Private takes precedence over the variable you declare as Public.

Implicit versus Explicit

You can declare a variable either implicitly, when you use it the first time, such as assigning a value to it, or explicitly, using a Dim, Private, or Public declaration statement.

If you declare a variable implicitly, Access declares it as a Variant data type.

However, it is a good idea to declare a variable explicitly. Declaring a variable explicitly helps you to reduce bugs in your code that occur when you type a variable name incorrectly.

To help you in coding VBA, in the IDE you can click Tools ⇨ Options. On the Editor page, you can then select the Require Variable Declaration option.

Scope

When you are talking about the scope of a variable, you are referring to which parts of an application can access the variable. For example, when you use the Dim statement in a routine, only that routine can access the variable: Function A cannot access variables that you declare in Function B.

If you declare the variable at the module level, in the Declarations section of a module with the Private statement, all routines in that module can access the variable. If you declare the variable in the Declarations section of a module with the Public statement, all code can access the variable.

VARIABLES (CONTINUED)

Data Types

You must specify the data type when you declare a variable. Some of the variable types, such as Integer, Long, and Currency, match the field data types.

You can declare the variables Text and Memo as type String. An example of code that declares a variable as type String is as follows:

```
Dim strDocName As String
```

The str prefix on the name of the variable is called a tag, and although it is not required, it is recommended. For a complete list of naming conventions, see Appendix A.

Special Variable Types

Some variables, such as Variant and Object types have a specific purpose.

Variant

The Variant type variable is the only one that accepts Null values. As a result, it is also the only variable type that can read data directly from the fields in tables. You can use the IsNull() function to determine whether a variable is Null. When you declare a Variant type variable, but do not assign a value to it, the variable is Empty. You can use the IsEmpty() function to determine whether a Variant data type variable is Empty.

Objects

There are a number of variable types that are references to objects in Access as well as other objects such as ActiveX controls. When you declare a variable of this kind, you are creating a reference, and not a copy of the control. You can use the Set command to assign the actual reference. For more information about Object variables, see Chapter 7.

CONSTANTS

Constants are values you can assign from within your application. You can specify the constant you create throughout the application. While in the Design view, if you need to update the constant, you only need to update it once in your application; all instances of the constant reflect the change. You can only change constants at design time.

Just like variables, constants can be different data types.

User-Defined Constants

You can use constants when you have values that are difficult to remember, and you want to create a more meaningful name. For example, you can use:

```
Const cColWidth as Double = 3.541
```

Now, wherever you need the value, you can type **cColWidth**. The compiler then replaces all occurrences of the constant with the value.

Built-in Constants

Both VBA and Access have built-in constants.

VBA Constants

VBA uses constants when you have to supply parameters for built-in functions.

VBA constants begin with the prefix vb. An example of using a VBA constant with a command is the MsgBox statement, which is discussed in the next section. Here are some of the constants you can see from the return value of the MsgBox: vbOK, vbCancel, vbAbort, vbRetry, vbYes, and vbNo. The actual values represented by the constants are 1 through 7, consecutively.

Access Constants

Access uses constants when working with methods of Access objects, such as forms and controls. You have also seen the use of constants with the various methods introduced from the DoCmd object in the last two tasks. The OpenForm parameters are examples of Access constants. You can recognize an Access constant by the prefix ac.

USING THE MSGBOX STATEMENT

The MsgBox statement is used almost as often as the DoCmd object. You can use the MsgBox statement to become more familiar with constants. The MsgBox statement's syntax can be either:

```
MsgBox Prompt, Style+Buttons, Title,
HelpFile, Context
```

or

```
vbMsgBoxResult = MsgBox(Prompt,
Style+Buttons, Title, HelpFile, Context)
```

You can use the MsgBox statement to either display a message or to ask for the user's input by supplying various buttons, and then return the user's choice.

Prompt is the text that you want to appear in the message box. The remaining parameters are all optional.

Style constants indicate the style for the message box. You can choose from the Style constants vbCritical, vbInformation, and vbQuestion. Each constant displays a different icon in the message box. Buttons represent the different combinations of buttons that the message box can display. A few examples are vbOKCancel, vbOKOnly, and vbYesNo.

You can add both the Style and Buttons constants to create various combinations for the message box. For example, if you want a combo box that asks a Yes/No question with Yes/No buttons, you can type **vbQuestion+vbYesNo** for the Style+Buttons parameters.

Title appears in the title bar of the message box. If you leave the title blank, "Microsoft Access" appears in the title bar. HelpFile and Context both specify what you want to do with Help, including the file used (HelpFile), and where to point in the Help file (Context).

vbMsgBoxResult is determined by whatever button the user clicks in the message box. For example, if the user clicks the Yes button, the vbMsgBoxResult is set to the equivalent of the vbYes constant.

USING MSGBOX AS A STATEMENT

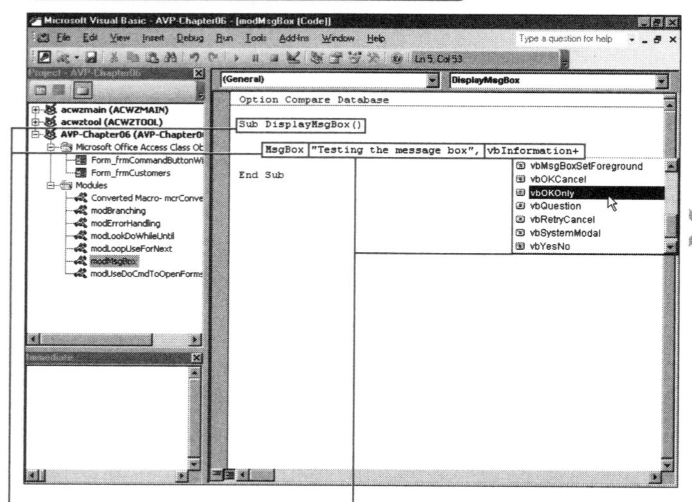

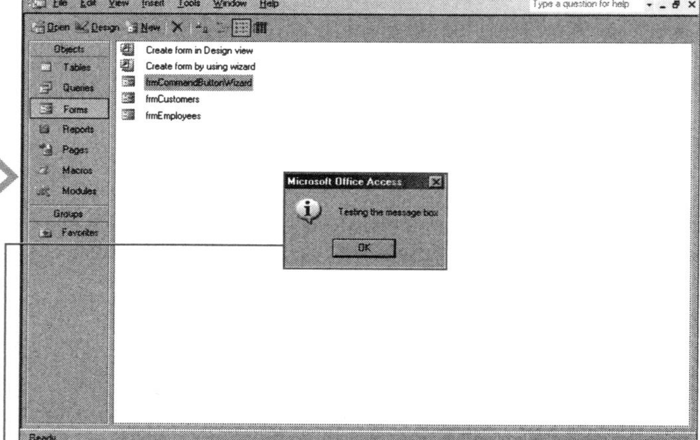

Note: This task uses modMsgBox in AVP-Chapter06.mdb on the CD-ROM.

1 In a module, create a new subroutine.

2 Type **MsgBox** and then a space.

3 Type the text to display in the prompt, and then **,**.

4 In the Intellesense constant list, select the type of message box to display, separating the Style and Buttons constants with **+**.

5 Fill out the Title parameter as desired.

6 Click the Run button ( ).

■ Access tests the new routine, and the message box appears.

■ Even if something other than the OK button is specified to be on the MsgBox, with this example nothing is being done with the result.

Extra

As you are typing the parameters, Intellesense can help you with the various constants. Use Intellesense while you build your MsgBox parameters. As you add each plus sign, +, the list of constants for the buttons appears.

Besides displaying text in the Prompt parameter, you can add breaks with multiple lines by using the vbCrLf constant. This adds a carriage return line feed character. Two of these constants add a blank line between lines of text. This makes your message boxes more useful to users, by allowing you to add enough text in the prompt of the message box to answer any questions users may have.

TYPE THIS:

```
MsgBox("Would you like to continue?" & _
          vbCrLf & vbCrLf & "Click Yes to continue.", _
          vbQuestion + vbYesNo)
```

RESULT:

```
Would you like
to continue?

Click Yes to
continue.
```

See the next section for more about the return value from the MsgBox statement.

USING MSGBOX AS A FUNCTION

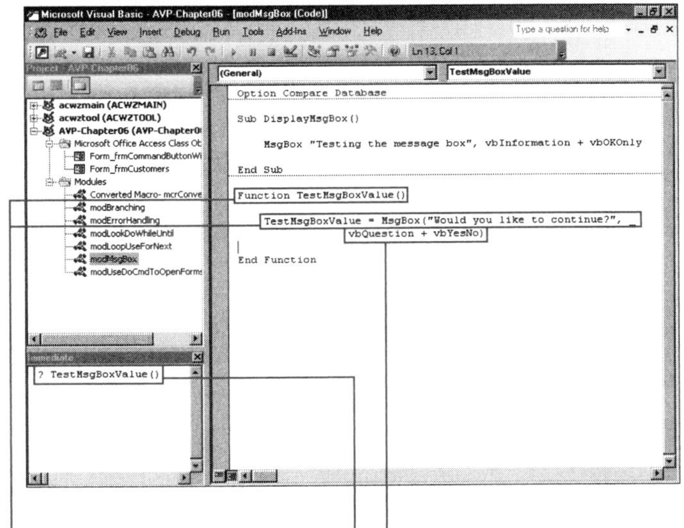

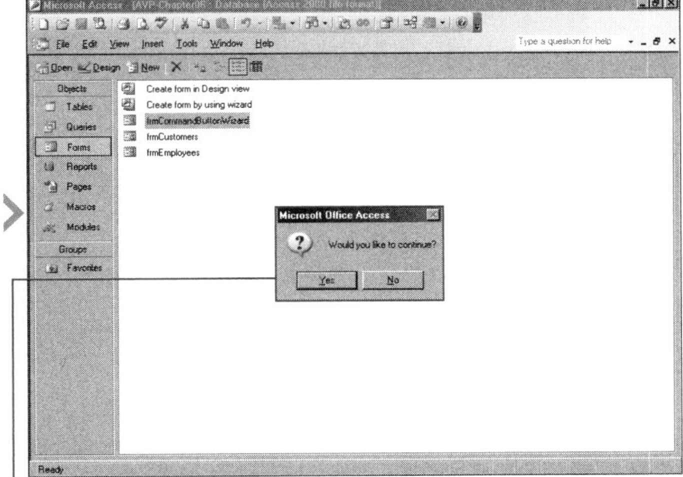

1 Open a module.

2 Type **Function**, a function, and then press Enter.

3 Retype the function, a space, **= MsgBox(**, and then the text you want to appear in the message box.

4 Type **_vbQuestion + vbYesNo** for the buttons parameter.

■ The underscore allows you to continue a line on the next line in the editor. VBA treats multiple lines as a single line.

5 Type **?**, a space, the function, and then **()**.

■ The message box appears. When you click Yes, the number 6 appears in the Immediate window. When you click No, the number 7 appears. These are the values returned and correspond to vbYes and vbNo.

CONTROL BRANCHING

When you include routines that perform various tasks in your applications, you can use control branching to access these routines, based on certain criteria.

Control branching uses two groups of statements for this purpose: the If Then...End If statement, and the Select Case...End Select statement. Which one you use depends on the number of branches you may need.

You can use branching statements with criteria to access the different routines. This decision-making process is similar to decision-making in real life. For example, when you check your mailbox, and see bills, you make a branching decision to pay the bills. In the syntax of an If Then...End If statement, the process looks like this:

```
If Bills = True Then
      'Pay the bill
End If
```

This statement is similar to an SQL statement, where Bills is the criteria. You can also combine criteria using And and Or.

If you have an alternative to Bills that includes everything else, then you can use the following:

```
If Bills = True Then
      'Pay the bill
Else
      'Everything else
End If
```

You can use the Select Case statement to examine a value in numerous ways:

```
Select Case Mail
     Case Bills
          '— Pay the bills
     Case Advertisements
          '— Throw in garbage
     Case Else
          '— Read
End Select
```

CONTROL BRANCHING USING IF THEN...ENDIF

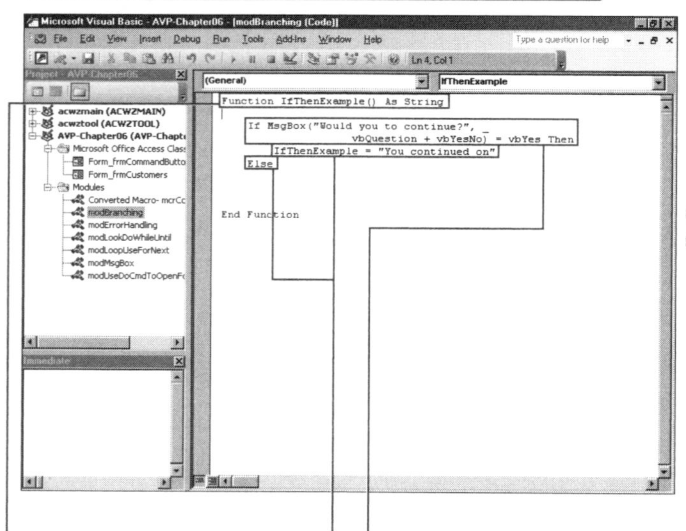

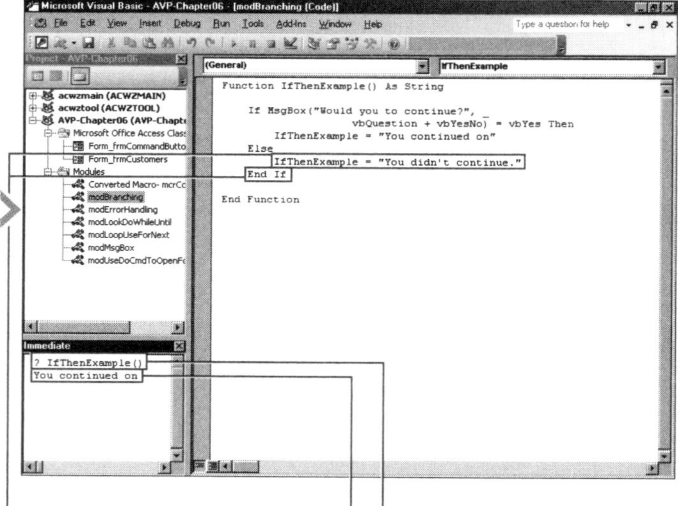

Note: This task uses modBranching in AVP-Chapter06.mdb on the CD-ROM.

1 Open a module, and then create a new function.

2 Type the If...Then statement comparing the MsgBox return value to vbYes.

3 Type the string you want to return from the function if the condition in step 2 is True, assigning it to the name of the function.

4 Type **Else**.

5 Type the string you want to return from the function if the condition in step 2 is False, assigning it to the name of the function.

6 Type **End If**.

7 Type ?, a space, the name of the function, and then parentheses.

■ A message box appears, and based on which button you click in the message box, a different message appears in the Immediate window.

Extra

You can use the Select Case statement to examine criteria in different ways. Along with comparing a single value as shown below, you can also examine ranges of values, just as you would with criteria in If...Then and SQL statements. Here are a few variations you can use for criteria on the Select Case statement lines:

CRITERIA	COMMENTS
"WA", "OR", "CA"	Same as "WA" Or "OR" Or "CA".
1 to 3	1 to 3 inclusive, similar to the Between clause.
1 to 3, 6, 8 to 10	1 to 3 inclusive, or 6, or 8 to 10 inclusive.
< 4, > 20	Less than 4 or greater than 20

You can also use the Case Else statement to cover any conditions that do not fall into the other Case statements. Note that when a condition is met, the code immediately goes to the End Select statement after executing the code in the Case statement code block.

You can nest branching statements within each other. This means that you can have If...Then statements with each other, and within Select Case statements. This gives you an unlimited means to solve any kind of branching issue.

In the Select Case line, you can use both literals, although this would not make much sense, and functions. Using functions is useful when you need to look at more than one value. You can perform a task that eliminates one value or another, and pass back the value that you want to compare.

CONTROL BRANCHING USING SELECT CASE ... END SELECT

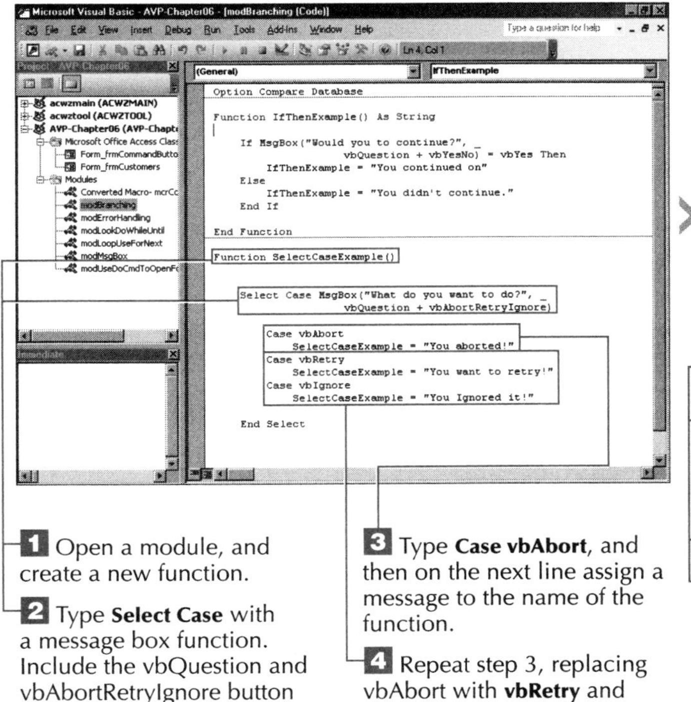

1 Open a module, and create a new function.

2 Type **Select Case** with a message box function. Include the vbQuestion and vbAbortRetryIgnore button constants.

3 Type **Case vbAbort**, and then on the next line assign a message to the name of the function.

4 Repeat step 3, replacing vbAbort with **vbRetry** and **vbIgnore**.

5 Type **End Select**.

6 Type **?**, a space, the name of the function, and then parentheses.

■ When you click the buttons displayed in the message box, a corresponding messages appears in the Immediate window.

LOOP USING FOR...NEXT

Loops are a common feature in coded application. With loops you can iterate through controls on a form, through the months in a year, or records in a table.

You can create a loop structure in your code using either the For...Next loop, or the Do While/Until loop. Which one you use depends on the task you want to perform.

You can use the For ... Next loop when you have a definite start and finish in the loop structure. The syntax for this loop is:

```
For Index = Start To Finish Step Increment
      '--code to perform
Next Index
```

In this code, Index is a variable that you use to track an incremental count. Start is an expression that represents the starting point of the values you want to increment. Finish represents the ending value, and can be a variable or literal value. Increment is a value that specifies what value you want to use to increment the loop count.

You can perform the loop in descending increments by setting the Start value to be larger than the Finish value, and setting the Increment value to a negative number.

You can also use the Index value inside the loop with the other code. For example, the following code displays the days of the week, starting with the current day:

```
Sub DisplayDays()
  Dim intDays As Integer
  For intDays = 0 To 6
    Debug.Print
WeekdayName(Weekday(DateAdd("d", intDays,
Date)))
  Next intDays
End Sub
```

The example uses function calls within function calls, a feature of coding that you will find less intimidating the more you write code. The example also uses Debug.Print. This method prints whatever you specify to the Immediate window and is useful for debugging purposes.

LOOP USING FOR...NEXT

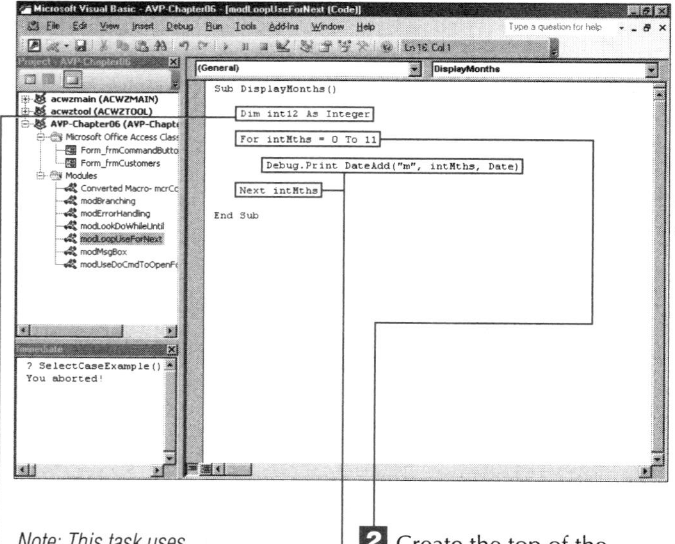

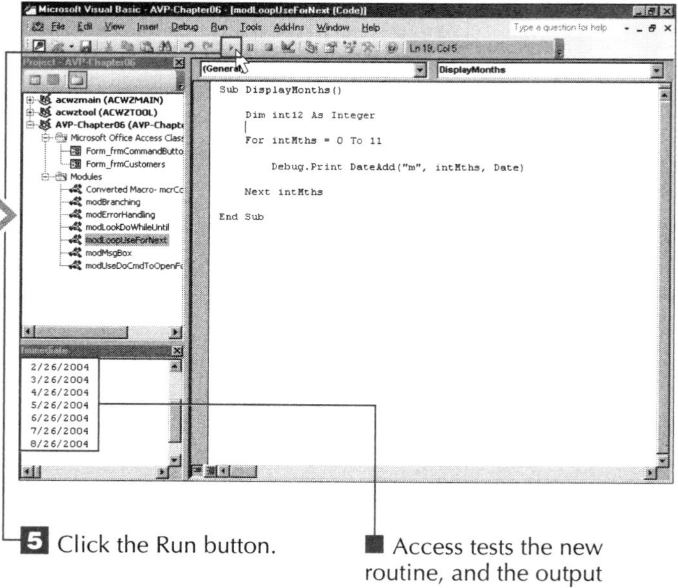

Note: This task uses modLoopUseForNext in AVP-Chapter06.mdb on the CD-ROM.

1 In a new subroutine, declare a variable as an Integer to be used for the index of the For…Next loop.

2 Create the top of the For...Next loop, using the variable from step 1.

3 Add the code to be run, printing into the Immediate window using the Debug.Print method.

4 Type **Next**, a space, and then the variable from step 1.

5 Click the Run button.

■ Access tests the new routine, and the output appears in the Immediate window.

LOOP USING DO WHILE/UNTIL

When you need to base the loop feature on a condition, and not on a finite value, then you can use the Do While/Until loop. There are two separate syntaxes for the Do While/Until loop. They are:

```
Do While Criteria
        '-- perform code
Loop
```

and

```
Do Until Criteria
        '-- perform code
Loop
```

where you can specify the same criteria that you would use in an If...Then or SQL statement.

The Do While loop continues to run while a condition is True, whereas the Do Until loop continues to run until a condition is True. Here is an example of using the Do Until loop:

```
Sub DisplayDaysUsingDoUntil(varDate As
  Variant)
    Dim intCount As Integer
    varCurrDate = Date
        Do Until varCurrDate = varDate
         Debug.Print varCurrDate
         varCurrDate = DateAdd("d", 1,
  varCurrDate)
    Loop

End Sub
```

Do While/Until loops are also very useful when you are working with records in a table. For more information about this, see Chapter 11.

A variation of these loops is Do ... While and Do ... Loop Until. When you use either of these loops, the application examines the criteria at the end of the loop instead of at the beginning. As a result, the loop always executes at least once.

LOOP USING DO WHILE/UNTIL

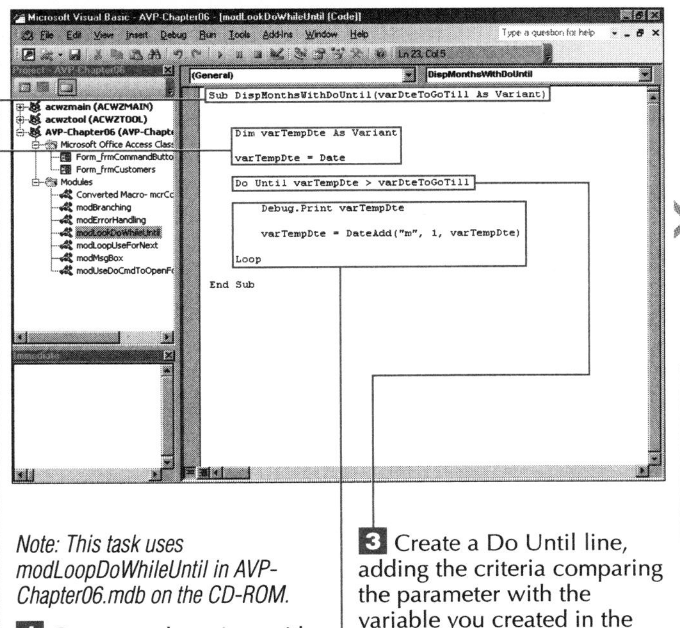

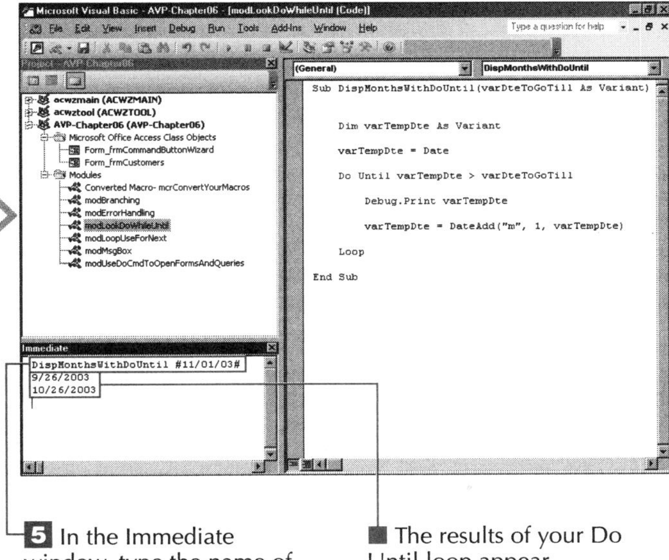

Note: This task uses modLoopDoWhileUntil in AVP-Chapter06.mdb on the CD-ROM.

1 Create a subroutine, with a parameter to compare.

2 Declare a variable, and assign it a base value.

3 Create a Do Until line, adding the criteria comparing the parameter with the variable you created in the routine.

4 Add the code to perform your tasks, and then add the Loop line.

5 In the Immediate window, type the name of the subroutine, passing the value to compare.

■ The results of your Do Until loop appear.

ADD ERROR HANDLING

One of the benefits of using VBA rather than macros is that you can add error handling to your code.

By default, Access does offer basic error handling, but it is not user-friendly. If your code produces an error in Access, a dialog box appears, telling you an error has occurred, and asks you if you want to end the application, debug the application, or need help to correct the error. This is a helpful feature when you are developing the application, but if other users work with the database, you do not want them to modify the code, which is what the debug option lets them do.

The basic subroutine format for error handling is as follows:

```
Sub TestErrorHandling()
        On Error GoTo Err_Test
            ' — Code with possible errors

     Exit Sub
Err_Test:
        MsgBox "Error Occurred"
    Exit Sub
    End Sub
```

You can activate error handling by using the On Error GoTo *errorlabel* statement. Next, you can add the code you want to test. After the main body of code, and before you add the error handler code, you can add an Exit Sub/Function statement. This is very important because if you do not add the statement, the error handling code will always execute, even when there are no errors.

The error handling code begins with a line label. You should name the label so that it tells you what the subsequent code is doing. You must also include a colon after the line label.

Next, you can add the code that you want to handle the error. For example, you can choose to display a message box, and then exit the routine by using the Exit Sub/ Function statement. You can also try to fix the error, and then use the Resume statement to execute the line of code that contains the error.

ADD ERROR HANDLING

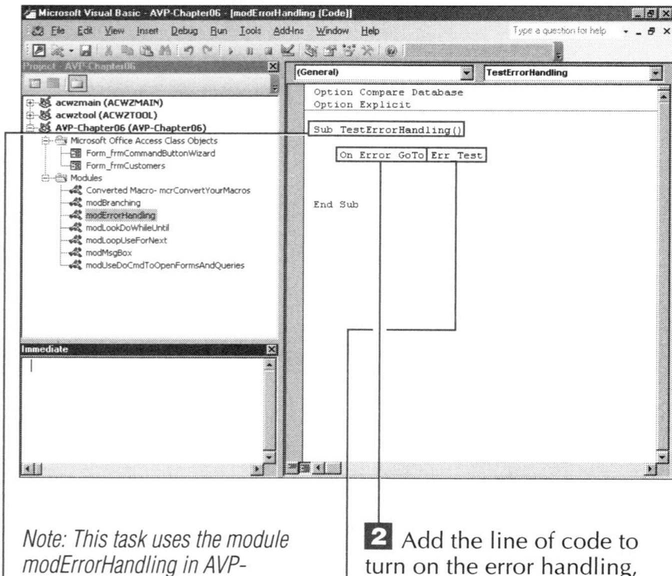

Note: This task uses the module modErrorHandling in AVP-Chapter06.mdb on the CD-ROM.

1 Create a new subroutine or function.

2 Add the line of code to turn on the error handling, using the On Error Goto statement.

■ Make sure you include the line label for the error handling code.

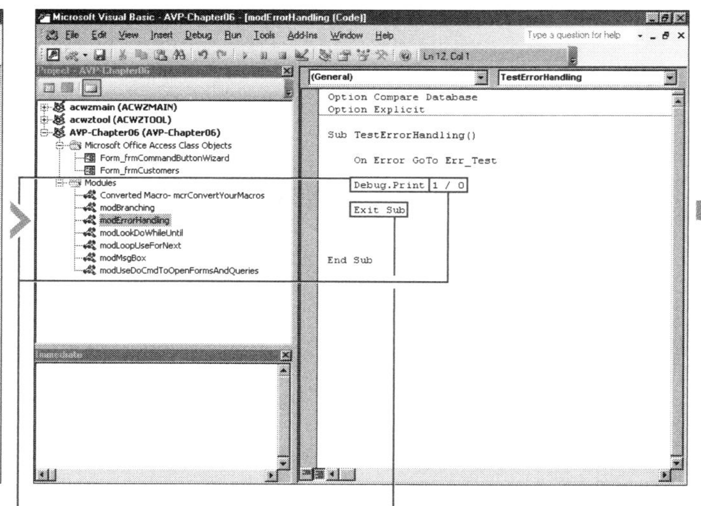

3 Add the regular code to be used in the routine.

■ If you want to test the error-handling abilities of the debugging program, you can purposely create an error. The code in this example attempts to divide by zero.

4 Add the Exit Sub/Function statement for whichever type of routine you are using.

Extra

You can include code in your existing error-handling code that customizes error response. For example, if you want your routine to continue executing even after an error is detected, you can use the On Error Resume Next statement. When the error occurs, it is ignored, and the next line of code executes.

You can also use the Resume Next statement to perform the next line of code after the line that contains the error. This is an alternative to the Resume statement, which takes you back to the line that contains the error.

Also, you can use On Error Goto 0 to cancel any current error handler. This is useful when certain errors are handled in this routine and others should be allowed to propagate up the call chain.

You can use a VBA object called Err that gives information about the current error that has occurred. The Err object contains various properties that describe the error. Some of the more useful properties are:

PROPERTY	PURPOSE
Description	Describes the error that occurred.
Number	Contains the error number of the error. You can trap for this condition, and handle errors differently, depending on the error, by using If...Then or Select Case statements.

Err.Number is reset to 0 by any On Error statement. Its value should be used or copied if needed before this statement.

You can find out which errors can occur by looking up Trappable Errors in Access Help. Access lists the error number and description.

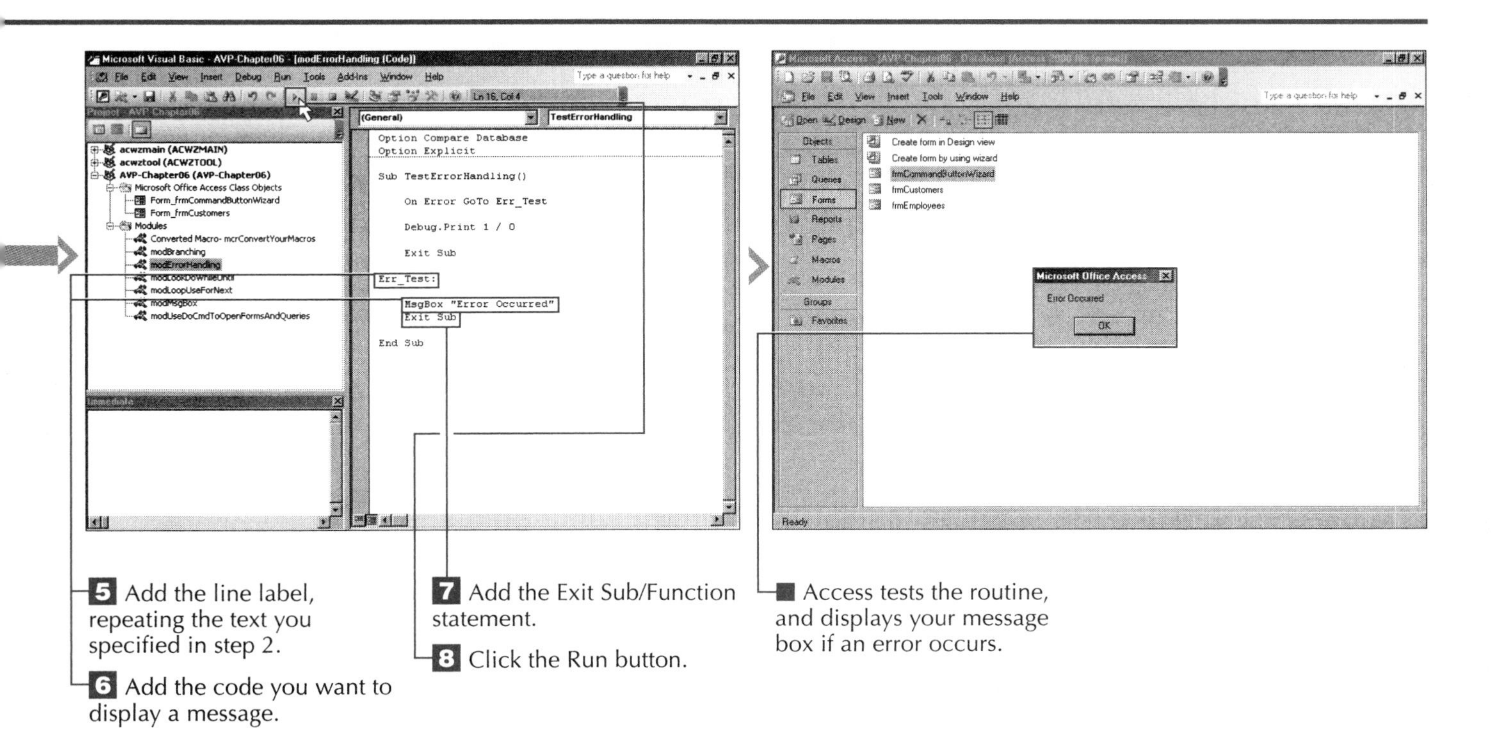

5 Add the line label, repeating the text you specified in step 2.

6 Add the code you want to display a message.

7 Add the Exit Sub/Function statement.

8 Click the Run button.

■ Access tests the routine, and displays your message box if an error occurs.

USING CODE BEHIND FORMS AND EVENTS

Code Behind Forms, or CBF, refers to the coding that takes place behind a form or report. Forms, reports, and controls also have Events you can program against them to further automate your database applications.

Note that both forms and reports have code behind them, but with different events. For more information about report coding, see Chapter 8.

VBA FORM CLASS MODULE

Each form has a module attached to it. By default, the routines in that module are only visible to that form, meaning they are private. There are several benefits to having your code behind your forms, for example:

- Using code behind your forms and reports is a great way to keep your code together. You do not need to look in different modules for routines.
- The code only loads into memory when you open the form, and is removed from memory when you close the form. This saves memory, unlike standard modules, which load into memory when you open the database application.
- When you copy a form from one database to another, the code goes with it.

However, when you have routines that are used by more than one form, you may want to store those routines in standard modules.

You can view these form modules, also called class modules, while you are in the form. You can use one of a number of methods to get into the form module. One way is to click the View Code button while highlighting the form in the database window. Another way is to click the View Code button while in Design view of the form. A third way is to click in the property sheet in the Events tab of the form or control for which you want to write or view code. For more about Events, see the next section.

Types of Routines in Form Modules

You can create functions and subroutines just as you can standard modules found in the Modules tab of the database window. The functions and subroutines that you create in the form module can be used by any of the other routines that are in the module.

Another type of subroutine is called the event subroutine. An event subroutine is a subroutine that you can write to respond to a specific event.

You can also create additional properties on your forms and reports. These custom properties allow you to expand the power of your reports. However, the creation and use of custom properties are beyond the scope of this book.

Scope and Lifetime

Scope allows you to see the variable or routine; lifetime indicates how long the variable or routine exists. When you are in a forms module, the scope and lifetime of Private variables are the same as routines, because everything is private to that module. You can have variables that are local to individual routines by using the Dim statement in the routine. For more information about scope and lifetime, see the section "Using Variables and Constants" in Chapter 6.

If necessary, you can also make a variable or routine public. When you specify a variable or routine to be public in a form or report, you must specify the form or report as well as the variable or routine.

EVENT-DRIVEN PROGRAMMING

The majority of the applications and programming languages that are created using the Windows platform usually involve event-driven programming. An event is something that occurs as a result of an action, either from the user, the application, or even the computer.

Events allow developers to automate their databases and have control over what happens when the users enter data, click a button, or move the mouse over a form. Events are programmed using event procedures.

Structure of an Event Procedure

All event procedures have a structure. They appear similar to other Sub procedures, because that is actually what they are. The structure of an event procedure looks like this:

```
Private Sub Object_Event(parameters)

End Sub
```

where the Object is either the form or control where you are programming the Event; and Event is, of course, the event. Parameters of event procedures are provided by Access, and the developer can use these parameters in the routine.

Form Events

At last count, there were 50 events for a form. However, you do not need to program all these events for every form. You only need to write code for an event when you need or want to use the event. Otherwise, the events are not fired.

While you are in a form, you can see events for that form by looking at the Event tab in the property sheet. The table shows some of the most common form events you can use, and their descriptions.

When an event can be canceled, you can have a parameter, called Cancel, passed to the event. To cancel an event, you can set the Cancel parameter to True. Canceling events is discussed further in the next section.

EVENT	OCCURS WHEN/DESCRIPTION
On Open	When you open a form, but before any records are displayed.
On Load	When you open a form, after the first record is displayed.
On Current	When you move to a new record in a form, including when you first open a form, after the load event.
Before Update	Before Access updates data to the table on which the form's recordset is based. You can cancel this event.
After Update	After Access updates data to the table on which the form's recordset is based.
On Close	When you close a form, but it is not yet unloaded.
On Unload	When you close a form, and the form is being unloaded. You can cancel this event.

Control Events

The type and number of events on controls may differ depending on the type of controls they are. For example, a command button has different events compared to a List Box control. Control events occur for individual controls before the form events occur.

The table shows some useful events on different controls. Note that the events may occur on other control types as well.

To see a full list of the controls, click the control with the Event page of the property sheet of the control opened.

EVENT	CONTROL TYPE	DESCRIPTION
Click	Command Button	When a user clicks a command button.
On Enter	Textbox	When a text box first receives focus.
Before Update	Textbox	Before a control updates the data to the recordset of the form. You can cancel this event.
After Update	Textbox	After a control updates the data to the recordset of a form.

WORK WITH EVENTS FOR FORMS AND CONTROLS

Events behind your forms and controls allow almost total control over your form. To program code for an event such as the On Open event, click the Builder button next to the event in the property sheet. In the Choose Builder dialog box, click Code Builder and then OK. Access creates a template and an event procedure for the event. You can type the commands you want the event procedure to perform. For a message box to display when a user opens a form, use this event procedure:

```
Private Sub Form_Open()
      MsgBox "Welcome to my form!"
End Sub
```

To create an event that opens a form when the user clicks a command button, you can use the On Click event:

```
Private Sub cmdOpenCustomer_Click()
      DoCmd.OpenForm "frmCustomer"
End Sub
```

In this procedure, cmdOpenCustomer is the object, in this case a command button, and Click is the event.

When you are programming an event, such as the Before Update event on a form or control, you can check to see if the data is as it should be, and, if not, you can cancel the event. When Access generates the event procedure shell, it includes the Cancel parameter. The example below contains additional code that cancels the event if the current date happens to be a specific date.

```
Private Sub Form_BeforeUpdate(Cancel As
  Integer)
      If Date() = "03/20/2003" then
            Cancel = True
      End If
End Sub
```

WORK WITH EVENTS ON FORMS

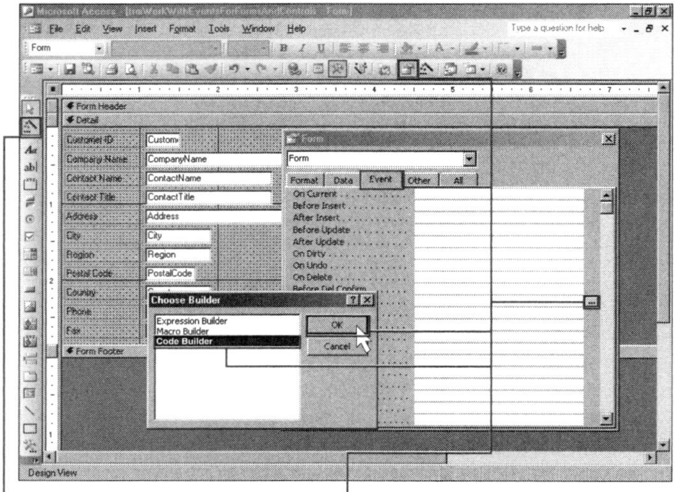

Note: These steps use frmWorkWithEventsForFormsAndControls in AVP-Chapter07.mdb on the CD-ROM.

1 Create or open a form in Design view, and then turn off the control wizards.

2 Click the Property Sheet button.

3 Click the Event tab.

4 Click the On Open property field Builder button.

5 Click Code Builder.

6 Click OK.

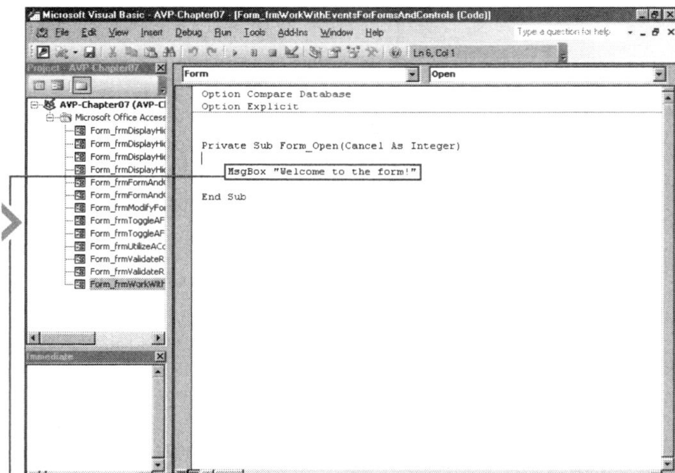

■ The code editor appears.

7 Type **MsgBox**, a space, and then the message you want to display when the form opens.

8 Save and close the form.

9 Reopen the form in View mode.

■ The message box appears.

Extra

If you only want to use event procedures for automation of forms and reports, you can bypass the Choose Builder dialog box and have Access create event procedures immediately. You can do this by clicking the Builder button (...) next to an Event field. The way to create event procedures immediately for forms and reports is to choose Options from the Tools menu while in the database window.

When the Options dialog box appears, click the Forms/Reports tab, and then check the Always use event procedures option, the third option from the bottom of the list.

Because you create an event procedure using Object_Event for the name of the procedure, you can easily look up the event in the form's module. While you are in the module editor, the left-hand combo box displays the name of the objects, forms, and controls. The combo box located at the top right-hand corner of the editor displays the names of the events. Choose the object first, and then the name of the event.

WORKING WITH EVENTS FOR CONTROLS

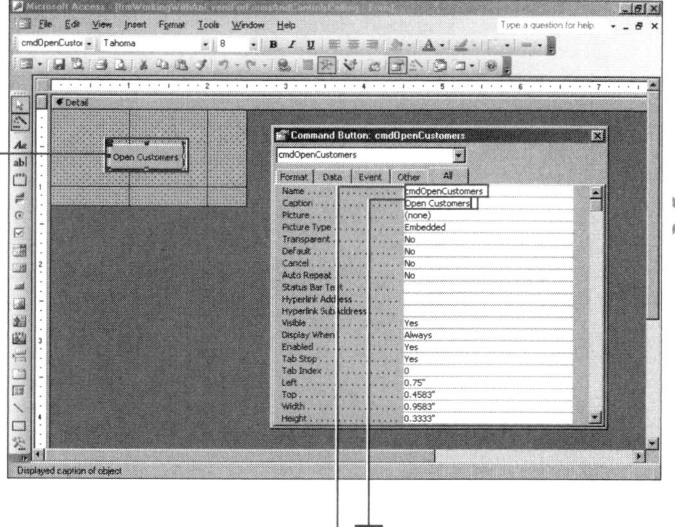

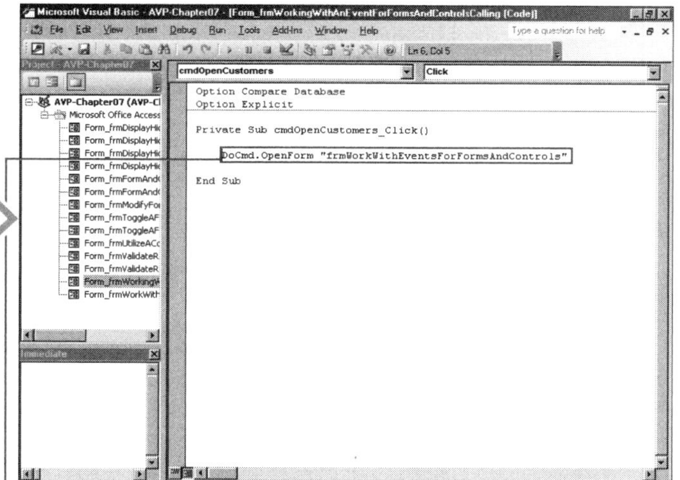

Note: These steps use frmWorkingWithAnEventForForms AndControlsCalling in AVP-Chapter07.mdb on the CD-ROM.

1. Create or open a new form in Design view.
2. Add a command button.
3. Type a caption for the command button.
4. Type a Name for the command button.
5. Create the event procedure for the On Click event of the command button.
6. Type **DoCmd.OpenForm**, a space, and then the name of the form you want to open.

■ This example uses a command to open a form that contains a message box.

7. Save and close the form.
8. Reopen the form, and then click the command button.

■ The form you named in step 6 appears.

SYNTAX FOR USING FORMS AND CONTROLS IN VBA

A powerful benefit of automating your database application is that you have complete control over your forms and controls. You can set the majority of the properties that you can set in Design mode, using VBA.

FORMS SYNTAX

To take advantage of the properties and methods for both forms and controls in VBA, you need to use the correct syntax. For example, you can set the caption of frmCustomer with this line of code:

```
Forms!frmCustomer.Caption = "New Caption
for Form"
```

This code follows the syntax of:

```
Forms!FormName.Property = value
```

where Forms is the collection of open forms. Note that it is not just the collection of all forms in the database, but of all open forms. FormName is the form to use. Property is the property to set. Most properties reflect the name you see in the property sheet, but without a space. Intellesense displays the various properties and methods, and helps you determine the property to use. Value is the value that you are assigning as the new caption.

The syntax displayed above is just one of the syntaxes you can use. Another way of working with form properties is to specify the form using an index, with either a numeric index or string, which is the name of the form. The syntax for this looks like:

```
Forms(index).Property = value
```

Applying this syntax to frmCustomer, you can type:

```
Forms(0).Caption = "New Caption for Form"
```

or

```
Forms("frmCustomer").Caption = "New
Caption for Form"
```

This last example is the preferred method because of its flexibility. When you use a numeric value for the index, you must know the number, and it is not very descriptive. Instead of the literal string of frmCustomer, you can make it a string variable, which makes this syntax flexible.

Another Form syntax you can use in form and report modules is to use the Me property to specify the current form behind which you are coding. For example, if you have a text box on the form for which you are coding, instead of using `Forms!frmCustomer!txtLastName`, you can use `Me!txtLastName`. If you want to change the caption of the form, instead of typing:

```
Forms!frmCustomer.Caption = "My Customer
form"
```

you can type:

```
Me.Caption = "My Customer form"
```

CONTROL SYNTAX

To specify the syntax for controls, you can just continue from the form's syntax. For example, if you want to assign a value of "Rubble" to a text box called txtLastName on frmCustomer, you can type the following:

```
Forms!frmCustomer!txtLastName = "Rubble"
```

When you specify an object you are creating, either a form or control, you can use the exclamation point, !, to separate it from the collection to which it belongs. You do not need to specify the controls collection for the form, because it is the default collection. The situation is the same for the Value property, which is the default property for a Textbox control. Otherwise you would type the last line of code this way:

```
Forms!frmCustomer.Controls!txtLastName.Va
lue = "Rubble"
```

MODIFY FORM AND CONTROL PROPERTIES AT RUNTIME

You can use the Form and Control properties for a variety of tasks. For example, you may want to set the Forms Caption property to show the name of the customer that you are editing.

If you want the main field to display the txtCompanyName control, you can program the On Current event as follows:

```
Private Sub Form_Current()
    ' Update the caption to the customer's
        company name
    Me.Caption = "Current Customer: " &
        Me!txtCompanyName
End Sub
```

You can also help the user to input data by adding event procedures at the control level. For example, you can automatically add a state based on the city a user enters. The code would look like this:

```
Private Sub City_AfterUpdate()
    ' Update the region based on the city
        entered.
    Select Case Me!txtCity
        Case "Seattle", "Spokane"
            Me!Region = "WA"
        Case "Los Angeles", "San Francisco"
            Me!Region = "CA"
        Case "New York"
            Me!Region = "NY"
    End Select
End Sub
```

In both of the event procedures above, a comment line gives anyone who reads the code a better idea of what is happening, and allows for future documentation.

MODIFY FORM AND CONTROL PROPERTIES AT RUNTIME

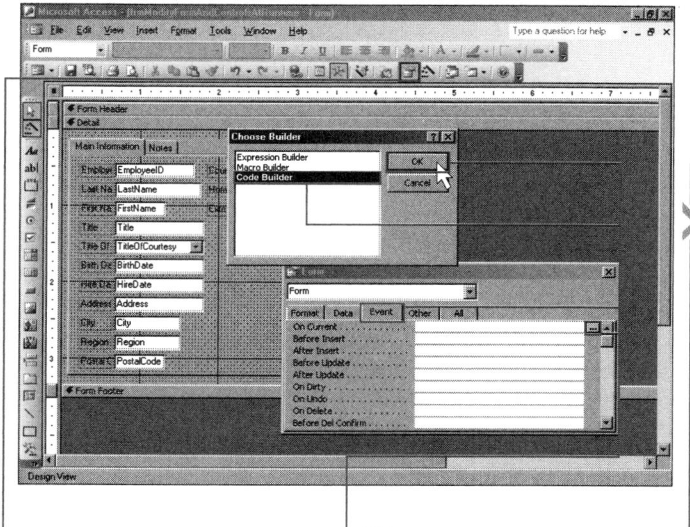

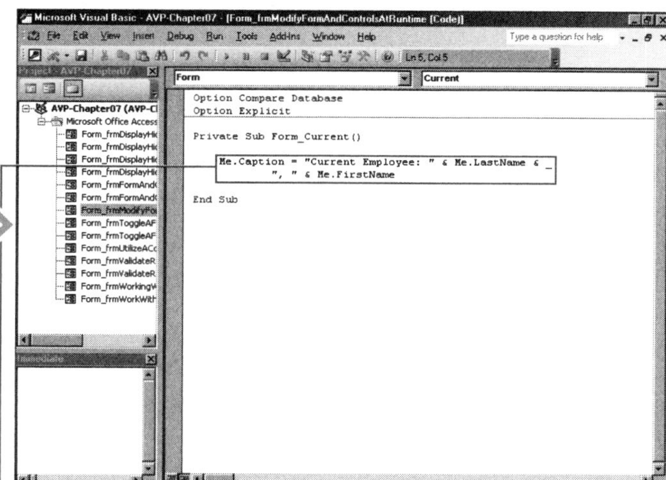

Note: This task uses frmModifyFormAndControlsAtRuntime in AVP-Chapter07.mdb on the CD-ROM.

1. Create or open a form in Design view.
2. Click the Property Sheet button.
3. Click the Event tab.
4. Click the Builder button.
5. Click Code Builder.
6. Click OK.

■ The code editor appears.

7. Add the event code to display the information you want in the Caption property field of the form.
8. Save and close your form.

■ When you reopen your form, your information appears in the title bar of the form.

USING FORM AND CONTROL VARIABLES

You can assign a variable to objects such as forms and controls. When you assign a value to a regular variable, Access makes a copy of the object in memory. When you assign a variable to a form or control, Access creates a reference, so that the object variable actually points at the original object. This means that when you update a property on the object variable, you also update the original object.

For example, if you want to create a variable to work with a form called frmCustomers, you can assign a variable just as you would for any type of variable:

```
Dim frm As Form
```

However, when you actually set the reference, you can use syntax similar to the following:

```
Set frm = Forms!frmCustomers
```

To set a property of the form through the variable, you can assign:

```
frm.Caption = "My New Caption"
```

The same rules apply if you were updating the property of the form directly. For example, if there is a control on the form, such as a text box called txtLastName, and you want to set it to "Rubble," you can use the following syntax:

```
frm!txtLastName = "Rubble"
```

You can also use the same syntax if you have a control you want to reference. The below example declares a control type variable, setting the reference to the txtLastName Textbox control, and then assigning False to the Visible property on the variable.

```
Dim ctl as Control
Set ctl = Forms!frmCustomers!txtLastName
ctl.Visible = False
```

USING FORM AND CONTROL VARIABLES

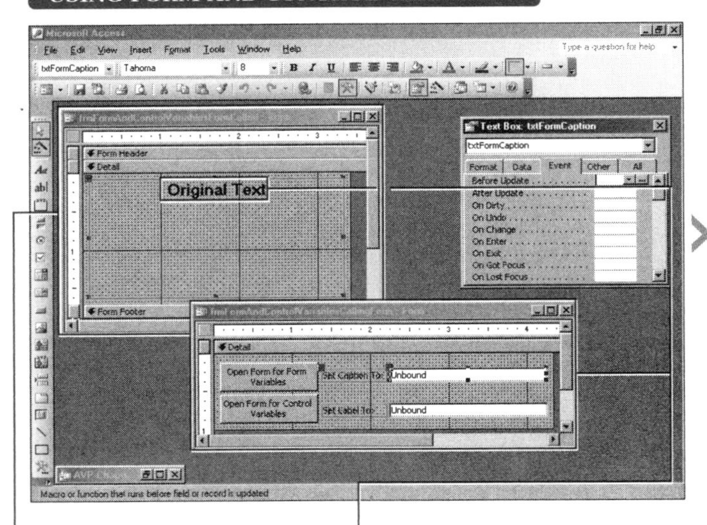

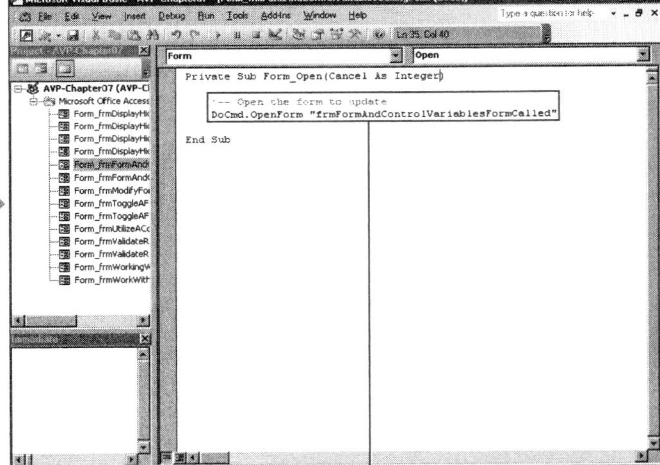

Note: This task uses frmFormAndControlVariablesFormCalled and frmFormAndControlVariablesCallingForm in AVP-Chapter07.mdb on the CD-ROM.

1 Create an unbound form with a label.

2 Type text in the caption of the form and label.

3 Create another form with two command buttons and text boxes.

■ The first command button and text box modify the Caption property of the form you created in step 1.

■ The second command button and text box update the Caption property of the label on the form you created in step 1.

4 In the code editor, create an event procedure for the On Open event of the form you created in step 1.

5 Add a DoCmd.OpenForm command, specifying the name of the form you created in step 3.

6 Add an event procedure to the On Click event of the first command button created in step 3.

Extra

When you know what type of control you want to use, you can be more specific in declaring the control type. For example, the steps below use the Textbox control type, and so you can also use the specific type:

```
Dim txt as TextBox
```

This enables Intellesense to give you more information about the available properties and methods. It also gives you better performance, because Access does not have to determine at runtime which type of control you are using. You can specify all of the standard Access controls, including ComboBox, ListBox, SubForm, SubReport, and TextBox.

When you use an object for a number of tasks in your code, you can use the With...End With statement. This statement can improve code performance, and can even make your code more readable. In the example below, although you can use the full form syntax, you can also use a Form variable:

```
With Forms!frmCustomer
      .Caption = "This is a Test"
      .Visible = True
      !txtLastName = "Rubble"
End With
```

With this code, you need to specify the "." or "!" as you would if you were using the full object syntax.

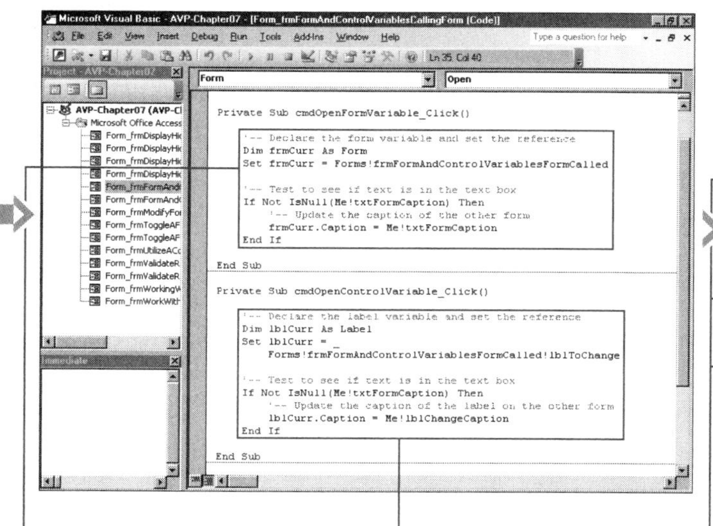

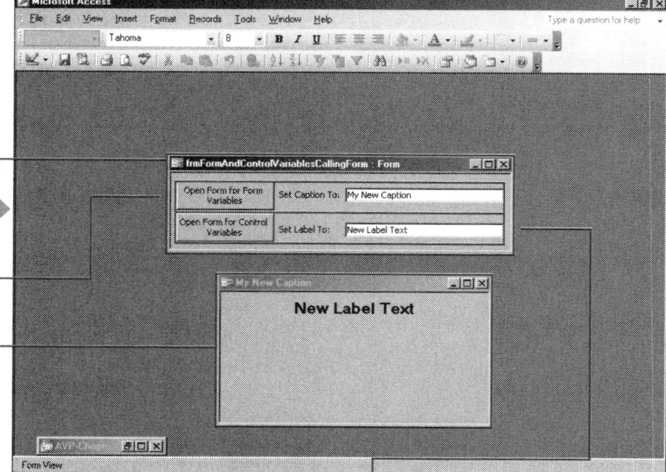

7 Type the commands to set a reference to the first form, and update the caption of the form.

8 Add an event procedure to the On Click event of the second command button you created in step 3.

9 Type the commands to set a reference to the label on the first form, and update the caption of the label.

10 Save and close both forms.

11 Reopen the first form, containing the two command buttons and text boxes.

■ The second form opens as well.

12 Update the text box next to the command button that updates the caption of the second form, and then click the command button.

13 Update the text box next to the command button that updates the caption of the label on the second form, and then click the command button.

■ The label and form captions are updated.

VALIDATE A REQUIRED VALUE BEFORE UPDATING

You can validate your data based on multiple fields by using the Before Update event of a form. You can test to see if one field is set to True, and that another field is filled in. If the field is not filled in, then you can display a message, move the focus to the field that you want filled in, and cancel the update. To do this, use the Cancel parameter to cancel the event. You can also use the SetFocus method, common to most input-type controls. The SetFocus method sets the focus to the control from which the method is called.

For example, a form may have a check box called chkUnionMember, based on the UnionMember field. If this check box is set to True, you can then make sure that the txtUnionMbrNumber Textbox control is filled in. If it is not filled in, then you can tell the user to fill in the txtUnionMbrNumber text box, set the focus to txtUnionMbrNumber, and cancel the event. The code for this is as follows:

```
Private Sub Form_BeforeUpdate(Cancel as
    Integer)
        If Me!chkUnionMember = True Then
                If IsNull(Me!txtUnionMbrNumber)
                  Then
                       MsgBox("This union
member needs his number filled in!")

Me!txtUnionMbrNumber.SetFocus
                       Cancel = True
                End If
        End If
End Sub
```

You can include as many of these types of validation as you need. Place the tests in the same order in the code as the tab order of the controls on the form.

While you can use the BeforeUpdate event of a control to validate data, if you never enter the control for which the BeforeUpdate event procedure is written, the code never executes.

VALIDATE A REQUIRED VALUE BEFORE UPDATING

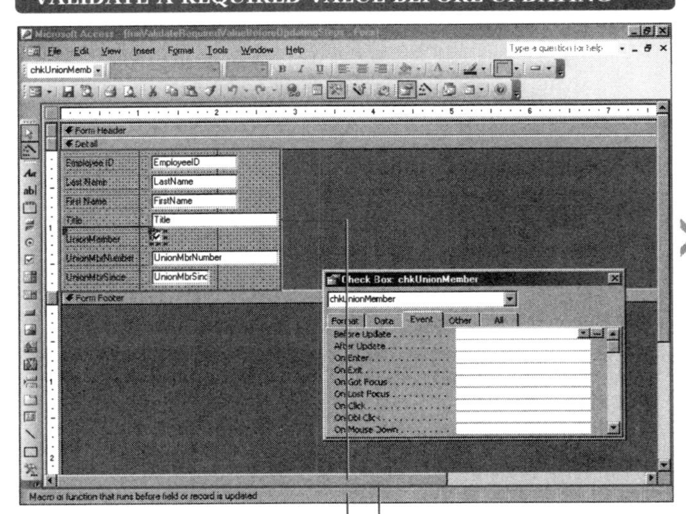

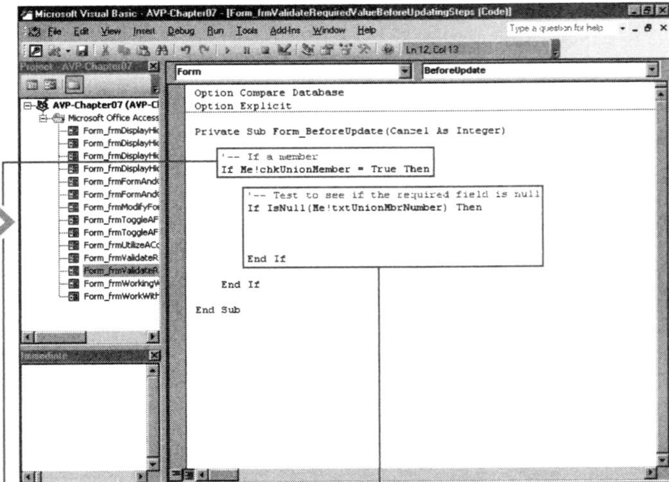

Note: This task uses frmValidateRequiredValueBeforeUpdatingSteps in AVP-Chapter07.mdb on the CD-ROM.

1 Create a form that includes the fields that you want to validate.

■ Be sure to name the controls so that you can refer to them in your code.

2 In the code editor, add an event procedure to the Before Update event of the form.

3 Type the If Then statement to test if the check box value is set to True.

4 Type the If Then statement to test if the required field is entered.

■ When you add multiple If Then statements, go from the outside in with logic and indentation.

Extra

You probably will have more than one required field for the user to fill in. The following code, used on frmValidateARequiredValueBeforeUpdatingExtra BeforeUpdate event, displays all the fields that the user must fill in, and sets the focus to the first field.

```
Private Sub Form_BeforeUpdate(Cancel As Integer)
    Dim strFields As String
    If Me!chkUnionMember = True Then
        If IsNull(Me!txtUnionMbrNumber) Then
            Me!txtUnionMbrNumber.SetFocus
            strFields = "Union Mbr Number"
        End If
        If IsNull(Me!txtUnionMbrSince) Then
            If Len(strFields) = 0 Then
                Me!Me!txtUnionMbrSince.SetFocus
            Else
                strFields = strFields & vbCrLf
            End If
            strFields = strFields & "Union Mbr Since"
        End If
        If Len(strFields) > 0 Then
            Cancel = True
            MsgBox ("This union member needs the following " & _
                "fields filled in:" & vbCrLf & vbCrLf & strFields)
        End If
    End If
End Sub
```

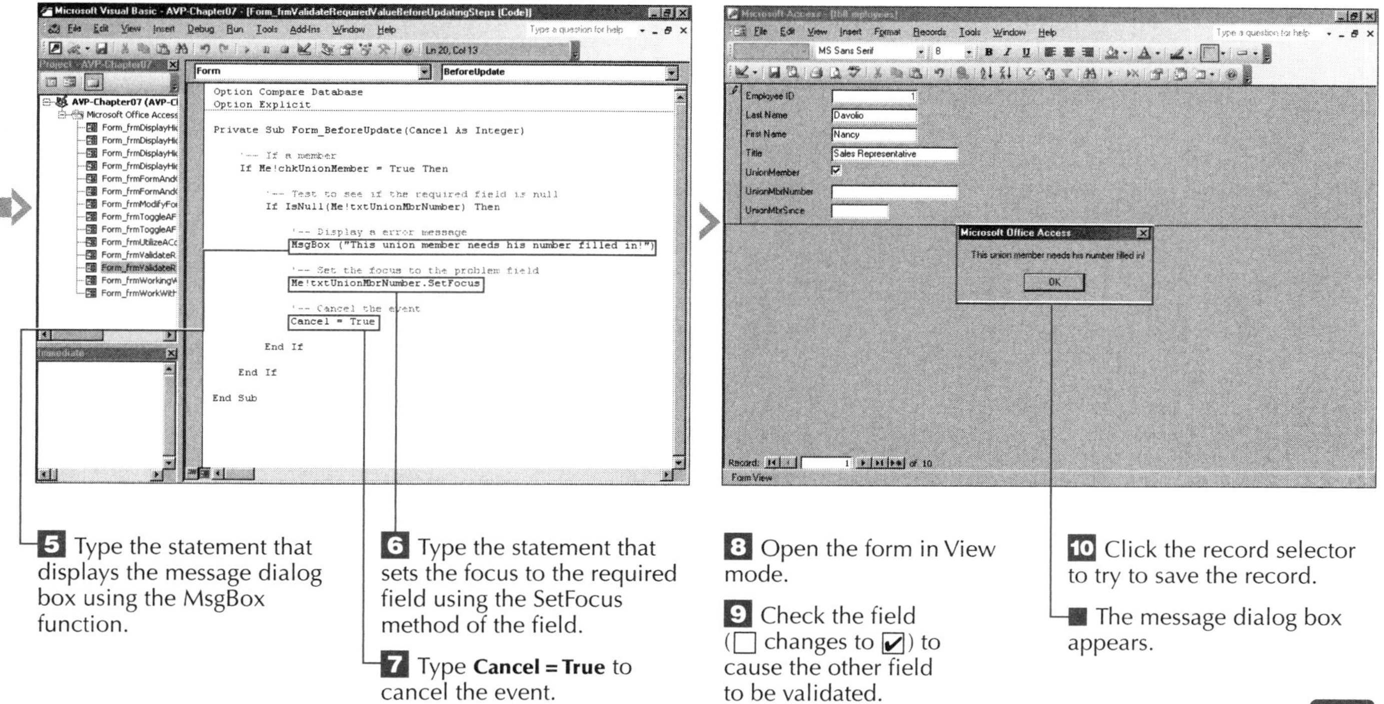

5 Type the statement that displays the message dialog box using the MsgBox function.

6 Type the statement that sets the focus to the required field using the SetFocus method of the field.

7 Type **Cancel = True** to cancel the event.

8 Open the form in View mode.

9 Check the field (☐ changes to ☑) to cause the other field to be validated.

10 Click the record selector to try to save the record.

■ The message dialog box appears.

WORK WITH DATA BEHIND A FORM

Bound forms are always bound to a record set, whether it is directly to a table, or to a query. You can manipulate the data behind the form using various controls in the form. You can also work with the data using VBA code. You can work with data behind a form by using the form's recordset.

RECORDSET OBJECT

A form's Recordset property is actually a recordset object that contains all of a form's data in rows, much like the Datasheet view of a table. There are properties and methods that you can use to move around the recordset and manipulate the data.

Recordset Object Properties

The most commonly used Record object properties appear here:

PROPERTY	DESCRIPTION
BOF	A Boolean type property that is True when you are at the beginning of the recordset.
EOF	A Boolean type property that is True when you are at the end of the recordset.
Fields	A collection of fields in the recordset. This is the default collection for the recordset object, so when you utilize a field in the recordset, use the syntax *recordsetobject!fieldname*.
Clone	A clone of the recordset.
Bookmark	A unique string value created for each record in a recordset for quick access.

Recordset Methods

The most commonly used Record object methods appear here:

METHOD	DESCRIPTION
FindFirst	Locates the first record matching a given criteria.
MoveFirst	Moves to the first record in the recordset.
MoveNext	Moves to the next record in the recordset.
MoveLast	Moves to the last record in the recordset.
MovePrevious	Moves to the previous record in the recordset.

CLONE A RECORDSET OBJECT

When you clone a recordset object, you create a second reference to the same set of data. This means that while you can move independently through the individual recordsets, they share certain features such as bookmarks. You can declare a Recordset type variable, and set the variable to the recordset.clone. You can use the following syntax to do so:

```
Set rsClonename =
Me.Recordset.Clone
```

where *rsClonename* is the name of the recordset variable you create.

BOOKMARKS

Bookmarks in recordsets are very much like the ones you use in a real book. You can use them to mark where specific records are in your recordset, allowing you to save the bookmark of the record to a string variable if you want, and to return to the record using that bookmark. The syntax for storing a bookmark to a string variable looks like this:

```
strVariable = recordsetobject.BookMark
```

To return to the bookmark, you simply reverse the statement:

```
recordsetobject.BookMark = strVariable
```

While you can store the bookmark in a string variable, it is not really a value that you can use for anything else. You can synchronize a recordset with the recordset's clone by setting the recordset's bookmark to the clone's bookmark.

UTILIZE A COMBO BOX TO LOCATE RECORDS

A combo box is a very useful control that allows the user to locate records in a form without having to use the Find command in the Edit menu. Instead, you can display a combo box at the top of the form, listing names or other meaningful information for the displayed value in the combo box.

Access has a wizard that creates the necessary code for this process. However, it is still a good idea to become familiar with this code. To create the combo box, you can click and drag a Combo Box control into the form with the control wizards toggled on.

In the first page of the wizard, Access displays the option "Find a record on my form based on the value I selected in my combo box." After you select this option, you can complete the rest of the wizard as described in Chapter 5.

After the wizard creates the control, Access generates the following for the After Update event of the new combo box.

```
Private Sub Combo24_AfterUpdate()
    ' Find the record that matches the
control.
    Dim rs As Object
    Set rs = Me.Recordset.Clone
    rs.FindFirst "[CustomerID] = '" &
Me![Combo24] & "'"
    If Not rs.EOF Then Me.Bookmark =
rs.Bookmark
End Sub
```

The first thing that occurs in the above code is the declaration of the Object called rs. Next, the code sets a reference to the clone of the recordset for the current form using rs. Every bound form has a recordset underneath it. You can set a reference to it, and manipulate it using code, just as you can in the form.

You can also see where the If...Then statement is used without the End...If statement. You can do this when you only have a single line to execute after the If...Then statement.

UTILIZE A COMBO BOX TO LOCATE RECORDS

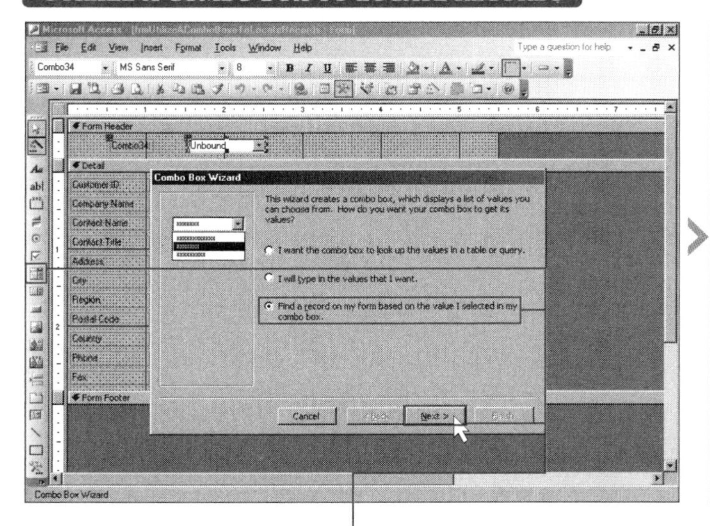

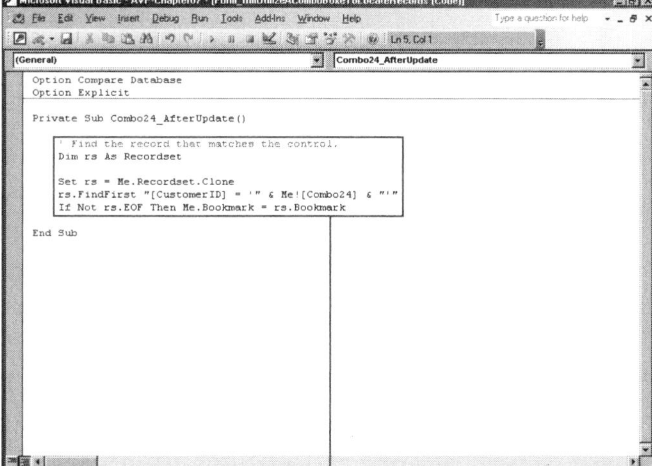

Note: This task uses frmUtilizeAComboBoxeToLocateRecords in AVP-Chapter07.mdb on the CD-ROM.

1 Create or open a bound form to which you want to add the combo box lookup.

2 With the control wizards on, click and drag a combo box control onto the form.

■ The Combo Box Wizard appears.

3 Select the third option.

4 Click Next.

5 Complete the rest of the wizard.

6 Select the combo box.

7 Click the Builder button (...) next to the After Update event of the combo box.

■ The code for the event procedure appears.

TOGGLE A FORM'S VIEWING OR EDITING

You may sometimes want to control what the users are able to do when they are in a form. For example, you may need to limit them to viewing the data on the form, or to editing the data. To do this, you must learn how to iterate through controls on a form, along with using other commands.

You can tell a form whether to allow the user to view or edit data when the form opens. To do this you can use an argument of the DoCmd.OpenForm method called OpenArgs. The OpenArgs argument is a string data type, and is reflected in the OpenArgs property of the form. Access does nothing with this property; it is purely for your use as a developer. You can use an If...Then statement in the event procedure of the On Open event in the form that the user opens. This statement tells you whether the word "View" has been passed to the OpenArgs property.

If Me.OpenArgs = "View", then you iterate, or loop, through each of the text boxes on the form, setting their Enabled properties to False, their Locked properties to True, and even changing their appearance by setting the SpecialEffect and BackStyle properties to 0.

You can use the For Each...Next object code block to loop through the collection. These statements let you loop through each item in a collection. An object variable of the type of item is declared just before the For Each...Next statement.

Inside the For Each...Next *object* code block, you can use If *object* TypeOf Is *objecttype* to make sure the type of control you are changing is a TextBox type.

CREATE THE FORM TO CALL THE TOGGLED FORM

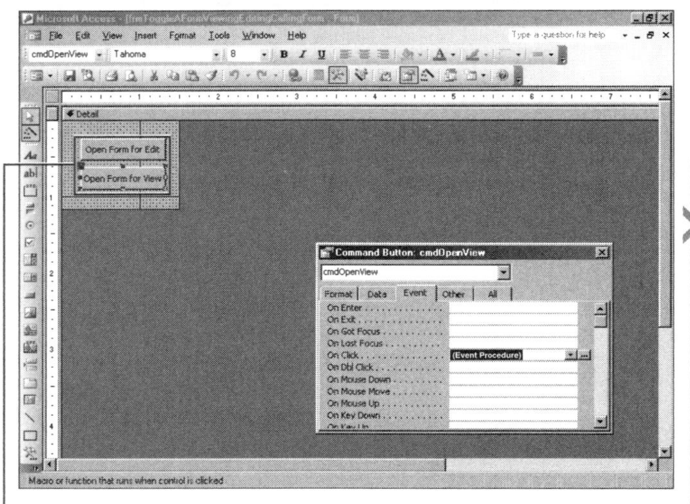

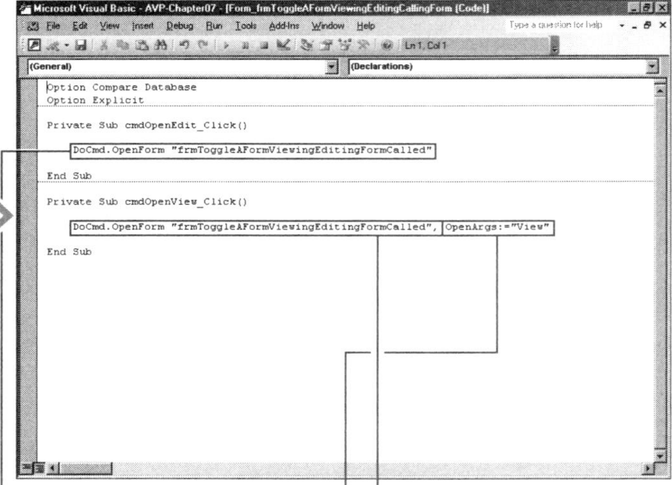

Note: This task uses frmToggleAFormViewingEditingCallingForm and frmToggleAFormViewingEditingFormCalled in AVP-Chapter07.mdb on the CD-ROM.

1 Create an unbound form.

2 Add two command buttons.

■ The first one is for opening another form in edit mode, the second for View mode.

3 Name the two buttons. For this example, the buttons are named cmdOpenEdit and cmdOpenView.

4 Add an event procedure for the On Click event of the button used to open a form for editing.

5 In the event procedure created in step 4, add a DoCmd.OpenForm command, specifying the name of the form that you will be creating in step 8.

6 Repeat steps 4 and 5 for the command button used for viewing the form.

7 Add the parameter of OpenArgs:="View" at the end of the DoCmd.OpenForm statement you created in step 6.

Extra

In addition to changing the individual control properties, you can set properties on the form that limit what the user can do. The properties you can set are AllowAdditions, AllowEdits, and AllowDeletions.

Add the commands just after the For Each...Next object code block, but before of the End...If statement. The commands you can use are:

```
Me.AllowAdditions = False
Me.AllowDeletions = False
Me.AllowEdits = False
```

After you type this code into the Form_Open event procedure and open the form in View mode, you should notice that the New Record button (▶*) in the Navigation buttons at the bottom of the form is now disabled. Also, you should not be able to edit or delete any records.

Along with using the controls' formatting properties to give visual clues, you can update the caption of the form to let the user know whether the form is in View or Edit mode. You can update the form's Caption property to display Edit Mode by default at the end of the caption. As a result, if a customer's form is being used, the caption should display: Customers – Edit Mode.

To display View mode, you can type the following command just after the If...Then statement used in the Form_Open event procedure:

```
Me.Caption = "Customers - View Mode"
```

CREATE THE FORM TO TOGGLE

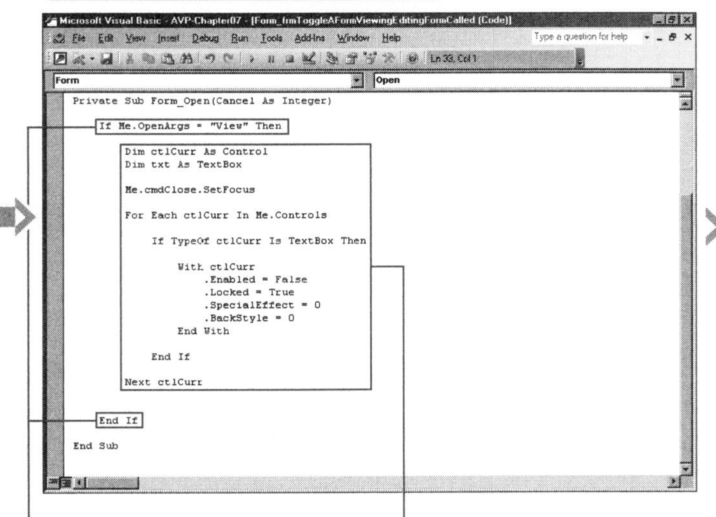

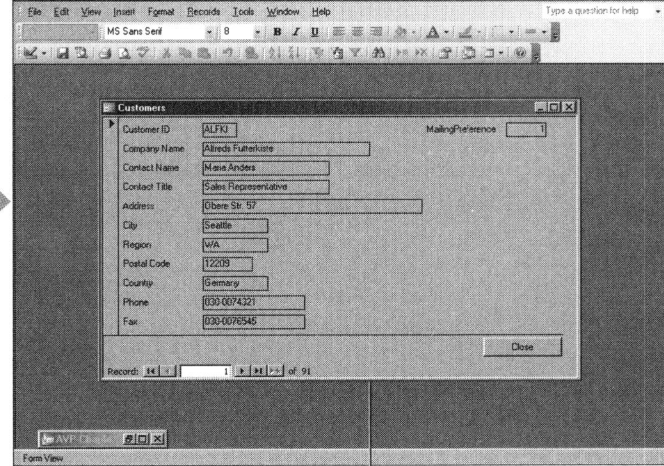

8 Create or open a bound form that has multiple bound text boxes on it.

9 Add the event procedure for the On Open event.

10 Type the If Me.OpenArgs Then statement, and add End If at the bottom of the routine.

11 Type the code as displayed in the figure.

■ Add a command button called button cmdClose if you do not have one. You need to have something to remove focus from the text boxes.

12 Open the form you created in step 1.

13 Click the command button you created in step 2 to view the form.

■ The second form appears, displaying fields that are not editable.

DISPLAY OR HIDE TAB CONTROL PAGES

There may be times when you want to limit the data that certain users can access. While you can do this using Access's security on your database, you can also limit user access with forms.

One way to limit user's access is to place your data on pages on a Tab control, and then hide or display the Tab control pages, depending on the user. You can use the Visible property on a Tab controls page object to hide or display Tab control pages.

You access the Page object through the Tab control's Pages collection. The Pages collection is the collection of individual pages belonging to the Tab control. The syntax for hiding a page on a Tab control is as follows:

```
TabControl.Pages(intPgNum).Visible = False
```

where TabControl is the specific Tab control you are using, and intPgNum is a zero-based integer that is the index to the page. For example, if you want to hide page 2 in a Tab control called tabInfo, then you can use the following code:

```
tabInfo.Pages(1).Visible = False
```

There are a couple of ways to specify which pages you want to hide for each user. One way is to place the users and the page numbers to which they have access in a table, and then loop through the records and set the pages they can use to Visible = True. The other, simpler way is to create a Select Case statement that looks at the user, and hides the appropriate tabs. This method is shown below.

DISPLAY OR HIDE TAB CONTROL PAGES

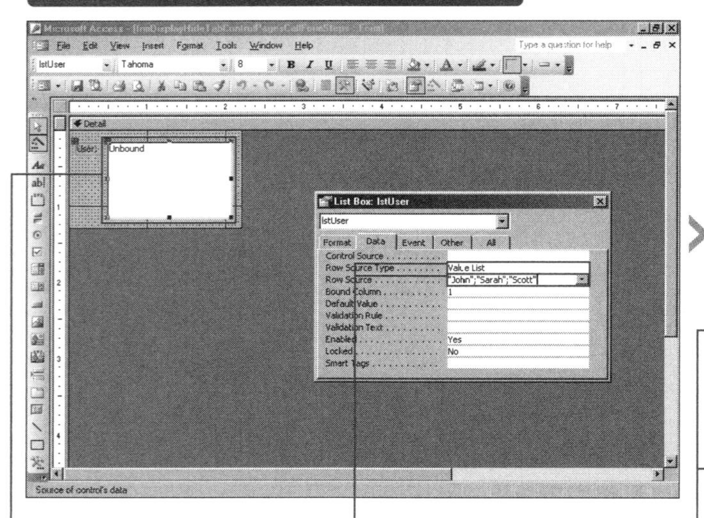

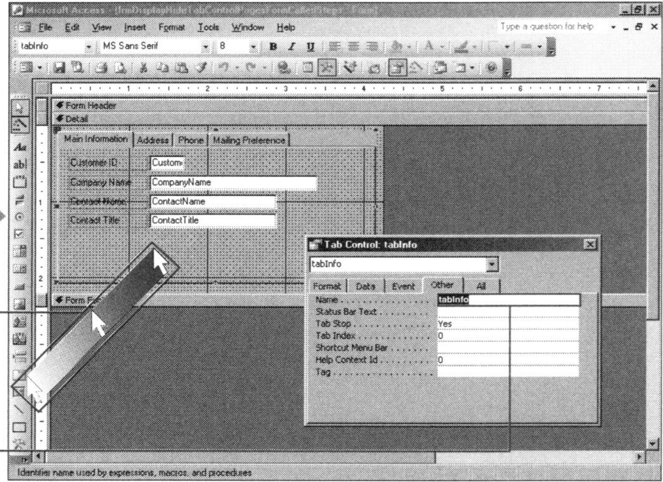

Note: This task uses frmDisplayHideTabControlPagesCallFormSteps and frmDisplayHideTabControlPagesFormCalledSteps in AVP-Chapter07.mdb on the CD-ROM.

1. Create a new form.
2. Add a list box to the form and name it.
3. In the Data tab of the property sheet, select Value List.
4. Type a series of names into the Row Source property field, surrounding each name with quotes, and separating them with semi-colons.
5. Save and close the form.
6. Create another form.
7. Add a Tab control to the new form, and then add the desired pages.
8. Assign a name to the Tab control.
9. Save and close the form.
10. Reopen the form you created in step 1.
11. Create an event procedure for the After Update event of the list box.

Extra

When you work with numeric indexes, such as pages in the Tab control, use constants for numeric values in your code. To use constants in the example on this page, you can change the code for the form with the Tab control to the following:

```
Private Const conPgMain As Integer = 0
Private Const conPgAddress As Integer = 1
Private Const conPgPhone As Integer = 2
Private Const conPgMail As Integer = 3
Private Sub Form_Open(Cancel As Integer)
Select Case Me.OpenArgs
     Case "John"
        Me.tabInfo.Pages(conPgAddress).
          Visible = False
        Me.tabInfo.Pages(conPgPhone).
          Visible = True
        Me.tabInfo.Pages(conPgMail).
          Visible = True
     Case "Sarah"
        Me.tabInfo.Pages(conPgAddress).
          Visible = True
Me.tabInfo.Pages(conPgPhone).Visible = False
        Me.tabInfo.Pages(conPgMail).
          Visible = True
     Case "Scott"
        Me.tabInfo.Pages(conPgAddress).
          Visible = True
        Me.tabInfo.Pages(conPgPhone).
          Visible = True
        Me.tabInfo.Pages(conPgMail).
          Visible = False
  End Select
```

The code specifies the conPgMain event even though it is not used. This makes it easy for you to use it in the future, and helps to document the code. Note that by putting the constant declarations in the declarations section of the module, you can add code to other routines and use the constants.

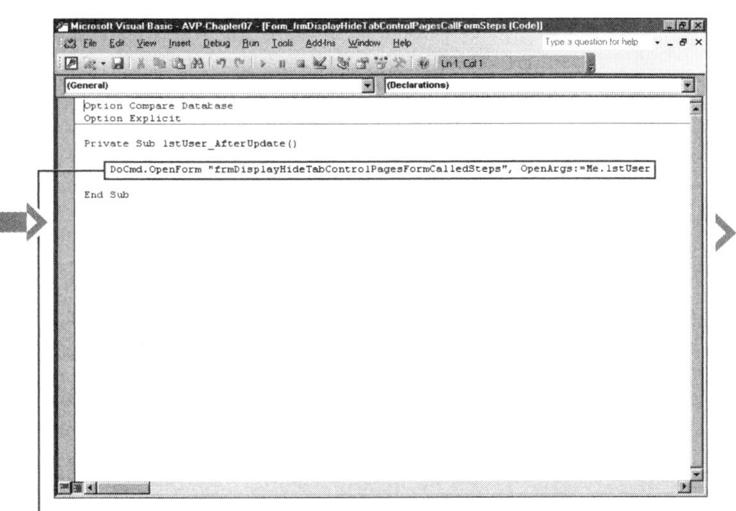

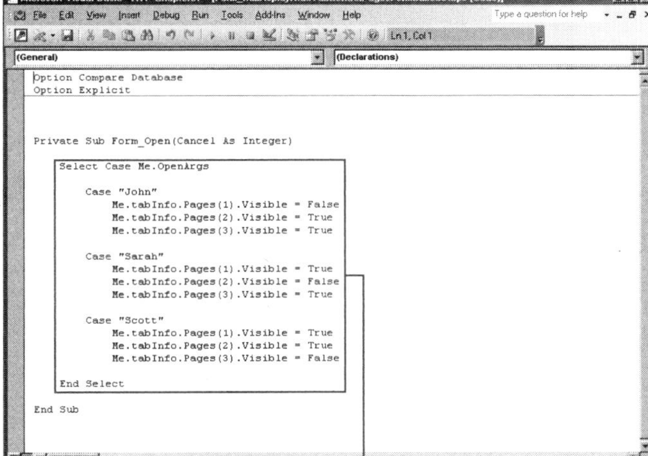

12 Type in a DoCmd.OpenForm statement, opening the tabbed form you created, and passing the current value of the list box using the OpenArgs parameter.

■ The OpenArgs parameter lets you pass a string value from one form to another form. Inside the called form, examine the OpenArgs property of the form for the string value that was passed.

13 Save and close the form you created in step 1 again.

14 Open the tabbed form.

15 Create an event procedure for the Open event of the form.

16 Add the code to examine the OpenArgs property, and hide or display the appropriate pages based on the value.

■ You can hide or display the appropriate pages based on the value passed using the OpenArgs property.

INTRODUCING ACCESS REPORTS

One of the most popular features in Access is the report writer. In fact, many companies use Access because it offers a wide range of report generation capabilities. You can create reports that are as simple as a listing of a table, or as complicated as a multiple-page loan document. You can create labels and other multi-column reports with the report writer, and even create reports that contain other reports.

As with forms, you can base a report on either a table or query. Also, as with forms, for better performance, base a report on a query, specifying only the fields you want to include.

The Access report writer is also referred to as a banded report writer. The bands are sections of the report you can create, based on the type of report you want.

SECTIONS OF A REPORT

Report Header/Footer Sections

These are optional for each report. You can use the report header for a cover page for the report, and the report footer for a summary page at the end of the report.

Page Header/Footer Sections

As with the report header/footer, these sections are optional. If you use them, they appear at the top and bottom of each page instead of just once in the report. You usually use the header for page heading information, such as when you want to repeat the name of the report and column headings. You can use the footer section for page numbers, as well as the date and time you generated the report.

Group Header/Footer Sections

Access allows you to specify groupings in your reports, such as grouping sales information by date or department. The header and footer sections let you summarize information about the group, and display aggregate values.

Detail Section

Every report has a detail section, even though it may not always be visible. If you are creating a bound report, individual records such as line items can be displayed. You can use the detail section for various purposes, depending on the type of report you are creating.

USING VBA BEHIND REPORTS

As with forms, you can use VBA behind your reports to automate some tasks. For example, you can hide an entire line of detail if a value is 0, or even calculate values while the application is running.

You can program VBA behind reports in the same way that you would with forms. This includes the use of event procedures, although instead of the over 50 events that forms have, you only use seven at the report level. You also have additional events at each section level, and for each of the controls that you use on the report.

You can set the various properties of controls and sections in reports just as with forms.

VIEWS OF A REPORT

There are three options for viewing a report. You can:

- Print the report to a printer, file, or other device such as a fax machine.
- View the report in Print Preview view. This mode lets you see what the entire report looks like.
- Preview the layout of the report. When you do this, you see how the report looks, but the data is not necessarily correct. You can also only view a few of the pages.

VARIOUS REPORT POSSIBILITIES

Access can generate a wide variety of reports for you. When you click the New button in the Reports list of the database window, you see a list of different types of reports Access generates.

REPORT TYPES THAT ACCESS CAN GENERATE

Report Wizard

The Report Wizard is fairly flexible for reports that you base on one or more record sources. There are various layouts and styles that you can specify. You can also use the wizard to specify various levels of groupings and sorting, presenting the user with a variety of report types. To create a report that uses a sub-report, you can select fields from related tables, and tell the wizard to create the report for you.

AutoReport: Columnar

AutoReport: Columnar takes a record source you specify and creates a report with the fields going down a page. The report uses the last style you specified using either the Report Wizard or the AutoFormat command of the Format menu in the Design view.

AutoReport: Tabular

AutoReport: Tabular takes the record source you specify and creates a report with the fields going across the page. The report uses the last style you specified using either the Report Wizard or the AutoFormat command of the Format menu in the Design view.

Chart Wizard

The Chart Wizard guides you through the steps that create a chart using Microsoft Graph. You can specify several features to use for your chart. The result is a read-only chart that the user cannot change interactively. To create a chart with interactive abilities, you can use the PivotChart feature. This is discussed in the next chapter.

Label Wizard

The Label Wizard helps you create mailing labels, as well as other types of labels, depending on what you want. The wizard offers a large number of standard mailing label dimensions, number of labels to print across and down the page, including the Avery standard for several Avery product numbers. You can use this wizard to arrange your information on the labels.

OTHER REPORT TYPES

There are a wide variety of report types you can create with Access reports. These include:

- Invoices: Using the sub-report feature, you can create a report that includes the main invoice information as well as item details on the invoice.
- Letters: You can create mail merges and forms where standard text is blended with data from your database.
- Complex documents: You can create documents that include a variety of sections that reflect your needs as well as the document type.
- Catalogs: You can create and maintain documents that include pictures and other documents.
- Documents to export to other applications: You can export a report that you create in the Access report writer into another application, such as Word, Publisher, or even as a document on a Web page.

TAKE ADVANTAGE OF THE REPORT WIZARD

You can use the Report Wizard to create either simple reports or more complex reports that use sub-reports. To use this feature, you can click the Reports topic in the database window, and then select Create Report Using Wizard from the top of the list of reports.

The first page of the Report Wizard lets you choose which record sources you want to use for the report. You can use either tables or queries, or both. If you pull fields from a record source, and then point to another record source in the Tables/Queries combo box, adding fields from the second record source, Access creates a report that uses sub-reports.

After selecting the fields you want to include in the report, you can move to the next page, which lets you specify the groupings for your report. When you specify groupings, you are displaying your data in order to detail one type of data, such as grouping a sales report by date of invoice. After selecting one or more fields on which you want to group, you can continue to the next page, where you can specify the sort order for the detail section of the report. You can also specify summary options on this page.

The next page of the Report Wizard lets you choose a layout for the report. Along with choosing portrait or landscape for your report format, you can choose to display the data in an outline or block style. On the next page, you can select the style of report you want to use, including Bold, Casual, Compact, Corporate, Formal, and Soft Gray.

The last page of the wizard lets you specify the title of the report, as well as whether you want to open the report in Design or Preview view after the wizard generates your report.

TAKE ADVANTAGE OF THE REPORT WIZARD

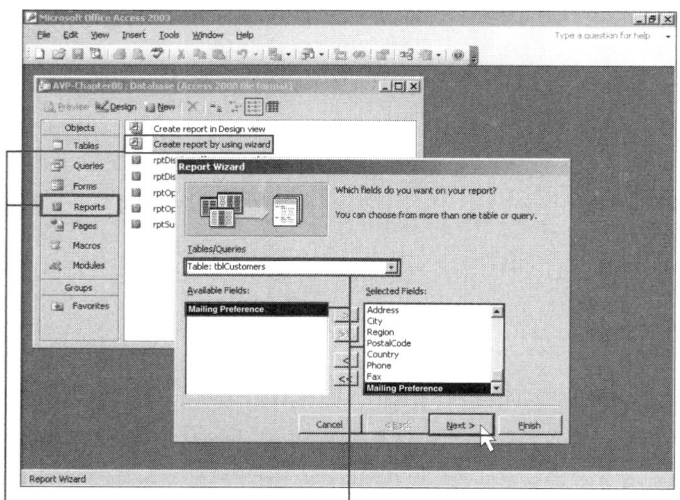

Note: This task creates rptTakeAdvantageOfTheReportWizard in AVP-Chapter08.mdb on the CD-ROM.

1 Click Reports.

2 Double-click Create report by using wizard.

3 In the first page of the Report Wizard, select the table to use as the record source for the report.

4 Double-click fields you want to include in the report.

■ The fields you select appear here.

5 Click Next.

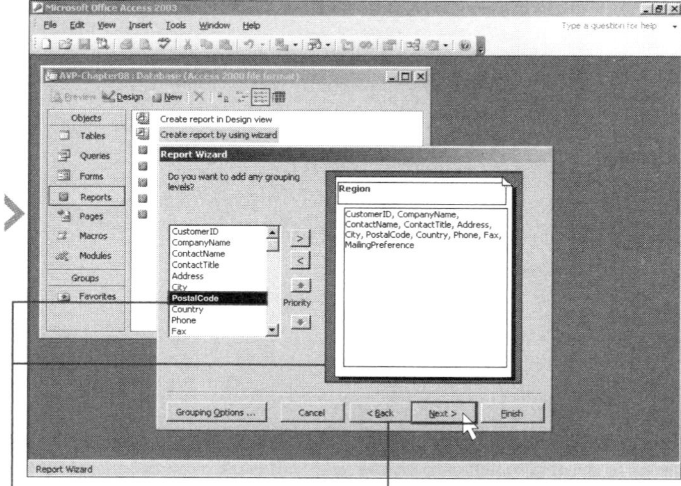

■ The grouping selection appears.

6 Double-click the fields you want to group by.

■ The fields that Access uses for grouping appear in bold, and the remaining fields indent.

7 Click Next.

■ The sorting page appears.

8 Select any fields on which you want to sort and whether you want each field to sort in ascending or descending order.

9 Click Next.

Extra

While in the Report Wizard, in the page that specifies grouping levels, you can specify some options after you select one or more fields on which you want to group. When you click a field to highlight it, you can then click the Grouping Options button. The Grouping Intervals dialog box appears, displaying all the fields you have specified you want to group on.

You can select the interval on which you want to group for each field. By default, the interval is Normal. Intervals can change, depending on the data type you are using to group on. Some of the different intervals for the various data types appear below:

DATA TYPE	INTERVAL
Text	Normal is all letters. You also have first letter, two initial letters, three initial letters, four initial letters, or five initials letters.
Numeric	Normal is 1. You also have 10s, 50s, 100s, 500s, 1,000s, 5,000s, or 10,000s.
Date/Time	Normal is day. You also have Year, Quarter, Month (the default), Week, Day, Hour, or Minute.

With these options, you have a great deal of versatility in using the grouping feature in your reports.

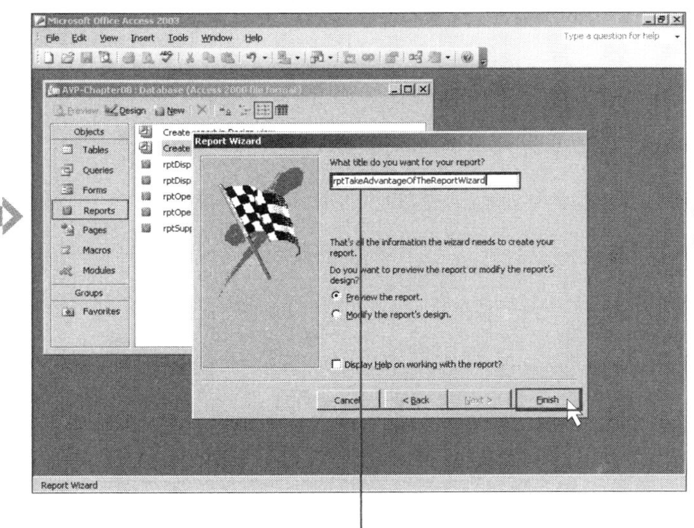

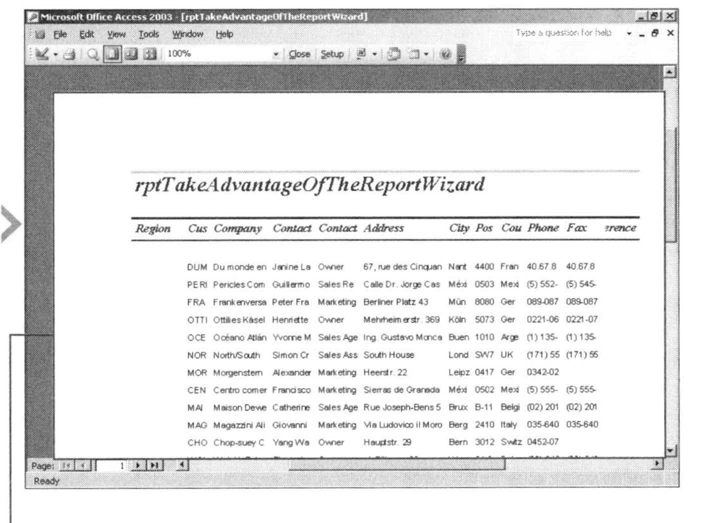

■ The page for selecting the layout appears.

10 Click Next to accept the defaults.

■ The page for selecting the report style appears.

11 Click Next to accept the default.

■ The final page of the wizard appears.

12 Type the title you want for the report.

13 Click Finish.

■ The new report appears.

■ In this example, a grouping was created using the region field, with a group header displayed.

CREATE A NEW REPORT

Normally, you can create a report using the Report Wizard, selecting the same style for each report you create. This is a great way to maintain a standard appearance in your reports. After you create a report, you can use the Report Designer to enhance the appearance of the report.

However, there are times when you may need to create a completely new report. To do this, you can choose the Create report in Design view option from the list of reports. A blank report appears in Design view.

If you are creating a report based on a record source, you must open the property sheet of the report, just as you would for a form, by choosing Properties from the View menu, or clicking the Property button. You can click the Data tab in the property sheet, and choose a record source.

As with forms, you have various properties, methods, and events that you can use, but they may vary, depending on the object you highlight in the report. The report has a particular set of properties, methods, and events, as does each section and control on a report.

After you create a report and select a record, you can click and drag fields from the field list just as you would on a form. If you want to create a report using columns, you can place a field on the report where you want it, highlight and cut the label, and then paste the label into the page heading section.

You can use the controls to align and size objects in your report just as you would when working on a form. In fact, most of the control types that you can use on a form can also appear in a report.

CREATE A NEW REPORT

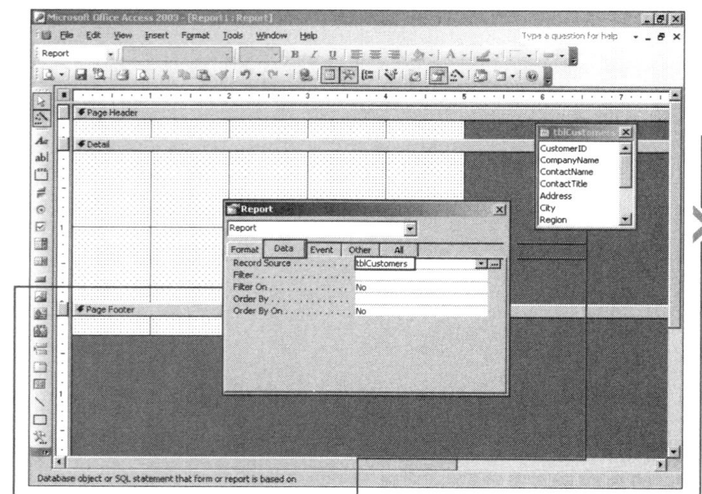

Note: This task creates rptCreateANewReportFromScratch in AVP-Chapter08.mdb on the CD-ROM.

1 Double-click Create report in Design view from the Reports object list.

■ A blank report appears in Design view.

2 Click View ➪ Properties Sheet.

3 Click the Data tab.

4 Click in the Record Source field, and select the table or query you want.

5 Click View ➪ Field List.

■ The fields available in the record source appear.

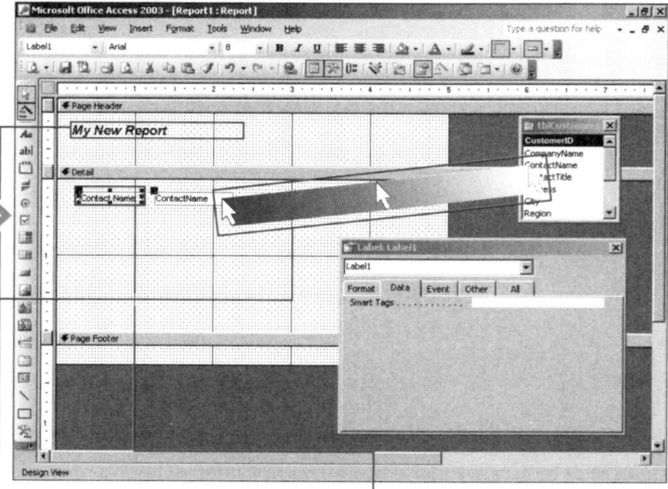

6 Add a label in the page header section, and type a title for the report.

7 Click and drag a field from the Field List into the detail section.

8 Select the label of the control.

Extra

You can reattach a label to a control if you accidentally remove the label. You can do this by clicking the label you want to reattach, and then clicking Edit ➪ Cut. Next, you can click the control to which you want to add the label, and click Edit ➪ Paste. The label attaches to the control. Keep in mind that you can have only one label per control.

If you have fields in the Textbox controls that contain text that can either be single or multiple lines, you can set the Can Grow property of the text box to True. Access expands the report, pushing the subsequent data down on the report. You can find the Can Grow property on the Format tab of the property sheet.

When you have repeating values, and you only want to show the first value, you can set the Hide Duplicates property to True. Then, if a field contains the same value that will be displayed in consecutive records, Access hides the value after the first appearance of the value.

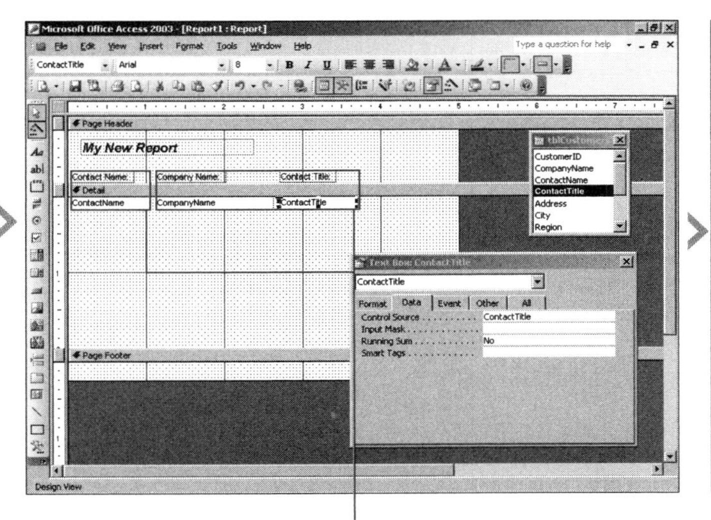

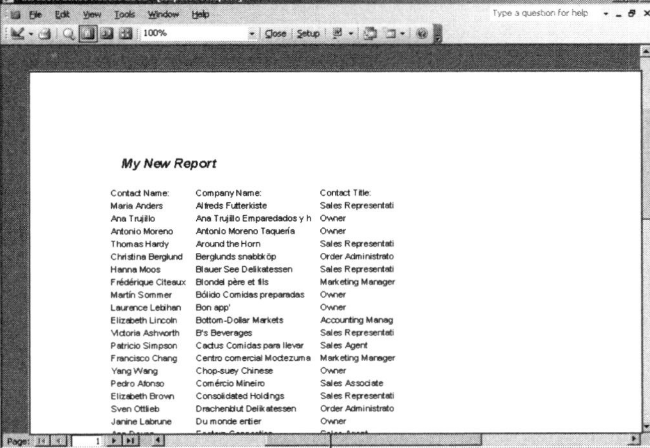

9 Click Edit ➪ Cut.

10 Click the page header section, and click Edit ➪ Paste.

11 Align the label and control over each other in their sections.

12 Repeat steps 7 to 11 for each field you want to include in the report.

13 Reduce the height of the detail section by clicking the pane splitter directly above the title bar for the page footer section. Drag the section boundary below the fields.

14 Click the View button ( ) to view the report.

- The new report appears in Preview view.

WORK WITH CALCULATED EXPRESSIONS

You can display calculated expressions in your reports in the same way that you would in forms. However, although it is best to create the calculated expressions at the form level when using them with forms, this is not as important with reports.

To create a calculated expression in a report, you can begin the expression with the equal sign, followed by the rest of the expression. Access imposes the same limits on expressions in reports as in forms. For example, you can call functions, but not subroutines. Also, you need to delimit your string literals with double quotes.

You can use expressions in various places in reports. In the report header section, you may want to use an expression to display the date range of the report. For example, if you have txtBeginDte and txtEndDte text boxes in a form called frmOpenReport, you can display those text box values with a literal string like the following:

```
="Reporting for the dates: &
Forms!frmOpenReport!txtBeginDte & " through
" & Forms!frmOpenReport!txtEndDte
```

You can also use calculated expressions in the detail section of the report. For example, if you have a Price field and a Quantity field, and you want to display the extended price, you can use the following expression in a new text box:

```
=[Price]*[Quantity]
```

The extended price is displayed for each record in the detail section.

You can use both user-defined and built-in functions in your expressions. For example, if you want to display the number of days between RequiredDate and ShippedDate, found in tblOrders, you can use the following expression:

```
=DateDiff("d",[ShippedDate],[RequiredDate])
```

Keep in mind that the fields you include in the expression need to be in the record source of the report.

WORK WITH CALCULATED EXPRESSIONS

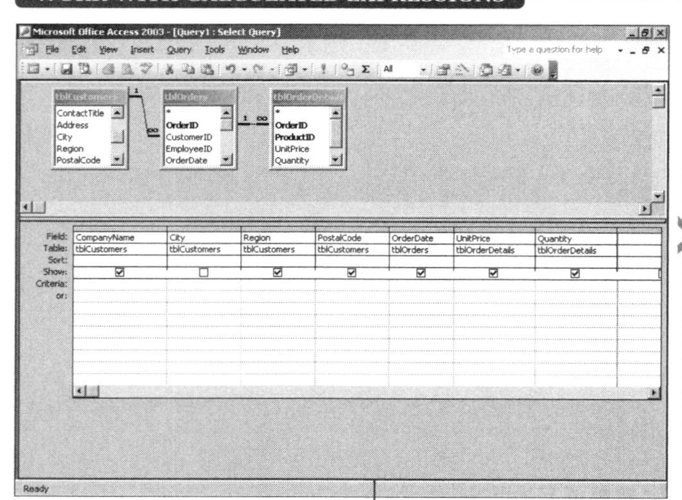

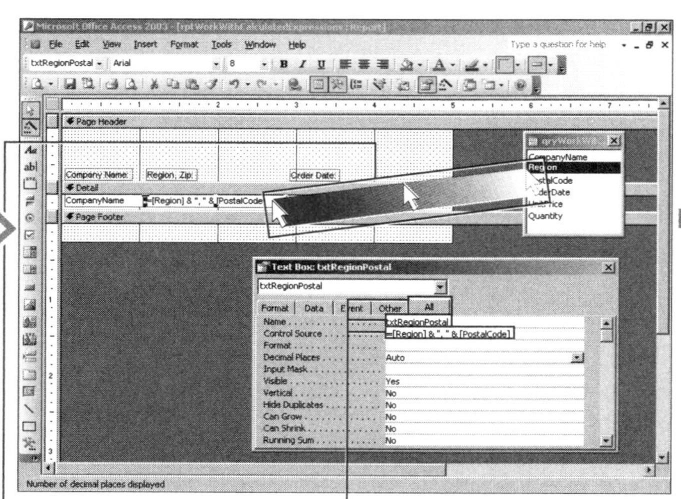

Note: This task creates rptWorkWithCalculatedExpressions in AVP-Chapter08.mdb on the CD-ROM.

1 Create a record source for the report, including fields to be used in the string and numeric calculated expressions.

2 Save and close the query.

3 Create or open the report to which you want to add the calculated expressions.

4 Add a Textbox control, placing it in the report where you want to display it.

5 Open the property sheet.

6 Click the All tab.

7 Type the name you want for the control in the Name property field.

8 Set the Control Source property to the string expression that you want.

Extra

Along with allowing you to create your own expressions, Access includes some built-in expressions that you can use when creating your reports. These expressions modify page numbers and the display of the current date. There are six different expressions you can create, shown below.

- Page Number
- Total Pages
- Page N of M
- Current Date
- Current Date/Time
- Current User

There are two ways to add these expressions to a report. The first way is to place the cursor in the section where you want to add the new control, and to choose either Page Numbers or Dates from the Insert menu. A dialog box appears, and you can choose the format of the particular type, page number, or date you want to display.

The second way to insert a built-in expression is to add a Textbox control, and then click the Builder button (...) next to the Control Source property field. The Expression Builder dialog box appears, and you can select Common Expressions from the object column, which is displayed in the first column on the right.

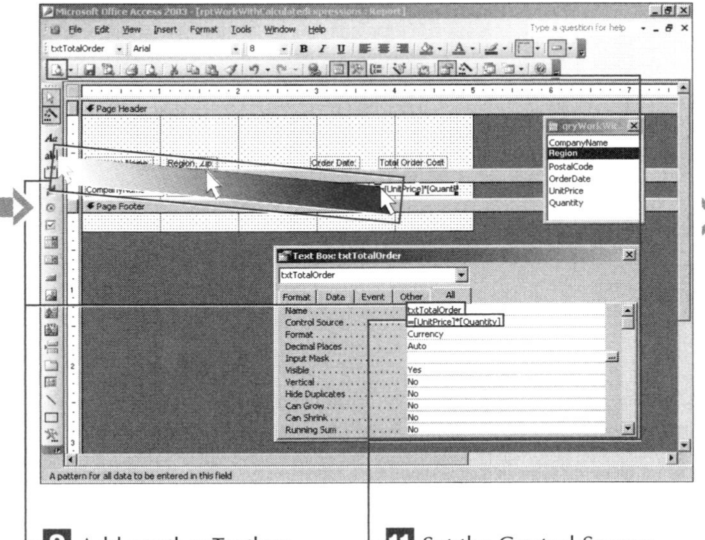

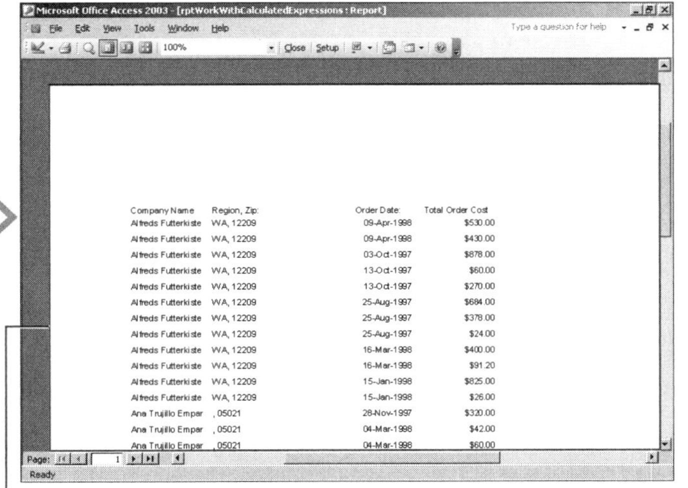

9 Add another Textbox control for the numeric value, and place it in the report where you want to display it.

10 Type the name you want for the control in the Name property field.

11 Set the Control Source property to the numeric expression that you want.

12 Click the View button.

■ The report appears with the calculated values.

■ In this example, the columns under the Region, Zip label and Total Order Cost label are both calculated.

HIDE ROWS BASED ON THE VALUE OF A FIELD

Access provides different events on reports that you can use to manipulate the properties of a report to suit your needs. For example, you may need to hide a line in the detail section if one or more values are 0 or Null.

As with forms, you can write code behind your reports to perform various tasks using VBA in report modules. You can use the On Format event for the detail section. The On Format event, available in each section in a report, occurs before Access formats a section.

Other events for each section are the On Print event, which occurs before the report writer prints each section, and the On Retreat event. The On Retreat event occurs as the report writer makes a second pass before actually printing the report. By making two passes, you can have expressions in the report that rely on values that the report writer does not print until later in the report.

In the On Format event, which is fired off for each detail record, you can add the following code:

```
Private Sub Detail_Format (Cancel As
Integer, FormatCount As Integer)
     If Me!FieldToTest = 0 Then
          Me.Detail.Visible = False
     Else
          Me.Detail.Visible = True
     End If
End Sub
```

where FieldToTest is the control, based on a field, that you are comparing to 0. Although it may appear that you only need to program for when you want to toggle the visibility to Off, you actually also need to toggle the visibility back to On. You can do this by including the second half of the If...Then...End code block.

HIDE ROWS BASED ON THE VALUE OF A FIELD

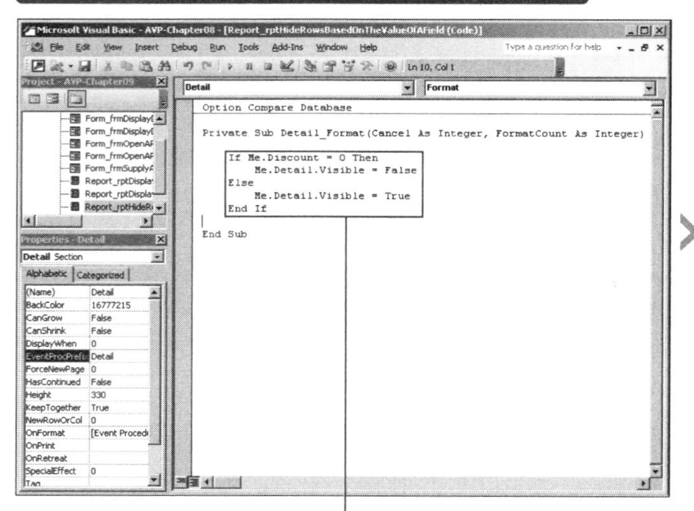

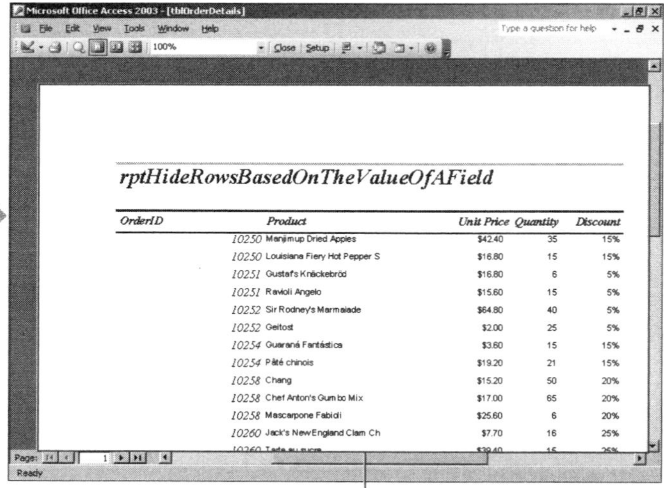

Note: This task creates rptHideRowsBasedOnTheValueOfAField in AVP-Chapter08.mdb on the CD-ROM.

1 Create or open a report in Design view, based on the record source you want to use.

2 After highlighting the gray bar of the detail section, open the property sheet and click the Events tab.

3 Create the event procedure for the On Format event.

4 Add the code specified in the figure, but reflecting your field.

5 Close the code editor.

6 Click the View button (▢).

■ The rows that meet the criteria of the If…Then statement do not appear in the report.

■ In this example, only those items that have a quantity greater than 0 will appear on this report.

SORT INFORMATION ON REPORTS

When you create a report, you may then want to sort the data in the report. For example, you may want to create a sort order using invoices by date.

Keep in mind that even if you set the sort order at the query level, if you are basing the report on a query, if the sort order of the report is different from the query level, the sort order you set in the query is not reflected when you preview or print the report. This is because you may hinder the performance if you set the sort order at the query level. However, if you do not set any groupings or sorting in the report, then the recordset level sorting appears in the report.

To confirm the sort order for a report, you can click View ➪ Sorting and Grouping while in the Design view of the report. The Sorting and Grouping dialog box appears, displaying the two columns, Field/Expression and Sort Order. You can select the field you want to use for the sort order in the Field/Expression drop-down list. You can then choose Ascending or Descending in the Sort Order column.

You can choose to have more than one field on which to sort. For example, you can print a report based on City and then LastName. To do this, you can use City as the top entry of the Sorting and Grouping dialog box, and LastName as the second entry.

Other properties appear in the lower half of the Grouping and Sorting dialog box. You do not need to use these properties for sorting, but you can use them when you manually specify groupings. For more information about manually specifying groupings, see the section, "Add Groupings to a Report."

SORT INFORMATION ON REPORTS

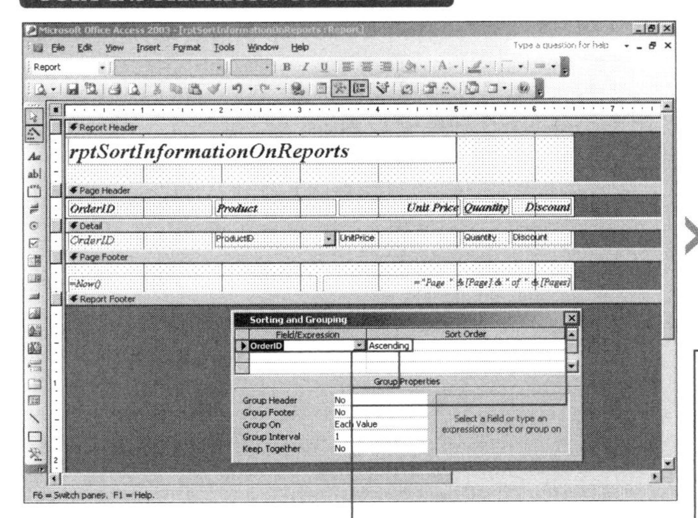

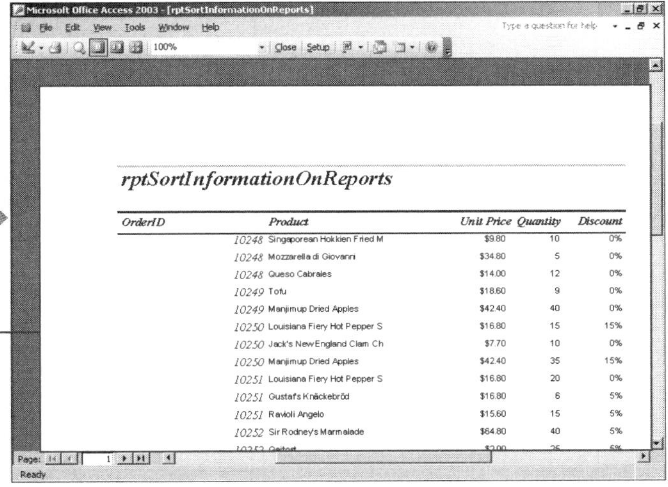

Note: This task creates rptSortInformationOnReports in AVP-Chapter08.mdb on the CD-ROM.

1 Create or open a form in Design view.

2 Click View ➪ Sorting and Grouping.

3 Type the name of the field you want to use in the Field/Expression column.

4 Set the Sort Order you want to use.

5 Close the Sorting and Grouping dialog box.

6 Click the View button.

■ Access sorts the report, based on the field you specified in step 3.

■ The report in this example was sorted on OrderID.

ADD GROUPINGS TO A REPORT

There is quite a bit more to take into consideration with regards to the organization of your data when adding groupings to reports over setting the sort orders. When you add groupings to a report, you are telling the report to group the data on specific fields or expressions, and by using additional properties, you are specifying the creation of group header and footer sections.

The properties you can use are: Group Header, Group Footer, Group On, Group Interval, and Keep Together. The first two properties create the appropriate header and footer sections. The Group On and Group Interval properties let you specify what fields to group on if it is not the whole value. The Keep Together property, when set to True, ensures that the entire group is kept on a single page, if possible.

To add groupings, you can click View ➪ Grouping and Sorting within the report you are designing. You can then select the fields or expressions you want to use for grouping. Next, you can choose whether to display the header or footer section, or both, for the group by checking the appropriate property. You can also set the intervals if you want.

After you close the Sorting and Grouping dialog box, the new sections appear in the report. You can now add fields to display header information, as well as add aggregate functions to display summary information. You can display summary information in either the group header or footer, depending on how you want your report to appear.

ADD GROUPINGS TO A REPORT

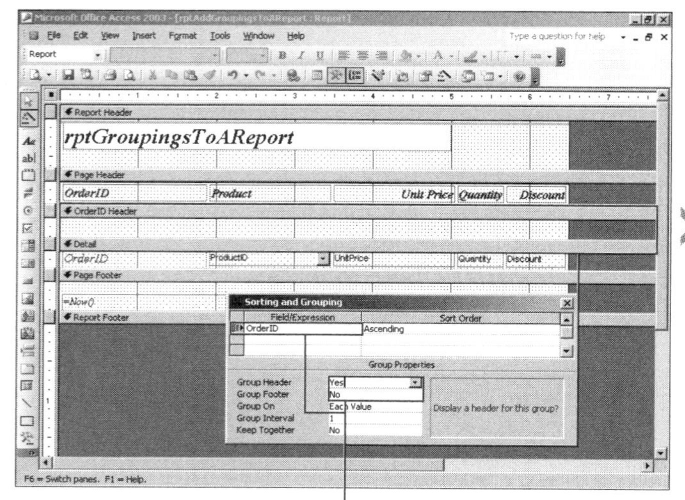

Note: This task creates rptAddGroupingsToAReport in AVP-Chapter08.mdb on the CD-ROM.

1 Create or open a form in Design view.

2 Click View ➪ Sorting and Grouping.

3 In the Sorting and Grouping dialog box, type the field name on which you want to group.

4 Type Yes or No for the new group header and footer sections to appear or not appear.

■ A new section appears on the report for the header and footer sections.

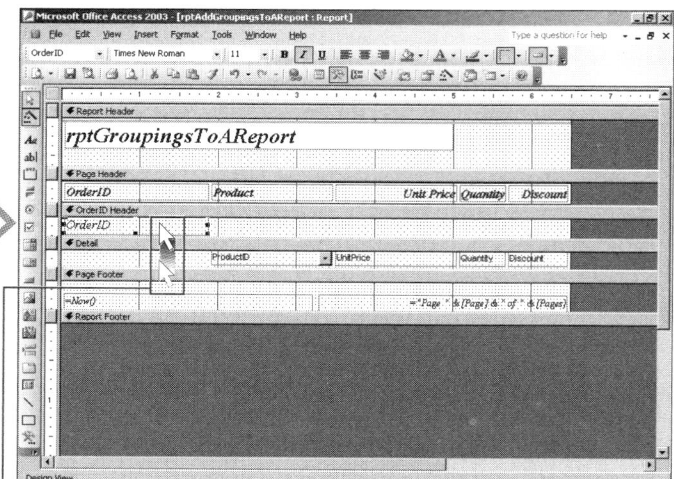

5 Move or add the field you want to display in the new section you have added.

■ In this example, the OrderID field moves from the detail section to the new group header section.

Extra

To add an aggregate value to a report, you can create an expression that uses one of the aggregate functions, such as Sum() or Count(). To display an aggregate function in a text box, you can use the following syntax in the Control Source property field:

```
=AggregateFunction(ValueToUse)
```

where AggregateFunction is the name of the aggregate function you want to use, and ValueToUse is the field you want to use in the expression.

Continuing from the example on this page, if you want to add a new text box to the InvoiceDate group footer section that summarizes the invoice amounts, you can type the following into the Control Source property field of the text box:

```
=Sum(InvoiceTotal)
```

You can also do the same thing at the report levels by using the same aggregate functions and fields. When you copy and paste the text box into the report footer, Access displays the totals for all the invoices in the report.

Similarly, you can display percentages for various sections by having one total control divide another total control. For example:

```
=grouptotal/reporttotal
```

This generates the percentage of a group total for the overall total, and appears in the group header or footer section.

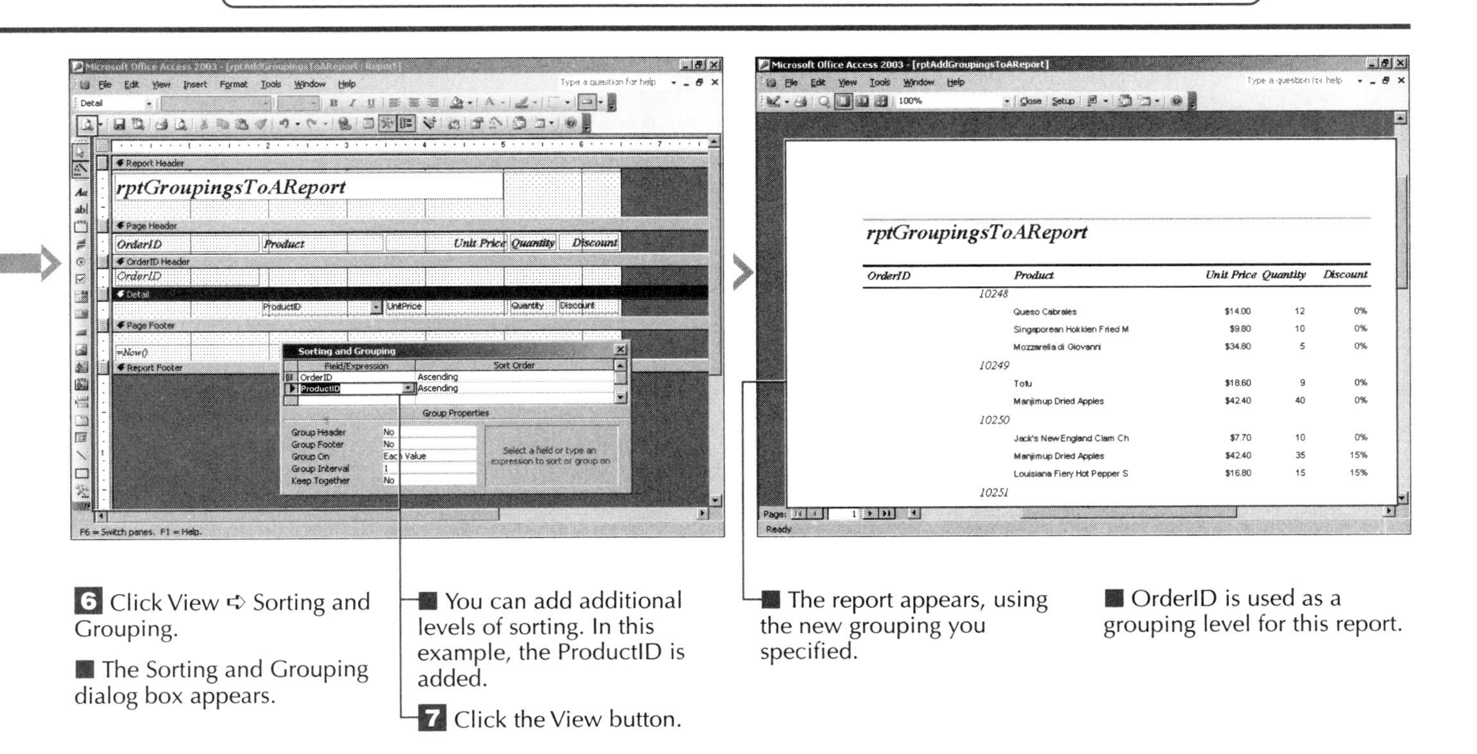

6 Click View ➪ Sorting and Grouping.

■ The Sorting and Grouping dialog box appears.

■ You can add additional levels of sorting. In this example, the ProductID is added.

7 Click the View button.

■ The report appears, using the new grouping you specified.

■ OrderID is used as a grouping level for this report.

OPEN A REPORT BASED ON A FORM FILTER

An important feature of a good database management system is the ability to take a report that presents all the records in a record source, and use that report against a smaller set of data using criteria you select. You can accomplish this a number of different ways.

You can apply filters to reports just as you can apply them to forms. However, while you need to use VBA or a macro to apply the filter to a report, you can apply the filter to a form using the user interface of a form.

You can use both the forms filter feature, and then VBA code to set the filter property of a report, based on the filter property of the form. To do this, you can create a form that displays the data you want to use as a base, such as tblCustomers. You can then add a command button with VBA code behind it.

In the code, you can use two of the form's properties: FilterOn and Filter. The code uses the IIF statement to supply the Where parameter for the Docmd.OpenReport method, as shown below:

```
DoCmd.OpenReport stDocName, acPreview, , _
IIf(Me.FilterOn, Me.Filter, Null)
```

The code checks to see if the filter is set to On for the form. If the filter is on, then the Filter property is passed, thereby restricting the records that are displayed. Otherwise, a Null value is passed, causing all records to be displayed.

No coding is required on the report side, which makes creating the report much easier; you achieve the same result with just one line of code. This technique is also easier to follow, because it does not matter which fields you use, because you are using the filter of the form.

OPEN A REPORT BASED ON A FORM FILTER

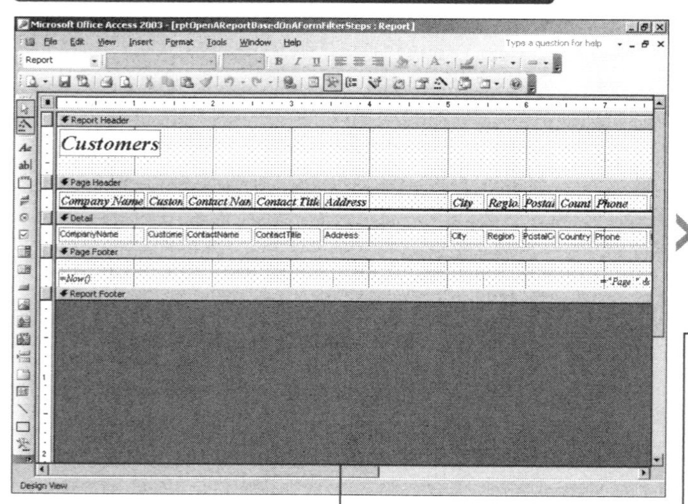

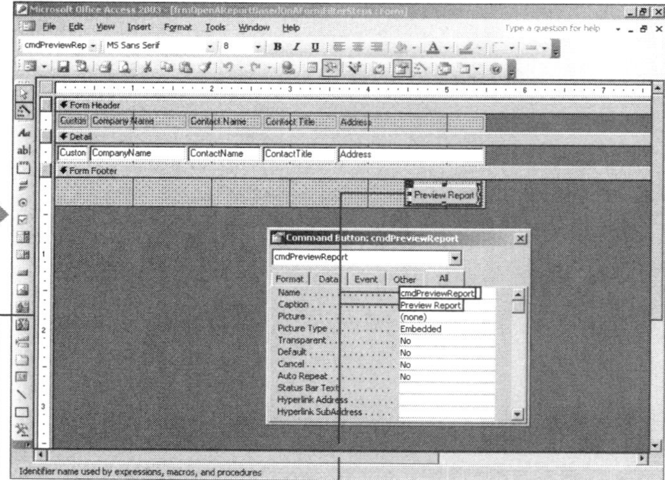

Note: This task creates rptOpenAReportBasedOnAFormFilterSteps in AVP-Chapter08.mdb on the CD-ROM.

1 Create a new report, adding the fields you want to display.

2 Click the View button to view the report; make sure it looks the way you want.

■ All records appear.

3 Create a new form, based on the record source you want.

■ In this example, the form is created in Continuous Form view, so that a row layout can be used, while still having a Form Header and Footer. You cannot do this in Datasheet view.

4 Add the command button that you want to use to open the report.

5 Type a name for the command button.

6 Type a caption for the command button.

Extra

Occasionally, you may accidentally filter out all the records in your report. If this happens, a blank report may appear, or worse, a report with #Error# displayed in the fields. To prevent this, you can add three lines of code, two in the On No Data event of the report, and one in the routine that opens the report.

The code you can use for the On No Data event looks like this:

```
Private Sub Report_NoData(Cancel As Integer)
    MsgBox "No Data to Report!"
    Cancel = True
End Sub
```

The On No Data event allows you to display a message when Access generates no data for the report, and to cancel the report.

When you cancel the report, Access generates an error for the DoCmd.OpenReport method that you use. To avoid displaying an error, you can use the On Error Resume Next statement, as in the following routine that calls the report:

```
Private Sub cmdPreviewReport_Click()

    On Error Resume Next

    DoCmd.OpenReport "rptOpenAReportBasedOnAFormFilterExtra", _
            acPreview, , IIf(Me.FilterOn, Me.Filter, Null)

End Sub
```

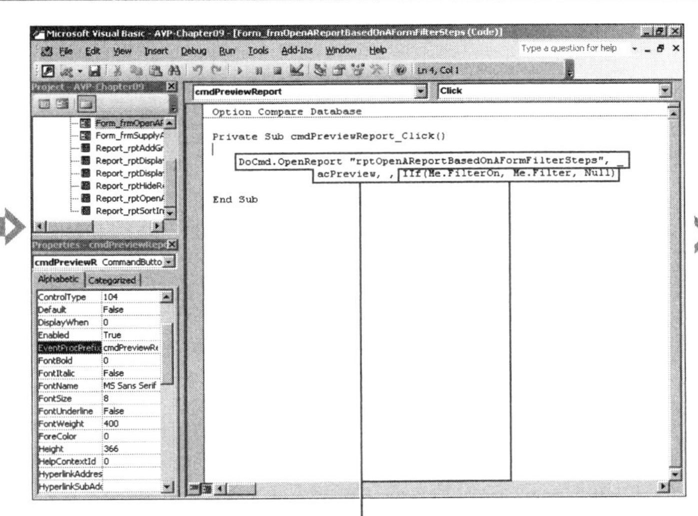

7 Create an event procedure for the On Click event of the command button you created in step 4.

■ The code editor appears.

8 Type the DoCmd.OpenReport statement with the report name, and acPreview to open the report you created in step 1 in preview mode.

9 Type **IIf(Me.FilterOn, Me.Filter, Null)** for the Where parameter of the DoCmd.OpenReport method.

10 From the form, click the View button ( ).

11 Place the cursor in the field that contains the value on which you want to filter in the form.

12 Click the Filter button ( ).

13 Click the command button you created in step 4.

■ The report appears, based on the filter you selected in your form.

■ The report displayed here limits the records to a single customer.

SUPPLY A PARAMETER USING A FORM

You can use a form to open a report using parameters to limit the records displayed on the report. To do this you must first create a form that you want to use to launch the report. In this form, you can add the control or controls that you want, to allow the user to input the criteria that Access can use to launch the report. These controls can be text boxes, combo boxes, or any type of field that you would use for standard input.

Next, you can add a command button that opens the report using the `DoCmd.OpenReport` method. For the `Where` parameter of the method, you can supply a criteria string which will include the input controls. This limits the data that displays in the report. The syntax of the `DoCmd.OpenReport` method looks like this:

```
DoCmd.OpenReport "reportname", _
acViewPreview, , "fieldname = '" &
Me.controlname & "'"
```

where reportname is the name of the report, fieldname is the field to compare to the desired value, in this case `controlname`, which is the name of the input control. Whether you use the quotes or other delimiters around your inputted data depends on the data type you use. Numeric data does not require delimiters; strings use quotes, and dates use the pound sign, #.

You can display the information in the report after the user enters the control in the form. To do this, you can add a Textbox control in the report, and set the control source of the text box to point to the control, or controls, that you use for input in the form.

You can use the following syntax to display the value that the user inputs:

```
=Forms!formname!inputcontrol
```

where formname is the name of the form that you use for opening the report, and inputcontrol is the control that you use for inputting the value.

SUPPLY A PARAMETER USING A FORM

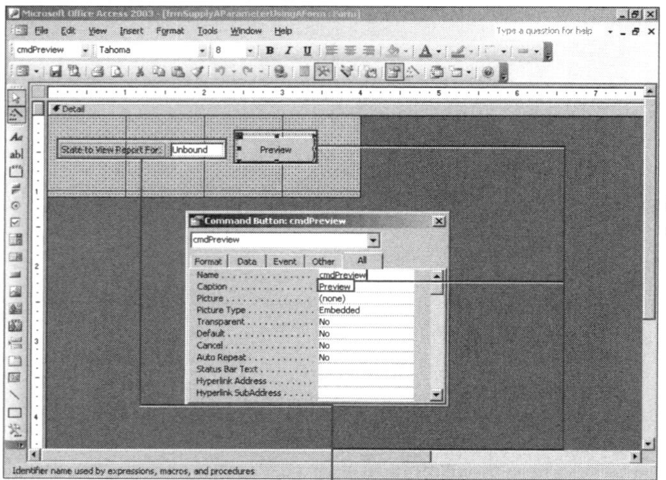

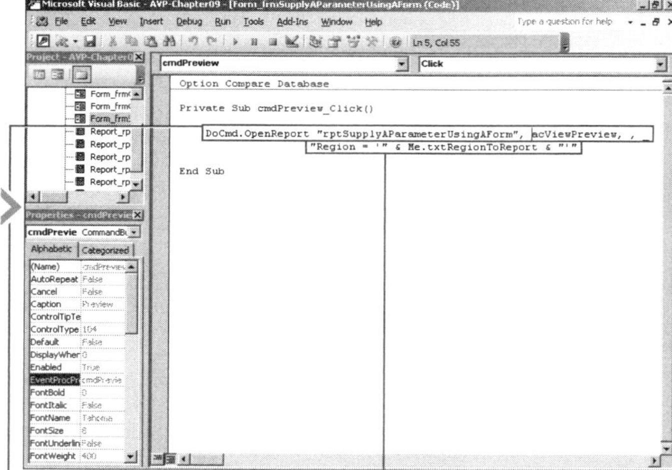

Note: This task creates rptOpenAReportBasedOnAFormFilter Steps in AVP-Chapter08.mdb database on the CD-ROM.

1 Create an unbound form.

2 Add an input control, and then name and label it.

■ This example adds the txtRegionToReport text box.

3 Add a command button, and name it in the Caption field.

4 Add an event procedure to the On Click event of the command button.

5 In the code editor, type in the Docmd.OpenReport command, specifying the report you want to create, and using acViewPreview.

6 Add the Where parameter, referring to the field and control to compare.

■ This example uses the condition "Region = '" & Me.txtRegionToReport & "'".

Extra

Another way to use criteria is to build a query on which to base a report. Within the query, you can then set the criteria of the field referencing the input control, which appears on the form you build. For the example on this page, you can create a query and set the criteria of the Region field to:

```
=Forms!frmSupplyAParameterUsingAForm!txtRegionToReport
```

You can then create the `DoCmd.OpenReport` command as follows:

```
DoCmd.OpenReport "reportname", acViewPreview
```

Which technique you use depends on your requirements. If you want to be able to print the full report without the criteria, then you can use the technique described on this page. Whichever technique you use, the actual report does not change, because the text box you create in the form still refers to the input control in the form.

You can use more that one parameter for criteria. If you need more than one parameter, you can simply add it to your form, and then refer to it either in the `DoCmd.OpenReport` method, or in the query.

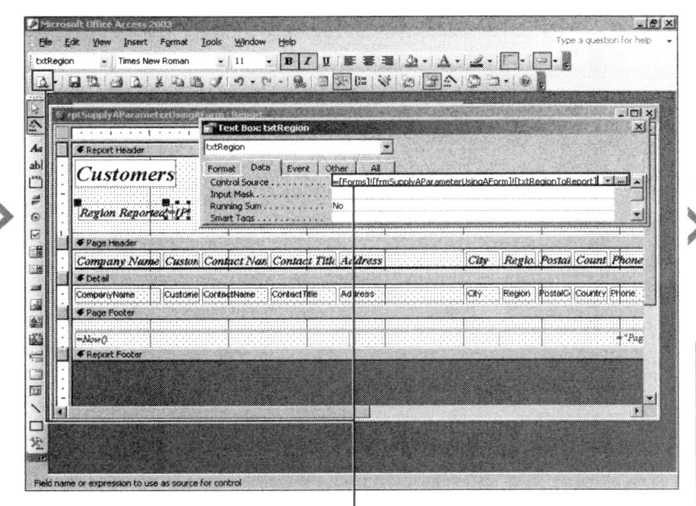

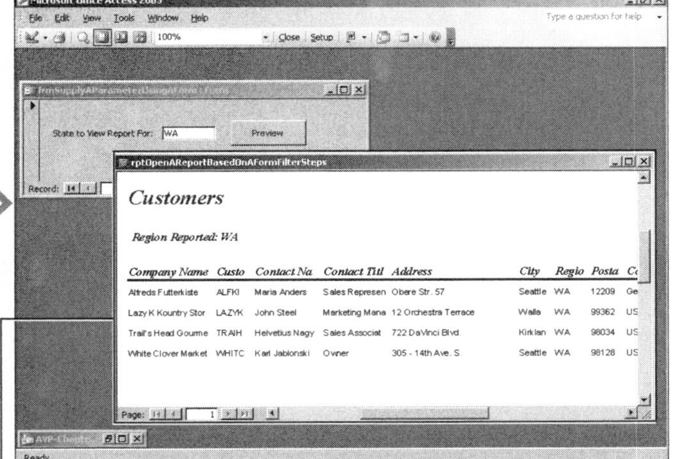

7 Create a report based on the record source you want to use.

Note: Be sure to include the field that you want to compare against in step 6.

8 Add a text box to the form.

9 Type the expression you want to use, referring to the form and control you created in steps 1 and 2.

■ This example uses the expression =Forms!frmSupplyAParameterUsingAForm!txtRegionToReport.

10 Click the View button.

■ The report appears, based on the item you specified in the form, with the value displayed.

■ For this example, all customers located in WA are displayed in the report.

DISPLAY DIFFERENT VIEWS OF THE SAME REPORT

When you create reports for users, invariably those users want different views of the report. Although you can copy a report and make the changes. Access gives you, and the users of your reports, the ability to create reports that show different views of the same data. These views include detail data, summary data, and a combination of detail and summary data. To display different views, you can create a form that includes an option group with the three view choices.

In the Open event of the report, you can toggle the visibility of various sections of the report, depending on the view that you choose. The syntax for setting the Visible property of the detail section to False would be: `Me.Detail.Visible = False`. To set the visibility of the group footer section, which displays the summary information, you can use: `Me.GroupFooter1.Visible = False`.

As you add more groups, Access names them sequentially. You can also name the group sections, using the Name property.

If you want to put together the Select Case statement and toggle the visibility of the various sections, you can use the following code in the report Open event:

```
    Select Case
Forms!formname!groupoptionname
          '-- Detail Only
          Case 1
               Me.GroupFooter1.Visible = False
          '-- Summary Only
          Case 2
               Me.Detail.Visible = False
          '-- Detail and Summary
          Case 3
    End Select
```

In the above code, nothing is done to the detail and summary, and Access displays all sections.

DISPLAY DIFFERENT VIEWS OF THE SAME REPORT

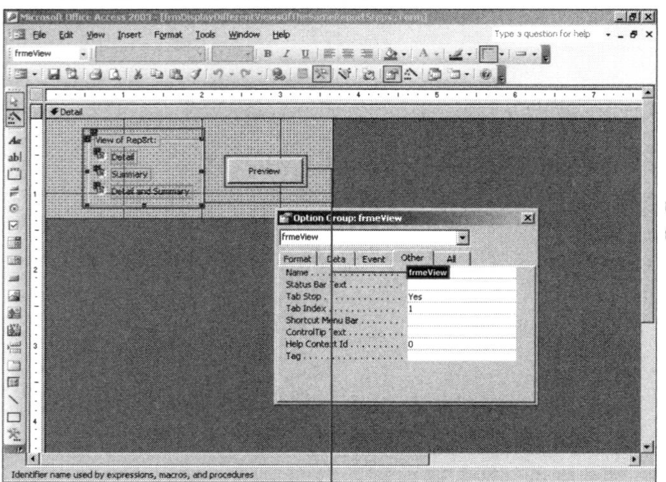

Note: This task creates rptDisplayDifferentViewsOfTheSameReportSteps in AVP-Chapter08.mdb on the CD-ROM.

1 Create an unbound form in Design view.

2 Add a group control, and then name and label it.

■ This example adds a text box named frmeView.

3 Add a command button, and name it in the Caption field.

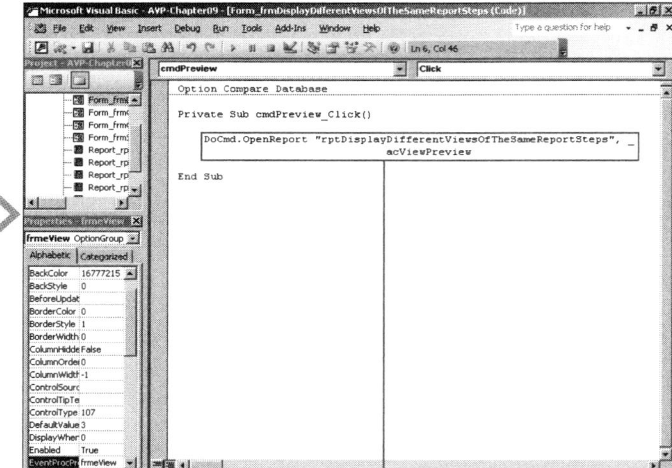

4 Add an event procedure to the On Click event of the command button that you created in step 3.

■ The code editor appears.

5 Type the Docmd.OpenReport command, specifying the name of the report you want to create, and using acViewPreview.

Extra

You can modify the case where just the summary is displayed by eliminating the labels for the column headings. To do this, you must first name the column heading labels, and then set the visibility of the labels to False. The code in the report where frmeView is Summary, which is the Case 2 section of code, would look like this:

```
        Case 2
            Me.Detail.Visible = False

            Me.CompanyName_Label.Visible =
False
            Me.OrderDate_Label.Visible =
False
            Me.OrderID_Label.Visible = False
            Me.Cost_Label.Visible = False
```

Because the Report Wizard creates the original report, it adds the names to the labels. You can view the report rptDisplayDifferentViewsOf TheSameReportExtra in the sample database AVP-Chapter08.mdb, located on the CD-ROM.

When your report appears, you can let the user know which view he is using. You can do this by inserting a Choose() function into the control source of a text box that you add to the report in the Report Header section. The actual Control Source property uses the following syntax:

```
=Choose(Forms!formname!groupoptionname,"Detail","
Summary",_
   "Detail and Summary")
```

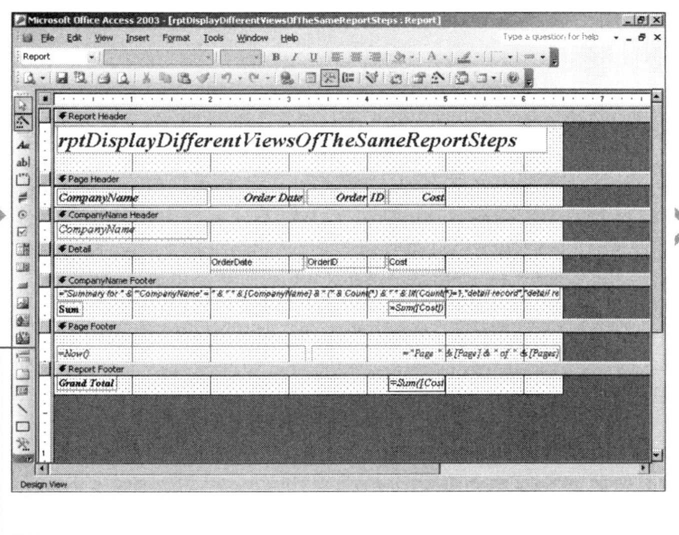

6 Create a report based on the record source you want to use.

■ This example uses the Report Wizard to create the report.

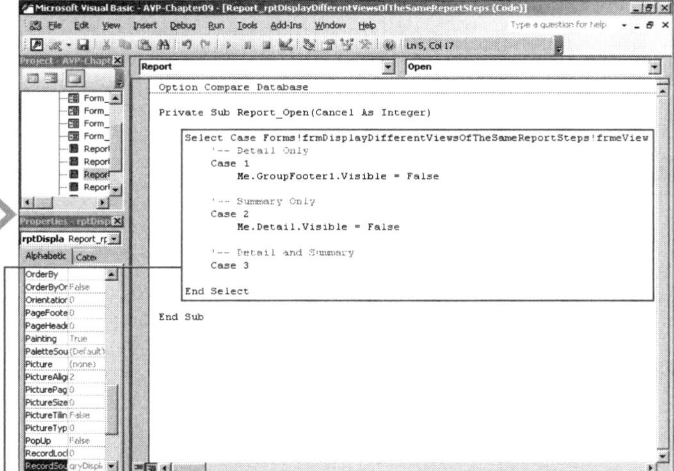

7 Type the code displayed in the figure, adding the name of your form and control for the Select Case line.

8 Save and close your report.

9 Open your new form, select a view you want, and then click the command button to open the report.

■ The report appears in the view that you specified in step 9.

INTRODUCING THE PIVOT TABLE AND PIVOTCHART

Pivot tables and PivotCharts are powerful tools that help you make strategic and tactical decisions. They not only convert transaction data into useful information, but they also allow you to determine the level of detail and how it appears. Pivot tables and PivotCharts can summarize and present data in a format familiar to management and accounting personnel, and then instantly reveal the underlying details that are vital to line management and workers. This ability to dynamically change the data display makes pivot tables and PivotCharts very appealing to end users. Being able to deliver such a versatile tool in custom applications is also a benefit to developers.

VIEWING ONE OR MANY RECORDS

Because you can change the layout and amount of detail that is displayed, you can use pivot tables and PivotCharts to enable a single record source to serve multiple purposes, for either a single user or to meet the diverse needs of many users. If the underlying query contains the appropriate fields, you can do all the filtering, sorting, and cross-tabulating that you want, directly in the pivot table or PivotChart. You can also quickly and easily switch between the PivotTable and PivotChart views — as well as to a more conventional view. This enables you to group and summarize data, or to display more details, a technique called drilling down, as appropriate for your immediate needs. For example: A sales manager can quickly identify the best and worst sales results for a given period, region, or category of sales; a salesperson can instantly confirm that he has received credit for all of his sales; and, a corporate buyer can look at sales trends for a region or product.

MULTIPLE VIEWS OF THE SAME DATA

A pivot table displays data in a grid, the body of which looks similar to a datasheet. Pivot tables allow the summary and analysis of data by the user. A PivotChart transforms the data into a graphical display. Both views enable the user to change the sorting and filtering criteria through the user interface. This is as easy as clicking and dragging a field from one place to another. Pivot tables and PivotCharts are now optional views for tables, queries, forms, in MDBs, as well as SQL server views, and stored procedures in ADPs. You can also save a pivot table or PivotChart as a report; however, report views are not interactive.

The most common type of data to be used for pivot tables and PivotCharts is time-series data, which indicates what has happened over a period of time. In addition to relaying current data, this type of reporting also lends itself well to trend analysis, regression analysis, and other statistical methods that facilitate using historical data to project additional data points into the future.

USES FOR PIVOT TABLES OR PIVOTCHARTS

Uses for Pivot Tables

The power of a pivot table comes from the ability to summarize large amounts of data into an easy-to-read, yet flexible, tabular layout. Pivot tables offer countless ways to summarize, group, filter, and display data. As the name implies, you can pivot the data by switching the fields that you use for the sources of the columns and rows. This allows you to view data in a format and order that may be more familiar to you, or to change to a format that reveals additional insights. For example, a sales manager can group sales data by region, product, or salesperson. The data can also be summarized by region, and then sales staff. It can quickly be changed to summarize the sales by sales staff, and to show the number of sales and total sales, including sales by product or by customer.

It is easy to display subtotals and grand totals for pivot tables. Because you can create subtotals for any grouping of data, a pivot table can easily display totals across the bottom and to the right of grouped data. In accounting, this is known as cross-footing. Cross-footing previously required Crosstab queries, but pivot tables offer an easier and faster way to produce these complex results.

Uses for PivotCharts

A well-designed PivotChart can summarize and reveal the meaning of the data contained in thousands, or even millions, of records. Charts are popular tools in management and marketing. In addition, because they quickly convey information, make vivid comparisons, depict patterns, and show trends, charts are excellent additions to presentations and other documents.

Access offers 12 chart styles, each containing from two to ten substyles, and including some three-dimensional styles. Also, it is easy to use multiple charts for comparing similar data for a series of items. Bar and column charts are among the most common charts you can create. Line graphs are excellent for trend analysis because they can clearly display change over time.

WAYS TO CREATE PIVOT TABLES OR PIVOTCHARTS

There are several ways to create pivot tables and PivotCharts. For example, clicking New on the Forms tab of the database window provides three ways to use a wizard to create a pivot table or PivotChart. The AutoForm: PivotTable and AutoForm: PivotChart features allow you to select one table or query as the record source from which the wizard opens a new form in the view you select. A more versatile option is to use the PivotTable Wizard, which allows you to include fields from multiple tables and queries in the record source. If you create a pivot table using the PivotTable Wizard, you may not need to create a special query for the record source. However, you need a Totals query if you want to display calculation results, such as extended price; or if you want to limit the results to certain records, such as a calendar year or a specific sales period.

In addition to specifically creating and saving a new form as a pivot table or PivotChart, you can also view existing database objects, such as forms, queries, and tables, as pivot tables and PivotCharts.

To create a pivot table from an existing form, you can open the form and then change the view by clicking View on the Menu bar and selecting PivotTable. Alternatively, when you open a form, the View command in the Form View toolbar also provides a drop-down list that includes both PivotTable and PivotChart. You can also right-click the title bar of the open form to select a different view. Similar options are also available for open tables and queries.

Because a well-structured table should contain only one subject, a single table is not usually a good record source for pivot tables and PivotCharts. However, a query typically links multiple tables and queries, and so it is an excellent record source for pivot tables and PivotCharts. You can select a saved query or create a new query and switch the views after placing the fields into the query grid.

USING THE PIVOTTABLE WIZARD

You can use the PivotTable Wizard to select fields from multiple tables and queries that you want to become the record source. This lets you avoid having to save a query just to use it as a record source. After you select the record source, the wizard creates a new blank form and opens it in the PivotTable view. The wizard also creates optional grouping criteria for date fields. When the form opens, you can place the appropriate fields into the various areas of the pivot table.

The main field types for pivot tables and PivotCharts include: Row fields, Column or Category fields, Total or Detail fields, Filter fields, and Series fields.

Row fields become the headings for the left side of the table or chart. The order of the row fields affects the grouping of the data. To track sales by employee, you can place the Employee field in the row area. Column or Category fields contain values that you want to use for columns. These fields appear at the top of a PivotTable and at the bottom of a PivotChart. They often represent a period of time.

Total or Detail fields contain values that you want to display and summarize. These often include fields for orders, invoices, and similar detailed data.

Pivot tables have an area designated for Filter fields. You can also filter records on a field that is not in the Filter fields area.

Series fields contain data that you want to plot, typically against the vertical axis. In charts, the data series appears as a line or a set of bars or columns, and is often identified in the legend. For example, employee sales for one year can appear in one column for each employee, or as a series of four quarterly columns for each employee.

USING THE PIVOTTABLE WIZARD

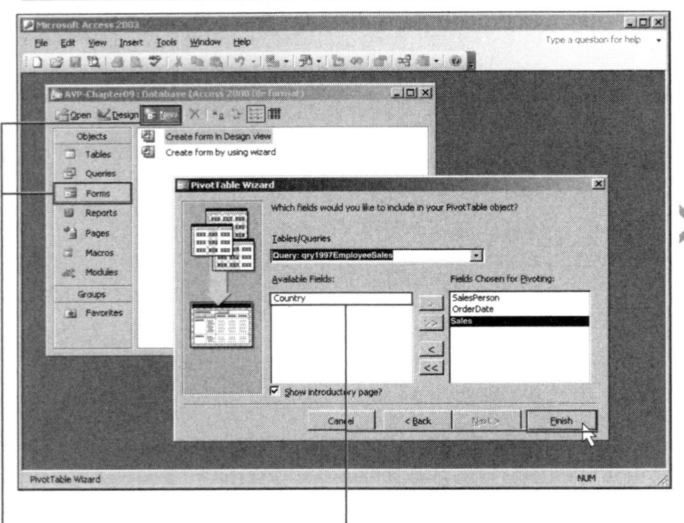

Note: This task uses PTfrmUseThePivotTableWizard in AVP-Chapter09.mdb on the CD-ROM.

1 Click Forms.

2 Click New.

3 In the New Form dialog box, select PivotTable Wizard, select a record source, and then click OK.

■ The PivotTable Wizard appears.

4 Double-click to select fields you want to include in the pivot table.

5 Click Finish.

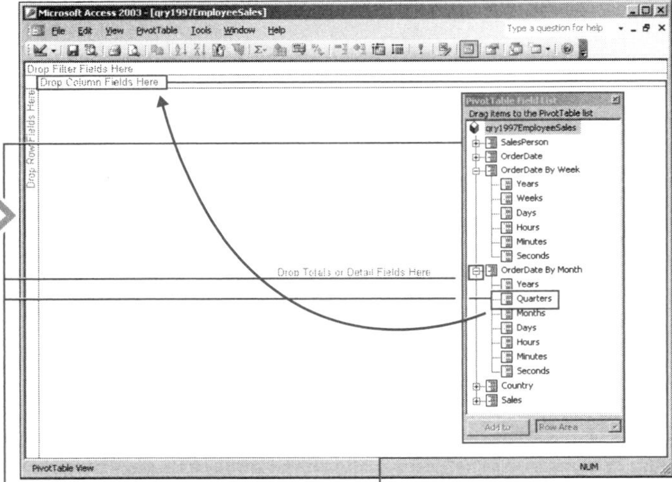

■ The PivotTable appears, with the field list displayed.

6 Click the plus icon to the left of OrderDate By Month to expand the list.

7 Click a date for the column area.

■ This task uses Quarters.

8 Drag the field you want into the table.

9 Click and drag other Row and Column fields from the Field List into the table.

■ A blue border appears around the area in which you place the field.

Apply It

You can use the PivotTable Wizard to select fields from multiple queries and tables. To do this, in the first page of the wizard, move the fields you want from the Available Fields list to the Fields Chosen for Pivoting list. Then, select a different table or query from the drop-down list and move the fields you want from the Available Fields list to the Fields Chosen for Pivoting list. Repeat this process until all the fields you want are included.

Using two Row fields instead of one greatly increases sorting and grouping options. For example, to report sales by a national marketing staff, you can use Employees and States. This way, in addition to seeing the total sales for each period, you can also see region-specific data. You can switch the row hierarchy to see how the sales staff ranks within a region. You can also dramatically change the emphasis by switching a column for a row. This is known as pivoting the table.

When you create a pivot table, the Totals cells remain empty. To calculate totals, click one of the Detail headings, and click the AutoCalc button (Σ). When you click the SubTotal button from the right-click menu, Access either hides or displays subtotals.

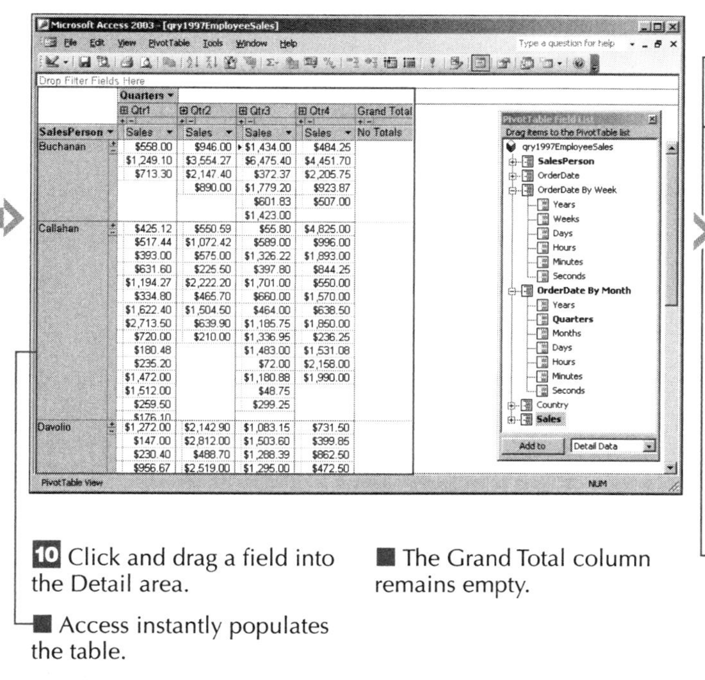

10 Click and drag a field into the Detail area.

■ Access instantly populates the table.

■ The Grand Total column remains empty.

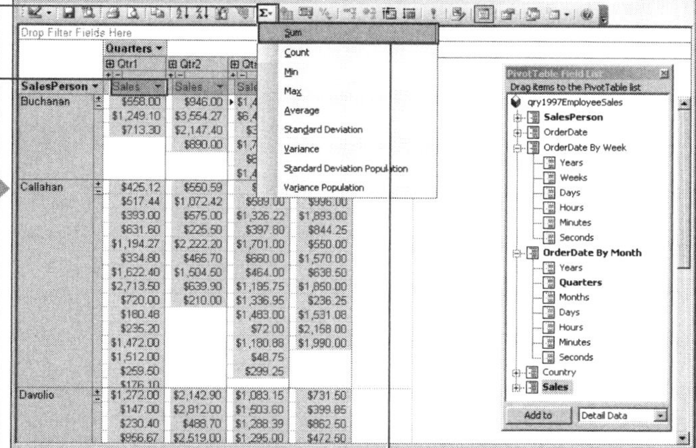

11 To create Totals, click a Column heading, and then click the AutoCalc button.

■ This task uses Sales as the Totals heading.

12 In the drop-down list, select Sum.

■ Access generates totals for sales and other numeric fields.

13 Save the form.

ADD A FILTER TO THE PIVOT TABLE

By default, the pivot table summarizes all data in the record source. By using a filter, you can limit the data that the pivot table summarizes and displays. For example, a top executive in a company may want to see the data for worldwide sales, while a regional manager may only want to see data for that region. The manager can limit the data that appears by moving the Country column to the filter area in the upper-left corner of the pivot table.

When you move a field to the filter area, it disappears from the row or column area. To filter by values in a field, you can click the filter drop-down arrow by the field name. From the list, you can select (All), which toggles between selecting and deselecting all the items in the list. After clearing the check boxes, you can select one or more values that you want to be represented in the table. By default, Access allows the selection of multiple values. However, when a field is in the filter area, you can also use the property window of that field to set it to allow only a single selection. This enables users to quickly switch between items without having to clear the check box.

You can also filter on fields that are in the rows and columns of a table. This allows a field to maintain a position in the table, while it also serves as a filter. The advantage of leaving the field in the grid when you make multiple selections is that the data still displays for each value. However, if you select multiple items in a field in the filter area, only the aggregate values display. In filtered fields, the filter drop-down arrow by the field name appears blue.

ADD A FILTER TO THE PIVOT TABLE

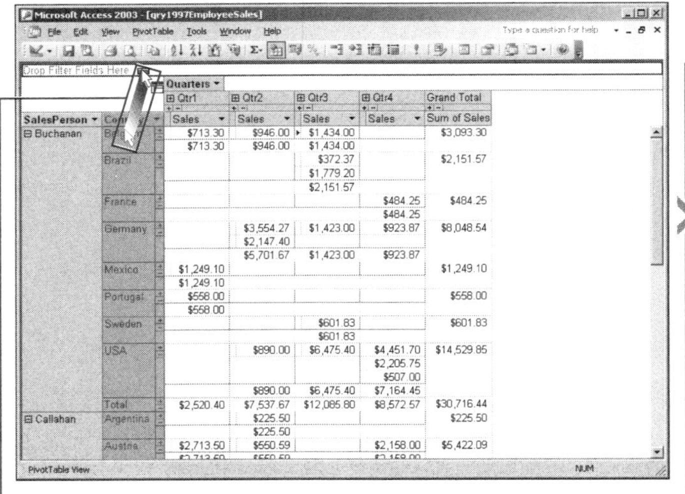

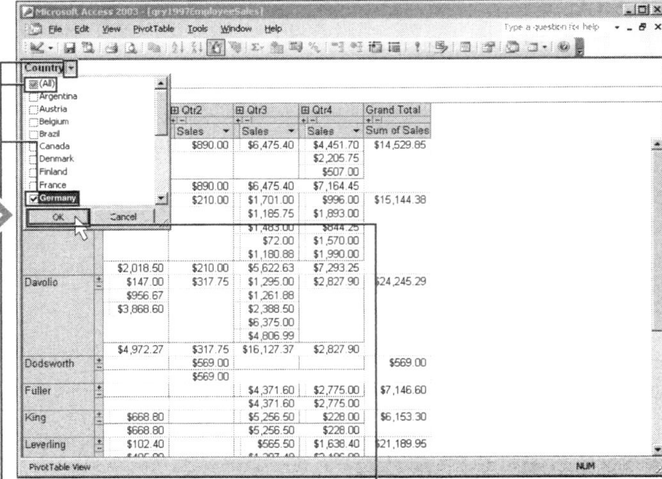

Note: This task uses the form PTfrmAddAFilterToThePivot Table in the database AVP-Chapter09.mdb on the CD-ROM.

1 Open a pivot table.

2 Click and drag a field to the Filter Fields area.

■ The blue border around the Filter Fields area, and the blue line on the table indicator to the right of the cursor, indicate where the field will appear.

3 Click the filter drop-down arrow in the label of the Filter field.

4 Check the (All) check box to deselect everything.

5 Click the check box for another item.

6 Click OK.

■ Because you selected only one item for your filter, the name of that item, Germany in this example, appears below the field label.

Apply It

You can use filters on multiple rows and columns to make it easier to locate and emphasize specific information. To add a filter to a row or column, click the filter drop-down arrow to the right of the heading. You can check the check box next to (All) to switch between selecting and deselecting all the values in that field.

Deselect everything (☐ changes to ☑), and then select three or four items from one field. Repeat this process for another row or column. Access limits the data that displays to the items you select. The results are more visually dramatic if you filter on rows and columns at the same time.

When you want to limit the data displayed on the pivot table, you can do so easily. Open a pivot table that has at least two fields in the row area. Ensure that you have not applied filters or hidden data. Click and drag the row field on the right to the Filter Fields area at the top of the table. Even though the totals do not change, there is now only one record for each value in the remaining row field. By moving the field to the Filter Fields area, you lose the ability to see the line item detail for that field.

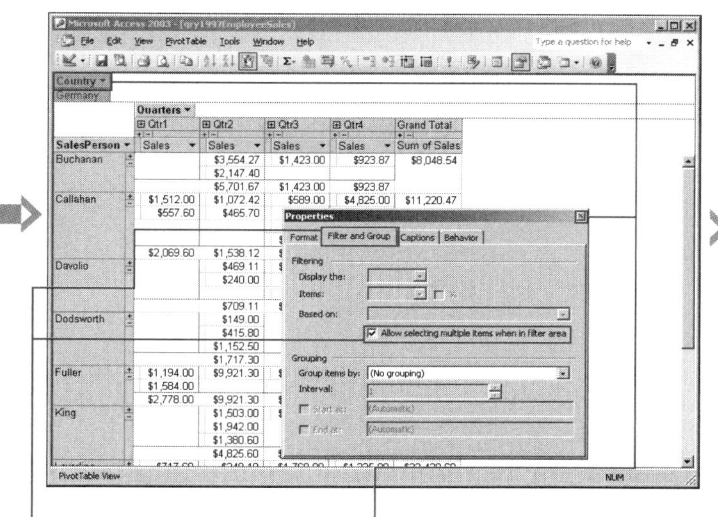

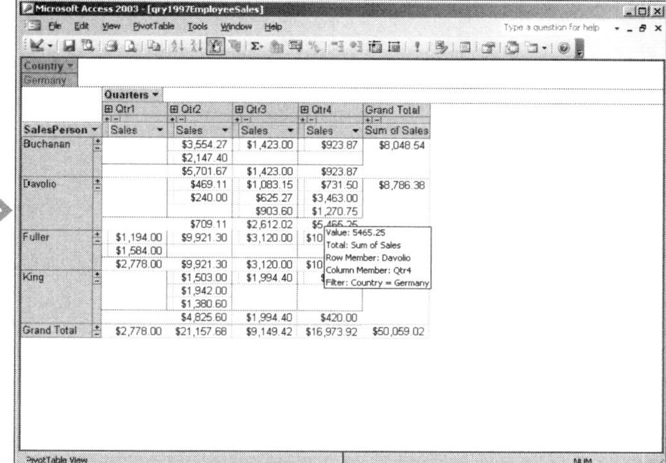

EXPEDITE FILTERING ON SINGLE SELECTIONS

7 Right-click the label of the Filter field you want to modify, and click Properties.

8 In the Properties dialog box, click the Filter and Group tab.

9 Check this option.

10 Click the Close button.

■ The filter drop-down arrow on the filter field label appears blue because an item is selected.

11 Click the filter drop-down arrow to select a different item from the drop-down list, and click OK.

12 Click the filter drop-down arrow in the Row Field.

13 In the drop-down list, check the (All) check box to deselect everything (☐ changes to ☑).

14 Click the check boxes for the other items you want (☐ changes to ☑).

15 Click OK.

16 Save and close the pivot table.

■ When you reopen the pivot table, it retains the layout and filters.

USING TOP/BOTTOM VALUES AND OTHER FILTERS

You can use advanced filtering and grouping techniques to control what data displays, and how it displays, in the pivot table. In addition to filtering data based on the records in the field, such as selecting specific employees, you can limit the records to the top or bottom values based on counts or percentages. For example, based on the sum of sales, you can identify the top two sales people for each quarter, or identify the sales regions that are in the bottom five percent. In addition to selecting records based on their ranking, you can also group items based on prefix characters, just as you can for a report.

You can specify top or bottom values by clicking the Show Top/Bottom Items button on the toolbar, or through the property sheet of the field. When you click the Show Top/Bottom Items button, you can select either Show Only The Top or Show Only The Bottom in the drop-down list, and then a count or percentage from the list; you can also type a value. The display instantly changes to reflect your choices. Clicking the Show Top/Bottom Items button and selecting Show All removes that filter and refreshes the display.

You can also customize the record set display by changing the properties of selected fields. To do so, you can open the Properties dialog box, right-click the field in the pivot table for which you want to specify filter criteria, and click Properties in the drop-down list. You can then click the Filter and Group tab, change the options you want, and close the property sheet.

You can work with filters by clicking the Show Top/Bottom Items button or the AutoFilter button, or by right-clicking the selected column heading and clicking the filter effect you want in the drop-down list.

USING TOP/BOTTOM VALUES AND OTHER FILTERS

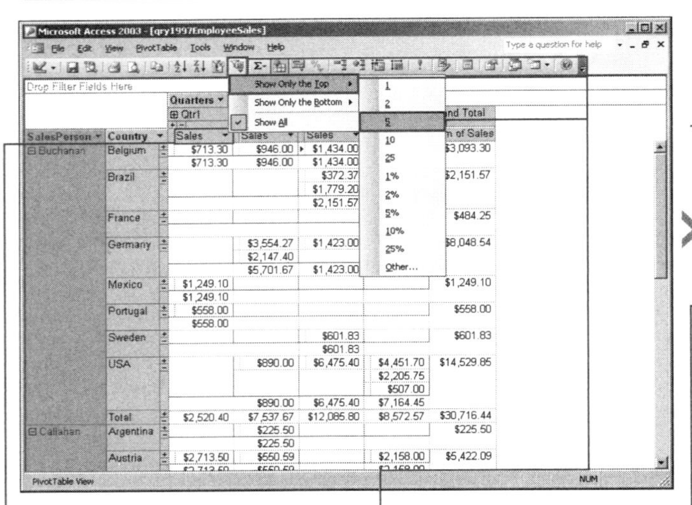

Note: This task uses PTfrmSpecifyTopBottomValuesandOtherAdvancedFilters in AVP-Chapter09.mdb on the CD-ROM.

1 Open a pivot table.

2 Click a Row Field heading to select the row.

3 Click the Top/Bottom button, and select the filter option you want from the drop-down list.

■ This example limits the display to the top five sales values based on the detail value.

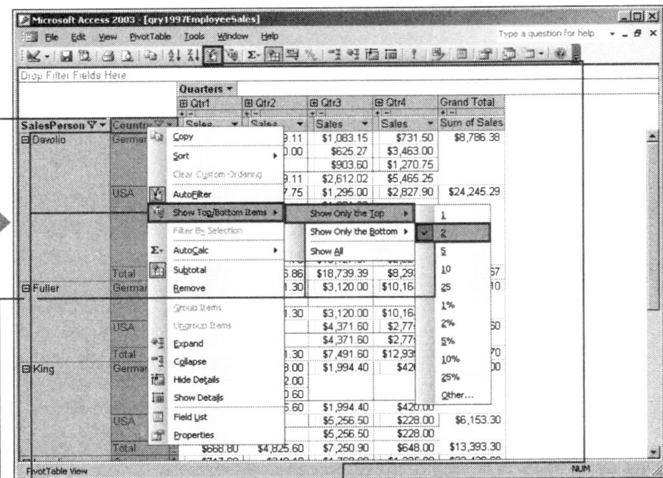

4 To further limit the display, right-click the Field heading of the secondary row and select Show Top/Bottom Items from the drop-down list.

5 Select the filter options you want.

■ This example shows only the top two items.

■ The filters are on the row field labels.

6 Click the AutoFilter button.

■ Access turns the current filter settings off.

Apply It

The PivotTable Wizard allows users to select fields from multiple queries and tables. It also allows you to include only selected fields rather than all the fields from the underlying object. In order to include fields from more than one table or query, select the desired fields from the first source and move them to the Fields Chosen for Pivoting box. Next, choose a different table or query from the drop-down list and select the desired fields. Continue this process until all the necessary fields are included. Notice that if the same field name comes from more than one table or query, the name of the table or query is listed with the field name.

Adding a second field to the row can greatly increase the options for sorting and grouping the data. For example, to report sales by a national marketing staff, you might also add the region field. That way, in addition to seeing each salesperson's total sales for each period, you could also see how each salesperson was doing in each region. You could also swap the hierarchy and see how the sales staff ranked within a region. You can then retrieve the top values for either field, and have a different set of records returned.

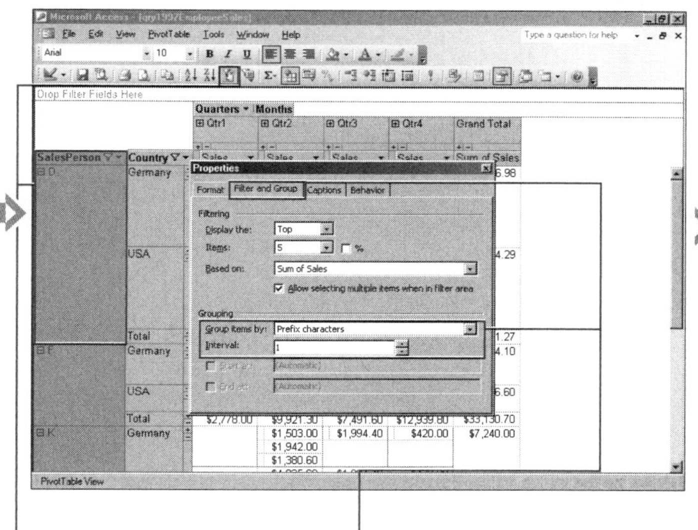

7 Click the AutoFilter button to turn the filters back on.

8 Right-click a field row heading, and then select Properties from the drop-down list.

■ The Properties dialog box appears.

9 Click the Filter and Group tab.

■ The existing filter is defined.

10 Select Prefix characters to group by, and an interval of 1.

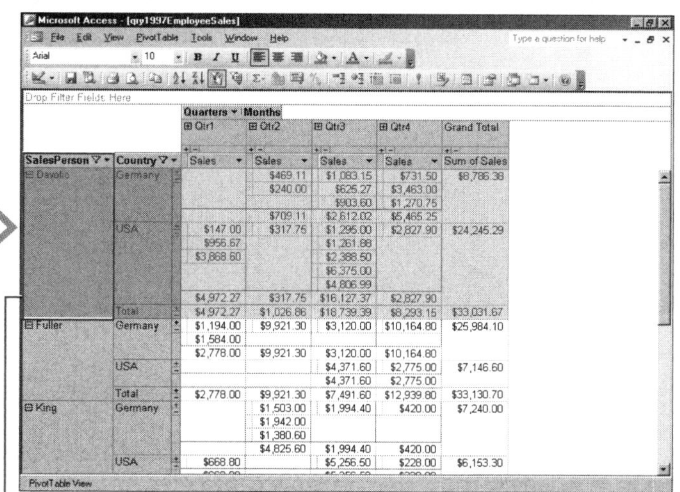

■ Access applies the new setting. Leave the Properties dialog box open.

11 In the same Row field heading, click the filter drop-down arrow.

■ The items are represented by letters, and all items are checked, although only the top five items appear.

12 Click Cancel.

■ The filter list closes for the field.

13 In the filter field properties, set the Group Items by property to No Grouping, and click Close.

■ The Properties dialog box closes.

DISPLAY SUMMARY/DETAIL DATA

You can use pivot tables in many different ways to filter, summarize, display, and hide data. The main difference between filtering and hiding data is that Access does not include filtered items in the aggregate totals in the table, while hidden items are still included in the calculations. When details are merely hidden, they are not removed or excluded.

There are several ways to display and hide data. One way is to use the plus and minus icons that appear on many of the labels. These icons indicate that you can display or hide details, for a selected record, row, or column. You can also display or hide data using the Show Details and Hide Details buttons on the toolbar, and by right-clicking an item and selecting Show or Hide from the drop-down list. The fastest way to display or hide lower-level details of a specific item is to select the item and click the plus or minus icons to the far right of the item label. To display or hide all the lower-level details for a row or column, you can select the row or column and click the Expand or Collapse button on the toolbar.

You can create a compact display by selecting each row heading and then collapsing the data. If there are multiple row fields, collapsing the far left field immediately summarizes the data and displays only one row for each value in the main field. This can provide a powerful executive summary that you can quickly access for more details. For example, you can right-click any value in the datasheet. When you select Show Details from the drop-down list, Access displays the underlying information for the value you selected.

DISPLAY SUMMARY/DETAIL DATA

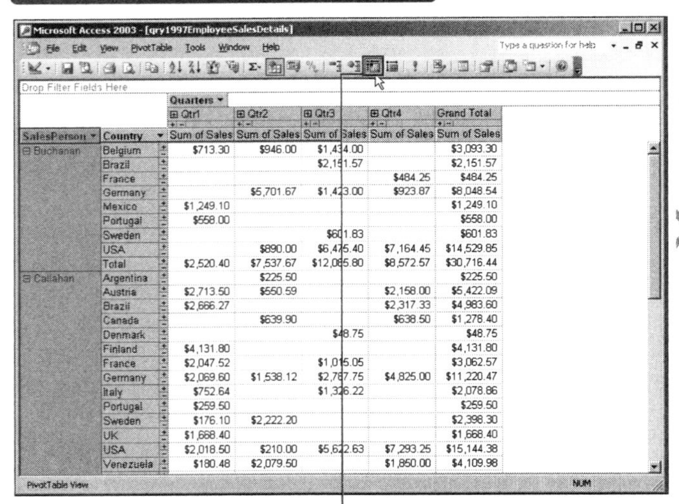

Note: This task uses the form PTfrmDisplaySummaryDetailData in the database AVP-Chapter09.mdb on the CD-ROM.

1 Open a pivot table with two fields in the row area.

2 Click the primary column heading to select the entire column.

3 Click the Hide Details button.

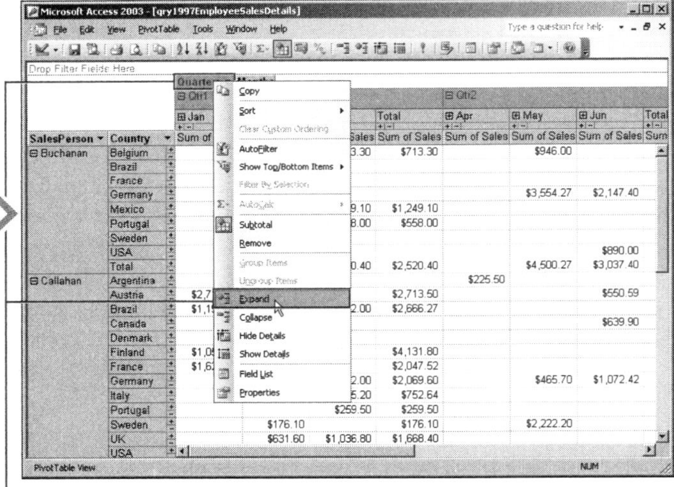

■ The table now summarizes the data by the secondary row column.

4 Right-click a column heading.

5 Click Expand.

■ Access automatically provides options for the date fields to group by day, week, month, quarterly, and even by hour.

■ By selecting Expand in the drop-down list, you are adding the next logical level of detail. For example, the level of detail goes from quarters to months, and from months to days.

Apply It

When you want to display or hide data, you should think of the direction in which your changes will occur. Expanding and collapsing parts of a table typically increases or decreases the number of rows that are displayed, respectively. For example, you may have two fields in the Row area, with the left field as the primary grouping. For each item in the left field, there may be several items in the right field. When you collapse the row on the left, it rolls up to display one row per primary row heading value. Thus, collapsing removes lower-level grouping. The Show and Hide Details commands display or hide columns, but do not affect the display of the row.

To demonstrate how you can use these tools together, open a pivot table that has two fields in the row area and only one row in the column area. Expand both rows by clicking the row heading. Collapse the far left row so that there is only one row for each field value by clicking the column heading. Show details for that row by clicking the Show Details button. Depending on the underlying data, several rows and columns may appear in the table. However, the records still only have one level of grouping and subtotals.

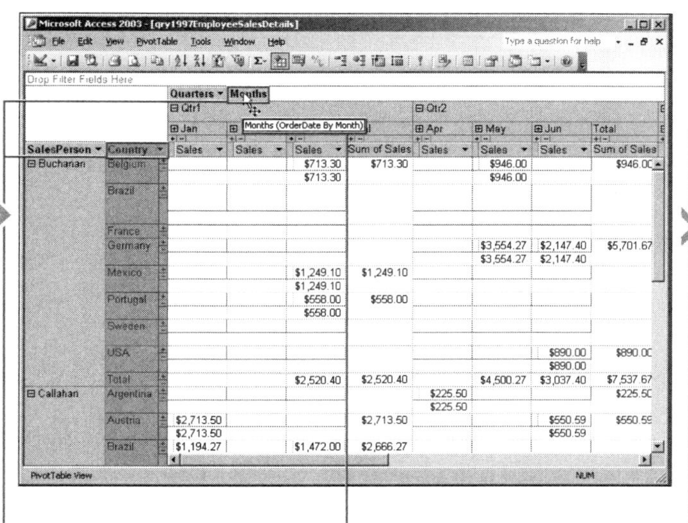

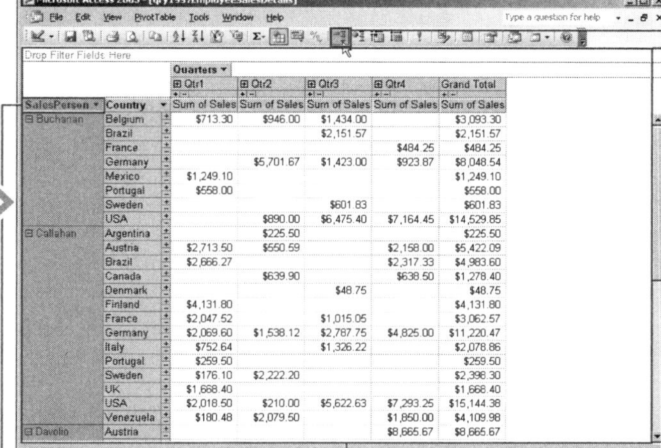

6 Click the secondary row heading to select the row.

7 Click the Show Details button.

■ As much detailed information as the underlying data provides appears.

8 Click the secondary column heading.

■ ↖ changes to ✥.

■ Access displays all available detailed information about the row.

9 Drag the heading from the table.

■ Access removes a level of detail from the table.

10 Right-click the primary row heading, and click Hide Detail in the drop-down list.

■ Access summarizes the data using the secondary row.

11 Click the primary row heading.

12 Click the Collapse button.

■ Access displays a summary level table with only one row per primary row heading value.

13 Save and close the form.

CREATE A SIMPLE PIVOTCHART FORM

While pivot tables allow you to research data, you can use PivotCharts to determine and convey larger trends to conduct trend analyses. The process for creating a PivotChart is similar to that for a pivot table. You must ensure that the necessary data is in the record source, which is typically a query.

The easiest way to create a PivotChart is to open a form that you have saved as a pivot table and to switch to the PivotChart view. This technique enables you to open the PivotChart with the same field placement and data that existed in the pivot table when it was last saved. The three most popular ways to switch the form views are: to open the drop-down list by right-clicking the title bar of the open form; to click the View command in the View button drop-down list; and, to click the View button on the main Access Menu bar. All three methods include PivotChart as an option.

You can also use the PivotChart Wizard to create a PivotChart based on a query or table. From the Forms tab of the database window, you can click New and select AutoForm: PivotChart. When you select a query or table, the wizard opens a new blank PivotChart. The form appears, and Access displays the Chart Field List. You must put fields into the chart before it can display any data. This process is very similar to that of creating a pivot table, where the column fields for pivot tables become the Series fields for PivotCharts.

CREATE A SIMPLE PIVOTCHART FORM

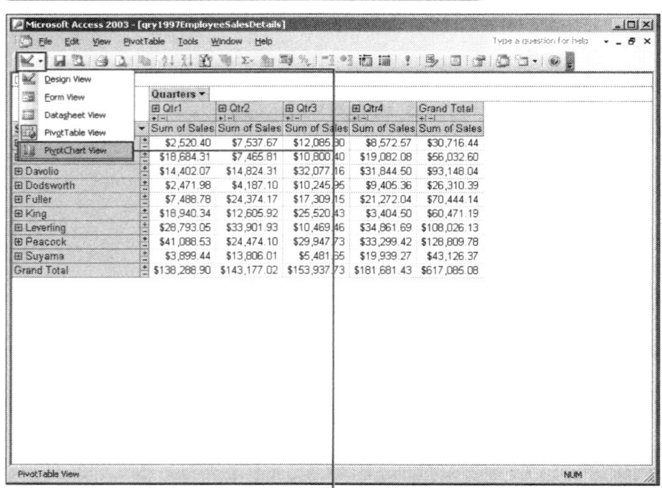

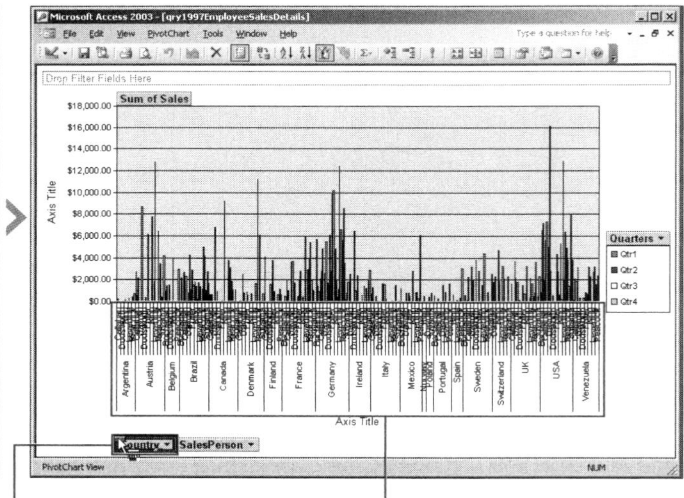

USING THE VIEW COMMAND

Note: This task uses the form PCfrmCreateASimplePivotChartFromPT in the database AVP-Chapter09.mdb on the CD-ROM.

1 Open an existing PivotTable form.

2 Click the View button.

3 Click PivotChart View from the drop-down list.

■ The column chart appears, displaying the data from the pivot table. Although there are two column fields, the details from the second column do not display.

4 Click and drag the Secondary Category to the left of the Primary Category.

■ Two levels appear on the x-axis of the chart.

5 Click the close button to close the form.

Apply It

By default, when a PivotChart opens, only the heading of the series or legend is displayed. You may find it useful to display the legend for most charts. Intuitively, you may right-click the heading to view the legend. However, right-clicking the heading offers options for working with the data, such as sort, expand, and collapse, rather than an option to display the legend. To display the legend, click the Show Legend button (▤) on the PivotChart toolbar. Access switches the display of the legend on or off. When the legend is displayed, Access highlights the Show Legend button in orange.

Instead of clicking and dragging fields into tables and charts, you can select the name of the field you want to add, and use the Add To button at the bottom of the Field List. Click the field you want to add. Click the drop-down list at the lower-right corner of the Field List, and select where you want to use the field. Click the Add To button. You can also use this technique to move fields from one area of a PivotChart or pivot table to another.

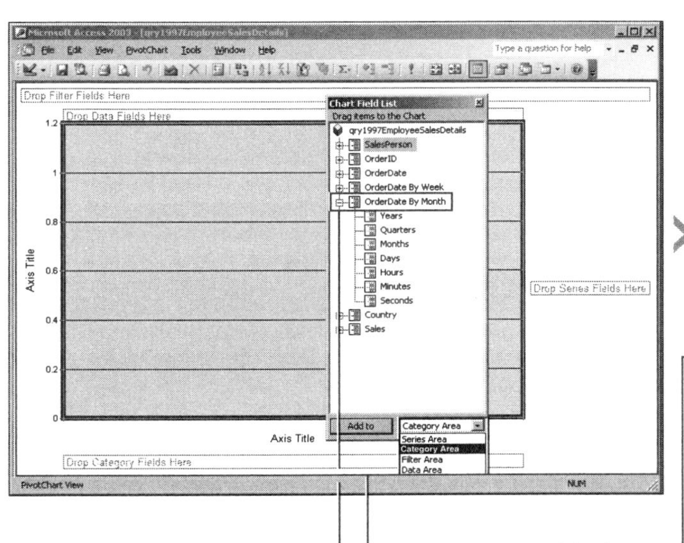

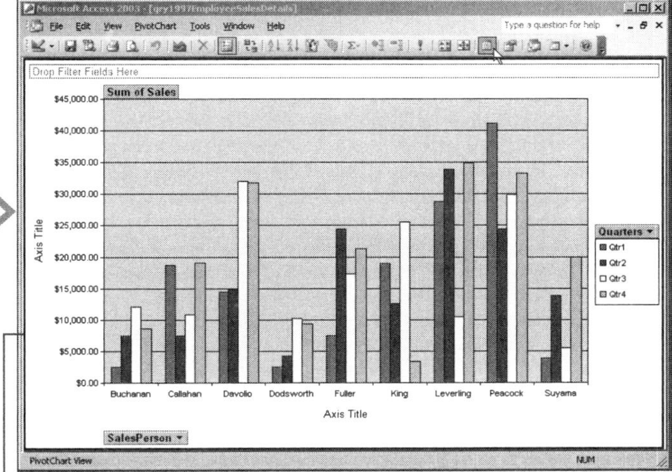

USING AUTOFORM: PIVOTCHART

1 In the database window, click Forms, New, and then AutoForm: PivotChart.

2 Double-click to select a query as the record source, and click OK.

■ Access creates a blank PivotChart, and it opens with the Field List displayed.

3 Click the plus icon to expand the OrderDate By Month list on the Field List.

4 Click and drag fields from the Fields list to the Series, Category, and Data areas.

■ Access creates the PivotChart.

5 Save and close the form.

DRILL, FILTER, AND GET DATA ON PIVOTCHARTS

PivotCharts have many of the same capabilities as pivot tables for summarizing and analyzing data. However, PivotCharts offer Drill Into and Drill Out features in addition to the Expand and Collapse features. You can only use the Drill Into and Drill Out features when you select a category item. The Drill Into features can have the same effect as filtering records. In fact, if you right-click a category label or column within a bar chart and then use the Drill Into feature, the records are filtered by that item. You can also select a category and use the Drill Into and Drill Out buttons on the toolbar.

PivotChart categories have a similar grouping hierarchy to PivotTable rows. The leftmost field is the primary grouping, and the categories move down in rank as they move to the right. When you Drill Into an item from a primary category, Access filters the records on that item and creates a chart showing the series information broken down by the secondary category. One of the benefits of automatically filtering a chart on a selected item is that a chart can quickly become unreadable when it displays too many details.

As with pivot tables, you can use conditional filtering and Autofiltering on PivotCharts. When you turn Autofiltering off, Access displays all data for all of the fields. Autofiltering retains the filter settings, so that when you turn it back on, it hides and displays the data in the way it previously appeared. It is important to turn AutoFiltering on and off at the appropriate times. A field retains filter settings when you move it within a PivotChart, or even out of and back to a PivotChart. You can quickly determine which fields are being filtered by looking for the filter drop-down arrows on field labels.

DRILL, FILTER AND GET DATA ON PIVOTCHARTS

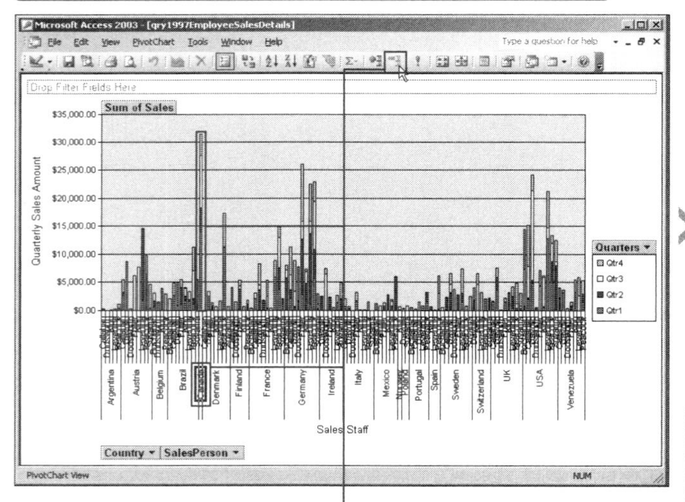

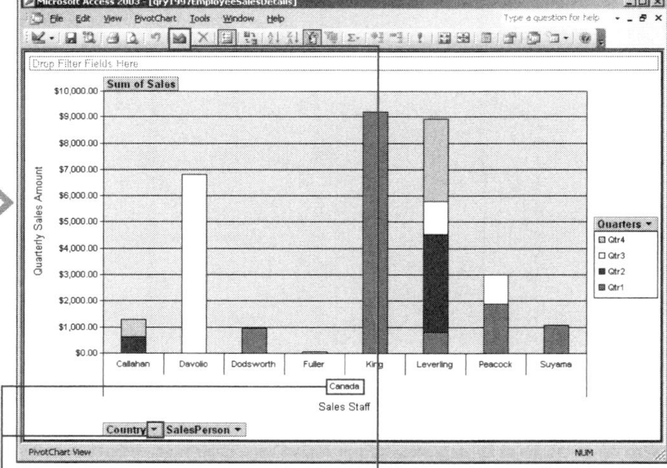

Note: This task uses PCfrmDrillingFilteringAndGettingDataOnPivotCharts in AVP-Chapter09.mdb on the CD-ROM.

1 Create a new PivotChart.

2 Arrange the hierarchy to create a complex chart.

3 Click a primary category item.

4 Click the Collapse button.

■ The record you selected collapses, creating a spike.

5 Right-click the spike, and select Drill Into.

■ The chart has a label that identifies the filter value — in this example, it is Canada. The chart breaks down the data, using the secondary category.

■ The filter drop-down arrow is blue for the primary category label.

6 Click the ChartType button, and then choose the new chart type.

■ By using a stacked column chart, Access depicts the series information with the colors on each column.

Apply It

After you Drill Out on a data series, you must use the Expand feature rather than the Drill Into feature to return to the previous chart layout. Open a column-style PivotChart with two category fields. Right-click one of the columns and click the Drill Out button (). Only the category with the selected column is affected. Right-click that column again and click the Drill Into button (). Rather than returning to the original display, Access now filters the data by the category and breaks it down into subcategories. To return to the original display, you can click the filter drop-down arrow for the Field button, check the All mark in the drop-down list (☐ changes to ☑), and click OK to remove the filter.

Right-click the same column and select Collapse from the drop-down list. The display appears the same as it was after you used the Drill Out feature. Right-click the column, and select Expand from the drop-down list. The chart returns to the original layout.

You can quickly display additional detail information by moving the mouse so that it hovers over a column. Access generates a pop-up window displaying the values of the series, the categories, and the appropriate totals.

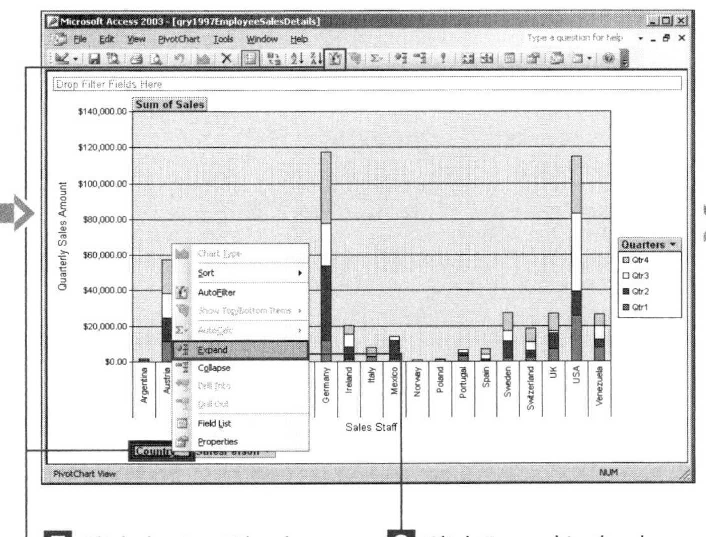

7 Click the AutoFilter button to remove the filters.

8 Right-click the primary category.

9 Click Expand in the drop-down list.

■ This example displays the quarterly and annual sales for each country.

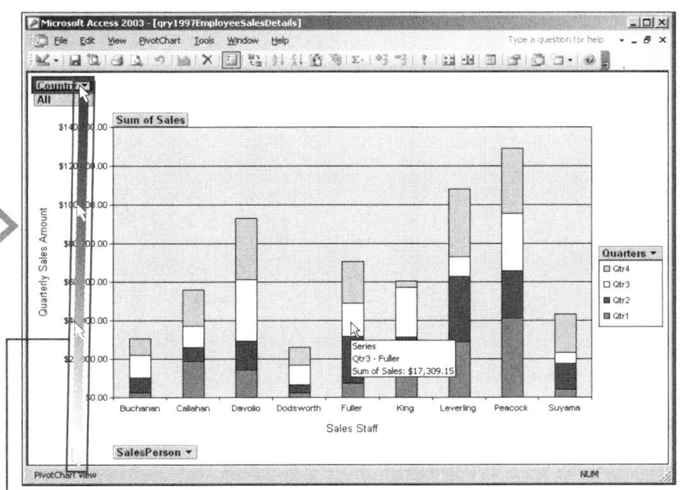

10 Click and drag the Primary Category into the Filter area.

■ This example displays the quarterly and annual sales by sales staff.

IMPORT OR LINK DATA

The ability to import and export data to and from many sources is a feature that contributes to the popularity of Access. In the past, when dBase and Paradox were competing applications, Access users could import and export data to and from those products with very little difficulty. Another revolutionary feature in those days was the ability to "link" tables from these other products.

With Access, you can link to other file types, such as Foxpro, SQL Server, and other Relational Data Management Systems, or RDMS, as well as import data from those file types. There are differences between linking and importing your data.

LINK DATA

When you link data, you are creating a reference from the database you are in, to the database, or file, where the data actually resides. When you create a link, an arrow appears in the icon for the file to which you are linked. You can perform most of the same tasks on linked data that you can on data that resides in your Access database. However, you cannot modify the structure of the linked table from your database; to do this, you must open the original file or database in which the data resides.

With linked data, when you modify fields and records, those changes appear in the original file to which you linked. Links are useful when you work with legacy data. Legacy data refers to data that is maintained by older systems, usually written in a programming language different from the one in which you are developing the current application. For example, a Medical Office Management system may have been built years ago using the FoxPro database application, another of Microsoft's databases. Now, the company that built the database system no longer exists, and while the old system can still perform most of the tasks that the administrative staff needs, there are new reports that you need to generate. You can create an Access database, link the tables in the old system to your database, and create new reports with Access.

You can split data from the database application, thereby creating two Access databases: a front-end database containing the application elements, and a back-end database containing data. Access even supplies a utility called the Database Splitter utility that facilitates this process. For more information about this utility, and the utility that you can use to manage linked tables, see the section "Split and Link an Access Database."

Along with Access tables, you can link other types of files, such as Excel spreadsheets, text files, and even lists from Windows Team Services. You can also link to SQL Server databases.

IMPORT DATA

Importing data is a little more straightforward. When you import data into Access, you make a copy of the data from the source file this copy now resides in Access. Any changes you make to the data do not appear in the original file.

You can import data from all the same file types to which you can link, and even a few more.

EXPORT DATA FROM ACCESS

In addition to being able to link and import data, with Access you can also export data. When you export data, you make a copy of the data into a specified format. As a result, this data is no longer connected to your Access database. If you want to refresh the data in your database using the exported data, you must re-import this data.

METHODS OF EXPORTING DATA

You can export any Access object. The way to export data from Access depends on the object.

Export from the File Menu

You can usually click File ➪ Export. Access asks you to choose the file format to which you want to export, and to where you want to export the data.

Mail Database Objects

You can click File ➪ Send To to attach tables to e-mail messages. You can use VBA code to do this, by incorporating DoCmd.SendObject.

Automation

You can use code to export portions of data, instead an entire table or query. For example, you can insert specific fields into a Word document without exporting the entire record, or multiple records, from Access.

FILE FORMATS FOR EXPORTING DATA

When exporting data, you can choose from the file formats listed below:

FILE FORMAT	DESCRIPTION
Access	Microsoft Access. If you specify a new database, Access creates the database and the object.
dBase	Database created originally by Borland. One of the first PC-based relational file formats.
Excel	Microsoft Excel. You can create worksheets from tables and queries in Access.
HTML	You can create static Web pages and include template pages for a standard appearance
Lotus	Now owned by IBM, Lotus is a spreadsheet format.
Paradox	A PC-based relational database file format.
Sharepoint Team Services	Collaborative Web site software for managing documents, projects, and data.
Text Files	Standard ASCII text file format. Nearly universal file format. Most systems read text files.
Windows SharePoint Services	New collaborative Web site software for managing documents, projects, and data.
Microsoft Active Server Pages	Create dynamic Web pages. Unlike static pages, where the data is not refreshed, you can refresh this data.
Microsoft IIS 1-2	A file format for creating dynamic Web pages.
Rich Text Format	A standard file format used by Word, which allows special codes for fonts.
Microsoft Word Merge	Creates a text file in the format compatible with the Word mail merge feature.
XML	The latest standard in data formats. Based on the HTML file standard, it allows data to be used by independent systems on and off the Web.
ODBC Databases	Open Database Connectivity allows third-party database providers to create drivers for their products. Examples are the SQL Server and Oracle.

USING WINDOWS SHAREPOINT SERVICES

Windows SharePoint Services, or WSS, is a fairly new technology that allows companies to create Web sites that are based on templates. These Web sites are specifically created for team collaboration. With a WSS site you can:

- Share documents
- Create lists
- Maintain discussions
- Perform surveys
- Maintain picture collections
- Create additional sub-sites
- Schedule meetings
- Track events, announcements, and tasks
- Perform many more tasks

Users can log on to the site, and depending on which permissions are set, these users can add items, make changes to existing documents, or join in a newsgroup discussion. Microsoft alone has over 80,000 internal WSS sites in use for team projects.

After the initial WSS site is created, modifying it to fit your needs is easy. After the administrator creates the site and gives you the necessary permissions, the administrator is no longer necessary. You can modify almost any aspect of the site that you need to without help from the administrator.

If you want to add functionality to your Web site, you can use libraries of features called Web Parts. While creating Web Parts requires development skill — because you create them using ASP.NET — you can use an existing Web Part by simply clicking and dragging it onto the Web site page to which you want to add it.

AN EXAMPLE OF A WINDOWS SHAREPOINT SERVICES SITE

An example of a WSS site can be a class site for students. Groups of students can work on various research projects in teams by having a subsite for each research project. For each project, they can assign tasks to the individual students, and schedule study or group project times. They can also keep all the working documents for the research projects on the site, and have all team members review the documents for modification. They can track various links to Web sites where they find research information, as well as supporting documents and pictures. They can also receive their grades on the site.

METHODS OF USING ACCESS WITH WSS

The majority of interaction between Access and WSS is the transferring of data between Access tables and WSS site lists.

From a WSS Site

While in the WSS site there are a few ways you can utilize Access. From a WSS site you can: export WSS site lists to Access tables; create links in Access to WSS site lists; and create Access reports based on WSS site lists.

From within Access

From within Access you can: export an Access table to a WSS site list; import a list from a WSS site into an Access table; and link to a WSS site list.

USING OFFICE PRODUCTS WITH WSS

All the products in Office 2003 work well with WSS. With some of the Office products, such as Word, Excel, Publisher, and PowerPoint, you can upload documents to a site, after which the site performs history tracking with check-in and check-out features.

With a new product called InfoPath, you can create a form and then upload the form to your WSS site. Users can then open your form on the site, and users can update the data through the form. You can even upload notes that you create in the new Office product, OneNote.

INTRODUCING XML

You can use the Extensible Markup Language, or XML, file format to either import or export data. XML is quickly becoming a standard for not only exchanging data between business systems, but also as base storage for some of the systems. An XML document can consist of a single table of information, or an entire database. Where you use HyperText Markup Language, or HTML, for displaying information, XML defines the data.

FILES THAT MAKE UP AN XML DOCUMENT

Unlike other file formats, XML documents can comprise more than one file. The table lists the extensions and descriptions of the files that are created when you export data to the XML format. Note that if you do not tell Access to format the data when exporting, Access does not create the last two files, XSL and HTM.

EXTENSION	DESCRIPTION
.xml	The XML data document. This is a static snapshot of the data.
.xsd	The schema file. This schema was based on the persisted table or query, and is in the W3C XSD standard.
.xsl	The presentation document. The XSL document specifies how the data in the XML is to be displayed, transforming the data for presentation purposes.
.htm	The final result. This combines the XML data files and XSL presentation together for use on the Web.

AN XML FILE

Much like HTML, XML files are made up of beginning and ending tags. Tags specify where to begin and end various commands. In HTML, they are used for formatting commands; in XML, for data elements, such as when fields and records start and stop. Below is an XML file created by exporting tblDVDs. This example is only the XML file: It contains the actual data. The specifications for the data are in the XSD file. Presentation specifications for the data are in the XSL and HTM files.

```
xml version="1.0" encoding="UTF-8" ?>

- <dataroot xmlns:od="urn:schemas-
microsoft-com:officedata"
generated="2003-07-22T12:55:53">

- <tblDVDs>

  <DVDID>1</DVDID>

  <DVDTitle>Memento</DVDTitle>

  </tblDVDs>

- <tblDVDs>

  <DVDID>2</DVDID>

  <DVDTitle>Aliens</DVDTitle>

  </tblDVDs>

- <tblDVDs>

  </dataroot>
```

Microsoft enhanced many of the XML features in Access. For example, smart tags use XML for accomplishing their tasks. You can import XML into or export XML from tables or queries. You can work in VBA using the Document Object Interface, or DOM. Data Access Pages use XML for creating islands of data from Access.

SPLIT AND LINK AN ACCESS DATABASE

When you are working in a database by yourself, it is not necessary to split the database. However, if you are working with other users in a database, and that database is on a file server, then for performance and integrity reasons you can split the database into two databases, the front-end and the back-end. The front-end contains the application elements — forms, reports, modules, and queries — and the back-end contains the data.

Access provides a utility called Database Splitter, which you can find under Database Utilities on the Tools menu. This utility asks you what you want to name the new database and where to save the new database. Access creates the database, copies all the tables into the new database, removes the tables from the original database, now the front-end database, and then creates a link to the tables in the new database.

If you look at the tables in your front-end database, you can see arrows on the icons for the tables. You can place the front-end database in a folder on the computer of each user, and place the back-end database in a folder on the server.

Because the path of linked tables is hard coded in the link of the front-end database, if you ever move the back-end database to a new location, such as a new server, you must re-link the tables to reflect the new location. You can re-link the tables with the Linked Table Manager, also a Database Utility that you can find on the Tools menu.

When you are in the Linked Table Manager, you can click the tables you want to link, or click Select All. After you click OK, the utility asks you to point to the new database and location to which you want to link. When you locate the database, you can click Open. The links are refreshed.

SPLIT AND LINK AN ACCESS DATABASE

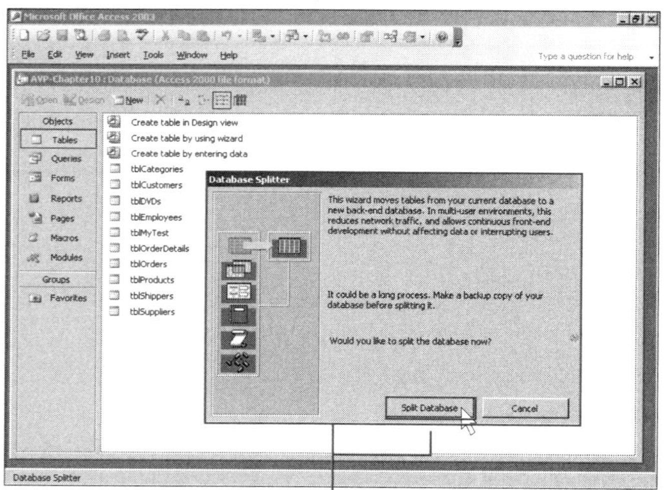

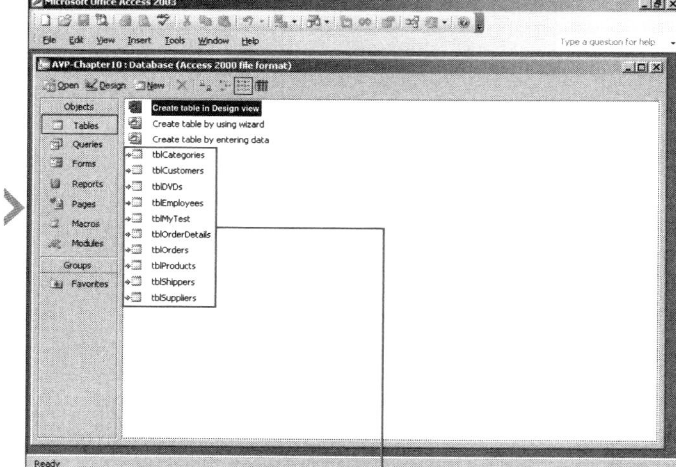

SPLIT AN ACCESS DATABASE INTO THE FRONT-END AND BACK-END

Note: This task uses the databases AVP-Chapter10.mdb and AVP-Chapter10_be.mdb on the CD-ROM.

1 Open the database that you want to split.

■ Be sure that the database contains tables.

2 Click Tools ➪ Database Utilities ➪ Database Splitter.

■ The Database Splitter Wizard appears.

3 Click Split Database.

■ The Create Back-end Database dialog box appears.

4 Make a note of the filename, and then click Split.

■ After a confirmation message box appears, all of the tables have blue arrows next to the icons.

Extra

When you have static lookup tables, it is a good idea to store them in the front-end database. This is because they do not have to be brought over the network, thus giving you better performance.

To do this, you must delete the link to the lookup table. Next, import the table into the front-end database from the back-end database.

When you need to update the lookup table, you must ensure that you update it in all the other front-end databases of other users. That is why you only want to store tables with static data in the front end, and not in lookup tables that need to be updated by others.

Another benefit of splitting a database into front-end and back-end databases is that when you need to modify various application objects, such as forms and reports, you do not have to worry about corrupting the data, because you store it in a separate database. However, keep in mind that when you modify a form or other application object, you need to make sure that you update the front-end databases on the computers of other users.

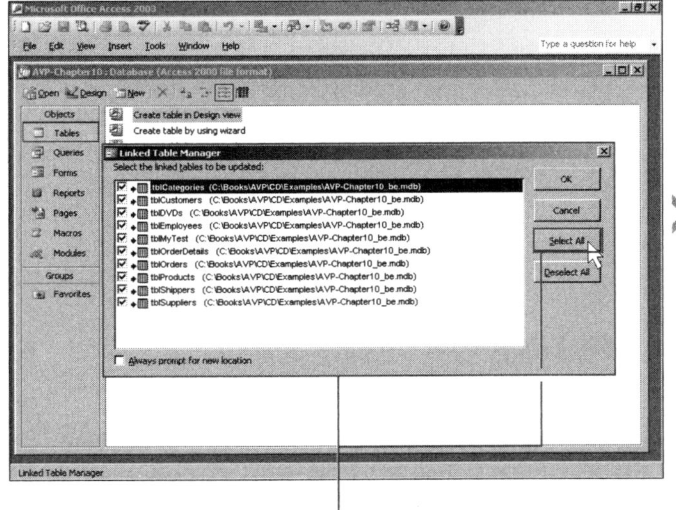

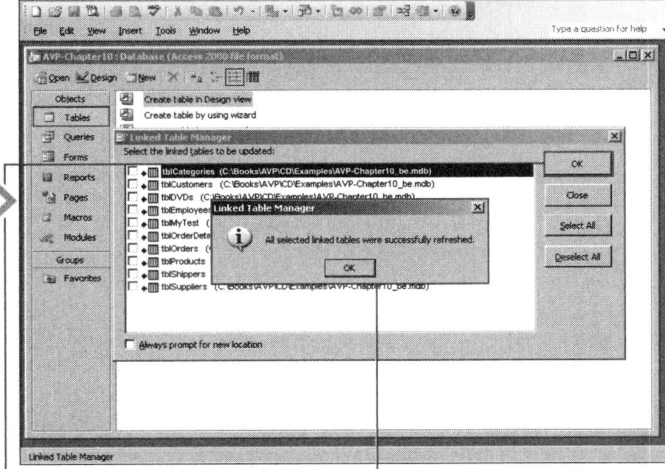

REFRESH LINKS USING THE LINKED TABLE MANAGER

1 Open a database you have split.

2 Click Tools ⇨ Database Utilities ⇨ Link Table Manager.

■ The Linked Table Manager dialog box appears.

3 Click Select All.

■ Access highlights all the tables.

4 Click OK.

■ If the database has moved to a new location, a dialog box appears, and asks you to locate the database.

■ A message box appears, and tells you that the links are refreshed.

IMPORT DATA FROM MICROSOFT EXCEL

Many users create worksheets using Microsoft Excel, only to realize later that they should have put the data in Access because they are using the data in a relational style. To address this problem, you can import the data to Access.

When you import the data from Excel into Access, you must then add a relational format, which is not used in Excel.

To import data from Microsoft Excel, you can choose Get External Data from the File menu, and then choose Import. The Import dialog box appears. You can then select Microsoft Excel (.xls) from the Files of type drop-down list, and locate the file you want to import. After you locate the file, you can click OK.

If there is only a single sheet in the XLS file, the first page of the Import Spreadsheet Wizard displays a sample of the imported data. If there is more than one sheet, then a page appears that lets you select the sheet or a named range.

With this wizard, you can specify whether you want the first row in the data to be the column headings. If you do, you can click Next.

The next page of the wizard asks whether you want to import the data into an existing table or a new table. If you are importing into an existing table, then you can click the Next button to proceed immediately to the last page of the wizard.

If you are importing a new table, then you can click Next to proceed to the next page in the wizard, which asks you to specify the name and index for each field you want to import. You can also choose to skip the field altogether and not import it.

The page after the individual field specification asks you to choose or create a Primary Key field for the new table. On the last page, you can specify the name you want for the new table, and whether you want to have Access analyze the table for normalization issues.

IMPORT DATA FROM MICROSOFT EXCEL

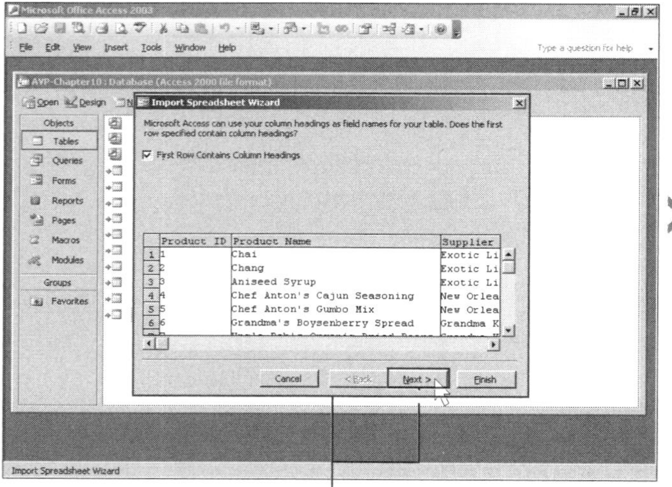

Note: This task uses AVP-Chapter10.mdb and xlsProducts.xls on the CD-ROM.

1 Click File ➪ Get External Data ➪ Import.

2 In the Import dialog box, choose Microsoft Excel (.xls) as the type of file.

3 Locate and select a worksheet.

4 Click Import.

■ The second page of the Import Spreadsheet Wizard appears.

5 Click Next.

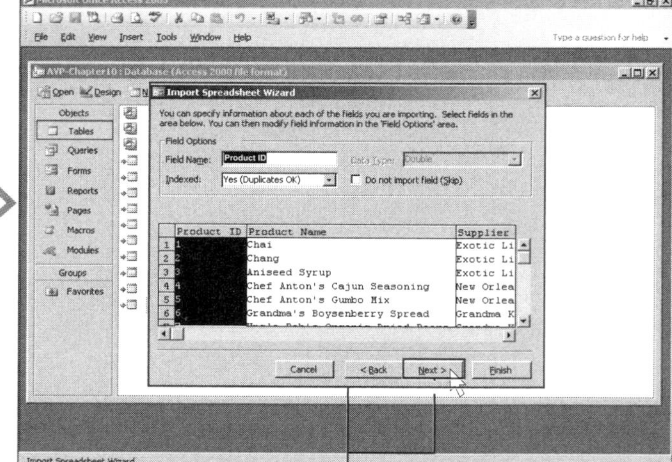

■ A new page appears, and asks whether you want to create a new table or add to an existing table. The default setting is for a new table.

6 Click New Table, and then click Next.

■ On the new page that appears, you can modify the fields.

7 Click Next.

Extra

Not only can you import data from Excel spreadsheets, but you can have Access examine the data and make sure it is organized in such a way to work optimally with your database. To accomplish this, check the I would like a wizard to analyze my table after importing the data option (☐ changes to ☑), located on the last page of the Import Spreadsheet Wizard, and then click Finish. After Access imports the table, a message box appears, asking you to verify that you want to analyze the new table.

After you click Yes, the Table Analyzer Wizard appears. The Table Analyzer Wizard examines your table, and offers solutions for various normalization issues that may occur when importing non-relational data.

The wizard addresses issues such as the creation of lookup tables so that you are not duplicating data in fields that may be contained in the lookup tables. This not only saves space, but also decreases the possibility of user error when you are managing data.

You can tell the wizard to either let you decide which fields you want to go into which tables, or you can let the wizard decide for you. The wizard shows you what it plans to do before it actually performs the task, so that you can either approve or disapprove changes.

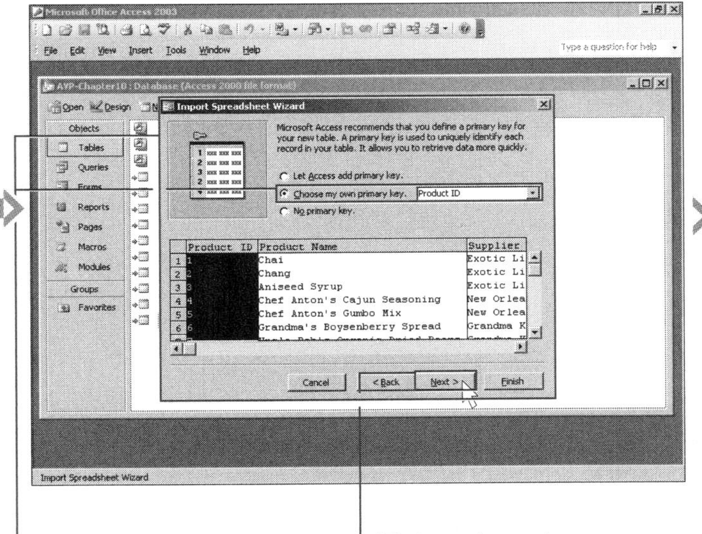

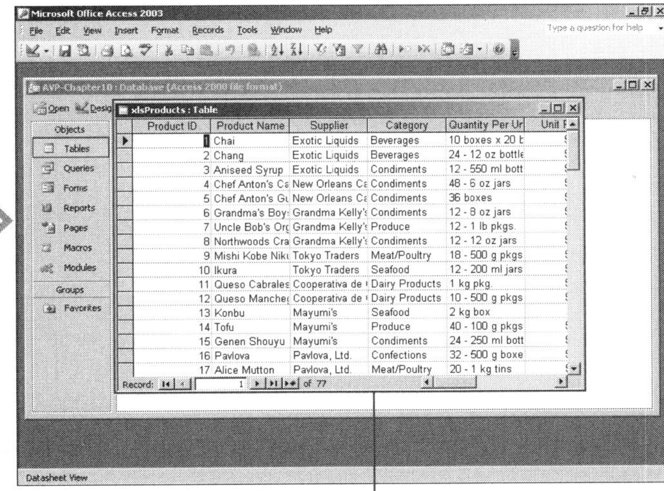

■ On this page you can specify the Primary Key field or create a new one.

8 Click Choose my own primary key, and select the field you want from the drop-down list.

■ If you do not have a primary key, skip step 8.

9 Click Next.

10 On the new page that appears, type the name you want for the new table.

11 Click Finish.

12 Double-click the new table in the list of tables in the database window.

■ The new table opens in datasheet view.

IMPORT DATA FROM TEXT FILES

When you import data that is in ASCII text files, you can choose one of two format types to import: Delimited or Fixed-Width. Many legacy systems only export using ASCII text format, so the ability to import using this format is necessary. Delimited means that each field included in the rows is separated, or delimited, by a specific character, usually a comma, a semicolon, a tab, or a space. Fixed-width means that the rows in the file are a specified length, as are each of the fields included.

Text values may be surrounded by specific characters, usually a single or double quote. Each row ends with a carriage return line feed. The wizard asks you to specify both the text qualifier and the field delimiters when you use the Text Import Wizard, but defaults are also given.

To import a text file, you can choose Get External Data from the File menu, and then Import. After selecting Text Files from the Files of type drop-down list, you can locate the file and click OK. The Import Text Wizard then appears.

You can now specify Delimited, which is the default, or Fixed Width. You can see an example of the data in the grid in the lower portion of the form. After you click Next, you can specify the delimiters. You can also specify whether or not the first row contains the name of the fields.

The rest of the wizard guides you through pages that are exactly like those in the Import Spreadsheet Wizard. This includes choosing to save the data in a new or existing table; field information and primary key information for new tables; and, the name for the new table.

You can even tell Access to analyze the table as soon as it is created.

IMPORT DATA FROM TEXT FILES

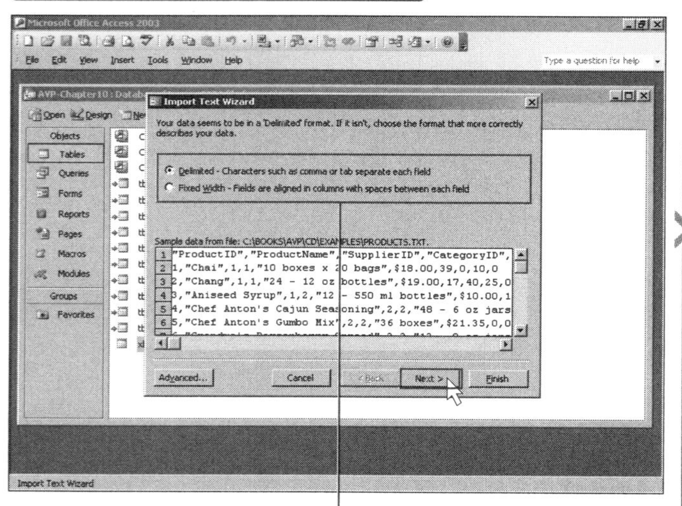

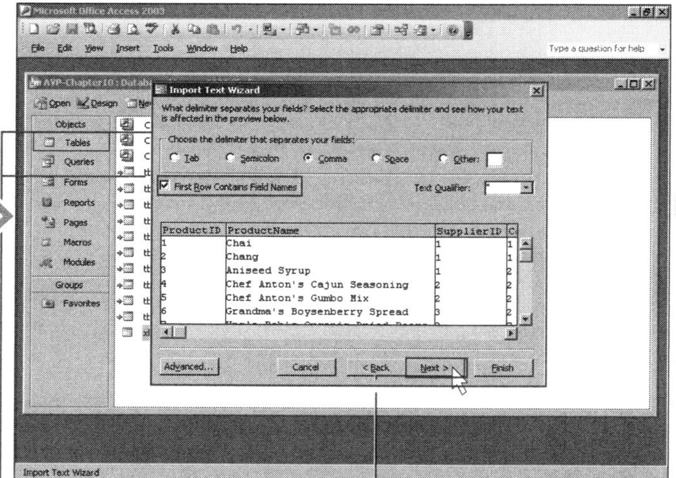

Note: This task uses AVP-Chapter10.mdb and txtProducts.txt on the CD-ROM.

1 Click File ⇨ Get External Data ⇨ Import.

2 In the Import dialog box, choose Text Files as the type of file.

3 Select a text file, and click Import.

4 On the first page of the Import Text Wizard, choose Delimited or Fixed-Width. This example uses the default setting, Delimited.

5 Click Next.

■ On the next page, you can specify delimiters and text qualifiers.

6 If the first row in the file you are importing contains fields, then click the First Row Contains Field Names check box.

7 Click Next.

■ A new page appears, and asks whether you want to use a new table or an old table. This example uses the default choice of new.

8 Click Next.

Extra

If you choose to use Fixed-Width importing, then you must specify the field width for each of the fields. When you select a file, and open it using the Import dialog box, Access decides whether it is a Delimited or Fixed-Width text file. If it is a Fixed-Width text file, then after the initial page, you can click Next to see how Access formats the data. Access uses a ruler, much like a Word ruler, which contains lines that signify breaks where the individual fields are.

After attempting to place the marks where it thinks they should be, the wizard allows you to add or remove breaks where you think best. The remaining pages of the wizard are the same as for the Delimited files.

The Import Text Wizard contains an Advanced command button. If you click this button, you can set up import specifications for importing files. This gives you the ability to create the specifications, and then use them when you import files in the future. You can also use the specifications when you import files using DoCmd methods such as TransferText.

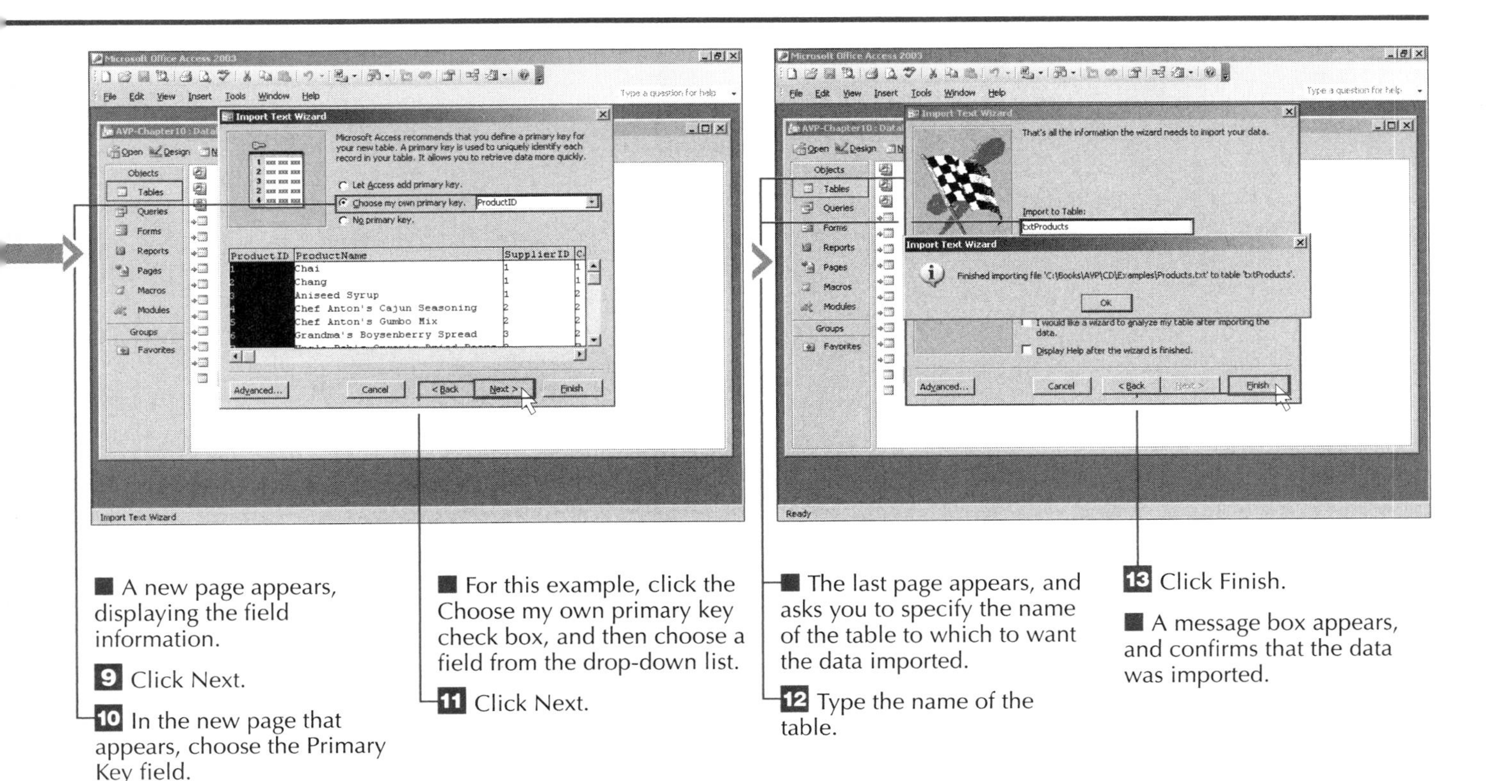

■ A new page appears, displaying the field information.

9 Click Next.

10 In the new page that appears, choose the Primary Key field.

■ For this example, click the Choose my own primary key check box, and then choose a field from the drop-down list.

11 Click Next.

■ The last page appears, and asks you to specify the name of the table to which to want the data imported.

12 Type the name of the table.

13 Click Finish.

■ A message box appears, and confirms that the data was imported.

IMPORT DATA FROM SQL SERVER

There are times when you may want to pull data out of an SQL Server database by importing it into Access. You may want a snapshot of the data without maintaining a link to the data. To import data from an SQL Server database, you must use a Data Source, or DSN. When you create a DSN, you are creating a file that tells Access the database file type to which you are connecting. Also, when you create a DSN for SQL Server, you must specify the SQL Server and database to which you are connecting. Lastly, you must specify which kind of security you want to use, either NT or SQL logon.

Note that in order to perform these tasks, you must have access to an SQL Server database. You can talk with your network administrators, and have them help you locate an SQL Server database that you can use. For this book, a locally installed version of SQL Server is used with the Northwind database that now comes with SQL Server Developer Edition or MSDE, which is the Microsoft SQL Server Desktop Edition. The Windows Integrated option is also used.

To import the SQL Server table, you can choose Get External Data from the File menu, and then Import. In the Import dialog box, you can choose ODBC Databases. The Select Database Source dialog box appears, where you can set up or choose the DSN you want to use. After you create or choose an existing DSN, which specifies the database, the list of tables in the SQL Server database is displayed, and you can choose which tables you want to import. You can also decide whether to select or deselect all tables in the database.

After you choose the tables and click OK, the tables appear in your list of tables in Access.

For more information on importing data from SQL Server, see the section "Link SQL Server Tables" in Chapter 1.

IMPORT DATA FROM SQL SERVER

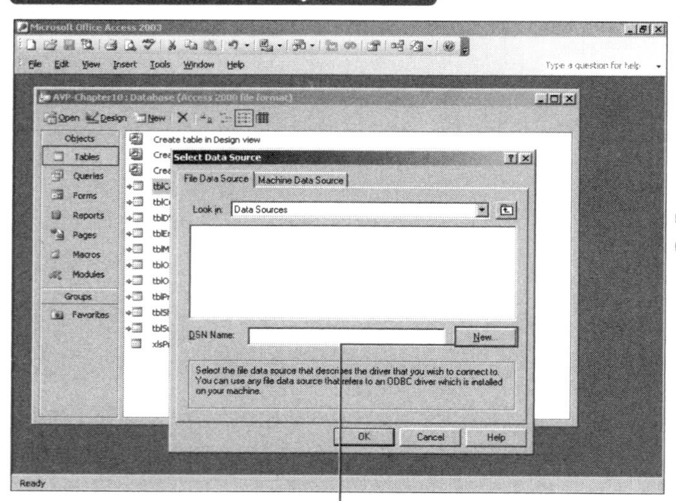

Note: This task uses AVP-Chapter10.mdb on the CD-ROM and an SQL Server version of Northwind.

1 Click File ⇨ Get External Data ⇨ Import.

2 In the Import dialog box, choose ODBC Databases as the type of file.

3 In the Select Data Source dialog box, click New.

4 In the Create Data Source dialog box, choose SQL Server as the data source, and then click New.

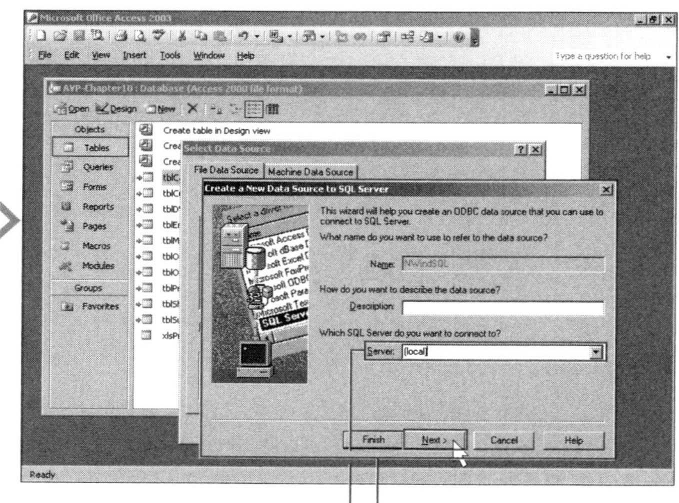

5 On the next page, type the name of the new data source and click Next.

6 On the last page of the Create Data Source dialog box, click Finish.

■ The Create a New Data Source to SQL Server dialog box appears.

7 Choose the SQL Server. This example uses the (local) version of SQL Server.

8 Click Next.

Extra

When you import data from SQL Server, Access converts the SQL Server data types over to Access data types. Here are some of the data type comparisons:

ACCESS DATA TYPE	SQL SERVER DATA TYPE
Yes/No	bit
Number (Byte)	tinyint
Number (Integer)	smallint
Number (Long Integer)	int
Number (Single)	real
(no equivalent)	bigint
Number (Double)	float
Currency	money; smallmoney
Decimal/numeric	decimal; numeric
Date/Time	datetime; smalldatetime
AutoNumber (Increment)	int (with the Identity property defined)
Text	varchar(n); nvarchar(n)
Memo	text
OLE Object	image

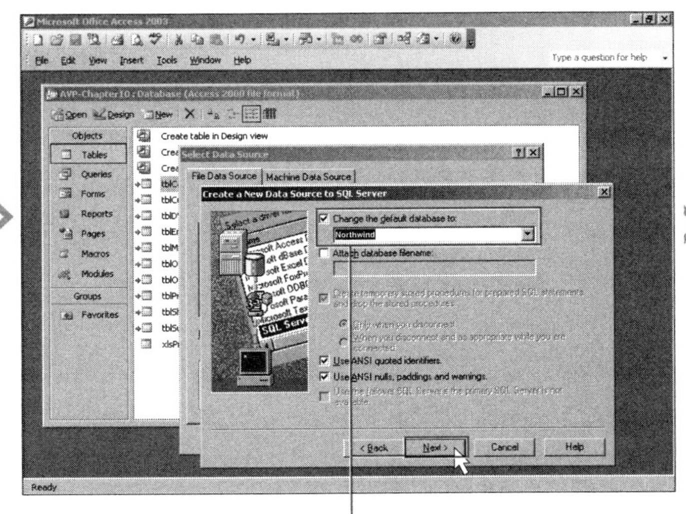

■ The next page asks you to specify the security you want to use. This example uses the default of Windows NT Authentication.

9 Click Next.

10 On the next page, choose the database you want to import from the tables.

■ This example uses the Northwind database.

11 Click Next.

12 On the last page of the wizard, click Finish.

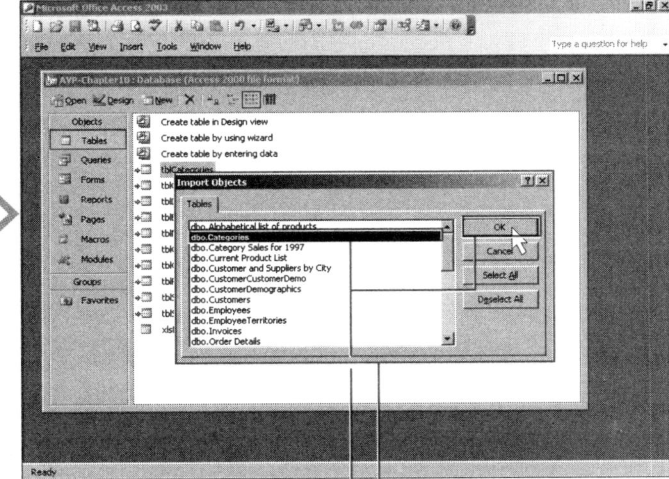

■ A summary page appears with information about the SQL Server database and the SQL Server itself.

13 Click OK.

14 In the Select Data Source dialog box, click the new DSN, and then click OK.

■ The Import Objects dialog box appears, displaying a list of tables for the database you specified.

15 Click the tables you want.

16 Click OK.

■ Access imports the tables.

IMPORT LISTS FROM WINDOWS SHAREPOINT SERVICES

There may be times when you are working with other people in your company, using a WSS site to collaborate. You may want to pull some information from a WSS list into your Access database. When you import WSS lists, unlike other file formats, you are not only able to import multiple lists at a time, but you can also import multiple views of the lists.

To import a view, you can choose Get External Data from the File menu, and then choose Import. Next, you can choose Windows SharePoint Services from the Files of type drop-down list. After you click Open, the Import from Windows SharePoint Services Wizard appears. The wizard asks you to specify the WSS site from which you want to import the lists. To ensure that you have access to a WSS site, you can ask your network administrator whether your company has a WSS site available.

The next page of the wizard asks you to specify the lists you want to import. The wizard also offers you an option for importing the IDs for lookup columns in order to be able to update the data. This option is set to True by default.

After you click Next, a new page appears, asking you select the views you want for each list that you import. The last page of the wizard displays the lists and views you have chosen. When you click Finish, Access imports the lists and views into Access tables with the name of *List:View*.

IMPORT LISTS FROM WINDOWS SHAREPOINT SERVICES

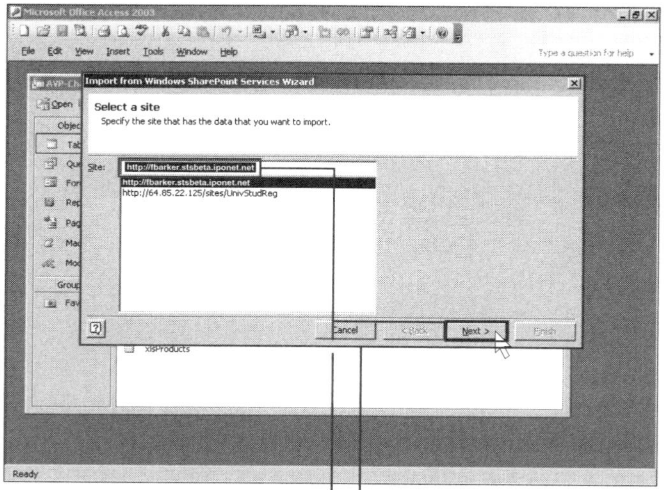

Note: This task uses AVP-Chapter10.mdb on the CD-ROM and a Windows SharePoint Services site.

1 Click File ➪ Get External Data ➪ Import.

2 In the Import dialog box, choose Windows SharePoint Services as the type of file.

■ The Import from Windows SharePoint Services Wizard appears.

3 Type the WSS site you want in the Site field.

4 Click Next.

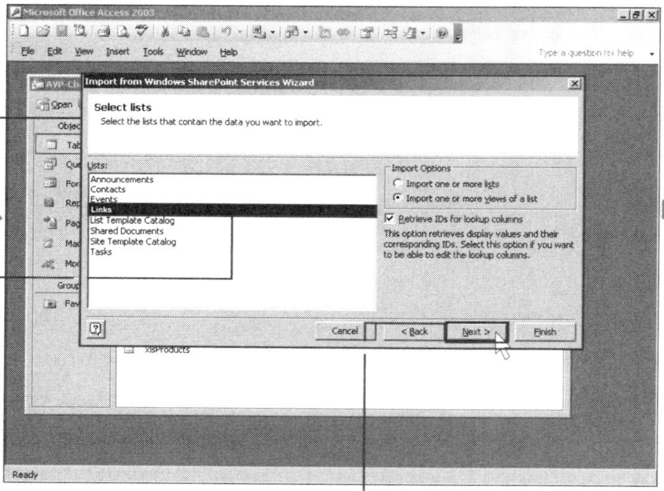

■ A logon dialog box appears.

5 Type the logon name and password, and then click OK.

■ The Select lists page appears.

6 Click the lists you want to import.

7 Click Next.

■ The Select Views page appears.

8 Click Next.

Extra

A very useful feature of Access and WSS is the ability to link to lists on the WSS site from within Access. When you do this, just as with other linked tables, the information you type into the link is immediately displayed on the site. This feature makes maintaining a WSS site even easier, because you can perform most of the maintenance of the data in the lists, including adding and deleting records, directly from within Access, where you and other users may be more comfortable.

To link to a list, you can choose Get External Data from the File menu, and then Link Tables. Next, you can select Windows SharePoint Services from the Files of type drop-down list. The Link to Windows SharePoint Services Wizard appears, which looks surprisingly like the Import from Windows SharePoint Services Wizard. In fact, they are identical except the word Link. You can follow the steps below, and your lists are then linked from WSS to Access.

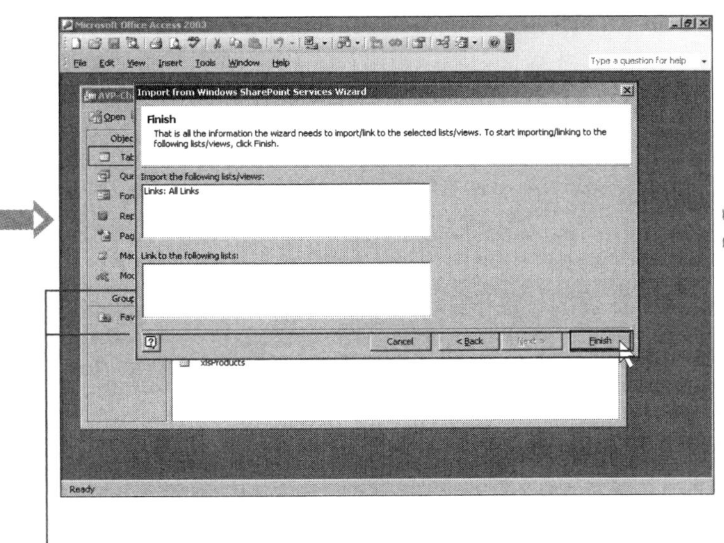

■ The last page of the wizard appears, displaying the lists and views you selected.

9 Click Finish.

■ A dialog box appears, confirming that Access has imported the list.

10 Click OK.

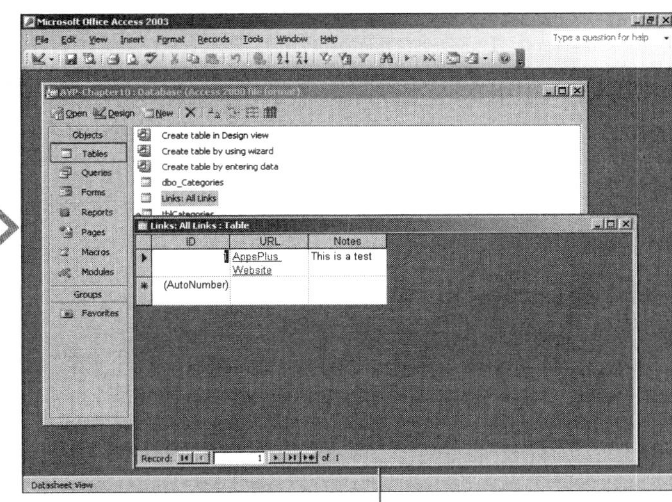

11 Double-click the new table in the database window to open the table.

■ The new table appears.

EXPORT, ANALYZE, AND E-MAIL DATA TO EXCEL

For every time you need to pull data into Access from Excel, you will probably just as often want to push data from Access into Excel for the number-crunching that Excel is so good at. When you export data to Excel, Access offers fewer options than for importing data from Excel. Unlike importing, where you can skip fields and change the names of the fields, when you export data, you simply select a table, and export it.

You do have the option of whether you want to send formatted or unformatted data. If you send formatted data, Excel specifies column headings in the resulting worksheet.

To export data, you can highlight the table or query you want to export, and choose Export from the File menu. You can choose one of the Microsoft Excel versions from the Save as type drop-down list. You can select the Save formatted check box and the Autostart check box, which appears when you click the Save formatted check box. If you choose the Save formatted option, then Excel shades the column headings with a different color to help them stand out from the other rows. When you choose both options, you are also telling Access to run Excel when the file is exported and to display the new worksheet.

Another way to create an Excel worksheet is to highlight a table, choose Office Links from the Tools menu, and then choose Analyze it with Excel. This is basically the same as exporting to Excel, while you are viewing the table.

Lastly, to e-mail data as an Excel worksheet, you can select a table or query, and then choose the Send To option from the File menu, followed by Mail Recipient (as Attachment). The Send dialog box appears, listing the various formats in which you can send the table. If you select Microsoft Excel 97-2003, and click OK, Access creates an e-mail with the new Excel worksheet as an attachment.

You can double-click the attachment to view it. Access creates the worksheet with the format option on, so the column headings are shaded.

EXPORT DATA IN EXCEL

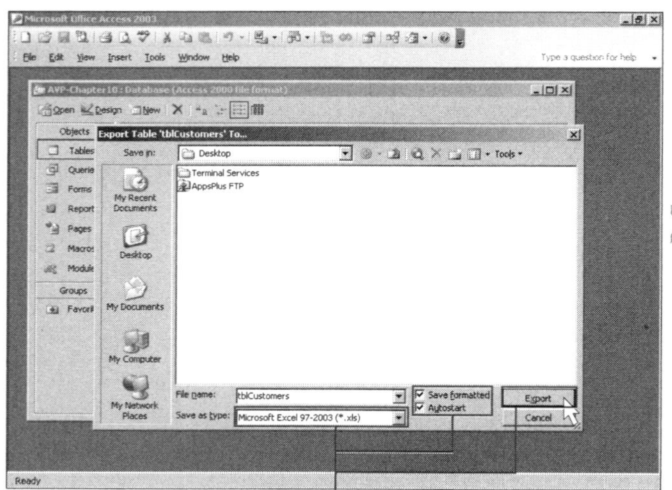

	A	B	C	D	
1	Customer ID	Company Name	Contact Name	Contact Title	
2	ALFKI	Alfreds Futterkiste	Maria Anders	Sales Representative	Obere Str. 57
3	ANATR	Ana Trujillo Emparedados y helados	Ana Trujillo	Owner	Avda. de la C
4	ANTON	Antonio Moreno Taquería	Antonio Moreno	Owner	Mataderos 2
5	AROUT	Around the Horn	Thomas Hardy	Sales Representative	120 Hanover
6	BERGS	Berglunds snabbköp	Christina Berglund	Order Administrator	Berguvsvägen
7	BLAUS	Blauer See Delikatessen	Hanna Moos	Sales Representative	Forsterstr. 57
8	BLONP	Blondel père et fils	Frédérique Citeaux	Marketing Manager	24, place Klé
9	BOLID	Bólido Comidas preparadas	Martín Sommer	Owner	C/ Araquil, 67
10	BONAP	Bon app'	Laurence Lebihan	Owner	12, rue des B
11	BOTTM	Bottom-Dollar Markets	Elizabeth Lincoln	Accounting Manager	23 Tsawasse
12	BSBEV	B's Beverages	Victoria Ashworth	Sales Representative	Fauntleroy Ci
13	CACTU	Cactus Comidas para llevar	Patricio Simpson	Sales Agent	Cerrito 333
14	CENTC	Centro comercial Moctezuma	Francisco Chang	Marketing Manager	Sierras de Gr
15	CHOPS	Chop-suey Chinese	Yang Wang	Owner	Hauptstr. 29
16	COMMI	Comércio Mineiro	Pedro Afonso	Sales Associate	Av. dos Lusía
17	CONSH	Consolidated Holdings	Elizabeth Brown	Sales Representative	12 Brewery
18	DRACD	Drachenblut Delikatessen	Sven Ottlieb	Order Administrator	Walserweg 2
19	DUMON	Du monde entier	Janine Labrune	Owner	67, rue des C
20	EASTC	Eastern Connection	Ann Devon	Sales Agent	35 King Geor
21	ERNSH	Ernst Handel	Roland Mendel	Sales Manager	Kirchgasse 6
22	FAMIA	Familia Arquibaldo	Aria Cruz	Marketing Assistant	Rua Orós, 92

Note: This task uses AVP-Chapter10.mdb on the CD-ROM.

1 Select the table to export from the list of tables in the database window.

2 Click File ⇨ Export.

3 In the Export Table dialog box, select Microsoft Excel 97-2003 from the Save as type drop-down list.

4 Check the Save formatted and Autostart check boxes.

5 Click Export.

■ Access launches Excel, and the new worksheet appears.

Extra

You can use VBA to export data into Excel spreadsheets. For example, to export a worksheet, you can use the DoCmd.TransferSpreadsheet method.

```
' Export the table to an Excel worksheet.
DoCmd.TransferSpreadsheet acExport, acSpreadsheetTypeExcel9, _
                           "tblCustomers", "c:\Customers.xls", True
```

You can also use acImport and acLink for the first parameter in the above method. The next parameter is the version number of Excel you want to use. You can also specify versions for Lotus, using Intellesense, which displays the different versions available. The next three parameters are the table you want to export; the file to which you want to export the table; and, whether to include headings.

To e-mail a spreadsheet, use the SendObject method of the DoCmd object.

```
' Email a spreadsheet
DoCmd.SendObject acSendTable, "tblCustomers", _
        "Microsoft Excel 97-2002 (*.xls)", "EmailAddress", _
        , , "test", "message"
```

The parameters in the above method are the object type you want to send; the name of the object; the format in which you want to send the object; and To, CC (blank), BlindCC (also blank), Subject, and message.

To see the full syntax for both of these commands, you can type them in the module editor, and Intellesense does its job by displaying all the parameters and their constants.

E-MAIL A TABLE AS AN EXCEL ATTACHMENT

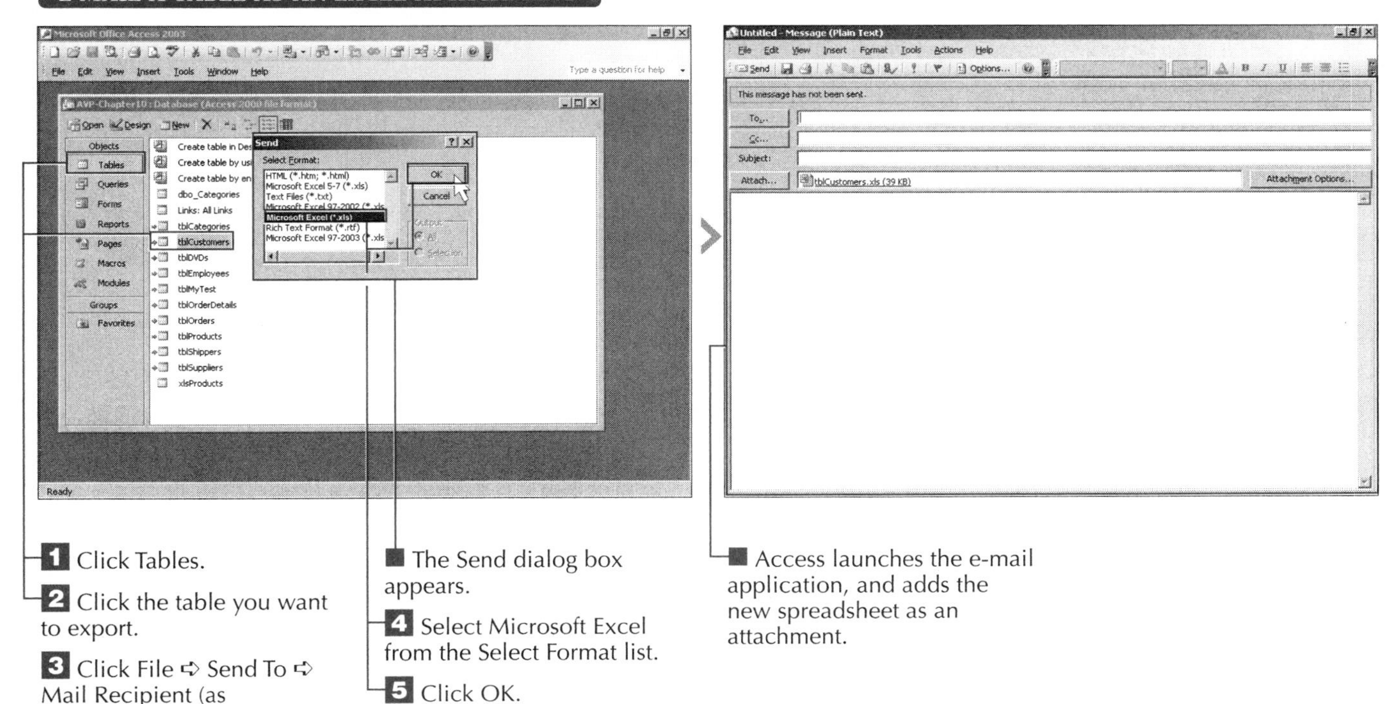

1 Click Tables.

2 Click the table you want to export.

3 Click File ➪ Send To ➪ Mail Recipient (as Attachment).

■ The Send dialog box appears.

4 Select Microsoft Excel from the Select Format list.

5 Click OK.

■ Access launches the e-mail application, and adds the new spreadsheet as an attachment.

EXPORT DATA AS TEXT FILES

There may be times when you need to export your data to a system that requires you to use ASCII text files. Access allows you to do this. Just as when you import data from ASCII text files, you must also specify delimiters when you export your data to text files.

Before exporting your table, it is a good idea to ask the recipient of the data the format in which he wants to receive the data. For example, if you send the data as a Fixed-Width text file, and the recipient requires a comma-delimited text file, then he may not be able to use your file.

After you specify the format for the text file, you can select the table you want to export. When you choose Export from the File menu, the Export Table To dialog box appears, and you can choose Text Files from the Files of type drop-down list. Note that if you select Format on this page of the wizard, then the resulting text file is in a plain-text format, not a data-text format.

After you specify the name of the new text file, you can click Export. The Export Text Wizard appears, and asks you to specify whether you want to create a Delimited or Fixed-Width text file.

Just as with the Import Text Wizard, if the text file is delimited, then on the next page you can specify the delimiters for the fields, as well as the text qualifier, and whether you want to include the field names in the first row of the new text file. If you select fixed-width, the wizard asks you to specify the field lengths by using the ruler, as discussed in the Extra section of the section "Import Data from Text Files."

The last page of the wizard asks you to specify the full path and filename for the new file.

EXPORT DATA AS TEXT FILES

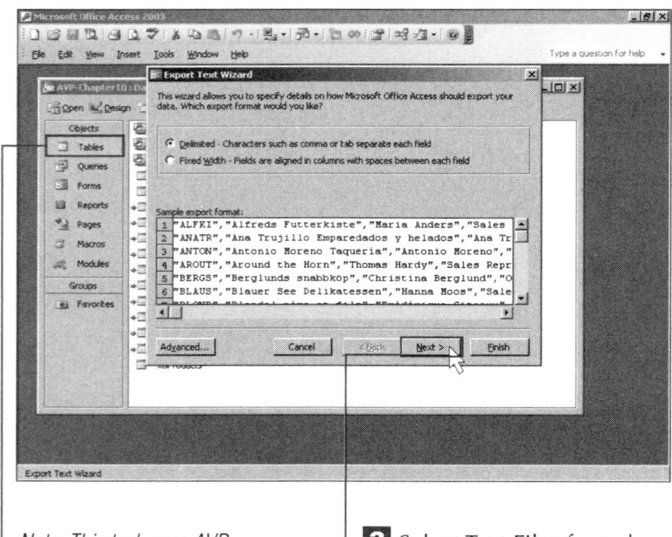

Note: This task uses AVP-Chapter10.mdb on the CD-ROM.

1 Click Tables, and then the table you want to export.

2 Click File ➪ Export.

■ The Export Table To dialog box appears.

3 Select Text Files from the Save as type drop-down list.

4 Type the name of the text file you want to create, select the folder, and click Export.

5 On the first page of the Export Text Wizard, click Next.

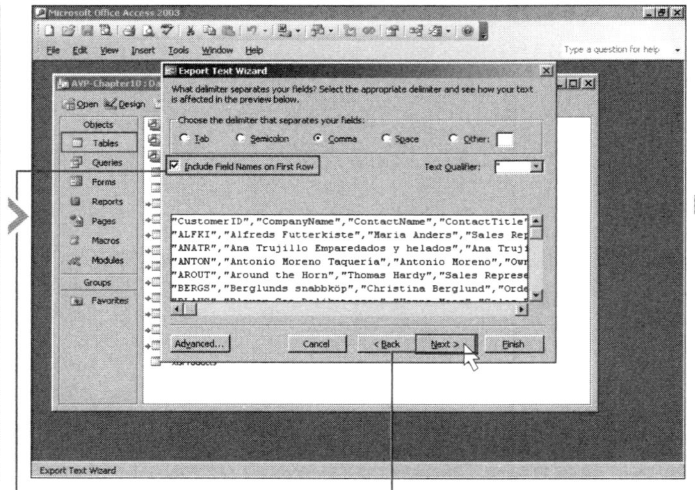

■ The next page of the wizard appears.

6 Check the Include Field Names on First Row check box.

7 Click Next.

Extra

Just as when you import text with the Import Text Wizard, there is an Advanced button in the Export Text Wizard. When you click the Advanced button, the Export Specification appears for the table you are exporting. If you intend to export a file more than once, and you need to use settings for that file that are different from the default settings, it may be a good idea to create a specification and save it.

With the Export Specification, you can set up various settings for the Delimited and Fixed-Width types. For delimited files, you can specify the delimiters and text qualifier.

More importantly, you can specify the language for which you want to export the data, including how you want to format date and time fields. This is very useful when you have data in the MM/DD/YYYY format, which is popular in the United States, and are sending it to Europe, where the DD/MM/YYYY format is popular.

You can even specify what you want to use for the decimal symbol with numeric values. You can also save your specifications for future use.

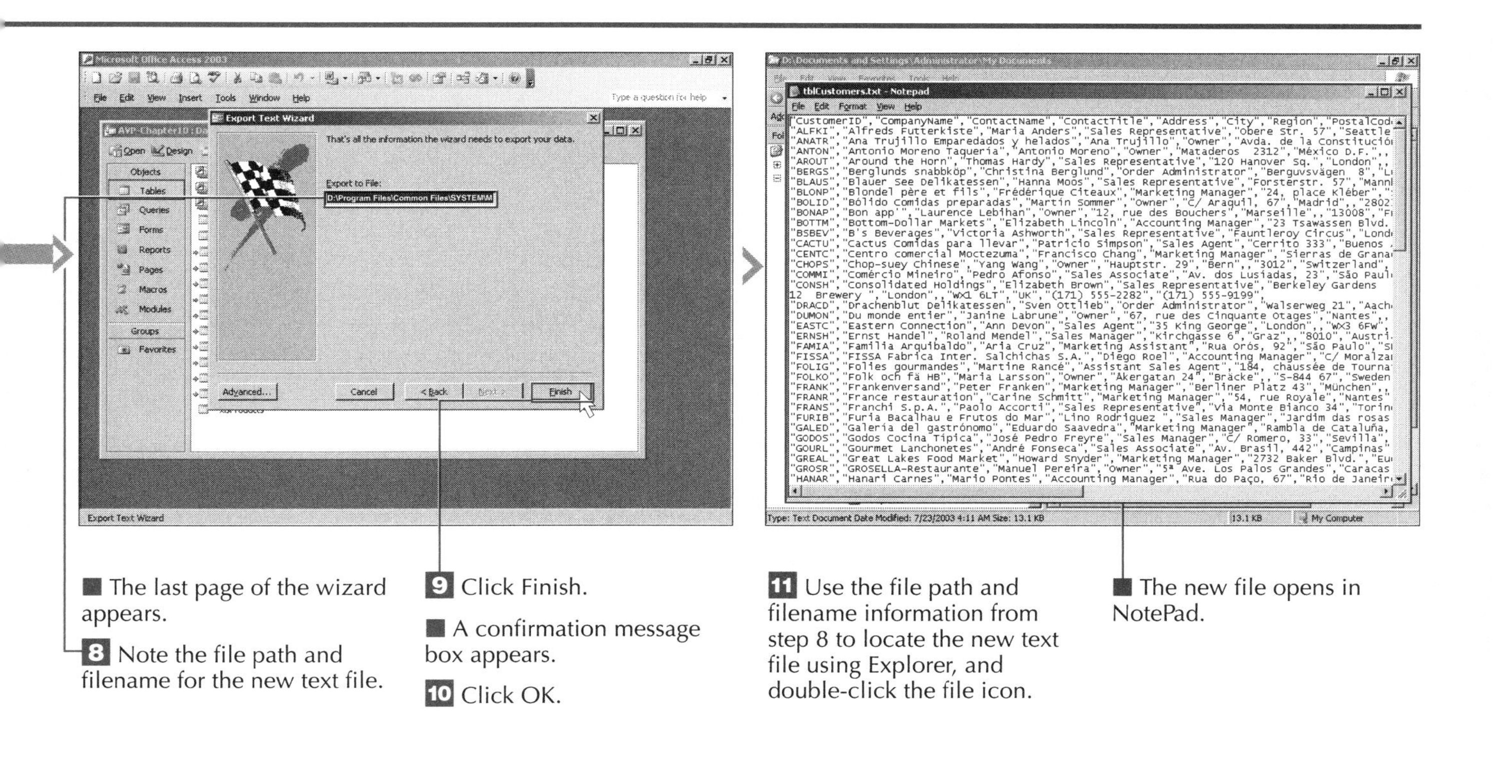

■ The last page of the wizard appears.

8 Note the file path and filename for the new text file.

9 Click Finish.

■ A confirmation message box appears.

10 Click OK.

11 Use the file path and filename information from step 8 to locate the new text file using Explorer, and double-click the file icon.

■ The new file opens in NotePad.

EXPORT DATA AS XML

Because XML is currently the fastest growing (in popularity) data file type, you may be required to export data from your Access database to XML. You can do that from Access.

Just as when you are exporting text files, you must determine what the recipient requires before you export your data to XML from Access. For example, the recipient may not need you to provide the presentation components, the XSL and HTM files, needing only the data and specifications components, the XML and XSD files. Fortunately, Access simply requires that you choose an option in the Export XML dialog box to do this.

You can select the table you want to export, and choose Export from the File list. When you choose XML from the Save as type drop-down list, and click Export, the Export XML dialog box appears. The Export XML dialog box gives you the choice of creating any or all of the following: Data (XML), Schema of the data (XSD), and Presentation of your data (XSL).

If you simply want to send some data to another user, and are not concerned with how the data appears on a Web page, you can select the options in the dialog box, and click OK. Access creates your files and saves them in the location you specify. However, if you want to specify additional information, you can click the More Options button in the dialog box. Another Export XML dialog box appears. This dialog box contains three tabs: Data, Schema, and Presentation. You can use these tabs to add more specific parameters to your data export, including exporting related tables into the new XML document.

When you finish, you can double-click the files that Access created to see how they look.

EXPORT DATA AS XML

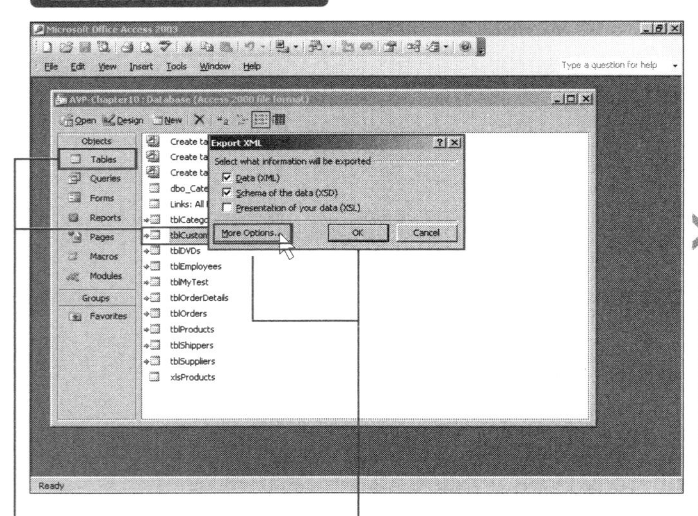

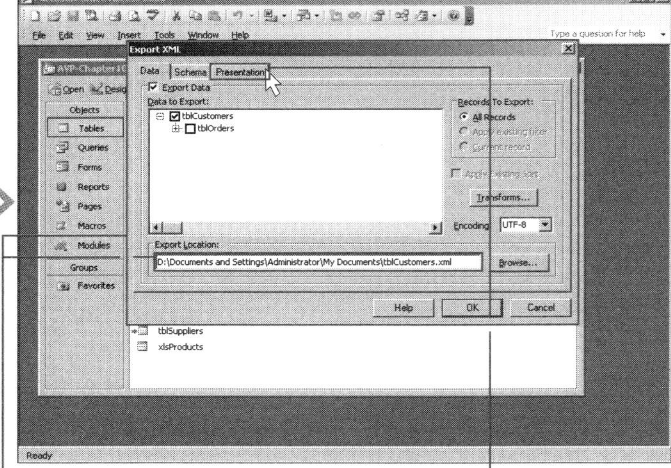

Note: This task uses AVP-Chapter10.mdb on the CD-ROM.

1 Click Tables.

2 Click the table that you want to export.

3 Click File ⇨ Export.

4 In the Export Table To dialog box that appears, select XML from the Save as type drop-down list.

5 Click Export.

■ The Export XML dialog box appears.

6 Click More Options.

■ Another Export XML dialog box appears.

7 Note the file path and filename for the new text file.

8 Click the Presentation tab.

Extra

You can include related tables with the data that you export to XML format. In the steps below, when you select a table that you know has related tables, you can click the More Options button in the Export XML dialog box.

The other Export XML dialog box that appears contains three tabs. A table also appears in the Export XML dialog box, beneath the table you have specified that you want to export. If you click the plus icon next to the table, additional tables appear if they are also related to your specified table.

Select any of the tables you want, and click OK in the Export XML dialog box. If you double-click the HTM file that Access creates, your data appears in the main table. However, if you open the XSD and XML files, they contain entries for the additional tables.

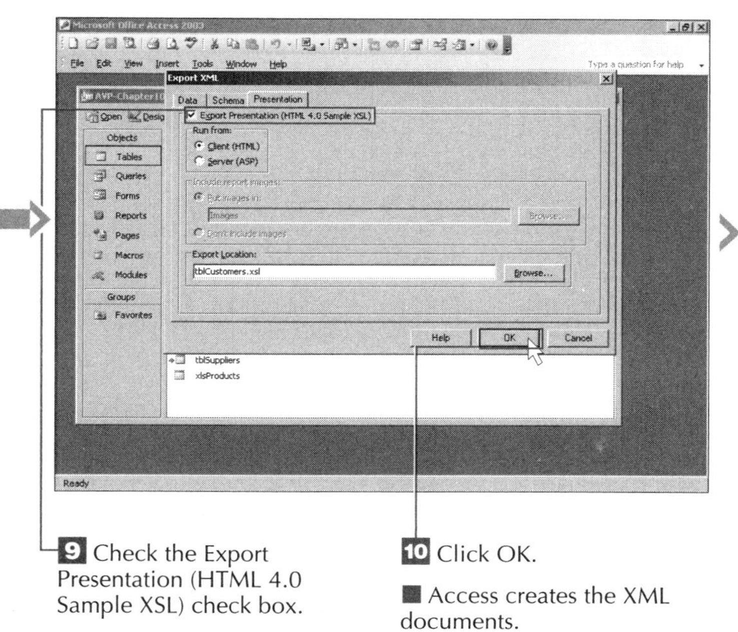

tblCustomers - Microsoft Internet Explorer

Address: D:\Documents and Settings\Administrator\My Documents\tblCustomers.htm

CustomerID	CompanyName	ContactName	ContactTitle	Address	City	Region	PostalCode	Countr
ALFKI	Alfreds Futterkiste	Maria Anders	Sales Representative	Obere Str. 57	Seattle	WA	12209	Germany
ANATR	Ana Trujillo Emparedados y helados	Ana Trujillo	Owner	Avda. de la Constitución 2222	México D.F.		05021	Mexico
ANTON	Antonio Moreno Taquería	Antonio Moreno	Owner	Mataderos 2312	México D.F.		05023	Mexico
AROUT	Around the Horn	Thomas Hardy	Sales Representative	120 Hanover Sq.	London		WA1 1DP	UK
BERGS	Berglunds snabbköp	Christina Berglund	Order Administrator	Berguvsvägen 8	Luleå		S-958 22	Sweden
BLAUS	Blauer See Delikatessen	Hanna Moos	Sales Representative	Forsterstr. 57	Mannheim		68306	Germany
BLONP	Blondel père et fils	Frédérique Citeaux	Marketing Manager	24, place Kléber	Strasbourg		67000	France
BOLID	Bólido Comidas preparadas	Martín Sommer	Owner	C/ Araquil, 67	Madrid		28023	Spain
BONAP	Bon app'	Laurence Lebihan	Owner	12, rue des Bouchers	Marseille		13008	France
BOTTM	Bottom-Dollar Markets	Elizabeth Lincoln	Accounting Manager	23 Tsawassen Blvd.	Tsawassen	BC	T2F 8M4	Canada

My Computer

9 Check the Export Presentation (HTML 4.0 Sample XSL) check box.

10 Click OK.

■ Access creates the XML documents.

11 Use the file path and filename information from step 8 to locate the new files using Explorer.

12 Double-click the HTM file that Access created.

■ Access launches Internet Explorer, and displays the data in HTML format.

EXPORT A TABLE TO WINDOWS SHAREPOINT SERVICES

If you are working with others and using a WSS site to collaborate, you will probably want to export some data from your Access database to the WSS site. Access helps you to do that. To export a table to a WSS site, you can choose Export from the File menu. In the Export dialog box that appears, you can choose Windows SharePoint Services from the Save as type drop-down list. The Export to Windows SharePoint Services Wizard appears.

Exporting to a WSS site is different from exporting to other formats, because you must specify the WSS site address. This means that you need to be able to access a WSS site. You can get the address from your network administrator. You can also change the name of the list to which you want to save the table, and add a description to be displayed on the site. After you enter the required information, and click Finish, a message box appears, indicating that Access has created the list.

After you click OK in the message box, Access launches your Web browser, and takes you to the logon page for the WSS site. When you enter the logon information, the new list appears in the WSS site. This indicates that the new list has been placed in the collection of lists on the site. As with other file types, after you export the data, it becomes a copy of the data, and no connection remains between the table in Access and the list located on the WSS site.

Note that when you export a table or query that contains an OLE field, such as a picture, the file does not export with the rest of the data. You must upload these files to a picture collection folder, and then direct users to them.

EXPORT A TABLE TO WINDOWS SHAREPOINT SERVICES

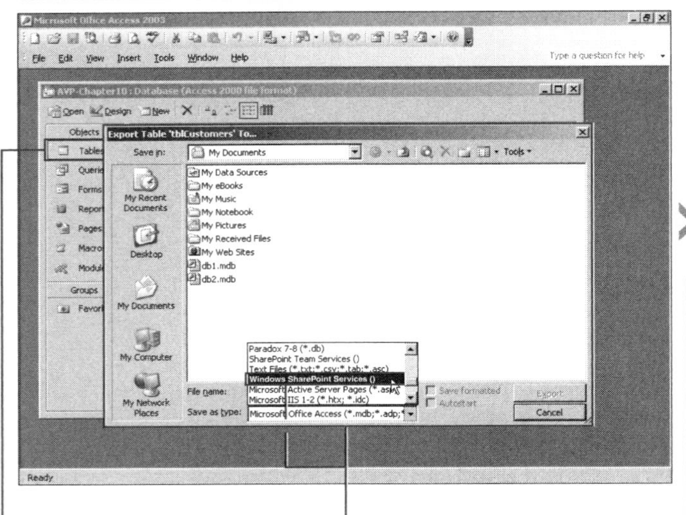

Note: This task uses AVP-Chapter10.mdb on the CD-ROM and a Windows SharePoint Services site.

1 Click Tables, and then click the table you want to export.

2 Click File ➪ Export.

■ The Export Table To dialog box appears.

3 Select Windows SharePoint Services from the Save as type drop-down list.

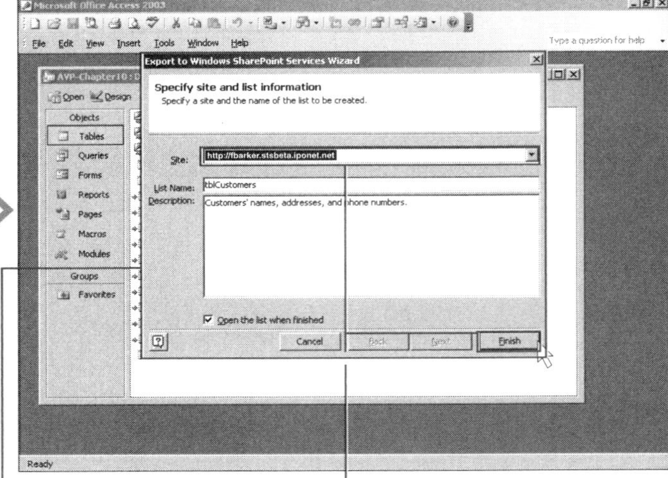

■ The Export to Windows SharePoint Services Wizard appears.

4 Choose the site to export the data to by typing the site address or by selecting it from a drop-down list if you have already been to the site.

5 Click Finish.

Extra

When you export a list to a WSS site, you can add the list to the Quick Launch bar, located on the left-hand side of your home page. To add the list from within the list, you, or the network administrator of the site, can click Modify settings and columns, which is located on the left-hand side of the page.

When you click the new list you have created, the properties appear for the list. Select Change general settings. You can now edit the various settings. Choose Yes for the Display this list on the Quick Launch bar option.

Make any additional changes you want to make to the list, and click OK when you have finished. Now, when you click Home on the top menu bar, the new list appears under the Lists group.

Because you cannot upload pictures to a WSS site, the list contains an extra column if you have included the picture column. The fields should be blank. To completely remove the column, select the column by clicking in the top of the column. Right-click and choose Edit/Delete Column from the menu that appears. In the Change Column page, click the Delete button at the bottom of the page. The column disappears.

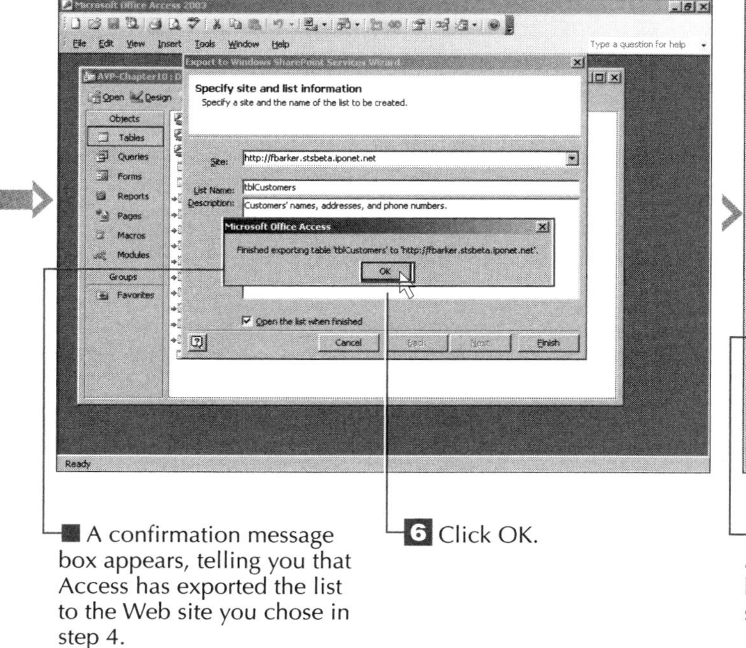

■ A confirmation message box appears, telling you that Access has exported the list to the Web site you chose in step 4.

6 Click OK.

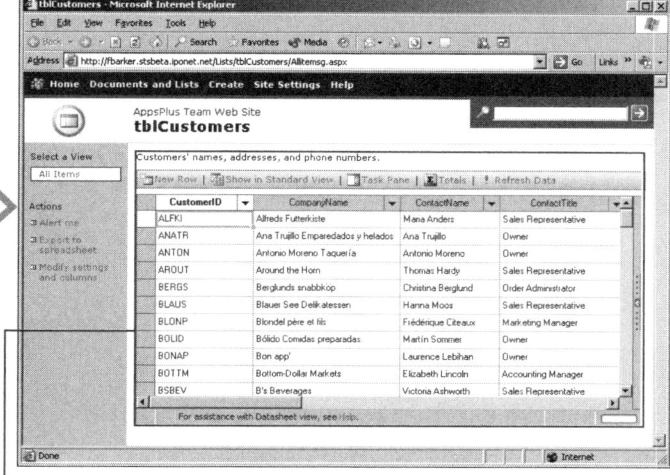

■ The list has been created, and Access launches the Web browser and takes you to the site automatically.

INTRODUCING ACTIVEX DATA OBJECTS

Over the years, Microsoft has provided many different methods for developers to work with data directly using code. Access has two methods you can use. The first method is Data Access Objects, or DAO, which was introduced in Access version 2.0 as a way for developers to work with data using code. Developers could open tables, update data in individual records, and modify the structures of the tables.

The second method is ActiveX Data Objects, or ADO, which was introduced in Access 2000. While DAO was introduced primarily for the Jet engine, an Access database engine, it was limited in Access data from SQL Server and from the Web. As a result, additional data access models were incorporated into Access, such as Remote Data Objects, or RDO. Access does not use RDO, but RDO is used by other languages, such as Visual Basic.

ADO was created to combine various features of the different data access models into two object models. Where DAO used dbEngine and Databases — Jet only — as the main objects, ADO allows you to specify Connection objects that can be any of the OLE database, or OLEDB, data providers. By using OLEDB directly through ADO, you are omitting a step, because with DAO you must use ODBC to access outside data sources such as the SQL Server.

ADO OBJECT MODELS

Just as Access has an object model that is made up of forms, reports, and controls, each of which have properties and methods you can use, ADO also has various objects that you can use to edit and work with your data. The two main object models, which consist of collections and objects, are the Microsoft ActiveX Data Objects library, or ADODB object model, which you can use for working with recordsets and data, and the Microsoft ADO Extended library, or ADOX object model, which you can use to work with security.

ADODB Object Model

The ADODB object model enables you to perform most of the data work that you need to do. The primary objects of the ADODB object model are:

OBJECT NAME	DESCRIPTION
Connection	You can use this object to open and maintain connections to the data. You can pass a string with the appropriate settings to specify the type of database, for example, SQL Server or Access. Also included is the path and name of the database, as well as any possible username and password. You can use the object with other objects such as Recordset and Command.
Recordset	Analogous to the datasheet in Access, this object is the data returned by an SQL string or query. You can move around recordsets using methods such as MoveNext and MovePrevious. You can also persist recordsets, which means that you can save them into separate files.
Command	This enables you to update queries that run using code. You can also use Command objects as sources for the creation of recordsets.
Parameters	Just as you can use parameters in the queries you execute, you can also add Parameter objects to the commands to supply parameters.
Fields	Recordsets have a Fields collection. Which fields are available depends on the data returned by the recordset.

ADO OBJECT MODELS (CONTINUED)

Declaring and Using ADO Objects

As with other objects you use with VBA, you must declare ADO objects. However, unlike some other objects, you must declare some of the ADO objects with the New keyword. This declaration creates a new instance of the object, so you can use the objects without using the Set statement. Below is an example of this statement with the Recordset object.

```
Dim rs As New ADODB.Recordset
```

where rs is the name of the Recordset variable you want to create. You can create other commands by using the CreateObject method of the commands with which they are used. The Object is one of the items you want to create. An example of this is the creation of a new parameter, as follows:

```
Dim par As ADODB.Parameter

Set par = cmd.CreateParameter
("parname")
```

where par is the name of the Parameter variable, cmd is the name of the Command variable, and parname is the name of the parameter as it appears in the Access query or the SQL Server stored procedure.

ABOUT ADO.NET

.NET is a Microsoft-developed platform that was created to make developing easier for both the Internet, using ASP.NET, and the Windows desktop environment, using Windows Forms. With .NET you can choose which language you want to use, such as Visual Basic .NET or C#.

The .NET platform uses ADO.NET for data access. ADO.NET is the latest data access method put forth by Microsoft, and unlike ADO, ADO.NET primarily works with disconnected record sets, using XML. By default, with ADO you need to use a Connection object, and keep it open during the entire time you are working with the data. With ADO.NET, ADO.NET opens the connection, data is retrieved into memory, and then ADO.NET closes the connection. When you need to update the data, ADO.NET opens the connection again.

While ADO.NET has some of the same objects as ADO, such as the Connection and Command objects, it uses objects other than the Recordset object for maintaining data. You can use ADO.NET with Access 2003, but ADO is recommended because the various controls are meant to work with ADO objects.

QUERIES VERSUS ADO

You may sometimes have to decide whether to use a query with DoCmd.OpenQuery or to use a VBA and ADO recordset. You may prefer to use a pre-built query to accomplish tasks, rather than opening a recordset and running through it record by record.

A query usually performs tasks more quickly; however, there are some tasks you cannot perform using only queries. For an example, see the Extra section in the section "Manage Records in Recordsets."

VIEW OR DESELECT LIBRARY REFERENCES

When using either the DAO or ADO libraries, references have to be set to the libraries. By default, Access sets a reference to both the DAO 3.6 Object Library and the ADO 2.6 Object Library. You may want to check the references, and possibly remove a reference, because you do not need to use both.

After you create a new database, you can check to see which libraries there are by first creating a new module, and then opening the module. This is because the libraries appear in the References dialog box, which you must access through the Tools menu when you edit modules.

When the References dialog box appears, the following libraries appear selected: Visual Basic For Applications, Microsoft Access 11.0 Object Library — which references are set will vary depending on what file format you use for your database — OLE Automation, Microsoft DAO 3.6 Object Library, and Microsoft ActiveX Data Objects 2.1 Library.

Keep in mind that if you deselect an item in the References dialog box, then your application may not compile correctly, and you may have to return to this dialog box to reactivate a library in the list.

If you are only going to be using ADO, you can deselect the Microsoft DAO 3.6 Object Library. After you deselect the library, you can close the dialog box. When you return to the References dialog box, the deselected reference does not appear at the top with the selected references.

If you need to reselect a library, you can scroll through the list and locate the name of the library to which you want to set a reference.

VIEW OR DESELECT LIBRARY REFERENCES

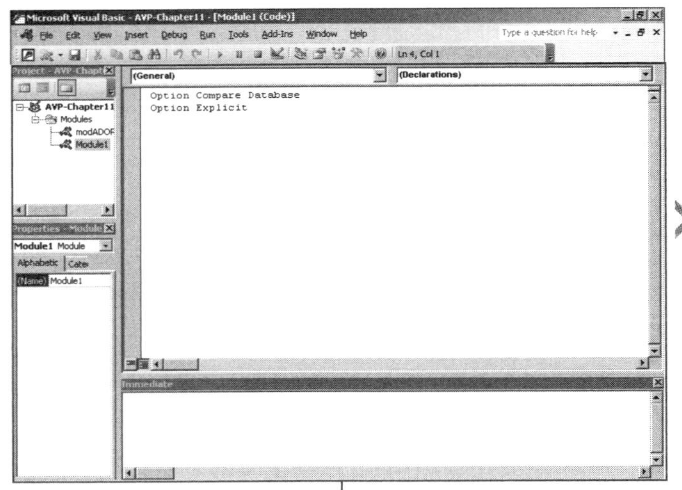

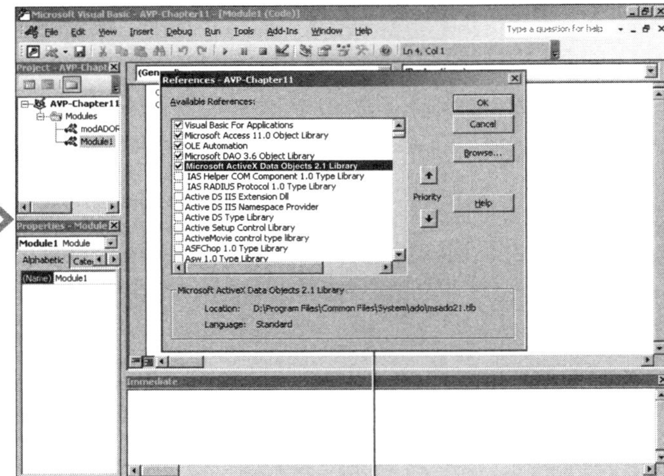

VIEW LIBRARY REFERENCES

Note: This task uses AVP-Chapter11.mdb on the CD-ROM.

1 Create or open a new database.

2 Click the Modules tab.

3 Click New.

■ A new module appears.

4 Click Tools ⇨ References.

■ The References dialog box appears, displaying a list of libraries, with the selected libraries at the top of the list.

Extra

When you use the various objects from the object models, you can use the library to specify the library from which the object came. For example, both ADO and DAO have Recordset objects, and if you select both library references, you can use the following code:

```
Dim rs as New Recordset
```

VBA uses the first library referenced in the list. While you can open the References dialog box and rearrange the list of references, which is a good idea, you may also want to include the library in the declaration of the object type.

Using the above example, if you want to use the ADO recordset rather than the DAO recordset, you can declare the variable as follows:

```
Dim rs as New ADODB.Recordset
```

where ADODB is the library name.

You should leave the DAO library reference selected in the References dialog box. This is because when you use recordsets from forms, the recordsets must still be DAO recordsets rather than ADO recordsets.

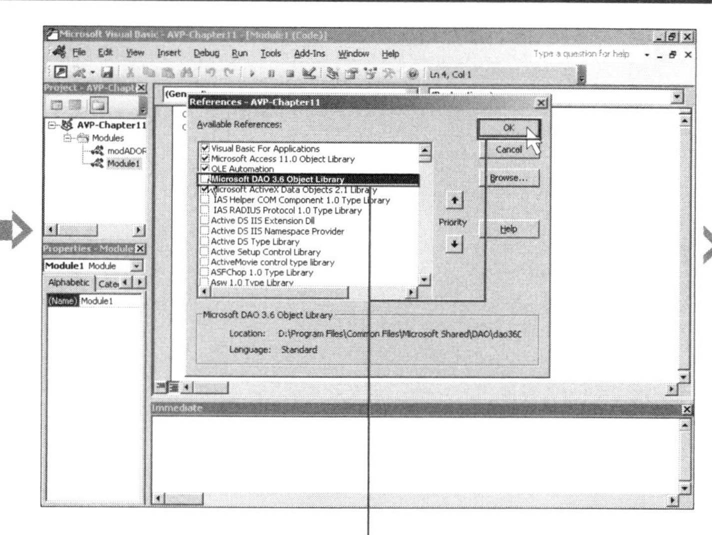

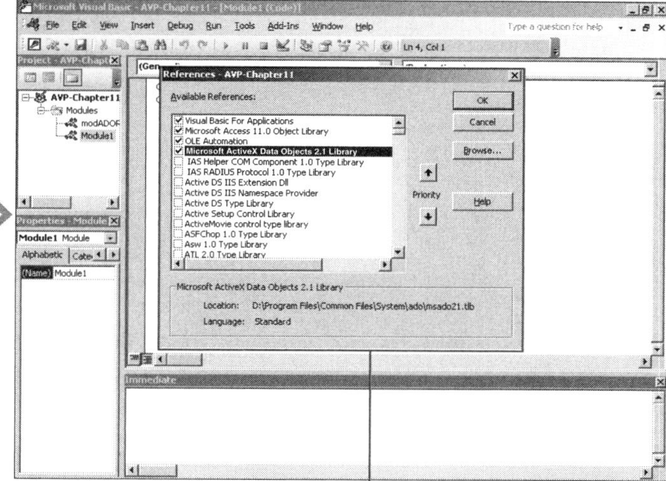

DESELECT LIBRARY REFERENCES

5 Locate the reference you want to deselect.

6 Click the check box to deselect the library reference.

7 Click OK.

■ The References dialog box closes.

8 Click Tools ⇨ References.

■ The References dialog box appears, with the deselected reference no longer at the top of the list.

CREATE AN ADO CONNECTION

One of the objects you use most often with ADO is the Connection object. The Connection object stores the information needed to open a connection to the data you are working with, and provides a method, called Open, to open the actual connection.

When declaring a new Connection object, use this:

```
Dim cnnName As New ADODB.Connection
```

where cnnName is the name you give to the Connection object. ADODB is added to the Connection object declaration to document your use of the ADO object. Using the object model name is very important when you use the Recordset object, because both the DAO and ADO objects have a Recordset object, and you can have problems if you want to use one type of access method over the other.

There are several ways to specify the connection string for the Connection object. You can use the CurrentProject. Connection object when you create a Connection object to a backend that is used with an ADP, and which could therefore be an SQL Server. The syntax appears as follows:

```
    cnnName.ConnectionString =
CurrentProject.Connection
```

If you want to specify a separate database from the current one you are in, you can specify the data provider you want to use, the name of the database, the user ID, password, and many other specifics, depending on the type of database you are using. Here is an example:

```
    cnnName.ConnectionString = _
      "Provider=Microsoft.Jet.OLEDB.4.0;User
ID=Admin;" & _
      "Data
Source=C:\Books\AVP\CD\Examples\AVP-
Chapter11BE.mdb;"
```

If you want to use the SQL Server database, use this:

```
   cnnNew.ConnectionString = _
"Provider='sqloledb';Data
Source='MySqlServer';" & _
        "Initial Catalog='Pubs';Integrated
Security='SSPI';"
```

CREATE AN ADO CONNECTION

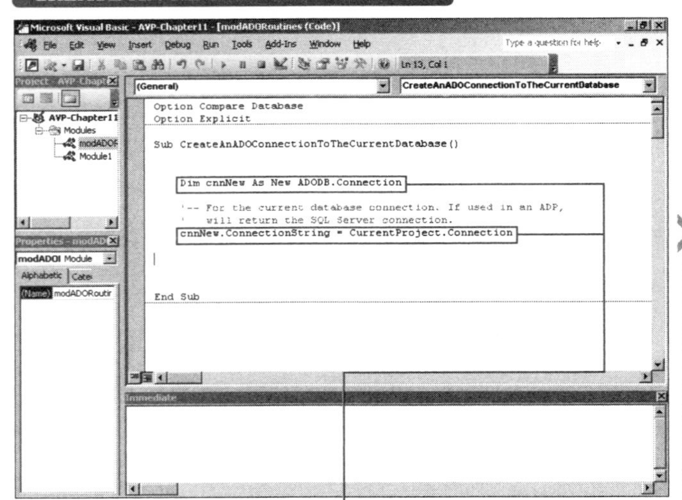

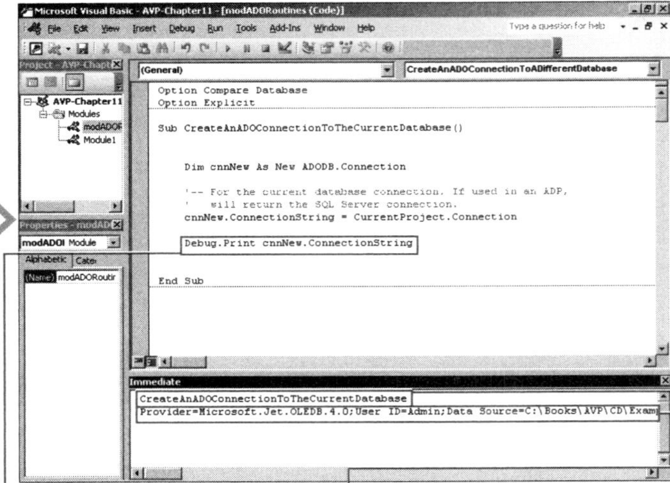

CREATE AN ADO CONNECTION TO THE CURRENT DATABASE

Note: This task uses modADORoutines in AVP-Chapter11.mdb and AVP-Chapter11BE.mdb on the CD-ROM.

1. Create a new subroutine.
2. Add the code for declaring the ADODB.Connection variable.
3. Add the code for assigning the ConnectionString property of the Connection object using the Connection property of the CurrentProject.
4. Type the Debug.Print command to print the ConnectionString property of the Connection object.
5. Click View ⇨ Immediate menu.
6. Type the name of the routine you created in the Immediate window, and press Enter.

■ The connection string appears in the Immediate window.

Extra

Your Access database, or project, has an AccessConnection property. To assign the AccessConnection property to the ConnectionString, you can use the following syntax:

```
    cnnName.Connection
String = Current Project.
Access Connection
```

You can use this property when you are working with data in Access forms, in order to allow the data to be updated. In fact, two data providers, OLEDB and Jet, are used, although you only use the Connection object.

If you want to use a connection to a separate a database more than once in your database application, you can save time by creating a centralized function, and returning the connection string from the function. The function looks like this:

```
Function CommonConnStr() As String

    '— Change this to point to your database.
    CommonConnStr = _
        "Provider=Microsoft.Jet.OLEDB.4.0;User ID=Admin;" & _
        "Data Source=C:\Books\AVP\CD\Examples\AVP-
Chapter11BE.mdb;"

End Function
```

You can then assign the connection as follows:

```
    cnnName.ConnectionString = CommonConnStr()
```

Now, if you need to change the name of the database, you only need to change the name in one location — the function — instead of in numerous places in the application.

You may be tempted to just hold on to the Connection object so that you do not need to open another one later. This should NOT be done when connecting to SQL Server.

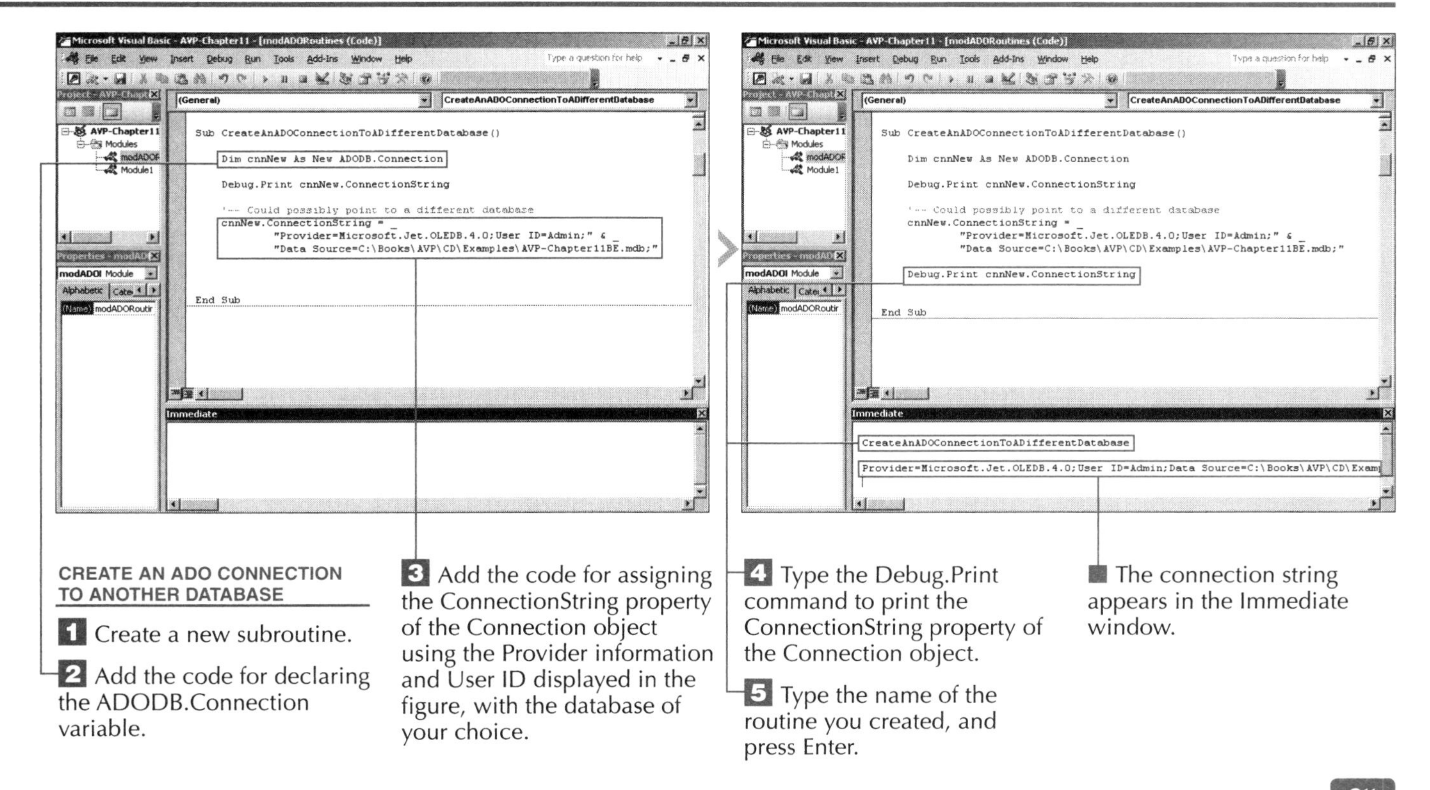

CREATE AN ADO CONNECTION TO ANOTHER DATABASE

1 Create a new subroutine.

2 Add the code for declaring the ADODB.Connection variable.

3 Add the code for assigning the ConnectionString property of the Connection object using the Provider information and User ID displayed in the figure, with the database of your choice.

4 Type the Debug.Print command to print the ConnectionString property of the Connection object.

5 Type the name of the routine you created, and press Enter.

■ The connection string appears in the Immediate window.

OPEN AN ADO RECORDSET

You can use the ADO Recordset object to view and manipulate data in your database, at a record or field level. The Recordset object has a number of properties and methods that make it easy to use.

In order to open a recordset, you must first declare it. To do this, you can use the New keyword, as well as specifying the use of the ADODB library. The syntax for declaring the Recordset object looks like this:

```
Dim rsName As New ADODB.Recordset
```

Now, when you open the recordset, you can use the Open method of the Recordset object. The syntax for the Open method looks like this:

```
rsName.Open Source, ActiveConnection,
CursorType, LockType, Options
```

where rsName is the name of the recordset variable. Source can be the SQL Select statement, a stored procedure call, a Command object, or a filestream object. In this chapter, you will use an SQL Select statement. ActiveConnection can be an open connection object. For example, you can use CurrentProject.Connection when using data in the same database. CursorType is dependent on whether or not you want to update the data with which you are working. The default constant is adOpenForwardOnly. To update and see other changes, you can use adOpenDynamic. If you are updating data, you may want to set the LockType parameter to the adOpenOptimistic constant. Options are used when the Source is a Command object.

An example of opening the tblCustomers table in the current database can be seen here:

```
rsNew.Open "Select * From tblCustomers", _
      CurrentProject.Connection,
adOpenDynamic, adLockOptimistic
```

This statement retrieves all the records from tblCustomers, and opens the recordset for editing. You can also see changes made by other users.

OPEN AN ADO RECORDSET

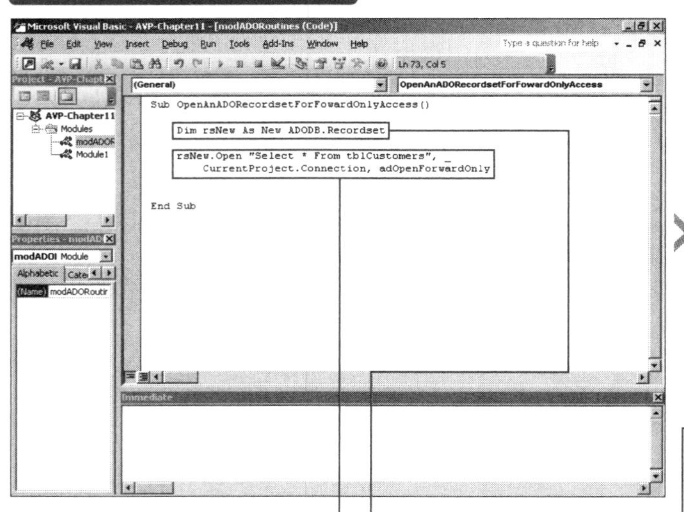

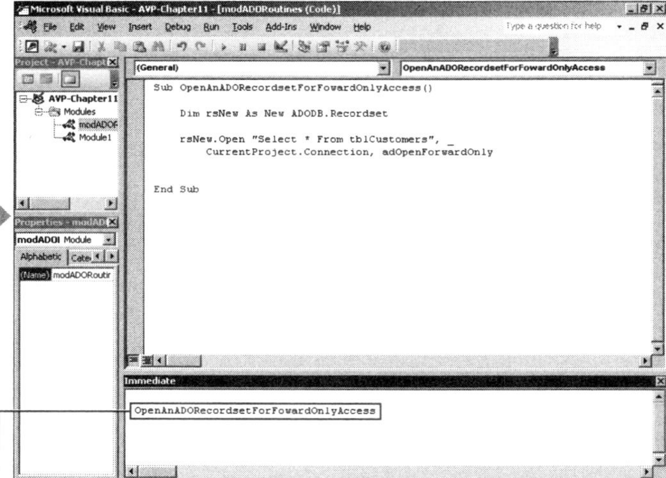

OPEN AN ADO RECORDSET FOR FORWARD-ONLY ACCESS

Note: This task uses modADORoutines in AVP-Chapter11.mdb on the CD-ROM.

1 Create a new routine.

2 Add the code for declaring the new ADODB.Recordset variable.

3 Type the code for opening the recordset using forward only access.

4 Type the name of the routine in the Immediate window, and press Enter.

■ Nothing should appear in the Immediate window when you press Enter.

Extra

Which cursor type you want to use depends on what you want to do with the recordset. The different cursor types appear below:

ENUMERATION	DESCRIPTION
adOpenDynamic	You can make changes to existing records, and add and delete records. You can also view changes that other users make.
adOpenForwardOnly	This is the default cursor type. It is a read-only type recordset, in which you can only move forward. This type gives you the best performance.
adOpenKeyset	You can make changes to existing records, and add and delete records. You cannot see changes that other users make.
adOpenStatic	A read-only snapshot type recordset in which you can move around. You cannot see any changes made by other users.
adOpenUnspecified	No cursor type is specified.

The LockType you use depends on what you are doing with the recordset. Below are the possible types:

ENUMERATION	DESCRIPTION
adOpenBatch Optimistic	Records are locked only when the Update method is called; this is for a batch of records, not individual records.
adOpenOptimistic	Records are locked only when the Update method is called.
adOpenPessimistic	Records are locked when they are edited, and until the Update method is called.
adOpenReadOnly	Records are read-only, and cannot be changed.
adOpenUnspecified	No locking type is specified.

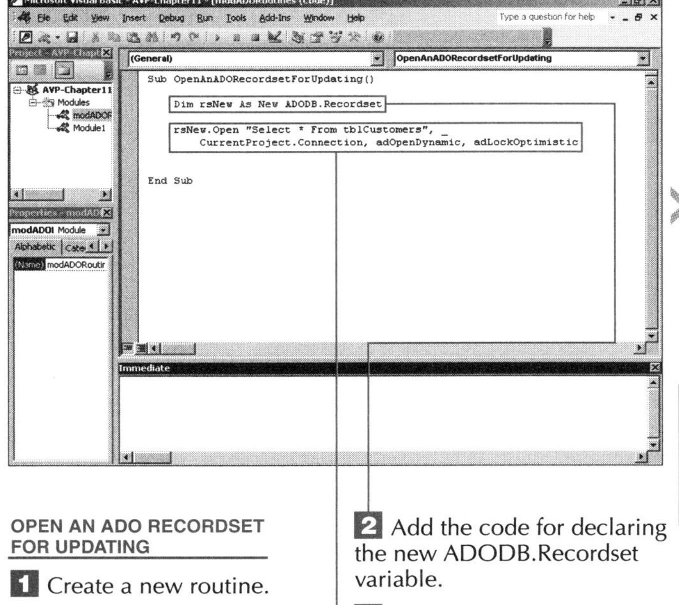

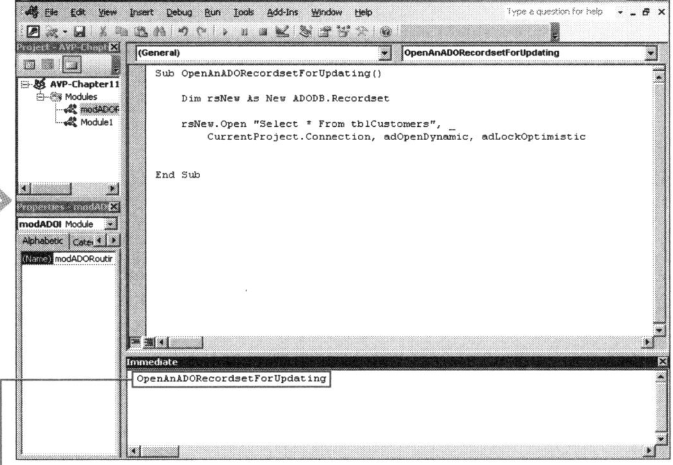

OPEN AN ADO RECORDSET FOR UPDATING

1. Create a new routine.
2. Add the code for declaring the new ADODB.Recordset variable.
3. Type the code for opening the recordset for updating.
4. Type the name of the routine in the Immediate window, and press Enter.

■ No messages appear, indicating that the recordset opened correctly.

MOVE AROUND AND DISPLAY DATA FROM THE RECORDSET

When you open a recordset, you can navigate through and display the data within the recordset. You can use several methods to move through the recordset, such as MoveNext, MovePrevious, MoveLast, and MoveFirst. The methods that are available depend on the cursor type you select for the recordset. For example, if you open the recordset with the adOpenForwardOnly cursor type, you cannot use the MovePrevious and MoveFirst methods, because you can only move forward.

The standard technique for moving through a recordset is to use the MoveNext method within a Do Until...Loop control structure. The criteria for the Do Until...Loop can be the End of File, or EOF, property of the recordset.

Inside the loop, in order to see the individual fields within each record, you can use the Fields collection. Each recordset has a Fields collection, just as forms have a Control collection. Because the Fields collection is the default collection for a recordset, you only need to specify the name of the recordset variable, followed by an exclamation mark, and the name of the field:

```
rs!fieldname
```

Just like controls on a form, you can use the number index of a field and use the parentheses to specify fields.

With the commands in this section and the previous section, you can now declare a recordset variable, and open the recordset. Next, you can create a loop that tests for the EOF property of the recordset to be set to True. Inside the loop, you can use the Debug.Print method to show the field you want to display in the Immediate window, using the rs!fieldname syntax. Lastly, you can use the Close method of the recordset to close the recordset when you are done with it.

MOVE AROUND AND DISPLAY DATA FROM THE RECORDSET

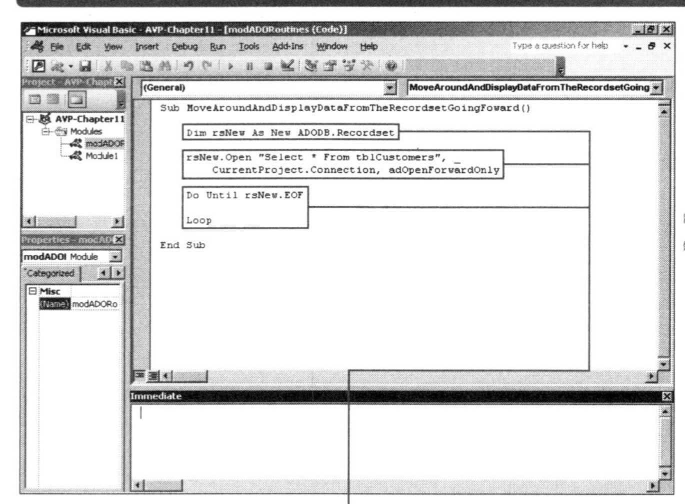

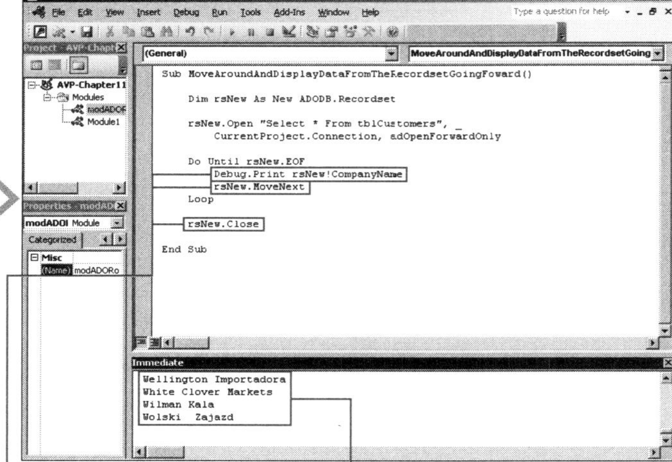

MOVE AROUND AND DISPLAY DATA FROM THE RECORDSET GOING FORWARD

Note: This task uses modADORoutines in AVP-Chapter11.mdb on the CD-ROM.

1 Create a new routine.

2 Add the code for declaring the new ADODB.Recordset variable.

3 Type the code for opening the recordset using forward only access.

4 Type the Do Until … Loop code, using the recordset variable and the EOF property.

5 Type the code to display the desired field in the Immediate window using Debug.Print.

6 Add the code to move to the next record.

7 Add the code to close the recordset.

8 Type the name of the routine in the Immediate window, and press Enter.

■ The field you specified appears in the Immediate window for each record.

Extra

To test if there are any records in the recordset, you can compare the EOF, End of File, and BOF, Beginning of File, properties at the same time. If they are both set to True, then there are no records located in the recordset. You can perform this test using an If Then statement:

```
If Not (rs.BOF And rs.EOF) Then
    ' — command to perform if there are records.
End if
```

It can be difficult to obtain an accurate record count using ADO recordsets if you do not know what you are looking for. Unlike DAO recordsets, which return an accurate record count if you call the MoveLast method of the recordset, ADO recordsets depend on the cursor type you are using.

Both DAO and ADO recordsets use the RecordCount property. However, with ADO, if you use a forward-only type recordset, the RecordCount property always returns a value of –1.

You get an accurate record count with static or keyset cursors. With a dynamic cursor, depending on the data source, Access returns either –1 or the actual count. If the Recordset object supports approximate positioning or bookmarks, it returns an accurate count, regardless of whether or not it is completely populated; otherwise, you must use the MoveLast method, which can hamper performance.

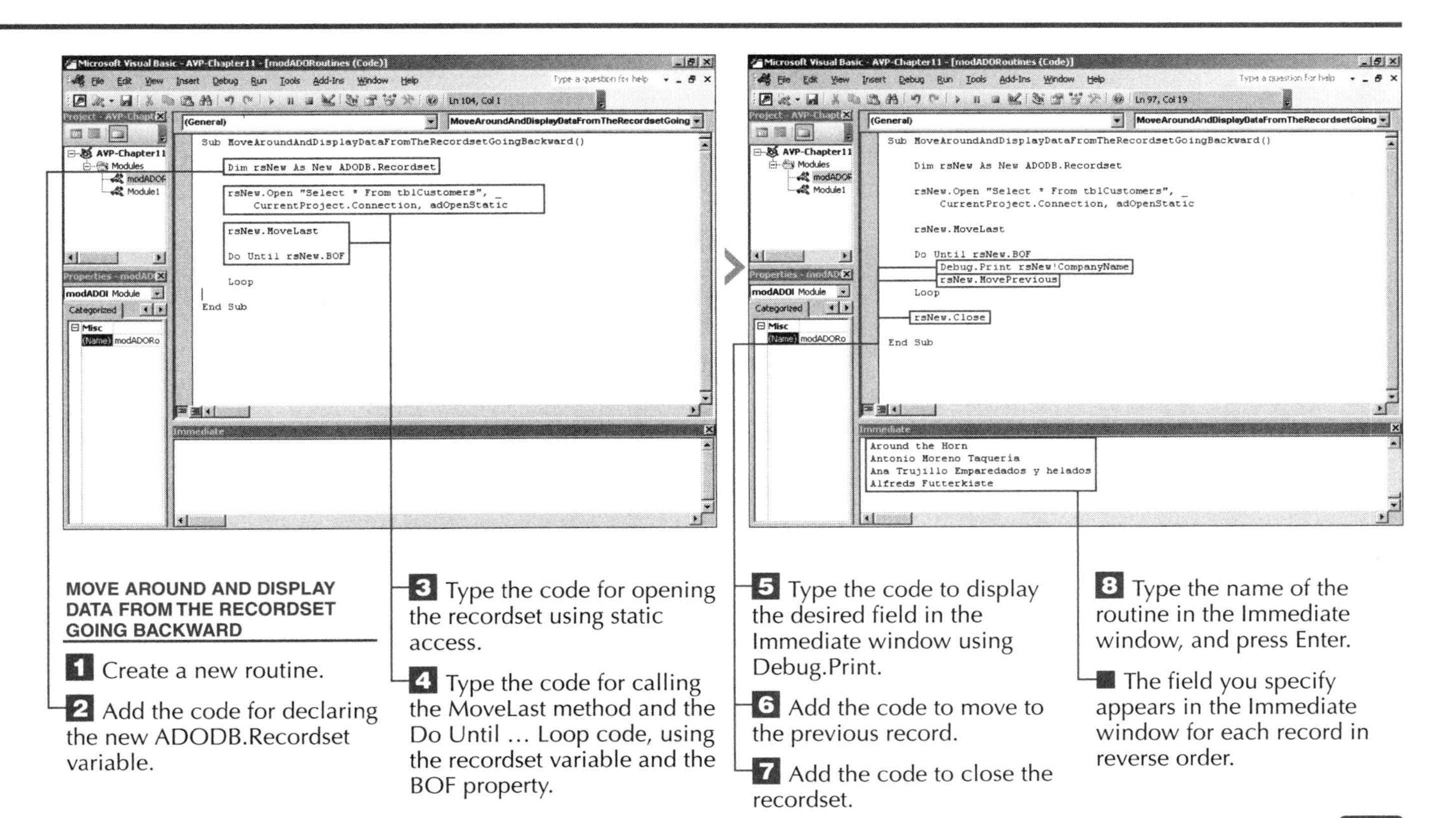

MOVE AROUND AND DISPLAY DATA FROM THE RECORDSET GOING BACKWARD

1. Create a new routine.
2. Add the code for declaring the new ADODB.Recordset variable.
3. Type the code for opening the recordset using static access.
4. Type the code for calling the MoveLast method and the Do Until … Loop code, using the recordset variable and the BOF property.
5. Type the code to display the desired field in the Immediate window using Debug.Print.
6. Add the code to move to the previous record.
7. Add the code to close the recordset.
8. Type the name of the routine in the Immediate window, and press Enter.

■ The field you specify appears in the Immediate window for each record in reverse order.

LOOP THROUGH A RECORDSET USING CRITERIA

While you can loop through a whole table, you can also loop through a subset of a table, examining only some of the data. For example, to look at Washington customers open the recordset as follows:

```
rsNew.Open "Select * From tblCustomers Where
Region = 'WA'", _
                    CurrentProject.Connection
```

You can then loop through all the records in the table, looking for rsNew.EOF = True, indicating the end of the recordset.

If you want to open the recordset with all the records, and then locate various criteria multiple times without reopening the recordset, you can do so using the Find method of the recordset, as well as compare the field, in this case Region, with the inputted values.

```
rs.Find Criteria, SkipRows, SearchDirection,
Start
```

where Criteria is a single-column comparison, but is not restricted to equal, =. You can use the other comparison operators, including >, <, and Like. You can use SkipRows to select the number of rows you want to skip before searching; the default is 0. SearchDirection can be adSearchForward (default) or adSearchBackward. The search continues until EOF and BOF, depending on the direction in which you search. Start is a Variant bookmark, which lets you start from a specific location within the recordset. You can use the MoveFirst method of the recordset to reset the location of the record pointer, in order to repeat the Find method.

You can also add code to trap for the EOF. For example, you can place the inner loop in the line of code:

```
If Not rsNew.EOF then
    ....
End If
```

If no records are in the recordset, the code will not fail.

LOOP THROUGH A RECORDSET USING CRITERIA

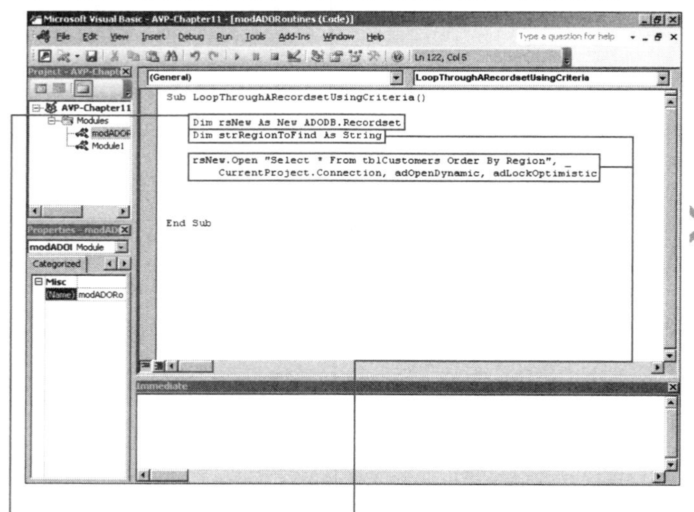

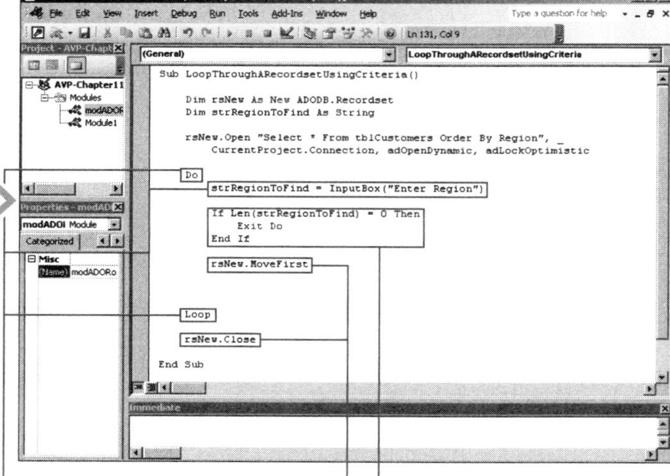

Note: This task uses modADORoutines in AVP-Chapter11.mdb on the CD-ROM.

1 Create a new routine.

2 Add the code for the new ADODB.Recordset variable.

3 Add the code for a string variable to store the user's choice of criteria.

4 Type the code to open the recordset using forward only access.

5 Add a Do … Loop structure with no criteria.

6 Add the code, using the InputBox() function to retrieve the current criteria the user wants to find.

7 Add the code to test the criteria inputted.

8 Add the code to move to the first record of the recordset, and add the code to close the recordset.

Extra

You can use the With...End With command with the code created in the steps to enhance the readability of the routine, and to reduce keystrokes. When you use the With....End With structure, you are telling VBA that whenever you are using a property or method with just the period or exclamation point, you are using that property or method of the object that you specified in the With statement.

```
Sub LoopThroughARecordsetUsingCriteriaExtra()
    Dim rsNew As New ADODB.Recordset
    Dim strRegionToFind As String
    With rsNew
        .Open "Select * From tblCustomers
Order By Region", _
            CurrentProject.Connection,
adOpenDynamic, _
        adLockOptimistic
        Do
            strRegionToFind =
InputBox("Enter Region")
            If Len(strRegionToFind) = 0 Then
                Exit Do
            End If
            .MoveFirst
            .Find "Region = '" &
strRegionToFind & "'"
            Do While !Region = strRegionToFind
                Debug.Print !CompanyName
                .MoveNext
            Loop
        Loop
        .Close
    End With
End Sub
```

Using the With...End With command increases performance, but you must also ensure that you increase readability as well. When the code extends beyond the boundaries of your screen, you may forget which variable you were using.

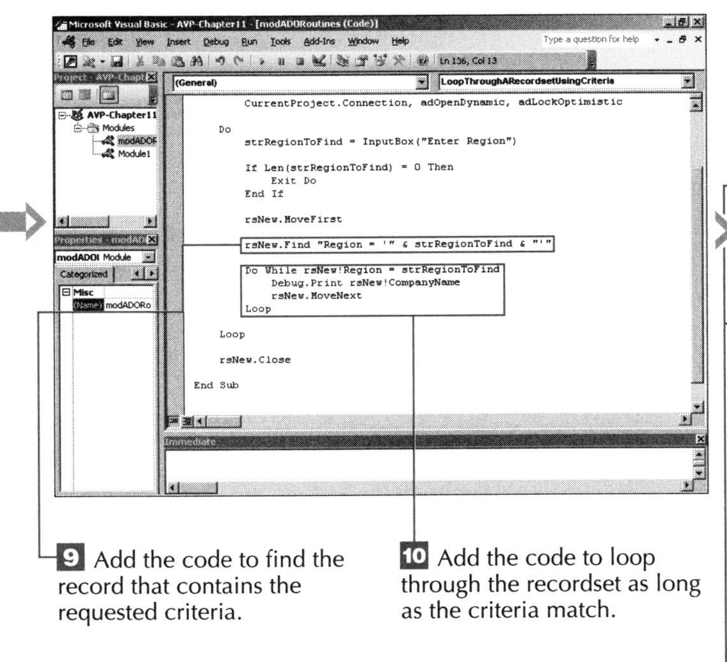

9 Add the code to find the record that contains the requested criteria.

10 Add the code to loop through the recordset as long as the criteria match.

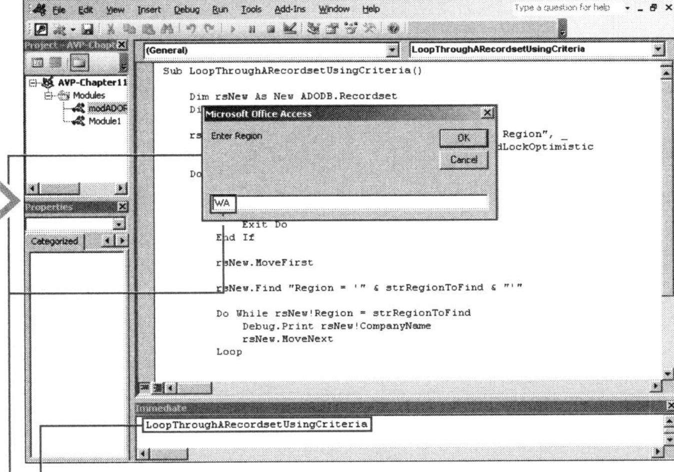

11 Type the name of the routine in the Immediate window.

■ The input box appears, displaying the prompt from step 6.

12 Type the criteria to look up.

■ The routine continues to display the input box, until you click Cancel, or OK, leaving the input field blank.

MANAGE RECORDS IN RECORDSETS

You can edit and update records individually when you need to. When you work in recordsets, you may need to edit one or more fields in your records, and add new records.

You can add new records using two recordset methods: AddNew and Update. You can use the AddNew method of the recordset to create a new row in the recordset and to add the data to the fields. You can use the Update method to update the recordset. For example, if you want to add new records and edit existing records in tblCustomers, you can open the recordset as usual, using criteria if you want to narrow down the returned records.

If you are opening a recordset just to add individual records, and the Primary Key field is an AutoNumber, then you can open the recordset where the testing 0 = 1. This causes the table to open without records, and records are not compared individually. For example, to open tblEmployees, use the OpenRecordset statement:

```
rs.OpenRecordset _
"Select * From tblEmployees Where 0 = 1", _
      CurrentProject.Connection,
adOpenDynamic, adOpenOptimistic
```

To add and update a new record, you can use this syntax:

```
rs.AddNew
      rs!FieldName1 = Value1
      rs!FieldName2 = Value2
      ' — Additional fields
rs.Update
```

If you edit a record, you do not have to use any particular edit method, because one does not exist. You can simply place the new values into the appropriate fields and call the Update method.

EDIT A RECORD

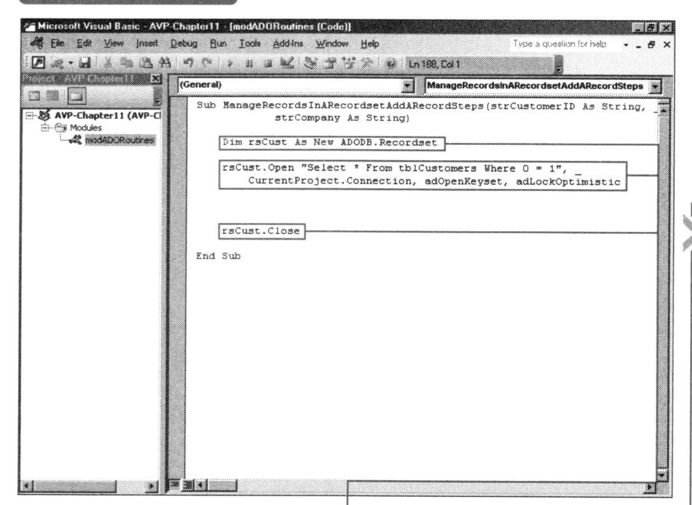

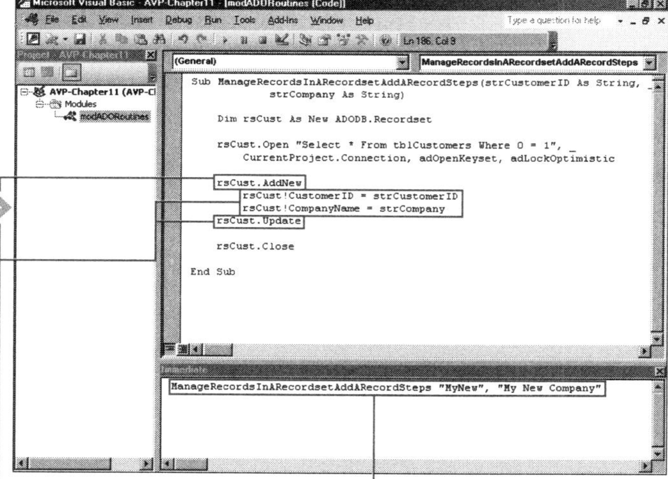

Note: This task uses modADORoutines in AVP-Chapter11.mdb on the CD-ROM.

1 Create a new routine, adding arguments for values to enter into the new record.

2 Add the code for the new ADODB.Recordset variable.

3 Add the code to open the recordset using updateable access with the criteria of the Primary Key field, set to a value that is not in the table.

4 Add the code to close the recordset.

5 Add the AddNew method.

6 Add the code adding the field entries.

7 Add the Update method.

8 Type the name of the routine, and then the appropriate parameters in quotes.

■ If you open the table, the new entry appears.

Extra

You can also use the Recordset object to delete individual records. To do this, open the recordset in one of the cursor types with update capability, such as adOpenKeyset and adOpenDynamic, and use one of the lock types, such as adLockOptimistic.

Because Access tables only work in the immediate update mode, and not in batch mode, when you call the Delete method of the recordset, the record is immediately deleted in the file. You should therefore confirm that the user actually intends to delete the record. The MsgBox statement, which prompts the user for this confirmation, is useful inside any loop you are using. The basic syntax for the Delete statement is:

```
    Dim rs As New ADODB.Recordset
    rs.Open Source, CurrentProject.Connection, adOpenKeyset, adLockOptimistic
    Do Until rs.EOF
             If MsgBox("The current record is: " & rs!Field & vbCrLf & vbCrLf & _
"Do you want to delete it?", vbQuestion + vbYesNo, _
"Confirm Deletion") = vbYes Then
             rs.Delete
         End If
   Loop
   rs.Close
```

This is a perfect example of using recordsets to complete a task that you cannot complete using queries.

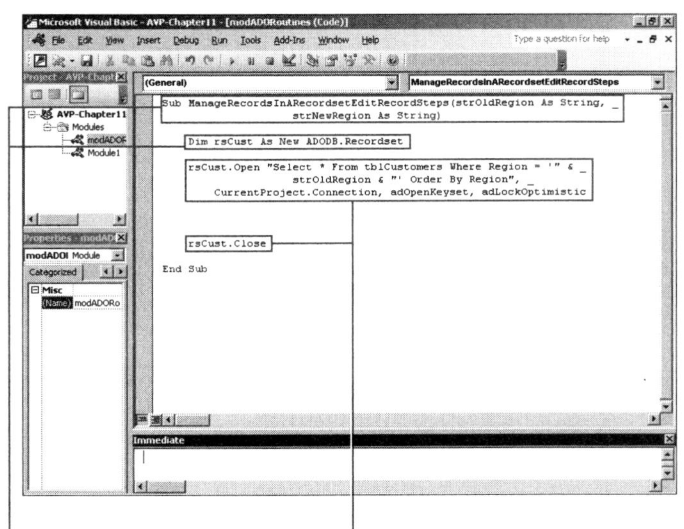

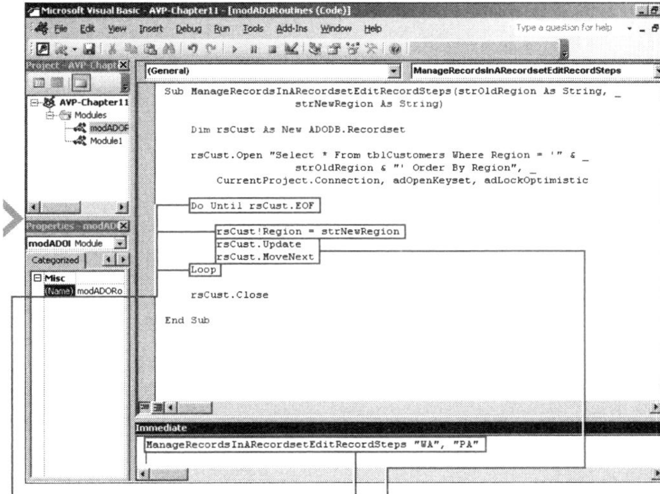

1 Create a new routine, adding arguments for values to compare the old criteria, and the new value with which you want to replace it.

2 Add the code for the new ADODB.Recordset variable.

3 Add the code to open the recordset using updateable access with the criteria of the old value.

4 Add the code to close the recordset.

5 Add the Do Until … Loop structure to check for the EOF property of the recordset.

6 Add the code to replace the old value in the appropriate field with the new value.

7 Add the Update and MoveNext methods.

8 Type the name of the routine, and then the old and new values in quotes.

■ You may need to check the data to see if the values were updated correctly.

EXECUTE A BULK QUERY USING THE ADO COMMAND

You can use the ADO Command object to perform bulk operations using action queries such as Update, Make Table, and Append. You can also create a Command object and open a recordset based on it by passing the Command object as the recordset Source in the Open method. This is useful if you intend to use the Command object more than once in a routine, because you can just reuse the Command object each time.

When using the Command object, you must first declare a variable for it as you would for other ADO objects, using the New keyword.

```
Dim cmdNew As New ADODB.Command
```

After declaring a new Command object variable, you can set the ActiveConnection property, and specify which type of command you want to execute by setting the CommandType property.

Before actually calling the Execute method of the Command object, you must set the final property, the CommandText property. This property is either an SQL statement — adCmdText — or the name of a query — adCmdStoredProcedure.

Finally, you can call the Execute method, which has some arguments that you can pass. The syntax is:

```
cmd.Execute RecordsAffected, Parameters, Options
```

where cmd is the name of the Command object. RecordsAffected is an Integer type variable that you can use to pass back the number of records that were affected — deleted, updated, or added. Parameters are any parameters that are in use. Options are various options that you can use. Which parameters and options you use depends on the type of database with which you are working. For example, with Access you do not need to use the parameters and options, but with SQL Server you may have to.

EXECUTE A BULK QUERY USING THE ADO COMMAND

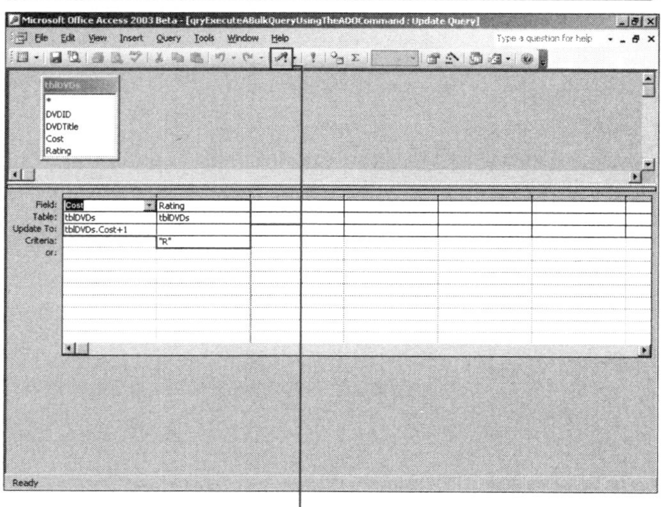

Note: This task uses modADORoutines in AVP-Chapter11.mdb on the CD-ROM.

1 Create a new query.

2 Make the query into an action query by clicking the Query Type button.

3 Specify the fields to update and use for criteria.

4 Save and close the query.

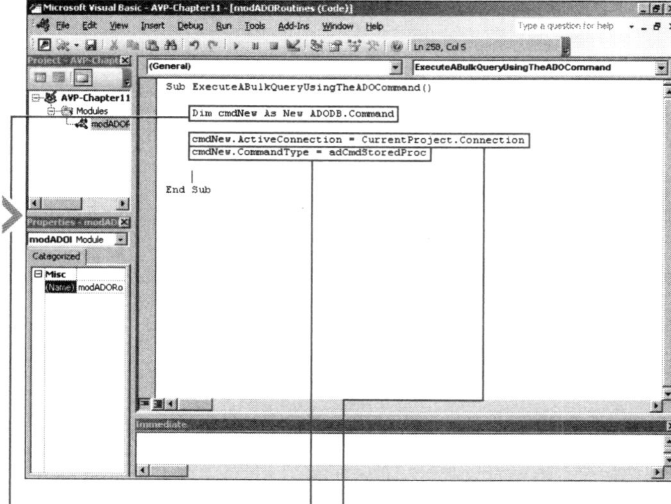

5 Create a new routine.

6 Add the code to declare the new ADODB.Command variable.

7 Assign the CurrentProject.Connection to the ActiveConnection property of the command object.

8 Specify adCmdStoredProc for the CommandType property of the command object.

Extra

The table contains descriptions of the constants for CommandType.

The most commonly used constants are adCmdText, which is an SQL string that you execute, and adCmdStoredProcedure, which is the name of a pre-built query in Access, and which stores procedures in an SQL Server.

You may want to set the CommandType property rather than having ADO use the adCmdUnknown constant, because ADO may make an incorrect choice. It may also return an error, and adversely affect performance.

CONSTANT	DESCRIPTION
adCmdFile	Specifies the name of a persisted recordset.
adCmdStoredProcedure	The name of a query in Access databases, stores procedures in an SQL Server database.
adCmdTable	The name of a table in the database.
adCmdTableDirect	The name of a table in the database, applied when you are using the results for a Recordset object. You can also use the Seek method on the results when the command is of type adCmdTableDirect.
adCmdText	SQL statement text.
adCmdUnknown	Chosen when you do not know the type of command being used. This is the default for the CommandType property.

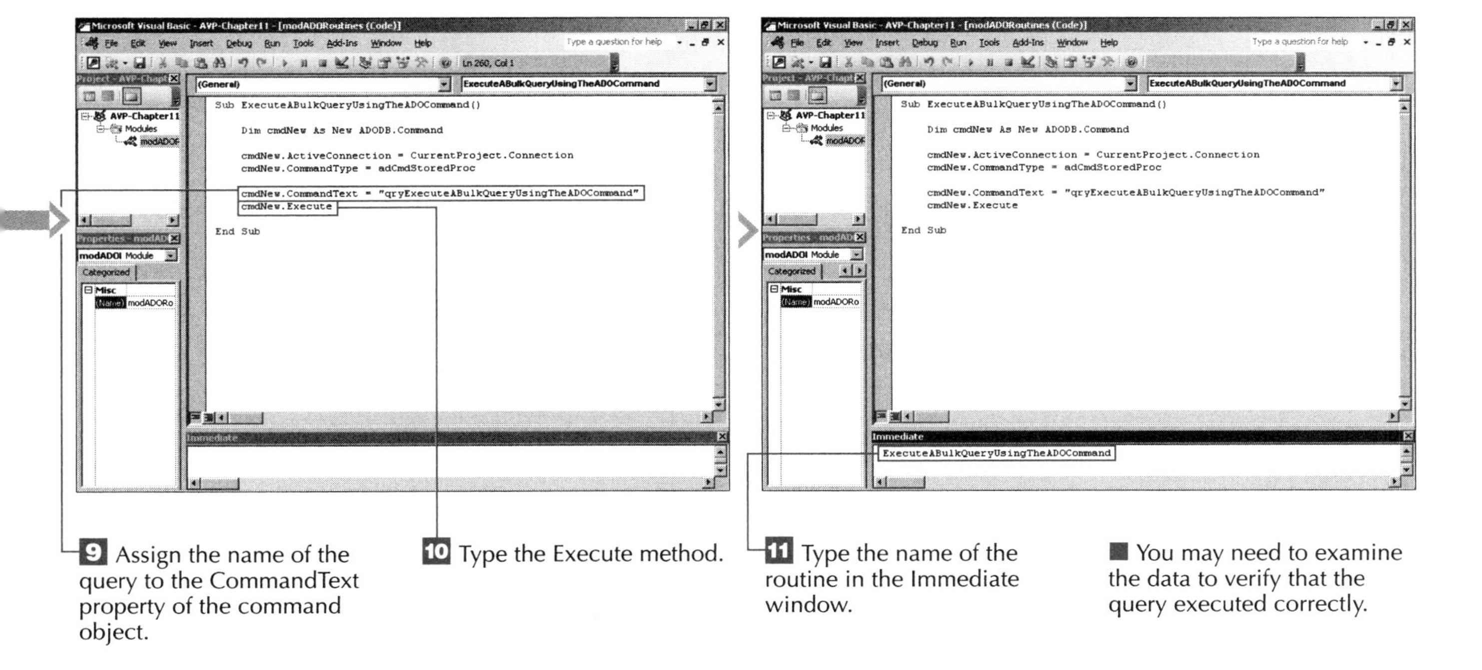

9 Assign the name of the query to the CommandText property of the command object.

10 Type the Execute method.

11 Type the name of the routine in the Immediate window.

■ You may need to examine the data to verify that the query executed correctly.

USING A PARAMETER WITH THE ADO COMMAND

When you use queries with Command objects, you can increase the power of the queries by using parameters with them. One way to add parameters is to include them when you call the Execute method. When you use this method, you include all the parameters in the Array() function. The call for the Execute method looks like this: `rs.Execute intNumRecs, Array(par1, par2).`

where par1 and par2 are the parameters to include. You can have as many parameters as you have in the query you are executing.

The other way to use parameters is to create Parameter objects and add them to the Command object. You can use the CreateParameter method of the Command object to create Parameter objects. The syntax for the various commands is:

```
    Dim par As ADODB.Parameter
    Set par =
cmd.CreateParameter(ParameterName, _
                        ParameterDataType,
ParameterType, ParameterSize)
    cmd.Parameters.Append par
    par.Value = Value
```

Both the ParameterDataType and ParameterType use enumerators with descriptive constants. ParameterDataTypes include adInteger and adChar. ParameterTypes include adInputParameter and adOutputParameter. For this task, you use adInputParameter for all the parameters.

You must call the Append method of the Parameters collection to add the parameter to the command. You must also ensure that you append the parameters in the same order they appear in the query.

USING A PARAMETER WITH THE ADO COMMAND INLINE

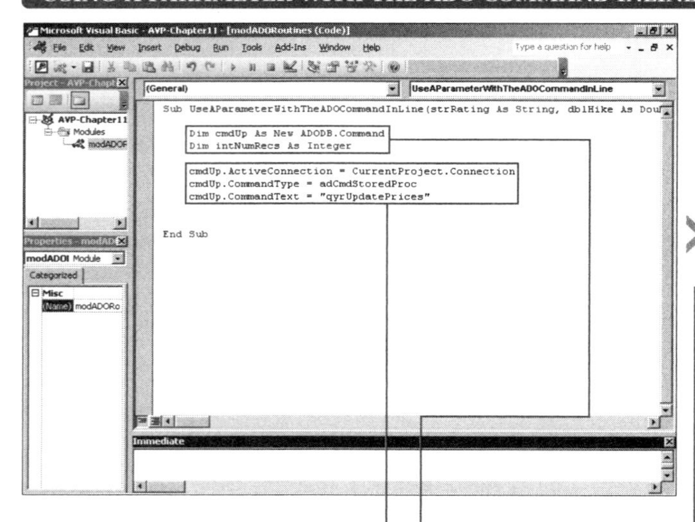

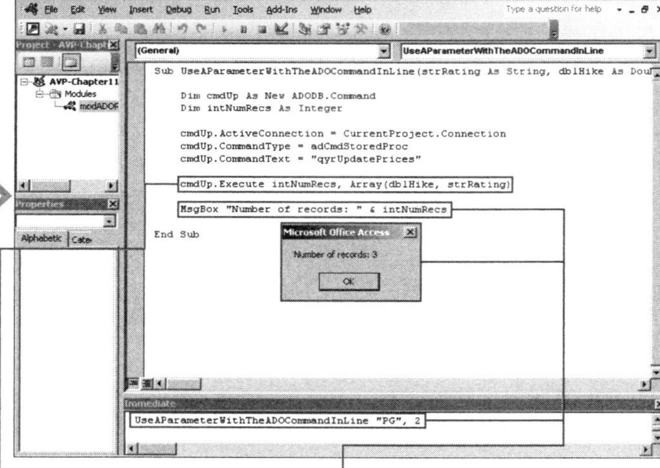

Note: This task uses modADORoutines in AVP-Chapter11.mdb on the CD-ROM.

1 Create the parameter query to run from the code.

2 Add a new routine, with the criteria to update another value, and the other amount to update.

3 Add the code for the new ADODB.Command and an Integer variable.

4 Add the code for the Command object set-up, with the name of the parameter query.

5 Add the code to call the Execute method of the Command object, with the Integer variable from step 3, and the Array() function, wrapping the two parameters to pass to the query.

6 Add the code for the MsgBox statement.

7 Type the name of the routine, and then the arguments.

■ A message box displays the number of records affected.

Extra

There are many ways in which you can supply the properties to the Parameter object. For example, you can supply the majority of the properties when you call the CreateParameter command, as shown below:

```
Set par =
cmd.CreateParameter(ParameterName, _
     ParameterDataType, ParameterType,
ParameterSize)
```

You can also set the parameter properties separately, on individual lines of code. This is useful for readability purposes as seen below:

```
Set par =
cmd.CreateParameter(ParameterName,
ParameterDataType)
par.Type = ParameterType
par.Size = ParameterSize
```

If you are not receiving enough information from Intellesense, you can open the Object Browser, and look up the object about which you need more information. To do this, in the module editor, choose Object Browser from the View menu.

Inside the Object Browser, you can choose ADODB in the project/library drop-down list, selecting the object for which you want to see the properties, methods, and events. When you highlight a property, method, or event, you can click the question mark at the top of the Object Browser, and help is displayed for the property, method, or event, with descriptions on how to use them.

USING A PARAMETER WITH THE ADO COMMAND WITH PARAMETERS

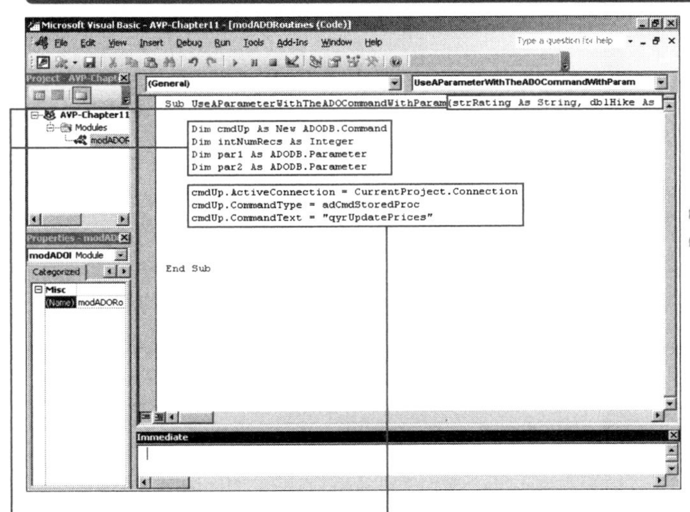


```
Sub UseAParameterWithTheADOCommandWithParam(strRating As String, dblHike As

    Dim cmdUp As New ADODB.Command
    Dim intNumRecs As Integer
    Dim par1 As ADODB.Parameter
    Dim par2 As ADODB.Parameter

    cmdUp.ActiveConnection = CurrentProject.Connection
    cmdUp.CommandType = adCmdStoredProc
    cmdUp.CommandText = "qyrUpdatePrices"

    Set par1 = cmdUp.CreateParameter("currHike", adDouble, adParamInput)
    cmdUp.Parameters.Append par1
    par1.Value = dblHike

    Set par2 = cmdUp.CreateParameter("currRating", adChar, adParamInput, 2)
    cmdUp.Parameters.Append par2
    par2.Value = strRating

    cmdUp.Execute intNumRecs

    MsgBox "Number of records: " & intNumRecs

End Sub
```

1 Add a new routine, with the criteria to update from another value, and the other amount to update.

2 Add the code for the new ADODB.Command, an Integer variable, and two Parameter variables.

3 Add the code for the Command object set-up, with the name of the parameter query to run, from step 1 on the previous page.

4 Add the code to create the first Parameter object, calling the CreateParameter method off the Command object, and adding the Parameter object.

5 Repeat step 4 for the second Parameter object.

6 Add the code to call the Execute method of the Command object, with the Integer variable from step 2.

7 Add the code for the MsgBox statement, and the query runs.

USING AUTOMATION TO CONTROL OTHER OFFICE PRODUCTS

Throughout this book, you use Access objects such as forms, reports, and controls. You also use the various objects found in the ADO object models, such as Recordset and Command objects, using VBA. Most of these objects have properties, methods, and events. When working with other Office applications, you will notice many similarities.

WHAT IS AUTOMATION?

Automation is a process where you can control different server applications from a controller application. You can use VBA and the various object models from within the controller application to manipulate the objects in the server application.

For example, you can use automation to generate an Excel spreadsheet from Access, with the controller application using data from a database. From within your Access database application, you can open Excel, use one of the default spreadsheets, create and format the columns, and then load the data into the columns from Access. You can also use the Excel Chart Wizard to generate a chart.

There are many ways to use automation in Office products. Here are some examples of how you can use automation within Access:

- Send form letters using Word with Access data. You can add an option to display a dialog box, and allow users to add or modify specific parts of the document.
- Take a report you create in Access, export it to Word, and add Word-specific features.
- Import your contacts from Outlook into your Access contact manager.
- Export your contacts from your Access contact manager into Outlook.
- Create Excel pivot tables based on detailed information from your Access database.
- Generate Excel graphs from Access data.
- Generate PowerPoint presentations using sales data from Access files.

Run Access from Other Office Products

Just as you can run other Office products from within Access using VBA and automation, you can also run Access from other Office products. You can use ActiveX Data Objects, or ADO, and Access objects just as you can from within Access, including the use of the DoCmd object to perform macro actions.

From within other Office products, you have full access to forms and reports. One of the common uses of Access is to create a report generator from Word or Excel, using one of these applications as the base application, and the database information from Access.

ActiveX Controls

ActiveX controls are mini-server applications that you can use inside your applications. Access is the controller application, while the ActiveX control is the server application. You can use server application properties, methods, and events using automation.

Other Applications

You can control other non-Microsoft applications as long as they adhere to the Automation standard. One example for the use of the Automation standard is the third-party ActiveX controls. You can use ActiveX controls in many different languages and applications because they are written to the Automation standard. Visio, a graphics utility, complied with the Automation standard before Microsoft purchased it.

USING OBJECT MODELS

Each Office application has proprietary object models consisting of collections, objects, properties, methods, and events. You can control other Office applications, such as Word, Excel, and Outlook, using their object models.

Reference the Libraries

Each object model is contained in a different library. As with the ADO libraries, you can find the various object models of an application by using the References dialog box from within the code editor.

You can have access to the object model after you add the library using the References dialog box. To use the various objects, you can declare variables for them, starting with the Application object.

Application Object

One object that all the object models have in common is the Application object. When you want to work with the object model, you must start with the Application object. The collections of properties, methods, and events vary for each application. You can examine the various collections of objects for the Application object using the Object Browser.

Declare the Variables

You must declare variables of the library just as you would declare variables with ADO objects. Some of the declarations require the use of the New keyword. With Automation objects, however, there are times when you will declare the variable, and then use the New keyword when you are actually using the object for the first time using the Set statement. The reason for this is that you postpone instantiating a copy of the server in memory until you actually need it.

Assigning the Variables

You can use the Set statement when you assign the objects. There are some cases where you can use the New keyword, and others where you cannot. Note that by including the New keyword, you are instantiating a new copy of Word. If you omit the New keyword, any current version of Word already open is used. This could cause some concern for the user, especially if your code deletes or modifies items in the current document.

Late Binding

There are some cases where you are not certain that the object model will be installed on the system on which you are installing your application. While this is not a big problem with the majority of the Office applications, there are some instances where it could be a problem. To solve this problem, you can do what is called late binding. Late binding means that you are not asking Access, or another controlling application, to know anything about the server application until you actually use it. As a result, you do not have to create a reference to the application in advance. When you create a reference at design time, this is known as early binding.

To use late binding instead of object models, you can declare the objects as Object. To set the variables, you can use the CreateObject command. For an Excel application object, you can use the following syntax:

```
Dim objExcel as Object

Set objExcel =
CreateObject("Excel.Application")
```

You can surround the code with error handling in case the application was not installed. When you do this, you will receive a reference error with the early binding method, and you can also get better performance.

Note that late binding can cause performance problems at runtime when used extensively. Early binding is faster. Also, programming errors that early binding will catch at compile time will not be caught until runtime using late binding. This is because the environment cannot validate your code against the object model until runtime.

CREATE A WORD DOCUMENT FROM ACCESS

You can create a Word document from Access that contains information from your database. Word has a rich object model that allows you to perform almost any task you need to do through automation. After the Application object, you can use the Documents collection to get to documents, and for creating a Word document and inserting text, the Range object.

Using the properties and methods of the Range object, you can manipulate ranges of text and perform tasks such as setting fonts, replacing data, and inserting and deleting text.

To open a document in Word from Access, first declare the variables you want to use. You can use the Application and Document objects, and declare them as follows:

```
Dim appWord As Word.Application
Dim docNew As Word.Document
```

Next, you need to create the objects using the Set statement. You can create the Application object in the standard way with the following statement:

```
Set appWord = New Word.Application
```

To set the document variable, you must add a new document to the Documents collection using the Add method, as follows:

```
Set docNew = appWord.Documents.Add()
```

After you set the variables for these objects, you can use the properties and methods for the objects. You can use the Range object, which is a property of the Document object. The Range object can contain a block, or range of text, letting you manipulate that text. You can use the InsertAfter method for adding text to a document, as follows:

```
docNew.Range.InsertAfter (strTextToAdd)
```

where strTextToAdd is a string variable or literal text.

You can set the Visible property of the Document object to True to make the Word application visible to the user.

CREATE A WORD DOCUMENT FROM ACCESS

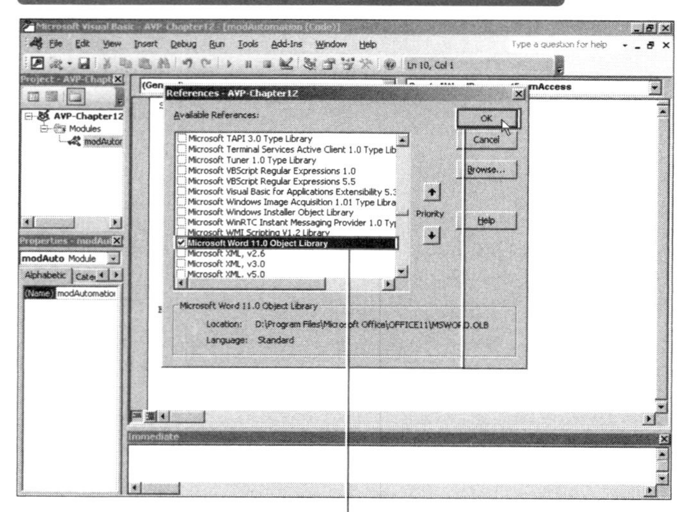

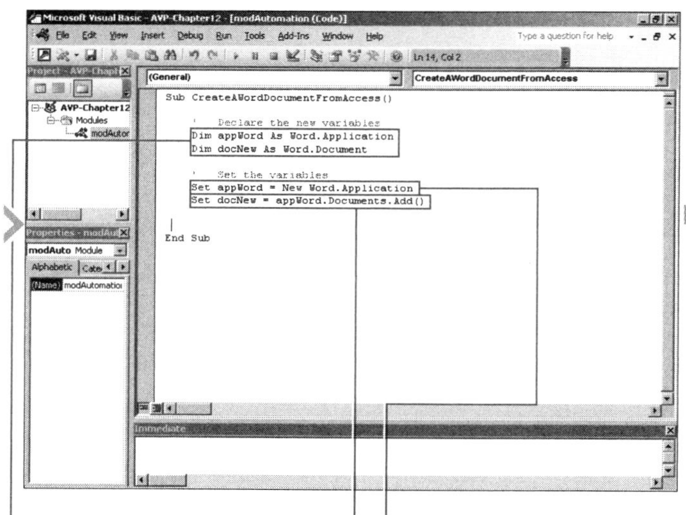

Note: This task uses modAutomation in AVP-Chapter12.mdb on the CD-ROM.

1 Create a new module.

2 In the code editor, click Tools ⇨ References.

■ The References dialog box appears.

3 From the list of Available References, select Microsoft Word 11.0 Object Library.

4 Click OK.

5 Type the code to declare the Application and Document object variables, such as: **Dim app*VarName* As Word.Application** and **Dim doc*VarName* As Word.Document**.

6 Type the code to set the new Word.Application: **Set app*VarName* = New Word.Application**.

7 Type the code to add a new document to the Documents collection of the Application: **Set doc*VarName* = appWord.Documents.Add()**.

Extra

You may sometimes want to create or open a document, modify it, print it, and save it, all without user intervention. There are a few ways to do this. For example, you can use the Close method of the Word Document object. The partial syntax of this method is as follows:

```
docVar.Close(SaveChanges, OriginalFormat, RouteDocument)
```

where docVar is the Document object, and SaveChanges is a variant that tells Word that it has the following choices: wdDoNotSaveChanges, wdPromptToSaveChanges, or wdSaveChanges. OriginalFormat specifies whether or not to save the document in the original format. The settings are, wdOriginalDocumentFormat, wdPromptUser, or wdWordDocument. RouteDocument routes the document to the next recipient.

Another way to avoid user intervention is to save a document, keep it open, and call the Save method of the Document object. This method simply saves the document as follows:

```
docVar.Save NoPrompt, RouteDocument
```

where NoPrompt is a True/False value and RouteDocument routes the document to the next recipient. When you use either the Close or Save method, you must set the Name property in advance.

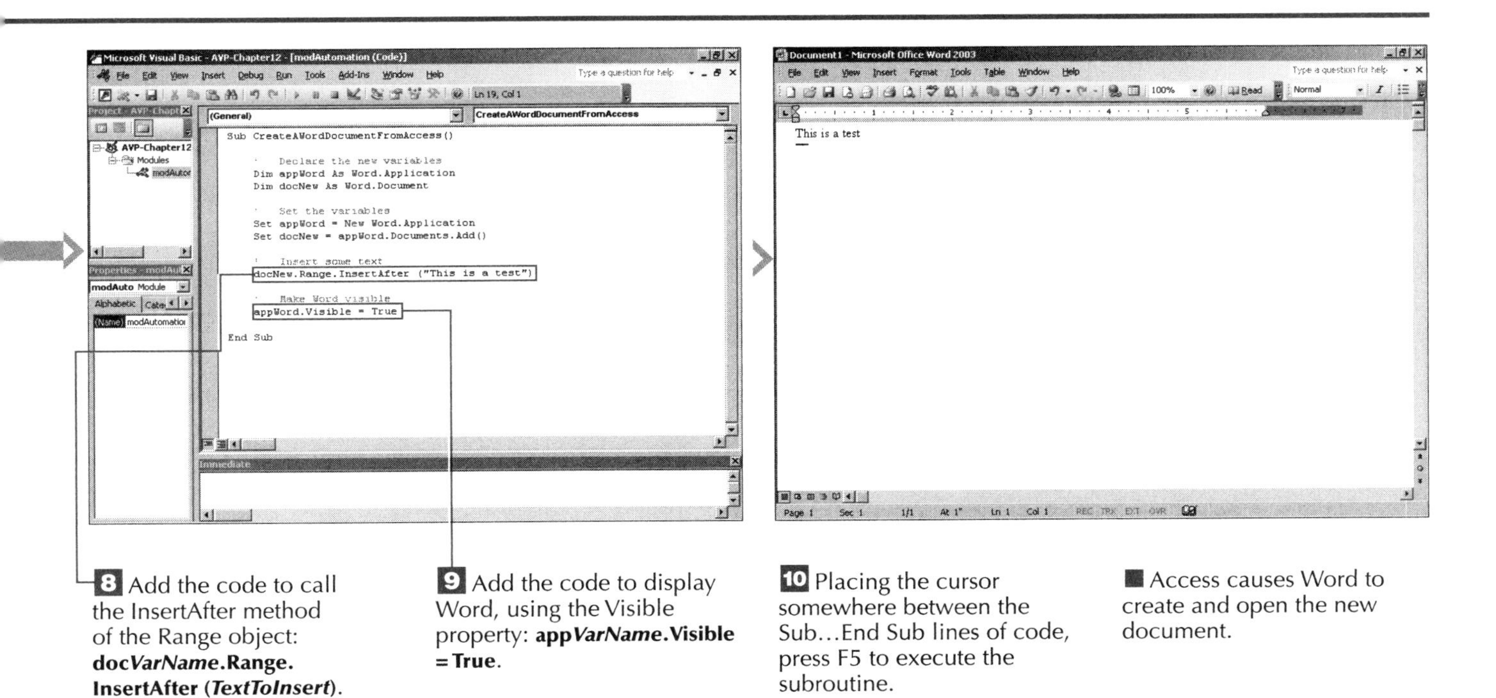

8 Add the code to call the InsertAfter method of the Range object: **doc*VarName*.Range. InsertAfter (*TextToInsert*)**.

9 Add the code to display Word, using the Visible property: **app*VarName*.Visible = True**.

10 Placing the cursor somewhere between the Sub…End Sub lines of code, press F5 to execute the subroutine.

■ Access causes Word to create and open the new document.

ADD A BOOKMARK TO A WORD DOCUMENT

When working with Word documents, one of the most common tasks to perform is the insertion of data from your database into the document. You can do this in a few ways. One of the simplest ways is to use the Mail Merge feature in Word, and pass it the name of a table or query. Another way is to use bookmarks in Word to specify where you want to move around within a document, or to insert text at specific places in the document.

To create bookmarks in a Word document, you must first launch Word. By default, Word creates a new document in which you can type the text you want.

If you are using bookmarks to mark locations within your documents to make it easier to move around, you can simply position the cursor in the general area where you want to go when you use a bookmark. However, if you want to use the bookmarks to mark specific locations for text insertion, you must position the cursor in the exact location.

After you position the cursor where you want to place the bookmark, you can choose Bookmark from the Insert menu. The Bookmark dialog box appears. You can add, edit, delete, and go to current bookmarks using this dialog box.

To add a bookmark, you must type a new name for the bookmark, and then click the Add button. Access adds the bookmark. To test the bookmark, you can close the dialog box, move to another position in the document, and then, using the Bookmark dialog box to select the bookmark you want, you can click Go To.

You can use the Word document and bookmarks you create in this section in the next section.

ADD A BOOKMARK TO A WORD DOCUMENT

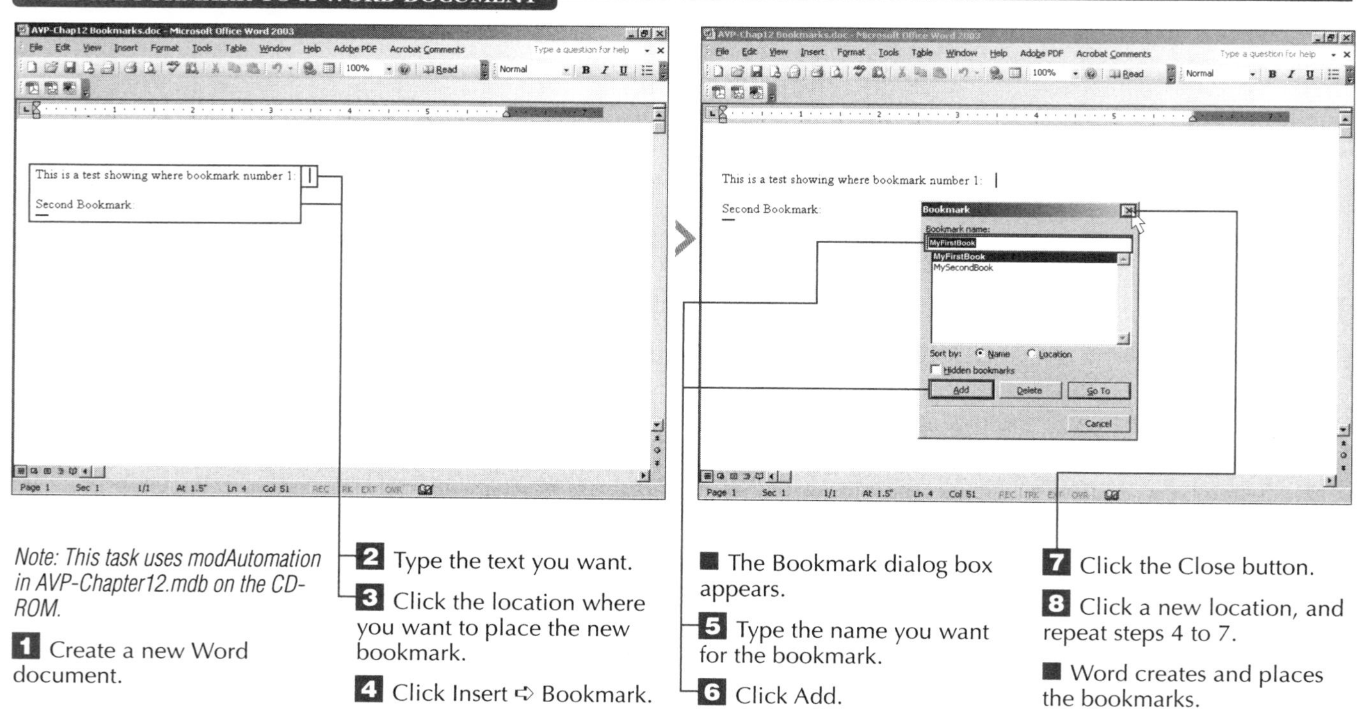

Note: This task uses modAutomation in AVP-Chapter12.mdb on the CD-ROM.

1 Create a new Word document.

2 Type the text you want.

3 Click the location where you want to place the new bookmark.

4 Click Insert ➪ Bookmark.

■ The Bookmark dialog box appears.

5 Type the name you want for the bookmark.

6 Click Add.

7 Click the Close button.

8 Click a new location, and repeat steps 4 to 7.

■ Word creates and places the bookmarks.

INSERT ACCESS DATA INTO A BOOKMARKED WORD DOCUMENT

After you create a Word document, you can use VBA to insert data from Access into the Word document. To do this, you can set a reference to the Word Library — for Office 2003, it is the Microsoft Word 11.0 Object Library.

You can use the Application, Document, and Range objects as well as the Bookmark collections. The Range object you use is derived from the bookmarks you created in the previous section.

You can use the Add method of the Documents collection to open an existing document and add it to the loaded documents. The syntax is as follows:

```
docCurr.Add(Template, NewTemplate,
DocumentType, Visible)
```

where docCurr is the document variable, and Template is the name of the template you want to use. Template can be the name of a regular document. NewTemplate is the name of a new template if you decide to create one. DocumentType can be one of the following: wdNewBlankDocument, wdNewEmailMessage, wdNewFrameset, or wdNewWebPage. The default is wdNewBlankDocument. Visible determines whether or not the document opens in a visible window.

Another new method you can use is the InsertAfter method of the Range object. You get the Range object from a Bookmark object by choosing a particular bookmark in the Bookmark collection. The index can either be an integer or a name you specify.

INSERT ACCESS DATA INTO A BOOKMARKED WORD DOCUMENT

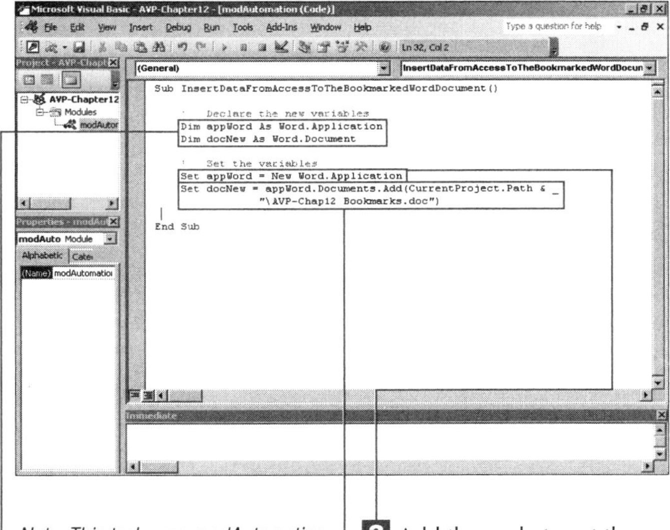

Note: This task uses modAutomation in AVP-Chapter12.mdb on the CD-ROM.

1 Add a new subroutine in your module.

2 Add the code to declare the Application and Document objects.

3 Add the code to set the Application object.

4 Add the code to add the new document to the Documents collections, using the Word document from the previous task.

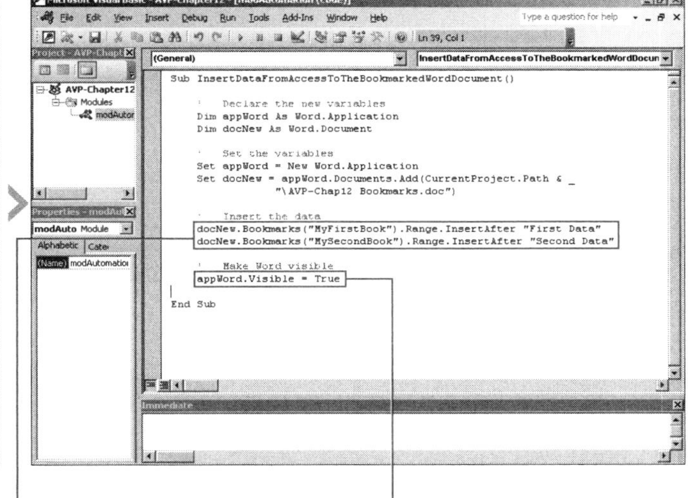

5 Add the code to call the InsertAfter method of the Bookmarks objects.

■ This example uses the names of the bookmarks assigned in the section "Add a Bookmark to a Word Document."

6 Type the code to make the Word application visible.

■ When you run this routine, Word opens the document with the new text inserted.

CREATE AN EXCEL SPREADSHEET FROM ACCESS

You can use Access data in Excel to augment data in a spreadsheet, or even to create entire spreadsheets. You can do this using Access, Excel, and Automation. In Excel, you can use Application, Workbook, and Worksheet objects. Like other object models, you can create objects from other collections and objects.

You can start with the Application object, and then add a new workbook to the Workbook collection, which is part of the Application object. Excel creates three worksheets by default. To use a worksheet within a workbook, you can assign the ActiveSheet property from the Workbook object to a Worksheet variable. The syntax is: `Set wksCurr = wkbCurr.ActiveSheet`.

You can now assign some of the cells. To do this, you can use the Cells array of the Worksheet object. To assign a value to individual cells, you can use the following syntax: `wksCurr.Cells(RowIndex, ColumnIndex) = Value`.

To assign values, you can use a For...Next loop to create the cells. The For...Next index variable indexes the RowIndex of the Cells array, as shown in the following syntax:

```
For intCurrRow = 2 To 10
        wksCurr.Cells(intCurrRow, 1) =
intCurrRow
      Next
```

These indexes are 1-based, not 0-based. The above code only assigns the intCurrRow as the value. You can also use values from a recordset; see the next section.

Finally, you can create a cell that sums up the values in the column. This is the standard Excel function, Sum. You can assign the Sum() to the value of the cell where you want it to appear.

CREATE AN EXCEL SPREADSHEET FROM ACCESS

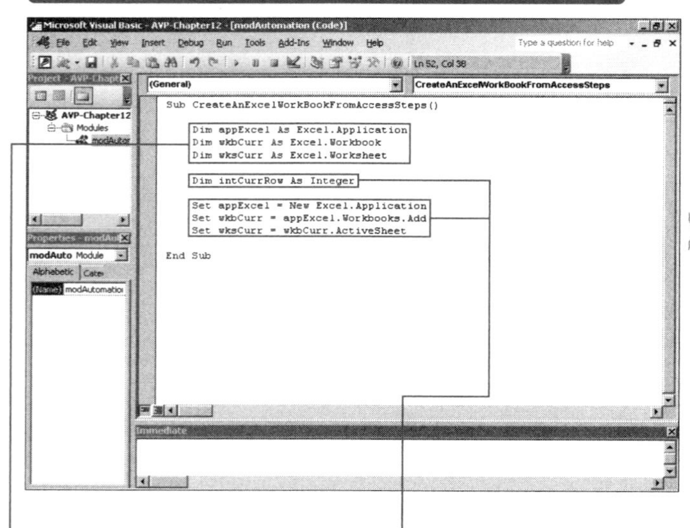

Note: This task uses modAutomation in AVP-Chapter12.mdb on the CD-ROM.

1 Create a new subroutine.

2 Add the code to declare variables for the Application, Workbook, and Worksheet variables.

3 Type the code for a variable to use as an index for the For...Next loop.

4 Type the code to set the objects.

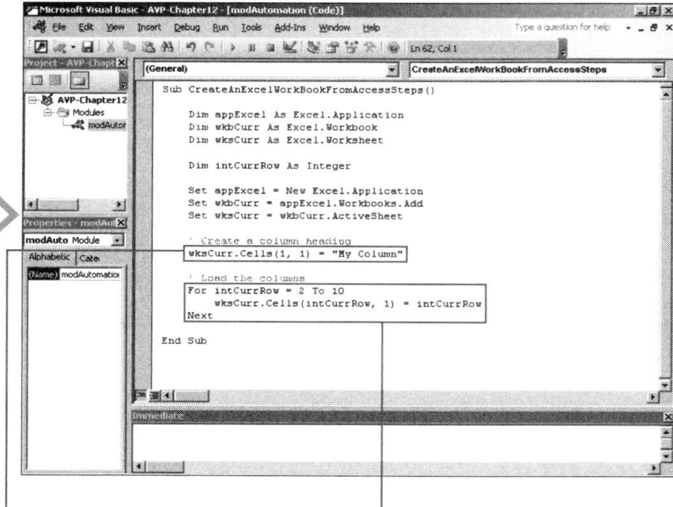

5 Add the code for the cell you want to use as the column heading.

6 Type the code to create the For…Next loop that adds the individual values into the cells.

Extra

When you are using an object repeatedly for several tasks in your code, you can use the With...End With control structure, making it unnecessary to repeat the object throughout the code. A section of the code from the steps has been revised below to use the With...End With control structure.

```
Set wksCurr = wkbCurr.ActiveSheet

With wksCurr
     ' Create a column heading
     .Cells(1, 1) = "My Column"

     ' Load the columns
     For intCurrRow = 2 To 10
          .Cells(intCurrRow, 1) = intCurrRow
     Next

     ' Add a cell to sum up the colum
     .Cells(11, 1) = "=SUM(A2:A10)"

End With
```

You can increase performance when using the With...End With statement. However, you may want to limit the amount of code you use this with statement, because having more than one screen length of code makes it difficult to read.

If you are performing all your tasks against the ActiveSheet, you can use the ActiveSheet with the With...End With statement instead of the variable. The With line of code would now appear as follows:

```
With wkbCurr.ActiveSheet
```

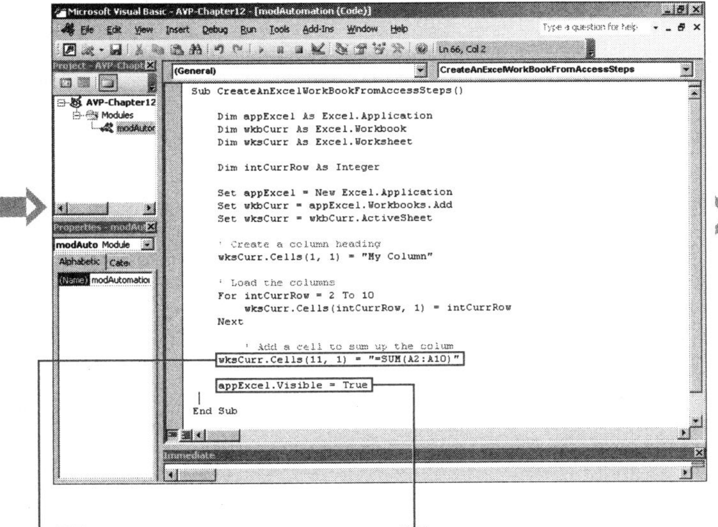

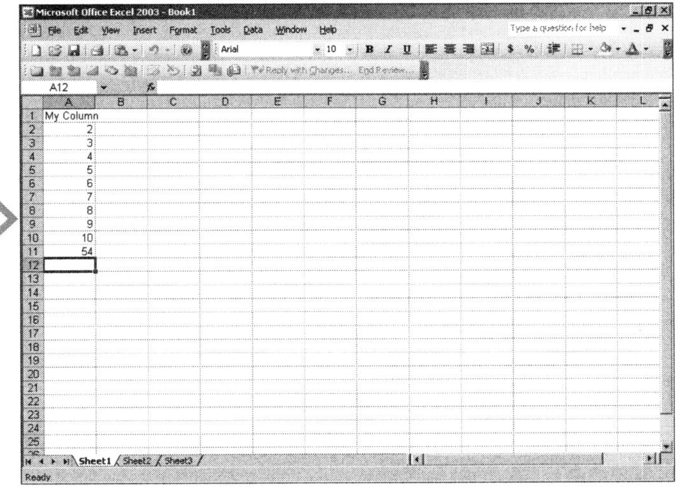

7 Type the code to create the cell containing the Sum() function.

8 Add the code that sets the Visible property of the Application object.

9 Click in the text between the Sub and End Sub lines, and press F5 to run the subroutine.

10 When you run this routine, Excel creates the spreadsheet, including the opened values.

LOAD RECORDSET DATA FROM ACCESS INTO EXCEL

There are many occasions for loading recordsets directly into spreadsheets. You can now use a method on the Range object called CopyFromRecordset, saving a lot of coding and enhancing performance over using loops.

With the CopyFromRecordset method, you can copy a recordset into your worksheet, starting with the first cell of the range. Access copies the columns in the recordset into the columns of the worksheet. To do this task you can use the Application, Workbook, Worksheet, Range, and Cell objects and collections.

After you create all the objects to your worksheet, you can take the Range object and call the CopyFromRecordset method, as shown here:

```
lngRows = wksCurr.Range("A2").
   CopyFromRecordset(rs)
```

where lngRows is the number of rows copied from the recordset, and wksCurr is the worksheet object. Range("A2") specifies the location where you want to start pasting the data into the worksheet. rs is the name of the recordset variable you are passing to the CopyFromRecordset method. There are two other arguments you can use with the CopyFromRecordset method: MaxRows and MaxColumns. These arguments allow you to limit the number of records and fields you can copy from the recordset to the worksheet.

Another method is AutoFormat, also found on the Range object. With the AutoFormat feature, you can format your columns using various formats. Below is an example of a range that you can specify by using lngRows:

```
wksCurr.Range("A1", "B" & lngRows +
1).AutoFormat
```

LOAD RECORDSET DATA FROM ACCESS INTO EXCEL

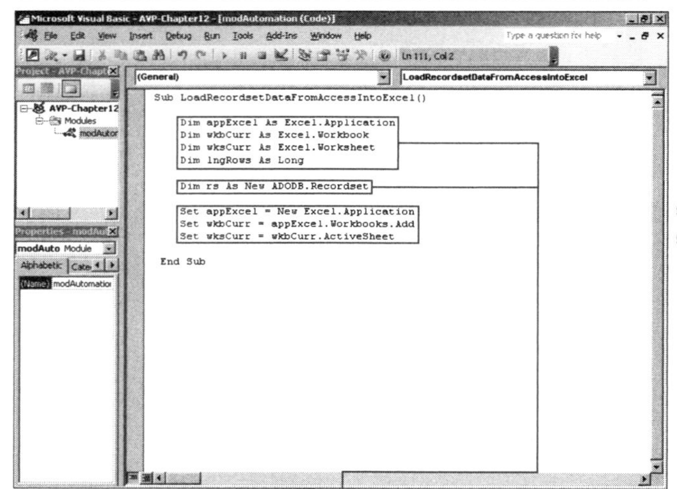

Note: This task uses modAutomation in AVP-Chapter12.mdb on the CD-ROM.

1 Create an Access select query or table to copy to Excel.

2 Create a new subroutine.

3 Add the code for variables for the Application, Workbook, and Worksheet variables.

4 Declare a variable for the copied records, and declare a new ADO recordset variable.

5 Type the code to set the objects.

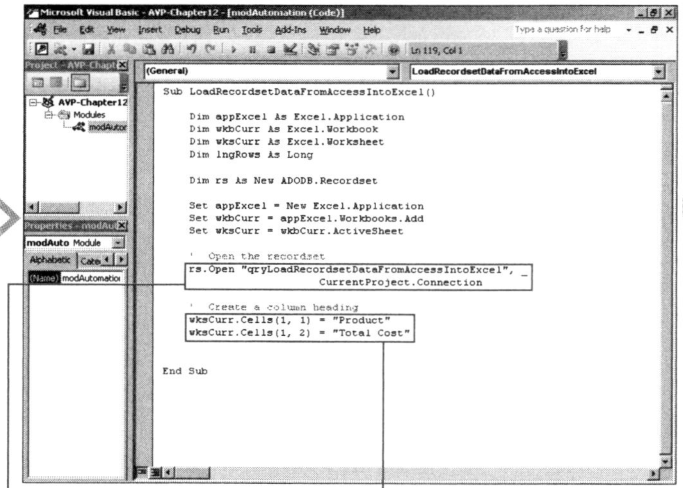

6 Use the Open method of the recordset object to open the query or table you created in Step 1.

7 Add the cells you want to use for column headings.

Extra

In using the AutoFormat method in the steps, you did not use parameters, allowing Excel to use the default values. If you want to use parameters with the AutoFormat method, you can use the following syntax:

```
object.AutoFormat(Format, Number, Font, Alignment, Border, Pattern, Width)
```

where Format is one of the AutoFormat standard formats. The rest of the parameters are self-explanatory.

Keep in mind that there are various methods and objects that you can use to call the AutoFormat method. The method that appears in the steps below is the best method because it controls the cells that you want to format.

However, when you use another method, such as from the Columns collection, where the syntax looks like this:

```
wksCurr.Columns.AutoFormat
```

you are telling Excel to automatically format the entire spreadsheet. As a result, instead of waiting for Excel to format just the range of cells, you are waiting for the entire spreadsheet to be formatted.

The problem with using the AutoFormat method of the Columns collection is that, by formatting the whole spreadsheet, you may be formatting areas that you may not want to format.

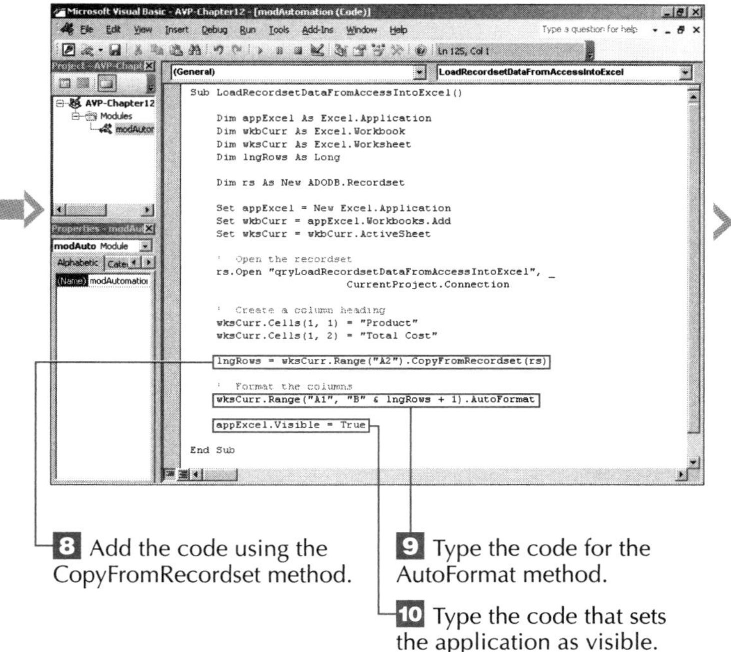

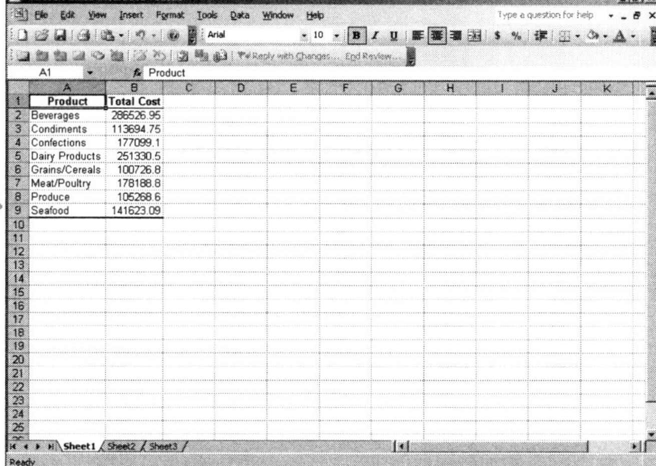

8 Add the code using the CopyFromRecordset method.

9 Type the code for the AutoFormat method.

10 Type the code that sets the application as visible.

11 Press F5 to run the subroutine.

■ When you run this routine, Excel creates the worksheet, including the data.

USING THE EXCEL CHART WIZARD FROM ACCESS

While Access has charting capability, it is somewhat limited. You can use Automation to take your relational data into Excel and Excel's charting capability. Excel is well known for the ability to create useful charts and graphs. Even with all of the new functionality in Access, such as the PivotChart, Excel is still better. There are some third-party graphics programs you can use to create graphs and charts in Access, but this book does not cover them.

Excel includes a Charts collection and object, found on the Application object. There is also a ChartObject that you can place on a spreadsheet, but this book does not cover that topic.

Excel helps you to create charts in a spreadsheet several ways. For example, you can set the various properties that Excel provides for Charts, or you can use the ChartWizard method from the Chart object to set the properties.

You can set up the data by creating worksheets and then loading data into the cells. You should not format the cells because you will only need to load them into a chart.

As with the prior Access to Excel tasks, you must set your queries up to lay the data out in Excel in a logical fashion, in this case laying out data in an x-y type method. For example, as shown in the steps, you can display the costs of products based on categories: Categories are used in the X-axis, and total cost in the Y-axis. Note that while the task actually uses the CategoryID, the Extra section shows how to pull in the Categories for the labels on the X-axis.

You can create a new Chart object, and then you can call the ChartWizard method to create the actual chart. The ChartWizard method can be a simple call, and Excel does the rest. The only thing you need to pass to the ChartWizard method is the source for the data, which, in this case, is the range of the other worksheet.

USING THE EXCEL CHART WIZARD FROM ACCESS

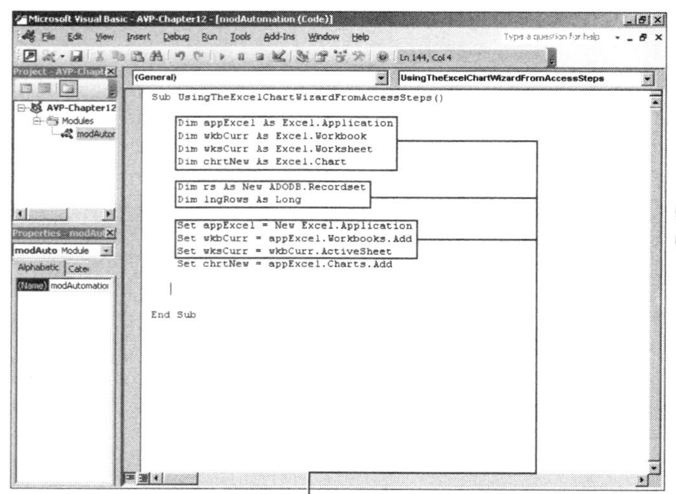

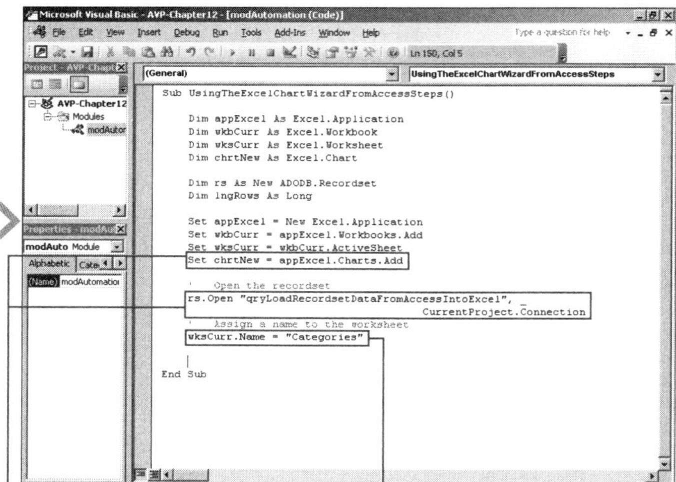

Note: This task uses modAutomation in AVP-Chapter12.mdb on the CD-ROM.

1 Create a new subroutine.

2 Add the code for variables for the Application, Workbook, Worksheet, and Chart variables.

3 Declare a variable for the copied records, and declare a new ADO recordset variable.

4 Type the code to set the objects.

5 Add the code that creates the new Excel Chart object.

6 Use the Open method of the recordset object to open the query or table you created in the last task.

7 Add the code that assigns a name to the worksheet.

Extra

The ChartWizard method contains parameters that you can use to enhance your chart.

```
chrtNew.ChartWizard(Source, Gallery, Format, PlotBy,
      CategoryLabels, SeriesLabels, HasLegend, Title,
      CategoryTitle, ValueTitle, ExtraTitle)
```

PARAMETER	DESCRIPTION
Source	Range object on which you base the report.
Gallery	Specify various chart types using xlChartType constants.
Format	One of the built-in AutoFormats.
PlotBy	Data is in rows or columns, xlRows or xlColumns.
CategoryLabels, and SeriesLabels	The number of rows within the source range that represent categoryseries labels.
HasLegend	If True, the chart includes a legend.
Title	The title text for the chart.
CategoryTitle, ValueTitle, ExtraTitle	The category and value axis, and extra title text.

Based on the call to the ChartWizard that appeared in step 8, a new call appears that displays the title.

```
chrtNew.ChartWizard wksCurr.Range("A2", "B" & lngRows + 1), _
CategoryTitle:="Category", ValueTitle:="Total Cost", CategoryLabels:=1
```

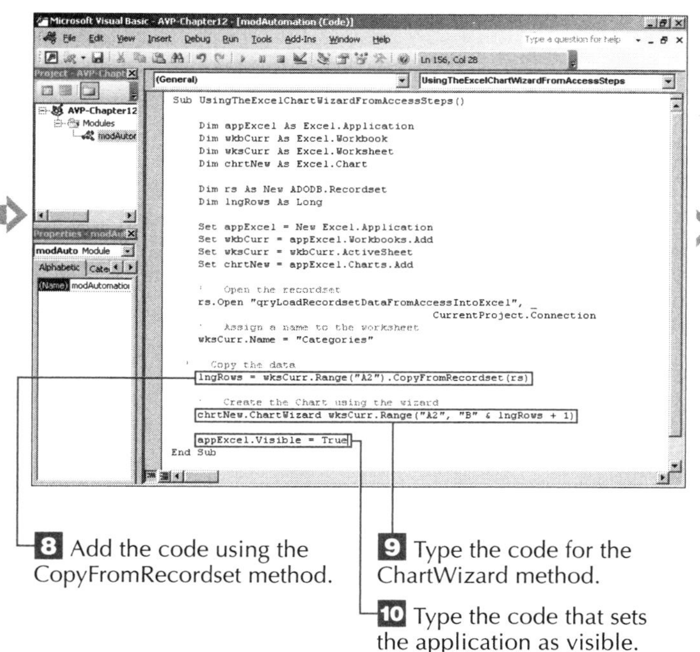

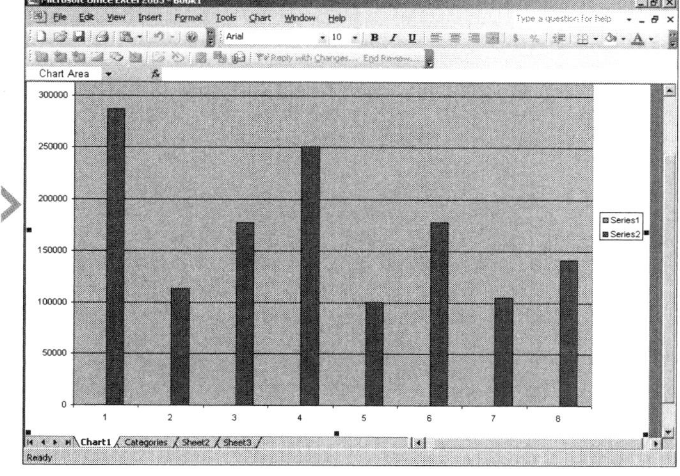

8 Add the code using the CopyFromRecordset method.

9 Type the code for the ChartWizard method.

10 Type the code that sets the application as visible.

11 Press F5 while in the editor to run the subroutine.

■ When you run this routine, Excel creates the chart, including the data from Access.

CREATE OUTLOOK E-MAIL FROM ACCESS

In some database applications you create using Access, it is very convenient to be able to create and send e-mail from within Access. When you need to perform simple e-mail tasks, you can use the SendObject method of the DoCmd object. See Chapter 6 for more about this method. For more complicated tasks, you can also use automation to work with the Outlook object model.

As with the other automation libraries, you can make the object library for Outlook accessible by adding a reference to the Microsoft Office Outlook 11.0 Object Library in the References dialog box. After you add the reference to the object library, you can declare a variable to the Application object. Just as with the other Office object models, Outlook objects are unique to the tasks you need to accomplish.

The first object is NameSpace, which you need to access the data within Outlook. You can declare the variable, and then set the variable using the GetNameSpace method of the Application object. You can create another object, the MailItem, by calling the CreateItem method and passing it in the constant that represents e-mail, which is oMailItem.

After you create the MailItem, you must set the properties you want, and then call the Display method. Some of the properties you can set are To, Subject, and Body. You can also call ResolveAll methods of the Recipients collection to resolve the e-mail names for you.

It may look like a lot of work, but after you have done it, modifying the method for your own purpose is fairly easy.

CREATE OUTLOOK E-MAIL FROM ACCESS

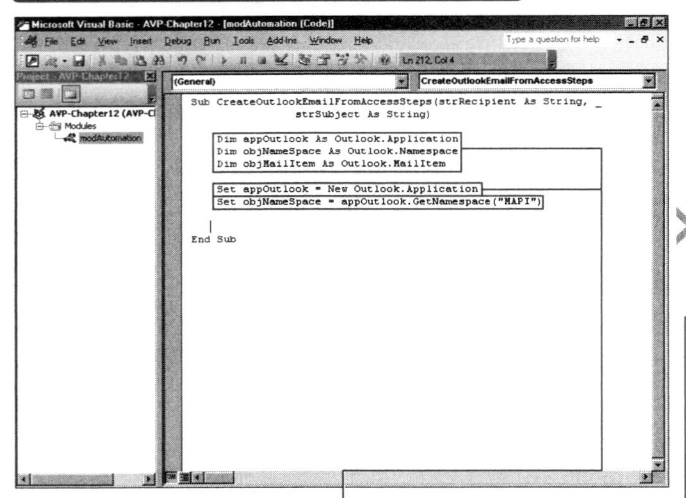

Note: This task uses modAutomation in AVP-Chapter12.mdb on the CD-ROM.

1 Create a new subroutine.

2 Add the code for variables for the Application, Namespace, and MailItem variables.

3 Type the code to set the Application object.

4 Add the code that calls the GetNamespace method, specifying MAPI in the parameter.

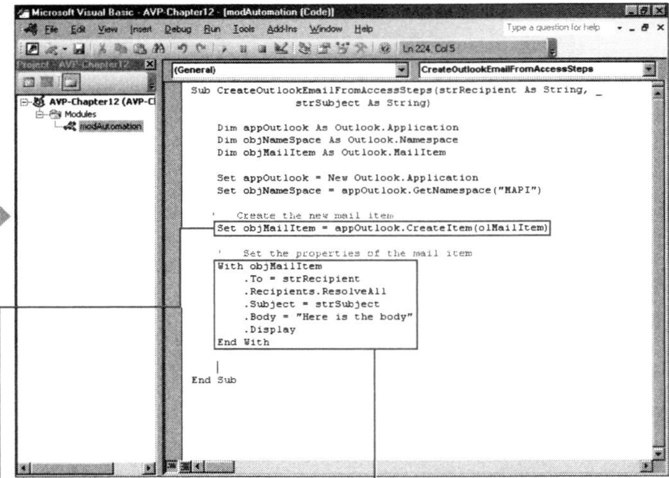

5 Type the code that calls the CreateItem method, assigning it to the object variable.

6 Type the code to set the properties of the new mail object.

Extra

You can create the MailItem, called the oMailItem in the steps. There are other items you can create, each with a particular set of properties and methods: AppointmentItem, ContactItem, DistListItem, JournalItem, MailItem, MeetingItem, NoteItem, PostItem, and TaskItem. To use these items, you declare a variable of the type you want, and then call the CreateItem method, passing the OlItemType constant, which is displayed when you use Intellesence. After you create the item, you can set the properties for the item, and then call the Display method to display the item, Send to send the mail item, or Save for other types of items. For example, you can modify the routine from this page to create a TaskItem:

```
Sub CreateOutlookTaskFromAccessExtra(strSubject As String, _
                  strTaskToPerform As String)

    Dim appOutlook As Outlook.Application
    Dim objNameSpace As Outlook.Namespace
    Dim objTaskItem As Outlook.TaskItem

    Set appOutlook = New Outlook.Application
    Set objNameSpace = appOutlook.GetNamespace("MAPI")

    Set objTaskItem = appOutlook.CreateItem(olTaskItem)

    With objTaskItem
        .Subject = strSubject
        .DueDate = Date
        .Body = strTaskToPerform
        .Display
    End With

    Set objTaskItem = Nothing
    Set objNameSpace = Nothing
    Set appOutlook = Nothing

End Sub
```

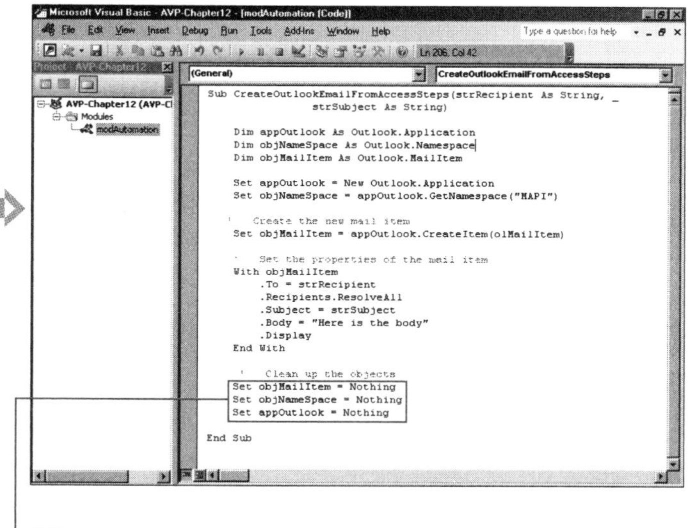

7 Type the lines of code to clean up the object variables.

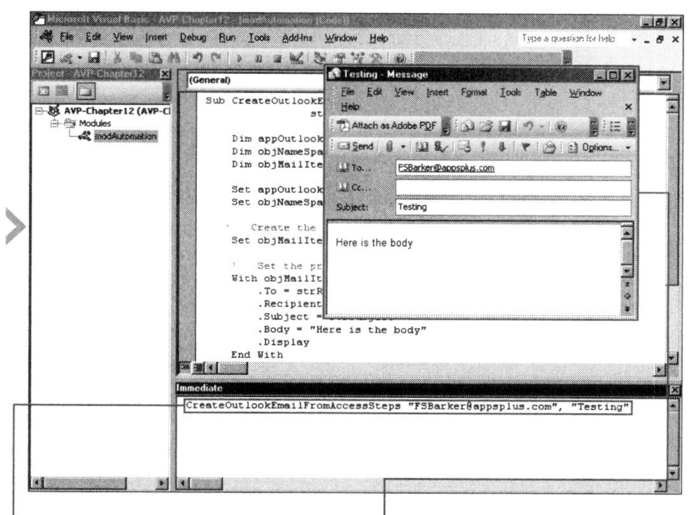

8 Type the name of the routine in the Immediate window, with the necessary parameters.

■ When you run this routine, Outlook creates the e-mail message.

WORK WITH SECURITY IN ACCESS

One of the most important considerations for any database management system is security. Because of this, Microsoft has added a security model in Access that is both complete and user-friendly.

There are several different ways in which you can provide security for your database. You can:

- Use a single database password for basic security
- Assign workgroup, user, and group permissions for database objects
- Secure VBA code and macros separately
- Encode your database or create an MDE file

SINGLE DATABASE PASSWORD FOR BASIC SECURITY

When Access first implemented security, you had to specify workgroups, users, and groups that could use the database. This was a very powerful but complex way of implementing security for an Access database.

However, Access developed a simpler way to implement security: a single password to get into a database. This system is both easy to set up and easy to reset.

WORKGROUP, USER, AND GROUP PERMISSIONS MODEL FOR OBJECTS

You may sometimes have more complex situations that arise when setting up your security. For example, you may want to allow users into your database, but to only see particular tables or queries, or to only see some of the data, but not be able to edit it. In this case, you must use the more extensive security system, involving workgroup, user, and group permissions.

To help you secure your database, Access now includes a wizard to guide you through setting up your database security. The straightforward user interface also helps you to maintain your users, groups, and objects permissions for users and groups.

Workgroups, Users, and Groups

In this security model, there is a new system database that Access uses. It is called system.mdw, by default. This database represents the workgroup, and stores the personal user IDs, or PIDS, and passwords of everyone in the workgroup. It also stores group information, such as who belongs to which groups. Groups have system IDs, or SIDs. The PIDs and SIDs that Access stores in the workgroup file make each workgroup file unique.

Access Object Permissions

After you create the workgroups, users, and groups, you need to assign permissions to your Access objects. Access stores the permissions, as well as the groups and users to which they belong, in the database. Which permissions are available depends on the object. For example, a table has different permissions than a form. Again, Access has an easy-to-use interface to help you assign permissions.

Activating Access Workgroup Security

Access workgroup security is already in place. The workgroup file is system.mdw, and the workgroup security has one user, Admin, and two groups, Admins and Users. All Admin users have the same PID. You can assign a password to the Admin, and then have the database ask for the password when a user wants to access protected objects in the database. For more about maintaining user information, including passwords, see the section called "Create and Assign Users to Groups."

SECURE VBA CODE SEPARATELY

With every version of Access, Microsoft improves your database security against data theft, and now viruses as well.

VBA Password

In Access 2000, Microsoft added a password to the VBA code, separate from the permissions available for the other objects. This password allows you to give your application to a user who is not secured, while still preventing them from accessing your VBA code.

The password for VBA is maintained in the VBA Integrated Development Environment, or IDE, and is separate from user passwords and the database password. It is another level of security, as well as complexity, that you can add to your database.

Trusted Macro Level

As with other Office applications that use VBA, you must now use trust levels to run your VBA code. This includes issuing certificates if you require a high level of security on your code.

Note that Macros, as used here, are not the classic Access macros, but are VBA routines that are used in other Office applications.

ENCODE YOUR DATABASE OR CREATE AN MDE FILE

Other ways to secure your database are to encode your database, or to create an MDE file.

Encode a Database

When you encode, or encrypt, your database, you are ensuring that if someone attempts to view your file in a word-processing application like Microsoft Word, they cannot access your data.

Because encoding significantly impacts the performance of your database, you should first ensure that it is necessary. One benefit from encoding is that it compresses the database; if you are copying the database over the Web, it reduces transfer time. However, because Windows offers a variety of compression utilities, this is not an issue.

Create an MDE File

Another way to secure your database is to create an MDE file, which you can identify by the .mde extension. When you create an MDE file, Access removes all source code, so users cannot modify or view the modules. However, this also means that users cannot edit forms and reports, because the forms and reports have code behind them.

Although many users create MDE files because they assume they will get better performance from the database files, this is not accurate. VBA must go through a compilation process that already removes the source code, and reduces the size of the database; as a result, converting it to an MDE file does not increase performance.

CREATE YOUR OWN SECURITY

This security method requires that you use your queries and forms to limit what the user can do. You can use VBA code to make tabbed pages invisible on forms, depending on who the user is. You can also control which users can edit the pages of a tabbed form, or even the entire form. See Chapter 7 for more about these techniques.

ABOUT WORKGROUP SECURITY TASKS

To fully understand the workgroup security model, and the various steps for creating each part of it, you should read through this chapter. However, Access includes a User-Level Security Wizard that guides you through the steps of creating a completely secured database. If you are in a hurry to get a database secured, see the section "Introducing the User-Level Security Wizard."

USING A SINGLE DATABASE PASSWORD

You can prevent users from accessing your database with a simple password at the database level. If users have the password, they can do what they want inside the database, unless you use additional security measures, such as using the VBA password. To add a single database password, you must open the database in exclusive mode. To do this, you can choose Open from the File menu without a database open. You can then highlight the database to which you want to add the password, and click Open Exclusive.

With the database now open, you can select Security from the Tools menu, and then Set Database Password. The Set Database Password dialog box appears. You must type the password twice for verification, and then click OK.

To test the database password, you must close the database. The next time you open the database, a Password Required dialog box appears. You must type the password, and click OK. If the password is correct, the database appears.

It is very important that you remember your password because if you lose it, you cannot access the database. This is also true for all the PIDs, SIDs, and other passwords.

If you want to remove the password requirement from your database, you can reopen the database in exclusive mode. Next, you can choose Security from the Tools menu, and then Unset Database Password. Access asks you to type the database password one more time.

If you want to change the password, you must first unset the password, and then set the database password again, using the new password.

USING A SINGLE DATABASE PASSWORD

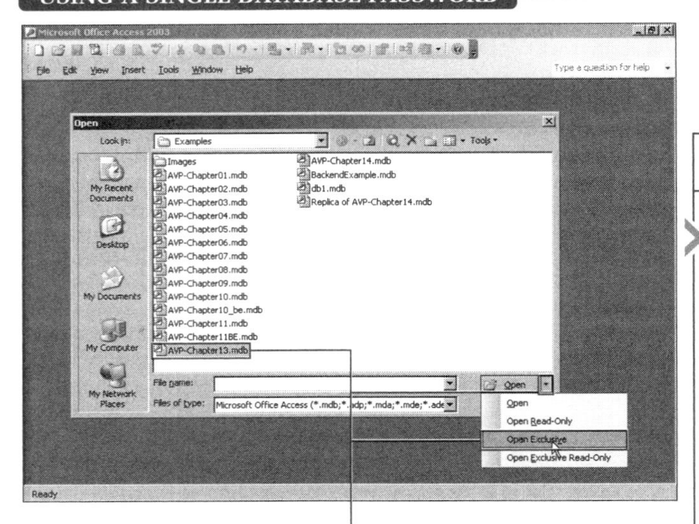

Note: This task uses AVP-Chapter13.mdb on the CD-ROM.

1 Click File ➪ Open.

2 Select the database for which you want to set the password.

3 Click the Open ▾.

4 Click Open Exclusive.

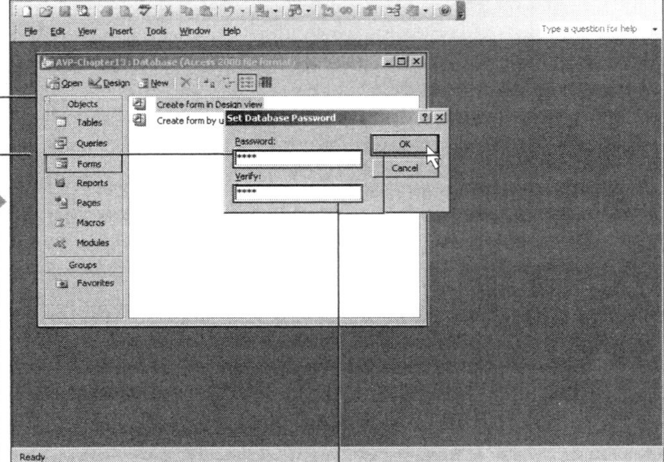

■ The database opens.

5 Click Tools ➪ Security ➪ Set Database Password.

■ The Set Database Password dialog box appears.

6 Type a password in the Password field.

7 Type the same password in the Verify field.

8 Click OK.

■ The next time you open the database, a password dialog box appears.

CREATE AN ACCESS MDE FILE

You can ensure that the VBA code in your database is secured by creating an MDE file. When you create an MDE file from an MDB file, your database VBA code is compiled, and the compiler removes the source code.

To create an MDE file, you must open your database in exclusive mode. You can now choose Database Utilities from the Tools menu, and then Make MDE File. The Save MDE File dialog box appears. You can locate the folder in which you want to place the new MDE file and assign it a filename. For convenience, you may want to leave the name of the new file the same as the database name from which you are making the MDE file.

You do not have to do anything with the original MDB file because the Make MDE File utility creates a new file. When you make any changes to the database, you must modify the original MDB file and then re-create the MDE file.

There are some things to keep in mind when you are creating MDE files. Regarding security, you need to set up permissions ahead of time with the MDB. This is because you cannot change permissions in an MDE file. Any security features that you add apply to the new MDE file, including database passwords. You must also know the VBA password in order to create the new MDE file. You cannot modify forms and reports, nor can you import new forms and reports into the MDE file. For additional information about security, you can refer to MDE security in Access Help.

CREATE AN ACCESS MDE FILE

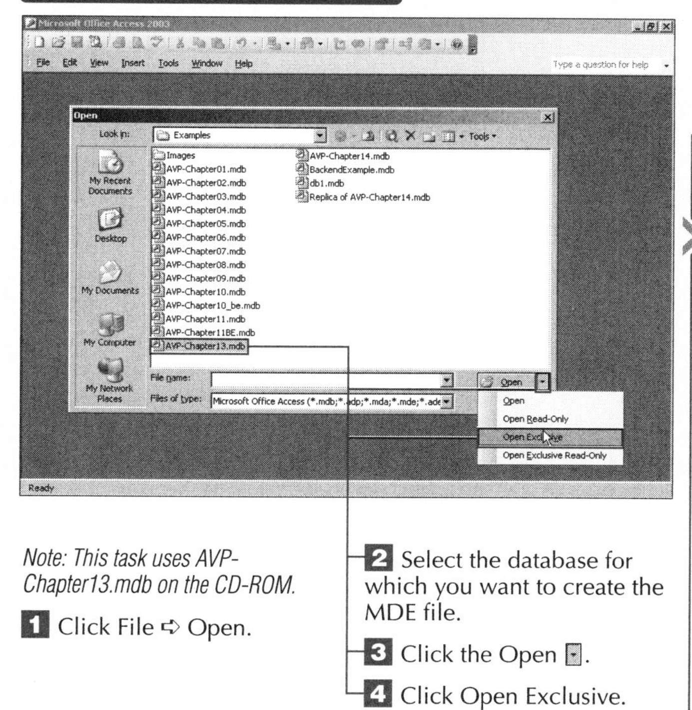

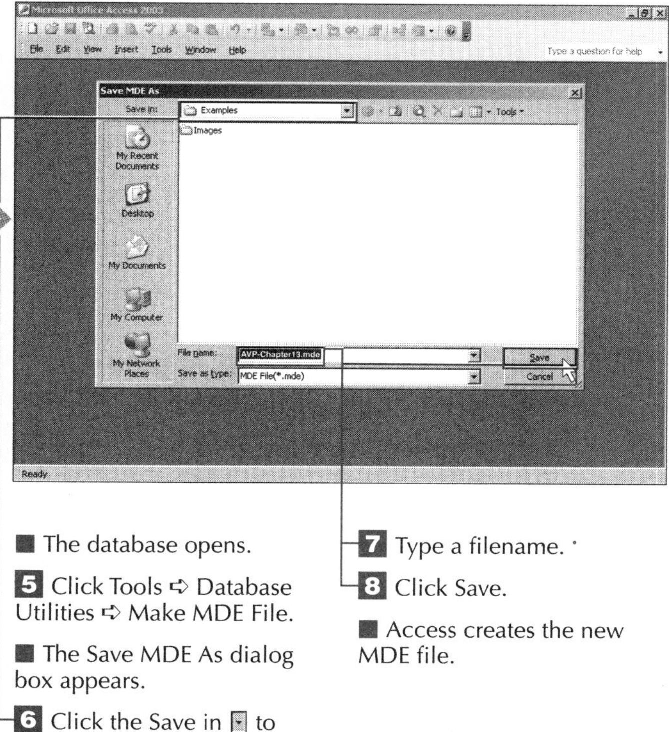

Note: This task uses AVP-Chapter13.mdb on the CD-ROM.

1 Click File ➪ Open.

2 Select the database for which you want to create the MDE file.

3 Click the Open ▾.

4 Click Open Exclusive.

■ The database opens.

5 Click Tools ➪ Database Utilities ➪ Make MDE File.

■ The Save MDE As dialog box appears.

6 Click the Save in ▾ to specify the location of the new MDE file.

7 Type a filename.

8 Click Save.

■ Access creates the new MDE file.

ENCODE AND DECODE A DATABASE

Surprisingly, anyone can use an application like Microsoft Word to access a secured database. By opening a database within Microsoft Word, a user can view and copy the data, although it will not appear as it does in Access.

You can encode a database to prevent users from viewing it in applications like Word. Of course, you must also secure the database with the security methods — such as assigning the database password and using the more extensive workgroup method — to prevent unauthorized users from opening the database in Access.

To encode your database, you can choose Security from the Tools menu, and then Encode/Decode Database. When the Encode Database As dialog box appears, you can choose the name and location you want for the new encoded file, and then click Save. Access creates the encoded database.

To decode the database, you can follow the same steps as for encoding the database. The Encode/Decode Database utility recognizes that the database is encoded and displays the correct dialog box for decoding the database.

Keep in mind that when you encode a database, you are going to experience a reduction in performance, although you should not notice the reduction in smaller databases. Because of this, few users encode databases. However, if you need high security for your database, encoding is a good idea.

ENCODE AND DECODE A DATABASE

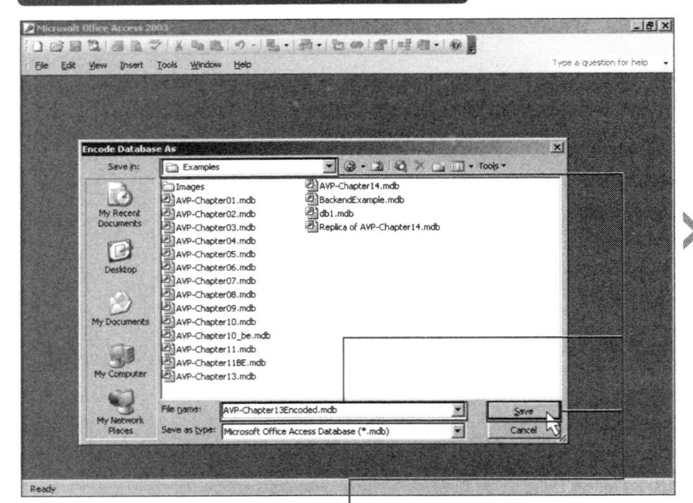

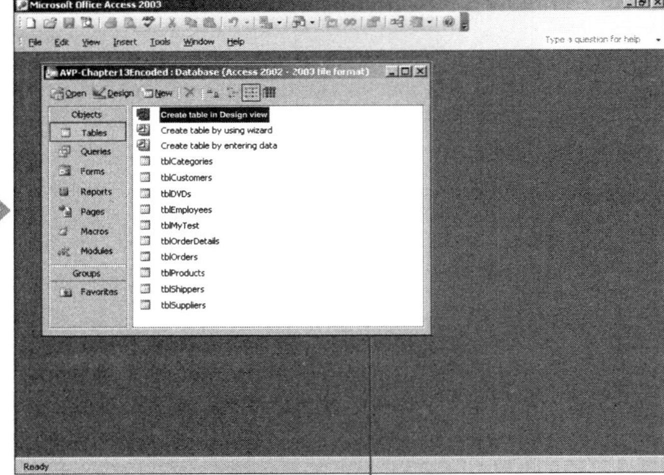

Note: This task uses AVP-Chapter13Encoded.mdb on the CD-ROM.

1 Open the database you want to encode.

2 Click Tools ➪ Security ➪ Encode/Decode Database.

■ The Encode Database As dialog box appears.

3 Click the Save in ▾ to specify the location of the new MDE file.

4 Type a filename.

5 Click Save.

6 Close the current database, and open the newly encoded database.

■ Access displays the new database.

■ To decode the database, repeat steps **1** and **2**. You can decode the database in the Decode Database dialog box.

SET THE PASSWORD FOR VBA CODE

If you do not want to create an MDE file, but you want to control which users have access to your VBA code modules, you can set a password on your code. The users can still modify forms and reports as necessary, and they can still create and import forms and reports.

To set the password, edit a code module for a form, report, or standard module. Inside the code editor, choose *NameOfDatabase* Properties from the Tools menu, where *NameOfDatabase* is the name of the database you currently have open. The Project Properties dialog box appears. When you click the Protection tab, a check box appears, labeled Lock project for viewing. When you select this check box, Access enables two password text boxes, one to enter a password, and the other to verify the password.

After you enter the password, the first time you go into a module or create a form or report, Access prompts you for a password. This also occurs if you add a command button to a form with the control wizards active. A message box appears, prompting you for the password, although it does not display a password dialog box. Access leaves the code editor open, so if you choose *NameOfDatabase* Properties from the Tools menu, then the password dialog box appears.

It is very important to remember the password because if you lose it, there is no way to get back in the modules. This is true of all Access passwords.

To remove the password, you can reopen the Properties dialog box for the VBA project, and deselect the Lock project for viewing check box.

SET THE PASSWORD FOR VBA CODE

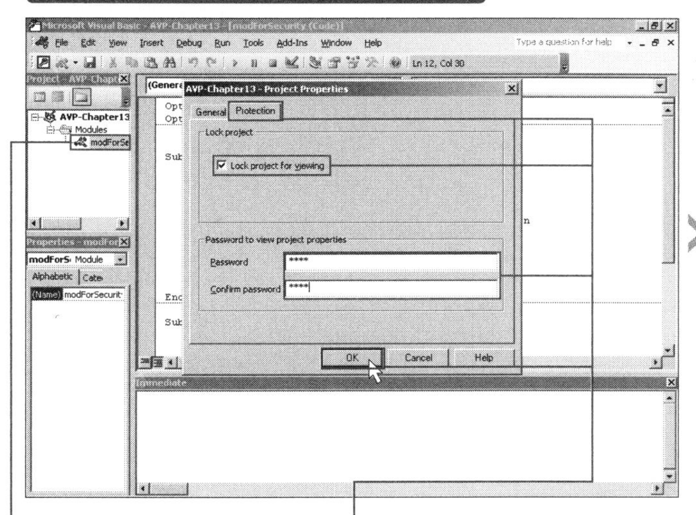

Note: This task uses AVP-Chapter13.mdb on the CD-ROM.

1 Open the database in which you want to set the password for the code.

2 Open a module by clicking the Code button, and click Tools ➪ Properties.

3 In the Project Properties dialog box, click the Protection tab.

4 Check Lock project for viewing.

5 Type a password in the Password and Confirm Password fields.

6 Click OK.

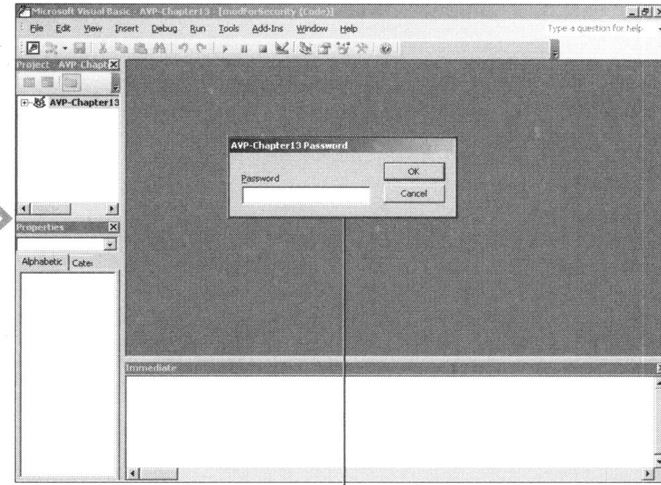

■ The database now has a password assigned to it.

7 Close the database, and then reopen it.

8 Open the module.

■ A Password dialog box appears.

WORK WITH WORKGROUPS

If you decide to use a more extensive version of security than encoding or passwords, you can start at the workgroup level. You can run the User-Level Security Wizard, which guides you through the creation of not only the workgroup, but also your users and groups.

If you decide to use the Access workgroup security feature, a situation may arise when you either need to switch workgroups or create a completely new workgroup. While neither of these tasks is particularly difficult, there are some things that you need to know. For example, the workgroup file is where Access stores the information for users and groups. If you have a group of applications that contain the same users and groups, then you can use a single workgroup for multiple applications. You can also use a single workgroup with a single application.

You can use the workgroup administrator to create and join workgroup files. To create a new workgroup, you can choose Security from the Tools menu, and then Workgroup Administrator. The workgroup administrator offers you three choices: Create, Join, and OK. To create a new workgroup, you can click Create.

If you click Create, a Workgroup Owner Information dialog box appears, allowing you to enter the name of the owner, organization, and workgroup ID. For the workgroup ID, you can use up to 20 characters and digits. When you create a workgroup ID, you must ensure two things: that the workgroup ID is unique, and that you record it somewhere. After you click OK, a Workgroup Information File dialog box appears, allowing you to specify the path and name of the workgroup file. The final dialog box confirms the information you have provided.

WORK WITH WORKGROUPS

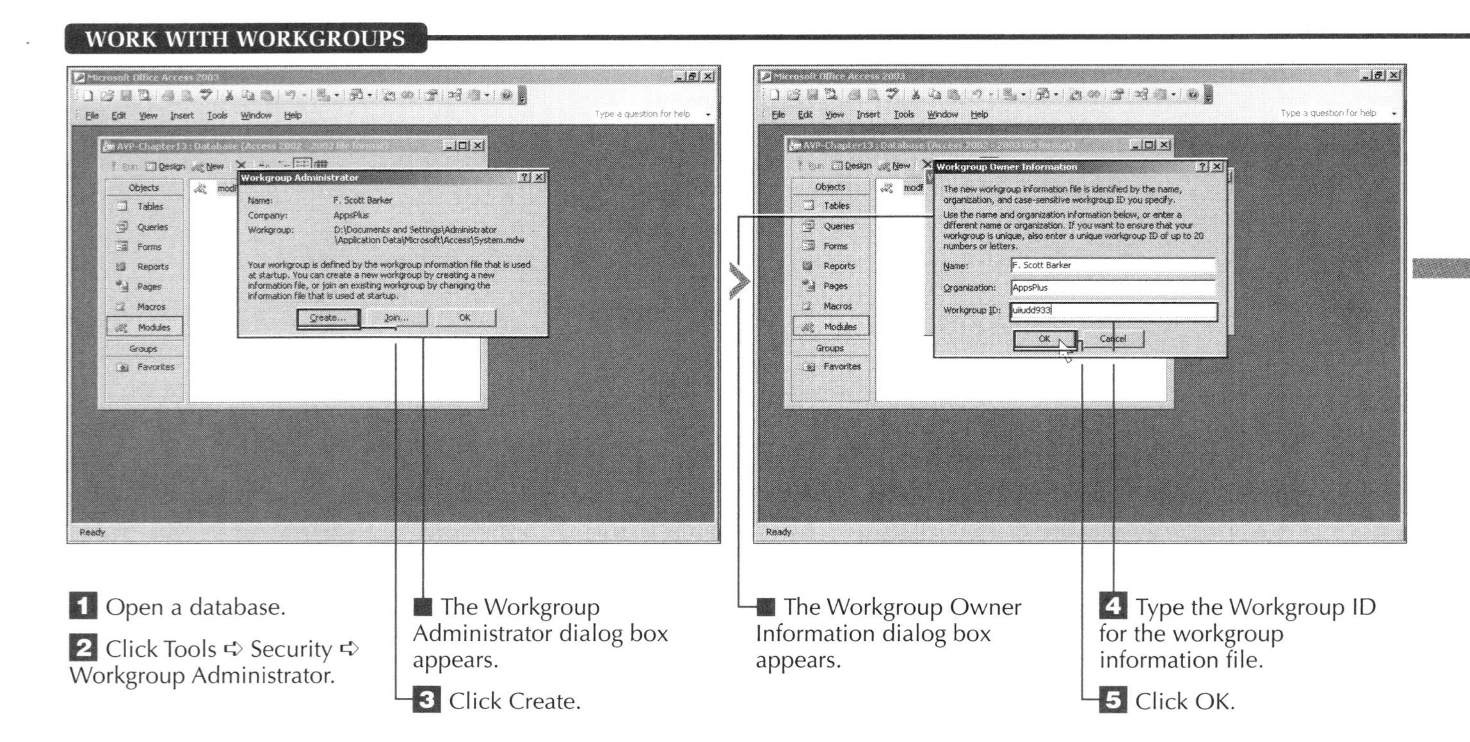

1 Open a database.

2 Click Tools ➪ Security ➪ Workgroup Administrator.

■ The Workgroup Administrator dialog box appears.

3 Click Create.

■ The Workgroup Owner Information dialog box appears.

4 Type the Workgroup ID for the workgroup information file.

5 Click OK.

Extra

Joining, or pointing to an existing workgroup is much easier than creating a new workgroup. To join a current workgroup, choose Security from the Tools menu, and then Workgroup Administrator. In the Workgroup Administrator dialog box, click Join. The Workgroup Information File dialog box appears, allowing you choose the workgroup file you want to join.

The workgroup file is located in various folders, depending on the version of Access you are using. By default, the current version stores the file in the D:\Documents and Settings*User*\ Application Data\Microsoft\Access folder, where *User* is the current user. You can also specify a more central location, such as on the server, so that all users who belong to the workgroup can have access to the workgroup file.

If you have multiple workgroups for your applications, you may prefer to open a workgroup file when you open an application, rather than specifically joining workgroups. When you join workgroups, you use the workgroup administrator to point to a workgroup file each time you want to use an application that uses a different workgroup. When you want to open a workgroup file with an application, you can create a shortcut, calling Access with the path and filename of the application. Include the /wrkgrp command line argument, with the path and filename of the workgroup file. You may also want to include the /user. An example shortcut that includes the workgroup file is as follows: C:\Examples\ MyDatabase.mdb / wrkgrp "D:\Documents and Settings\Administrator\ Application Data\Microsoft\Access\System.mdw" /user FSBarker.

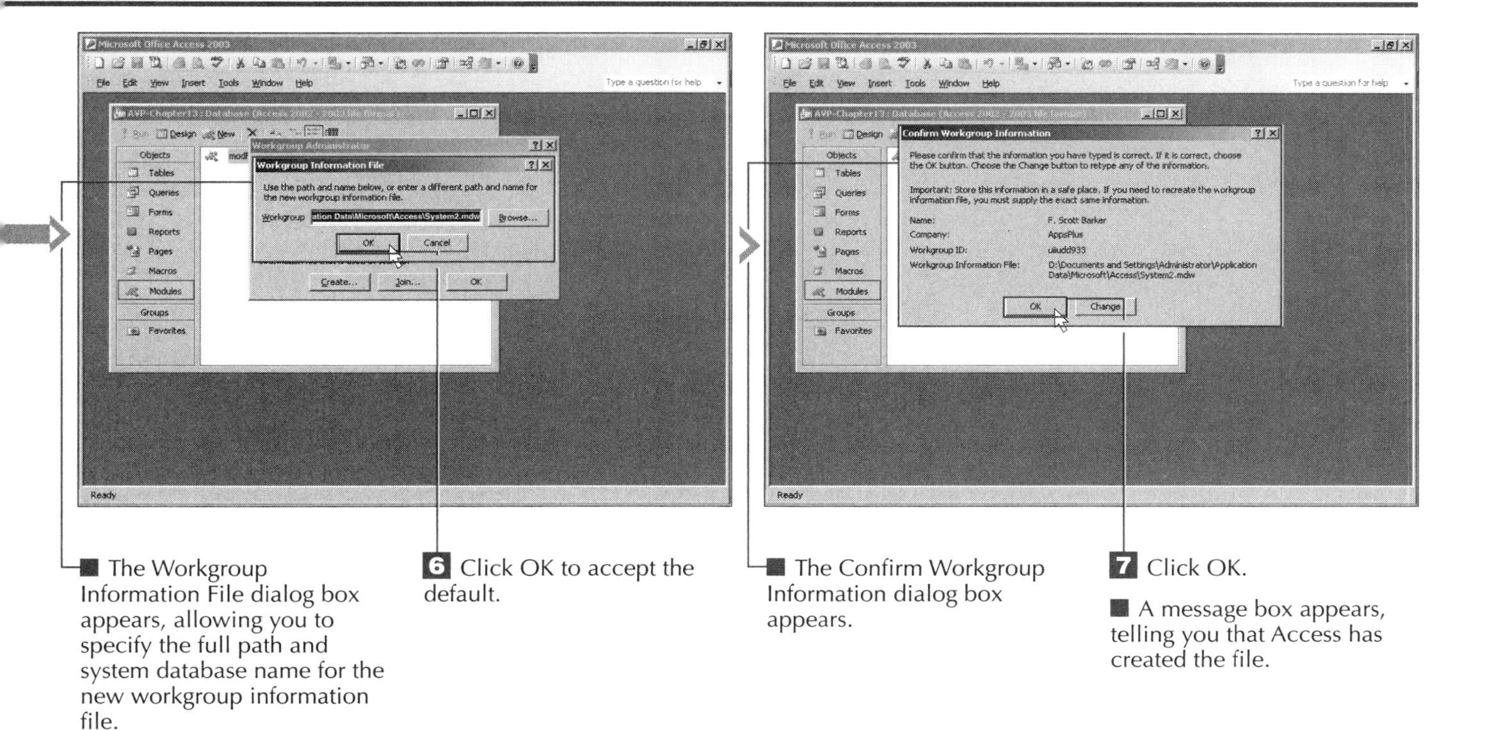

■ The Workgroup Information File dialog box appears, allowing you to specify the full path and system database name for the new workgroup information file.

6 Click OK to accept the default.

■ The Confirm Workgroup Information dialog box appears.

7 Click OK.

■ A message box appears, telling you that Access has created the file.

CREATE GROUPS

After you create a workgroup, you can add groups to take advantage of the powerful workgroup security features. Groups enable you to assign the same permissions for objects such as forms and reports to different users. Rather than having to assign permissions for each object at the user level, you can assign the permissions to the group, and add the users to the group to which they belong.

It is best to determine the structure of your groups and users ahead of time, so that you can plan them logically. To add a group, you can choose Security from the Tools menu, and then User and Group Accounts. The User and Group Accounts dialog box appears, with three tabs: Users, Groups, and Change Logon Password. See the next section for more information about the Users tab.

The Change Logon Password tab allows you to change the password for a user who is currently logged on. This is where you change the password if you want to activate Access's security. By changing the initial ADMIN password from blank to something else, Access then presents a logon dialog box from that time forward.

If you click the Groups tab, a drop-down list of current groups appears. Below the field for the drop-down list are two buttons, New and Delete. When you click New, the New User/Group dialog box appears.

In the New User/Group dialog box fields, you can enter the Name of a group and a Personal ID, or PID. The PID will consist of 4–20 characters or digits. You must remember to make the PID unique and also to write it down so that you do not forget it. You can click OK to accept the name and PID. The New User/Group dialog box closes, and Access adds the group to the drop-down list in the Groups tab. When you finish adding all the groups you want, you can click OK to exit the User and Group Accounts dialog box.

CREATE GROUPS

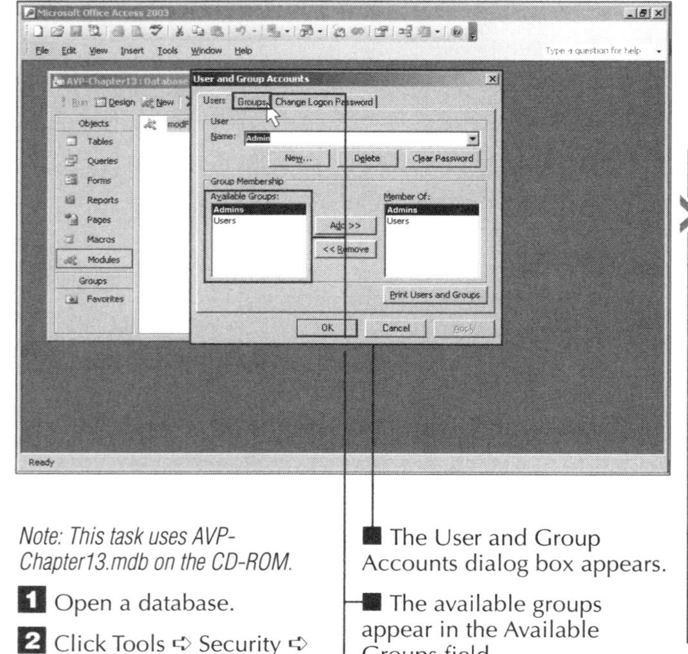

Note: This task uses AVP-Chapter13.mdb on the CD-ROM.

1 Open a database.

2 Click Tools ➪ Security ➪ User and Group Accounts.

■ The User and Group Accounts dialog box appears.

■ The available groups appear in the Available Groups field.

3 Click the Groups tab.

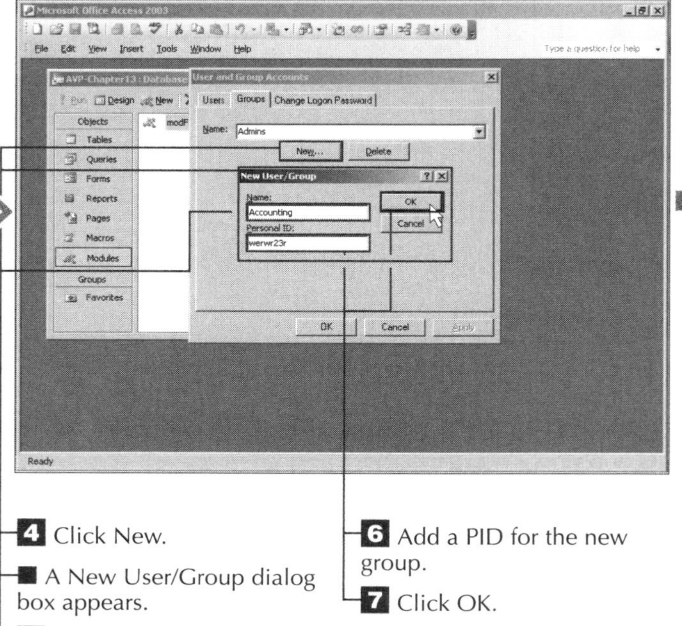

4 Click New.

■ A New User/Group dialog box appears.

5 Add a name in the Name field.

6 Add a PID for the new group.

7 Click OK.

Extra

You can access the user, group, and permissions information using VBA code. Use the Microsoft ADO Ext. 2.8 for DDL and Security objects library. DDL in this case stands for Data Definition Language. After you add the reference for this library, you will have access to various objects that you can use.

To display all of the groups in a database, begin by declaring a variable for a new Catalog object. Next, declare a Group variable object, without specifying the New keyword, because you will be using the variable with a For Each...Next control structure. The For Each ... Next is first described it in Chapter 7, in the section "Toggle a Form's Viewing or Editing."

Now, assign the Connection property of the current project to the ActiveConnection property of the catalog.

Finally, loop through each of the groups in the Groups collection of the catalog, displaying the name of the group in the Immediate window. You can see the code below:

```
Sub CreateGroupsExtra()
    Dim catCurr As New ADOX.Catalog
    Dim grpCurr As ADOX.Group
    catCurr.ActiveConnection = CurrentProject.Connection
    For Each grpCurr In catCurr.Groups
        Debug.Print grpCurr.Name
    Next
End Sub
```

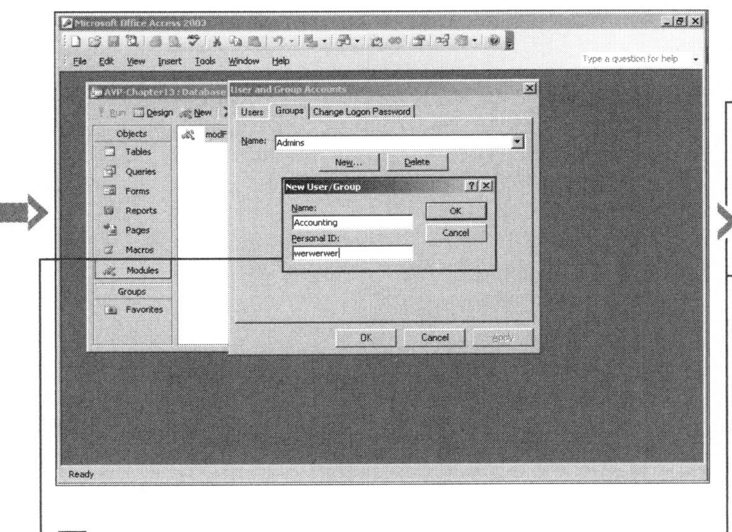

8 Repeat steps 4 to 7 for each group that you want to add.

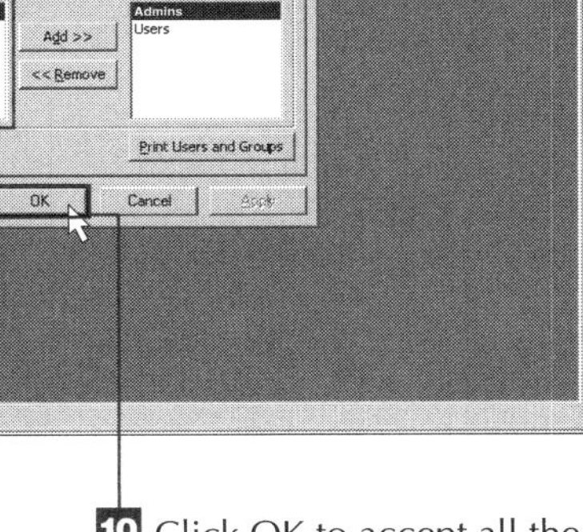

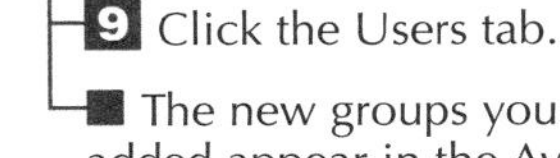

9 Click the Users tab.

■ The new groups you have added appear in the Available Groups field.

10 Click OK to accept all the changes and close the dialog box.

CREATE AND ASSIGN USERS TO GROUPS

In order to control who has access to your database, and take advantage of security, you need to create users. You can create individual users in the same way that you would create groups. However, users and groups are not the same; after you create a user, you must assign that user to a group, and have the user choose a password.

To create a user, you must choose Security from the Tools menu, and then User and Group Accounts. The User and Group Accounts dialog box appears, displaying the Users tab by default. To create a new user, you can simply click the New button in the User section of the tab. The New User/Group dialog box appears, allowing you to specify a Name and Personal ID for the new user. You can use up to ten characters or digits in the PID, and you should write down this information to ensure that you do not forget it. You can then click OK to accept the new name and PID.

After you add a new user, Access displays the name of the new user at the top of the User Name drop-down list. Below the User section is the Group Membership section, where you can assign groups to the current users.

Users can belong to more than one group, so you should be sure to assign users to all the necessary groups. For example, you may want to assign a user to both the Accounting and Investments groups, giving the user the permissions of both groups. See the next section for more information about permissions.

To do this, you must select the group that you want to assign in the Available Groups field. Next, you must click the Add button. The group moves from the Available Groups field to the Member Of field. When you click OK, Access makes the user a member of all groups that you added to the Members Of field.

CREATE AND ASSIGN USERS TO GROUPS

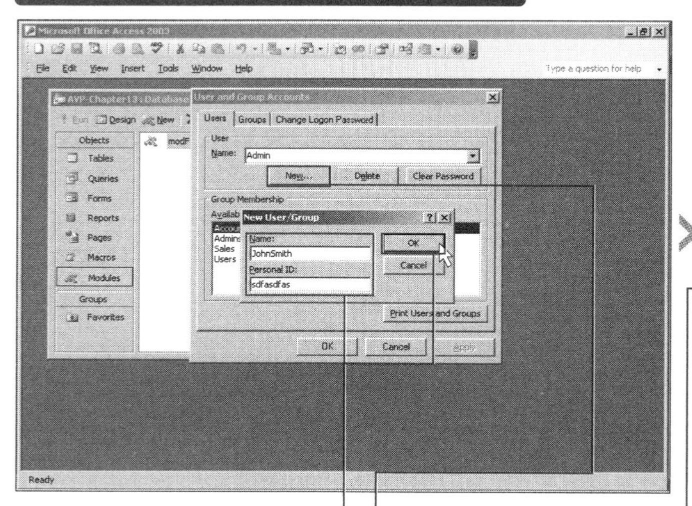

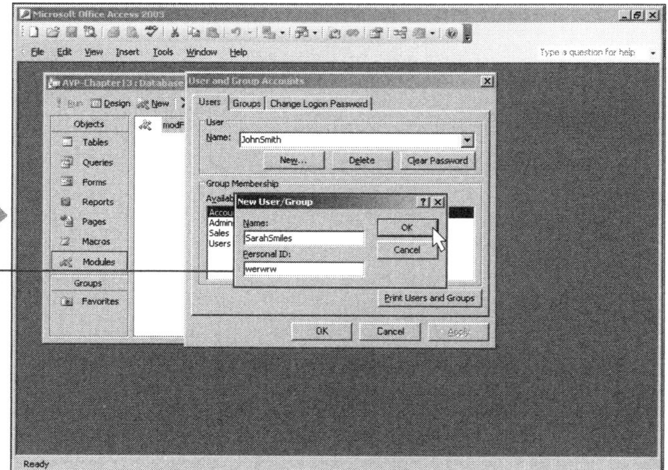

CREATE USERS

Note: This task uses AVP-Chapter13.mdb on the CD-ROM.

1 Open a database.

2 Click Tools ➪ Security ➪ User and Group Accounts.

3 In the User and Group Accounts dialog box, click New.

4 In the New User/Group dialog box, type a name for the new user in the Name field, and then type a PID in the Personal ID field.

5 Click OK.

6 Repeat steps 3 to 5 for each user you want to create.

Extra

Continuing with the previous task's Extra section, you can work with User information in VBA code, just as you can with the Group information. To do this you must use the Catalog object, as you did last time, along with the Users collection and User object, replacing the use of the Groups collection and Group object.

When you use the code below, Access displays the name of each user in the Immediate window. Along with the names of each user, you will see internally used users, such as Creator and Engine.

```
Sub CreateAndAssignUsersToGroupsExtra()
    Dim catCurr As New ADOX.Catalog
    Dim usrCurr As ADOX.User
    catCurr.ActiveConnection =
CurrentProject.Connection
    For Each usrCurr In catCurr.Users
        Debug.Print usrCurr.Name
    Next
End Sub
```

To print a list of users and groups, you can click the Print Users and Groups button, located at the bottom of the Users tab, in the User and Group Accounts dialog box. When you click the Print Users and Groups button, the Print Security dialog box appears.

In the Print Security dialog box, you can choose to print users and groups, users only, or groups only. When you click Print, Access sends the list directly to the printer, without a screen preview or print dialog box.

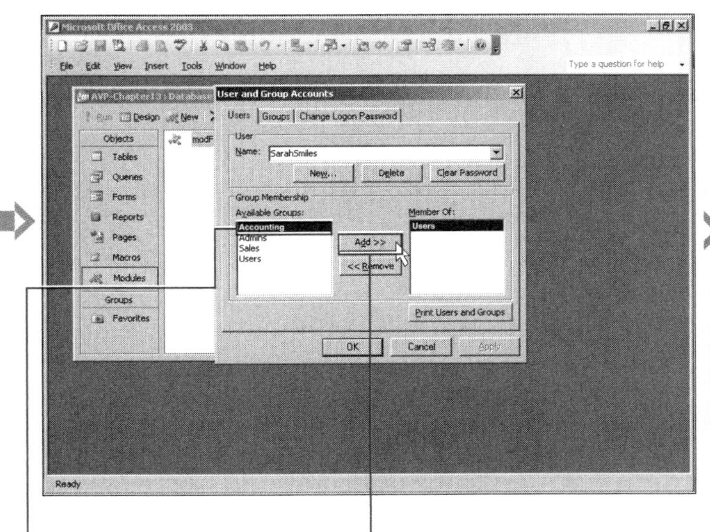

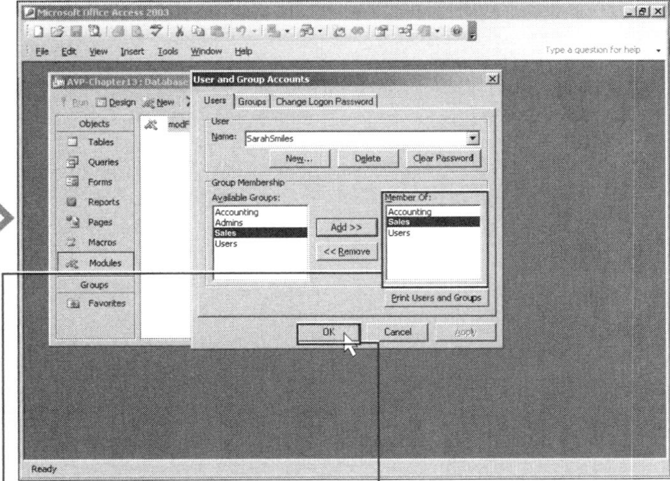

ASSIGN USERS TO GROUPS

■ Access assigns the default Users group to every new user that you create.

7 Select a group in the Available Groups field that you want to assign to the user that is displayed in the User Name field.

8 Click Add.

■ The group you select appears in the Members Of field.

9 Repeat steps 8 and 9 for each group that you want the user to belong to.

■ Access assigns all of the groups that you specified.

10 Click OK to accept the changes and close the dialog box.

ASSIGN PERMISSIONS

When you create users and groups, and assign the different users to different groups, you are making it possible for the users to log on to the appropriate databases. In order to allow users to work with the database files, you must also assign permissions to the various groups.

Although you can assign permissions to individual users, it is better to assign permissions to groups, instead. This is because assigning permissions for each user as you add them can become a time-consuming and complex process. By assigning group permissions, you only need to assign a user to the group to set the correct permissions for that user.

When you are assigning permissions to groups and users, whichever has the least restrictive permissions, the user, or a group the user belongs to, for an object is the set of permissions that Access uses.

To assign permissions, you can choose Security from the Tools menu, and then User and Group Permissions. The User and Group Permissions dialog box appears, letting you specify which groups or users can have which permissions. You can change Permission types based on the object type.

When you click Groups in the List options, the Permissions tab changes from displaying users in the field above, to displaying groups, and vice versa. You can select the Object type that displays in the Object field by selecting the Object type you want from the Object Type drop-down list. After you select an object and a user or group, you can select which permissions you want that user or group to have for the object by selecting or deselecting the specific permission check boxes at the bottom of the dialog box.

You can save time when assigning permissions for new objects that you create by setting the default beforehand. After you set permissions, you can test the objects by assigning a particular user, and working with the various objects.

ASSIGN PERMISSIONS

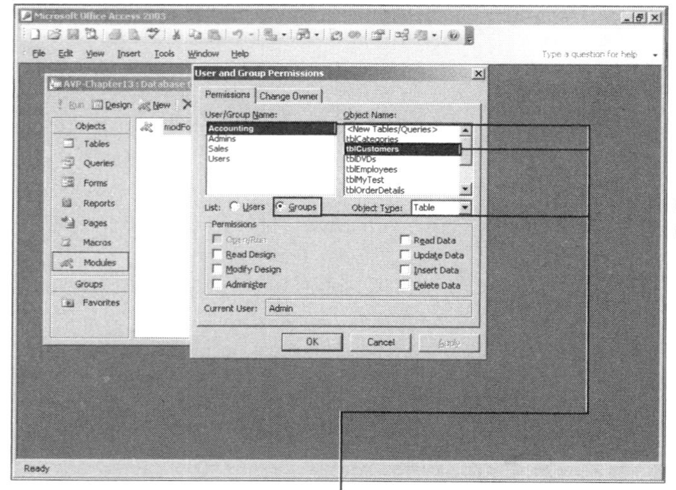

Note: This task uses AVP-Chapter13.mdb on the CD-ROM.

1 Open a database.

2 Click Tools ⇨ Security ⇨ User and Group Permissions.

■ The User and Group Permissions dialog box appears.

3 Click Groups.

4 Select a Group and Object to which you want to assign permissions.

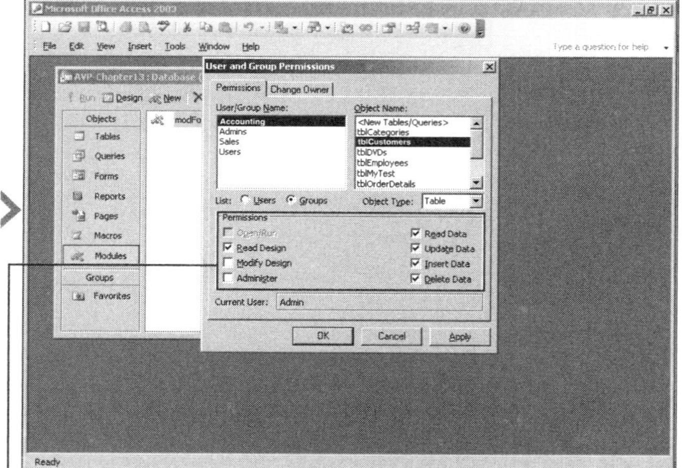

5 Click the check boxes next to the permissions you want for the selected group and object.

Extra

After you create your new groups, users, and assigned permissions, you need to create a new Admin user, giving it a name like SuperAdmin, and assigning it to the Admins group by repeating the steps in the section "Create and Assign Users to Groups." Next, remove the original Admin user from the Admins group, by repeating steps 1 to 3 of the previous section, except clicking the Delete button in step 3. Finally, remove all permissions from the Admin user by repeating steps 1 to 5 below, except deselecting all check boxes in step 5. By deleting the original Admin user, you are making your database truly secure. This is because every copy of Access has an Admin user, with the same PID. However, the Admins group is unique for each copy of Access, so that the Admins group is safe.

When you create an object while you are logged on as a particular user, Access makes that user the owner of the object. Owners have administrative rights to the different objects that they create. At some time, you may need to change the ownership of objects. You can do so by opening the User and Group Permissions dialog box, and clicking the Change Owner tab. You then simply select the objects you want to change, and specify the new owner.

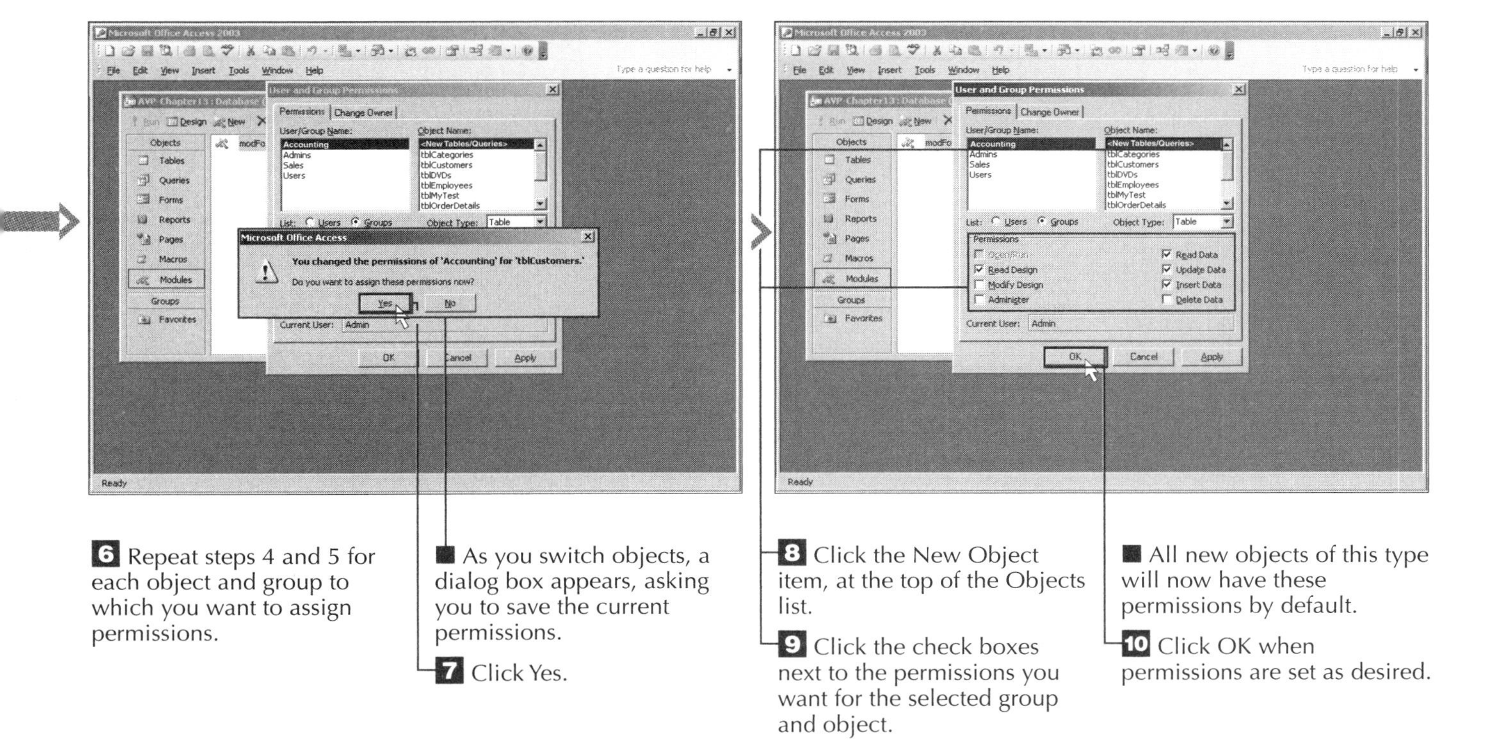

6 Repeat steps 4 and 5 for each object and group to which you want to assign permissions.

■ As you switch objects, a dialog box appears, asking you to save the current permissions.

7 Click Yes.

8 Click the New Object item, at the top of the Objects list.

9 Click the check boxes next to the permissions you want for the selected group and object.

■ All new objects of this type will now have these permissions by default.

10 Click OK when permissions are set as desired.

INTRODUCING THE USER-LEVEL SECURITY WIZARD

Because setting up security for your database can be difficult the first time you do it, Microsoft has created a wizard to guide you through the process. By running the Access User-Level Security Wizard, you can set up your database security both quickly and easily.

Although the wizard allows you to quickly secure the database from unauthorized users, you may also unintentionally secure it from yourself as well. However, the last step in the wizard is to specify a backup for your database: You can access the backup if you can no longer access the secured database.

To run the User-Level Security Wizard, choose Security from the Tools menu, and then User-Level Security Wizard. The first page of the wizard asks you to either create a new workgroup file, or to use a current one if it exists, other than the default system.mdw file. Because the system.mdw file is the same file that comes with all copies of Access, it is a good idea to create a new one.

Because you are creating a new workgroup file, the wizard next asks you for the information that it needs to create the file. The wizard supplies most of the entries necessary. You can also specify whether or not to make the new workgroup file the default, or to create a shortcut to the database. See the Extra section in this task for more information about creating a shortcut.

The next page in the wizard asks you to specify the objects for which you want to set permissions. If you leave objects deselected, the security level is set to low, allowing full access to them. Next, the wizard displays a list of possible predefined groups that you can use in your workgroup. You can simply place check marks by the groups that you want to include.

INTRODUCING THE USER-LEVEL SECURITY WIZARD

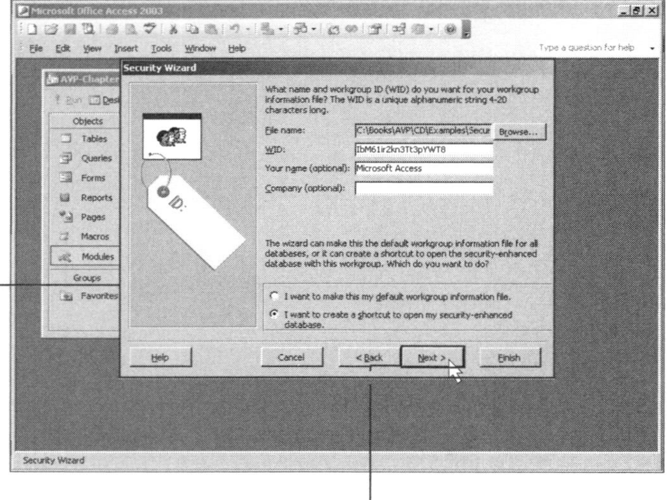

Note: This task uses AVP-Chapter13.mdb on the CD-ROM.

1 Open a database.

2 Click Tools ➪ Security ➪ User-Level Security Wizard.

■ The Security Wizard dialog box appears.

3 Click Next to accept the default settings for the creation of a new workgroup file.

■ The page displaying the workgroup information appears.

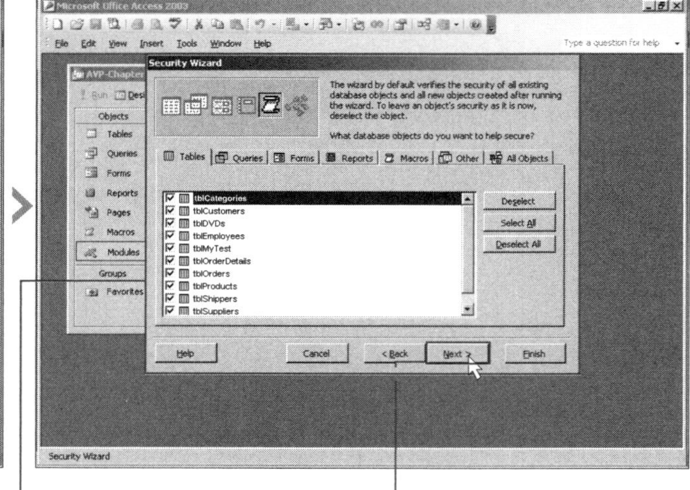

4 Click Next to accept the default settings.

■ The page for specifying which objects you want to include appears. By default, all of the objects are selected.

5 Click Next to accept the default settings.

Extra

In the workgroup file page of the User-Level Security Wizard, you can create a shortcut to the new workgroup file.

When you create a shortcut to the database, it allows the database to use the workgroup file for an instance of an Access application, rather than joining the workgroup file. You may need to switch workgroup files if you work with unsecured databases, and the shortcut is a good idea because most small databases that you work with may not be secured. You can read more about assigning workgroup files in the prior section, "Work with Workgroups."

An excellent feature of the User-Level Security Wizard is that if you forget something earlier in the security setup process, you can go back in the wizard and address it. For example, if you forget to make a note of the name of the workgroup file you created, you can click the Previous button a few times until you come to the workgroup file page.

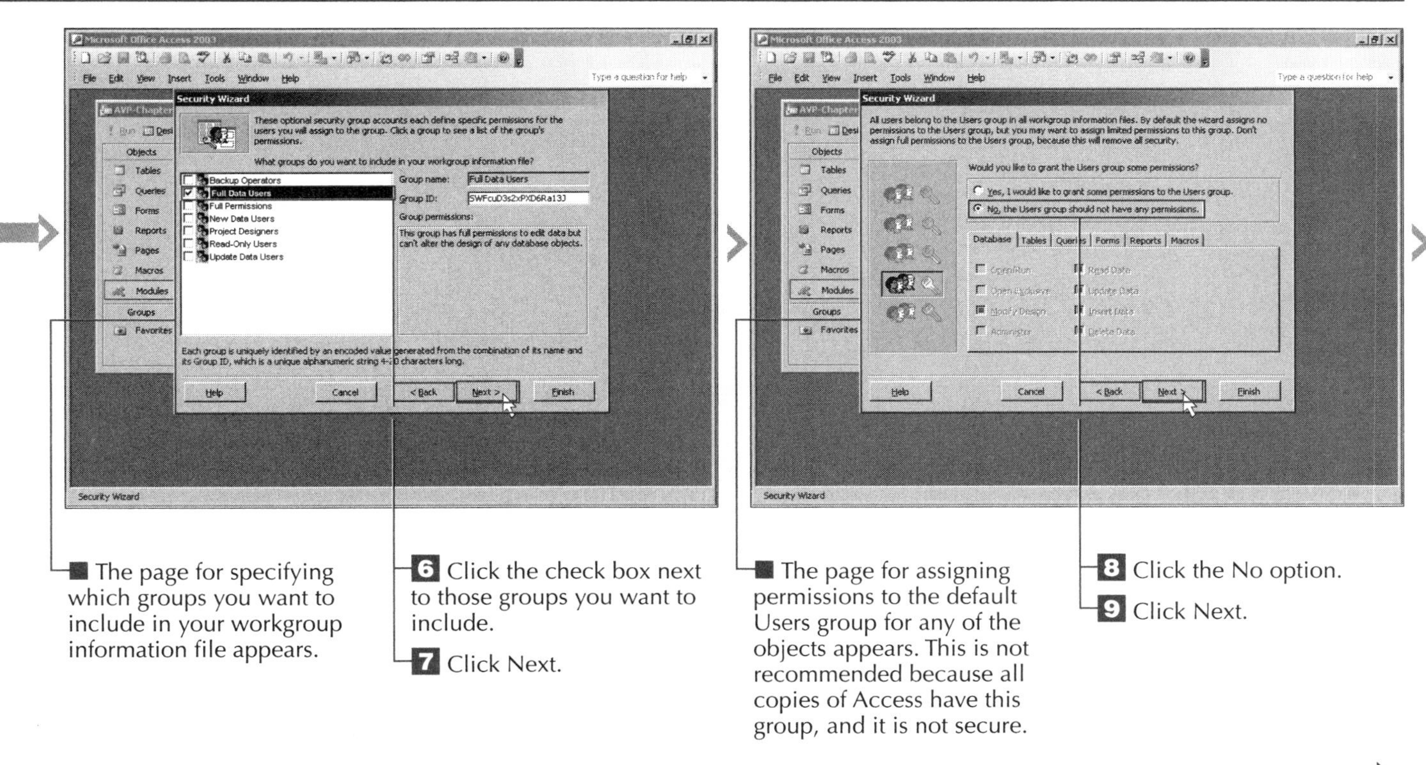

■ The page for specifying which groups you want to include in your workgroup information file appears.

6 Click the check box next to those groups you want to include.

7 Click Next.

■ The page for assigning permissions to the default Users group for any of the objects appears. This is not recommended because all copies of Access have this group, and it is not secure.

8 Click the No option.

9 Click Next.

CONTINUED

INTRODUCING THE USER-LEVEL SECURITY WIZARD (CONTINUED)

The next page of the User-Level Security Wizard allows you to specify whether or not you want to give permissions to the Users group. The Users group is one of two built-in groups in Access. All copies of Access have the same Users group with the same PID, and as a result, they are not secure. You should assign limited permissions to this group. Alternatively, you can decide not to give permissions, and just use the groups that you selected in the previous page of the wizard.

The next page of the Security Wizard then asks you to specify the users you want to add. After you add the users you want, you can click the Next button. The next page allows you to assign the users to groups. The wizard allows you to specify whether you want to assign multiple users to a group, or a user to multiple groups.

By default, Access adds a user named Administrator. This is because the built-in Admin user is not secured, and should not be used. When the wizard is finished, the Administrator user takes the place of the Admin user, with full administrative privileges, and the Admin user has no administrative privileges. The Administrator user is also assigned by the wizard to the Admins group.

The wizard now prompts you to make a backup of your database before it is secured. It is mandatory to make a backup of the database, and the wizard asks you where you want that database on your system. Access displays a report, and prompts you to reopen the database with the new workgroup file.

INTRODUCING THE USER-LEVEL SECURITY WIZARD (CONTINUED)

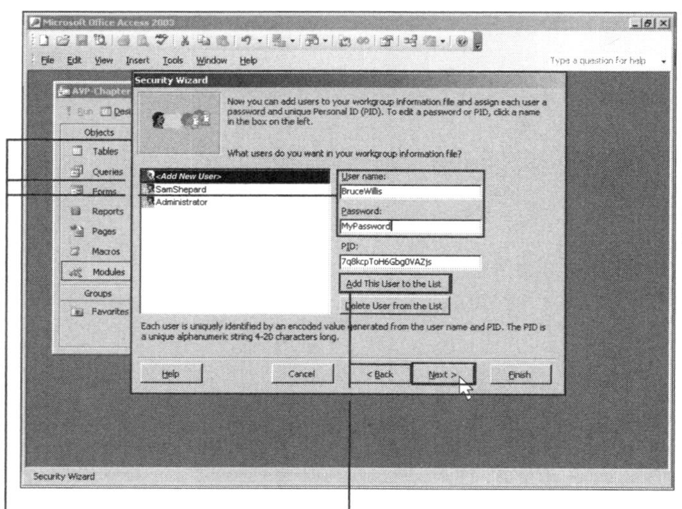

■ The page that allows you to add users appears.

10 Click Add New User in the Users list.

11 Type the username and password.

12 Click Add This User to the List.

13 Repeat steps 10 to 12 for each user you want to add.

14 Click Next.

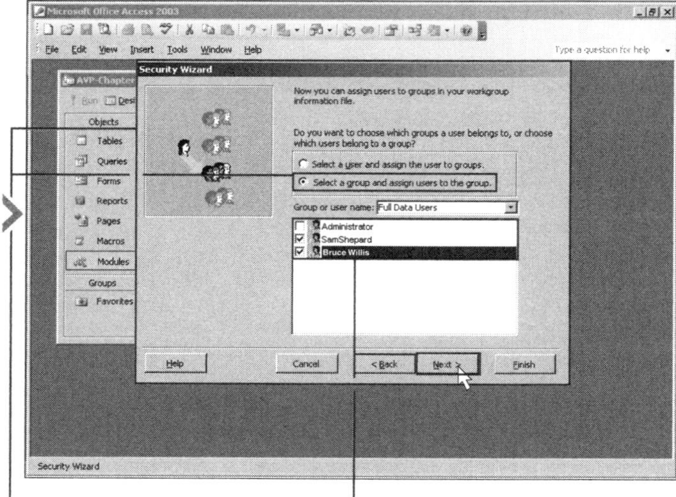

■ The page for assigning permissions appears.

15 Click the Select a group and assign users to the group option.

16 Click the check box next to the users you want to assign (☐ changes to ☑).

17 Click Next.

Extra

When the Security Wizard finishes setting up security for your database, it prints out a comprehensive report that lists all the necessary security settings, such as users, groups, and permissions. The wizard can also generate the report in a snapshot format for you to keep in a safe place along with all your other administrative files on your server or computer. It is a good idea to print a copy of the report to place it into a notebook or folder in a secure place.

When the Security Wizard is finished, you should locate the file that the wizard created as your backup, and move this file to a secured place, such as a safe or file cabinet. This is because you do not want to leave this file in the same folder as the secured database because all users with access to the folder can then access this file. You can recognize this file by the .ext extension.

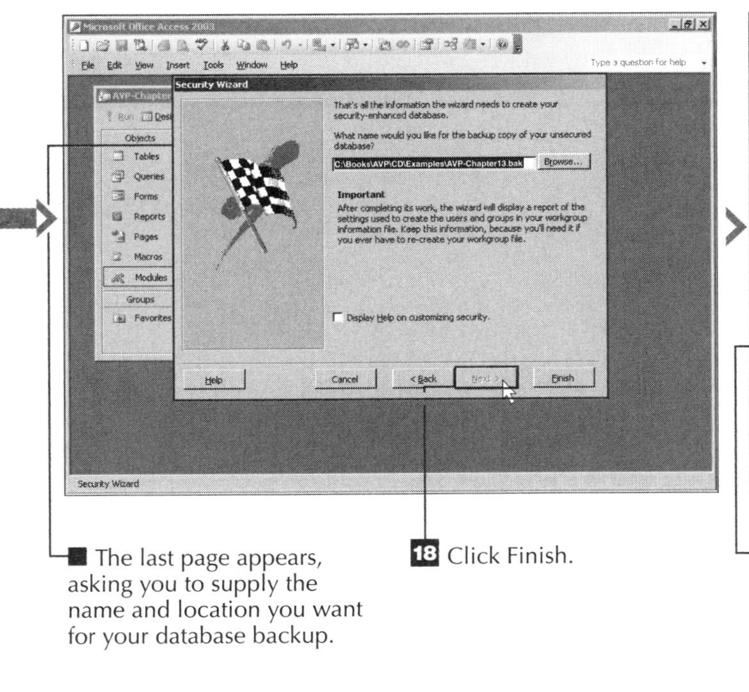

■ The last page appears, asking you to supply the name and location you want for your database backup.

18 Click Finish.

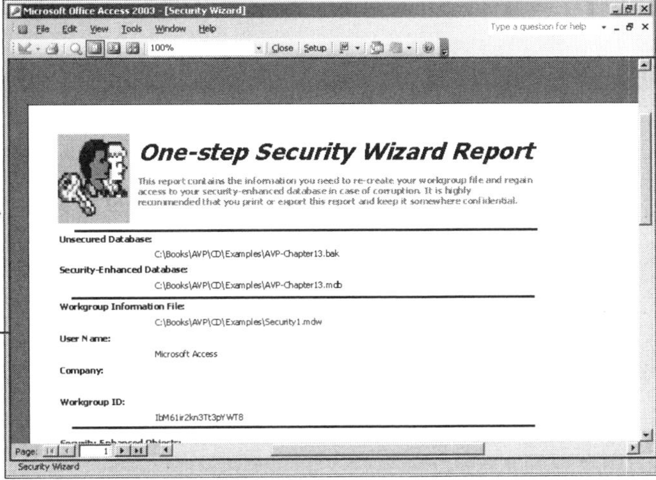

■ Access secures the database and generates a report.

19 Close the report.

■ Access asks if you want to save the report in a snapshot format.

20 Click Yes.

■ Access saves the report in a snapshot format.

INTRODUCING REPLICATION

Although many Access users have never heard of it, replication enables users to make copies of their databases. They can then make changes to the copies. Access can update both the original and the copies with data from each other.

ELEMENTS OF REPLICATION

Replicas

The copy of the database is called a replica, and the original database is the called the Design Master. While you can change data in any replica, and in the Design Master, you cannot change the design of the objects, such as forms, reports, and tables, in the Design Master.

Synchronization

The process of updating a replica is called synchronization. You can synchronize your database in different ways: either using the menus, using VBA code, or using the Replication Manager, available from the Office Downloads Web site.

Data Conflict Resolution

Sometimes you may make changes to two different replicas on the same record or field at the same time, creating a data conflict in which one replica overrides the other replica. If this happens, then a Data Conflict Resolution Wizard appears the next time you open the overridden database.

REPLICATION METHODS

Using the Menus

You can use a menu option called Replication in the Tools menu. This option has a number of utilities for every phase of replication, from creating replicas to synchronizing and resolving conflicts.

There are a couple of other menu options, such as recovering the Design Master. This is useful when your original Design Master becomes corrupt. By using the recovery utility, you can assign one of the replicas as the Design Master.

The other menu option is to use the Partial Replicate Wizard. This wizard helps you to specify a filter for replicating and synchronizing replicas. For example, if you have a sales force divided into regions, you can give a salesperson a replica that contains only the data for their region.

Briefcase

Using replication in Access can be as simple as creating a new Briefcase on your computer, and dragging your database into the new Briefcase. The Briefcase feature has been available to users since Windows 95. You can use Briefcase to make copies of various Office application documents. By dragging the applications into the Briefcase, you can later update the original from the copy, as well as update the copy from the original. Access enables you to synchronize, even if both versions have changed. Other Office documents, such as Excel spreadsheets, only update if both have not been changed.

Using VBA

You can use VBA to perform any of the tasks that you can do using the menus and Briefcase, including creating replicas, synchronizing, and handling data conflicts. You can also use VBA to work with partial replication, and with the filters and synchronization.

CREATE A REPLICA USING MENUS

You can create a replica by using the menus in Access. While in the database you want to replicate, you can choose Replication from the Tools menu, and then Create Replica.

A message box appears, telling you that Access must close the database before it can be replicated. A dialog box then asks you if you would like to make a backup of your database before you make it your Design Master. It is a good idea to make a copy of your database.

When you make a copy of your database, Access uses the name of the database and adds the .bak extension. The copy appears in the same folder as the original database. Your current database now changes to the Design Master.

Note that the dialog boxes that ask you to make a backup, and to specify which replica you want to be the Design Master, only appear the first time you replicate the database. If you create a replica using the Briefcase, and then create another replica using the menus, these dialog boxes do not reappear. For the purpose of this task, the database was reset so that you can see all the message boxes as they appear.

If you want to create a partial replica, you can choose Replication from the Tools menu, and then Partial Replica Wizard. With this wizard you can create a new partial replica, or modify the filters for an existing partial replica.

You can create replicas from other replicas; however, you cannot create a full replica from a partial replica, or from a replica with the replica type of Not Replicable. For more information, see the section "Create a Replica Using VBA."

CREATE A REPLICA USING MENUS

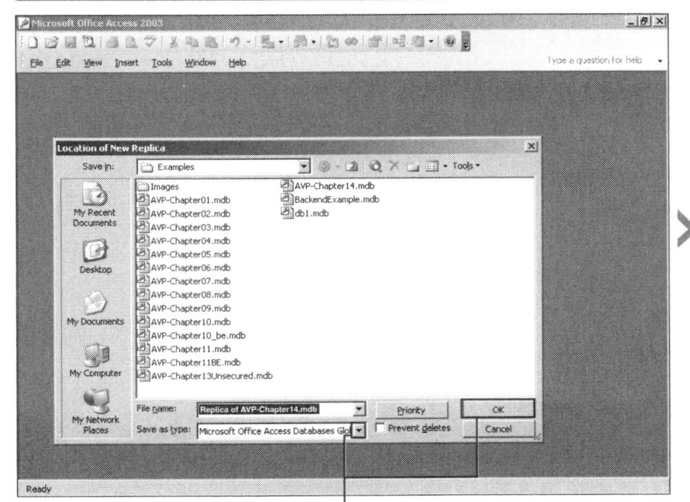

Note: This task uses AVP-Chapter14.mdb on the CD-ROM.

1. Open a database.
2. Click Tools ➪ Replication ➪ Create Replica.
3. Click Yes to close the database to replicate it.
4. Click Yes to back up your database.
5. In the Location of New Replica dialog box, click the Save as type ▾ to specify the location of the replica.
6. Click OK.

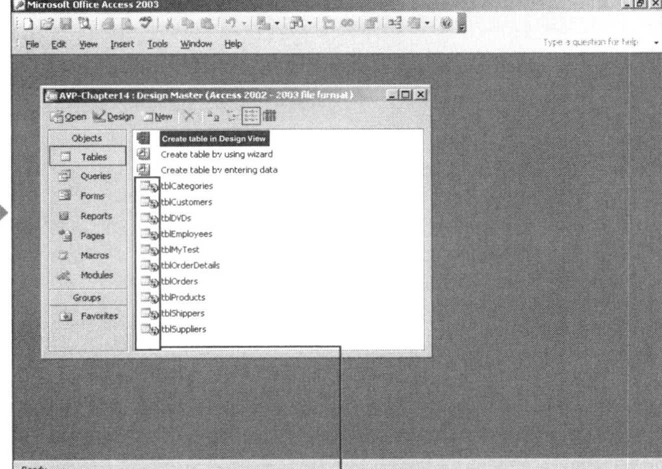

■ A message box appears, telling you the names and locations of the new Design Master and replica.

7. Click OK.

■ Access replicates the database, and you are returned to the database window.

■ The replication symbol appears next to all of the object icons in the database.

CREATE A NEW BRIEFCASE TO REPLICATE A DATABASE

If you often bring work home, but also have other users working in your database at the same time, you can use Briefcase to replicate your database. Before you can use Briefcase to replicate your database, you must create a new Briefcase.

Briefcase is a little-known, but very useful, utility in Windows. In previous versions of Windows, you could find Briefcase on the desktop, but even then, few people used it. Now, to use Briefcase, you must select the folder or location where you want to store the Briefcase, and right-click the folder or location. In the drop-down list, you can choose New, and then Briefcase. A new Briefcase appears in the location you specify.

After you create the Briefcase, you can replicate your database by dragging it from the original location and dropping it into the Briefcase.

When you drag the database into the Briefcase, Windows asks you a few questions that help it to create the Design Master and the replica. It first warns you that you are changing the database to be replicable, and introduces some of the issues that may arise from this change. If you choose to continue, Windows asks you if you want to create a backup database. This is recommended. Windows then asks you which database you want to have as the Design Master, the original or the Briefcase version.

You can now change the data in either the original or the Briefcase by right-clicking the Briefcase and selecting update. Windows then asks if you want to merge changes.

CREATE A NEW BRIEFCASE TO REPLICATE A DATABASE

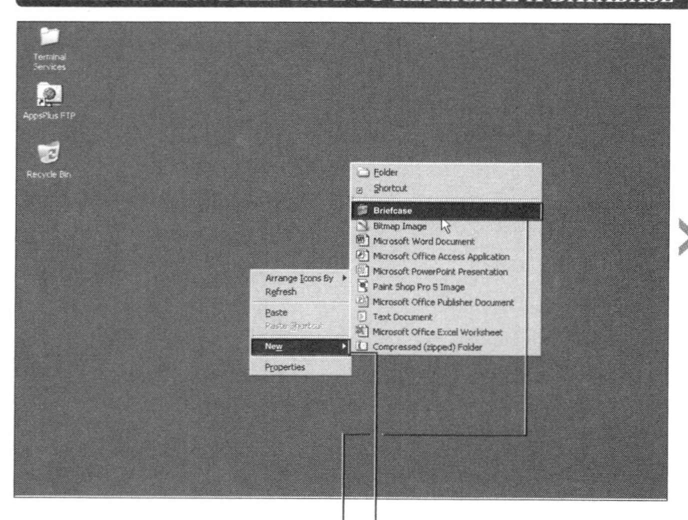

CREATE A NEW BRIEFCASE

Note: This task uses AVP-Chapter14.mdb on the CD-ROM.

1 Right-click in the location you want to place the new Briefcase.

2 In the drop-down list that appears, click New.

3 Click Briefcase.

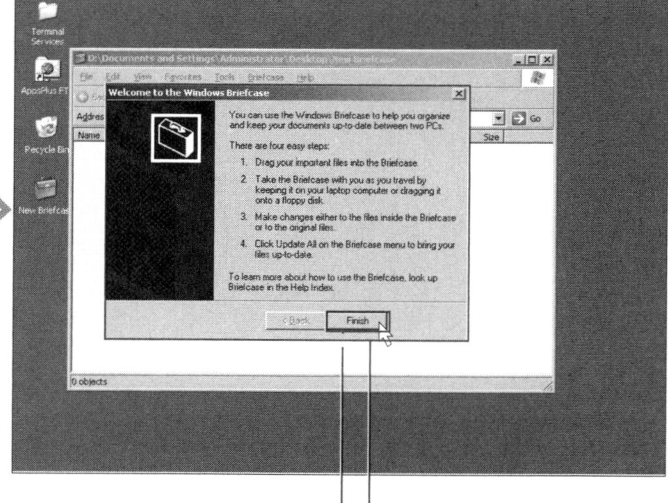

■ This example places the Briefcase on the desktop.

4 Double-click the Briefcase.

■ A welcome message appears.

5 Click Finish when you have read the message.

Extra

Changes occur in a database when you make the database replicable. Below are a few of the changes:

- Access increases the size of your database significantly.
- Access adds hidden fields to each of your tables for tracking record level changes.
- Access adds hidden system tables for replication.
- Access changes AutoNumber fields that are synchronous to random. The reason for this is that if the AutoNumber fields remain synchronous, then you may have many data conflicts due to all the copies assigning the same unique numbers. The random number is generated so that conflicts are very unlikely to happen.
- A new icon appears for your tables in the database window.
- Each object in Access has a property called Replicable, so you can replicate some objects and not others. To use the Replicable property, select the object, right-click, and choose Properties from the drop-down list. Choose Replicable from the property sheet that appears.

You should not notice a big change in performance.

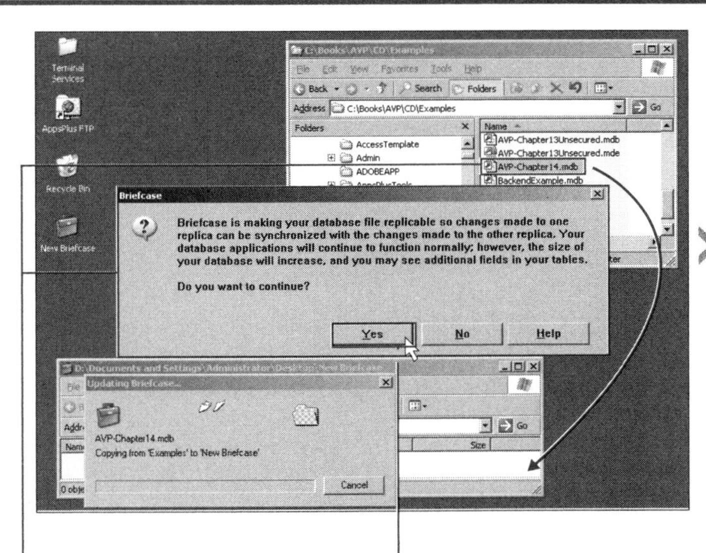

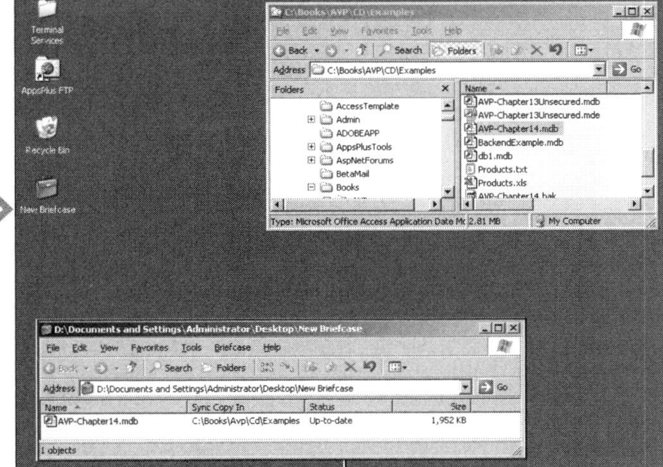

REPLICATE A DATABASE WITH THE BRIEFCASE

1 Using Explorer, click and drag the original database icon to the Briefcase.

■ A dialog box appears, warning about the changes that will occur in the database, and verifying that you want to continue.

2 Click Yes.

■ The next dialog box asks if you want to back up the database.

3 Click Yes.

■ A dialog box appears, asking which copy you want to designate as the Design Master, the original copy or the Briefcase copy.

4 Click OK to accept the default, which is the original copy.

■ The new database appears in the Briefcase.

SYNCHRONIZE YOUR REPLICAS

After you create your replicas, you may want to synchronize them. To synchronize your replicas, you must have access to all the replicas you want to synchronize. This means that they must all be logged onto the network, or through the Internet. Internet replication is a topic that is beyond this book's coverage.

You can now choose Replication from the Tools menu, and then Synchronize. The Synchronize Database dialog box appears. It displays an option group labeled Synchronize. The first choice in the option group is a drop-down list of the other replicas in the replica set. You can choose a replica from the list and click OK.

Below the OK and Cancel buttons, there is a Browse button that you can use to locate a replica that has been moved. If you locate a database, and it is not part of the replica set, Access knows that it is not part of the replica set, based on the values Access entered in the new tables created specifically for replication.

Located below the first Synchronize option is a check box labeled Make 'replica path and name' the Design Master. This check box lets you designate a replica in the drop-down list as the new Design Master. Keep in mind that you can only have one Design Master.

There are two other option buttons that are disabled in the Synchronize Database dialog box. You can use these options when you are using a synchronizer. Synchronizers enable you to schedule a time when you want to synchronize all your replicas. In this case, you would specify that either one or all synchronizers synchronize all replicas.

SYNCHRONIZE YOUR REPLICAS

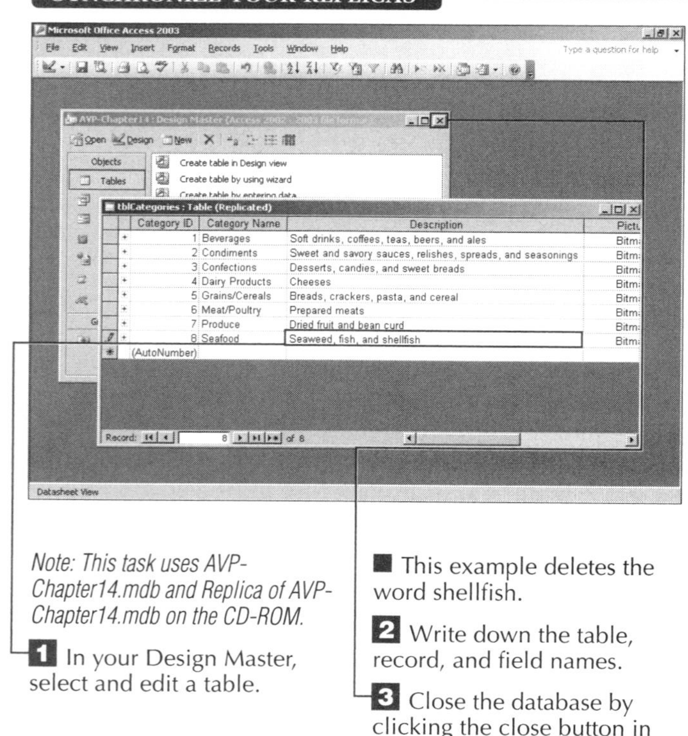

Note: This task uses AVP-Chapter14.mdb and Replica of AVP-Chapter14.mdb on the CD-ROM.

1 In your Design Master, select and edit a table.

■ This example deletes the word shellfish.

2 Write down the table, record, and field names.

3 Close the database by clicking the close button in the Access main window.

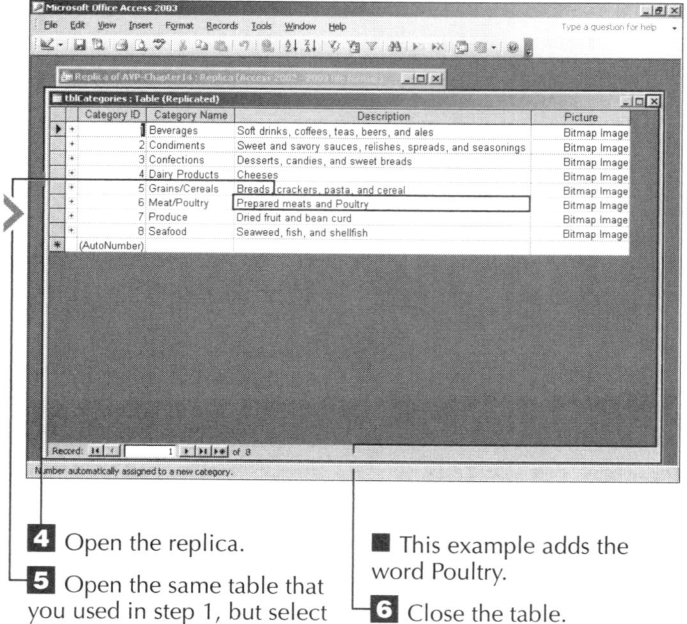

4 Open the replica.

5 Open the same table that you used in step 1, but select and edit a different record.

■ This example adds the word Poultry.

6 Close the table.

Extra

You can test the synchronization feature of Access. To do this, you must open the first database that you assigned as the Design Master. Make some changes in the database, such as changing values in obvious fields. Close the Design Master.

You can now open the replica of the database. With the replica opened, open the same table that you did in the Design Master, and make some changes in the table. Be sure to change values in different fields only. Changing values in the same record and field results in data conflict, which is discussed in the next section.

Next, while in the database window, choose Replication from the Tools menu, then Synchronize Replicas. In the Synchronize Database dialog box, choose the first option, and choose the Design Master. When you open each of the copies, they are identical.

The Replication Manager is a separate utility that shipped with the Microsoft Office Developer Edition, prior to Office 2003. You can download the Replication Manager at http://office.microsoft.com/Downloads/default.aspx. The Replication Manager allows you to manage your replica sets graphically, and includes setting up schedules for synchronization.

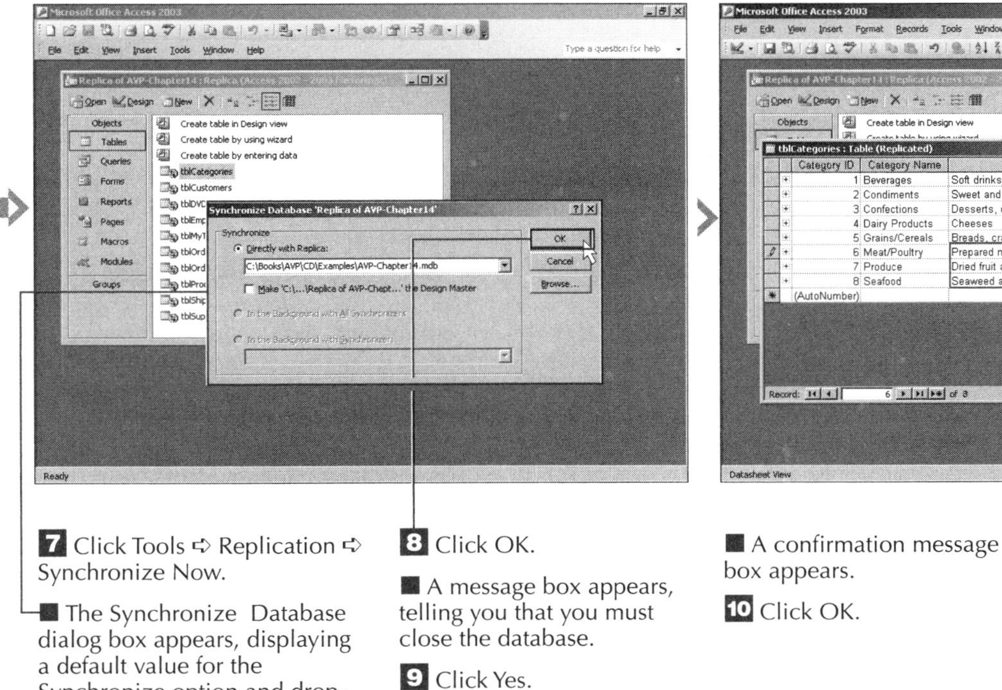

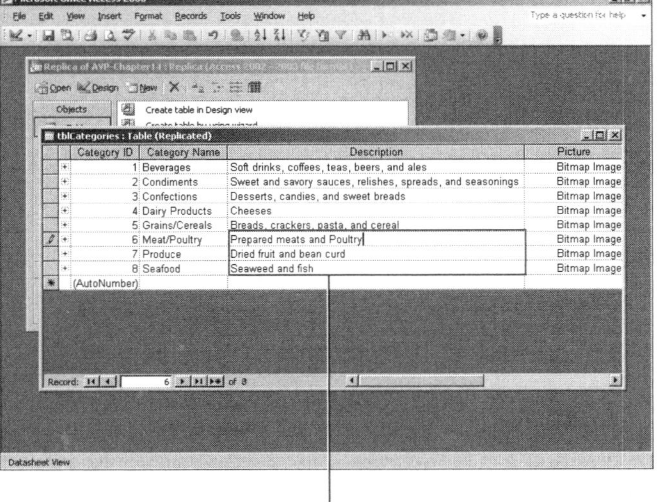

7 Click Tools ➪ Replication ➪ Synchronize Now.

■ The Synchronize Database dialog box appears, displaying a default value for the Synchronize option and drop-down list.

8 Click OK.

■ A message box appears, telling you that you must close the database.

9 Click Yes.

■ A confirmation message box appears.

10 Click OK.

11 Open the table that you edited in both databases.

■ Both changes have taken effect.

RESOLVE DATA CONFLICTS

When users make changes in replicas to the same fields, and in the same records, data conflicts result. When conflicts occur, the user who has a lower priority rating receives a message box with a message stating that the replica set he is using has conflicts from synchronizing with other members. It then asks whether the user wants to resolve the conflicts. If the user clicks Yes, then the Microsoft Replication Conflict Viewer dialog box appears.

You can use the Microsoft Replication Conflict Viewer dialog box to handle conflicts for both Jet databases and the SQL Server. The first page of the dialog box displays a list of conflicts that have occurred. There are various conflicts that can occur, but the most common is synchronization.

If you double-click a conflict, the main page of the conflict viewer appears. Two records are displayed: the record that overrides, and the record that is overridden. On the overridden record, all the fields that you can edit are enabled. This allows you to make changes to the data to resolve the conflict. You can also see all the fields in the records, or just the fields that have conflicts.

The dialog box allows you to handle the conflict in a number of different ways: You can physically change the data and accept the changes; you can accept the changes based on the overriding record; or you can postpone the resolution altogether. There is also a check box option that allows you to log the error for later use.

Interestingly, the user with the lower priority rating in the original data conflict actually has control over the ultimate solution to the data.

RESOLVE DATA CONFLICTS

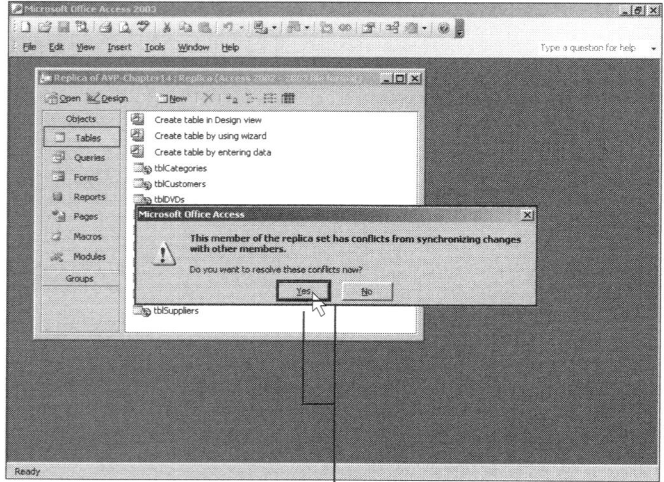

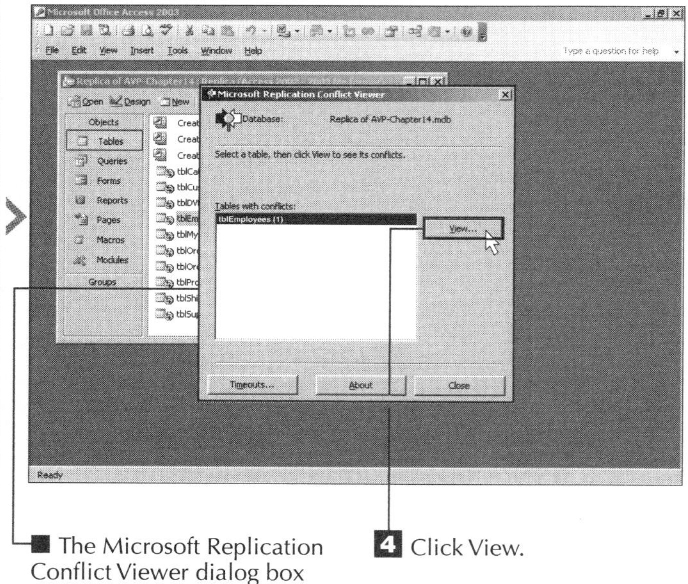

Note: This task uses AVP-Chapter14.mdb and Replica of AVP-Chapter14.mdb on the CD-ROM.

1 Repeat steps 1 to 9 in the previous section, except select and edit the same table, record, and field in each database replica.

2 Open both of the databases.

■ The replica that is overridden displays a message box, asking whether you want to resolve the conflict.

3 Click Yes.

■ The Microsoft Replication Conflict Viewer dialog box appears.

4 Click View.

Extra

There are various types of errors that can occur, some from data conflicts, and some from synchronization. Below are some of the specific types:

TYPE	DESCRIPTION
Locking	Occurs if you are attempting synchronization when a record is locked.
Referential Integrity	There are three types: On Delete — deleting of foreign key records; On Update — foreign key records do not exist; and Foreign Key — invalid primary key involved in another conflict.
Simultaneous Update	Occurs if the same row and field have been updated. This is by far the most common conflict.
Table-Level Validation	Occurs if a field in a record has a value that does not match the table validation rule.
Unique Key	Occurs if two different records have the same unique value. This is the reason why you use Random for AutoNumber.
Update-Delete	Deletes are processed first; as a result, if an update occurs on the same record, an error occurs.

The Microsoft Replication Conflict Viewer now handles all of these data and synchronization conflicts. In prior versions of Access, some of the errors caused problems that included forcing you to start over from the beginning with a new Design Master. Since the release of Access 2000, many of these issues have been resolved.

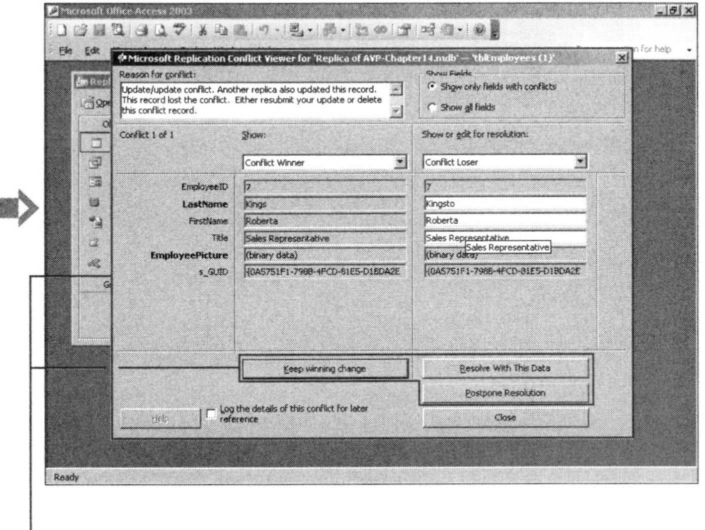

■ The Conflict Viewer displays the individual conflict.

5 Click the button for the method you want to use to resolve the conflict.

■ This example selects the Resolve With This Data option.

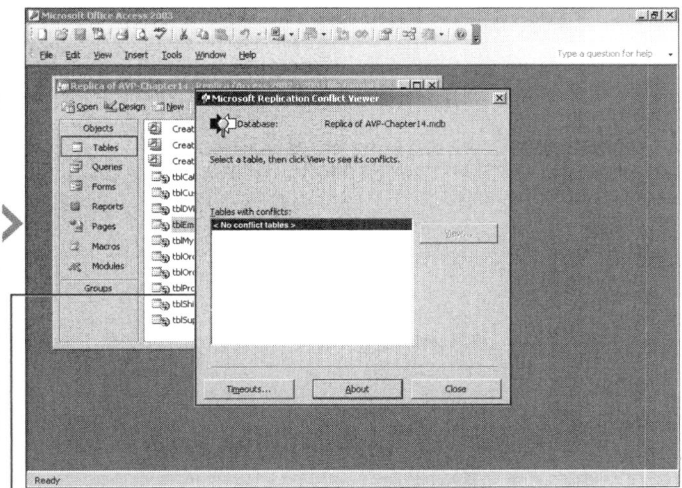

■ The original Conflict Viewer dialog box appears, indicating that no conflicts remain.

CREATE A REPLICA USING VBA

You can create a replica using VBA almost as easily as when you use the menus. There are only a few commands you need to learn to perform all the replication tasks. You must first perform a few extra steps, because the commands to perform the various tasks are contained in an ADO library called Microsoft Jet and Replication Objects 2.6, or JRO.

To use the ADO library, you must set a reference by choosing References from the Tools menu while in the code editor. Locate the library in the list and select it. You can now use the various objects. You will most often use the Replica object from the JRO library. Just as with other ADO objects, you can declare the Replica object with the New keyword. The code looks like this: `Dim rpl As New JRO.Replica`.

You can use one property and one method to create the replica. First, type the ActiveConnection property of the Replica object, which you must set to the connection property of the database of which you are making a replica. If this is the first replica you are making, then make sure that the database is replicable by using the MakeReplicable method: `rpl.MakeReplicable`.

However, you can only do this from another database, because you need to open it exclusively. For the purposes of this task, first create a replica using the menus as described in the section "Create a Replica Using Menus."

Next, you add the CreateReplica method of the Replica object. The syntax for the CreateReplica method is:

```
rpl.CreateReplica(ReplicaName, Description, ReplicaType ,
        Visibility , Priority , Updatability)
```

where ReplicaName is the name of the new database — replica — and Description describes the new database. ReplicaType is one of four values: jrRepTypeNotReplicable, jrRepTypeDesignMaster, jrRepTypeFull, and jrRepTypePartial. Visibility is the property that allows you to see the replica, and Priority is the priority level for the replica. Updatability is one of two values: jrRepUpdFull or jrRepUpdReadOnly.

CREATE A REPLICA USING VBA

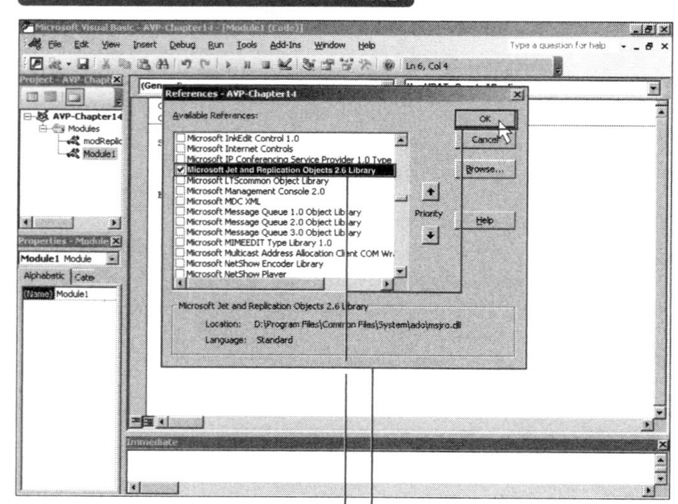

Note: This task uses AVP-Chapter14.mdb and Replica of AVP-Chapter14.mdb on the CD-ROM.

1 In the Design Master, create a new module and subroutine.

2 Click Tools ➪ References.

■ The References dialog box appears.

3 Scroll through the Available References list, and check Microsoft Jet and Replication Objects 2.6 Library.

4 Click OK.

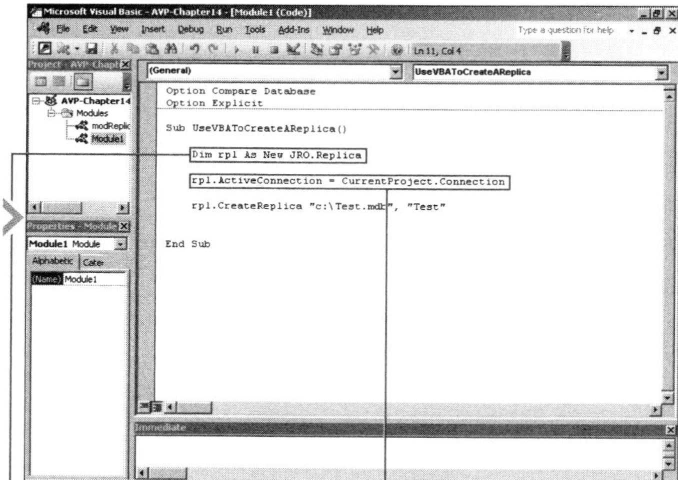

■ You can now work with replication using VBA.

5 In the new subroutine you created, type the code to declare a new Replica object variable: **Dim *rpl* As New JRO.Replica**.

6 Type the code that assigns the connection string of the design master: ***rpl*.ActiveConnection = CurrentProject.Connection**.

Extra

You can use a method called MakeReplicable to make a database replicable. When you call this method, Access performs all of the steps that are necessary to change a database into a Design Master.

The syntax for the MakeReplicable method is as follows:

```
rpl.MakeReplicable(ConnectString ,
ColumnTracking)
```

You can use ConnectString instead of the ActiveConnection property of the Replica object, to override it. If you set this property to True, which is the default setting, then ColumnTracking specifies that you want to have conflicts tracked down to the column level; otherwise, conflicts occur at the row level. Both ConnectString and ColumnTracking are optional.

There is a collection on the Replica object called Filters. When you create a replica with the type of jrRepTypePartial, you can set up the filter's collection to replicate based on the filter. You can also use referential integrity. For example, if you have a filter on the tblCustomers table where the region equals the region of a salesperson, then all the orders and related records are replicated and synchronized as well.

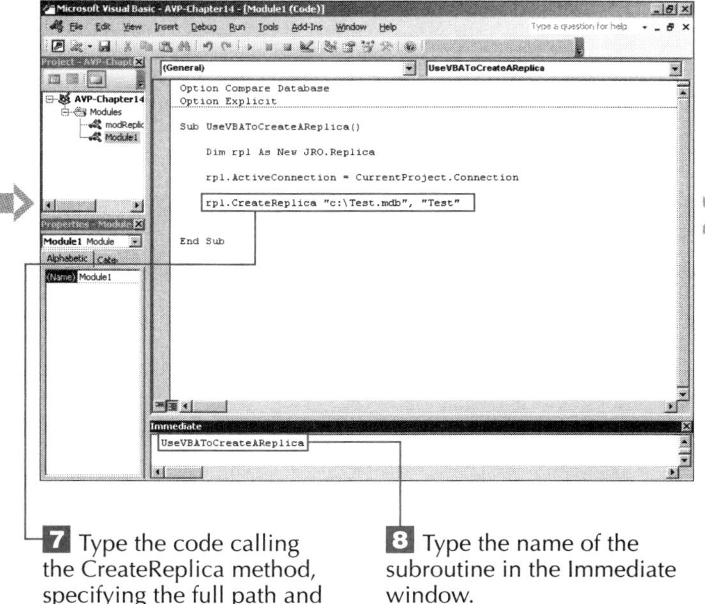

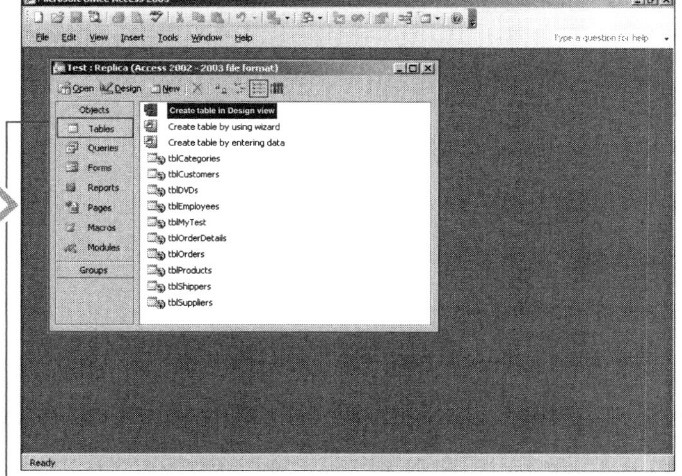

7 Type the code calling the CreateReplica method, specifying the full path and name of the new replica, and a description.

■ You are now ready to test the routine.

8 Type the name of the subroutine in the Immediate window.

9 Locate and open the new replica.

■ The new replica appears.

SYNCHRONIZE REPLICAS USING VBA

When you use VBA to control the synchronization of your replicas, you can create seamless interfaces where the user does not need to use the menus to synchronize replicas himself. You can use VBA to declare a replica object, and then set the ActiveConnection property. After you do this, you can call the Synchronize method for the replica object to synchronize the current replica, or the replica that you specify by the connection string that you assign to the ActiveConnection property.

The syntax for the Synchronize method is as follows:

```
rpl.Synchronize(Target, SyncType , SyncMode)
```

where Target is the file path and name of a replica, the name of a synchronizer, or the name of an Internet server. This example uses the file path and name of the replica. SyncType can be one of the following: jrSyncTypeExport, jrSyncTypeImport, or jrSyncTypeImpExp, which is the default. SyncMode is the method of synchronization, which can be: jrSyncModeDirect, jrSyncModeInternet, or jrSyncModeIndirect, which is the default.

If you use the default value, jrSyncModeIndirect, you must use a synchronizer, which can only be set and used with the Replication Manager. However, if you are synchronizing using dialup, then updates are handled like a mail drop. When you use the other mode, jrSyncModeDirect, both replicas are opened at the same time. This method is faster on a LAN, but if you are using a WAN or dialup, the jrSyncModeIndirect method is recommended. The jrSyncModeInternet type is used strictly for the Internet.

The example below uses the jrSyncModeDirect type, which allows the direct replica to be synchronized directly, rather than through the Internet, or by using a dropbox method, which is what the indirect method uses.

SYNCHRONIZE REPLICAS USING VBA

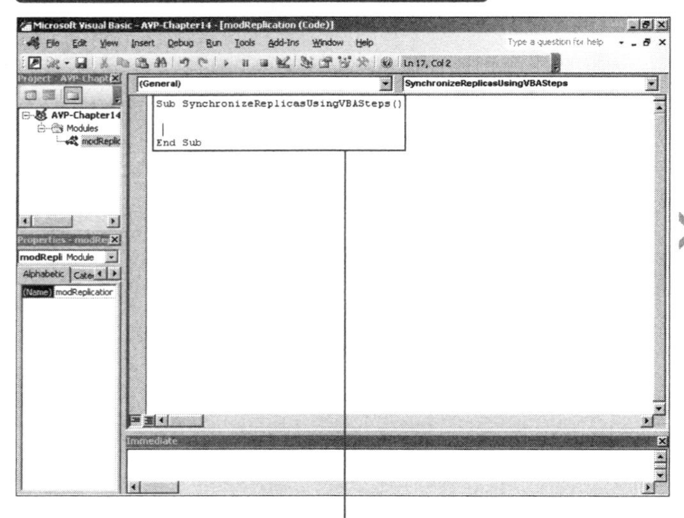

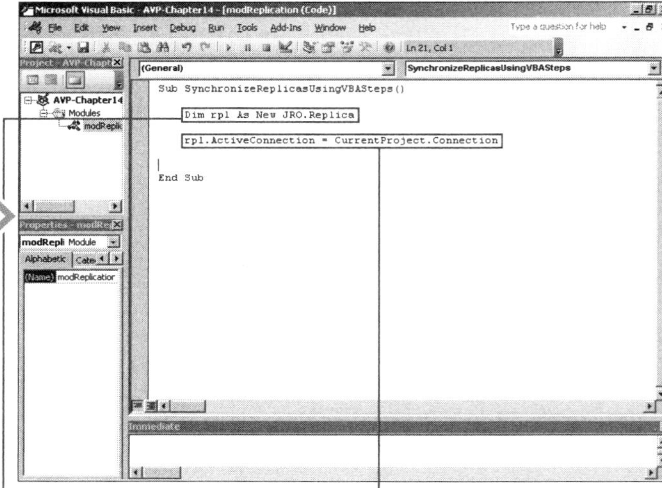

Note: This task uses AVP-Chapter14.mdb and Replica of AVP-Chapter14.mdb on the CD-ROM.

1 Repeat steps 1 to 9 in the section "Synchronize Your Replicas."

2 Switch back to the Design Master by clicking the Access icon at the far right of the module toolbar.

3 Add a new subroutine.

4 Add the code to declare a new Replica type object variable.

5 Add the code to assign the ActiveConnection property.

Extra

You should wrap all the code that you are creating for replication in error handling code. This is because you will be confronted with network-related and other issues that may frequently cause errors to occur, possibly more frequently than any other development you do with Access, except Automation.

You can give the user an error message and the opportunity to retry the synchronization, as follows:

```
Sub SynchronizeReplicasUsingVBAExtra()
    Dim rpl As New JRO.Replica

    On Error GoTo SyncErr
    rpl.ActiveConnection = CurrentProject.Connection
    rpl.Synchronize "c:\test.mdb", jrSyncTypeImpExp, jrSyncModeDirect
        MsgBox "Replicas Synchronized"
    Exit Sub
SyncErr:
    If MsgBox( _
      "An error has occurred attempting to synchronize the replica." & _
        vbCrLf & vbCrLf & "Would you like to try again?", _
        vbQuestion + vbYesNo, "Retry Synchronization?") = vbYes Then
            Resume
    Else
            Exit Sub
        End If
End Sub
```

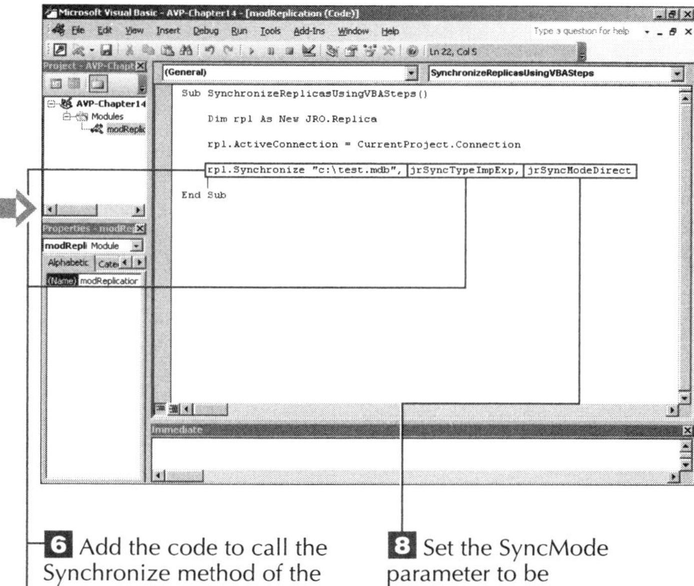

6 Add the code to call the Synchronize method of the replica object.

7 Set the SyncType parameter to be jrSyncTypeImpExp.

8 Set the SyncMode parameter to be jrSyncModeDirect.

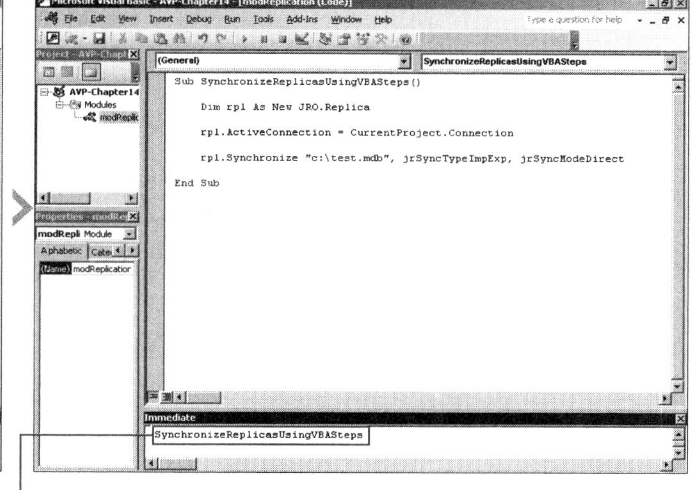

9 Type the name of the routine in the Immediate window.

■ The data is now synchronized between the two replicas.

10 Open the table that you edited to verify that the replicas were synchronized correctly.

ACCESS AND THE INTERNET

With every version of Microsoft Office, the Office applications have been improved in order to provide a convenient way to place your data on the Web.

You can use several languages, such as HTML and XML, to take advantage of developing Internet technologies.

XML OVERVIEW

Extensible Markup Language, or XML, is to data what HTML is to presentation. You can use XML tags to specify various elements of the data, such as fields, their data types, and other properties. XML uses separate documents to form the data that you use. XML allows different business systems to work with data in a common format. Read more on XML in Chapter 10.

HTML OVERVIEW

The primary language of the Internet is HyperText Markup Language, or HTML. You can use HTML to specify how to display information in your browser using a beginning and ending tag, <HTML> and </HTML>. All the information for your Web page goes in between these tags. HTML code is not case sensitive. Common beginning and ending HTML tags and their function appear in the table. An example of a simple HTML page appears here:

```
<html>
   <head>
        <title>This is the Header</title>
   </head>
   <body>
        <p>This is my HTML page </p>
   </body>
</html>
```

HTML TAG	DESCRIPTION
<a></a>	Designates a hyperlink. You can use these tags within other tags, such as <p></p>, so that a portion of the text is used for linking to addresses within the current page or other pages.
<body></body>	Designates the page's body, which contains the majority of the document information.
 	Adds a line break. This tag does not require a closing tag.
<div></div>	Divides up the page, and specifies text that appears in the division header.
<head></head>	Specifies the heading of the page.
<html></html>	Designates the beginning and ending of an HTML document.
<img>	Designates an image file. You can surround this tag with <a></a> to create a graphic hyperlink. This tag does not require a closing tag.
<p></p>	Designates the beginning and ending of a paragraph.
<script></script>	Specifies script languages such as vbscript and jscript that perform tasks beyond the capabilities of HTML.
<strong></strong>	Designates a larger format for a font.
<table></table>	Creates a table. Within these tags you can use other tags, such as <tr></tr>, for table row, and <td></td>, for table data.
<title></title>	Specifies the text that you want to appear in the title bar of the browser window.
<ul></ul>	Designates a bulleted list. To specify the list items, surround each item with <li></li>, or list item, tags.

ACCESS FEATURES FOR THE INTERNET

Access has several features that make your Office experience more accessible to the Web, whether you are placing data on a Web site, or integrating Web features, such as hyperlinks and Data Access Pages, into your Access interface.

Unbound Hyperlinks

Some of the first features added to Access for the Internet were new control properties called Hyperlink Address and Hyperlink SubAddress. These two properties allow you to specify the Uniform Resource Locators, or URLs, which are addresses for various Web sites on the Internet, as well as files on your system. The Hyperlink Address control property allows you to specify other types of files, such as Word documents and Excel spreadsheets. The Hyperlink SubAddress control property allows you to specify a worksheet or range in Excel or Word. The controls that can contain hyperlinks are the Command Button and the Image and Label controls. For more about unbound hyperlinks, see the first section, "Set the Hyperlink Properties of Controls."

Hyperlink Data Type

For convenience, it is useful to add hyperlinks to unbound controls on forms, as well as to be able to store hyperlink data in tables. When you store values in the tables using the Hyperlink data type, you can specify the text you want to display, the main hyperlink address, and the subaddress. When you use the Hyperlink data type field on a form, it changes as the records change. For more about using the Hyperlink data type, see the section "Add and Use a Hyperlink Field in a Table."

Using Hyperlinks with VBA

You may sometimes need to work with hyperlinks using VBA code. With VBA you can follow hyperlinks that are located in tables, and the user does not necessarily need to even click them. For more about this, see the section "Using VBA to Follow a Hyperlink."

Export Objects to HTML

All the objects used for data, or editing and viewing data, can be exported to the Web as HTML pages. This includes tables, queries, forms, reports, and Data Access Pages. For more about publishing data to the Web, see the section "Publish Access Data to HTML."

Data Access Pages

Data Access Pages are a way to create a Web interface to use Access data. Access includes an interface that contains a Data Access Pages editor. When you create Data Access Pages, you are creating HTML Web pages that are bound to data. Access even provides a wizard, which you can see in the section "Using the Data Access Page Wizard."

Other Internet Features

Another Internet feature in Access is XML utilization. XML uses Smart Tags, and you can program XML using VBA, as well as import and export XML. You can use XML Web Services to let you import data, as well as functionality, from the Web.

SET THE HYPERLINK PROPERTIES OF CONTROLS

Hyperlink properties give you the ability to change images, labels, and text box controls into hyperlinks. Access provides a couple of methods for setting the hyperlink properties. You can open the property sheet for the controls, and go to the Format tab. The Hyperlink Address and Hyperlink SubAddress properties of controls are displayed in the property sheet.

In the Hyperlink Address field, you can type the URL of a Web site, or a file path and a filename on your local area network. For the Hyperlink SubAddress property, you can type the range or a named range for Excel.

While you can add the information directly into the properties, there are times when you may not have the exact information you need. When this occurs, you can click the Builder button beside the two properties, or right-click the control and choose Edit Hyperlink from the Hyperlink menu. The Edit Hyperlink dialog box appears. Note that if this is the first time going into the hyperlink, the dialog box is named Insert Hyperlink.

The Edit Hyperlink dialog box assists you in editing hyperlinks. Along the left side of the dialog box is a toolbar that lists choices of what you want to link to. They include Existing File or Web Page, Object in This Database, Create New Page, and E-mail Address.

The middle section of the Edit Hyperlink dialog box varies, depending on the option you choose in the Link to toolbar. When using the Existing File or Web Page option, you have the choice of Current Folder, Browsed Pages, and Recent Files. You can also type the URL. If you are working with objects in the current database, you can use a control listing the objects in the database.

You can use the Create New Page link to make a new Web page. You can also use the E-mail Address link to help you type all the information you need to send an e-mail.

ADD A LABEL HYPERLINK CONTROL

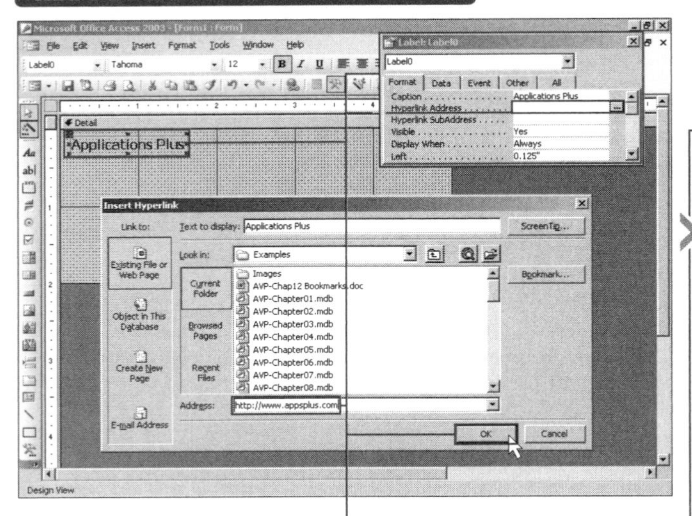

Note: This task uses frmSetTheHyperlinkPropertiesOfControls in AVP-Chapter15.mdb on the CD-ROM.

1 Create or open a form in the Design view, and add a text label to the form.

2 Click the label, and open the property sheet to the Format tab.

3 Click in the property field, and click the Builder button.

4 Type the hyperlink URL.

5 Click OK.

6 Open the form in Form view.

7 Click the label.

■ The browser opens, and displays the Web site you specified in step 4.

Extra

When you work with hyperlinks, you can specify different options as to how they display. To specify hyperlink options, choose Options from the Tools menu in the database window. When the Options dialog box appears, click the General tab. In the General tab at the bottom left, is a Web Options button.

Click the Web Options button. The Web Options dialog box appears, where you can specify the Hyperlink Color, Followed Hyperlink Color, and whether or not to underline the hyperlinks. After you make your changes, click OK twice to close the dialog boxes.

You can also set the Hyperlink Base. The Hyperlink Base is a relative path from which you can base all your hyperlink addresses. It can be a file path, intranet, or Internet address. To set the Hyperlink Base, choose Database Properties from the File menu. At the bottom of the Summary page, you can see the Hyperlink Base. You can use this to set the relative path of all hyperlinks in the database.

ADD AN IMAGE HYPERLINK CONTROL

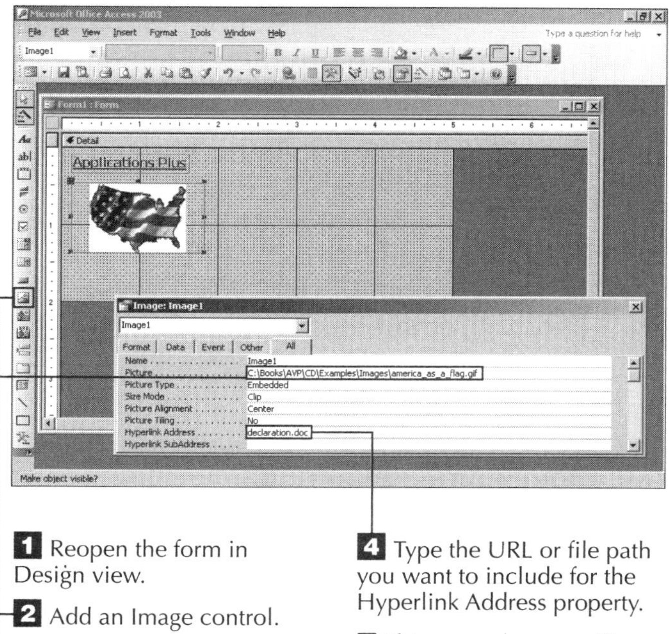

1 Reopen the form in Design view.

2 Add an Image control.

3 Set the image you want to use as the Picture property.

4 Type the URL or file path you want to include for the Hyperlink Address property.

■ This example uses a file path and filename.

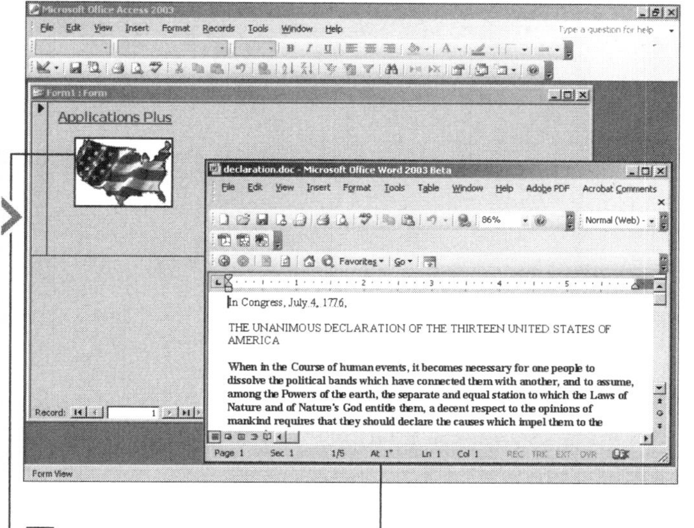

5 Open the form in View mode.

6 Click the image.

■ The Web site or file you specified in step 4 opens.

ADD AND USE A HYPERLINK FIELD IN A TABLE

It is very convenient to store a variety of hyperlink types, such as Web site information and e-mail addresses, in your database. Adding a field with the data type of Hyperlink is similar to adding other data types. You can add the field to the table you want by opening the table in Design view and entering a name for the new field. From the Data Type drop-down list, you can choose Hyperlink. You can then add the caption to the field, and save the table.

To add data to the new hyperlink field, you can open the table in Datasheet view, and place the cursor in the field. You can right-click, and choose Edit Hyperlink from the Hyperlink menu.

Another way to edit the hyperlink is to type the address directly into the field. Hyperlink addresses can have up to four parts. These parts are separated by the number sign, #:

```
DisplayText#Address#SubAddress#Screentip
```

where DisplayText is the text that you want to display; Address is the URL, or full file path, such as e-mail address, depending on the type of hyperlink you are creating; SubAddress can be a range in a spreadsheet; and Screentip is displayed when a user moves their mouse over the field.

To edit the field after it is in place, you can use the Edit Hyperlink dialog box. To use the hyperlink, you just need to click it.

ADD AND USE A HYPERLINK FIELD IN A TABLE

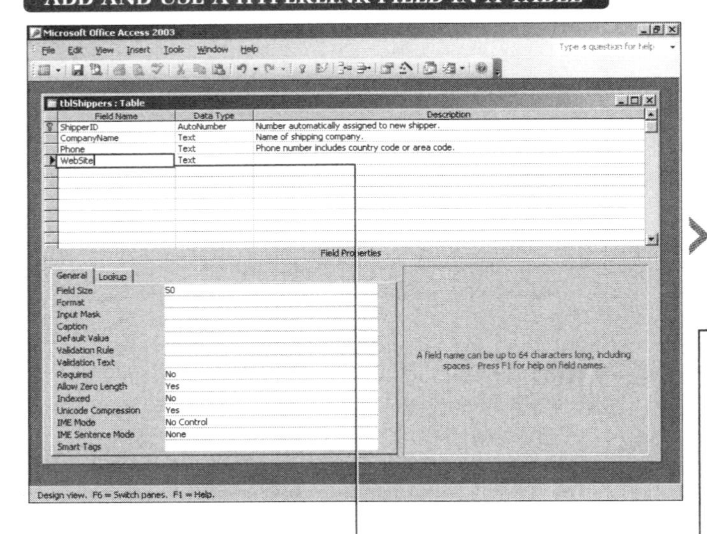

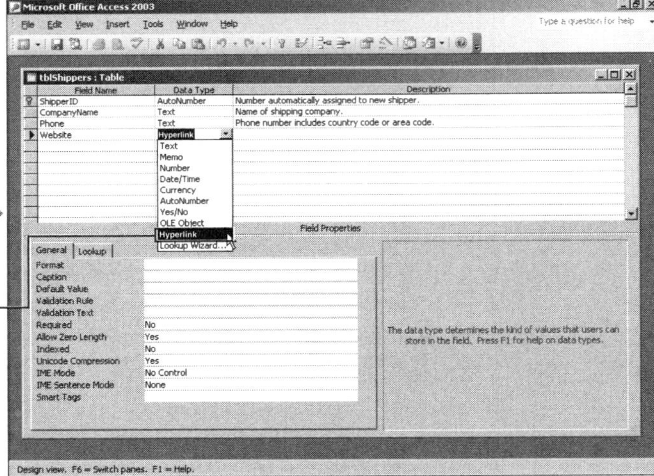

ADD A HYPERLINK FIELD IN A TABLE

Note: This task uses frmAddADataTypeOfHyperlink ToATable in AVP-Chapter15.mdb on the CD-ROM.

1 Create or open a table in the Design view.

2 Click in a field and type a field name.

3 Click in the Data Type field, and select a hyperlink from the drop-down list.

4 Save and close the table.

Extra

You can divide up hyperlink addresses using the pound sign, #. In addition, there are various types of hyperlink addresses you can use, depending on what you want to do. For example:

- You can use http:// to specify an Internet address.
- You can use mailto: to specify an e-mail address.
- You can use file: with a full path and filename to specify files on your local network.

Here are a few other things to keep in mind:

- If you use the standard URL starting with http://, Access adds the pound signs on each end of the URL.
- If you leave the Hyperlink SubAddress field blank, and you do not include the http:// prefix in the hyperlink address, Access places it there for you, along with the pound signs.
- If you are pointing to an object in the database you are currently in, you do not have to specify anything in the Hyperlink Address property field. You can just specify the object type and object name in the Hyperlink SubAddress property, such as table tblCustomers.

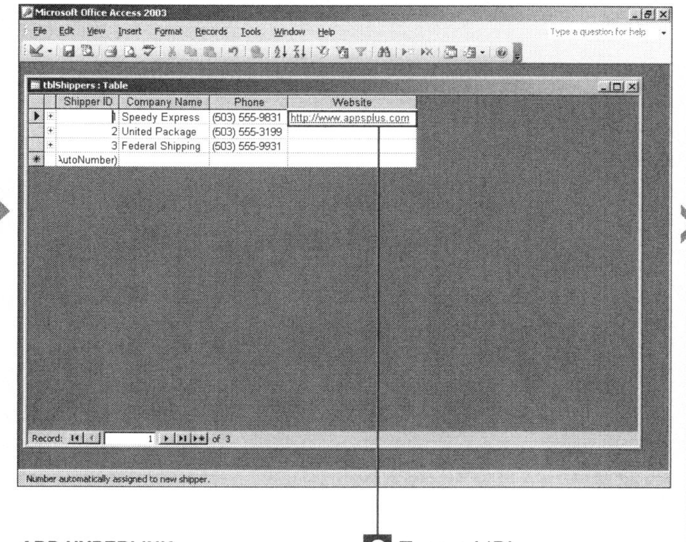

ADD HYPERLINK DATA TO A TABLE

5 Open the table that contains the new hyperlink field.

6 Type a URL.

7 Click the new URL.

■ The Web browser launches and displays the Web site.

USING VBA TO FOLLOW A HYPERLINK

You may sometimes want to follow a hyperlink using VBA code. VBA code is useful for allowing the user to type in where they want to go, or to have more control over following the hyperlinks.

The FollowHyperlink method of the Application object in Access allows the user to type the hyperlink address they want to follow. The reason it is called FollowHyperlink is that VBA follows the hyperlink, regardless of the type of hyperlink. For example, when you follow a hyperlink to an e-mail address, a new mail message opens. If you follow a hyperlink to a Word document, Word opens and displays the linked document. If you specify a Web site with the http:// prefix, then the Web site displays in your default browser. The syntax of the FollowHyperlink method is as follows:

```
    Application.FollowHyperlink(Address,
SubAddress, NewWindow, AddHistory,
ExtraInfo, Method, HeaderInfo)
```

where Address is the main address used for the hyperlink. SubAddress can be the range of cells in a Excel workbook, or a bookmark in a Word document. NewWindow determines whether to open a new window for the browser or to use the window that is already open. AddHistory specifies whether to add the value in Address to the browser history. ExtraInfo allows you to specify a query for a URL. Method is either msoMethodGet or msoMethodPost, and is used with ExtraInfo. HeaderInfo specifies header information.

For this task, you set up a form, allowing the user to enter the address he wants to follow. You can include code to ensure that the user has entered a value into the text box for the address.

USING VBA TO FOLLOW A HYPERLINK

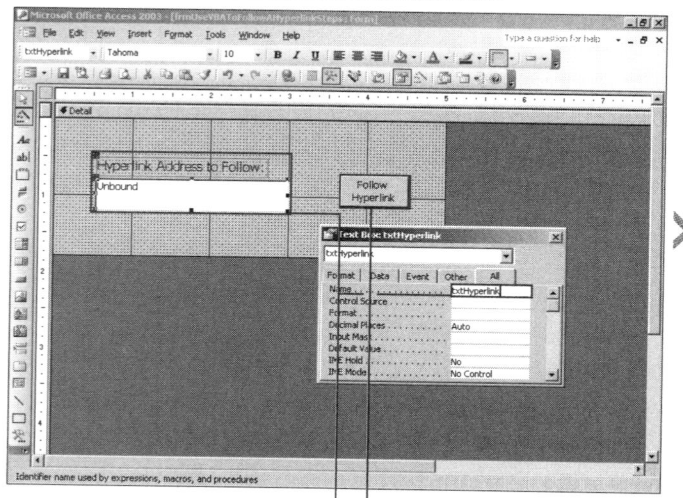

Note: This task uses frmUseVBAToFollowAHyperlinkSteps in AVP-Chapter15.mdb on the CD-ROM.

1 Create a new unbound form.

2 Add a command button, label the button, and name it.

3 Add a text box and label.

4 Type a name for the text box.

■ This example uses the name txtHyperlink.

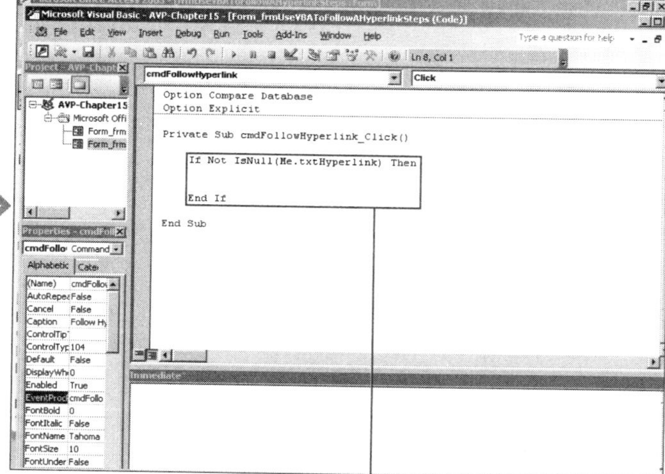

5 Add an event procedure to the click event of the command button.

■ The code editor opens.

6 Add an If..Then … End If structure check to see if the text box is not null: **If Not IsNull(Me.*controlname*) Then**, followed by two hard returns, and then **End If**.

Extra

To create a form that does not break if a user enters an invalid address, you need to add error-handling code to the code that checks if the user has entered some text. To do this, you have two options.

You can use an On Error Resume Next statement to ignore the error and continue the routine. Or, you can use a simple On Error GoTo label statement.

To use the second option, you can create an error handler that displays an error message. This example shows a message box containing the description of the error, and then exits the routine.

```
Private Sub cmdFollowHyperlink_Click()

    On Error GoTo FollowHyperlink_Err

    If Not IsNull(Me.txtHyperlink) Then

        Application.FollowHyperlink Me.txtHyperlink

    End If

    Exit Sub

FollowHyperlink_Err:

    MsgBox Err.Description
    Exit Sub

End Sub
```

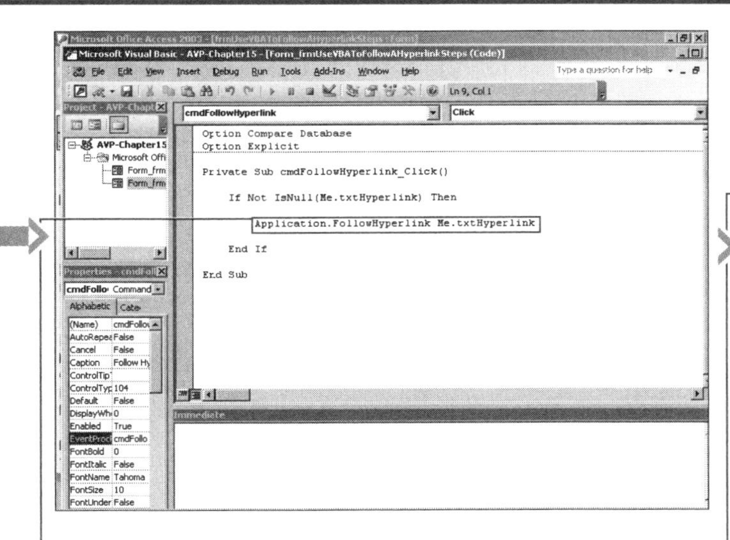

7 Type the Application.FollowHyperlink command using the text box: **Application.FollowHyperlink Me.*controlname***.

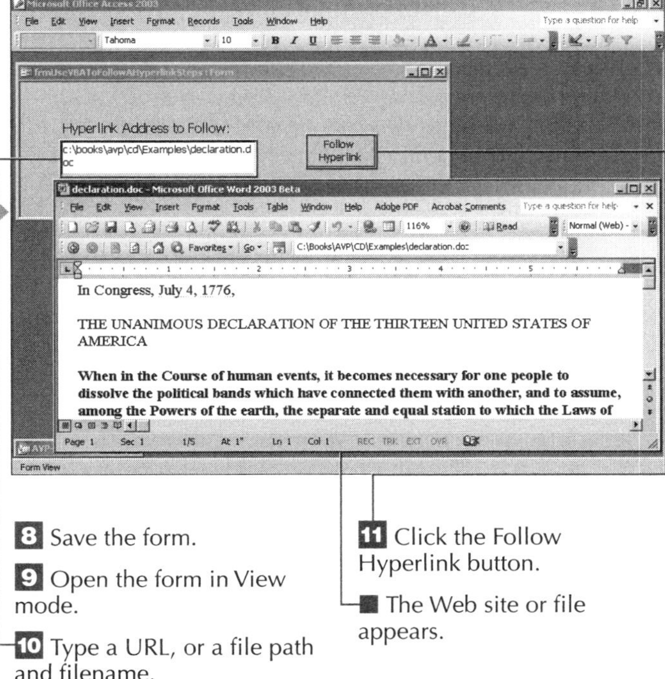

8 Save the form.

9 Open the form in View mode.

10 Type a URL, or a file path and filename.

11 Click the Follow Hyperlink button.

■ The Web site or file appears.

PUBLISH ACCESS DATA TO HTML

There are a few ways to publish your data on the Internet. One of the simplest ways is to take a table and export it to HTML by choosing Export from the File menu. In the Export Table dialog box, you can choose HTML Documents from the Save as type drop-down list. You can also choose to format the table you export; the resulting data appears in a table type format with borders included.

Before Access generates the HTML page, a dialog box appears, asking if you want to include an HTML template. An HTML template is an HTML document that can contain a company logo or anything else you may want to include on Web pages that you generate for your data.

Another way to publish Access data is to publish your reports on the Web. After you create your report, you can choose Export from the File menu. In the Export Table dialog box, you can choose HTML Documents from the Save as type drop-down list. You can also choose to format the table you export. Again, this option displays the data in a table type format with borders included. Before Access generates the HTML page, a dialog box appears, asking if you want to include an HTML template.

When you create your HTML document, also called a Web page, you cannot edit the page because the data is no longer connected to the database in any way; it is completely static.

To use the new Web page, you can simply copy the HTML file to the Web folder of your Web site. You can then link to the page.

EXPORT A TABLE AS AN HTML PAGE

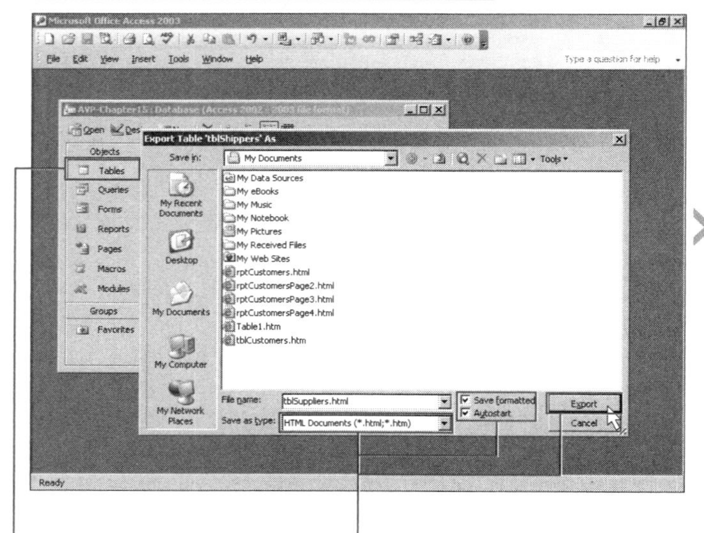

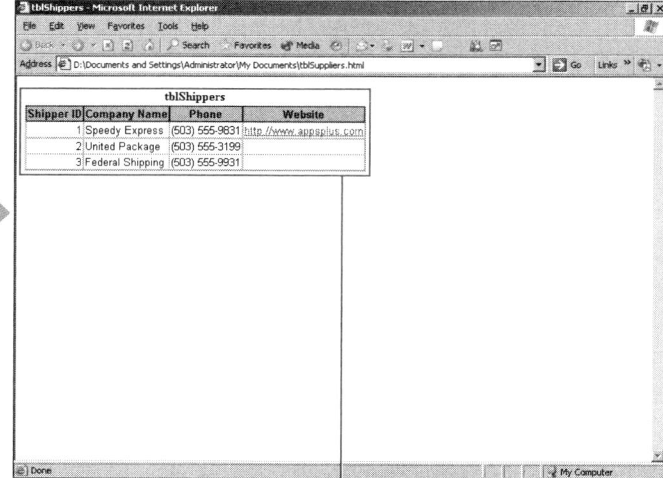

Note: This task uses AVP-Chapter15.mdb on the CD-ROM.

1 Click Tables, and click the table you want to export.

2 Click File ➪ Export.

3 In the Export Table As dialog box, select HTML Documents from the Save as type drop-down list.

4 Check Save formatted and Autostart.

5 Click Export.

■ The HTML Output Options dialog box appears.

6 Click OK.

■ The table appears in the browser window.

Extra

Access allows you to specify a standard appearance for data you publish to the Web by specifying templates. A template is an HTML document that includes special comments. Access uses these comments to place the data into the template to create the final HTML document. The special comments in the example below are: `<!–ACCESSTEMPLATE_TITLE–>` and `<!–ACCESSTEMPLATE_BODY–>`. The entire code for the template is as follows:

```
<html>
   <head>
      <title> <!–ACCESSTEMPLATE_TITLE–> </title>
   </head>
   <body leftmargin="50" >
       <strong>My Example Template</strong>
       <!–ACCESSTEMPLATE_BODY–>
       <br>
       <br>

   </body>
</html>
```

To use the template with the data, export the object as an HTML document using Export from the File menu, and then choosing HTML Documents from the Save as type drop-down list. In the HTML Output Options dialog box, check the Select an HTML Template check box. You can then click the Browse button, and choose your HTML template file.

EXPORT A REPORT AS AN HTML PAGE

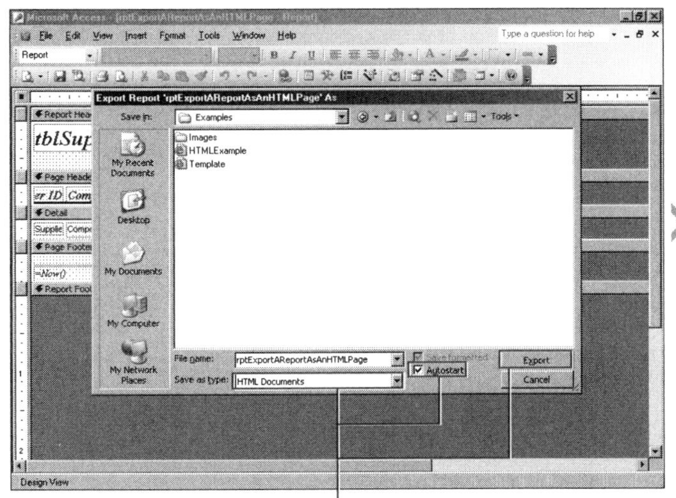

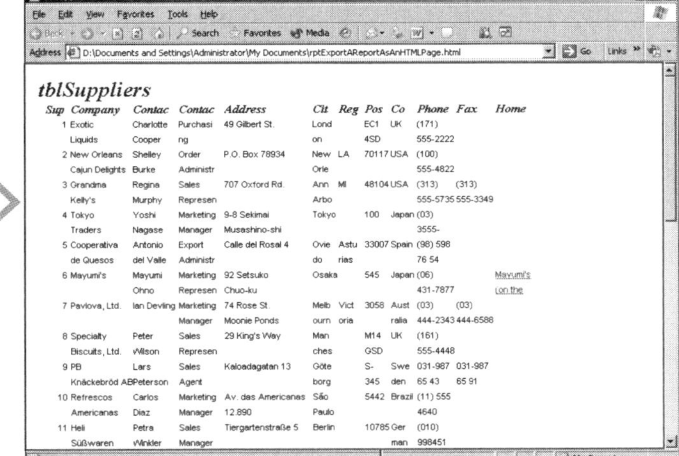

1 Click the report you want to export or open the report in the Design view.

2 Click File ➪ Export.

3 In the Export Report As dialog box, select HTML Documents from the Save as type drop-down list.

4 Check Autostart.

■ The Save formatted check box is already selected.

5 Click Export.

■ The HTML Output Options dialog box appears.

6 Click OK.

■ The report data appears in the browser.

USING THE DATA ACCESS PAGE WIZARD

You can use Data Access Pages, or DAPs, to put your Access data on the Web. There are several ways to create Data Access Pages. On the Pages tab, you can choose from the following options: Create data access page in Design view, Create data access page by using wizard, and Edit Web page that already exists. This task covers the use of the wizard.

To create a Data Access Page using the wizard, you must choose the Create data access page by using wizard option from the list on the Pages tab. The Page Wizard appears, asking you to specify on which tables or queries you want to base your new Data Access Page. After choosing a record source, you can also select the fields you want to include. Note that if you choose more than one record source with fields from the additional record sources, Access asks you to choose the table that is unique; you can only use that table, including the fields.

After you choose your record source, you can click the Next button. You can then choose the fields on which you want to create groupings. After clicking Next, you can choose the fields, if any, on which you want to sort.

When you click Next again, the last page appears, allowing you to name the Data Access Page. You can also specify a theme you want to use and whether to open the page in the Design view or open the form in the browser. You can then click Finish.

When you create the Data Access Page, you are actually creating a separate HTML file, with a link that is created inside your Access database. If you move the file, you must relocate the link, which Access prompts you to do.

USING THE DATA ACCESS PAGE WIZARD

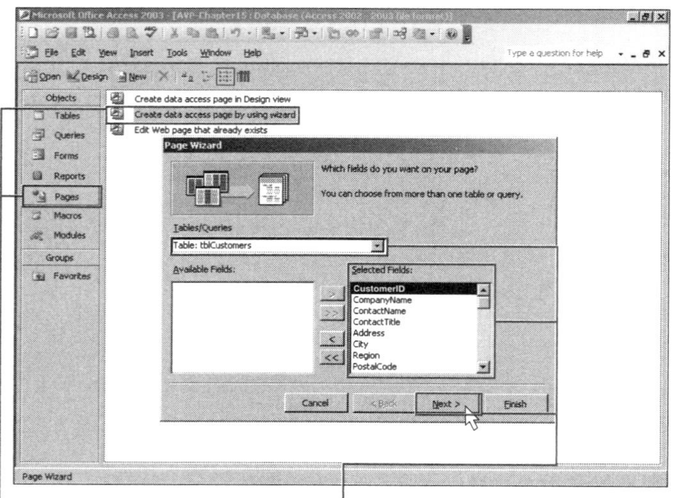

Note: This task uses dapUseTheDataAccessPageWizard in AVP-Chapter15.mdb on the CD-ROM.

1 Click Pages.

2 Double-click Create data access page by using wizard.

■ The Page Wizard appears.

3 Select the table you want to use for the Data Access Page.

4 Select the fields you want to include for the new Data Access Page.

5 Click Next.

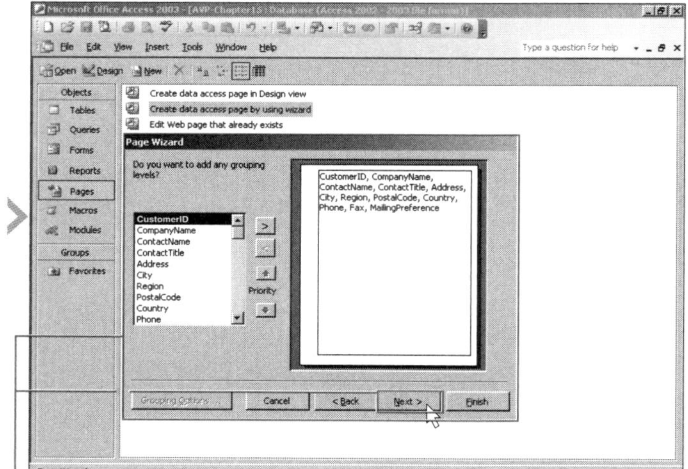

■ The Grouping page of the wizard appears, letting you choose fields on which to base the groupings of the page. The default is none.

6 Click Next to accept the default.

■ The page for setting the sort order appears, letting you choose fields on which to base the sort order of the page. The default is none.

7 Click Next to accept the default.

Extra

The last page of the wizard allows you to specify a theme. Themes let you give Web pages a uniform appearance throughout the Web site. Microsoft FrontPage provides the themes you can use with Data Access Pages. You can use Microsoft FrontPage to create Web sites.

When you are in the last page of the Data Access Page Wizard, select the check box next to the Do you want to apply a theme to your page option (☐ changes to ☑). After you click Finish, Access creates the page and displays it in Design view, and the Theme dialog box appears.

The Theme dialog box allows you to choose various themes that you can apply to your Data Access Page. For example, you can choose vivid colors, active graphics, and a background image. As you look through the various themes in a list box, a sample appears for each theme. When you find a theme you like, click OK. You can also click the Set Default button if you want to use that theme for additional pages.

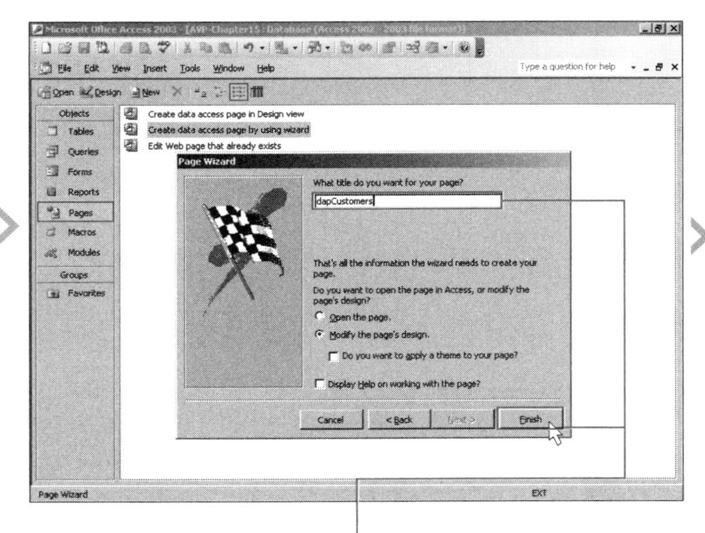

■ The last page of the wizard appears, allowing you to specify the name of the Data Access Page.

8 Type the name you want.

9 Click Finish.

10 Click the View button (▤).

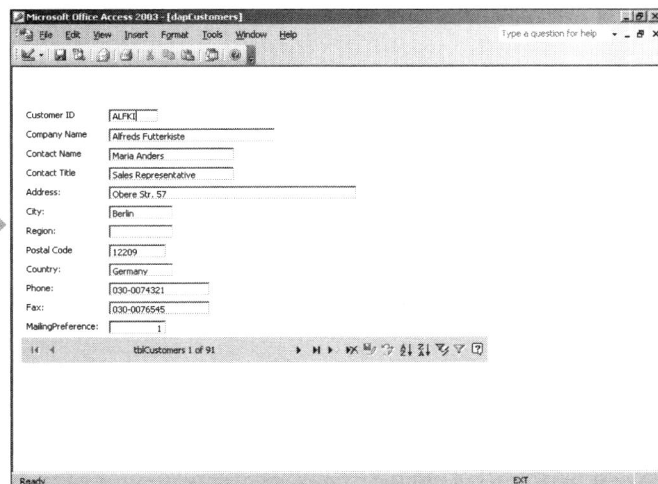

■ The new Data Access Page opens in Design view.

CONVERT FORMS AND REPORTS TO DATA ACCESS PAGES

When you create a database that contains many forms and reports, you may also want to use the form or report on the Web. You can use Access to convert your forms and reports to Data Access Pages.

When you begin converting forms and reports, you may want to start with simple ones. This is because more complicated forms require more modifications to make the Data Access Pages work properly.

To convert a form, you must first create the form. After you create the form, you can right-click in the form, and then choose Save As from the drop-down list. The Save As dialog box appears, allowing you to save the form as another form, as a report, or as a Data Access Page. When you choose the Data Access Page option, and click OK, the New Data Access Page dialog box appears.

The New Data Access Page dialog box allows you to specify where you want to place the new Data Access Page HTML file. Most users want to locate the pages under the database. This option makes it easier to locate the files when you need to move them.

After you convert the form to a Data Access Page, the new Data Access Page appears in the browser. You can open it in Design view to modify it, if necessary. You can also move the Data Access Page to your Web site. See the Extra section to update your Data Access Page when you move your database.

CONVERT A FORM TO A DATA ACCESS PAGE

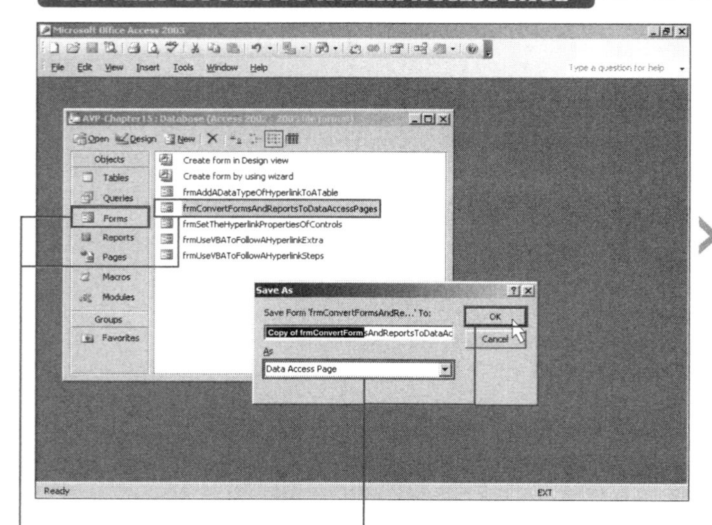

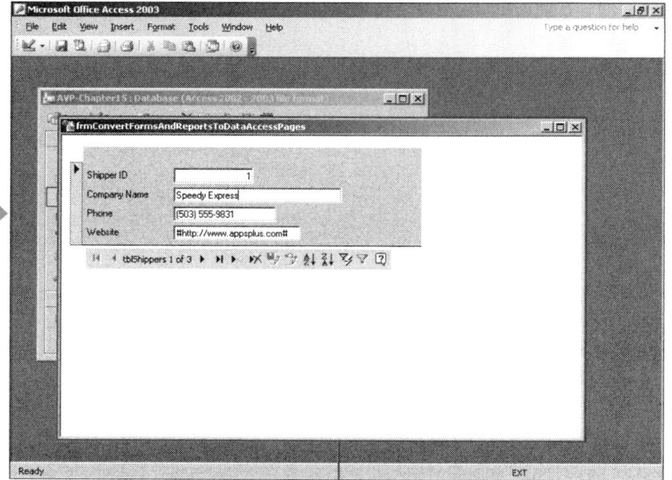

Note: This task uses frmConvertFormsAndReportsToDataAccessPages in AVP-Chapter15.mdb on the CD-ROM.

1 Click Forms.

2 Right-click the form you want to convert to a Data Access Page.

3 Choose Save As from the drop-down list.

■ The Save As dialog box appears.

4 Select Data Access Page from the As drop-down list.

5 Click OK.

■ The new Data Access Page dialog box appears, asking you to specify where you want the new page.

6 Select the folder where you want to place the new Data Access Page.

7 Click OK.

■ The new Data Access Page appears.

Extra

You may want to move the database that you use for your Data Access Page. When you do this, you can change the connection information by first opening the Data Access Page in the Design view. You can then choose Field List from the View menu. The Page Connection properties icon ( ) appears at the top left-hand corner of the Field list. When you click this icon, the Data Link Properties dialog box appears.

The Data Link Properties dialog box opens to the Connection tab, and allows you to point to the database in the new location.

Besides pointing to a new database location, you can also specify the username and password. The default is Admin with no password. Access uses this default for all databases. Access gives you the option of saving the password, and of testing the connection by using a command button.

The other tabs allow you to specify other types of databases such as an SQL Server database.

CONVERT A REPORT TO A DATA ACCESS PAGE

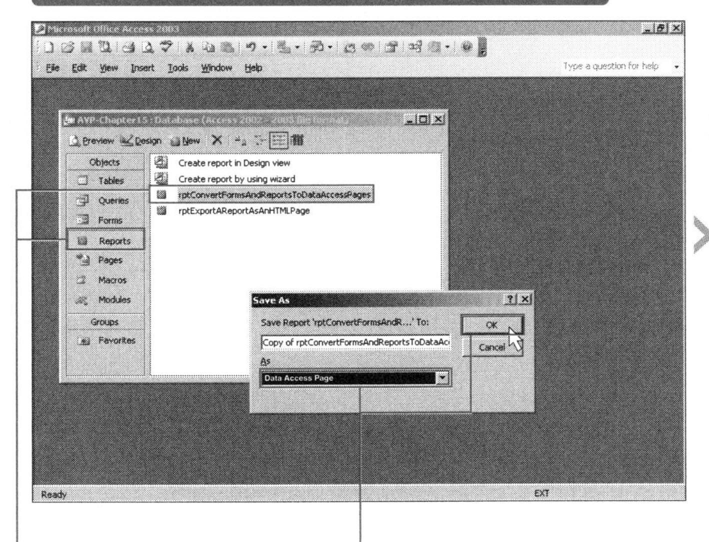

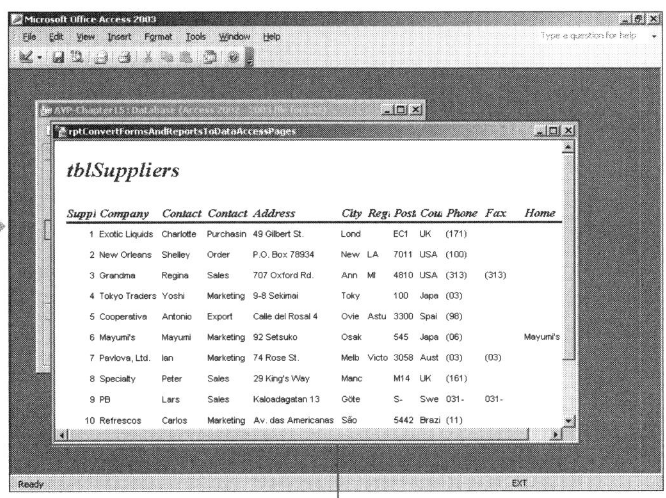

1 Click Reports.

2 Right-click the report you want to convert to a Data Access Page.

3 Choose Save As from the drop-down list.

■ The Save As dialog box appears.

4 Select Data Access Page from the As drop-down list.

5 Click OK.

■ The new Data Access Page dialog box appears, asking you to specify where you want the new page.

6 Select the folder where you want to place the new Data Access Page.

7 Click OK.

■ The new Data Access Page appears.

APPENDIX

LESZYNSKI NAMING CONVENTIONS FOR MICROSOFT ACCESS

Developers generally feel both an appreciation for, and an ambivalence towards, naming conventions. They feel ambivalent because they often see these standards as slowing the development process, increasing the size of object names and files, and stifling true programming creativity. However, their appreciation for conventions comes from their understanding that, without order, every project could transform into incoherent spaghetti code and spaghetti objects, in Access terminology. Spaghetti in this case refers to code and objects that use various ways of naming objects, thereby creating a confusing environment when you try to work on the application. As a result, most developers understand the need for an ordered approach to development, while at the same time they want a system that is not too intrusive.

A system that is comprehensive and applied consistently also tends to be mildly intrusive. For example, to apply a naming convention to your objects, you must follow a certain naming method every time you type an object name. However, the small pain of typing extra keystrokes produces a large gain. For example, beginning the names of your queries with the qry tag helps you to distinguish your queries from your tables, saving time.

Creating naming conventions takes a great deal of research and testing. You can take several different approaches when naming objects. For a complete discourse on designing your own naming convention, see *Access Expert Solutions* by Stan Leszynski, published by Que Corporation.

This appendix outlines the Leszynski Naming Conventions, or LNC, a set of standardized approaches to naming objects during Access development. These naming conventions were originally developed by Mr. Leszynski to help those who work primarily in Access development. He also developed them to address a need that existed in the marketplace due to a lack of consensus about development styles among leading Access developers.

LNC provides common standards for developers who work with multiple Microsoft development tools. Access, Visual Basic, Excel, SQL Server, and other Microsoft products have more in common in their post-2000 versions than in any previous versions. Consequently, this Access version is very compatible with the LNC development style for all of the Microsoft application development products, as detailed in the separate set of conventions, Leszynski Naming Conventions for Microsoft Solution Developers. LNC has been used as the foundation for the code examples in the Microsoft Access and Jet documentation for many years.

The terms, naming conventions, style, and LNC are used interchangeably throughout this appendix.

Version 99.1, for Access 1.x, 2.x, 7.x, 8.x, 9.x, 10.x, and 11.x.

TAGS FOR DATABASE WINDOW OBJECTS

This table lists the Level One tags for Database window objects. Note that only one tag exists for each object type.

Although Level One is the simplified naming model, it is necessary to provide tags to identify subform and subreport objects specifically. The distinction between objects and subobjects is critical for non-developers who navigate by using the Database window. Because it is not appropriate to open subforms and subreports directly from the Database window, they must be clearly identified and grouped by using tags.

OBJECT	TAG
Class	cls
Command Bar	cmb
Data Access Page	dap
Form	frm
Macro	mcr
Module	bas
Query	qry
Report	rpt
Subform	fsub
Subreport	rsub
Table	tbl

TAGS FOR FORM AND REPORT CONTROL OBJECTS

The next table lists the Level One tags for control objects on forms and reports. These Level One control tags provide no differentiation of control type other than to distinguish labels, which do not interact with the user, from controls that can display or modify data. This level of detail is not adequate for applications where VBA code is written behind forms or reports, but it can be a convenience with macro-centric applications.

CONTROL	TAG
Label	lbl
Other types	ctl

Keep in mind that Level One tags are very important. Some expressions on forms and reports cannot be evaluated when the name of the control is the same as the name of a table field in the object recordset. For example, if you were to use the following expression as the control source for a report control named Qty, in a report whose record source also contained a Qty field, then the report would display an #Error message, rather than the proper calculation:

```
=IIf([Qty]<100,"Low",[Qty])
```

This code creates what is called a circular reference, where Access does not know whether to evaluate [Qty] in your expression as the table field with that name, or the control with that name. You can solve the problem by giving the report control a different name from the bound field name, such as txtQty.

The next two tables list the Level Two tags for control objects on forms, reports, and Web pages. All control tags are three characters long. A different tag is provided for each control type, both built-in and standard OLE controls. VBA code written behind forms and reports using this convention reflects the control type in the event procedure names — for example, cboState_AfterUpdate. The automatic sorting provided by this notation in the Access module design window can be very helpful during development.

Controls on Data Access Pages are not necessarily objects in the Access object model, as is the case for controls on forms and reports. As a result, the specific type of control used on a Web page built in Access may come from a DLL, may be one variety of a single, multifaceted control type, or may be created with HTML statements. This structure is evident in the TypeOf column in the following table.

CONTROL	TAG	TYPEOF
Bound HTML (Web page)	bht	MSOBoundHTML
Bound hyperlink (Web page)	bhl	MSOBoundHTML
Bound object frame	frb	BoundObjectFrame
Button (command bar)	btn	CommandBarButton
Chart (graph)	cht	ObjectFrame
Check box	chk	CheckBox
Check box (Web page)	chk	Input
Combo box	cbo	ComboBox
Command button	cmd	CommandButton
Command button (Web page)	cmd	Button
Custom control	ocx	CustomControl
Drop-down list (Web page)	cbo	Select
Expand (Web page)	exp	ExpandControl
Hotspot image (Web page)	iht	Img
Hyperlink	hlk	**
Hyperlink (Web page)	hlk	A HRef
Image	img	Image
Image (Web page)	img	Img
Label	lbl	Label
Label (Web page)	lbl	MSTheme-Label
Line	lin	Line
Line (Web page)	lin	HR
List box	lst	ListBox
List box (Web page)	lst	Select
Movie (Web page)	mov	Img
Office chart (Web page)	cht	Chart
Office pivot table (Web page)	pvt	PivotTable
Office spreadsheet (Web page)	sht	Spreadsheet
Option button	opt	OptionButton
Option button (Web page)	opt	Input
Option group	grp	OptionGroup
Option group (Web page)	grp	FieldSet
Page (tab)	pag	Page
Pages (tab)	pgs	Pages
Page break	brk	PageBreak

CONTROL	TAG	TYPEOF
Record navigation (Web page)	nav	RecordNavigationControl
Rectangle	shp	Rectangle
Rectangle (Web page)	shp	MicrosoftAccessRectangle
Scrolling text (Web page)	mqe	Marquee
Section	sec	Section
Subform/Subreport	sub	Subform
Tab	tab	TabControl
Text box	txt	TextBox
Text box (Web page)	txt	TextArea
Toggle button	tgl	ToggleButton
Unbound object frame	fru	ObjectFrame

**Hyperlink is actually a ComboBox, CommandButton, Image, Label, or TextBox.

VBA OBJECT BASE NAME LENGTHS

There is not an LNC rule that limits variable name length, but common sense dictates that variable names longer than 15 or 20 characters waste a lot of keystrokes at each use. For procedure names, the VBA module editor shows just over 20 characters of a procedure name by default, so this number is suggested as the target maximum procedure name length.

You should abbreviate VBA object base name elements wherever possible by using a standardized abbreviation table. You can extend LNC by creating your own standard abbreviations, as well. You should create and use standardized terminology in your applications wherever possible.

COMPOUND VBA OBJECT BASE NAMES

Procedure base names follow the construction ObjectVerb, where the Object portion describes the primary object type affected — often the same as the primary argument — and Verb describes the action. This style sorts functions and subs by their target object when shown in ordered lists, as follows:

FormCtlHide

FormCtlShow

FormPropAdd

FormPropGet

FormPropSet

This sort order is preferable to the commonly used alternative with VerbObject construction:

AddFormProp

GetFormProp

HideFormCtl

SetFormProp

ShowFormCtl

Tags are required for the following VBA objects: variables, type structures, and constants. Optional tags are also available for some types of procedures. By definition, if you are a Level One user, then LNC assumes that you are not writing Visual Basic code. If you are creating procedures, then you are a Level Two user and should always apply Level Two tags and prefixes to database objects as well as VBA objects.

Base names are optional in some Level Two constructions. When you are programming in VBA in Level Two, you always require the tag element, but the BaseName is optional for local variables only. For example, a procedure that declared only one form object variable can legitimately use the variable name frm, which is a tag without a base name. Type structures, constants, and variables that have module-level or public scope must have both a tag and base name.

Tags for Variables

Visual Basic variable tags are noted here, and grouped by type of variable. Tags for collection variables are made by adding "s" after the tag for the object type stored in the collection.

Tags for Visual Basic Data Variables

VARIABLE TYPE	TAG
Boolean	bln
Byte	byt
Conditional Compilation Constant	ccc
Currency	cur
Date	dtm
Double	dbl
Enum	enm
Error	err
Integer	int
Long	lng
Object	obj
Single	sng
String	str
User-Defined Type	typ
Variant	var

The Conditional Compilation Constant, Error, and User-Defined Type items are not true data types — created with Dim name As type — but rather are programming concepts. A Conditional Compilation Constant variable is a flag of type Boolean, an Error variable is a Variant created with the CVErr() function, and User-Defined Types are unique constructs.

The LNC style for using enumerated constants is to make them verbose and descriptive by referring to the name of their parent. The Enum declaration shown here provides an example:

```
Public Enum penmMenuLoca   ' Location of
new menu items

  penmMenuLoca_Top = 0       ' At the top
of menus

  penmMenuLoca_Bottom = 1   ' At the
bottom of menus

End Enum
```

Tags for Visual Basic Object Variables

OBJECT	TAG
Access.Application	accapp
ADODB	ado
AllDataAccessPages	dpgs
AllDatabaseDiagrams	dias
AllForms	frms
AllMacros	mcrs
AllModules	bass
AllQueries	qrys
AllReports	rpts
AllStoredProcedures	prcs
AllTables	tbls
AllViews	qrys
Application	app
Assistant	ast
Collection	col
CommandBar	cbr
CommandBars	cbrs
Control	ctl
Controls	ctls
CustomControl	ocx
CustomControlInReport	ocx
DAO.DBEngine	daodbe
DataAccessPage(s)	dap(s)
DoCmd	doo
Excel.Application	xlsapp
Excel.Chart	xlscht
Excel.Sheet	xlssht
Form	frm
Forms	frms
Graph.Application	gphapp
GroupLevel	lvl
MAPI.Session	mpimps
Menu bar	mbr
Menu (generic)	mnu
Menu (popup/shortcut)	mct

Tags for Visual Basic Object Variables (continued)

OBJECT	TAG
Menu (submenu/drop-down)	msb
Module	bas
Modules	bass
MSProject.Application	prjapp
MSProject.Project	prjprj
OfficeBinder.Binder	bndbnd
Outlook.Application	otlapp
PowerPoint.Application	pptapp
Reference	rfc
References	rfcs
Report	rpt
Reports	rpts
SchedulePlus.Application	scdapp
Screen	scn
Section	sec
SQLOLE.SQLServer	sqlsvr
TeamManager.Application	mgrapp
Toolbar	tbr
Word.Application	wrdapp
Word.Basic	wrdbas

Tags for ActiveX Data Object Variables

OBJECT	TAG
Command	cmd
Connection	cnn
Error(s)	err(s)
Field(s)	fld(s)
Parameter(s)	prm(s)
Property(ies)	prp(s)
Recordset	rst

Although, as noted earlier, a tag by itself is a legitimate variable name, the variable tag int is a reserved word and cannot compile in VBA — it requires a base name.

Prefixes for Variables

You can categorize the prefixes for Visual Basic variables into two groups: prefixes for scope, and all other prefixes. The following prefixes are ordered by increasing, or broader, scope:

PREFIX	SCOPE
No prefix	Use no prefix for variables that are local to a procedure.
s	Place this prefix before locally declared variables in a procedure with a Static statement.
m	Use this prefix for module-level variables declared with Dim or Private statements in the Declarations section of a module.
p	Use this prefix to denote variables declared as Public in the Declarations section of a form or report module. Such variables are publicly available to other procedures in the same database only.
g	Use this prefix to denote variables declared as Public in the Declarations section of a standard module. These variables are truly global and may be referenced from procedures in the current database or other databases.

When you use scope prefixes, you must always place them at the beginning of a variable name, and before any other prefixes.

In addition to scope, prefixes can identify other characteristics of variables, as follows:

PREFIX	SCOPE
a	Use this prefix to denote a variable that is declared as an array, including a ParamArray argument in a function.
c	Place this prefix before constants that you define.
e	Use this prefix for a variable that is an element of a collection. These variables are usually part of a For Each...Next loop structure.
i	Use this prefix to denote a variable — usually of type Integer — that serves as an index into an array or an index counter in a For...Next loop.
o	Place this prefix before object variables that reference Automation servers through late binding — an object variable — where the tag denotes the type of server.
r	Use this prefix for variables that are arguments, or parameters, passed into a procedure and declared as ByRef, or not declared as either ByRef or ByVal — including a ParamArray — which implies ByRef.
t	Use this prefix to describe a variable that is declared as a user-defined type structure. The variable should inherit the base name from the original declaration for the type.
v	Use this prefix for variables that are arguments, or parameters, passed into a procedure and declared as ByVal.

Allowable Prefix Combinations

Because a prefix provides a very detailed description of a variable, the number of allowable prefix combinations is limited, as shown below.

ANY ONE OF THESE	CAN COME BEFORE THIS
s, m, p, g, r, v	a
m, p, g	c
s, m, p, g, r, v	e
s, m, p, g, r, v	i
s, m, p, g, r, v	ia
s, m, p, g, r, v	o
m, p, g	t

Naming Constants

Access 95 introduced sweeping changes in the use of constants. The changes most relevant to naming conventions include the following:

- A constant can now be assigned a data type when the constant is defined.
- All constants have been renamed and contain a tag of ac, db, or vb to identify their primary functional area.
- Constants can now be created with the Variant data type.

When creating constants, you must use a scope prefix — if appropriate — the prefix c, and the suitable tag for the data type of the constant. To properly synchronize the tag and the data type, you should not let Access assign the type; instead, you should always use the full Const name As datatype syntax.

Constants require a unique prefix when declared Public in a widely distributed application to prevent name contention.

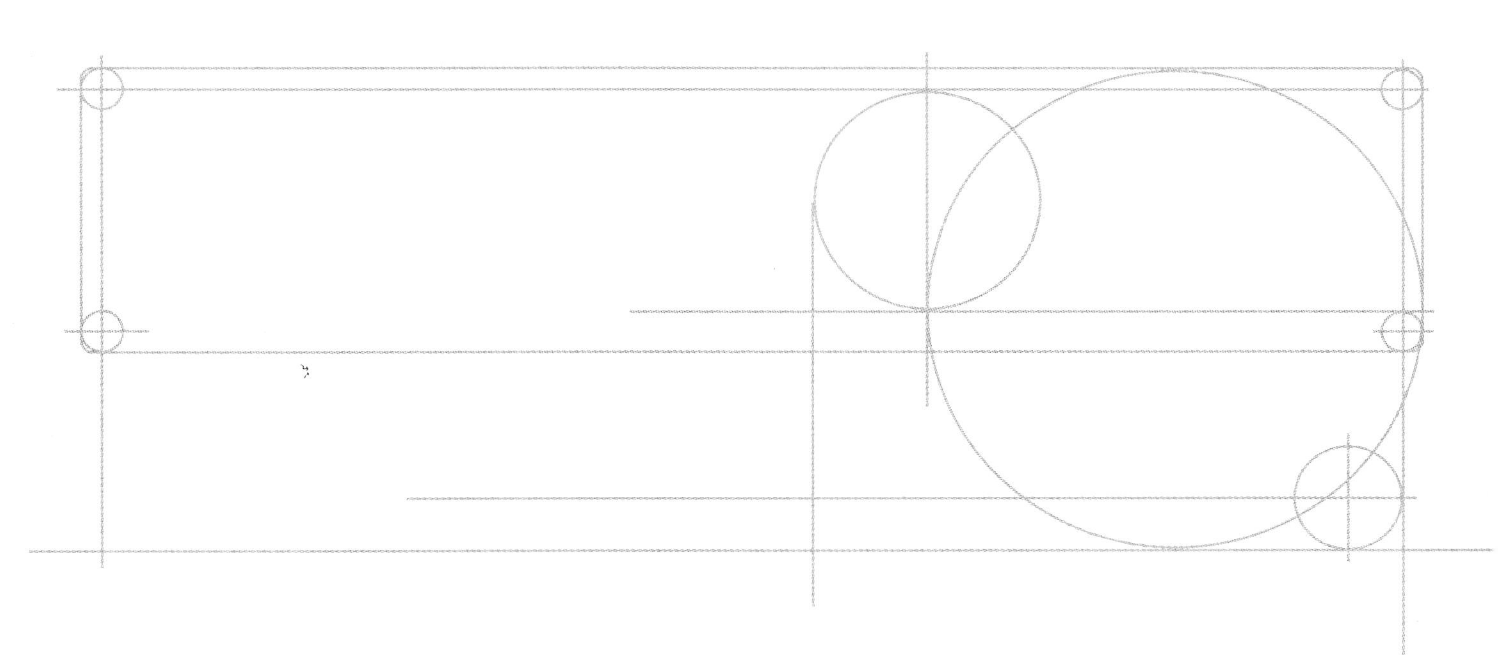

WHAT'S ON THE CD-ROM

The CD-ROM included in this book contains many useful files and programs. Before installing any of the programs on the disc, make sure that a newer version of the program is not already installed on your computer. For information on installing different versions of the same program, contact the program's manufacturer. For the latest information, please refer to the ReadMe file located at the root level of the CD-ROM.

SYSTEM REQUIREMENTS

To use the contents of the CD-ROM, your computer must have the following hardware and software:

For Windows 9*x*, Windows 2000, Windows NT4 (with SP 4 or later), Windows Me, or Windows XP:

- A Pentium processor running at 120 MHz or faster
- At least 32MB of RAM; for best performance, at least 64MB is recommended
- An Ethernet network interface card, or NIC, or a modem with a speed of at least 28,800 bps
- A CD-ROM drive
- Access 2003

AUTHOR'S DATABASE FILES

These files contain all the sample code and objects from the book for each chapter. You can open the files directly from the CD-ROM, or you can copy them to your hard drive and use them as the basis for your own projects. To find these files on the CD-ROM, open the D:\Chapters folder. You can then find the Microsoft Access MDB files labeled for each chapter.

ADOBE READER VERSION

The CD-ROM contains an e-version of this book that you can view and search using Adobe Reader. You cannot print the pages or copy text from the Adobe Reader files. The CD-ROM also includes an evaluation version of Adobe Reader.

INSTALLING AND USING THE SOFTWARE

For your convenience, the software titles appearing on the CD-ROM are listed alphabetically.

Adobe Reader

For Windows 95/98/NT/2000. Freeware.

Adobe Reader allows you to view the online version of this book. For more information on using Adobe Reader, see the section "Using the E-Version of this Book" in this appendix. For more information about Adobe Reader and Adobe Systems, see www.adobe.com.

FMS Access Utilities

For Windows 95/98/NT/2000/XP. Demos.

FMS is the premier developer and distributor of Access utilities. Included on the CD are demos for Total Access Memo, Total Access Analyzer, Total Visual SourceBook, Total Access Components, Total SQL Statistics, Total Access Startup, Total Access Speller, Total Access Statistics, Total ZipCode Database, Total Visual Agent, Total Visual CodeTools, Total SQL Analyzer PRO, and Total Access Admin.

SPEED Ferret

For Windows 95/98/NT/2000/XP. Demo.

Product works on all versions of Access.

SPEED Ferret is a powerful search-and-replace utility for Microsoft Access databases. This version of SPEED Ferret runs in demo mode until the user purchases and installs the license key. The demo mode does not allow you to save your files, and half of the search results are obscured by asterisks.

ADDITIONAL LINKS

www.appsplus.com

You can reach the author, F. Scott Barker, at his company Web site, AppsPlus.

www.query.com

You can purchase a full version of the Leszynski Naming Conventions at this Web site. See Appendix A for more information.

TROUBLESHOOTING

The programs on the CD-ROM should work on computers with the minimum suggested system requirements. However, some programs may not work properly.

The two most likely reasons for the programs not working properly include not having enough memory, or RAM, for a program that you want to use, or having other programs running that affect the installation or running of a program. If you receive error messages, such as Not enough memory or Setup cannot continue, try one or more of the methods below, and then try running the software again:

- Turn off any anti-virus software.
- Close all running programs.
- In Windows, close the CD-ROM interface and run demos or installations directly from Windows Explorer.
- Have your local computer store add more RAM to your computer.

If you still have trouble installing the items from the CD-ROM, call the Wiley Publishing Customer Service phone number: 800-762-2974 (outside the U.S.: 317-572-3994). You can also contact Wiley Product Technical Support at www.wiley.com/techsupport.

USING THE E-VERSION OF THIS BOOK

You can view *Access 2003: Your visual blueprint for creating and maintaining real-world databases* on your screen using the CD-ROM included at the back of this book. The CD-ROM allows you to search the contents of each chapter of the book for a specific word or phrase. The CD-ROM also provides a convenient way of keeping the book handy while traveling.

You must install Adobe Reader on your computer before you can view the book on the CD-ROM. The CD-ROM includes this program for your convenience. Adobe Reader allows you to view Portable Document Format (PDF) files, which can display books and magazines on your screen exactly as they appear in printed form.

Adobe Reader is a popular and useful program. There are many files available on the Web that are designed to be viewed using Adobe Reader. Look for files with the .pdf extension. For more information about Adobe Reader, visit the www.adobe.com/products/acrobat/readermain.html Web site.

To view the contents of this book using Adobe Reader, display the main menu of the CD-ROM by double-clicking the eBook folder and then eBook.pdf. Click the eBook link, click Install, and then select the chapter of the book you want to view.

USING THE E-VERSION OF THE BOOK

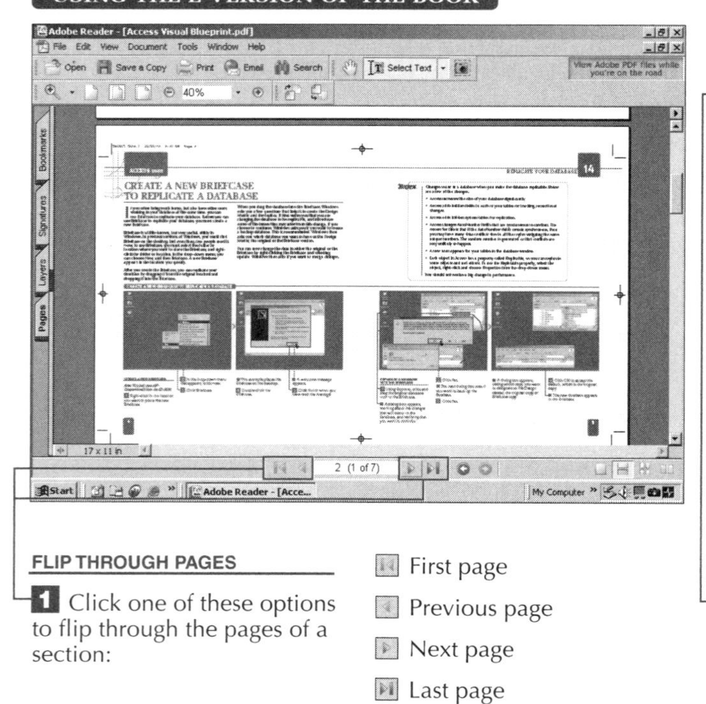

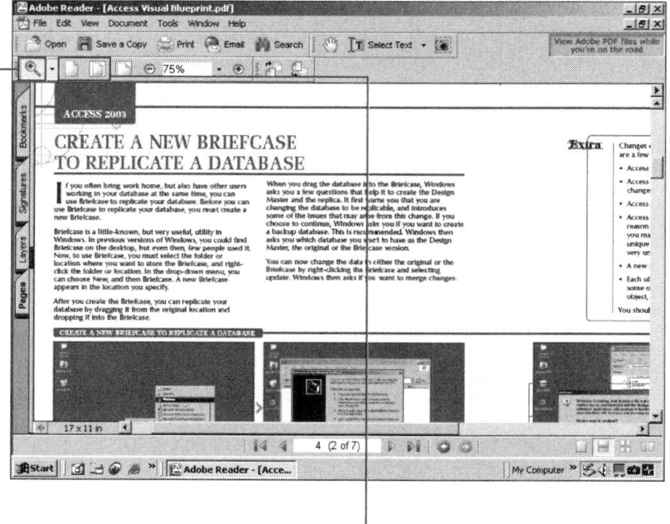

FLIP THROUGH PAGES

1 Click one of these options to flip through the pages of a section:

- First page
- Previous page
- Next page
- Last page

ZOOM IN

1 Click the Zoom In button to magnify an area of the page.

2 Click the area of the page you want to magnify.

■ You can click one of these options to display the page at 100% magnification ( ) or to fit the entire page inside the window ( ).

Extra

To install Adobe Reader, insert the CD-ROM into a drive. In the screen that appears, click Software. Click Adobe Reader and then follow the instructions on your screen to install the program.

You can make searching the book more convenient by copying the PDF files to your computer. To do this, display the contents of the CD-ROM and then copy the Book folder from the CD-ROM to your hard drive. This allows you to easily access the contents of the book at any time.

When you search for text, the text that Adobe Reader highlights may be difficult to read. To make highlighted text easier to read, you can turn off the font smoothing capabilities of Adobe Reader. In the Adobe Reader window, click Edit ⇨ Preferences. Click Display on the left side of the Preferences dialog box. In the Smoothing area, click Smooth (☐ changes to ☑), and then click OK.

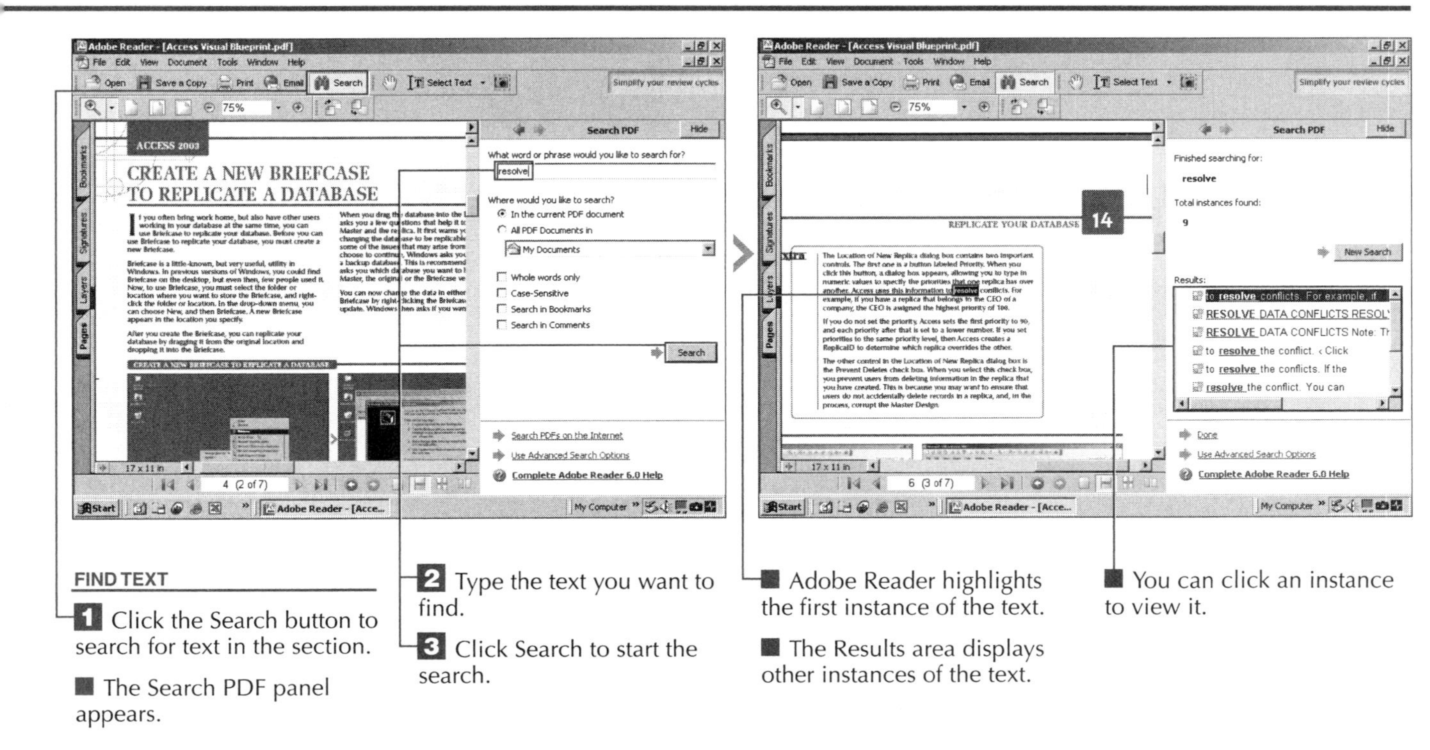

FIND TEXT

1 Click the Search button to search for text in the section.

■ The Search PDF panel appears.

2 Type the text you want to find.

3 Click Search to start the search.

■ Adobe Reader highlights the first instance of the text.

■ The Results area displays other instances of the text.

■ You can click an instance to view it.

APPENDIX

WILEY PUBLISHING, INC. END-USER LICENSE AGREEMENT

READ THIS. You should carefully read these terms and conditions before opening the software packet(s) included with this book "Book". This is a license agreement "Agreement" between you and Wiley Publishing, Inc. "WPI". By opening the accompanying software packet(s), you acknowledge that you have read and accept the following terms and conditions. If you do not agree and do not want to be bound by such terms and conditions, promptly return the Book and the unopened software packet(s) to the place you obtained them for a full refund.

1. **License Grant.** WPI grants to you (either an individual or entity) a nonexclusive license to use one copy of the enclosed software program(s) (collectively, the "Software") solely for your own personal or business purposes on a single computer (whether a standard computer or a workstation component of a multi-user network). The Software is in use on a computer when it is loaded into temporary memory (RAM) or installed into permanent memory (hard disk, CD-ROM, or other storage device). WPI reserves all rights not expressly granted herein.

2. **Ownership.** WPI is the owner of all right, title, and interest, including copyright, in and to the compilation of the Software recorded on the disk(s) or CD-ROM "Software Media". Copyright to the individual programs recorded on the Software Media is owned by the author or other authorized copyright owner of each program. Ownership of the Software and all proprietary rights relating thereto remain with WPI and its licensers.

3. **Restrictions on Use and Transfer.**

(a) You may only (i) make one copy of the Software for backup or archival purposes, or (ii) transfer the Software to a single hard disk, provided that you keep the original for backup or archival purposes. You may not (i) rent or lease the Software, (ii) copy or reproduce the Software through a LAN or other network system or through any computer subscriber system or bulletin-board system, or (iii) modify, adapt, or create derivative works based on the Software.

(b) You may not reverse engineer, decompile, or disassemble the Software. You may transfer the Software and user documentation on a permanent basis, provided that the transferee agrees to accept the terms and conditions of this Agreement and you retain no copies. If the Software is an update or has been updated, any transfer must include the most recent update and all prior versions.

4. **Restrictions on Use of Individual Programs.** You must follow the individual requirements and restrictions detailed for each individual program in the What's on the CD-ROM appendix of this Book. These limitations are also contained in the individual license agreements recorded on the Software Media. These limitations may include a requirement that after using the program for a specified period of time, the user must pay a registration fee or discontinue use. By opening the Software packet(s), you will be agreeing to abide by the licenses and restrictions for these individual programs that are detailed in the What's on the CD-ROM appendix and on the Software Media. None of the material on this Software Media or listed in this Book may ever be redistributed, in original or modified form, for commercial purposes.

5. **Limited Warranty.**

(a) WPI warrants that the Software and Software Media are free from defects in materials and workmanship under normal use for a period of sixty (60) days from the date of purchase of this Book. If WPI receives notification within the warranty period of defects in materials or workmanship, WPI will replace the defective Software Media.

(b) WPI AND THE AUTHOR(S) OF THE BOOK DISCLAIM ALL OTHER WARRANTIES, EXPRESS OR IMPLIED, INCLUDING WITHOUT LIMITATION IMPLIED WARRANTIES OF MERCHANTABILITY AND FITNESS FOR A PARTICULAR PURPOSE, WITH RESPECT TO THE SOFTWARE, THE PROGRAMS, THE SOURCE CODE CONTAINED THEREIN, AND/OR THE TECHNIQUES DESCRIBED IN THIS BOOK. WPI DOES NOT WARRANT THAT THE FUNCTIONS CONTAINED IN THE SOFTWARE WILL MEET YOUR REQUIREMENTS OR THAT THE OPERATION OF THE SOFTWARE WILL BE ERROR FREE.

(c) This limited warranty gives you specific legal rights, and you may have other rights that vary from jurisdiction to jurisdiction.

6. **Remedies.**

(a) WPI's entire liability and your exclusive remedy for defects in materials and workmanship shall be limited to replacement of the Software Media, which may be returned to WPI with a copy of your receipt at the following address: Software Media Fulfillment Department, Attn.: *Access 2003: Your visual blueprint for creating and maintaining real-world databases*, Wiley Publishing, Inc., 10475 Crosspoint Blvd., Indianapolis, IN 46256, or call 1-800-762-2974. Please allow four to six weeks for delivery. This Limited Warranty is void if failure of the Software Media has resulted from accident, abuse, or misapplication. Any replacement Software Media will be warranted for the remainder of the original warranty period or thirty (30) days, whichever is longer.

(b) In no event shall WPI or the author be liable for any damages whatsoever (including without limitation damages for loss of business profits, business interruption, loss of business information, or any other pecuniary loss) arising from the use of or inability to use the Book or the Software, even if WPI has been advised of the possibility of such damages.

(c) Because some jurisdictions do not allow the exclusion or limitation of liability for consequential or incidental damages, the above limitation or exclusion may not apply to you.

7. **U.S. Government Restricted Rights.** Use, duplication, or disclosure of the Software for or on behalf of the United States of America, its agencies and/or instrumentalities "U.S. Government" is subject to restrictions as stated in paragraph (c)(1)(ii) of the Rights in Technical Data and Computer Software clause of DFARS 252.227-7013, or subparagraphs (c) (1) and (2) of the Commercial Computer Software - Restricted Rights clause at FAR 52.227-19, and in similar clauses in the NASA FAR supplement, as applicable.

8. **General.** This Agreement constitutes the entire understanding of the parties and revokes and supersedes all prior agreements, oral or written, between them and may not be modified or amended except in a writing signed by both parties hereto that specifically refers to this Agreement. This Agreement shall take precedence over any other documents that may be in conflict herewith. If any one or more provisions contained in this Agreement are held by any court or tribunal to be invalid, illegal, or otherwise unenforceable, each and every other provision shall remain in full force and effect.

INDEX

B

C

INDEX

D

INDEX

F

G

H

I

J

L

M

N

S

T

U

V

W